THE OXFORD ILLUSTRATED HISTORY OF
THE RENAISSANCE

The historians who contributed to *The Oxford Illustrated History of the Renaissance* are all distinguished authorities in their field. They are:

FRANCIS AMES-LEWIS—Birkbeck, University of London

WARREN BOUTCHER—Queen Mary University of London

PETER BURKE—University of Cambridge

GORDON CAMPBELL—University of Leicester

FELIPE FERNÀNDEZ-ARMESTO—University of Notre Dame

PAULA FINDLEN—Stanford University

STELLA FLETCHER—University of Warwick

PAMELA O. LONG—Independent scholar

MARGARET M. McGOWAN—University of Sussex

PETER MACK—University of Warwick

ANDREW MORRALL—Bard Graduate Center

PAULA NUTTALL—Victoria and Albert Museum

DAVID PARROTT—University of Oxford

FRANÇOIS QUIVIGER—The Warburg Institute

RICHARD WILLIAMS—Royal Collection Trust

The editor and contributors wish to dedicate this volume to Matthew Cotton.

THE OXFORD ILLUSTRATED HISTORY OF

THE
RENAISSANCE

Edited by

GORDON CAMPBELL

OXFORD
UNIVERSITY PRESS

OXFORD
UNIVERSITY PRESS

Great Clarendon Street, Oxford, OX2 6DP,
United Kingdom

Oxford University Press is a department of the University of Oxford.
It furthers the University's objective of excellence in research, scholarship,
and education by publishing worldwide. Oxford is a registered trade mark of
Oxford University Press in the UK and in certain other countries

First Edition published in 2019

Impression: 1

Published in the United States of America by Oxford University Press
198 Madison Avenue, New York, NY 10016, United States of America

British Library Cataloguing in Publication Data
Data available

Library of Congress Control Number: 2018939297

ISBN 978–0–19–871615–0

Printed in Italy by
L.E.G.O. S.p.A. Lavis (TN)

CONTENTS

Introduction

GORDON CAMPBELL

THE Renaissance is a model of cultural descent in which the culture of fifteenth- and sixteenth-century Europe is represented as a repudiation of a medieval world in decline in favour of the revival of the culture of ancient Greece and Rome. The parallel religious model is the Reformation, in which the church is represented as turning its back on corruption and decline in favour of a renewal of the purity of the early church. In both models, there had to be an intervening middle period between the glorious past and its revival. The idea of the Middle Ages (*medium aevum*) was introduced to European historiography by the Roman historian Flavio Biondo in 1437, and quickly became a commonplace. Thereafter European history was conventionally divided into three periods: classical antiquity, the Middle Ages, and the modern period. The biblical metaphor of rebirth was first applied to art by Giorgio Vasari, who used the term to denote the period from Cimabue and Giotto to his own time. It was certainly an inordinately slow birth.

The broadening of the term 'renaissance' to encompass a period and a cultural model is a product of the nineteenth century, albeit with roots in the French Enlightenment. That is why we use the French form (*renaissance*) rather than the Italian (*rinascità*) to denote this rebirth. In 1855 the French historian Jules Michelet used the term 'Renaissance' as the title of a volume on sixteenth-century France. Five years later Jacob Burckhardt published *Die Cultur der Renaissance in Italien* (The Civilization of the Renaissance in Italy), in which he identified the idea of a Renaissance with a set of cultural concepts, such as individualism and the idea of the universal man. Vasari's designation of a movement in art had become the term for an epoch in history associated with a particular set of cultural values. These issues are explored in detail in François Quiviger's chapter on 'The Civilization of the Renaissance', which explores the afterlife of Burckhardt's concept of individuality in more recent notions of self-fashioning and gender fluidity, and in the complex notion of the 'self'.

The model of the Renaissance has evolved over time. An older generation of historians had a predilection for precision: the Middle Ages were deemed to have begun in 476 with the fall of the Roman Empire in the West and concluded with the fall of Constantinople in 1453, when Greek scholars fled to Italy with classical manuscripts under their arms. This book subverts those easy assumptions at every turn, but the contributors nonetheless assume that the model of a cultural Renaissance remains a useful prism through which the period can be examined. That model has been challenged by those who prefer to think of the fifteenth and sixteenth centuries purely in terms of a temporal period called the Early Modern period. This idea is, of course, as fraught with ideological baggage as is the term Renaissance, and embodies narrow assumptions about cultural origins that may be deemed inappropriate in a multicultural Europe and a globalized world.

This is a book about the cultural model of a Renaissance rather than a period. That said, it must be acknowledged that while this model remains serviceable, it also has limitations. The idea of a Renaissance is of considerable use when referring to the scholarly, courtly, and even military cultures of the fifteenth and sixteenth centuries, because members of those elites were consciously emulating classical antiquity, but it is of little value as a model for popular culture and the everyday life of most Europeans. The idea of historical periods, which is emphasized by the use of centuries or rulers as boundaries, is particularly problematical in the case of the Renaissance, because a model that assumes the repudiation of the immediate past is insufficiently attentive to cultural continuities.

Such continuities are sometimes not readily apparent, because they are occluded by Renaissance conventions. Shakespeare is a case in point. He was in many ways the inheritor of the traditions of medieval English drama, and he accordingly divided his plays into scenes. Printed conventions, however, had been influenced by the classical conventions in Renaissance printing culture. Horace had said that plays should consist of neither more nor less than five acts ('Neue minor neu sit quinto productior actu fabula', *Ars Poetica* 189). Shakespeare's plays were therefore printed in five acts, and so were appropriated into the classical tradition. In 1863, three years after Burckhardt had published his book on the Renaissance, the German playwright Gustav Freytag published an essay on drama (*Die Technik des Dramas*) in which he advanced the thesis that a five-act structure (exposition, rising action, climax, falling action, denouement) can be discerned in both ancient Greek drama and in the plays of Shakespeare. The model of the Renaissance was thereby imposed on the structure of Shakespeare's plays (and of the plays of the ancient Greek playwrights). This influence may also be seen in the early quartos of Shakespeare's plays. The inclusion of classicizing genres (comedy and tragedy) on the title-pages (such as *A Pleasant Conceited Comedy called Love's Labour's Lost* and *The Most Excellent and Lamentable Tragedy of Romeo and Juliet*) would seem to be the promotional work of the publisher, not the author. When Shakespeare's colleagues decided to assemble a posthumous collection of his plays, they chose to publish them in a folio format, which was the form normally associated with the publication of classical texts. Within this famous folio, the plays were organized in three genres: comedy, tragedy, and history, the last of which was borrowed from an ancient non-dramatic genre. By such means publishers obscured the roots of Shakespeare's plays in vernacular English drama, and so appropriated his work to the model of the Renaissance. The plays do reflect innovative classical influences as well as cultural continuities with the Middle Ages. Many of the chapters in this book address the blend of continuity and innovation in the culture of the period.

The model of the Renaissance still affects the European sense of its past. In England, for example, secondary schools do not teach the language of England's past—Anglo-Saxon—because our line of cultural descent is deemed to originate in ancient Greece and Rome; traditional schools therefore teach classical Latin, and sometimes ancient Greek. The humanists of the Renaissance believed that classical Latin was pure and medieval Latin corrupt, and so taught classical Latin; we do the same today. In the case of Greek, we are much more precise. We do not teach Homeric Greek or Byzantine Greek or modern Greek, but rather the Greek of Athens in the fifth century BCE. In this sense, we are inheritors of the Renaissance.

Renaissance humanists are the subject of Peter Mack's chapter, which traces the contours of humanism from its origins in Italy (especially Padua) and the seminal figure of Petrarch before turning to the humanist scholars of fifteenth-century Italy and the slightly later humanists of northern Europe and Spain. The humanist movement represented by these scholars had a transformative impact on the educational initiatives of the Renaissance, and also left its mark on academic disciplines such as philosophy, history, and classical scholarship.

Humanism was also important for national literatures. The burgeoning of vernacular literature, accelerated by the technology of print, produced a distinguished corpus of literature in many languages. This literature, much of which is indebted to classical models, is the subject of the chapter by Warren Boutcher. Latin was the language of educated discourse, but throughout this period it faced a fast-growing rival in vernacular writing, which created new literary cultures amongst a plethora of lay publics. In some cases classical genres were retained for writing in vernaculars, so the period is replete with examples of epics and tragedies written in national languages. The language of the international republic of letters was Latin, but the hegemony of Latin as the learned language of Europe was increasingly challenged by French, the language that also produced what might be claimed as Europe's most distinguished body of vernacular literature.

The idea of the Renaissance has slowly evolved since the nineteenth century. There was an assumption (now an embarrassment) that Europe was the centre of the world, that Europeans had discovered other parts of the world and brought civilization to the uncivilized. Now we speak of cultural encounters, and acknowledge that there were complex cultural exchanges. These issues are explored in the chapter on the global Renaissance by Peter Burke and Felipe Fernandez-Armesto, who describe the interfaces between the European Renaissance and the cultures of the Byzantine Empire, the Islamic world, Asia, the Americas, and Africa. Travellers, including missionaries, disseminated European ideas and in turn were influenced by the cultures in which they found themselves. Print enabled words and images to become vehicles of culture, and travellers brought artefacts back to Europe. There had been many renaissances in various parts of the world, but the European Renaissance was the first global Renaissance.

Within Europe, in forms such as architecture, the traditional model of a cultural movement beginning in Italy and Flanders still has much to commend itself, as long as lines are not drawn rigidly. Italian Renaissance architecture spread well beyond Italy: the Belvedere in the garden of the Hradčany in Prague is a wholly Italianate building, as are the Palace of Charles V in the Alhambra, the Boimi Chapel in Lviv (now in Ukraine), and the reconstructed royal palace in Visegrád (Hungary). There are also striking examples of cultural hybridity, such as the arcaded galleries (with local and Venetian elements) around the squares in Zamość (Poland), the Orthodox decoration of the interior of the Palace of Facets in the Moscow Kremlin, and the Islamic strain in Spanish architecture after the Reconquista. Nor are Renaissance buildings confined to Europe. The debt to Italy in the architecture of Juan de Herrera is readily apparent in the Escorial, but Italian forms and Herreran monumental severity also characterize the early cathedrals in the Spanish Empire, notably Mexico City, Puebla, and Lima.

THE BELVEDERE SUMMER PALACE (1538–63) in the garden of the Hradčany in Prague was designed by Paolo Stella, an Italian architect and sculptor. The sandstone reliefs on the building are the work of Italian masons. The Belvedere is the earliest wholly Italianate building to have been built north of the Alps.

THE CATHEDRAL BASILICA OF ST JOHN THE APOSTLE AND EVANGELIST IN LIMA, Peru
(1598–1622), was designed by the Spanish architect Francisco Becerra, who had previously
designed Pueblo Cathedral in Mexico (1575). The two towers show the influence of Juan de
Herrera's Escorial, near Madrid. The interior aisles are Renaissance in style.

In the twenty-first century, the model of the Renaissance is characterized by its
breadth, but also the elasticity of its temporal boundaries. Italianists characteristically
regard the death of Raphael in 1520 and the Sack of Rome in 1527 as marking the end of
the High Renaissance. Students of the Spanish Golden Age, on the other hand, see the
period of Spain's artistic and literary zenith as beginning in the 1490s (the Reconquista
concluded in 1492) and extending to the early seventeenth century, with the death of
Lope de Vega in 1635. The advantage of treating the Renaissance primarily as a cultural
phenomenon rather than a period is that such temporal discrepancies are easily
accommodated. The chapters in this volume will therefore describe the history (especially the cultural history) of a long Renaissance, and one with permeable boundaries.

The study of the Renaissance is dominated by the history of art and architecture.
Two chapters in this volume attend to the seminal centres of art and architecture, and to
their influence. Francis Ames-Lewis's chapter is centred on Italy and beyond, and Paula
Nuttall and Richard Williams discuss the art and architecture of the Northern Renaissance in Flanders and beyond. Francis Ames-Lewis considers the access that Italian
Renaissance artists and architects had to the art and architecture of classical antiquity,
and how they interpreted those models for contemporary clients. Burckhardt's vision of
the Renaissance as centred on man rather than God is used as the starting point of the

discussion of the human form in Renaissance sculpture and portraiture. Italian Renaissance painting was indebted to survivals from classical antiquity, but perhaps more importantly, drew on the classical notion of mimesis, the imitation of nature. The contemporary models that were examined through the prism of mimesis included the work of North European artists, notably in Flanders.

The chapter on the art and architecture of northern Europe, by Paula Nuttall and Richard Williams, focuses on the effect on local traditions of the ideas of the Renaissance. The fifteenth and sixteenth centuries are treated separately, because the leaky watershed of 1500 marks a shift in the relationship between northern and southern art. In the fifteenth century, the art of northern Europe was in small measure influenced by developments in Italy, but the dominant change was a series of innovations in the north that paralleled or preceded comparable shifts in Italian art. In the sixteenth century the relationship changed, as the burgeoning humanist movement in the north began to facilitate direct Italian influence on the art of the north, which increasingly reflected the classical ideals of the Italian Renaissance. These divisions between north and south are not always sharp, partly because artists and architects were mobile, so there were Flemish artists working in Rome and Italian artists working in northern and central Europe, and artistic relations between centres such as Venice and Nuremberg facilitated constant exchanges.

From a twenty-first-century perspective, the fifteenth and sixteenth centuries seem to be dominated by wars and religion—and by wars arising out of confessional differences. It would be a mistake, however, to think of religion and warfare in terms of our own experience. Religion provided a language not only for articulating belief in God, but for many matters for which we would now use the language of politics or human emotion. The artistic image of the Madonna and Child, for example, was a centuries-old devotional image with pagan roots in the depiction of Isis and Horus, but at the hands of Renaissance (initially Venetian) artists, it became an intensely human image of a mother and her infant son.

Conversely, the art of the period can reflect strands of spirituality in the Renaissance. The crucifixion panel in Grünewald's Isenheim Altarpiece depicts the tortured body of Jesus on the cross, his skin covered with sores, his hands twisted with the pain of the nails, and his feet contorted by the single nail driven though them. The painting was originally hung in a monastic hospital that cared for the dying, and patients who gazed at the body of Jesus would not have thought of it in theological terms (seeing, for example, the three nails as an image of the Holy Trinity), but as a reflection of their own afflictions, and possibly as an affirmation that grace can survive the destruction of the body. Stella Fletcher's chapter on religion is an account of the spiritualities that characterize such belief, and of the refractions of those spiritualities in the art of the Renaissance.

Europe was continuously at war in the years covered by this volume, but there was neither large-scale destruction nor vast numbers of casualties by comparison with the wars of the twentieth century. In Renaissance Europe, many more people died of

MATHIS GOTHART NITHART (GRÜNEWALD), central panel of the Isenheim Altarpiece (1512–15). On the left the Virgin Mary is held by St John the Evangelist, and Mary Magdalene kneels in prayer. On the right John the Baptist points to Jesus, holding a scroll that reads (in Latin) 'he must increase but I must decrease' (John 3:30).

plague, and of childbirth, than were killed in battle. War could be brutal, but it was also regarded as an art, a subject explored in David Parrott's chapter on 'War and the State'. Machiavelli stood at the head of a long succession of theorists, many of whom saw war through the prism of the wars of classical antiquity. War was driven by aggrieved rulers who were motivated by considerations of honour, reputation, and vindication. The nature of warfare evolved constantly throughout the period, partly because of developments in weaponry and fortifications, but also because of the changing nature of armies and navies.

The study of the arts in the Renaissance has traditionally been focused on what are traditionally known as the fine arts: painting, sculpture, architecture, music (i.e. composition), and poetry. These are all spheres in which artists of the Renaissance produced some of the finest creations of European civilization. This preoccupation with the fine arts in subsequent centuries has, however, often played down the importance of other areas of creative endeavour. The distinction between the fine arts and the decorative arts that first emerged in the mid-eighteenth century, for example, established a hierarchy of taste: the fine arts were intended to give pleasure, while the decorative arts (then known as the mechanical arts) were deemed to be merely useful. Easel painting was a fine art, but the painting of figures on pottery was decorative; the exteriors of buildings (including their gardens) were the product of the fine art of architecture, but the interiors (including layout as well as fittings and furnishings) were decorative art; sculpting in marble was a fine art, but ivory-carving and wood-carving were crafts. Such distinctions persist in modern attitudes, and unhappily suppress popular awareness of some magnificent works of art, such as Benvenuto Cellini's salt cellar, now in the Kunsthistorisches Museum in Vienna. The virtuoso craftsmanship of this small piece, which was commissioned by King Francis I of France, melds decorative elements from the Fontainebleau School with sculpted figures in the idiom of Italian Mannerism. Such works of art have not captured the

BENVENUTO CELLINI, gold and enamel salt cellar (1540–3). The female figure of Tellus represents earth; the temple beside her held pepper. The male figure of Neptune represents the sea; the ship beside him held salt. The figures in the base represent the winds, the times of the day, and human activities.

public imagination because they are not classified as fine art. During the Renaissance, however, artists were members of craft guilds, and in many languages the terms 'artist' and 'artisan' were used interchangeably.

The chapter by Pamela Long and Andrew Morrall on craft and technology sets aside modern distinctions between art and craft, and indeed illuminates the convergence of artisanal and learned cultures during the Renaissance. The figures on Cellini's salt cellar are classical gods drawn from the learned tradition. This detail is indicative of an important phenomenon, which is the integration of the classical renewal that lies at the heart of the Renaissance into the design of crafts. Aristocratic patronage facilitated the transition of classical themes from the learned world to crafted objects ranging from tapestries to tableware. The trades that produced the craft and technology of the period were often innovative in fields such as agriculture, shipbuilding, military technology, and fortification.

Traditional narratives of the scientific revolution tend to run from Copernicus (a heliocentric cosmology) to Newton (a universe governed by scientific laws). Just as the Renaissance was deemed to begin in 1453 with the fall of Constantinople, so the scientific revolution that heralded the birth of modern science was deemed to begin in 1543, the year in which Copernicus' *De revolutionibus orbium coelestium* (On the Revolutions of the Heavenly Spheres), Vesalius' *De humani corporis fabrica* (On the fabric of the human body), and the German translation of Leonhart Fuchs's *De historia stirpium* (On the History of Plants) were published. Paula Findlen's chapter on 'The Renaissance of Science' presents these accomplishments as the culmination of developments in science and medicine in the course of the Renaissance. The humanist re-examination of the science and medicine of classical antiquity promoted debates about how best to explain the nature of the universe, the place of human beings within it, and the physiology of the human body.

The aspects of the cultural life of the Renaissance that are most difficult to recover include the performing arts, which come alive at the moment of performance but leave little evidence of the experience of those who witness them. Some performance spaces survive, such as the Teatro Olimpico in Vicenza, as do written accounts, financial records, musical scores, pictorial representations, and a range of artefacts, and performances can in some measure be reconstructed from such materials. Margaret McGowan's chapter on the performing arts focuses on festival, music, drama, and dance, and shows how these forms are shaped by the knowledge of classical antiquity promoted by the humanist scholars of the Renaissance. This is a theme that animates and connects all the chapters in this volume.

THE TEATRO OLIMPICO IN VICENZA (1580–4) was designed by Andrea Palladio and Vincenzo Scamozzi. The stage and semi-circular seating were inspired by the description of an ancient theatre in Vitruvius' *On Architecture*. The perspectival scenery was a Renaissance innovation based on the work of Sebastiano Serlio. The theatre is still used for plays and concerts.

CHAPTER 1

Humanism and the Classical Tradition

PETER MACK

RENAISSANCE humanism was a scholarly movement which profoundly changed
European society and intellectual life. By the end of the sixteenth century the educational reforms instigated by the humanists had altered the lives and ways of thinking
of elites throughout Europe and the New World of America. Even today our ideas of
proportion and beauty in buildings and literary works are deeply influenced by
classical ideals revived and transformed in the Renaissance.

Humanists occupied themselves with a range of studies centred on curiosity about
the world of classical antiquity. They aspired to write Latin prose like Cicero, to study
and interpret Latin literature, to collect manuscripts of ancient writers and to use those
manuscripts to improve their texts, to learn Greek, to understand ancient Greek poetry
and philosophy, and to write poetry and history which followed classical models. They
were hungry for facts about the history, customs, and beliefs of the ancient world, and
they tried to use their knowledge to guide conduct in their own time. They sought to
make their discoveries about pagan classical literature and thought compatible with their
Christian beliefs. Above all their goal was to become, and to enable others to become
better people, through their understanding of the greatness of the classical past.

Renaissance humanism sponsored a revolution in education. In the historian Paul
Kristeller's influential definition, humanistic studies (*studia humanitatis*) by the mid-
fifteenth century 'came to stand for a well-defined cycle of studies', which included
grammar, literary studies, rhetoric, poetics, history, and moral philosophy. But this was
the core rather than the limit. Scholars trained in humanistic subjects turned their
attention to improving texts and translations of the Bible, to political theory, to other
fields of philosophy, including cosmology and the nature of the soul, and to theology.
The Florentine Marsilio Ficino (1433–99) was as much a humanist in his attempt to
make Platonic philosophy part of Christianity as he was in his translations from Greek
into Latin for Cosimo de' Medici. The theorists and supporters of the Reformation and

the Counter-Reformation were trained by humanists and in their turn encouraged the growth of humanistic education.

Renaissance humanism relied heavily on the work of medieval scribes and scholars. If the Carolingian scribes had not copied classical manuscripts in the ninth and tenth centuries there would have been very few old Latin manuscripts for humanist scholars to 'discover' and disseminate. If Latin had not been revived in the ninth century and then continued to be taught as the learned language of Europe throughout the later Middle Ages there would have been no basis from which humanists could urge a return to the standards of classical Latinity. Medieval scholars and rulers created the universities and the Europe-wide network of learning which Renaissance humanists later adorned. Although humanist scholars tried to enhance their significance by denigrating the preceding Middle or Dark Ages, modern scholars acknowledge continuities between medieval and Renaissance learning. We need to insist that there was change but that in many cases it began gradually. The texts and teaching methods of early fifteenth-century humanist grammar schools differed only in some emphases from medieval schools, but by the middle of the sixteenth century the difference had become much greater. Writers like Machiavelli and Montaigne are unthinkable in the Middle Ages and are the direct products of humanist approaches to the ancient world.

Although the origins of Renaissance humanism lay with Paduan teachers of letter-writing and independent scholars like Petrarch (1304–74), the crucial support for the early development of humanism came from noble and civic patronage. Owning a library of classical texts or employing an ambassador who could deliver a competent neo-classical Latin oration became a matter of prestige for Italian cities and courts, which were soon imitated in that regard by the magnates and kings of other European countries. The success of humanists in persuading first the civil servants and then the rulers of Florence and Rome of the external publicity value of classical learning was essential to the diffusion of the humanist movement. Humanists occupied important administrative and diplomatic posts. They became chancellors of cities and states; some even became popes. They sometimes succeeded in displacing the hereditary nobility to become the trusted counsellors of rulers.

The spread and development of humanism depended on schools. It is a characteristic of northern European humanism, which in many ways surpassed Italian humanism after about 1500, that the most important humanists devoted themselves to the reform of schools and to writing new textbooks. Secular and religious princes were in a position to found new schools and colleges, and to reform the syllabus of existing institutions of learning. The Renaissance is marked by widespread writing about educational reform and by the elaboration of new programmes for many schools which in the sixteenth century had many shared features, both across the newly developing nation-states and across Europe as a whole. These educational reforms were the most far-reaching, enduring, and influential legacy of humanism.

A further crucial motor for the development of humanism was provided by the invention and diffusion of printing. Although manuscripts remained more beautiful and more prestigious in terms of aristocratic collecting well into the sixteenth century, the advent of print made it possible to circulate a newly discovered or newly improved text rapidly and uniformly throughout Europe. The reduction in the price of books made it possible for scholars and students to own several texts on the same subject where previously they might have been content with one. The Europe-wide distribution achieved by printers in the major centres like Venice, Paris, Basel, and Frankfurt gave authors of new Latin scholarly works the incentive of knowing that their ideas could be spread very rapidly throughout Europe.

As the nation-states became more powerful, the educated elite, including scholars, operated in a series of bilingual worlds, in which Latin was the international language of political and scholarly communication but the local vernacular was the language of the courts and of political power. The male elite was educated in Latin but they increasingly expressed themselves publicly in Italian, French, German, Spanish, and English. An Elizabethan bishop would write against the continental Roman Catholics in Latin and against the local puritans in English. Important and influential though neo-Latin instructional works were, the enduring legacy of humanism lies in vernacular literature, treatises, and Bible translations.

Origins of humanism and Petrarch

Latin learning and classical Latin literature could hardly have survived in Western Europe without the activities of Irish and English monks in the sixth to eighth centuries. They cultivated Latin grammar, collected, read, and copied classical Latin texts, and eventually re-exported Latin learning to the European continent in the time of Charlemagne (768–814). The towering figures here were Bede (673–735), who wrote Bible commentaries, grammar textbooks, and works on chronology as well as his Latin *Ecclesiastical History of the English People* (731), and Alcuin (c.740–804), who was called from the centre of learning at York to help Charlemagne establish new monastic schools in his empire, in France, Germany, and northern Italy. In the ninth century the monasteries founded by Anglo-Saxon missionaries produced copies of most of the classical Latin texts which have survived, many of them written in the new Caroline minuscule script, which later humanists misidentified as the ancient Roman handwriting, and reproduced in the italic and roman typefaces we still use today. For many of the classical Latin texts which we read today, a single copy had survived into the ninth century, when most of them were recopied in sufficient quantities to increase their chances of recovery. Lupus of Ferrières (c.805–62) collected, copied, and collated manuscripts, encouraging his friends and pupils to do likewise. What was recovered in the ninth century was never truly lost again; while some texts languished safe but uncopied in monastic libraries, others were recopied, especially in the great Benedictine monastery of Montecassino in the eleventh and early twelfth centuries. From the monasteries Latin spread to courts and universities, becoming the international language of learning and high-level church communication. But this form of Latin was still a living language, much influenced by the local vernaculars and in many ways unlike the careful artistic Latin prose of classical writers like Cicero.

A second crucial factor in the revival of ancient learning was the political life of Italian city-states in the thirteenth and fourteenth centuries. By 1250 cities like Padua, Florence, Venice, and Siena had established republican systems of government in which political speech-making was an important part of the fabric of city life. At the same time as the essential foundations of modern accountancy and international banking were being laid, many merchants in these cities were wealthy enough to demand a role in political activities. While he was in exile in France, Brunetto Latini (*c*.1225–93), first Chancellor of the Florentine republic and teacher of Dante, wrote an Italian translation of part of Cicero's rhetorical textbook, *De inventione*, with a commentary which made connections to the art of letter-writing. At almost the same time *Rhetorica ad Herennium* was translated into Latin by Guidotto da Bologna. Latini valued what Cicero and other classical writers could teach but, in spite of his own Latin learning, he believed that Cicero's teachings should be made available to readers of the vernacular.

In the twelfth century, interest in classical rhetoric had taken a different turn with the compilation of arts of letter-writing which combined instructions for writing various types of official letter in Latin with observations based on classical Latin rhetoric. From the late eleventh to the late fourteenth century dozens of letter-writing manuals (*artes dictaminis*) were composed and the teaching of Latin letter-writing flourished as part of a practical training for officials and notaries at the margins of medieval universities, notably Bologna. According to one school of thought the earliest humanists were the heirs of the writers of *artes dictaminis*. Another school of thought, in contrast, sees the early humanists as asserting the value of classical models in an age of anti-classicism. The context here would be the anti-classical polemics of the Bolognese professor of *dictamen*, Boncompagno da Signa (1165–1240).

The first of the humanists was the Paduan notary Lovato Lovati (1241–1309), who read widely in classical lyric poetry and composed Latin verse epistles, a treatise on classical Latin poetic metre, and a short commentary on Seneca's tragedies. Lovati's pupil, the Paduan notary and diplomat Albertino Mussato (1261–1329) wrote in Latin a defence of poetry, a history modelled on Livy, and a verse tragedy, *Ecerinis*, modelled on Seneca's tragedies, which warned his fellow citizens against tyranny. These Paduan early humanists exhibited an enthusiasm for classical literature, a wish to understand it better, and a desire to imitate Latin literature in their own private and literary writings. In their public letters they continued to follow the models of the medieval *ars dictaminis*.

Opposite: SIMONE MARTINI, Frontispiece to Petrarch's Vergil. Petrarch commissioned this frontispiece from the great Sienese painter Simone Martini in Avignon around 1336 for his manuscript of Vergil's works. The frontispiece shows Vergil writing, the commentator Servius opening the curtain, and three figures representing Vergil's three great poems, the *Aeneid*, the *Georgics*, and the *Eclogues*.

Ytala pclaros tellus alis alma poetas/
Sz tibi grecos redic hic attingere metas.

Serimus altiloqui regens archana maioms.
Ut pateant duubz pastoribz atoz colonis.

MRacia uenplen tus tilia aagms fineis
Saue rolta forutunil nudato a salut pmpri

Francesco Petrarca (Petrarch) was the outstanding scholar and writer of his generation. The son of an exiled Florentine notary, he soon abandoned his own legal studies and took advantage of the accumulation of French and Italian manuscripts of Latin texts around the papal court in Avignon. He collected and copied manuscripts, putting together the most complete version of Livy's history available in his day and personally correcting it by comparing it with other manuscripts. His Livy is the famous British Library Harley manuscript 2493, later owned and corrected by Lorenzo Valla. In Avignon, Petrarch commissioned from Simone Martini the frontispiece for his Vergil, showing Vergil, Aeneas, and the ancient commentator Servius at the top, with scenes illustrating the subjects of the *Eclogues* and *Georgics* below. He also found manuscripts of Cicero (the oration *Pro Archia* and the *Letters to Atticus*) and Propertius. His own list of his favourite books includes Cicero, Seneca (*Moral Epistles* and *Tragedies*), Valerius Maximus, Livy, Macrobius, Aulus Gellius, Vergil, Lucan, Statius, Horace (especially the *Odes*), Juvenal, St Augustine, Boethius, and a Latin translation of Aristotle's *Ethics*. He owned a manuscript of Homer's *Iliad* but he never succeeded in learning enough Greek to read it. In Latin Petrarch wrote letters (in prose and verse), philosophical treatises, pastoral poems, and an unfinished epic, *Africa*, on the life of the Roman general Scipio Africanus. He strove to uphold classical standards of Latin expression and wrote biting critiques of the misguided thinking and poor use of Latin by scholastic philosophers and British logicians. He was the first post-classical author to publish collections of his letters. Petrarch's name lives today because of his Italian poetry and particularly for his *Canzoniere*, the collection of poems celebrating his love for Laura, which was much imitated by fifteenth- and sixteenth-century Italian, French, and English poets.

To the following generation of humanists Petrarch served as an important model in several different ways: for the breadth of his curiosity about the ancient world; for his wide knowledge of Latin literature and his attempt to relate this knowledge to his own experience; for his discovery of new manuscripts and new texts and his attempts to improve the texts of works he knew; for his attempts to write Latin poems and letters worthy of comparison with classical Latin; for his critique of scholastic Latinity; and for his ambition to learn Greek.

Italian humanism of the fifteenth century

Coluccio Salutati (1331–1406), Chancellor of Florence for thirty years, was among Petrarch's correspondents. Like Petrarch he sought to improve the texts of Latin authors and built up a large library, uniting for the first time for centuries Cicero's *Letters to Atticus* with the newly discovered *Letters to his Friends*, a Carolingian manuscript found in the cathedral library of Vercelli in 1392. He also owned the oldest complete manuscript of the poet Tibullus and one of the three primary manuscripts of Catullus. His private letters imitated Cicero's. He established Greek teaching in Florence when he persuaded Manuel Chrysoloras (1350–1415) to lecture at the university between 1397 and 1400. Chrysoloras taught Greek to the next generation of Florentine humanists and encouraged them to make translations from Greek into Latin, not according to the old word by word method but attempting to formulate the ideas expressed in the Greek text in good Latin sentences. He composed a grammar (*Erotemata*) for the use of Western European students, which became the first Greek grammar to be printed (in 1471) and was used by Erasmus and Reuchlin. Salutati also engaged Giovanni Malpaghini (1346–1422) to teach rhetoric in Florence. According to the historian Ronald Witt, this was the decisive point at which public letter-writing began to prefer classical models of Latin epistolography over the medieval *ars dictaminis*.

Among Chrysoloras's pupils was Leonardo Bruni (1370–1444), who translated Aristotle's *Politics* and *Ethics* into a Latin which fitted with humanist theories of translation and ideas of Latin style. He also translated nine of Plutarch's *Lives* and several of Plato's dialogues, including *Phaedo, Apology,* and *Gorgias* into Latin. He used Greek historians such as Polybius and Xenophon for his Latin historical compilations *On the First Punic War, On the Italian War,* and *Commentaries on Greek Matters.* Bruni later became Chancellor of Florence and wrote in Latin a *Praise of the City of Florence* (1404) and a *History of the Florentine People in Twelve Books* (1416–44). He wrote Italian biographies of Petrarch and Dante. Bruni organized a programme of Italian translations of his Latin works. His *On the First Punic War* was the subject of five separate Italian translations in the fifteenth century and survives in 120 vernacular manuscripts. It was printed twelve times in Italian before 1600, as against five Latin editions. Evidently there was a great demand for Roman history in the vernacular. Although Bruni's scholarship and history were firmly based on his knowledge of Greek and his commitment to a good classical Latin style, he believed in using the vernacular to spread the benefits of humanist learning.

Another pupil of Chrysoloras was the great educator Guarino Guarini (1374–1460), who followed his master back to Constantinople (1403–9) in order to perfect his Greek and to acquire manuscripts of Greek texts. Guarini ran a private school in Verona (1419–29) and then established a court school in Ferrara (1429–60). The emphasis of his teaching was on giving pupils knowledge about all aspects of the ancient world, teaching them Greek, and helping them to acquire a Latin writing style which approximated to classical standards of expression. His method of reading focused on style, and on teaching his pupils to collect vocabulary, maxims, and literary examples of the employment of figures of rhetoric for use in their own compositions. He also put considerable emphasis on teaching his pupils the principles of classical rhetoric, the art of composing speeches and other texts. He wrote a new commentary on the anonymous *Rhetorica ad Herennium*, which most people up to the middle of the sixteenth century believed to have been the work of Cicero, and which had been the most important first primer of rhetoric since the Middle Ages and continued to be so. His commentary focused on the literal teaching of the text, commented in detail on its language and style, provided contextual information from ancient history, and gave examples from Cicero's orations, especially *Pro Milone*, which showed the use of the doctrines. He makes many references to Cicero's rhetorical works and to the first-century Roman rhetorician Quintilian. His method of grammar school teaching was

THE COPY OF THE COMPLETE TEXT OF QUINTILIAN'S *The Orator's Education* which Poggio Bracciolini found in a monastery in St Gall, Switzerland. Most medieval manuscripts contained an incomplete version of the text. This eleventh-century manuscript was soon copied by Poggio so that other humanists could have access to the complete Quintilian.

diffused by the account of his school written by his son Battista. Guarino's near contemporaries Pier Paolo Vergerio (1368/70–1444) and Gaspare Barzizza (1360–1430) wrote works on education and grammar teaching which promoted the humanist approach to grammar school teaching.

The greatest of the manuscript recoverers, Poggio Bracciolini (1380–1459), was also a member of Salutati's circle, though not a pupil of Chrysoloras. As a papal secretary Poggio attended the Council of Constance (1414–17) which ended the schism in the papacy. From Constance in 1415 Poggio made an expedition to the Burgundian monastery of Cluny, where he found an ancient manuscript of five of Cicero's speeches, two of which were previously unknown. In 1416 and 1417 he went to St Gall, where he found a text of Lucretius, a complete Quintilian, Asconius' commentary on five of Cicero's speeches, as well as texts by Silius Italicus and Manilius. On later manuscript collecting expeditions he found eight previously unknown speeches of Cicero, Statius' *Silvae*, and Petronius' *Trimalchio's Feast*. Besides his extraordinary discoveries of old manuscripts and new texts, Poggio was very influential in improving texts and circulating them. Inspired by his example, Gerardo Landriani found Cicero's *Brutus* and the complete texts of his *De oratore* and *Orator* in 1421. Other discoveries around this time included the minor works of Tacitus and several new comedies by Plautus.

The growth of humanism depended on the support of wealthy and powerful patrons who received dedications, founded libraries, and commissioned manuscripts and translations. Because they were convinced of the value to the city of classical scholarship and stylish Latin writing, such patrons formed an influential network of support which encouraged scholars and educational reforms. One crucial aspect of this support was the founding and support of public libraries. Niccolò Niccoli (1364–1437) was the son of a rich cloth merchant and a member of social circles associated with humanism. As a protégé of Salutati who copied manuscripts around 1400 alongside Poggio, he played a role in the development of the humanistic script, based on the Caroline minuscule, which was the medium for many attractive and readable humanist manuscripts. Niccoli persuaded Florentine magnates to employ humanist scholars as tutors to educate their children and collected ancient cameos and sculptures, and, above all, manuscripts. Poggio's correspondence shows how he helped Niccoli acquire copies of old manuscripts. Although he could not read Greek, Niccoli owned 146 Greek manuscripts which were eventually, in pursuance of his wishes, incorporated in a public library in the Dominican convent of San Marco. The Florentine bookseller Vespasiano da Bisticci (1421–98) once organized forty-five scribes to produce 200 volumes in less than two years for Cosimo de' Medici (1389–1464) for the library of the Badia of Fiesole. The list of books for copying was compiled by the humanist Tommaso Parentucelli (1397–1455), who later became Pope Nicholas V. In the 1470s Vespasiano organized copying of manuscripts for the library of Federico di Montefeltro in Urbino. This collection was later incorporated in the Vatican library established by Nicholas V in the 1450s. Nicholas V commissioned Latin translations of many Greek authors, including Thucydides, Herodotus, Xenophon, Theophrastus, Ptolemy, and

AN ELEVENTH-CENTURY GREEK MANUSCRIPT OF PLATO'S dialogues which was in Florence in the fifteenth century when the later pages of the manuscript were written to complete the collection. It was probably one of the manuscripts which came from Constantinople in the fifteenth century and which preserved the Greek text of Plato for printing and study in Western Europe.

Strabo. As a participant in the Council of Constance, Cosimo had helped finance Poggio's book-collecting expeditions. He was able to use such contacts to enrich his own library with classical texts and new discoveries. In 1492 his grandson Lorenzo de' Medici (1449–92) dispatched Janos Lascaris on a journey to various Byzantine provinces to collect Greek manuscripts. He returned with more than 200. On Lorenzo's death the family library made available to the citizens of Florence consisted of over 1,000 volumes.

Ottoman threats to the Byzantine Empire and the eventual fall of Constantinople in 1453 led to more contacts between East and West and to the migration westwards of many scholars and manuscripts. Basilios Bessarion (1403–72) first came to Italy as a member of the Greek delegation to the Council of Ferrara-Florence (1438–45), which aimed to reunite the Western and Eastern churches. After he settled in Italy and was made a Cardinal his house in Rome became a centre of Greek studies. He built up an exceptional library of Greek manuscripts which he donated to the city of Venice as the basis of a public library and so that Greek émigrés might have access to as complete a library of Greek texts (including Christian texts) as possible. Cardinal Bessarion made a new Latin translation of Aristotle's *Metaphysics* and used philological arguments based on original Greek manuscripts to resolve problems of theological controversy and in the text of the Bible.

The greatest scholar of the first half of the fifteenth century was probably Lorenzo Valla (1407–57), who was born into a family associated with the papal court, and worked for King Alfonso the Magnanimous while he was establishing his rule over Naples, before returning to Rome in 1447, first as papal *scriptor* and later as apostolic secretary and professor of rhetoric. During the 1430s Valla conceived and began to publish a series of works which he revised throughout his career, improving them as his knowledge of Latin and Greek literature increased. His dialogue *On the True Good* (1431) attacks conventional Christianizing Stoicism by opposing to it an original amalgam of Christianity and Epicureanism. Inspired by the disagreeable experience of teaching rhetoric at the law-dominated University of Pavia, *Refoundation of Dialectic and Philosophy* (1439) attacks the basis of Aristotelian logic and metaphysics and proposes in its place a simplified logic operating in everyday language, which for Valla was the language of Cicero and Quintilian. Valla continues with Petrarch's sweeping and often unfair attacks on the barbarous Latin and impenetrable complexity of Scholastic philosophers. In his view arguments should be expressed with clarity using classical Latin vocabulary and constructions, checked against the usage of the best authors. His most successful work, *Elegantiae* (1441), reformulates the rules of Latin syntax and the usage of Latin vocabulary on the basis of analysing examples from the whole corpus of Latin literature. One of Valla's aims was to recover the distinctions between closely related words which had been observed in classical Latin but had been lost by medieval writers. These additional distinctions made it possible to think more precisely in Latin and to follow the thought of the classical authors more carefully. In *On the Donation of Constantine* (1440), Valla shows on historical, linguistic, and rhetorical grounds that the document which purported to transfer power over the Roman Empire to the papacy was a later forgery and could not possibly have been written at the time of Constantine. His *Annotations on the New Testament* (1443) corrects the Latin of the Vulgate translation (the official Bible of the Roman Catholic Church) by comparing it with manuscripts of the original Greek text. In 1447 Valla completed his *Emendations on the Text of Six Books of Livy*, the result of a careful study of manuscripts of books 21–6.

Knowledge of the newly discovered complete text of Quintilian was fundamental to all Valla's works, which are based on close investigation of classical Latin usage and on the application of principles taken from rhetoric. Valla was active in textual criticism and the collation of manuscripts, as evidenced by his work on Petrarch's copy of Livy. Valla's thorough knowledge of Greek was the inspiration for his work on the text of the New Testament and for his Latin translations of Thucydides and Herodotus. His translation of Thucydides is still important to editors because Valla had access to a manuscript tradition which is now lost. The translation is so exact that scholars can reconstruct places in which he has amended his Greek text on the basis of the manuscript he consulted. Valla was unafraid to draw controversial conclusions from his linguistic discoveries. Much of his effort was devoted to criticisms of Aristotelian and scholastic philosophers and to controversies with other humanist scholars including Poggio. In his own lifetime and immediately afterwards Valla was a controversial figure whose views could be ignored and several of whose major works (including *On the True Good*, the *Refoundation of Dialectic and Philosophy*, and the *Annotations on the New Testament*) were unknown or little circulated. The exception was his grammatical masterpiece, the *Elegantiae*, which was an important reference work both in Italy and northern Europe in the sixteenth century, with forty-five manuscripts surviving and 152 printed editions before 1620.

Valla's pupil Niccolò Perotti (1429–80) composed an unfinished commentary on Martial, *Cornucopia or Commentaries on the Latin Language*, which is in effect a dictionary of a good part of the Latin language. His *Rudimenta grammatices* (1468) became the basic humanist Latin grammar, insisting on classical standards of expression. It includes a humanist version of the treatise on letter-writing and, in later editions, rules for the composition of Latin verse, which makes it a complete elementary course in Latin. It was printed 115 times before 1500 and a total of 133 times up to the last printing in 1535. The earlier editions are mostly from Italy (and especially Venice) and Paris; the later ones mainly from Germany.

In contrast to Valla's life of wandering and controversy, the translator and philosopher Marsilio Ficino (1433–99) spent most of his life in Florence supported by Medici patronage. Cosimo de' Medici commissioned from him Latin translations first of the *Hermetica*, Greek texts which apparently preserved ancient Egyptian theologico-magical wisdom, completed in 1463, and then of all Plato's *Dialogues*, published in 1484. Ficino eventually added translations of the major Neoplatonic philosophers Porphyry, Iamblichus, and Plotinus. He wrote commentaries on several of Plato's dialogues,

PETRARCH'S COPY OF LIVY WITH VALLA'S ANNOTATIONS. Petrarch was largely responsible for gathering together the surviving books of Livy's *History of Rome*. Petrarch personally copied some thirty folio pages of this manuscript and added annotations. This manuscript of Livy was later owned by Lorenzo Valla, who annotated its text and compared it with other manuscripts.

including *Parmenides, Sophist, Philebus, Timaeus, Phaedrus,* and *Symposium*. His original works included *Platonic Theology: On the Immortality of the Soul* (1474), which seeks to prove the immortality of the soul through analysis of its attributes, to refute rival accounts of the soul's mortality, and to reconcile Platonic views of the soul and the afterlife with Christianity, and *Three Books on Life* (1489), a largely medical work based on the ancient theory of the four humours, which included descriptions of some magical processes of healing involving astrology and amulets. Ficino believed that Plato's works (and indeed the *Hermetica*) incorporated earlier wisdom (the so-called Ancient Theology) which God had entrusted to Moses, Solomon, and the Egyptians and which could be used to supplement both the Old Testament and the later and more complete revelation of his plans conveyed through the life and teaching of Jesus. Ficino was a healer, a priest, and a philosopher as well as a translator. His syncretic philosophy combining Christianity, Platonism, and magic was one of the distinctive achievements of the Renaissance. For most Renaissance readers Ficino's Latin translations of Plato, usually published with his commentaries, were the principal means of access to Plato's thought. His translation of Plato was first printed in 1484 in an unusually large edition (for the time) of 1,025 copies which sold out within six years. Plato was not printed in Greek until 1513. Ficino's Latin translations and interpretations of Plato and of the Neoplatonists had an immense influence on Renaissance thought, literature, and culture.

Angelo Poliziano (in English, Politian, 1454–94), the greatest classical scholar of the fifteenth century, was educated in Florence. Lorenzo de' Medici took him into his household as tutor to his children, in which guise he appears leading his charges to greet their father and his political associates in the fresco by Domenico Ghirlandaio in the Sassetti Chapel of the Church of Santa Trinita, Florence. Poliziano was a fine poet in both Italian and Latin, and lectured on classical literature at the University of Florence. His Latin letters were treated as models of style by sixteenth-century teachers and were quoted and cited alongside Cicero's letters in many Renaissance letter-writing manuals. His greatest work of scholarship was the *Miscellanea*, a collection of studies of varying length on particular scholarly issues, mainly improvements in the text of various Latin authors on the basis of a collation of manuscripts or a comparison with Greek sources. The book also included short essays on miscellaneous topics such as the origin of the names of the days of the week, the invention of purple, and the correct spelling of the name Vergil. He knew Greek very well and was able to use the text of the Greek poet Callimachus to emend a corrupt passage in one of Catullus' (Latin) poems, which he recognized as being based on it. Poliziano examined and collated old manuscripts of Terence, Vergil, and Seneca. In his manuscript collations on printed texts he used sigla abbreviations (individual letters or other short forms identifying particular manuscripts) to distinguish between the different manuscripts he was using. He constructed arguments based on the history of manuscripts, showing for example that the received text of Cicero's *Letters to his Friends* depended on a lost manuscript in which some of the quires had been bound together in the wrong order. He took an interest in post-classical authors in both Latin and Greek.

DOMENICO GHIRLANDAIO, *The Confirmation of the Franciscan Rule*, Sassetti Chapel, Santa Trinita, Florence. In the foreground Angelo Poliziano, as tutor, leads his pupils up to greet their father, Lorenzo de' Medici.

He knew Greek well enough to compose Greek epigrams and, unlike earlier Italian humanists, to make improvements in the texts of Greek authors. He interested himself in disciplines allied to philology such as the study of ancient coins and inscriptions. Poliziano originated methods and lines of approach in manuscript studies and textual scholarship which came to full fruition only centuries later. Even though he never published an edition of a classical text, modern classicists regard Poliziano as the greatest scholar of the fifteenth century and one of the most significant in the history of their discipline.

Count Giovanni Pico della Mirandola (1463–94) was a precocious polymath who knew Greek, Latin, and Hebrew. He is famous for offering to defend 900 theses on religion, natural philosophy, and magic against all critics in Rome in 1486, before the pope halted the exercise. The theses represent an attempt to reconcile Platonic, Aristotelian, Christian, and Jewish knowledge. Pico was a friend of Poliziano, and later also of Savonarola, and was supported by the patronage of Lorenzo de' Medici. He wrote a vernacular commentary on Benivieni's *Canzone*, itself based on Ficino's interpretation of Plato's *Symposium*. His principal published work was the *Heptaplus*, a cabbalistic interpretation of the first twenty-six verses of Genesis. Pico was the first Christian to have extensive knowledge of the Cabbala, which he owed to the Jewish scholars who taught him Hebrew. His *Oration on the Dignity of Man*, originally intended to introduce the defence of his theses, presents man as essentially free to choose between animal and angelic forms of life, while urging that the individual should choose the latter in order to attain moral transformation, intellectual knowledge, and eventually union with the infinite. Like Ficino he believed in the doctrine of ancient theology, which regards the knowledge of Orpheus, Pythagoras, Zoroaster, and Moses as an earlier form of divine wisdom to be used alongside the Christian revelation.

The arrival of printing in Italy gave a fresh impetus to the development and diffusion of humanism because it enabled many identical copies of classical texts and new works of scholarship to be produced rapidly and distributed throughout Europe. Cicero's *De oratore* was the second book to be printed in Italy (the first was an ancient grammar text) when Arnold Pannartz and Konrad Sweynheim set up their press in the Benedictine Abbey at Subiaco in 1465. Between 1465 and 1475 almost all the classical Latin texts appeared in print in Italy, not all of them in very good editions. Printing made it possible for scholars to build up comprehensive working libraries relatively quickly. Printed books facilitated collation of manuscripts, as we see for example in Poliziano's manuscript annotations on the Rome 1473 edition of the elder Pliny's *Natural History*. Printing made classical texts available in quantities impossible before. By the end of the fifteenth century nearly 200 editions of Vergil and over 300 of works by Cicero had been printed, mainly in Italy. From 1494 to 1515 the scholar-printer Aldus Manutius (*c.*1450–1515) produced a great series of classical editions in Venice, including the first editions of many Greek texts, such as the complete works of Aristotle (1495–8), Sophocles, Euripides, Herodotus, Thucydides, Demosthenes, and the Greek rhetoricians. By 1515, thanks largely to Aldus, all the major classical authors were in print in serviceable and often beautiful editions. Venice's role as an international centre of trade and printing meant that new editions could circulate rapidly throughout Europe. Thanks to fifteenth-century Italian scholarship and printing, the future of classical texts and the linguistic and scholarly knowledge needed to interpret them had been secured.

Northern European humanism 1470–1530 and Spain

Humanism in northern Europe developed out of contacts with Italy in the fifteenth century. Humphrey, Duke of Gloucester (1391–1447), commissioned a Latin translation of Aristotle's *Politics* from Leonardo Bruni, which was delivered in 1433. Pier Candido Decembrio (1392–1477) dedicated his translation of Plato's *Republic*, completed in 1441, to Duke Humphrey and assisted him in building up the collection of classical manuscripts which he donated to Oxford University. In the fifteenth century students from the Netherlands, Germany, Spain, and Britain frequently travelled to Italy to study law and medicine. Some of these students acquired a taste for humanistic learning which they brought back to their own countries and which led to reforms in the teaching of Latin and the beginnings of Greek teaching. Where earlier northern humanists had had to study in Italy in order to learn Greek, by about 1490 it was possible to learn Greek in northern Europe, with the result that many important northern humanists of the sixteenth century, such as Erasmus, More, Vives, and Melanchthon, either never went to Italy or went there only when they were already fully educated.

The first important Dutch humanist, Rudolph Agricola (1444–85) went to Pavia to study law in 1469. He soon gave up his law studies to devote himself to improving his Latin style and his knowledge of classical Latin literature, acting as an unofficial tutor in

QUENTIN MASSYS, Portrait of Erasmus, Hampton Court. This is most likely the portrait which Erasmus sent, together with a companion portrait of the printer Pieter Gillis, to his friend Thomas More in 1517, to commemorate their friendship.

humanist subjects to other Dutch and German students who helped support his further studies. In 1475 he moved to Ferrara in order to learn Greek. For a time he was employed as an organist by Count Ercole I, who frequently engaged musicians and composers from the Low Countries. Agricola played a part in the official ceremonies of both Italian universities, giving public Latin orations at the installation of three rectors (Pavia, 1472–4) and for the inauguration of the university year (Ferrara, 1476).

In all Agricola spent ten years in Italy and it was there that he conceived and began to write his masterpiece, *On Dialectical Invention* (1479), which was inspired by the advanced teaching in Latin composition he had been giving to his northern fellow students, who were already masters of arts when he began to teach them. *On Dialectical Invention* presents a new approach to the process of planning a text, setting out from a reconsideration of the principles of communication in the light of examples from classical Latin poems and orations. Thus Agricola always foregrounds the need to convey a message to a particular audience in the most persuasive way and investigates the ways in which passages from classical literature have been shaped to achieve this end. He developed new principles for planning texts from a combination of doctrines taken from rhetoric and dialectic textbooks. The analysis of examples of effective writing in the light of the general principles of communication is at the heart of Agricola's project. With its original treatment of the topics of invention, the relationship between narrative and argument, the arousal of emotion, and the organization of texts, *On Dialectical Invention* is the most original rhetoric text of the Renaissance and one of the five most important works ever written on the subject. It also includes instructions for making dialectical analyses of texts, which Agricola later exemplified in his commentary on Cicero's *Pro lege Manilia* and which became a sub-genre of northern humanist literary commentary. Agricola's contribution to rhetorical theory may be compared with those made by Valla and Poliziano to classical philology.

On his return to Frisia, Agricola became town secretary of Groningen. His personal fame among northern students and the travel required by this diplomatic post enabled him to inspire other would-be humanists in the Low Countries. He helped Alexander Hegius (1433/40–98), who was one of Erasmus' teachers, learn Greek, and he wrote a letter on the humanist educational programme, *On the Formation of Studies* (1482), to the composer Jacques Barbireau (1455–91), who had tried to persuade him to open a humanistic school in Antwerp. This letter also includes instructions for compiling commonplace books in which pupils would record phrases, arguments, and stories from their reading for reuse in their own compositions. Agricola's instructions for what became one of the staples of grammar school training were later elaborated by Erasmus and Melanchthon. His last years in Heidelberg were devoted to the study of Hebrew and to religious writings in support of his pupil Johann von Dalberg (1445–1503), who was Bishop of Worms and Privy Councillor to the Elector Palatine.

William Grocyn (c.1449–1519) and Thomas Linacre (c.1460–1524) were both private pupils of Poliziano in Florence. Grocyn returned to establish Greek teaching in Oxford in the 1490s, while Linacre went on to study medicine in Padua. Linacre helped Aldus Manutius with the publication of the Greek Aristotle. He later won fame for his Latin translations of works by Galen and for his works on Latin grammar. Johann Reuchlin (1455–1522) learned Greek from Chrysoloras's *Erotemata* and taught Greek in Tübingen in the 1480s. He wrote a Latin dictionary (1478) and composed comedies in Latin (1498, 1504). He was the first northern humanist to interest himself in Hebrew, perhaps as a result of time spent with Johann von Dalberg in Heidelberg in the 1490s. He collected Hebrew manuscripts, wrote a dictionary and grammar of Hebrew in Latin (1506), the first Christian to do so, and composed Latin dialogues on the Cabbala (1494, 1517).

Erasmus of Rotterdam (?1469–1536; see portrait on page 27) became the most prominent European intellectual of the early sixteenth century. He provided programmes for founders of schools and collaborated closely with printers to improve the texts of classical writers in circulation and to ensure the availability of his own works. He made notable contributions to the study of the Bible and developed a European network of correspondents whose studies he encouraged and corrected through his letters. The establishment of grammar schools concentrating on classical literature and on promoting classical standards of Latin composition and the acquisition of Greek was crucial to the success of the humanist movement in northern Europe. Erasmus contributed decisively to the syllabus of the new grammar schools with his tract *On the Method of Study* (1511), which was often printed with Agricola's *On the Formation of Studies* and other humanist texts on education. Erasmus produced textbooks and editions for school use (including editions of the most elementary readers such as the *Distichs of Cato*), offering a model which many first-rate northern humanists followed, of concerning themselves with educational theory and working to provide textbooks which would further the humanistic movement in grammar schools.

Erasmus wrote *On Copia* (1512), which one might gloss as 'on abundance of subject matter and expression', the most successful rhetoric book of the sixteenth century, for St Paul's School in London, founded by John Colet (1467–1519), Dean of St Paul's and one of Erasmus' strongest supporters in England. The book provides a series of well-explained methods of varying a pre-existing text, using the tropes of rhetoric and the topics of invention, along with examples and collections of alternative expressions for much-used phrases. Erasmus designed the book for grammar-school pupils as a preparation for the classical rhetoric manuals by Cicero and Quintilian. *On Copia* puts particular emphasis on the use of description, comparison, examples, and axioms within texts. It teaches pupils the method of constructing commonplace books. Erasmus' *On Writing Letters* (1521) taught practical letter-writing, one of the principal composition exercises in the grammar school, adapting classical rhetorical teaching to modern conditions. It provided a great deal of helpful advice on self-presentation in relation to an audience, which pupils could have used in their own writing of letters and speeches as well as in the conduct of their everyday lives.

Erasmus' *Adages* (first published in 1500) is a dictionary of classical Latin proverbs, intended to assist pupils in understanding texts and to provide them with materials with which to embellish their own writings. When Erasmus had acquired a better knowledge of Greek he published with Aldus Manutius in 1508 a much expanded version incorporating proverbs from Greek texts and exploring the connections between proverbs in both languages. He always emphasized the value of proverbs in preserving and conveying ancient moral teaching. The further expanded edition of 1515 incorporated long essays on moral and political topics in which Erasmus showed the way in which proverbs and techniques of amplification could be used to compose impressive and persuasive arguments.

In 1505 Erasmus published for the first time Lorenzo Valla's *Annotations on the New Testament*. Since he believed that an improved Latin text of the New Testament would help recall the church to its former purity, he set about making a Greek text on which to base a new translation of the Bible intended to correct errors in the Vulgate. He studied Greek New Testament manuscripts available to him in England in 1512–13 and the writings of the Church Fathers in search of improved readings. In Basel in 1515–16 he had access to five Greek manuscripts, but he based most of his readings on a twelfth-century manuscript of no great value. Nevertheless his publication of his *Novum Instrumentum* in 1516, which included a Greek text, a new Latin translation, and annotations interpreting the text, marked a new era in biblical scholarship. Text, translation, and annotations were further improved in subsequent editions. Erasmus strengthened the evangelical message with his *Paraphrases* on the books of the New Testament, which use the techniques of rhetorical amplification to make his audience understand and feel the force of the Christian message. Erasmus' Greek text was the basis for translations of the New Testament by Martin Luther (1483–1546) into German (1522), by William Tyndale (c.1494–1536) into English (1526), and by the translators of the King James Version (1611).

Erasmus was also active as an editor of patristic and classical texts. His somewhat faulty edition of the works of Seneca appeared from Basel in 1515 and his much better edition of St Jerome in 1516. His Seneca was greatly improved in its second edition of 1529, for which he had access to better manuscripts and made many more emendations. Erasmus enriched Latin literature with his mock encomium *The Praise of Folly* (1511), which promoted his brand of evangelism based on a recognition of the simple and revolutionary teaching of Christ and a rejection of the worldly prudence of the established church, and with his dialogues and his many letters to his wide circle of friends. To receive a letter from Erasmus, and for that letter to be published in one of his printed volumes, was a much sought-after honour for scholars and noblemen. Since Erasmus was hostile to many of the same failings of the church, such as the sale of indulgences, he was at first sympathetic to Luther and refused to attack him. Later he clarified his adherence to Catholic doctrine, asserting the importance of the freedom of the will against Luther's theology of predestination. Although he remained faithful to Rome, even moving from Basel when it became Protestant in 1529, his attacks on the church hierarchy and his insistence that the methods of philology be applied to the Bible and the Church Fathers encouraged a critical approach to the religious establishment. Unintentionally he was one of the forerunners of the Reformation.

Printing was first established in France, in Paris, in 1470. In 1471 the works of Sallust were printed. By 1478 there was a press in Lyon which later became a centre of humanistic and classical printing. From the 1470s Italians were appointed to lecture at the University of Paris and Greek teaching was available there from about 1476, though it was greatly strengthened by the work of Janos Lascaris (c.1445–1535) from 1495. Lascaris was also involved in organizing the royal library and in procuring Greek manuscripts from Milan. Jacques Lefèvre d'Étaples (c.1460–1536) began to study Greek around 1480. In 1490 he wrote an introduction to Aristotle's *Metaphysics*. In 1492 he visited Florence and was influenced by both Ficino and Giovanni Pico della Mirandola. Thereafter he made humanist Latin translations of and introductions to the principal works of Aristotle (1506) which remained the staple of university teaching in Paris, combining this with an interest in Hermetic and Platonic texts. He also published an edition of the Psalter (1509) and of St Paul's *Epistles* (1512) with careful explanations of the situation in which Paul was writing and the literal meaning of the text. Lefèvre shared Erasmus' commitment to the study of Greek and to classical standards of Latin style but he was more traditional and supported both the Aristotelian university syllabus and the church's interpretation of scripture.

Guillaume Budé (1468–1540) was a man of independent means who devoted himself to scholarship from about 1491. He learned Greek in Paris and published four translations of treatises by Plutarch (1503–5). He became a royal secretary in 1497 and was Francis I's Master of Requests (1522–40) and Director of the Royal Library. His *Annotations on the 24 Books of the Pandects* (1508) approaches a legal text from the point of view of philology and philosophy. He uses the legal text as a historical source to reconstruct the reality of life in ancient Rome. His book was also a scathing attack on scholastic jurisprudence which treated Roman law as a universally authoritative system rather than a human artefact which was created and adapted in response to particular historical circumstances. Budé was the founder of legal humanism which was further developed by the Italian scholar Andrea Alciati (1492–1550), who taught at universities in France from 1518 and who became famous for his publications on emblems (a genre involving a symbolic image, explanatory verses, and a motto) from 1531. Budé's second great work of scholarship was *On the Unit* (1515), a deeply scholarly and controversial investigation of the value of all measurements and coins in the ancient world, based on both a thorough knowledge of all the sources and a practical sense of the ways in which measures and values operate. His *Commentaries on the Greek Language* (1530) is a work of lexicography which was later incorporated in Henri Estienne's Greek–Latin dictionary, *Thesaurus of the Greek Language* (1572). Budé was influential in persuading Francis I to establish in 1530, and pay the salaries of, the 'Royal Lectureships', originally two in Greek, two in Hebrew, and one in Mathematics, and which were the origin of the Collège de France.

Sir Thomas More (1477/8–1535) was a friend of Erasmus, with whom he made Latin translations of Lucian around 1506, and a strong supporter of humanistic learning in England. From a legal career he turned in 1517 to royal service under Henry VIII, eventually reaching the eminence of Lord Chancellor in 1529. He wrote an English biography of the Italian humanist Giovanni Pico della Mirandola (1510) and a humanistic history of the reign of Richard III in English and Latin (1514–18). His most famous work was the Latin *Utopia* (1516), in which he launched a new genre of fiction and described a communistic form of political organization based on an Erasmian combination of Plato and Christianity. Through his household, and his association with Juan Luis Vives, he promoted the education of women in classical subjects. He was irrevocably opposed to the Reformation and to Tyndale's translation of the Bible into English, which he persecuted. He serves as an example of a statesman devoted to and motivated by Christianity and the study of the classical world, who found time for scholarship and writing.

Juan Luis Vives (1492–1540) left Valencia to study in Paris in 1508 and went from there to Bruges in 1512, where he met More in 1520. More helped him when he came to England, where Vives taught Greek at Oxford and worked as tutor to Princess Mary from 1527. He wrote a commentary on St Augustine's *City of God* (1522), which he dedicated to Henry VIII. Most of his works were published after his return to Bruges in 1528. They include a survey of the state of learning in various subjects, *On the Causes of*

Tho: Moor L'Chancelour

HANS HOLBEIN THE YOUNGER, watercolour sketch of Sir Thomas More. Holbein, who later became in effect court painter to Henry VIII, was introduced to the royal circle by Thomas More. This lifelike sketch was probably made as a preparation for an oil portrait of More.

the Corruption of the Arts (1531), which was followed by his proposals for a reorganization of the teaching of the principal subjects, *On Teaching the Disciplines* (1531), very successful elementary dialogues for pupils learning Latin, the *Colloquia or Practice of the Latin Language* (1539), and an important and influential treatise on letter-writing (1534). He also composed important works on the education of women (1524) and on ways to tackle the problem of poverty (1525). He wrote a book on the nature of the soul, *On the Soul and Life* (1538), and studied the emotions. He composed a series of texts on rhetoric and dialectic, including an original synthesis of rhetorical doctrine adapted to modern conditions and organized around the idea of style, *On the Method of Speaking* (1533), which did not enjoy much influence. Vives was a fine stylist and an original thinker who was active across a range of curriculum subjects and who demonstrated notable social concerns.

Philipp Melanchthon (1497–1560) studied at Heidelberg and Tübingen, where he began to teach. In 1518 he was appointed Professor of Greek at Wittenberg, where he became the leading light of the university and lectured on an astonishing range of classical and biblical texts, including Homer, Vergil, Cicero's orations and *De oratore*, Terence, Paul's Epistles, especially Romans, and Aristotle's *Ethics* and *Physics*. His lectures resulted in many printed commentaries (some of them based on notes his pupils took on his lectures) and in the *Epitome of Moral Philosophy* (1538). Melanchthon played a crucial leadership role in reforms of Wittenberg University and of many German grammar schools and universities. His influence on the curricula of Protestant German schools and universities was very strong, as evidenced by his epithet 'the preceptor of Germany'. He wrote a series of influential textbooks on rhetoric and dialectic, which emphasized the connections between the two subjects and tried to combine coverage of the main Aristotelian and Ciceronian doctrines with incorporation of some of the new insights of Agricola and Erasmus. His crucial contribution was to emphasize both Christianity and an education in classical languages and literature by recognizing their different but complementary spheres. Once one understood the overwhelming centrality of grace, one could allow a place for pagan learning as helpful within the necessarily less important concerns of this world. Working alongside Luther, Melanchthon made crucial contributions to the development of Protestant theology, as the main author of the Augsburg Confession (1530) and through the different editions of his *Theological Commonplaces* (1521–59), where he sought to give clear statements of the essential doctrines of Protestant Christianity on the basis of biblical texts. The work was organized logically from such central topics as sin, law, grace, Christ, and God. Melanchthon created and provided the basic textbooks for an educational system which combined Christianity with humanist learning.

Although Italy led the way with printing of classical texts in the fifteenth century, it now seems that printers in the north of Europe, and especially in Paris, took over the leadership in humanistic printing early in the sixteenth century. According to Andrew Pettegree's figures, France, Germany, Switzerland, and the Netherlands accounted for 104,000 editions in Latin and Greek between 1450 and 1600, compared with 39,600 for Italy. Green and Murphy identify 338 editions of Cicero's rhetorical works printed between 1500 and 1600 in northern Europe, compared with 73 editions from Italy. Paris alone printed 153 editions, compared to Venice's 57. Northern printers also published very large numbers of new Latin works on humanistic subjects, for example there were 165 editions of Erasmus' *De copia* between 1512 and 1569, only 12 of them from Italy (all from Venice). The early sixteenth century also saw great scholarly printers establish their reputations in northern Europe, such as Amerbach and Froben in Basel and Gryphius in Lyon. The French scholar-printer family of Robert and Henri Estienne published the first editions of the Greek historians Eusebius, Dionysius of Halicarnassus, and Dio Cassius, a Latin dictionary (1531), and a Greek dictionary (1572). The establishment of the Frankfurt book fair no doubt helped to establish the pre-eminence of northern European printers in the international trade in classical and humanistic texts.

Even more crucial for the future development of humanism in Europe was the establishment of new schools and universities and the reform of the curriculum of existing ones. In 1517, under the influence of Erasmus and other humanists interested in applying philology to the Bible, Trilingual Colleges were founded at Louvain and

Alcalá to teach Latin, Greek, and Hebrew to students. New colleges founded at Oxford, such as Corpus Christi (1517) and St John's College (1555), expressed humanist ideals and focused on teaching Greek and studying the best classical authors. Francis I's establishment of the royal lectureships in Greek and Hebrew in 1530, and Henry VIII's appointment of Regius Professorships in Greek at Cambridge (1540) and Oxford (1541) illustrate the same trend. By the late sixteenth century Oxford and Cambridge offered a fixed curriculum founded on the study of logic, based on the Latin translation of Aristotle, rhetoric, and classical literature, often involving Greek, which could be extended in a range of different directions depending on the interests of individual students and their tutors.

Across Europe grammar schools were founded whose primary aim was to teach classical standards of Latin expression and increasingly over the century also Greek. Pupils were taught to read, write, and speak Latin through study of a range of moralizing texts, such as *The Distichs of Cato* and *Aesop's Fables*, through conversational dialogues, such as the *Colloquies* of Erasmus and Vives, and through study of Terence's *Comedies*. They followed a course in the best examples of the main genres of Latin literature: Cicero for letters, Vergil and Horace for lyric poetry, Vergil and Ovid for epic, Caesar or Sallust for history, and Cicero's *De officiis* for moral philosophy. They were taught to write Latin letters through imitation of Cicero and using a letter-writing manual such as the one by Erasmus or the one presented in the later sections of Perotti's grammar. Many of them wrote examples of the short genres such as narrative, fable, description, and speech for a character set out in Aphthonius' *Progymnasmata*. Many of them used Erasmus' *De copia* to enrich their style. In some cases, notably in the worldwide network of Jesuit schools, this was followed by study of modern and classical rhetoric textbooks. Latin education was the medium for training the future elite to express themselves effectively both in the international medium of Latin and in the local vernacular. Classical poetry, proverbs, ethics, and history provided the storehouse of maxims and narratives which would educate the virtuous public man and enable him to persuade and entertain his peers. Increasingly a classical education came to be seen as a valuable accomplishment for noble and royal women (and for the daughters of scholars), as we see from the examples of Queen Elizabeth I (1533–1603) and of Margaret Roper (1505–44), the daughter of Thomas More.

Humanism took hold relatively late in Spain, though some Spanish intellectuals of the fifteenth century, such as Alonso de Cartagena (1384–1456), who translated Latin works into Spanish, and Alfonso de Palencia (1423–92), were influenced by developments in Italy. The first notable Spanish humanist was Antonio de Nebrija (1444–1522). He wrote a Latin grammar (1481), a Latin–Spanish dictionary (1492), and the first grammar of the Spanish language (1492), as well as works on Spanish history, in both Latin and Spanish, and rhetoric. Like Valla he worked on the text of the New Testament, aiming to use Greek manuscripts to improve the vulgate translation. He believed that similar procedures should be applied to the Vulgate Old Testament through study of Hebrew manuscripts. Nebrija was one of the contributors to the

Complutensian Polyglot Bible (completed 1517, first printed 1522), compiled at the University in Alcalá by a team financed by Cardinal Francisco de Cisneros (1436–1517), who bought many old Greek and Hebrew manuscripts for their use. This Bible printed Hebrew, Greek (the *Septuagint*, third to second century BCE), and Latin texts of the Old Testament, together with the Syriac text of the first five books and its own Latin translation at the foot of each page, and Latin and Greek texts of the New Testament. The sixth volume of the edition consisted of Hebrew, Greek, and Syriac dictionaries (Syriac is a dialect of Aramaic, the language spoken by Jesus). Spanish scholars from converted Jewish families were largely responsible for the Old Testament editing and translating. The publication of this edition was an extraordinary achievement of scholarship and typography.

In the sixteenth century Spanish scholars were active and often eminent in many traditional and innovative aspects of classical studies. Hernán Núñez de Guzmán (*c.*1473–1553) collected and compared manuscripts, edited Theocritus and Seneca, and proposed improvements to the texts of Pomponius Mela (1543) and Pliny the Elder (1544). Juan Ginés de Sepúlveda (*c.*1490–1573) translated Aristotle's works into Ciceronian Latin, studied the Roman calendar, wrote histories, and defended the Spanish conquest of America and the subjugation of the Amerindian population. Antonio Agustín (1517–86) was the pioneer of the historical study of Roman law, who edited the sources on the basis of primary manuscript scholarship and studied ancient inscriptions and coins. Francisco Sánchez de las Brozas (1523–1600) wrote philological commentaries on Vergil, Horace, Ovid, and Ausonius. As a pioneering grammatical theorist, he argued for reform of the humanist approach to grammar to include principles based on logic and analogy alongside observation of classical Latin usage. Benito Arias Montano (1527–98) returned to the biblical traditions of Spanish scholarship as the principal editor of the great Antwerp polyglot Bible (1569–73). This Bible improved the texts of the Complutensian Polyglot in significant ways and set the future direction of biblical studies by treating the Bible as a work of literature which needed to be understood in its historical context, just as one might treat a classical text.

But Spain's most important contribution to the development of humanism was made through its global empire and particularly through the educational activities of the Society of Jesus. After St Ignatius of Loyola (1491–1556) converted from a military to a religious life in 1522 he studied Latin and theology first in Alcalá and then in Paris. In Paris he attended the lectures of humanist scholars. Humanist approaches to rhetoric inform the *Spiritual Exercises* (1548). The Society of Jesus which he founded in 1539 always emphasized the importance of a classical education. In the definitive *Order of Studies of the Society of Jesus* (1599), which fixed procedures that had been developing since the 1550s, the complete course would take a student from the elementary stage to the equivalent of a degree in theology. The upper section comprised a three-year course in philosophy (principally logic, natural philosophy, and metaphysics, but also including mathematics and ethics) and a four-year course in theology (based mainly on the works of St Thomas Aquinas, but including Hebrew, Scripture, and training in the practicality of serving a parish). The lower section had five grades: three levels of grammar, humanity, and rhetoric. In the early years the focus was on Latin and Greek grammar and on writing Latin in imitation of Cicero. Students read Cicero's letters and philosophical works, Ovid's *Heroides*, Vergil, Aesop, and Chrysostom, followed by Caesar, Sallust, Livy, Horace's *Odes*, orations by Cicero and Isocrates, St Basil and Plutarch. Study of Soarez's *Rhetorica* was followed up in the fifth year by reading the rhetorical works of Cicero, Quintilian, and Aristotle and analysing speeches by Cicero and Demosthenes in the light of rhetorical theory. Jesuit education embraced the elites of the cities across the world where they worked as well as aiming to train priests. Jesuit schools spread the doctrine that training in classical languages, literature, and history should be the basis for elite education across the whole world and was widely imitated by secular educators.

The broader impact of humanism

Humanism had an immense influence on a range of disciplines including education, philosophy, historiography, classical and literary scholarship, and neo-Latin and vernacular literature. It made a huge contribution to many of the most important writings of the Western tradition, for example Castiglione, Machiavelli, Ariosto, Tasso, Rabelais, Ronsard, Montaigne, Spenser, and Shakespeare. It touched every aspect of intellectual life and guided the way in which education and scholarship developed right up to the present.

In the sixteenth century the theory of education and the proper development of the ruler and his advisers became topics of very widespread interest and concern. The experienced diplomat Baldassare Castiglione (1478–1529) modelled his description of the ideal courtier, *The Courtier* (1528), on Cicero's *De oratore*. The perfect courtier needs grace and good judgement. He must avoid affectation and cultivate a certain nonchalance. He must be loyal, brave, skilled in arms, and must make a good first impression. He should know Latin and Greek, poetry, oratory, and history and be effective in writing verse and prose, especially in the vernacular. He should acquire musical accomplishments and know enough about the visual arts to judge them well. The ability to speak and write well is one of the chief requirements. The courtier needs knowledge as a basis for speech, and the ability to organize his ideas and express them in words which are carefully chosen, impressive, and well joined together. In everything he says and does he must consider carefully the place, the audience, its timeliness, and the reason for doing it. The dialogue ends with Bembo's evocation of Platonic love, urging the courtier to move upwards from the love of the beauty of an individual woman to love of divine goodness. Castiglione's idealized description of the early sixteenth-century court of Urbino is rooted in his appreciation of classical literature and philosophy. In his *The Book Named the Governor* (1531), the royal clerk Sir Thomas Elyot (*c.*1490–1546) combines a humanist educational programme with a digest of the moral knowledge required in a counsellor. The young nobleman must learn Latin and

Greek and must read a wide range of poetry, especially Homer, Vergil, and Ovid. He should study classical and humanistic dialectic and rhetoric, especially Aristotle, Agricola, Quintilian, Cicero, and Erasmus. These studies will help him to learn ethics, politics, and expression from his reading in oratory, history, and philosophy. Elyot's discussions of the moral virtues in books 2 and 3 combine moral axioms and narratives and collect material obtained by a rhetorical and ethical reading of classical and modern texts. Elyot's assumption throughout is that the boy will learn in Latin but that his practical work as a counsellor will be conducted in English.

At the heart of Renaissance education, rhetoric sat alongside the study of ancient languages and literatures. Classical education helped create a civic society among the elite, built on a shared fund of moral axioms and narratives and founded on the expectation that reasons would be given for actions and that rulers would persuade and on occasion be persuaded. The letter-writing manuals composed in northern Europe in the sixteenth century emphasized the range of occasions on which one might need to write or speak, the primary importance of thinking about the addressee, and the freedom which the writer enjoys in relation to the content of the letter. Iberian Counter-Reformation preaching manuals placed new emphasis on delivery, on the arousal of emotion, and on the persona which the preacher should cultivate. A renewed focus on style and amplification was promoted by manuals of the tropes and figures printed for the grammar school market. Late sixteenth-century rhetoric learned from and linked with humanist dialectic, teaching persuasive argument expressed in a Latin of a classical quality rather than in the restricted and formulaic language of scholastic logic. Where Melanchthon emphasized the connections between rhetoric, dialectic, and the analysis of classical texts, Peter Ramus (1515–72) wrote twin manuals of rhetoric and logic short enough to be summarized on a page so that pupils could move rapidly from the rules of the arts to learning how they worked in practice through reading Cicero's speeches and Vergil's poems. Sixteenth-century rhetoric moved into the vernacular, with most of the major languages acquiring manuals of letter-writing, such as Pierre Fabri's French *Great Art of True Rhetoric* (1521), which also included a general rhetoric and a poetics, Angel Day's *English Secretary* (1586); of preaching, for example Francesco Panigarola's Italian *Method of Composing a Sermon* (1584); and of rhetoric and dialectic, exemplified by *The Rule of Reason* (1551) and *The Art of Rhetoric* (1553), both by the Elizabethan diplomat and secretary of state Sir Thomas Wilson (?1525–81). An understanding of rhetoric remains central to any study of the Renaissance and the history of modern disciplines.

Later humanism made contributions to philosophy beyond its traditional preoccupation with moral philosophy. Most importantly it began to attack the dominance of the Aristotelian model. Humanists collected, edited, translated, and studied a wide range of texts by non-Aristotelian ancient philosophers, Epicureans, Stoics, and sceptics, but above all Plato and his followers. Philological work on the ancient philosophical texts was itself a contribution to philosophy. As well as showing the true richness of the philosophical inheritance from antiquity, humanists increasingly focused on the internal problems within Aristotle's philosophical system and the difficulties of reconciling Aristotle's ideas with Christianity. Some Renaissance philosophers had even greater difficulties in disproving claims of heresy in their own philosophies, often based on Platonism. Nicholas of Cusa (1401–64) was a cardinal of the Catholic church who collected manuscripts containing the works of ancient philosophers. He was a Platonist, especially dedicated to the writings of Pseudo-Dionysius the Areopagite (which were in fact written around 500 CE) and Proclus. Nicholas knew Poggio and Niccolò Niccoli and was interested in Hermeticism. His thought insisted on the infinity of the divine in contrast to the limitations of the human intellect. He believed that learned ignorance, aware of one's own limitations, was the best approach to thinking about God. His Platonism led him to take an interest in theories of number, measure, and proportion.

The immortality of the soul was an important topic for humanist philosophers. Marsilio Ficino had asserted the immortality of the soul through its ontological status, on account of its being self-moving, substantial, divine, and immaterial. Following Proclus he saw the human soul as a mediator between the higher and lower worlds and as striving for union with God through its very nature. Pietro Pomponazzi (1487–1525) published his work *On the Immortality of the Soul* in 1516. He saw the soul as the medium between mortal and immortal things, insisting that the intellect and sense perception (which is undoubtedly material) are inextricably linked. The soul must perform abstraction from material things, hence it is itself posed between the material and the immaterial, partaking of the immaterial but dependent on the body. In opposition to St Thomas Aquinas, he argued that Aristotle's *De anima* presented the individual soul as mortal and was therefore inconsistent with Christianity. He maintained that the separation of philosophy and theology enabled him to believe in the immortality of the soul while pursuing arguments which left the question more open. Although he had taken care to insist on his submission to the doctrines of the church, his opponents accused him of undermining the crucial Christian doctrine of the immortality of the soul.

Later sixteenth-century south Italian philosophers developed imaginative new cosmologies. Bernardino Telesio (1509–88) believed that natural philosophy needed to be developed on the basis of sensory experience and natural principles without reference to metaphysics or theology. He believed that matter was inactive and that the principles of heat and cold were the basis for motion in the universe. He regarded space as distinct from the material of the bodies it contains and as finite. He was anxious to point out the problems in Aristotelian cosmology but he followed it in many of the details of his system, including geocentrism and the idea of celestial spheres. Giordano Bruno (1548–1600) followed Copernicus' heliocentrism and envisaged a universe which was infinite and homogeneous, full, and containing an infinity of worlds. All bodies in the universe are formed of the four elements dear to the Greek philosophers, earth, water, air, and fire. Celestial bodies are divided into stars and planets (every planet must be linked to a star) according to the proportion of the four elements.

Seeing the infinite universe as a complete unity left little room for a Christian God. The church condemned Bruno for his theories and burned him in Rome on 17 February 1600. Tommaso Campanella (1568–1639) was a Platonist and, on the central issue of the importance of heat and cold for understanding all bodies, a follower of Telesio. He criticized Aristotle's doctrines of form and matter, of the four elements, and of the distinction between natural and violent motion, preferring to rely on sense experience. In his view every being in the world had sense which could choose between what would help and harm it and would therefore ensure its self-preservation. In animals life and cognition depend on the *spiritus* which acts as a medium between the soul and the external world. The Italian scholar Germana Ernst explains that, for Campanella, 'Every sensation is a form of "contact" on the part of the *spiritus*, that enters into a relation, via various sense organs, with the exhalations, motions and light coming from external objects. The sensations that the *spiritus* experiences are the source of all cognition: memory, imagination, reason and the intellect itself, which is nothing but weakened and distilled sense.' Campanella was tried for treason and heresy and managed to avoid the death penalty only by feigning madness. He developed his philosophical system during his long years in prison. Renaissance cosmology could not be confirmed empirically, but its rejection of the Aristotelian model and its insistence on the intellectual freedom of the philosopher may have helped prepare the ground for the scientific revolution.

Humanists themselves brought about a revolution in the writing of history, through a combination of reading of the Greek and Roman historians, a wide-ranging curiosity about the ancient world, and determination to think independently. Biondo Flavio (1392–1463) combined critical scholarship and humanist erudition with a flair for narrative which imitates Livy. He was the first historian to make systematic use of archaeological evidence. His *Roma instaurata* (1443–6) investigates the topography of ancient Rome and the surviving Christian monuments, while *Italia illustrata* (1448–58) surveys the history and geography of the peninsula. His *Decades of History from the Decline of the Roman Empire* (1439–53) provides a history of Europe from 410 to 1442 based on more than fifty sources, including letters and charters as well as chronicles. Niccolò Machiavelli (1469–1527) achieved lasting fame for drawing lessons about political conduct from a pragmatic analysis of ancient and contemporary history in his *The Prince* (1514) and *Discourses on the First Ten Books of Livy* (1515–19). Machiavelli wrote in Italian but he took his inspiration from ancient historians. In 1520 he was commissioned to write *The Florentine Histories*, telling the story of the city from its origins to 1492, with a preliminary book on Italy from the fall of the Roman Empire to 1434. He used a range of mainly secondary sources while adding the orations and the political analysis which he found in the Greek historians Thucydides and Polybius.

Francesco Guicciardini (1483–1540) was a Florentine lawyer and diplomat who worked for the papacy (1513–27), rising to become ruler of the province of Romagna (1523). His *History of Italy*, written after his retirement in 1537, surveys the history of the peninsula from 1490 to 1534. He makes use of many documentary sources and of all the experience of his political career to write a detailed history involving a complex array of interlocking narratives, enlivened with his shrewd insight into the causes of human behaviour. Guicciardini regarded the period he surveyed as a catastrophe for Italy caused by the ambition and short-sightedness of its rulers. His Tacitean cynicism and insight are demonstrated by a comment on his employers in his *Dialogue on the Government of Florence*:

> I don't know anyone who dislikes the ambition, the avarice, and the sensuality of priests more than I do . . . Nevertheless, the position I have enjoyed with several popes has forced me to love their greatness for my own self-interest. If it weren't for this consideration, I would have loved Martin Luther as much as I love myself—not to be released from the laws taught by the Christian religion as it is normally interpreted and understood, but to see this band of ruffians reduced within their correct bounds.

Humanism inspired new histories within national traditions, such as Thomas More's *History of Richard III* and Edward Hall's *Union of the Two Noble and Illustre Families of Lancaster and York* (1548). Contemporary history in Latin was represented by works like Aeneas Silvius Piccolomini's (1405–64) *Commentaries*, which contain a good deal of material on the expansion of the Turks as well as on this pope's own eventful life, and the *History of his own Times* (1620) by Jacques Auguste de Thou (1553–1617). De Thou presented a comprehensive account of European history from 1543 to 1607, based on careful research in the sources he collected in his substantial library. His object was to present an unbiased work. His history is scrupulously exact and written in a lively and elegant style. The popularity of history in the Renaissance prompted some authors to attempt histories of a wider world than the national or European histories which were familiar to them. Some of these accounts were excessively reliant on medieval chronicles but others gathered first-hand information from travellers and soldiers. The Spanish language *General History of the Indies* (1552) by Francisco López de Gómara (*c*.1511–*c*.1566), which Montaigne used for information about Peru and Mexico, will serve as an example. Renaissance historians also began extensive work on the theory and methods of writing history, as in Jean Bodin's (1530–96) *Method for Easy Understanding of Histories* (1566).

Although the principal classical authors had all been printed by around 1530, classical scholarship and textual criticism continued to make advances in the sixteenth century. Pier Vettori (1499–1585) made the first edition of Clement of Alexandria (1550) and the first complete edition of Aeschylus (1557), adding 700 lines to previous texts of *Agamemnon*. In his edition of Aristotle's *Rhetoric* (1549) he understood the value of medieval Latin translations in editing a Greek text, as he was able to show that the manuscript from which William of Moerbeke had translated around 1270 was close to the readings of the oldest and best manuscripts available to Vettori and therefore used readings which could be inferred from it. Francesco Robortello (1516–67) produced an important edition of Aristotle's *Poetics* (1548) and the first edition of Longinus' *On the Sublime* (1552). He also wrote a short dissertation on the principles of textual emendation, classifying the different ways in which emendations could be proposed and giving examples of each. This is the first systematic discussion of the theory of textual criticism. The French scholar Denys Lambin (1520–72) made editions of Horace (1561), Lucretius (1563), and Cicero's complete works (1565–6). His edition of Lucretius was particularly successful as it was based on a ninth-century manuscript which remains one of the two most important authorities. For Cicero's letters he used an excellent manuscript which is now lost and for whose readings modern editors must rely on Lambin and his contemporaries. Joseph Justus Scaliger (1540–1609), a Huguenot working in Leiden, wrote a commentary (1574) on Antonio Agustín's text of Festus' *On the Significance of Words* in which he was able to use his knowledge of archaic Latin, a recently discovered manuscript of Servius' commentary on Vergil, and scholarship on Roman law to introduce many improvements in the text, mainly by brilliant conjectures. His thorough and careful emendation of the text of Manilius (published with commentary in 1579) on the basis of a thorough study of ancient astronomy enabled that text to be understood far better than before. In later years he formulated a new basis for the history of the ancient world by reconstructing their systems of chronology. Justus Lipsius (1547–1606) moved between Louvain and Leiden. He made famous editions of Latin prose writers, Tacitus (1574; revised to great effect in 1607) and Seneca (1605). He maintained wide-ranging historical interests and wrote monographs on ancient warfare, amphitheatres, and topics related to Stoicism, which he sought to revive.

Alongside this editorial and scholarly work there was more attention to the reading and teaching of central literary texts, especially Vergil, Ovid, and Cicero. Many commentaries were composed especially in northern Europe. Renewed attention to Aristotle's *Poetics*, by the late sixteenth century often studied in Greek, and the discovery of Longinus' *On the Sublime* helped to stimulate a flourishing of literary theory, especially in Italy, and often composed in the vernacular. Julius Caesar Scaliger (1484–1558), an Italian living in France and the father of Joseph Justus, in his Latin *Seven Books of Poetics* (1561) surveyed existing poetry in the light of Horace, Aristotle, and Plato. He sought to understand the ways in which poets use words to imitate the world and he insisted on the creativity of their arrangements of words, proposing that poets create a second nature, for the purpose of teaching delightfully. According to Ann Moss he makes a critical methodology out of comparing different poets' treatment of similar subjects. Lodovico Castelvetro (c.1505–71) expresses his views on poetry through a lengthy Latin commentary on Aristotle's *Poetics* (1570), in which he tries to correct Aristotle's mistakes. He believed that Aristotle needed to distinguish more carefully between different types of imitation. He thought that poetic imitation was intended to delight the audience and especially the general populace. He believed that a theory of history needs to precede a theory of poetry and that the power of invention determines the excellence of a poet. He focused on the ways in which a poet could make subject matter vivid to an audience and, against the Platonists, he favoured art over *furor*. He initiated the strict interpretation of the unities which would characterize French neo-classical drama criticism. The great epic poet Torquato Tasso (1546–95) wrote in Italian *Discourses on the Art of Poetry* (1562–5), which he later revised and enlarged as *Discourses on the Heroic Poem* (c.1587). Tasso insists on the different objectives of epic and tragedy, arguing that epic needed to elicit wonder, both in its narrative and in the style in which it is written. The epic poem needs a great and unified action (hence his criticism of Ariosto); it should mingle tragic solemnity with lyric grace; it must be magnificent and marvellous but also lifelike. Some of his positions, and the arguments he makes against other theorists, are distorted by the need to prove the perfection of his own epic. Sir Philip Sidney (1554–86) probably wrote his *Defence of Poetry* around 1584. He aims to synthesize Aristotle, Plato, Horace, and Scaliger, proving the value of poetry to the commonwealth, and insisting on its superior effectiveness in moral teaching, in comparison with history and philosophy. The poet's main aim must be to create ideal speaking images of virtue, but he delights the audience by his creation of new and marvellous worlds. In comparison with his eloquence in developing ideas borrowed from continental theorists, Sidney's observations on the state of poetry in England are conventional and over-pessimistic. He rejects the ambitious and mixed forms which will be the glory of English Renaissance drama but he points the way to understanding Spenser's aims and inclusions in *The Faerie Queene*.

Two related sub-genres within debates about literary theory were the argument about imitation, and the question about whether and how best to write in the vernacular. Fifteenth-century humanists had written in Latin both as the universal language of scholarship and in order to demonstrate their excellence as Latin stylists. Recapturing the ability to write in the language of Cicero, utilizing the full resources of the classical Latin language, was one of the great aspirations of the humanists. But humanist scholars could also see the limitations of an excessive focus on Cicero. In a controversy with Paolo Cortesi, Poliziano in 1485 preferred to imitate different models and above all to write like himself. Copying Cicero's sentence structures and vocabulary is lifeless. The sceptical philosopher Gianfrancesco Pico (1470–1533) upheld the same position in letters of around 1512 to Pietro Bembo (1470–1547), who asserted in reply that imitation was central to all forms of human activity, and that if one was inevitably going to imitate then one should imitate only the best. Erasmus entered the controversy in a decisive way with his criticism of the style of many of his contemporaries and his mockery of the project of imitating Cicero in his *Ciceronianus* (1528).

Bembo was also one of the promoters of writing in the Italian vernacular rather than in Latin, in order to increase the value of one's native tongue. His *Prose on the Vernacular Language* (1525) proposed that Italian writers should imitate the language of Petrarch and Boccaccio rather than current Tuscan or their own dialect. Following the lead of Bembo and using many of the arguments put forward by Sperone Speroni (1500–88) in his *Dialogue on Languages* (1542), Joachim Du Bellay (c.1525–60) in his *Defence and Glorification of the French Language* (1549) argues that languages need to be cultivated in order to improve and that this must be achieved by translation and by creating original compositions. Since there are no existing native models, French writers will have to imitate the Greeks and Romans.

Later in the sixteenth century there was a vogue for imitating Seneca and Tacitus rather than Cicero, but in his *Instruction in Letter-Writing* (1591) Justus Lipsius argues that while boys should learn to imitate Cicero, grown-ups can add the study of Sallust, Seneca, and Tacitus to their continued reading of Cicero. He believed that one should imitate the spirit of writers one admires while remaining true to one's own voice.

The humanist movement produced a very substantial modern literature in Latin, most notably in the mock encomium of Erasmus' *Praise of Folly*, the fictional dialogue of More's *Utopia*, and in the novel *Argenis* (1621) by John Barclay (1582–1621). Humanist writers excelled in Latin letters (e.g. Petrarch, Poliziano, and Erasmus) and in epigrams (Marullo, Poliziano, Sannazaro, and Secundus). They wrote Latin epics (Petrarch, Vida, Sannazaro), elegies (Beccadelli, Pontano, Secundus, Du Bellay), and pastorals (Petrarch, Mantuan, Sannazaro). They composed Latin comedies (Reuchlin, Macropedius), tragedies (Mussato, Muret, Buchanan), and psalm paraphrases (Petrarch, Gilles de Delft, Macrin, and Buchanan). Above all they wrote histories and philosophical works in Latin prose. Many of these works are now being recovered for the European literary heritage through translations and parallel texts. Since these works represent a substantial part of the total literary output of the Renaissance and since they have many great merits, one of the tasks of literary scholarship in the next fifty years will be a proper appreciation of the merits of neo-Latin literature and its relations to classical literature and the Renaissance literature of the vernacular languages.

Even more striking is the impact of humanist learning and education on vernacular literature. Much of the greatest vernacular literature of the sixteenth century was written in deliberate imitation of classical forms: the pastoral poetry of Tasso, Guarino, Montemayor, and Spenser; the satire of Ariosto, Aretino, Marston, and Jonson or the epics by Ariosto, Trissino, Ronsard, Tasso, Spenser, Camoens, and Milton. Much vernacular literature combines literary forms under the inspiration of the classics; hence epic romances, pastoral dramas or novels, comedy which incorporates romance alongside Roman models, and tragedy which differs creatively from Senecan or Euripidean models. Some of the most significant original literary works of the Renaissance are unthinkable without the contribution of humanism. Rabelais's *Gargantua and Pantagruel* is founded on knowledge of Greek and on anti-scholastic satire. Montaigne's invention of the form of the essay owes an enormous debt to his humanist training and to his reading of Plutarch's *Parallel Lives* and *Moralia*, Seneca's *Moral Epistles to Lucilius*, and Roman poetry. Spenser's intertwining of Platonic and Christian thought and Jonson's comedy of humours depend entirely on their classical education. Shakespeare learnt how to develop his source material, whether it was taken from chronicles, romances, or Plutarch, through his careful reading of Ovid and Vergil and his study of Erasmus' *De copia*.

Renaissance humanism made a lasting contribution to many different aspects of European culture. It played a crucial role in the recovery of classical literature and the growth of scholarship. It made a central and lasting contribution to educational theories and school syllabuses. It revolutionized the study of the Bible and helped to encourage the fundamental questioning of church authority which led to the Reformation. By learning from classical examples humanism changed the practice of writing history, widened the scope of historiography, and in effect invented political theory. Renaissance humanism had a vast and enduring impact on European literature and the visual forms of narrative which have developed from it. Renaissance recovery of tragedy, comedy, and epic and Renaissance combinations between genres still contribute to the production and understanding of most of the narrative and poetic cultural forms we practise today.

CHAPTER 2

War and the State, c.1400–c.1650

DAVID PARROTT

'A prince, therefore, should have no other object or thought, nor acquire skill in anything, except war, its organization and its discipline.'

Machiavelli, *Il Principe*, chapter 14

Bellicosity

NICCOLÒ Machiavelli's trenchant assertion might appear out of place in a study of Renaissance Europe. The Renaissance is associated with concepts of rationality and civility, and primarily concerned with the development of human potential; the converse of the uncontrolled destructiveness and atavistic violence of warfare. Indeed, key figures of the Renaissance such as Erasmus and Thomas More can be cited for their condemnations of warfare as immoral, ungodly, and the frivolous sport of an idle and vicious ruling class.

Yet Renaissance Europe was not simply a period of artistic, intellectual, scientific, and economic development; it was also an era of endemic warfare which wrought seismic changes upon its political, social, and economic development. Humanist scholars and writers, artists and scientific practitioners not only accepted warfare as an intrinsic part of their world, they were deeply engaged with the challenges and opportunities that war posed for rulers and states. A defining characteristic of the Renaissance was reverence for the classical past as a means to interpret or recreate the present. The history of ancient Rome was at the centre of this process: humanist education was in thrall to the great histories of the classical world—Caesar, Livy, Tacitus, Plutarch—which were substantially accounts of military leadership, battles, and wars under the Roman Republic and Empire. The culture of the Renaissance, as Machiavelli's work demonstrates, was steeped in the study of warfare, whether practical discussions of the 'art of war', or with the relationship of war to politics, rhetoric, and morality. But all this simply added to an already bellicose political and social environment.

War in fifteenth- and sixteenth-century Europe was not seen as some unnatural event, forced upon an international order whose normal condition was peaceful coexistence and stability. Organized warfare was accepted as a normal and unavoidable—if still for the majority of the population, undesirable—state of affairs. Many frontier societies were constructed around informal military organization. Village communities on and behind the Hungarian border with the Ottoman Empire were always semi-mobilized as irregulars and raiding parties, as were the populations of Lithuania or Livonia, or indeed their Muscovite opponents, who faced in addition the need to defend themselves against Tatar raids from the south and east. The world of the Spanish Reconquista of the Moorish kingdom of El Andalus was one of decades-long mobilization of local communities heavily composed of irregular soldiers, ancestors of the *conquistadores* who were to bring a similar militarized communal culture to the Spanish New World. Even more stable societies could degenerate into such 'frontier' states. Large regions of France during the wars of religion from the 1560s to the 1590s fragmented into communities defined by their confessions, who waged irregular warfare against local rivals and would-be aggressors.

But even in contexts where the external military threat appeared less considerable, there were obstacles to establishing communities in which peaceful coexistence was the norm. Family, kinship, and other informal associations bound people together more tightly than any abstract loyalty to state or ruler. Mobilizing support from family or kin groups to pursue violence via feud or vendetta touched on deep-rooted loyalties and obligations: the kin group was the primary mechanism for favour and advancement, for sharing resources in difficult times, and for defending the honour of group members. Violence was the honourable response to failures of deference and could come in the form of a challenge to a duel, spontaneous interpersonal violence, or the mobilization of kin to wage a vendetta against the family of the offending party.

This obsession with honour and recognition of status, and (the high threshold for) the tolerance of retributive personal or collective violence, extrapolated easily into international warfare. Rulers did not regard avoiding war as inherently desirable; indeed they regarded the pursuit of peace at the cost of their international reputation and personal prestige as more damaging than resorting to war—even in cases where the chances of military success appeared slight. The Spanish monarchy was well aware of the operational difficulties and expense of campaigning against its rebellious subjects in the Low Countries. Restarting the war with the Dutch Republic in 1621 at the expiry of the Twelve Years Truce was more likely to involve further rounds of crippling expense and indecisive siege warfare than any outright victory. However, the truce had been deemed dishonourable and damaging to the reputation of the monarchy, so the decision to restart war had been a foregone conclusion for a half-decade before 1621.

Preoccupations with honour, reputation, and vindication were the common values of early modern rulers and elites. Throughout this period the vast majority of European states were ruled as hereditary principalities or kingdoms, where the assertion of family right and inheritance was the basis of sovereignty. Legitimacy came from the blood line, while territory and its populations belonged to the ruler as a dynastic inheritance and as family property. Externally as well, dynasticism was the currency in which international relations were conducted: territorial rights were established through familial or marital inheritance. This effectively negated any notion that the state had an abstract and autonomous existence which might require the ruler to pursue goals of general security or prosperity, and to avoid war when it threatened these.

Dynasticism was no less a force in the other types of early modern states. If hereditary monarchies and principalities characterized Western and Mediterranean Europe, elective monarchies were typical in eastern and northern Europe, and were perhaps most prestigiously embodied in the imperial title of Holy Roman Emperor and in the papacy. A body of electors, whether the *szlachta* of Poland, the magnates of Hungary or Bohemia, the seven Electoral Princes of the Holy Roman Empire, even the College of Cardinals, might seem to project other sets of interests into the formulation of state policy. Yet once elected, most such rulers sought to pursue family interests as the primary motivation for foreign policy. This could be in the form of international antagonisms or agreements: the long-standing claims of the Polish Vasa kings against the rival branch of the Vasa in Sweden, for example; or the willingness of Habsburg Holy Roman Emperors to be drawn, sometimes reluctantly, into family agreements with the Spanish Habsburgs from the 1600s. It could also be seen in the attempts of elected rulers to use the resources of the state to advance immediate family interests. Most infamous, of course, were the attempts of successive Renaissance popes from the Borgia, Alexander VI (1492–1503), through to Paul III Farnese (1534–49), to acquire permanent family territories carved out of the Papal States and their dependencies. Such ambitions rarely failed to have bellicose consequences.

The drive towards dynastic imperatives was less direct in the third type of Renaissance state, the various republics surviving in Italy, the Free (i.e. autonomous) imperial cities in Germany, the Helvetic cantons, and, from the 1580s, the Dutch Republic of the seven 'United Provinces'. Yet to examine the power structure and policies of the second great Italian republic, that of Genoa, is to see a handful of powerful, intermarried families controlling the institutions of the city and its policies throughout the early modern period. The result was a 'collective' family policy which sought to build their private wealth and international status on a close and consistent military and financial alliance with Habsburg Spain. Republics and city states had frequently developed a political language of inclusivity and citizenship during the later Middle Ages, expressed through symbolism in art and architecture, civic ritual and pageantry, and shows of collective involvement in decision-making. Yet numerous ruling families eroded the effects of this, ensuring that in political reality the policies of the city-state reflected priorities which were similar to those of hereditary or elective monarchies. The Medici family spent the fifteenth century accruing power and influence within the republican government of Florence. Though they used the language of community and service to the Republic to represent their political role, few believed that the Medici were truly

TINTORETTO, *Venice—The Doge invoking support of Virgin Mary.*

'first among equals'. The upheavals of the French invasions of Italy after 1494 offered an alliance of ordinary citizens and rival great families the opportunity to force the Medici from the city. But the continuing struggles in Italy subsequently permitted the Medici to return, backed by Spanish military power, and in 1530 they converted the Republic into a hereditary duchy.

International relations were thus substantially shaped by the interests and decisions of rulers acting on behalf of what they perceived as their dynastic or family interests. The same volatile concerns with honour, reputation, and status that shaped interpersonal violence in the early modern state were thus extended into the conduct of international relations. European bellicosity was shaped by a further factor. The essential characteristic of the European ruling class was its self-identity as the second estate of the *bellatores*, whose status was inextricably linked to warfare and fighting. The enduring means to validate or consolidate noble status was through military service in war, individual feats of arms, or, at the very least, association with the trappings of warfare in visual representation, architecture, dress, and behaviour. The European ruling class was interested too in the opportunities that warfare brought for recognition and advancement of status. Rulers themselves were, of course, part of this culture: their claim to pre-eminence amongst their own nobilities was, with rare exceptions, based on military leadership and martial self-projection.

Reasons for conflict

As in any other historical period, the main reasons for conflict between states were enduring and familiar: the quest for security against present or future threats to territory or regime; the strategic advantages to be gained from conquering or controlling additional territory; the resources and revenues that these lands and peoples might bring—whether for the ruler and the government, or as a means to reward a military and administrative elite.

However, in terms of particular and public motivations for warfare in Europe from 1400 to 1650, pride of place would go to the assertion or defence of territorial claims based on the inheritance and marital rights of ruling families. Recommencing in the early fifteenth century, the dynastic ambitions of the English house of Lancaster profited spectacularly from a civil war between the Burgundian and Armagnac branches of the French house of Valois. Once the Burgundians abandoned their English allies and made peace with the French crown, the days of English power in France were numbered, and by 1453 they had been driven out of all but the remaining bridgehead of Calais. Dynastic tensions nonetheless mounted as the dukes of Burgundy expanded their territories through judicious marriage, inheritance, and conquest: there was a real possibility that the duchy would come to dominate the first-rank European powers. But when Duke Charles the Bold (1433–77; ruled 1467–77) sought to make good his claim to Lorraine, an important addition to the jigsaw of territorial acquisitions, he encountered not merely the resistance of the Duke of Lorraine but his Swiss allies. The annihilation of the Burgundian armies by the Swiss in 1476–7 and the death of Charles in battle led to the division of Burgundy between Louis XI of France and the House of Habsburg. Louis XI (1423–83; ruled 1461–83) asserted that the province of Burgundy itself reverted to France since the Valois Burgundian line was now extinct in the male line; the Habsburg claims, above all to the Burgundian Netherlands, were based on the marriage of Charles the Bold's sister to Maximilian of Habsburg, who was to be elected Holy Roman Emperor in 1508.

The prospect of extended wars over the Burgundian succession was deferred for a few decades by a new dynastic preoccupation, the claims that Charles VIII of France held over the kingdom of Naples. Invading Italy in 1494 and exploiting the divisions and opportunism amongst the various Italian rulers, Charles reached Naples virtually unopposed, dispossessed the Aragonese ruling dynasty, and had himself crowned king in early 1495. This triggered a series of major wars for control of territory in Italy between the French and Spanish monarchies, the Austrian Habsburg rulers, and the various major Italian states, that were to last, on and off, until 1559.

Between 1516 and 1519 the Austrian Habsburg lands, the Burgundian inheritance, the states of Spain, and the imperial title were all subsumed into the extraordinary dynastic 'composite monarchy' of Charles V of Habsburg (1500–58; ruled 1519–56), the ultimate expression of the dynastic legitimation of sovereignty. Charles's inheritance refocused the struggle from Italy into a wide-ranging duel between Habsburg and Valois

ALLEGORY OF THE ABDICATION OF CHARLES V by Frans Francken the Younger (1581–1642).

monarchies, and further war zones encompassed, above all, the lands of the old Duchy of Burgundy. The scale and length of these Habsburg–Valois wars steadily increased through the first half of the sixteenth century, culminating in the largest and costliest of these conflicts, that between 1551 and 1559, which was waged across Italy, in Germany, on the Netherlands' frontiers, and over the Mediterranean. Both powers were driven to the brink of financial collapse by 1557, while Charles V, literally worn out by the struggle to defend the Habsburg *Monarchia*, staged a spectacular abdication ceremony at Brussels in 1556, where he divided the monarchy between his brother Ferdinand (1503–64; ruled 1558–64), who received the lands and rulerships in central Europe and was elected Emperor, and his son Philip II (1527–98; ruled 1556–98), who was granted Spain, Italy, and the Netherlands.

The treaty of Cateau-Cambrésis which ended the Habsburg–Valois dynastic struggle in 1559 was a watershed in west-central Europe, and the inauguration of a period in which dynastic motives for warfare competed and combined with the second major motivation for conflict, the proliferation of confessional antagonisms. Religious conflict had been a key factor in justifying warfare elsewhere in Europe from the outset of the period. Foremost amongst these conflicts throughout the fifteenth and sixteenth centuries was the attempt of European powers to prevent the rise of the Ottoman Empire as the major force in south-east Europe and in the Mediterranean. The period from 1389 to 1529 was marked by almost uninterrupted Ottoman success in deploying their superior resources, manpower, and military organization in conquests which brought them to the gates of Vienna in 1529, and established their permanent control south of a line which ran through Croatia, partitioned Hungary, and continued onwards through Ukraine to the Black Sea. The pressure was no less successfully applied to the European presence around the coasts and the islands of the eastern Mediterranean, and indeed the great Christian victory at Lepanto in 1571 did more to consolidate Ottoman and Western spheres of influence in the Mediterranean than to signify any decisive transformation in the military balance of power.

But the pursuit of Ottoman imperialism, though perceived as an existential threat to much of east-central Europe, was not the only enduring source of confessional conflict. Religious differences justified the wars waged by the Grand Duchy of Lithuania and its dynastic ally, Poland: on the western borders this involved conflict with the Prussian-based Catholic Order of the Teutonic Knights, and in the east with the Orthodox Muscovites. The defeat of the Teutonic Order at Grunwald in 1410 massively reduced the threat in the west, but still left a lengthy struggle with the rulers of Muscovy. This was fought both on the borders between Lithuania and territory claimed by the Muscovite rulers as part of their ancient inheritance of Rus, and later over control of Livonia and surrounding territory with access to the Baltic. The struggle for control in Livonia was also to draw in the Scandinavian kingdoms of Denmark and Sweden; from the 1520s the conversion of the rulers of both these states to Lutheranism gave an additional level of confessional antagonism to the conflicts.

The emergence of an entirely new set of confessional conflicts in the Christian West was most obviously tied to the impact of the Lutheran Reformation and the subsequent Protestant reformers, above all Jean Calvin and his followers. But a foretaste of the schismatic potential of reformed ideas was provided a century earlier by the Hussite wars in Bohemia which broke out in 1419, four years after Jan Hus's execution for heresy at the Council of Constance. Though the movement was contained within Bohemia, Hussite beliefs remained a powerful force, and underpinned both Protestant ideas and resistance as they spread from Germany in the sixteenth century. The revolt of the Lutheran German princes against Emperor Charles V's attempts to reimpose Catholicism was challenged and seemingly defeated in 1547 after the battle of Mühlberg. But new Protestant unrest amongst the princes, strongly backed by France, defeated and humiliated Charles in 1552 and gained the legal establishment of Lutheran religious practice in the German territories. Even more lastingly disruptive to Western peace was the emergence of militant Calvinism in France and the Netherlands, and the attempts of the French and Spanish monarchies to repress this threat to Catholicism. The struggle in France lasted over thirty years, 1561–95, and during these decades minimized France's involvement in international conflict. That the kingdom did not suffer dismemberment at the hands of a Spanish-backed Catholic movement, intent on dethroning Henri IV, the first Bourbon—and initially Protestant—ruler of France, was largely due to Spain's own confessional problems in the Netherlands. Here a potent combination of Protestant grievances and the territorial resistance of peoples and elites to heavy-handed Spanish government and taxation had sparked off a revolt in 1567–8. This conflict was to last until a final settlement was reached in 1648, and involved from 1579 the division of the Netherlands between the seven 'United Provinces' and the loyalist southern provinces of the Spanish Netherlands.

As the war between Spain and the United Provinces continued, the focus shifted away from a land-based struggle attempting to redraw the frontier between North and South. Dutch enthusiasm for developing and expanding the conflict was focused upon the potentially rich spoils from attacking the commercial and territorial transoceanic empires of both Habsburg Spain and, thanks to Philip II's rights of inheritance, Habsburg Portugal. This refocusing of the war against the Habsburgs into not just a maritime but an extra-European dimension represented a decisive shift in the character of European warfare. Associations of Dutch political, financial, and maritime interests attacked the Spanish and Portuguese colonial empires for commercial and economic advantage. Rival trading fleets competed in colonial markets that were supposedly the monopolies of Spanish merchants; trading bases and forts were captured and competing centres of commercial operations established; Portuguese or Spanish settlements were looted or destroyed, while Spain retaliated against Dutch and English outposts. Even before Spain and Portugal and their empires had been united by the dynastic union of 1580, maritime and other clashes between their overseas empires had been avoided and downplayed as much as possible. But the struggle with the Dutch, the English, and the French was to create an entirely new, global dimension to European warfare, and for the first time generated wars which were explicitly wars of trade and economic control.

The climax of European conflicts during this period was reached in 1618 with the opening of what was to become the Thirty Years War (1618–48), three decades of continuous conflict which engulfed central and Western Europe, successively drawing in every major European state. As with the outbreak of the First World War in 1914, historians have traditionally divided between those who see the Thirty Years War as a terrible accident and those who see it as a virtually unavoidable consequence of political and religious developments over the previous half-century. The determinists have a strong case in that the motives for the war straddle both dynastic and confessional conflict. The war was another revolt against Habsburg dynastic rulership, in this case the Habsburgs' political relationship to the elective monarchy of Bohemia. But the principal flashpoint in Bohemia was the determination of the Protestant noble majority to contest any Habsburg attempt to expand the powers of the Catholic Church and to retrench previously conceded religious freedoms. Yet given the dynastic mindset of most of the international community, the revolt was treated by most states in 1618 as an internal matter falling within the legitimate sphere of action of the duly elected Austrian Habsburg ruler of Bohemia. Only the precipitate action of the Calvinist Palatine-Elector, Frederick V, in accepting the Bohemian crown from rebel leaders who had declared the Habsburg Ferdinand II deposed, turned the conflict outwards, and started the chain of events that led to a European conflagration. Yet even after the war had spread across central and Western Europe there were a number of points at which the Austrian and Spanish Habsburgs and their Catholic allies came close to imposing general peace on their terms. The factor which finally destroyed the best chance of ending the war in 1635 was the intervention of France: under Louis XIII and Cardinal Richelieu the old French rivalry with the House of Habsburg was to be renewed via a twenty-five-year war waged from 1635 to 1659 in Italy, Flanders, Lorraine, the Mediterranean, and on the Pyrenean frontiers. France's alliances with Habsburg enemies, the Calvinist Dutch Republic and Lutheran Sweden, emphasized the overwhelmingly dynastic motivation of this last phase of the Thirty Years War.

The conflict between France and Spain continued until 1659, but the other belligerent states had finally achieved an uneasy peace at the Congress of Westphalia in 1648. The agonizing slowness in reaching this settlement, given that the main negotiators had assembled in Osnabrück and Münster back in 1643, did not, as is often asserted, reflect collective rethinking of the nature of sovereignty, national identity, or aspirations to create a European balance of power. Such entrenched myths about 1648 have been presented as the culmination of an earlier evolution of 'Renaissance' states, based on principles of territorial sovereignty and the secularization of politics. The reality of the Westphalian negotiations was considerably more prosaic: the supposed beneficiaries of a new concept of territorial sovereignty, especially the German princes, gained no more autonomy from the Westphalia settlements than they had possessed before; religion continued to play a major role in international politics into the eighteenth century. It was not such principles that made the negotiations so painful and protracted, but the practical problems of coordinating a peace congress with scores of interested participants, rather than conducting the bilateral, 'dynastic' negotiations typical of most previous settlements. Moreover, the leading negotiators at the conferences behaved with a consistent opportunism and gamblers' recklessness in order to serve the immediate territorial interests of rulers whose concern with any abstract international state-system was minimal.

The changing character of war

In what ways did European warfare change over these 250 years, and what impact did this have on the states which were engaged in war? For many decades the discussion about military change has been focused on the notion of an early modern 'military revolution', which decisively transformed both the waging of war and the relationship between warfare and the authority and effectiveness of the state. Originating in 1955 with a celebrated article written by Michael Roberts, the 'military revolution' thesis brought together technological and organizational change, the increase in the overall size of armies, and the integration of military administration and organization into a larger pattern of state-building. Though a brilliant synthesis, its critics have argued that the original thesis was too narrowly focused on a few technological changes, above all, infantry firearms; it was too prone to neglect military developments and initiatives outside a narrow remit of territorial case studies; and in assessing states' responses to military change it was too wedded to a traditional model of administrative centralization and bureaucratic modernization.

This period of Renaissance warfare has also been linked into a larger, and indeed global, 'gunpowder revolution'. Like its 'military' counterpart, however, the 'gunpowder revolution' is also problematic in seeking to present what was actually a long-term and haphazard evolutionary process in terms of one or two transformative moments. The casting of artillery, initially firing stone shot but increasingly making use of more effective iron cannonballs, was the first practical development following from the successful manufacture of gunpowder. Very gradually the trade-off between the effectiveness of artillery and its weight, cumbersomeness, and unreliability improved. Both the Ottoman capture of Constantinople in 1453 and the successful drive of the French to expel the English from Normandy and Aquitaine in the 1450s are associated with the deployment of artillery. When Charles VIII invaded Italy in pursuit of his Neapolitan crown in 1494, much was made of the artillery train which accompanied his army and whose existence persuaded Italian cities and towns to open their gates to the French without resistance. In reality, Charles demonstrated a virtually universal law of siege warfare: that the willingness of a garrison or population to resist has less to do with the quality and defensibility of their fortifications than with their assessment of the capacity of the besieging army to block any attempts to lift the siege by a relieving force.

Further technical improvements during the sixteenth century saw better-made, less cumbersome artillery pieces deployed on the battlefield as well as in siege works. Yet this was far from transformative. Down to the Thirty Years War the numbers of cannon generally available to an average-sized campaign army remained small: the French army of 23,000 men at the Battle of Rocroi in 1643 possessed only twelve cannon against a similar-sized Spanish force with eighteen. In those armies in which the numbers of cannon increased, it was at the lightest end of the scale, guns firing a ball weighing three pounds or less, with much more limited range and impact. The occasional importance of well-placed batteries of guns on particular battlefields still needed to be traded off against the overall reduction in the army's mobility, the inflexibility of a battery once set up on the battlefield, and the heavy expense and logistical demands of maintaining artillery trains.

Two developments had led to the proliferation of artillery. Though in practice there were other factors at work in determining their defensibility, the notion that artillery had suddenly rendered the traditional walls of medieval cities, towns, and castles redundant had a powerful influence on European rulers. Castles and fortified cities were statements of the sovereignty and prestige of rulers; their loss to an enemy was a personal affront over and above any strategic or economic consideration. The advent of siege artillery gave a powerful stimulus to a series of experiments with new fortification techniques, abandoning curtain walls and high towers in favour of low-lying, immensely thick walls and ramparts. A series of further experiments concerned the defence of these low-lying walls. The favoured solution involved various forms of angled bastions projecting outwards from the walls and providing covering fire against enemy siege forces trying to move up against the defences. These were further defended by elaborate sets of equally low-lying outworks, and sometimes by an attached or separate 'star-fortress'—essentially a defensive strongpoint made up of five, six, or more angled bastions.

The cost of such new fortification was immense; rather than a straightforward brick/stone construction, the new system required land-clearances, the remodelling of terrain, and a combination of stone, brick, and earth in quantities far greater than anything previously constructed. Moreover, the defence against an enemy army was not intended to be passive; the siege works, artillery batteries, and raiding parties were to be held back by counter-battery fire from artillery set into the walls and bastions. Even though the reality of the deployment usually fell short of the original plans, the growth of new fortifications and their vast scale nonetheless represented a huge driver for the production and deployment of artillery.

The new fortifications became as integral to the self-perception of rulers as the great medieval castles had been: they were symbols of sovereignty as much as a court and palace, the striking of coinage, or the exercise of justice. Rulers spent heavily not just on the building of these supposedly invulnerable fortifications, but to emblazon them with escutcheons and other family symbols that projected dynastic pride and sovereign status as well as military prowess. Indeed the symbolism was so powerful that associations with new military architecture were deliberately deployed in other contexts: the Italian princely house of Farnese, for example, built their sixteenth-century palace at Caprarola upon a pentagonal, 'star-fortress' base.

Militarily, however, the development was perhaps less decisive than its expense and its impact on artillery production might suggest. For many lesser princes and for independent city-states, the attraction of using limited resources to build a single prestigious fortification system was strong. The effects could be exactly the reverse of those anticipated: the Gonzaga dukes lavished money on the fortifications of Mantua, and above all on the creation of a super-fortress at Casale in their second duchy of Monferrato, standing on the western frontiers of Spanish Milan. Far from providing protection for Monferrato, the fortress at Casale attracted the military attention of both Spain and France from the moment it was constructed in the 1590s until it was finally razed by treaty in 1695. State-of-the-art fortifications without troops on the ground to drive off besieging armies would, at best, only protract the inevitable surrender of the garrison. In the case of the Republic of Siena, overspending on the city's new fortifications in the 1540s/1550s deprived it of the financial resources to resist Florentine aggression and ensured its political extinction.

THE FARNESE PALACE OF CAPRAROLA, central Italy, constructed by Giacomo da Vignola 1559–73.

The spread of permanent, new-style fortifications was patchy. Where they were regarded by local rulers as adding prestige and security to what were already seen as key locations, they reached into Eastern and Northern Europe. In the 1560s, for example, the Livonian Knights of the Sword constructed three angled bastions to strengthen the defences of Narva. However, such expensive and prestige-signalling construction was in general less evident in the east; the strongpoints and towns on the Hungarian borders relied on local resources and techniques for strengthening fortifications with extra earthworks and temporary bastions or forts.

The second transformative role for gunpowder and artillery was at sea. The classic Mediterranean warship remained throughout this period the galley: shallow-draught, low-lying ships, equipped with sails but which relied, in manoeuvring, coastal operations, and in battle, on banks of up to 120–40 oarsmen per galley. Traditional tactics had relied on ramming and boarding, but the addition of one heavy cannon and 2–4 lighter weapons mounted in the bows added firepower to galley warfare. The devastating effects of cannon-fire on these lightly built ships and their vulnerable concentrations of manpower became a significant factor in battle. The longevity of the galley in warfare when contrasted with the greater robustness and cost-effectiveness of the

THE SIEGE OF JÜLICH, 1621–2, by Pieter Snayers shows both the new-style defences of the town and the temporary siege works, including temporary 'star-forts', that the Spanish have erected along their siege lines.

sailing warship owes much to this capacity to combine limited but effective firepower with the manoeuvrability and flexibility offered by the oarsmen.

However, the more obvious symbiosis between artillery and navies came in the form of the ocean-going warship, ultimately the galleons of the later sixteenth century and their successors. Small numbers of cannon had initially been deployed in the poop and stern of ships to provide firepower, but without the accuracy of the bow-mounted guns in galleys. As these ships grew in size, combining square and lateen sails for better speed and manoeuvrability, shipbuilders innovated by mounting cannon along their flanks. At first these batteries were placed on the upper deck, but shuttered gun ports permitted the cannon to be mounted lower in the ship, improving stability. By the mid-sixteenth century the capital warships of the various European powers had the principal battery of guns mounted along both sides of a covered lower deck.

At this point it was still possible to combine the functions of warship and merchant vessel. A single row of guns below decks was compatible with the internal disposition of an ocean-going merchant ship. However, the logic of deploying shipboard firepower as the principal means of waging naval war encouraged progressively heavier armaments. Rather than simply mounting guns along a single deck, new generations of warships became gun-platforms, with two, sometimes three, decks of cannon. This opened a clear gap between purpose-built warships and merchant ships with military

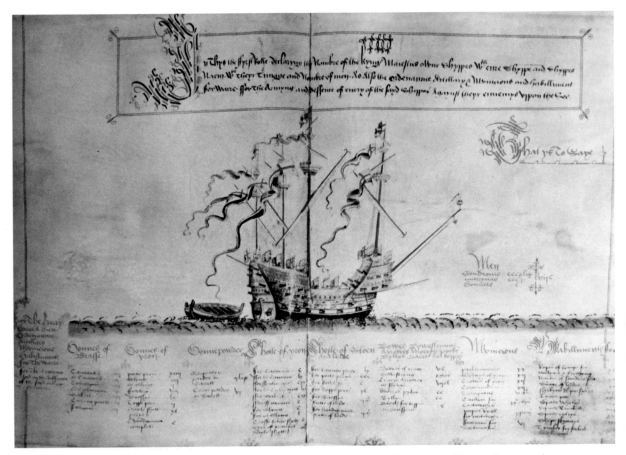

THE *GREAT HARRY* IN THE ANTHONY ROLL, a record of ships in Henry VIII's navy created by Anthony Anthony.

potential. The need to absorb close-range fire from similarly armed enemy ships, and indeed the internal recoil from such massive gun batteries, demanded thicknesses and quantities of timber in the initial construction that were incompatible with the economies of building and operating merchant ships. In the 1580s the *Sao Martinho*, a purpose-built Portuguese galleon that served as the flagship of the Spanish Armada in 1588, already carried 48 heavy guns on two main gun decks, while the English *Sovereign of the Seas*, launched in 1637, carried 102 guns on three decks.

This concentration of artillery represented a huge financial expenditure, even though ships' guns tended to be cast in cheaper iron rather than bronze. A single warship with 40–60 guns carried considerably more artillery than would accompany a field army of 20,000–30,000 men. Like fortifications, warships became linked with dynastic pride and self-projection. From the early sixteenth century this determined a drive towards size, armament, and decoration that were by no means optimal. Henry VIII's flagship, the *Henry Grace à Dieu* (or *Great Harry*), at nearly 1,500 tonnes and carrying

43 cannon was heavier and more heavily armed than any other English warship when launched in 1514. From the outset the ship handled badly, and played a limited role in naval operations until a drastic remodelling in 1536. The *Vasa*, symbol of Gustavus Adolphus's Swedish monarchy, capsized and sank after her launch in the harbour in Stockholm in 1628: her 64 cannon and high stern, encrusted with elaborate dynastic iconography, had made her dangerously unstable.

Even if practicality and utility were on occasions sacrificed to the personal priorities of rulers, the symbiosis of warship design and artillery transformed the projection of naval power around the European coasts, but above all into the extra-European world. The capacity of European states to establish, link together, and fight over European colonies, whether around the African coasts, the New World, the Far East, or the Pacific, was unthinkable without this technology. The financial and organizational burdens implied by such shipbuilding and ship-arming technology were substantial: by 1650 large-scale, purpose-built dockyards and naval ports were commonplace, and probably the largest industrial and commercial enterprises of the period.

Less time needs to be spent on what has, paradoxically, absorbed the greatest attention in traditional accounts of the advent of gunpowder. The infantry handgun, after a large number of experiments with weight of shot, barrel length, and firing mechanism, reached its most developed form in the heavy musket of the late sixteenth and seventeenth centuries, fired by applying a length of lighted match to the powder-charge in the musket breech. Lighter *carabins* or *calivers* were also developed, and frequently issued to dragoons (horse-borne infantry). Cavalry were often armed with pistols, employing the more sophisticated (and expensive) wheel-lock firing mechanism, in which a spark struck from a flint ignited the powder.

In relation to modern debate, and especially the role that infantry firearms play in justifying the arguments for a 'military revolution', it is important not to separate firearms from a much wider set of tactical issues. All infantry firearms down to the end of this period were grossly inaccurate and had a range no greater—and often considerably less—than traditional longbows and crossbows. The outer limits of effectiveness for the heaviest musket from this period was around 100 metres; even in the hands of experienced soldiers a musket took between ninety seconds and a full two minutes to load, prime, and fire. If the musket had virtues to offset against these disadvantages, it was that it was simple to drill soldiers in its basic use, and it required no particular physical prowess beyond the ability to support its weight with the aid of a forked rest; when fired, its shot had a penetrative power far beyond any other missile weapon.

Muskets and other infantry firearms were not some isolated innovation in the development of warfare, capable of changing the course of conflict simply by their existence. They were a part, and by no means the most important one, in a much larger series of experiments and developments in battlefield tactics and organization in which the essential issues were the respective strengths of the offensive and defensive.

At the beginning of the fifteenth century the primary offensive weapon system remained the mounted, heavy-armoured knight. The weight and intimidating power of a charge of heavy cavalry, arrayed in a deep formation, equipped with lances and armoured to deflect most indirect hits by arrows or other projectiles, remained a formidable force on the battlefield. Certain defensive formations—notably the English army's linking of highly skilled longbowmen and dismounted men-at-arms—could hold their own against either heavy cavalry or an attack of armoured knights on foot, as at Agincourt (1415) and Verneuil (1424). But these were exceptions which proved the general rule, and heavy cavalry remained a potent weapon, especially against infantry forces who were not in well-prepared positions and did not contain a solid core of experienced troops.

There were nonetheless drawbacks entailed in depending on an armoured force of knights/men-at-arms as the cutting edge of offensive tactics. This was a hugely expensive and specialized military system: a single heavy cavalryman, equipped with full armour, provided with carefully bred warhorses, and requiring a support staff, represented a substantial capital investment. To the expense was added the issue of training: the skills required to deploy weaponry while wearing heavy armour on horseback required practice from early youth; new heavy cavalry could not just be mustered or purchased at will. Armoured knights were less effective when fighting a war of manoeuvre, against an enemy unprepared to fight a conventional battle or prepared to use fortifications or terrain to secure their positions. Moreover, the tight link between social origins and this style of warfare created a sense of exclusivity which rendered cooperation between the equestrian elite and the commoner troops within armies difficult. The contempt with which the military elite regarded the ordinary troops in their own armies stood in contrast to the chivalric courtesy which they practised towards enemies of a similar rank, especially when the latter could yield substantial ransoms.

Some attempt to resolve the problems of inflexibility and cooperation can be seen in the flourishing of both the mercenary 'great companies', and their evolution by the fifteenth century into the forces of the Italian *condottiere* commanders. Brought together from the debris of forces fighting in France in the fourteenth century, the original companies, most notably the White Company of John Hawkwood (*c.*1360–90), integrated different types of soldier more effectively into a single force. Men-at-arms were accompanied by mounted archers, longbowmen, and other infantry. Their strength, and by Hawkwood's time their marketability, depended on cohesion born of shared military experience: they brought a flexible combination of weaponry, and were capable of acting together as a tight-knit force in very different combat environments. In the struggles amongst the smaller territorial states in Italy, the companies and their *condottiere* successors offered a much more effective and flexible solution to rulers' military ambitions and local defence than attempts to construct over-specialized forces of heavy cavalry.

The trend towards hiring specialists from outside a particular society was to gather momentum in the second half of the fifteenth century. The greatest transformation in this respect also meant a shift in offensive tactics from reliance on heavy cavalry to the rise of the massive infantry pike square. This deceptively simple weapon system was pioneered in the Swiss cantons. Relying on the mass and impact of ordinary foot soldiers, packed together in units of typically around 4,000 men, the Swiss combined newly recruited peasants with the experience of a significant core of veterans. Armed with a mixture of pikes up to 6–7 metres long, long-handled axes, and broadswords, the majority of soldiers in the centre of the block contributed little more than weight to the impact of the unit. However, the result was a force that either as a single unit or multiple great squares could smash through any formation of enemy cavalry or infantry. The destruction of the Burgundian army's traditional heavy cavalry by the Swiss in 1476–7 inaugurated a long period in which the Swiss pike-square was the most sought-after weapon system in west-central Europe.

Competition with the Swiss came from the *Landsknechte*, mass infantry forces recruited in the German lands from the late fifteenth century and deploying the same fighting techniques. It might be assumed that this massive reduction in the unit cost per soldier from armoured cavalryman to peasant pikeman would be reflected in the overall cost of war. But rather like the English longbowmen whose specialized training began in early youth, the group cohesion, rough-and-ready soldiers' democracy, and strong local identities within the great infantry squares proved impossible for any other communities to imitate. The costs of hiring Swiss mercenaries and German *Landsknechte* remained high; the elaborate costumes of the soldiers, their reputation for conspicuous consumption and profligacy, advertised their marketability as a skilled workforce. The rulers of major states eagerly sought their services regardless of cost: no French army after 1515 was made up of fewer than 50 per cent *Landsknechte* and Swiss mercenaries; during the 1550s the proportion of mercenaries regularly approached 80 per cent of French armies whose overall strength totalled 30,000–40,000 men.

For all their effectiveness as an offensive force on the battlefield, these dense, deep formations were vulnerable to artillery. The heavy casualties inflicted on the Swiss at Marignano just outside Milan in 1515 were mainly due to the effects of French cannon. Moreover, even when the infantry squares broke through the enemy lines, it was difficult for these troops to follow up to pursue and rout a retreating enemy. It took the Swiss a third battle, at Nancy, definitively to smash the Burgundian forces which had been able to regroup after suffering shattering losses at Grandson and Morat. Above all, focusing on specialized, expensive mercenary infantry was problematic if military operations involved siege warfare rather than a massed engagement in the open field. Both Swiss and German mercenaries considered digging siege works was beneath their dignity, while employing them for the routine activities of enforcing a blockade of a city or fortress was absurdly extravagant. They were also the soldiers notoriously least likely to tolerate the shortfalls of pay which were an almost inevitable aspect of any protracted siege.

Two contemporary developments in different parts of Europe led an evolution away from the giant pike-square as the optimum means to pursue offensive tactics. The first

THE VICTORY OF THE SWISS PIKE-SQUARES AT GRANDSON, 1476, from the *Schilling Chronicle*.

of these, largely neglected by historians, was the evolution of more effective cavalry tactics. The redundancy, for all but ceremonial purposes, of heavy-armoured cavalry was evident by the early sixteenth century. However, lighter, more mobile cavalry were still used in offensive roles. Attention has been focused on the supposed ineffectiveness of new types of Western European cavalry, especially units of German *Reiter*, medium-armoured cavaliers. By riding up in sequence to enemy infantry units and successively discharging pistols at close range, they hoped to cause enough confusion, damage, and panic in an enemy force to break up their unit and allow ranks of cavalry behind to press home the advantage. In the hands of well-drilled and experienced cavalry, these tactics could prove decisive, as they did at the Battle of Mühlberg in 1547 when Charles V's *Reiter* routed German Protestant infantry and cavalry. However, against experienced and cohesive infantry units this tactic was unlikely to achieve a breakthrough. Increasingly in Western armies of this period, cavalry units of this sort were deployed on both flanks of armies, and fought against other cavalry units deploying a similar mixture of firearms and hand-to-hand combat. These engagements were not so much the physical clash of tight-packed bodies of cavalry as chaotic melees in which individual cavalry fought in small groups until one side wavered or broke. A breakthrough could then offer the possibility that the victorious cavalry would regroup and could outflank or panic the infantry centre of the enemy army. This was the case at the Battle of Ivry in 1590 won by Henri IV of France and his cavalry against his French opponents in the Catholic League; it became the pattern of numerous battles in the later Thirty Years War.

Still more important were developments in Eastern Europe. These were partly in response to the armies of the Ottoman Empire, which contained a very large component of light and medium-armoured cavalry, the *sipahi* forces, raised through a form of feudal levy from the Ottoman landholders or *timariots*. The parallel development within the Polish–Lithuanian dynastic union during the sixteenth century was the hussar: these were also medium-light cavalry, armed with a lance, a long straight sword, and a bow, which on horseback was lighter and far more effective than a cumbersome, short-range firearm. Reliant, like the *sipahi*, on speed and manoeuvrability, massed units of hussars could break into infantry formations, using their lances and long swords against the defensive pikes, and intimidating musketeers whose opportunity to fire and reload against fast-advancing cavalry was limited. Such cavalry, fluid in their formations and manoeuvring, were far from easy targets for any enemy counter-strike. Copied in Hungary and supplemented by the even lighter cavalry, the *croates, cravattes*, and sometimes units who described themselves as cossacks from nearer the Ottoman frontiers, the military future for cavalry lay in these styles of forces. After a series of battles in Polish Prussia during the mid-1620s where Swedish infantry were badly mauled by Polish cavalry-dominated armies, Swedish resistance finally collapsed altogether in the face of an assault by Polish hussars and light cossack cavalry at Honigfelde in 1629. It was not the case that cavalry were overshadowed by infantry, let alone replaced altogether. By the later decades of the Thirty Years War, the overall proportion of cavalry in armies regularly exceeded the infantry, often by a proportion as high as two-thirds to one-third. Cavalry were seen as

FRANCIS I (1494–1547; ruled 1515–47).

the linchpin in commanders' operational plans, offering striking power, speed, surprise, and the ability to follow up initial military advantage far more effectively than infantry.

That cavalry was anything but an obsolete military arm in the century from 1550 to 1650 reflects the considerable discussion and uncertainty about the role of infantry firearms in the structuring of contemporary armies. The Swiss and *Landsknechte* down to the 1520s had tended to neglect firearms in favour of brute impact and *armes blanches,* but the next generation were more ready to see benefits from the new weaponry.

The Spanish *tercios* composed of 3,000 infantry when they were first deployed in the 1530s—a century later reduced to around 1,500—were more or less equally divided between pikemen, swordsmen/halberdiers, and musketeers. They represented the first systematic attempt to deploy firearms within infantry formations. In the right circumstances musket fire could certainly be used to considerable effect: the Spanish musketeers sheltering behind a low park wall and in the woods at the Battle of Pavia in 1525 slaughtered a large proportion of the French cavalry force, unhorsed King Francis, and ensured his capture.

Individual successes could not, however, disguise the essential problem: the extreme vulnerability of free-standing musketeers to any assault by enemy infantry or cavalry. For musketeers to be effective they had to be brought out of tight-packed, deep formations, and deployed in lines. But with the limited range of their weapons, their slow firing rate, and the open order required to avoid accidents with match and powder, they needed protection, which could be provided most effectively by a solid wall of pikemen, able to wield their 3–4-metre spears to fend off cavalry or infantry attacks, and then to launch their own offensive 'push of pike' to drive off enemy forces. Throughout this period the highly prized infantry, the 'double-pay men', were those armed with pikes: they bore the brunt of hand-to-hand fighting, and the cohesion of the infantry depended on their steadiness of nerve and experience.

Nonetheless, the conviction gained momentum through the sixteenth century that infantry firearms might prove decisive in the right conditions, whether on the battlefield, in sieges, or in the waging of 'small' or irregular warfare. How far this made a virtue of necessity is open to question: most armies drew on pools of unskilled manpower and needed to make use of this resource quickly and for no more than one or two campaigns. Equipping these recruits with muskets or other handguns was the only practical option. The process took another step forward in the later sixteenth century with the fashionable notion that if the musketeers could be drilled to discharge their muskets in sequence by rows, then retire to the back of the formation to reload in prescribed sequence, it might be possible to ensure a continuous hail of musket-fire directed at an advancing enemy. This infantry manoeuvre, the celebrated countermarch, was attributed to the self-publicizing efforts of the military commanders of the Dutch Republic, Maurice and Frederick-Henry of Orange-Nassau, but was probably in use in the Spanish *tercios* during the 1590s, a few years before its deployment by the Dutch. Such manoeuvres fed the dangerous illusion that infantry firepower alone, delivered from slow, unreliable, and inaccurate muskets, might be sufficient to defeat an enemy without having to engage in hand-to-hand struggle where cohesion, experience, and acquired skills would almost certainly prove decisive.

The progressive increase in the numbers of musketeers until they composed two-thirds of typical infantry units, against one-third of pikemen, compounded these problems. Although innumerable experiments were conducted to find a formation that would allow extended lines of musketeers to be protected by adequate forces of pikemen, the simple truth was that the concerns to maximize firepower and simultaneously to provide weight and cohesion in defence and attack could never be made compatible. Reducing the overall size of units, as some reformers attempted, ensured that linear deployment of musketeers did not create a single, widely extended front, but it also meant that units of only 200–300 combined musketeers and pikemen were intensely vulnerable to the weight and momentum of assaults by units, such as the *tercios*, that were three or four times larger. It took the *tercio*-sized regiments of the Habsburg/Catholic League army less than an hour at Breitenfeld (1631) to pulverize the forces of the Elector of Saxony, drawn up in small, elaborately integrated units. That the army of Gustavus Adolphus of Sweden, fighting alongside the Saxons, transformed the outcome of the battle was not because the Swedes had got the equation of firepower and weight/cohesion 'right'. It was because the high proportion of experienced Swedish, Scots, and German veterans serving in the army manoeuvred themselves with exemplary skill and discipline to smash through the weakened centre of the enemy army.

New military technology, whether warships and fortresses or the effective deployment of weapons, was one of the challenges that warfare presented to rulers and their governments in this period. But it needs to be integrated into two other, obviously related issues. The first was the growing scale of warfare, the increasing size of armies and navies. The second was the challenge of paying for and administering armies and navies that were not merely larger but had grown into more complex institutions.

The growth of military establishments across Europe between 1400 and 1650 is by no means a monolithic process. It is important to draw a distinction between the size of individual armies or navies on campaign and in battle, and the size of overall military establishments. Individual examples of armies on the battlefield might appear to support a claim that these increased dramatically. At Agincourt in 1415 Henry V probably mustered 9,000 troops against 12,000 in the French army. At Pavia in 1525, the French forces numbered around 23,500 against Charles V's army of 23,000. Yet earlier battles on a larger scale can easily be cited: it seems likely that both the Christian alliance and the Ottomans fielded armies of around 15,000–16,000 troops at the Ottoman victory of Nicopolis in 1396, while at Varna in 1444 it is suggested that the victorious Ottoman army may have numbered up to 60,000 and the Christian forces 20,000. Moreover, numbers on the battlefield do not continue to increase after the early sixteenth century: during the Thirty Years War the crucial Battle of Lützen in 1632, at which Gustavus Adolphus lost his life, was fought between a Swedish army of 19,000 and an imperial army of 17,000. Throughout these two centuries it was rare to mass field armies on the battlefield or at a siege totalling over 25,000 men. Significantly, the largest single engagement in this period, and indeed down to the 1690s, was a battle at sea: at Lepanto in 1571 some 68,000 sailors, oarsmen, and soldiers in the Christian fleet of 212 galleys and other vessels fought against 80,000 combatants in 250 Ottoman galleys.

Yet particular armies on campaign, in battle, and at sieges do not tell the whole story. Across this period there was a considerable increase in the overall size of military

GIORGIO VASARI'S PAINTING OF THE BATTLE OF LEPANTO.

establishments across Europe, taking into account the maintenance of multiple armies, the provision of reserves, garrison troops, and all types of naval forces. The most probable explanation for this was political. The pressure of the Ottoman Empire, first of all in south-east Europe and then as a naval power in the Mediterranean, had a huge impact in shaping the scale of the military responses of its European opponents. The Ottoman military machine, based on the resources of a huge territorial agglomeration stretching from Cairo to Baghdad, and from Aden to Belgrade, was able to maintain permanent troops and temporary levies well in excess of 100,000 men. Thanks to a relatively efficient logistical system, large parts of this military establishment could be projected into war zones, focused in particular campaign theatres for sieges or battles, while additional contingents of reinforcements and reserves could be deployed from the military resource pool. In the 1526 Ottoman campaign in Hungary, the forces under the command of Suleiman numbered over 60,000 troops, and more could be allocated from across the empire to make good losses and to consolidate gains. This was well over twice the size of the army that the Hungarians and Bohemians had mobilized for the campaign, and largely accounts for their crushing defeat at Mohacs in that year.

States aiming to resist the Ottoman military system needed to increase the size of their own military establishments. This was the case amongst the Eastern European powers, explaining in part the dynastic union between Poland and Lithuania, and that between Hungary and Bohemia. By 1579 the paper strength of the Polish–Lithuanian military establishment stood at 56,000. In central and Western Europe the key figure in directing resistance to Ottoman expansion from the 1520s was the Habsburg ruler Charles V. His position as heir to the composite monarchy linking the Austrian, Burgundian, and Spanish inheritances, and his election as Holy Roman Emperor, provided him with a military resource base not seen in the West since the fall of the Roman Empire. Charles V's ability to mobilize these imposing resources was felt by his chief Western enemy, Valois France. At the time of the siege of Metz and the war against France in the 1550s Charles V possessed a military establishment of between 100,000 and 150,000 men. France, the most populous and wealthiest territorial state in Europe, in turn increased her own mobilization of military resources, waging a succession of wars simultaneously in up to three independent campaign theatres in the decades from the 1530s.

The clash of the major powers—the Ottomans, the Habsburg *Monarchia*, and France— had its impact in turn on second-rank states. War on land and sea against the Ottomans squeezed Venice to the limits of her resources, forcing her to maintain land forces of 30,000 to 35,000 through much of the sixteenth century, and to raise her establishment of combat-ready galleys from 25 up to 100 vessels between 1400 and 1600. Henry VIII invaded France in 1544–5 in alliance with Charles V with an English army (including German *Landsknechte*) of 40,000 troops.

Charles's dynastic *Monarchia*, though it ratcheted upwards the military commitment of both his allies and enemies, was ultimately unsustainable, as the partitioning of his territories following his abdication demonstrated. His son and successor to the Spanish territories, Philip II, may never have mobilized military resources as great as those of his father, though the contribution of the Spanish crown in the later sixteenth century to the growth of European military establishments was arguably as important. This can be seen most clearly in Philip's creation and maintenance of an unprecedentedly large permanent army of occupation in response to the revolt of the Netherlands beginning in 1568. The Army of Flanders, the largest single element of Spain's military establishment until the mid-seventeenth century, typically numbered between 60,000 and 80,000 men. This permanent army of both field troops and garrisons was partly sustained by the Spanish crown's new-found wealth from the silver of the New World. But more significantly for other European states, it was also financed by locally extracted war taxes, or 'contributions', levied both on territory in the Netherlands

deemed to be occupied, and in areas where the army was simply reinforcing established authority. As the Dutch Republic consolidated its independence and increased
its wealth, partly through its own colonial ventures, its own military establishment was
increased to levels that could safeguard the seven provinces against this threat. Other
rulers might have sought to follow the Spanish example, but were hampered by their
comparative lack of financial resources. The 'Long Turkish War' of 1593–1606, fought
in Hungary between the Ottomans and a Habsburg-directed coalition of Catholic
troops, provided some opportunities to experiment with larger military establishments
maintained through locally extracted taxes and war contributions. But for the majority
of central European powers the opportunity to maintain unprecedented military
establishments without driving themselves into bankruptcy came with the Thirty
Years War. During these decades of continuous war the techniques of sustaining armies
through funding which did not depend exclusively on the rulers' own resources or tax
revenues were considerably developed: the levy of 'contributions' or war-taxes extracted
by the armies became more sophisticated, while the 'plunder economy' of arbitrary
military exploitation flourished. The Austrian Habsburg rulers and Holy Roman
Emperors Ferdinand II and Ferdinand III maintained total strengths of 50,000–60,000
troops under arms from the 1620s onwards; even a second-rank state like Bavaria
maintained a military establishment of 20,000 men from 1635. None of this would have
been possible without the financial opportunities—albeit also the dangers—opened up
by extended and continuous warfare. As ever, once these thresholds of scale had been
passed, apart from sporadic, short-term retrenchments, the pattern of overall increase
was clear and irreversible.

Rulers thus responded to a series of particular circumstances and initiatives by
choosing, or being obliged, to increase the scale of their military activities. But as
indicated, these competitive decisions to increase the numbers and the scale of armies
and navies had financial consequences. This problem of the rising numbers and cost of
troops was compounded by the financial consequences of technological change. If
firearms provided a cheap way of equipping large masses of infantry, the power, shot,
and match that they expended in ever larger quantities were a major burden, often as
costly as the basic bread/biscuit rations which many armies sought to provide for their
troops and sailors. War also meant gaining access to and paying for manufacturing
capacity, whether this was for building specialized warships in dockyards, constructing
massive new fortifications, cannon-founding, or the manufacture of other weaponry. It
meant contracting for the stockpiling and supply of foodstuffs, munitions, transport
vehicles, and draught animals. As armies grew larger, the expense of these elements
grew inexorably, as did the organizational challenges of coordinating manufacturing
processes, the movement of goods, and their supply to armies.

How were these financial and administrative demands to be met? The traditional
historiography of this period has traced a quasi-Darwinian link between the drive to
ensure the survival of the state through the effective management of warfare and the
development of a more centralized and powerful state administration. War and state-

building are thus intimately linked: a mass of initiatives supposedly aimed at central-izing and streamlining government administration, improving tax collection and developing the tax base, taking direct control of great areas of military organization such as recruitment, supply, and relations with the civilian population, are all attrib-uted to the growing pressure of warfare on rulers. The response to these military challenges must have led to the development of the centralized and bureaucratic modern state, the only organizational force capable of meeting the new challenges of warfare.

The reality behind these state-building theories was rather different. The whole period was one of experimentation, not with centralized state-building but with the outsourcing of military functions and organization, and ultimately of military finan-cing, into the hands of contractors and entrepreneurs, some of whom may have been the subjects of rulers, some from outside their domains. Certain elements of the management of war were contracted without hesitation or exception. The provision-ing of food rations to land armies or sailors; the manufacturing, stockpiling, and distribution of munitions; the purchases of weapons, clothing, and other military hardware: all these were placed either in the hands of the commanders of individual military units or ships, or were handled by larger-scale supply contractors. These latter might, for example, negotiate contracts with governments to provide biscuit rations to the entire Spanish galley fleet for one or more campaigns, or to supply munitions to all the Venetian garrisons along the Adriatic. Such contractors might be supervised by state administrators: the Venetians deployed members of the Senate as *proveditors* to investigate the fulfilment of supply contracts on land or at sea. But these were not areas that the state wished to control directly. They recognized that the networks of personal, family, and local contacts possessed by private merchants and manufactur-ers, the technical and mercantile know-how accrued through professional activity, and the flexibility and quality of their access to private credit made contracting far superior to reliance on state-employed administrators. For all the rhetoric from military com-manders and government ministers about lazy, corrupt, and incompetent suppliers, it was widely recognized that the skills brought to the complex, volatile business of purchasing grain or saltpetre, to arranging bread-making and distribution to armies on the march or within enemy territory, to stockpiling adequate but not excessive magazines of powder or match, were better handled by those who had a professional background in other mercantile operations.

The same applied to almost everything connected with armaments manufacturing, from basic pikes and muskets through to first-rate warships and massive projects for urban fortification. For crucially, though the scale of warfare was progressively expanding in this period, the demands of military supply were almost never sufficient to justify the existence of dedicated industrial complexes. Even the *Arsenale* in Venice, the classic example of a state-controlled shipyard, made up a lot of its business by private contracting to build and supply merchant galleys and sailing ships. Across Europe, soldiers' arms, equipment, and munitions were produced in small, non-specialized private workshops. The skill and experience of the military contractors lay in their ability to aggregate the capacity of numerous small-scale masters to fulfil large munitions contracts, to ensure some basic uniformity and quality control, and to arrange the collection, amassing, and distribution of the product.

None of this outsourcing of the logistical and hardware aspects of warfare was controversial to contemporaries. In the rare cases where reliance on private enterprise versus state control was explicitly discussed, as it was in sixteenth- and seventeenth-century Spain, the case for the greater effectiveness and cheapness of private contracting was conceded without much real debate. The case made by Spanish councillors and courtiers for direct administration was about prestige: it played on the implicit challenge to the king's reputation of outsourcing functions in a matter as intimately linked to royal sovereignty as the waging of war. And in supplying and equipping the armies this had limited traction, whether with the Spanish crown or other contemporary rulers. Where it became potentially controversial was in the provision of the armed forces themselves.

As we have seen throughout this period, many of the major military innovations— whether the *condottiere* companies, the Swiss and the *Landsknechte*, the German *Reiter* and various kinds of Eastern European light cavalry—were provided via specialized groups of mercenaries, hired by rulers who recognized their importance and skills as military specialists. Such mercenaries might be seen as 'foreign', though where identity and allegiance was determined by the identity of a dynastic ruler this was difficult to establish: it is questionable whether Charles V, ruler by dynastic right over a vast composite monarchy, ever hired a 'mercenary', if by mercenary is implied the service of someone who was not a subject from one of his numerous territories. What was distinctive about such groups of mercenary specialists, however, was that they were raised and maintained by their regimental colonels or company captains, and were not directly under the authority of the state's military administrators, even if they were subject to the generals. The soldiers were recruited, frequently equipped, fed, and paid by their colonels/captains, who exercised powers of discipline and justice over them. To some extent, therefore, overall command of an army involved negotiation with these officers: the interests of such military contractors certainly could not be taken for granted, as generations of French commanders forced to negotiate with Swiss units in French service discovered; Swiss fighting quality was almost never in question, but the terms and conditions attached to other aspects of service in the army could lead to clashes and disputes that were rarely won by the French generals.

However, a much more general phenomenon was gathering pace and reached a climax in the Thirty Years War: this was the willingness of rulers to contract out the raising and management not just of specialized troops, but of most of the soldiers serving in their armies, in the same way that they also contracted out the equipping and operations of the ships in their navies. Here the issues were directly concerned with finance and organization. Buying units of Swiss mercenaries was extremely expensive: very large payments in advance of recruitment and at the beginning of service were yet another aspect of the 'sellers' market' that such specialists successfully operated. Hiring Italian *condottieri*, Swiss, or *Landsknechte* did nothing to relieve the financial strains imposed on rulers by their military activities. However, as the sixteenth century progressed and periods of continuous military conflict grew lengthier, a more general form of military enterprise provided rulers and state administrations with much greater financial relief. Military service had maintained its high social cachet even as armies grew larger; investing financially in military activity as well as simply accepting military command was attractive to wealthy and socially ambitious subjects. In return for absorbing the costs of raising and equipping his troops and taking on the administrative burdens of the assignment, the colonel of a regiment, sometimes even company captains, would be granted control of appointment to the lesser officerships in his unit and a high level of autonomy in its running. He would also be the recipient of a 'salary' once campaigning began that reflected not just his wages as a serving officer, but reimbursement for his initial 'investment' in setting up his unit of infantry or cavalry, getting it to the army, and paying its initial wages. The same systems could be applied in the operations of navies: the Spanish galleys in the Mediterranean were either run under contract as entire squadrons by Genoese, Ragusan, or Neapolitan and Sicilian noble families, or the individual galleys were operated by their captains against negotiated lump-sum payments. And almost everywhere a large part of states' naval activity was based on licensed privateering, a system which transferred almost all the financial risk to the shipowners and their investors in return for the right to profit from prizes captured from the enemy's navy or merchant fleets.

The benefit to the ruler and his states was evident: the huge expenses and administrative challenges of recruiting and equipping an army or navy, paying the initial (and usually the largest) bonuses and wages to the troops, could all be outsourced to the financial credit and organizational efforts of the officers. Only once the army had come into being and started operations would the state start to become liable for the costs of the military, and by this time it was hoped, sometimes with justification, that these costs could be recovered from war taxes—those contributions on territory that the army was now occupying. The aim was to minimize the direct calls on the state's own limited revenues and resources. In cases, for example the Swedish royal army's 1631 expansion into territory around the Baltic and Germany, this system could be spectacularly successful, shifting the costs of warfare almost entirely away from the Swedish population and onto the lands occupied by the Swedes. War, in Gustavus Adolphus's words, could pay for itself—via the invested resources of his officers, who became stakeholders in the successes of Swedish conquest and imperialism.

Without this capacity to outsource a mass of the costs and the organizational burden of war into the hands of military contractors, it is doubtful that European states could have sustained the direct burden of fighting lengthy and larger-scale wars. Government administration remained either skeletal or, as in France, had expanded as a patrimonial system based on the sale of government office. These administrations had a limited capacity to tax, coordinate resources, or adjust to unprecedented organizational burdens. Their weakness was paralleled by the capacity of privileged and wealthy elites in most states to obstruct demands from rulers for taxation or other forms of revenue extraction. In this context the rulers' preparedness to delegate military authority and financial responsibility could tap a rich seam of enthusiasm amongst their elites. Buying into military command was a potentially remunerative investment: the profits to be gained from high levels of war taxes, loot, ransoms, and even the astute management of a military unit or warship might be considerable, even taking into account the levels of risk. At least as important, it was an investment which carried far higher social prestige than normal commercial activity: it was possible both to make a fortune and to gain or consolidate status from engaging in the quintessentially noble activity of military command. Not only was the market for raising troops immense and robust, the limited financial resources of many of the potential officers were supplemented by financial backers from the banking and mercantile worlds, partly because the investment was attractive, partly because the cachet of nobility and social status could rub off even on those indirectly involved.

Under these propitious circumstances, the scale of the enterprises could grow to a point where they became almost independent of the formal mechanisms of the state. The Dutch East and West India Companies (1602, 1621) were the largest and, especially in the case of the earlier VOC (the Dutch East India Company), most successful examples of military outsourcing in this period, maintaining private fleets, troops, garrisons, and fortifications out of the profits of their commercial activities and shareholder investment. Yet in expanding their colonial holdings, strengthening commercial and political links with the centre, and defending the colonies against other European powers, they were undertaking a large measure of the state's foreign policy. In contrast, the huge, privately contracted army created for Emperor Ferdinand II by Albrecht von Wallenstein in the mid-1620s proved less stable. Although the army, based on a huge exercise in mobilizing private capital, gave the emperor unprecedented authority over the states of the Empire at the height of the Thirty Years War, it proved financially unsustainable: the burdens that were laid upon occupied territory in an attempt to recover the levels of investment by subcontracting officers and their financial backers were impossible to maintain. The hostility generated amongst the princes of the Empire by the burdens of the army persuaded the emperor—whose own priority was a predictably dynastic ambition to persuade the Prince Electors to designate his son as heir apparent to the imperial title—to dismiss Wallenstein. Yet even after this first, and indeed a subsequent, failure of Wallenstein's system, military enterprise continued; the legacy was the smaller-scale, more adaptable but no less entrepreneurial imperial armies that followed after 1634, which were able to sustain the war effort against the Habsburgs' enemies down to 1648.

Far from driving a process of bureaucratic and centralizing state-building, the costs and demands of war in this period were leading to the wholesale retreat of state authority from the military sphere. If the burdens of unprecedented warfare and military change were met, it was largely through the initiative, organization, and finance of the state's subjects, acting as both private creditors and organizers of the rulers' armies.

Renaissance responses

How were changes in the character, scale, and culture of war perceived by contemporary theorists and commentators? We have seen that humanist writers, steeped in the historical and political writings of the classical world, for the most part had little hesitation in embracing a culture of bellicosity. Yet precisely this immersion in the wars and armies of Greece and Rome led inevitably to attempts to compare and to draw contrasts between the warfare of the past and the present. It was tempting to use examples and models from the classical past either to suggest solutions to the military challenges of the present, or to argue for the fundamental changes which divided the military issues of the past from today's warfare. Commentators were no less interested in the role the state ought to play in organizing and waging warfare, not least in matters related to mercenaries and the potential to mobilize citizen populations for warfare. Finally, and in a break with the notion that writers and theorists were at one in embracing the desirability of war, there was a significant interest in the moral and cultural problems that contemporary warfare generated, and in particular a search for new restraints on warfare.

How much could be learnt about modern warfare from a study of the ancients? Machiavelli's *Art of War*, published in 1521 and during his lifetime his best-known and most influential work, asserted that the main problem with the waging of modern war was precisely that it had departed so capriciously and unnecessarily from the priorities and experience of ancient armies, above all those of Republican Rome. The surviving military texts of Claudius Aelian and Flavius Vegetius Renatus were enthusiastically endorsed as defining authorities on military good practice. Machiavelli's position was shared by other traditionalists: these variously echoed him in sweeping aside the impact of changes brought about by artillery or fortifications, in being sceptical of all weapons—whether firearms or bows—which detracted from hand-to-hand combat, in giving limited attention to cavalry, and in ignoring the possibilities of sea power and amphibious operations. Machiavelli's argument for the superiority of classical armies was essentially focused on morale, not on weaponry, and his concern was to recreate the discipline and order of the Roman armies. From this Roman-style discipline would follow the drill and systematic training that would, he assumed, turn a shiftless rabble of recruits into a cohesive and successful army.

As artillery, infantry firearms, and new-style fortifications proliferated, so theorists' dismissal of these as trivial or irrelevant encountered scepticism and resistance. By the later sixteenth century a large proportion of all published manuals on the art of war were taken up with complex diagrams, line drawings, and technical descriptions to demonstrate artillery ballistics and the geometry of constructing angled bastions. Yet where traditional 'classisizing' treatises such as the *Art of War* held their ground with

FRONTISPIECE FROM WALLHAUSEN'S *L'art militaire pour l'infanterie* (1615).

later generations was in the argument that soldiers' military effectiveness was chiefly the product of externally imposed discipline and systematic drill and training. This argument became the key to a whole new generation of writings, founded above all on Justus Lipsius' *Six Books of Politics* (1589). Lipsius' work was the starting point for subsequent theorists who sought to create elaborate systems of drill and tactical deployment via instruction manuals. The well-disciplined, obedient, and austere soldier presented as Lipsius' moral ideal became the blank canvas on which systematic weapons drill and ever more elaborate tactical formations could be imposed. Such ideas were especially linked with the extended Calvinist ruling family of the Orange-Nassau, and their various initiatives to transform the organization of Dutch and German princely armies. Both the well-known volume by the engraver Jacob de Gheyn, depicting the stage-by-stage process of loading and firing muskets and calivers, and the handling of pikes, and the extensive series of publications on drill and the tactical deployment of troops by Jacobi of Wallhausen, are testimony to this Orange-Nassau interest in systematizing the training of soldiers.

Others remained unconvinced that such externally imposed systems could prove effective. Sir Roger Williams, experienced commander in the Netherlands, voiced a common scepticism when he defended the importance of military skills learnt directly through practice and imitation, arguing that the real determinant of military effectiveness was the proportion of veteran troops in an army or a regiment. For Williams the most successful armies were those, like the Spanish Army of Flanders, in which a significant body of troops was kept together long enough to acquire its distinctive military culture based on shared identity and experience, and the transmission of that experience as practical knowledge and example.

This, however, was a truth which military theorists from Machiavelli onwards, and to some extent also their masters, did not want to hear. Machiavelli and subsequent generations of Renaissance theorists were driven by a positive enthusiasm for Roman ideals of discipline and order. But they were also wrestling with a negative emotion: their humanist disdain for the widespread use of mercenary soldiers. A sustained thread through Machiavelli's works is an extreme hostility to mercenaries, which to him meant any soldier who is hired as a military professional by a princely ruler or republican government, and a fortiori any such soldier who is obviously 'foreign'—not a subject of that ruler. Machiavelli leaves no argument unturned in his bid to persuade his reader that only a tyrant or a short-sighted madman would rely on mercenaries. For Machiavelli, such soldiers are intrinsically craven, having no interest in delivering military successes which would make their role redundant, and still less in sacrificing themselves for someone who is only a paymaster. Their commanders are more dangerous to their employers than the enemy, and their ambitions will always be to supplant those who pay them to fight their wars. Machiavelli could make much of the celebrated, but unusual, case of the *condottiere* Francesco Sforza, who after the extinction of the Visconti dynasty exploited the weakness of the short-lived Ambrosian Republic to have himself proclaimed Duke of Milan. Much of Machiavelli's argument,

FRANCESCO SFORZA,
the model of the
'over-mighty mercenary'.

itself unoriginal, was plagiarized, reiterated, and developed by other writers throughout the period, and touches a virtually timeless set of intuitive responses and prejudices
about the nature of those who are willing to offer their military services for hire.

Machiavelli's republican sympathies further strengthened his antipathy towards
mercenaries, since for him the essence of civic virtue was the willingness of the free
citizens of a republic to serve the public interest in war. To rely on mercenaries is to
deprive the citizen of his right and duty, and to encourage the collapse of civic spirit
which Machiavelli so deplored in contemporary society. Again, Machiavelli's sympathies are echoed in Lipsius, who also speaks of the virtues of an armed citizenry who
fight only when required and then return to civil pursuits. And in contrast to Machiavelli, who lauded the belligerence and warrior-virtues of a citizen army, others like
Thomas More saw the dependence on a citizen army as a means to limit war, since it
would only be mobilized to defend the interests of the state, not to fuel the capricious
ambitions of a ruler.

As they struggled to meet the costs of warfare, such arguments for the virtues and
effectiveness of a militia appealed to rulers for a different reason. They offered the
prospect of being able to raise a large force based on citizen conscription for a fraction

of the costs of hiring professional soldiers. This superficially enticing theory had one great flaw: reluctant peasants from the Florentine countryside, even more reluctant citizens from Italian and German cities, combined with vagrants and criminals from across European societies, were unlikely to be translated into outstanding soldiers by attempts to apply Roman ideals of citizenship, discipline, and rote-taught military drill. From the militia of Florentine *contadini* trained by Machiavelli and routed by Spanish veterans at the sack of Prato in 1512, to the ignominious disbandment of the Bavarian militia in 1632, denounced by Elector Maximilian as 'entirely useless and without effect', the deployment of militias as recommended by military theorists was an unmitigated failure. Only in Sweden did a system of military service bring impressive results and lighten the fiscal burden for the crown. But what was created in Sweden from the sixteenth century was in reality a system of permanent peasant conscription, and simply ensured a steady supply of cheap recruits into the multinational, highly professional Swedish army. If there was a lasting legacy of Machiavelli's belief that ideal republics were better suited to waging war than princely regimes, it lay not with the creation of militias but in the enduring interest in the manner in which republican governments, however oligarchic in practice, could nonetheless legitimize their demands for military expenditure more effectively than principalities. The extent to which both Venice and the Dutch Republic could obtain resources that allowed them to punch above their apparent military weight was not missed by contemporary commentators.

Not all debate in this period was about making war more effective and sustaining its increasing scale and duration. One major challenge confronted by Renaissance Europe was to find new or reinforced arguments seeking to constrain warfare. Despite the predominant stress on bellicosity, Europe in 1400 had inherited a series of concepts and norms which actively sought to prevent war and, if that proved impossible, to constrain the ways in which it was waged. The concept of Christendom, the notion of a universal state co-ruled by pope and emperor as heirs to the classical Roman Empire, offered a potent argument for both the pursuit of peace and the reconciliation of conflict within the Christian world. Violence and military ambition should be directed towards targets outside Christendom, above all as crusades against the threat of Islam. In consequence, Christian theology and ethical teaching, while they by no means espoused pacifism, did seek to define and promulgate the circumstances under which war could be justly undertaken (*jus ad bello*) and the ways and means by which it could be waged once begun (*jus in bello*). Through the notion of laws of war, theologians sought to define and secure the rights of non-belligerents and to establish some principles of proportionality in the use of violence and destruction to achieve military objectives.

Both these bases were under threat in this period. The concept of Christendom crumbled under the impact of the successive Reformations of the fifteenth and sixteenth centuries. While the ideal of Christendom was by no means intellectually or culturally dead by 1650, it had lost any strength as an appeal to practical restraint in wars waged between European states. Charles V's reign offered a few enthusiastic supporters of imperial authority the possibility that a 'universal monarchy' might be created in place of a divided Christendom, one where a single dynastic power enjoyed such preponderant authority that no group of other powers would be able to challenge the authority of the dynastic 'superstate', which could then enforce peace on its own terms across Europe. Even following the huge prestige garnered by Philip II after Lepanto in 1571, the Spanish monarchy never seemed likely to achieve this European preponderance, though the ideal continued to be celebrated by theorists such as Tommaso Campanella.

With the decline of Christendom came the linked concern that the laws of war were increasingly marginal to a large proportion of the conflicts being waged by Europeans. The virtual permanence of Christian–Islamic conflict; the intensifying of wars against the Orthodox in the east; the division of Catholic Europe into rival confessional camps reaching its climax in the Thirty Years War; the contact between the *conquistadores* and pagan civilizations in the New World: all of these encounters potentially fell outside existing restraints resting on the common identity of Christian soldiers fighting in 'just' wars. One response to this challenge, that of the so-called Salamanca School of rigorous scholastic enquiry, took traditional just war theory and sought to test and extend it in relation, above all, to the issue of the Spanish conquests in the New World. Under Francisco de Vitoria and his pupils, notably Francisco Suárez, rights of conquest, appropriation, and forcible conversion of Amerindian peoples and extirpation of their cultures were exposed to intense and legalistic scrutiny, in which the conclusions in almost all cases favoured the existing rights of the native peoples. In a European context where Spanish authorities were anxious to justify their conquests in the New World without a base of dynastic legitimacy to draw upon, these arguments were not simply brushed aside. Seeming to conform at least outwardly to stricter applications of just war theory in relation to conquered peoples was a Spanish priority for several decades from the 1540s.

A more radical approach to the challenge of establishing widely relevant laws of conduct both *ad* and *in bello* was offered by Hugo Grotius, above all in his *Three Books of the Laws of War and Peace* (1625). Faced with the extent that confessional strife undermined claims for the validity of laws of war based on religious authority, Grotius sought to establish a set of universal constraints on war based upon natural law. Such universal laws, he argued, were functional necessities for the operation of any type of social life, and even for the minimal association required by international relations. They were, he argued, founded on the fundamental human right of self-preservation and a prudential prohibition against wanton injury. Grotius' aim was to establish precepts that should be accepted: 'even though we should even grant...that there is no God, or that he takes no care of human affairs'. Grotius had good reason to fear involvement in theological controversy, and such ideas were advanced with caution. As commentators have pointed out, Grotius' attempt to universalize laws of behaviour, whether in civil society or in the context of international war, emerges as a minimalist set of assertions about *jus in bello*, even if he is more forthright about limiting the circumstances in which war can justly be waged against another state or people.

That Grotius was writing in the midst of the Thirty Years War tends to underline the inevitably limited impact of such attempts to constrain violence through law. The last word might still belong to Erasmus, writing his *Complaint of Peace* (1521) almost exactly a century earlier:

> Sit down, before you draw the sword, weigh every article, omit none, and compute the expense of blood as well as treasure which war requires, and the evils which it of necessity brings with it; and then see at the bottom of the account whether, after the greatest success, there is likely to be a balance in your favour.

CHAPTER 3

Religion

STELLA FLETCHER

ANY period of Christian history can be appreciated by studying the built environment of Rome, but the pilgrim who seeks to understand the nature of Christianity at the height of the Renaissance could do worse than visit the Vatican's Stanza della Segnatura, frescoed by Raphael for Pope Julius II (r. 1503–13) between 1508 and 1511. Pride of place is given to the *Disputa*, which ostensibly depicts a learned disputation about the Blessed Sacrament, but is effectively a lesson in the broader tenets of the Christian faith. In the style of an apse decoration at the east end of a basilical church, it presents the heavenly Church Triumphant in an imaginary hemisphere, above the clerics and laymen of the earthly Church Militant, who inhabit a mathematically precise world of squares and right angles. In the heavenly realm the Trinity appears on the central axis: God the Father is attended by a goodly company of angels; beneath him Christ in Majesty is flanked by the Virgin Mary and John the Baptist; lower still, the Holy Spirit in the form of a dove appears between the open Gospel books of Matthew, Mark, Luke, and John. They are attended by alternating New and Old Testament figures, St Peter exchanging glances with Adam, the protomartyr St Stephen gazing in rapture beyond the radiant Moses with his tablets of stone. Directly beneath the Trinity is a monstrance containing the host, which retains all the physical attributes of a wafer but has become transformed into the body of Christ. The monstrance stands on an altar, that mysterious transformation having taken place in the holy sacrifice of the mass, the eucharistic sacrament. Around the altar, the four Doctors of the Church—Gregory the Great in a papal tiara, red-robed Jerome with his crouching lion, Ambrose of Milan and Augustine of Hippo in episcopal mitres—consult their own works in an attempt to explain these sacred mysteries to the rest of humankind. The group standing behind Augustine includes the thirteenth-century Dominican theologian St Thomas Aquinas, in black, and the Franciscan St Bonaventure, dressed as a cardinal. The prominently positioned pontiff to Bonaventure's left is his fellow Franciscan Sixtus IV (r. 1471–84), Julius II's uncle and inspiration. Behind Sixtus are the sharp features of laurel-crowned Dante, his presence serving as shorthand for the three potential destinations believed to await the human soul after the death of the body: heaven for the blessed, hell for the damned, and purgatory, where earthly sins could be purged to fit souls for heaven. Finally, as words and ideas are represented on the right of the *Disputa*, so the left foreground is devoted to the visual arts: the Dominican painter Fra Angelico assumes a superior air as he glances towards a book held by the architect Donato Bramante, who leans on a balustrade every bit as sturdy as the churches he designed in Milan and Rome.

The Trinitarian faith of Renaissance Christians dated back to the early Church and is most clearly expressed by the fourth-century Nicene Creed: 'I believe in one God, the Father almighty . . . in one Lord Jesus Christ, the Only Begotten Son of God . . . and . . . in the Holy Ghost, the Lord, the giver of life.' Christians have generally found it difficult to give equal weight to each of the Trinity's three Persons; Renaissance Christianity was clearly Christocentric. One measure of this is provided by the extant Oxford and Cambridge colleges founded in the fifteenth and sixteenth centuries, for dedications

THE TRINITY IS DEPICTED down the central axis of Raphael's *Disputa* (1509–10). God the Father is attended by angels, the Son is flanked by saints, and the Holy Spirit mediates between heaven and earth, where the sacrament of the altar is keenly discussed by a host of eminent theologians.

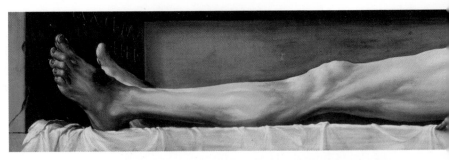

CADAVER TOMBS WERE CREATED throughout Western Christendom in the medieval and Renaissance periods. Hans Holbein the Younger developed that model in his painting of *The Body of the Dead Christ in the Tomb* (1520–2). The decaying flesh is deliberately realistic, even if the length of the body is exaggerated.

to the Trinity are easily outnumbered by those to its Second Person. Elsewhere, Christ was lauded as king of republican Florence in the 1490s and again in the 1520s, when coins were minted bearing the words 'Jesus Rex Noster et Deus Noster'. His significance as the Saviour of fallen mankind is explained in the Creed: 'For us men and for our salvation he came down from heaven…and became man. For our sake he was crucified…he suffered death…and rose again on the third day…He ascended into heaven.' Although the technicalities of salvation went on to polarize religious opinion and divide Christendom, pre-Reformation devotion centred on Christ's incarnation— God assuming human form—and his physical suffering on the cross. This physical emphasis derived from the vividness of the Franciscans' preaching about the Crucifixion and their promotion of re-enactments of the Passion, whether as plays or in following the Stations of the Cross. These, in turn, help to account for the emotional intensity to be found in Grünewald's Isenheim Altarpiece (1512–16, Musée d'Unterlinden, Colmar) or the graphic depiction of a taut, wounded body in Holbein's *Dead Christ* (1520–2, Öffentliche Kunstsammlung, Basel). Thus the prevailing character of Christian devotion was emotionally intense but also intensely physical and appreciated through the senses. Thanks to his ascension, all that could potentially remain on earth of Christ's physical body was the blood shed at the Crucifixion or, less plausibly, the relics of his circumcision. Phials of the Holy Blood were kept at Bruges and elsewhere. Similarly, pieces of the True Cross could be found and venerated throughout Christendom. The fragment belonging to the Venetian *scuola grande* (confraternity) of S. Giovanni Evangelista was associated with a sequence of miracles, in consequence of which Gentile Bellini and five other artists were commissioned to celebrate it in nine richly detailed canvases (1496–1501, Accademia, Venice). As the foremost church of Western Christendom, St Peter's Basilica in Rome was home to a particularly remarkable and no less miraculous relic, a cloth on which Christ's face appeared after it was used to wipe blood and sweat from his face as he carried the cross to Calvary. To this was added the tip of the Holy Lance with which the centurion pierced Christ's side, a gift to Innocent VIII (r. 1484–92) from the Ottoman sultan Bajazet in 1492.

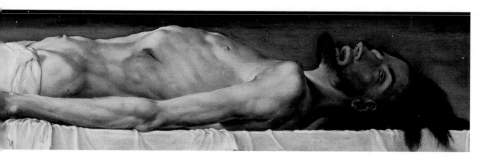

Pilgrimages to and the veneration of relics were both deplored by the Dutch scholar Desiderius Erasmus, who maintained that these acts impeded true piety. He belonged to an alternative but no less Christocentric Renaissance tradition, as spiritual as the other was physical. In terms of texts it can be traced back to *De imitatione Christi* (c.1418–27), a devotional manual which encourages believers to emulate Christ in their daily lives and seek unity with him through the Blessed Sacrament. It is attributed to Thomas à Kempis and is the most famous expression of the spiritual movement known as the *Devotio Moderna*. Erasmus inherited this tradition through his early education with the Brethren of the Common Life at Deventer, and his *Enchiridion militis Christiani* (written 1501) has a similar purpose to *The Imitation of Christ* (*De imitatione Christi*). The ultimate imitation of Christ was a martyr's death. Few Renaissance men and women were called to meet that fate, making Erasmus' friend Thomas More exceptionally isolated as he faced the prospect of it during his imprisonment in 1534–5. One of the texts he composed in prison, *The Sadness of Christ*, is a reflection on Christ's agony in the Garden of Gethsemane and demonstrates how More used Christ's submission to the Father's will to prepare himself for death. Stripped of cultural accretions, this is what it meant to be a Christian.

As his earthly parent, Mary was a major beneficiary of the emphasis on Christ's humanity. By the fifteenth century she had become the Mater Dolorosa, the sorrowful mother keeping vigil at the foot of the cross, as opposed to the majestic figure of Byzantine tradition. In 1423 the cult of Our Lady of Sorrows acquired its own feast day, 15 September. The Bible itself being relatively short on Mary's biographical details, gaps were filled with reference to the apocryphal Gospels of James and Pseudo-Matthew, in consequence of which fifteenth-century painters, including Ghirlandaio and Carpaccio, depicted the Virgin's birth, her presentation in the Temple, and her marriage, complete with Hebrew inscriptions, earrings, and bearded high priests, gleaned from observation of Jewish communities in the cities of Italy. Biblically inspired Annunciations, Visitations, Nativities, and Presentations of Christ were the stock-in-trade of Renaissance artists, but arguably even more distinctive of the period were paintings associating Mary with roses: those of Lochner and Schongauer depict the Madonna seated in brightly flourishing rose gardens, while Dürer's *Madonna of the Rose Garlands* (1506, National Gallery, Prague), assisted by the Christ child, distributes garlands to representatives of the Church Militant, led by Pope Julius II and Emperor Maximilian I. The roses represent the rosary beads which were popularly thought to have been given by the Virgin to St Dominic, who stands to her right in the painting, beads fingered by the faithful as they prayed the *Ave Maria* 150 times. Caterina Cornaro, the former queen consort of Cyprus, can be seen holding a rosary in Gentile Bellini's *Miracle at the Bridge of S. Lorenzo* (Accademia, Venice), part of the cycle made for S. Giovanni Evangelista.

Dominic's prominence is no accident, for Marian devotions were nothing less than a battleground for Renaissance friars, Dominicans championing the rosary while Franciscans and Carmelites insisted that Mary was herself conceived without sin in order to be the mother of the sinless Christ. There was considerable popular devotion to her immaculate conception, but no official doctrine because Dominican theologians remained resolutely opposed to it. The Franciscan pope Sixtus IV sought to advance the immaculist cause, but even his bull *Grave nimis* (1483) admitted that the Church had yet to reach a definitive teaching. This remained the case for another four centuries. In the meantime, Mary's sinlessness was inferred in the belief that she had ascended bodily into heaven, where she was crowned as its queen, as depicted by Titian in his *Assumption of the Virgin* (1516–18) for the Franciscans of S. Maria Gloriosa dei Frari in Venice. Vast numbers of pilgrims made their way to Marian shrines at Regensburg, Walsingham, and elsewhere but, as with Christ's ascension, the paucity of physical relics prompted them to be resourceful. Thus the most striking physical survival of Renaissance devotion to the Virgin is to be found at Loreto, near the Adriatic coast of what were then the Papal States. In the 1290s her house—the Holy House—was allegedly transported there from Nazareth by angels, though the earliest written account of this dates from *c*.1470. Thereafter, Pope Sixtus' nephew Girolamo Basso della Rovere appointed Carmelite friars to guard the shrine and commissioned a programme of architectural and decorative improvements that was continued by their Franciscan-educated kinsman, Julius II.

Franciscan emphasis on Mary's marriage had the consequence of establishing her husband, Joseph, as a figure of equal significance, at least in that single episode. Indeed, a relic said to be the Virgin's wedding ring was kept at Perugia, where the future Pope Sixtus was elected minister general of the Franciscans in 1464. Just as Sixtus' papal election allowed him to promote the cult of the Immaculate Conception, so it also enabled him to highlight Joseph, who, for the first time, was allocated a feast in the Roman calendar. There followed a glut of church dedications to St Joseph, who came to be depicted actively protecting Mary and the young Jesus, rather than as the bumbling dotard of popular plays. More particularly, the local artist Pietro Perugino was commissioned to paint the marriage of Joseph and Mary for the cathedral of Perugia (*c*.1500–4, Musée des Beaux-Arts, Caen), with suitable emphasis on the ring.

After Mary and Joseph the most culturally significant member of Christ's earthly family was John the Baptist. Piero della Francesca's *Baptism of Christ* (*c*.1450, National Gallery, London) and Lucas Cranach's numerous versions of Salome with the saint's head on a platter are clearly inspired by the biblical account of his life but, as with Mary, there were alternative sources. The fourteenth-century Pisan friar Domenico Cavalca used Eastern Christian texts to write a life of John that included various scenes from his childhood, including a meeting with the Holy Family when they returned from their flight to Egypt. Cavalca enjoyed a receptive readership in neighbouring Florence, which had assumed the Baptist as its patron saint after the city was liberated from the Goths on his feast day, 24 June 401. That civic patronage accounted for the frequency with which Florentines from Lorenzo Giberti and Donatello to Leonardo da Vinci depicted John in their chosen media, but it was Cavalca who ensured that he was captured at an ever younger age as the fifteenth century advanced.

In depictions of Jesus' adult ministry, such as the miraculous draught of fishes (Luke 5:1–11) or the Last Supper, his disciples inevitably play supporting roles. Peter's brief period of prominence, between the Resurrection and the emergence of Paul as apostle to the gentiles, is caught in Masaccio's Brancacci Chapel frescos (1420s, S. Maria del Carmine, Florence), but even in Rome, where he was martyred, key-carrying Peter was regarded as half of a double act with sword-wielding Paul. Thus, St Peter's Basilica was unquestionably the city's premier pilgrimage destination, but those pilgrims who sought the jubilee indulgences which were made available roughly every twenty-five years throughout the Renaissance period had to complete a circuit of all Rome's major pilgrimage churches, including S. Paolo fuori le Mura and S. Maria Maggiore. At least 100,000 pilgrims are thought to have visited Rome in the jubilee years of 1525 and 1550, suggesting that numbers may have been even higher before some potential pilgrims turned Protestant. In 1462 St Peter was required to share the limelight with another apostle, his brother Andrew, whose head was conveyed from Patras when the Ottomans overran Greece and was brought into Rome on Palm Sunday. According to the account provided by Pius II (r. 1458–64) in his memoirs, it was given the most theatrical of receptions, in the course of which the Greek cardinal Bessarion spoke on behalf of Andrew and Pius responded as heir to Peter.

If Jesus' male disciples received relatively little attention from Renaissance artists, the same could hardly be said of red-haired, scarlet-clad Mary Magdalen, weeping piteously at the foot of the cross in Grünewald's Isenheim Altarpiece or cradling Christ's head in Botticelli's *Lamentation over the Dead Christ* (1490–2, Alte Pinakothek, Munich). Even in her reformed state there was something disorderly about Mary Magdalen, as Donatello's harrowing sculpted depiction of her (1453–5, Museo dell'Opera del Duomo, Florence) suggests. Thus she has no place in the harmonious heavenly hemisphere of the *Disputa*. Her repentance for a past sinful life (Luke 8:2) was Mary of Magdala's principal attraction for preachers and their audiences, but her story had become distorted over centuries of retelling, so that, from Gregory the Great onwards, she was taken to be one and the same as the unnamed prostitute of Luke 7:36–50 *and* Mary of Bethany, the sister of Martha and Lazarus, in John 11–12. At the elite end of the cultural spectrum, Mary Magdalen was Bishop William of Waynflete's patron of choice when he founded a college at Oxford in 1458, but the cult of this composite figure was most intense at Sainte-Baume, near Marseille, where, it was believed, she had lived in a cave, covered only by her long hair and fed by angels. Successive kings of France were patrons of the shrine, which was visited by Francis I (r. 1515–47) in 1515 and his mother, Louise of Savoy, the following year. Another pilgrim was the scholar Jacques Lefèvre d'Étaples, who was troubled by the slur on Mary of Bethany's character by the supposition that she was a prostitute. In his *De Maria Magdalena* (1518) Lefèvre distinguished the three women whose identities had become so confused. A pamphlet war ensued, between those who condemned this attack on the Church's traditional teaching and those who defended Lefèvre's attempt to discern the historical truth. Finding himself condemned as a heretic, Lefèvre retreated into the contemplation personified by Mary of Bethany.

Even more popular than Mary Magdalen in the Renaissance period was Catherine of Alexandria, who was supposed to have lived in the fourth century, to have spurned earthly marriage, defended her Christian beliefs against fifty philosophers, and been martyred for her faith. Among female heads of Florentine households in 1427 Caterina was easily the most popular name (148 individuals), followed by Antonia (84) and Margherita (65). Despite the lack of evidence that Catherine ever existed, the thirteenth-century hagiographer Jacopo da Voragine included a 1,600-word account of her life and martyrdom in his *Legenda aurea*. This work was translated into the various vernaculars and printed to meet popular demand, the English printer William Caxton's *Golden Legend* (1483) providing but one example. Nor was the fifteenth century short of its own hagiographers, including Antonio degli Agli, whose *De vitis et gestis sanctorum* expanded Catherine's story to 2,500 words. For painters Catherine's main attraction was her reputation as a mystic 'bride of Christ'. Memling's altarpiece for the Sint-Janshospitaal in Bruges (c.1479) shows the Christ child placing a wedding ring on Catherine's finger in the presence of John the Baptist and John the Evangelist, the hospital's patrons, St Barbara, and angel musicians.

Many other images of virgin martyrs found natural homes in communities of clois-tered women. A notable exception is Carpaccio's nine-panel St Ursula cycle (1497–8, Venice, Accademia), which was commissioned by a Venetian confraternity and follows the saint's odyssey from Brittany to Rome and Cologne, and from martyrdom to heavenly glory. Here, as elsewhere, Carpaccio appears to convey a wealth of realistic detail, while nevertheless capturing something of the intangible spiritual lives of his contemporaries. Nowhere is this more obvious than in his *Apparition of the Ten Thousand Martyrs* (c.1515, Venice, Accademia; see page 90). The setting is the Venetian monastic church of S. Antonio di Castello, where a classically inspired altarpiece gives an idea of how such works were introduced into buildings of contrasting architectural style. Miniature ships and other ex-votos, tokens of thanks for answered prayers, can be seen among the beams. The small kneeling figure in white is Francesco Ottobon, prior of S. Antonio, who, in 1511, had a vision of the 10,000 Roman Christians who had allegedly been martyred on Mount Ararat. Like the prior, we see them enter the church in pairs, carrying crosses. They process towards the altar and are blessed by St Peter. The post-antique centuries

THIS RELIQUARY BUST OF St Thekla is typical of the wooden polychrome work produced in Renaissance Germany, but it is unlikely to have contained relics of a woman whose story is told in the apocryphal *Acts of Paul and Thecla*. The lioness and column reflect the nature of her martyrdom.

brought relatively few new Christian martyrs, exceptions being Thomas Becket in the twelfth century and Peter Martyr of Verona in the thirteenth, both of whom enriched Christian culture with verifiable relics and new pilgrimage destinations, in Canterbury and Milan respectively. Throughout the Renaissance period saints' body parts (primary relics) and objects associated with them (secondary relics) continued to be venerated in elaborate reliquaries, among which polychrome busts are especially characteristic of the period. The faith placed in the healing powers of relics is well illustrated by the case of the French king Louis XI (r. 1461–83), who had the episcopal ring of St Zenobius sent from Florence in 1482 in the hope that it would prolong his life.

In the *Disputa* Raphael's balanced treatment of the four Doctors of the Church gives no hint that Jerome caught the spirit of the age as the others did not. This Jerome had been extracted from his study, where Renaissance artists frequently depicted him at work on the Latin Bible known as the Vulgate. In that enclosed setting he was often given the features of scholarly contemporaries, including Lefèvre d'Étaples and the mid-fifteenth-century archbishop of Florence, Antonino Pierozzi. Jerome's spiritual and artistic attractions went further, for his personal austerity chimed with Renaissance

VITTORE CARPACCIO'S *Apparition of the Ten Thousand Martyrs* (c.1515) was commissioned by Ettore Ottobon after his uncle Francesco Ottobon, prior of S. Antonio di Castello, Venice, experienced a visionary dream of the 10,000 Christian soldiers who were said to have been martyred on Mount Ararat some centuries earlier.

ideas of sanctity and allowed artists to present his emaciated form kneeling penitentially in the desert. His promotion of virginity and monasticism inspired five new monastic congregations in the later fourteenth century alone, his Mariology bore considerable fruit, and his distinctive attribute, the tame lion, presented its own artistic challenge, though presumably less so for Venetians, whose patron, St Mark, was himself symbolized by a lion. Jerome's birth near Aquileia made him particularly popular in nearby Venice, where Lorenzo Bastiani's *Funeral of St Jerome* (1460s–1470s, Venice, Accademia) survives from a cycle made for the Scuola di S. Girolamo, and Carpaccio's cycle for the Scuola di S. Giorgio degli Schiavoni (c.1502–7) includes the jolly *St Jerome and the Lion*, another funeral scene, and the considerably rarer subject of *St Augustine in his Study*, in which Augustine attempts to write a letter to Jerome at the very moment of the latter's death in 420 and finds his room bathed in a miraculous light.

Jerome was clearly an inspirational figure for artists, scholars, and members of monastic orders, but a better guide to popular ideas of sanctity in the Renaissance period is to identify the cults that flourished locally after the deaths of holy men and women but failed to gain formal recognition by the wider Church. In this category we find the

DOMENICO GHIRLANDAIO, *St Jerome in his Study* (1480). This subject was popular in the
Renaissance period. One such painting, attributed to Jan van Eyck, was owned by Lorenzo de'
Medici (1449–92) and appears to have been the model for Ghirlandaio's fresco, commissioned
by members of the pro-Medicean Vespucci family.

English Lancastrian king, Henry VI, who was killed by his Yorkist enemies in 1471
and had allegedly performed 174 miracles by 1500, the French Franciscan prelate Élie
de Bourdeille, who became the object of a cult at Tours, and the Dominican friar
Girolamo Savonarola, who was burned for heresy in 1498 and whose ashes were

thrown into the Arno at Florence to prevent them being venerated as relics by his ardent followers. All were at least potential candidates for formal canonization, but introducing the papacy into the process meant venturing into the world of politics and diplomacy. In the 1520s Henry VI's cause was investigated by papal agents but abandoned at Henry VIII's break with Rome, while Savonarola's was utterly hopeless as long as his Florentine disciples were political enemies of the Medici popes Leo X and Clement VII. The best opportunities had passed.

Scores of fifteenth- and sixteenth-century Christians have been beatified (declared 'blessed') or canonized as saints. For the purposes of formal canonization, popes from Martin V (r. 1417–31) to Adrian VI (r. 1522–3) were inclined to favour long-dead candidates. It also helped to be male: Rose of Viterbo (d.1252) and Catherine of Siena (d.1380) formed a minority of two. Princes were easily outnumbered by men of more humble birth. Model bishops such as Osmund of Salisbury (d.1099) fared fractionally better. Patriotism was evident in the canonization of Bellinus, a twelfth-century bishop of Padua, by the Venetian pope Eugenius IV (r. 1431–47) and that of Catherine by the Sienese pontiff Pius II, but the surest route to veneration at Renaissance altars was to have been a Franciscan friar. Sixtus IV canonized his order's protomartyrs, Beraldus of Carbio and companions, who were martyred for preaching in Morocco in 1120, and Bonaventure (d.1274), with whom Sixtus identified as a theologian and (sometime) cardinal. Martyrdom was hard to achieve while the secular powers were conspicuously reluctant to engage in crusading initiatives, but by 1516 the Ottoman sultan Selim's spectacular military successes against fellow Muslims suggested that he would soon turn his forces towards Christendom, so Leo X's canonization of another seven Franciscans, martyred in north Africa in 1227, represented a statement of crusading intent. Similarly, when Adrian VI canonized Benno (d.1106), the overtly pro-papal bishop of Meissen in Saxony, Martin Luther recognized it as a response to his own anti-papalism in the same region. After 1523 there were no further canonizations until 1588, when a fifteenth-century Franciscan lay brother, Diego of Alcalá, was raised to the altar by Sixtus V in a gesture of support for Philip II of Spain on the eve of his armada's expedition against Protestant England.

Only five men had the distinction of both living in and being canonized in the Renaissance period. Just six years after his death in 1444, Bernardino of Siena's canonization by Nicholas V (r. 1447–55) was the quickest, and was followed by those of Vicente Ferrer by his Valencian compatriot Calixtus III (r. 1455–8), the Neapolitan Francesco di Paola by Leo X, and those of Casimir of Poland (Kazimierz Jagiełłończyk) and the Florentine Antonino Pierozzi by Adrian VI. The last case had the fingerprints of Giulio de' Medici (soon to be Clement VII) all over it. Ferrer effectively pulled strings on his own behalf by prophesying the papal election of Alfonso Borja, the future Pope Calixtus, while Bernardino enjoyed the favour of successive popes, and Pius II lauded Pierozzi as one who 'conquered avarice, trampled on pride, was utterly unacquainted with lust and most abstemious in food and drink'. However, secular patronage was also crucial in three of the canonizations. Most obviously, King Sigismund I of Poland petitioned

FRANCESCO DI GIORGIO MARTINI,
St Bernardino Preaching from a Pulpit
(*c*.1473–4), is a small image, little larger
than a postcard, painted in tempera
on parchment. More ambitious
versions of the same subject show the
Observant Franciscan friar preaching
to vast open-air crowds who are
enthralled by his homely style.

Pope Leo on behalf of his brother's cause. Francesco di Paola ministered to the dying
Louis XI in 1483 and remained in France thereafter. French lobbying for his canonization
presumably stifled the chances of the no-less-saintly Bourdeille. Finally, the two Medici
popes inherited their great-grandfather Cosimo's devotion to Pierozzi, who was prior of
the Florentine Dominican convent of S. Marco when Cosimo had his own cell there.

Setting aside the politics of canonization, these five cases confirm the Renaissance
preference for mendicant saints, Ferrer and Pierozzi being Dominicans, Bernardino an
Observant Franciscan—that is, one who strictly 'observed' the founder's rule—and
Francesco di Paola a cave-dwelling hermit who took his inspiration from Francis of
Assisi and founded his own order of friars, the Minims. Casimir was a layman who
refused to marry; like the others, he cultivated a life of austere piety, dying at 26. He
showed no obvious interest in the work of his tutor, the historian Jan Długosz. Nor
did the saintly friars concern themselves with secular culture; indeed, they were
positively hostile towards the classical revival. Fra Antonino and Fra Bernardino
were so highly regarded that the stationer Vespasiano da Bisticci could not resist
writing biographical sketches of them, even though they owned nothing and
could make no purchases from him. Antonino was a scholar, but Bernardino

devoted his life to preaching the gospel clearly and simply to large urban audiences throughout central and northern Italy, encouraging them to adore the Holy Name of Jesus—'IHS'—surrounded by a distinctive sunburst.

Bernardino sought to promote unity between all Franciscans, but his very popularity meant that the Observance gained new members and opened new houses while the more scholarly, less austere Conventuals found themselves on the defensive. The opportunity for a Conventual resurgence came in 1471 with the papal election of the minister general, Francesco della Rovere. As Sixtus IV, he attempted to subject the Observants to Conventual authority, but was thwarted by the Observants' numerical strength and their secular support. Indeed, it took him eight years to secure Bonaventure's canonization in the face of Observant opposition. The Franciscan family grew increasingly estranged and was formally divided in 1517. A further split followed when the stricter Capuchins splintered off in 1528. The Conventuals may have lacked momentum, but they can nevertheless be associated with some remarkable artistic achievements. The decoration of Sixtus' new chapel in the Vatican, the Sistine, was heavily influenced by Franciscan scholarship and traditions, including the order's comparison of its rule with the Law of Moses. Elsewhere, the main Franciscan house in Venice, the Frari, acquired two important altarpieces in quick succession: Titian's soaring *Assumption* and the same master's *Pesaro Madonna* (1519–26), which features St Peter as patron of the Franciscans, together with St Francis himself and St Anthony of Padua.

The Dominican Fra Angelico created some of the tenderest religious images of the fifteenth century, while his confrères in the Order of Preachers retained their reputation as theologians, guardians of spiritual orthodoxy. To that end Dominicans served as inquisitors and as masters of the Sacred Palace, the pope's theologians. Among the latter was the Spaniard Juan de Torquemada, a compatriot of St Dominic. In the 1430s Torquemada's patron, Eugenius IV, found a refuge with the Florentine Dominicans at S. Maria Novella and was instrumental in introducing a Dominican Observant community to S. Marco in the same city. Among Pierozzi's successors as prior of S. Marco, Savonarola was particularly notable for his missionary zeal, inspiring vocations among the leading Florentine families as well as an outpouring of religious enthusiasm across the social spectrum, especially among women. Savonarola polarized opinion, acquiring critics as fervent as his supporters. Indeed, an anti-mendicant thread can be traced from Lorenzo Valla's critical *De professione religiosorum* (c.1441), through the accusations of hypocrisy made by Leonardo Bruni and Poggio Bracciolini', to the antics of the money-grubbing Fra Timoteo in Machiavelli's play *Mandragola*. What they were not— as later commentators such as Jacob Burckhardt might have us believe—were grotesque 'medieval' throwbacks. Whether in terms of vocations, scholarship, or attracting audiences to their sermons, the friars were an integral part of Renaissance culture.

The mendicants' mission to the laity obliged them to be prominent in cities. Monks, on the other hand, had always separated themselves from the world, retreating into the desert or finding substitute deserts on islands or mountaintops. For the most part, Western European monks followed the Rule of St Benedict and were therefore

Benedictines. Cluniac and Cistercian houses survived as testament to earlier monastic reform movements, but it was the Carthusians in their house-like cells spaced around vast cloisters that particularly inspired the patronage of fifteenth-century French and Italian elites. The monumentally proportioned Certosa di Pavia was built for the Visconti and Sforza dukes of Milan and that at Ferrara for the Sforza ally Borso d'Este, who retained his own cell there. In 1521 there were 206 active Carthusian houses throughout Europe, including the London Charterhouse, where Thomas More found spiritual refuge from the pressures of his legal and governmental career. This tally suggests that there was genuine enthusiasm among Luther's contemporaries for an order which had the reputation of never having required reform.

From the Venetian lagoon there emerged a monastic reform movement that spread throughout the states of Italy. In 1404 the patrician Ludovico Barbo founded a congregation of secular canons—priests who did not live under a rule—on the small island of S. Giorgio in Alga. This community included Barbo's kinsman Gabriele Condulmer, the future Eugenius IV. Four years later Barbo became abbot of the Benedictine monastery of S. Giustina at Padua, where his reforms encouraged Christ-like living in the manner of the north European *Devotio Moderna*. Indeed, S. Giustina became one of the main centres from which the *Imitation of Christ* was distributed in the pre-print era. Barbo was subsequently called to reform the Roman house of S. Paolo fuori le Mura and that of S. Giorgio Maggiore, Venice, before reluctantly accepting the bishopric of Treviso, but it was his work at S. Giustina that inspired a movement. Monastery after monastery allied itself to S. Giustina, thereby creating a reformed congregation within the Benedictine Order.

For another small band of Venetian patricians the islands of the lagoon were neither remote nor austere enough. In 1510 Paolo Giustiniani travelled to the mountains of Tuscany and was inspired to join the hermits at Camaldoli. He soon persuaded his friends Sebastiano Zorzi and Pietro Querini to join him, though another, Gasparo Contarini, chose to remain in the world and achieved distinction as a diplomat and a cardinal. Fired with enthusiasm for the purity of the eremitical life, Giustiniani and Querini composed exhaustive reform proposals for the entire Church in the *Libellus ad Leonem X* (1513). Their programme included heavy censorship of printed works and a complete clampdown on books for the laity. This level of austerity was not unique to Camaldolese hermits, for Giastiniani's and Querini's contemporaries Gian Pietro Carafa and Gaetano Thiene took a similarly uncompromising line. From its foundation in 1524, their Theatine Order was devoted to strict liturgical observance and personal austerity, the brethren surviving by means of freely given gifts. After the imperialist sack of Rome in 1527 Carafa sought refuge in Venice and was still there nine years later, when he encountered the Basque nobleman Ignatius of Loyola. Ignatius was impressed by the Theatines' piety, but would have preferred them to abandon the cloister and take on a public, missionary role. Spaniards were particularly familiar with religious orders undertaking specific missions on the fringes of Christendom and doing so with a military discipline: the knights of Calatrava, Santiago, and Alcántara flourished during the Christian Reconquista of Iberia, and the Mercedarians were dedicated to ransoming Christians held captive in Muslim lands. Carafa's family included a number of prominent Knights Hospitaller, but there was little overlap between his vision for the Church and that of Ignatius. Apparently rebuffed by the Theatines, Ignatius and his followers devoted themselves to teaching the faith to European children and on extra-European missions, receiving papal recognition as the Society of Jesus in 1540.

The 1530s saw the birth of a female order that united the spirituality of the *Imitation of Christ* with practical works, especially religious instruction. This was the Company of St Ursula, the brainchild of Angela Merici of Brescia. The Ursulines flourished, suggesting that they met a need that was not satisfied by retreating into the cloister, but more traditional options nevertheless remained available. One woman who had more need than most of such a retreat was Jeanne de France, the rejected wife of Louis XII (r. 1498–1515), who founded a new order, dedicated to the Virgin of the Annunciation, after the king had their marriage annulled so that he could wed his predecessor's widow, Anne of Brittany. Our sources for female piety being heavily weighted towards this social apex, some of the best surviving examples of the prayer books—books of hours—used by elite women are those made for that same Queen Anne, ranging in size from *grandes* to *très petites*. Other well-known examples were made for Duchess Marie of Burgundy and Bona Sforza, the Milanese queen consort of Poland. These manuscript volumes contain a simplified version of the divine office sung at specific hours by monastic communities and said by the secular clergy. Their owners, whether female or male, sought to emulate the clergy by habitually reading the prayers, alone or in groups. Anne of Brittany's private oratory survives at Loches and it is easy to imagine her there, kneeling in prayer and reading from one of her smaller volumes. The advent of printing ensured that books of hours became accessible lower down the social hierarchy, leaving the piety of elite women to be distinguished by other means. Marguerite d'Angoulême, sister of Francis I and queen consort of Navarre, was notable for her religious poetry, as was the Roman widow Vittoria Colonna, *marchesa* of Pescara. Their younger contemporary Katherine Parr, wife of England's Henry VIII (r. 1509–47), composed prose works on religious themes, including a paraphrase of the *Imitation of Christ*. Pious literature created a bond between these women of the highest rank: Marguerite and Vittoria were correspondents in the 1540s, the same decade in which Henry's daughter Elizabeth translated Marguerite's *Miroir de l'âme pécheresse* as a gift for Katherine, her stepmother. They shared the same religious culture, suggesting that it was merely a matter of political expediency that Marguerite and Vittoria died as Catholics, Katherine and Elizabeth as Protestants.

Opposite: ANNE DE BRETAGNE AT CONFESSION (*c.*1492–5) is one of Jean Poyer's miniatures in the prayer book commissioned by Anne of Brittany, wife of Charles VIII of France, to aid the spiritual development of their eldest son. The other illustrations depict angels, prophets, saints, biblical episodes, and pious legends.

onfiteor deo et beate
marie virgine et bea
to francisco et beato gieco

All Christians were obliged to perform corporal works of mercy: feeding the hungry, giving drink to the thirsty, clothing the naked, lodging the homeless, visiting the sick, ransoming the captive, and burying the dead. Few individuals could afford to make much of a difference to the sum of human suffering, though exceptions included the Burgundian chancellor Nicolas Rolin, who founded the Hôtel-Dieu to serve the sick and needy of mid-fifteenth-century Beaune. More often than not, charitable works were corporate activities, including initiatives prompted by mendicant preaching in the cities of Italy. Such were the *monti di pietà*, funds into which those who could afford to do so made pious donations and from which those in need received loans at manageable rates of interest. Pre-dating the *monti*, lay confraternities responded charitably to the poor harvests, pandemic plague, and social dislocation of the fourteenth century, and subjected themselves to flagellation in the hope of appeasing a presumably angry deity. By the fifteenth century the sense of crisis had passed, but confraternities remained in being, albeit with an emphasis on mutual assistance and a more discerning attitude towards needy non-members. Of the hundred or so confraternities in *quattrocento* Florence, a minority existed for charitable purposes, while others were united by devotional practices, the singing of *laude*, or the organization of festivals. Some were specifically for artisans, women, or children. In Venice members of different trades or foreign communities were united by membership of particular *scuole*, the larger of which—*scuole grandi*—provided charitable services on behalf of the government. However, increasing proportions of their resources were spent on building and decorating lavish meeting houses, such as that of the Scuola Grande di S. Marco by the Lombard masters Pietro Lombardo and Mauro Codussi.

Before Lombardo and Codussi, Filippo Brunelleschi created perfectly proportioned sacred spaces, including the first centrally planned Renaissance chapel (at S. Maria degli Angeli, Florence), and Leon Battista Alberti applied a triumphal arch to a church façade (Tempio Malaestiano, Rimini). Other classically inspired designs, such as Masaccio's fictive barrel vault in S. Maria Novella, Florence, have never existed in more than two dimensions. Beyond Italy, Renaissance-style churches or, at least, façades, can be found as far afield as Coimbra and Moscow, with notable examples including the funerary chapel of Cardinal Tamás Bakócz at Esztergom and Sigismund I's chapel in Wawel Cathedral, Kraków. If the Renaissance in Hungary and Poland meant applying the elements of Roman pagan architecture to Christian buildings, in Rome itself churches already existed in the shells of antique buildings. Thus the domed Pantheon doubled up as S. Maria Rotonda, a Dominican church was built over the temple of Minerva, and others were dotted around the Forum and over the Palatine Hill. In 1482 Christian antiquity was recalled when work began on the church of S. Pietro in Montorio and, again, in 1502 when Bramante was commissioned to add a smaller structure to the side of that church, over the spot where it was believed that St Peter was crucified. This circular, domed *tempietto* was modelled on the classical temple of Hercules Victor, on the opposite bank of the Tiber, and was originally intended to be surrounded by a circular portico supported by another sixteen columns, the whole arrangement being

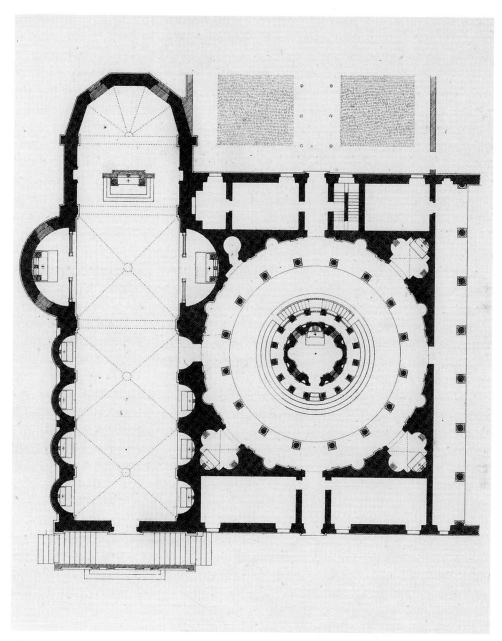

The Roman church of S. Pietro in Montorio, standing on the supposed site of St Peter's martyrdom, was reconstructed under the patronage of Isabella of Castile and Ferdinand of Aragon. Donato Bramante's Tempietto (*c*.1502) is in the adjacent courtyard, but the surrounding circular colonnade seen in this plan was not realised.

designed to reflect the centrality of Peter to the Church. The thinking behind the Tempietto was expressed on a considerably grander scale in the rebuilding of St Peter's Basilica. When Nicholas V envisaged a replacement for the Constantinian basilica he thought in terms of a Latin-cross floor plan with a long central axis. It was Bramante who produced an architectural reflection of Nicholas's centralizing vision for the papacy: a Greek cross in a square, covered by a dome similar in scale to that of the Pantheon. The foundation stone was laid by Julius II in 1506. From the austere end of the Christian spectrum Bramante's grand design was praised by the Augustinian hermit Egidio da Viterbo, who wanted God to be adored in a magnificent edifice and for that building to be in Rome, the Latin Jerusalem. Egidio was not alone in comparing St Peter's with Solomon's Temple in Jerusalem. Indeed, with the New Testament lacking any architectural emphases, Old Testament-inspired Temple comparisons proliferated during the sixteenth century, from Calvinist *temples* in France to Philip II's monastery-palace of El Escorial.

Of all the Renaissance paintings of church interiors, only Rogier van der Weyden's *Seven Sacraments* altarpiece (1445–50, Koninklijk Museum voor Schone Kunsten, Antwerp) shows the rites of baptism, confirmation, penance, eucharist, holy orders, matrimony, and extreme unction being performed side by side within a single space. It captures a stage in the steady reduction of these ritual signs of spiritual grace, which had once been more numerous and which sixteenth-century Protestants reduced to two, baptism and eucharist.

The Church taught that baptism was a precondition for salvation. This explains the zeal with which it was forced on 'converts' after the incorporation of Muslim Granada into Christian Spain in the 1490s, though they were presumably even less conversant with the tenets of their new faith than were the Jews throughout Spain who accepted baptism and then carried on observing the full range of Jewish practices. Otherwise, high levels of infant mortality ensured that baptism was performed as soon as possible after birth. Henry VIII's daughter Mary was baptized when two days old, her half-siblings Elizabeth and Edward at three days. Thus it was highly exceptional when, in 1449, Cosimo de' Medici's eldest grandson, Lorenzo, was not baptized until five days after his birth. Van der Weyden's priest holds the baby over the font while two men and two women stand by. These are presumably the father, two godmothers, and one godfather, indicating that the baby is a girl. This illustrates good practice, as established by various ecclesiastical councils, but such was the significance of patronage in Renaissance society that numbers of godparents tended to mushroom. Lorenzo de' Medici may have had as many as twenty-one of them, but Henry VIII exercised pious restraint by choosing four godparents for Princess Mary and three for Prince Edward. Baptism also involved patronage on a higher level in that the vast majority of children were given saints' names. The Florentine tax assessment known as the *catasto* is our best guide to the relative popularity of given names. In 1427 the most common boys' names were Giovanni and Antonio, reflecting the city's devotion to its patron, John the Baptist, and the influence of the mendicants, including St Anthony of Padua.

ROGIER VAN DER WEYDEN'S *Seven Sacraments* Altarpiece (1445–50) provides a succinct lesson in the tenets of Christianity and in how to live a devout and orderly life. From left to right around the Crucifixion group, the sacraments of baptism, confirmation, penance, eucharist, ordination, marriage, and extreme unction are depicted.

Behind the baptismal group on Van der Weyden's left-hand panel a bishop confirms an adolescent boy, introducing him to a fuller experience of the Holy Spirit. In reality, episcopal non-residence could result in confirmation candidates waiting years for this rite, while the elite's ready access to bishops meant that their infants were confirmed immediately after baptism. Beyond the painting's model bishop, a man confesses his mortal sins to a priest, who confers absolution. Confessors were guided through the process by manuals such as Antonino Pierozzi's popular *Confessionale*, which was available in print from the 1460s onwards. Such volumes were particularly valued when seminaries for the training of priests were still highly exceptional institutions. Candidates for priesthood, as illustrated on Van der Weyden's right-hand panel, had received minor orders, were already ordained deacons, and had reached a minimal age of 24. It did not follow that clerics who attained high office in the Church were in priestly orders, for Francesco Todeschini-Piccolomini (Pius III) and Giovanni de' Medici (Leo X) were not ordained until after their papal elections. Much rarer than clerics attaining high office without priestly orders were those who entered the clerical state as widowers. Marriage existed before and outside Christian culture, so required a little more ingenuity—or Jerome's translation of the Greek *mysterion* as 'sacramentum' (Eph. 5:32)—to put it on a par with baptism, but the presence of Jesus at Cana (2 John 1–11) and other scriptural references to marriage were enough to give it Christian significance and to render divorce unthinkable. Greek philosophers and Christian sages alike argued for the superiority of celibacy over marriage, Jerome going so far as to give virginity a numerical score of 100 per cent, against which he rated widowhood at 60 and marriage at a mere 30. On the extreme right of the *Seven Sacraments* altarpiece a loyal wife awaits the more blessed but otherwise precarious state of widowhood while a priest anoints her dying husband, whose bed is positioned somewhat improbably in the south aisle of the church.

A Crucifixion scene occupies the foreground of Van der Weyden's central panel, with Christ's sacrifice cleverly mirrored in the more distant celebration of the eucharist. The vast majority of such celebrations were spoken low masses, such as we see here, for there is no congregation and the priest is accompanied only by his server. Perhaps he is saying a soul-mass, endowed for the benefit of particular souls in purgatory. At the opposite end of the liturgical scale were sung high masses, for which numerous Renaissance settings survive, including eighteen by the widely acclaimed Josquin Desprès and the earliest extant requiem, by Johannes Ockeghem. Van der Weyden catches the eucharist at its most solemn moment, when the priest elevates the consecrated host. As in the later *Disputa*, the lesson in orthodoxy is that the wafer's substance has been miraculously 'transubstantiated' into the body of Christ, even though it retains the same shape, colour, and taste. The case of a thirteenth-century Bohemian priest who doubted this much-performed miracle was depicted by Raphael in his Vatican fresco of the *Miracle of the Mass at Bolsena* (1512–14, Stanza di Eliodoro): the priest's doubts were dispelled when the host began to bleed in his hands. Raphael brings us closer to the altar than does Van der Weyden, but a better rendering of the priest's experience is provided by the anonymous *Mass of St Hubert* (c.1485–90, National Gallery, London). Clearly displayed on the altar are the three objects required for the celebration of mass: a square linen corporal, a saucer-like paten to hold the host, and a chalice for the wine. In all three paintings the celebrant is correctly vested in a full-length white alb covered by a decorated chasuble, and the altars are suitably clothed with white linen and decorated frontals. A very different eucharistic lesson is told by Paolo Uccello in the six small scenes of his *Profanation of the Host* (c.1468, Galleria Nazionale delle Marche, Urbino), in which a Christian woman steals a consecrated host in order to repay her debt to a Jewish moneylender. Their scheme is discovered: the woman is condemned to hang and the Jew is burned alive. Although Jews had long since been expelled from France, where the story originated, they did live and lend money in Italian cities, but there were no cases of host desecration there, making Uccello's choice of subject all the more remarkable.

In the annual liturgical cycle a complex sequence of fixed and movable feasts associated with the life of Christ overlapped the densely populated list of saints' days. Feasts began with vigils the previous evening and the 'octaves' of major ones were marked eight days after the relevant vigil. Best practice was established in Rome and its guardian was the papal master of ceremonies. Between 1483 and 1528 this office was held successively by Johannes Burchard and Paride Grassi, both of whom kept detailed diaries of the liturgy celebrated in St Peter's Basilica, the Sistine Chapel, and the Roman 'station' churches visited by the *cappella papale*. The Church's year began with the penitential season of Advent, the four Sundays of which were occasions for preaching in the papal chapel by Dominican, Franciscan, Augustinian, and Carmelite friars. In 1494 Advent preaching determined the course of Florentine politics. The Medici had been exiled on 9 November, leaving a power vacuum. Throughout Advent Savonarola preached a series of sermons on the Psalms, in the course of which he strayed into political territory and inspired the creation of a new, more inclusive constitution. Christmas brought a flurry of liturgical activity: vespers on 24 December and three masses from midnight onwards. By Christmas 1497 Savonarola had been excommunicated by Alexander VI (r. 1492–1503), so took this festal opportunity to defy the pope by celebrating the three masses and leading a procession outside S. Marco. The liturgical pace hardly slackened for the feast of St Stephen (which witnessed the assassination of Duke Galeazzo Maria Sforza when he visited Milan's church of S. Stefano in 1476), St John the Evangelist (which could include a papal foray across Rome to the city's cathedral church, S. Giovanni in Laterano), and Holy Innocents, on 26, 27, and 28 December respectively.

The Christmas season continued through to the Purification (2 February), but it was Epiphany (6 January) that struck the loudest chord with Renaissance elites, because the visitors who brought gifts of gold, frankincense, and myrrh to the Christ child were traditionally said to be kings. Charles VII of France (r. 1422–61) had himself depicted as one of their number. This deflected attention from an alternative interpretation of the visitors as 'magi', oriental astrologers. According to the Florentine Marsilio Ficino's undated sermon *De stella magorum*, an angel announced the birth of Jesus by taking the form of a comet, putting astrology at the very heart of God's covenant with man. The Magi recognized the comet or star's significance which, argued Ficino, proved the existence of a parallel non-Jewish revelation of God's will. It is not known whether Ficino's sermon was written for the Florentine Compagnia de' Magi, the confraternity which met at S. Marco and whose principal activity was the organization of occasional pageants re-enacting the visit of the Magi. By the 1460s these were highly elaborate affairs, with each king or magus beginning his journey in a different quarter of the city, meeting in the piazza della Signoria, and processing together to S. Marco.

The Epiphany was significant in Florence because it also marked the baptism of Jesus by the city's patron saint, but the Medici acquired a particular devotion to the Magi by two more specific routes: first, the exile of the Magi-loving Strozzi family in 1434 created a devotional vacancy; then, Cosimo's association with the Dominicans at

S. Marco brought him into contact with the Magi cult already centred there. The Magi were painted on the wall of Cosimo's cell in the convent and the creator of that fresco, Benozzo Gozzoli, was subsequently commissioned to decorate Cosimo's chapel in the Palazzo Medici with the *Journey of the Magi*, each magus and his companions appearing on a separate wall, paralleling the confraternity's processions through the city. They meet at Filippo Lippi's *Adoration of the Magi* altarpiece. Surely it was this Medicean devotion to the Magi that caused the baptism of Cosimo's grandson Lorenzo to be delayed until 6 January. When the Medici were themselves exiled in 1494 the Compagnia de' Magi ceased to function, but Savonarola briefly ensured that the cult remained active at S. Marco, even if a re-enactment of the Magi's visit was held behind closed doors in January 1498. Even in the papal chapel Epiphany was celebrated with a Florentine twist, for the friars chosen to preach at vespers were Servites, members of an order that originated in Florence.

The next liturgical season opened with the pentitential act of receiving ashes on Ash Wednesday, but not before the riot of worldly indulgence that was Carnival. Again, Florentine history offers some of the more notable Carnivals of the Renaissance period, because Savonarola reacted against the prevailing culture by encouraging his followers to construct bonfires of 'vanities' in 1497 and 1498. Thereafter, the five Sundays of Lent were opportunities for Dominican, Franciscan, Augustinian, Carmelite, and Servite friars to preach in the papal chapel. Aspects of the chapel's Lenten timetable could depend on the relative fortunes of these orders, so that the Franciscan Sixtus IV refused to celebrate the Annunciation (25 March) at the Dominican church of S. Maria sopra Minerva, where it doubled up as the patronal feast, venturing instead to the more distant Augustinians at S. Maria del Popolo. After Sixtus' death, the natural order was restored, in addition to which the Dominicans' protector, Oliviero Carafa, also persuaded his fellow cardinals to visit the Minerva on feast of St Thomas Aquinas (7 March).

On Palm Sunday the great drama of Holy Week began with processions recalling Jesus' entry into Jerusalem. Thursday brought remembrance of the Last Supper, complete with the ritual washing of feet. Events leading up to the Crucifixion were revived on Good Friday in penitential processions, the faithful queuing up to venerate the wood of the Cross. Often there was little distinction between sacred liturgy and secular entertainment, though the performance of Passion plays was not restricted to this season. Devotions inspired by the brief period between the Crucifixion and the Resurrection can be seen in attempted recreations of Jerusalem's church of the Holy Sepulchre, the most obvious Renaissance example being Alberti's Rucellai Sepulchre in the Florentine church of S. Pancrazio. In liturgical and dramatic terms Easter was an anticlimax. The impact of the symbolic 'new fire' was limited by it being lit in daylight on Holy Saturday, after which the first mass of Easter could be celebrated as soon as Saturday morning, rather than in the early hours of Easter Sunday, as has been the case since the mid-twentieth century. This lack of drama reflects the tone of the Gospel accounts, particularly John's, which provides many details for the Crucifixion and falls away thereafter, but it also explains why Renaissance artists have left us so many

Crucifixions, Descents from the Cross, and *Pietà*, but relatively few depictions of the risen Christ. A striking exception can be found in Sansepolcro, where Piero della Francesca effectively celebrated his home town in a *Resurrection* fresco (1460s, Museo Civico, Sansepolcro).

Emphasis on the Crucifixion continued in feasts dedicated to the Invention of the Cross (3 May) and its Exaltation (14 September). The former recalled the Empress Helena's discovery of the wood that had formed the Cross, relics subsequently housed in the Roman church of S. Croce in Gerusalemme. From 1478 the cardinal-priest of S. Croce was Pedro González de Mendoza, whose birthday happened to fall on 3 May. Mendoza's devotion to the True Cross was almost overwhelming: his foundations included the Colegio Mayor de S. Cruz at Valladolid and the hospital of S. Cruz at Toledo, his confessor was Tomás de Torquemada, prior of S. Cruz in Segovia, and he chose to be buried next to the altar of St Helena in his cathedral at Toledo. Mendoza was with the Spanish monarchs Ferdinand and Isabella when the city of Granada, capital of the eponymous Muslim kingdom, fell to their forces on 2 January 1492, and again four days later when the king and queen made their formal entry into the city, the Cross now raised triumphantly above its walls. According to the diarist Stefano Infessura, news of this great Christian victory reached Rome on 1 February, on which day a miracle occurred: workmen at S. Croce in Gerusalemme happened to remove some plaster in the roof of the church to reveal a lead box on which the contents were declared to be the TITULUS CRUCIS. It had been placed there in the 1140s. The *titulus* itself is a piece of wood, *c.*25 cm by 14 cm in size, bearing incised letters in three rows and three languages, Latin, Greek, and Hebrew or Aramaic. Although incomplete, the text is clearly intended to say 'Jesus of Nazareth, king of the Jews'.

The summer season witnessed a sequence of movable, Christocentric feasts: Ascension, Pentecost, Trinity, and Corpus Christi. Marking the descent of the Holy Spirit and thereby making the Trinity complete, Pentecost was second only to Easter in terms of significance. Corpus Christi commemorated the institution of the eucharist and, like Trinity, was of relatively recent vintage as a feast of the Universal Church. At the popular end of the spectrum, Corpus Christi processions and plays made the most of summer weather, though the heat could also contribute to outbreaks of violence on these occasions. Among the fixed feasts, SS Peter and Paul (29 June), the Assumption of the Virgin (15 August), and her Nativity (8 September) were the most notable. Roman diarists allow us to distinguish standard practices from exceptional ones, such as the zeal with which Sixtus IV observed the Marian feasts at the height of the plague season, when many curialists preferred to absent themselves from Rome altogether. The remainder of the liturgical year, which included the feasts of St Michael and All Angels (29 September), All Saints and All Souls (1 and 2 November), and St Andrew (30 November), was comparatively quiet.

The strict formality of the liturgical calendar worked well in a Church led by canon lawyers, for whom religion could be reduced to the quantifiable mechanics of formal observance. Among the fifteenth- and sixteenth-century popes, only three—Sixtus IV,

THE GOSPEL LECTIONARY BL ROYAL 2 B XII is a liturgical book created in England *c*.1508.
It contains sixteen miniatures to mark the beginning of readings for major feasts, in this case
Corpus Christi. The circular host is the body of Christ and the chalice contains his blood.

Adrian VI, and Sixtus V (r. 1585–90)—were doctors of theology, but at least three times
as many held doctorates in civil and canon law. Most popes were Italian and theology
was a low priority in Italian universities, which specialized in law. Indeed, the premier
university in the Papal States, Bologna, had no professor of theology. Study of the
subject in Italy tended to be associated with the mendicant friars, so it is no coincidence
that Sixtus IV was a Franciscan and Sixtus V a Dominican. Beyond the Alps, Paris was

the pre-eminent centre for theology, with Cologne, Leuven, and Oxford also notable. Adrian VI was a product of Leuven. All the universities shared the same approach to theology, which was legalistic in that theological texts were subjected to the laws of logic, with a view to identifying the truths they contained. In that sense theology was no different from the other disciplines, for logic was applied to medical and legal texts in the relevant faculties. Collectively, this approach is known as Scholasticism. It dictated the academic experience of all scholars throughout the Renaissance period, but subsequent attention has tended to focus on the minority who considered its legalism to be a source of spiritual sterility. These were men whose study of classical literature caused them to value rhetoric over logic and to argue that eloquence could engender wisdom, that good style could inspire good morals. From their study of the 'humane' letters, as opposed to Scripture, these scholars were posthumously identified as 'humanists'. There was no love lost between humanists such as Ulrich von Hutten, who satirized the theologians of Cologne in his *Epistolae obscurorum virorum* (1515–17), and traditional theologians, who dismissed the classical scholars as 'mere grammarians'. That latter assessment was not entirely without justification, for Christian humanists were united by their interest in textual scholarship, rather than by any theological or philosophical opinions.

Humanists particularly appreciated the Fathers of the Church because the latter were steeped in classical literature and could therefore be regarded as the Christian counterparts of literary giants such as Cicero. Interest in patristic texts was a convenient way of uniting Greek and Latin culture, exemplified by the translations of Basil the Great, John Chrysostom, Athanasius, and Gregory of Nazianzus made by the Florentine Camaldolese monk Ambrogio Traversari. In the decades prior to 1453 and Constantinople's fall to the Ottoman Turks generations of Greek scholars settled in Italy, among them the prelate Bessarion, who participated in the ecumenical Council of Ferrara-Florence (1438–45), and Giorgios Trapezountios (George of Trebizond), who translated Basil, Gregory of Nyssa, and Gregory of Nazianzus into Latin. The first printed edition of a Greek patristic text in Latin translation appears to have been that of Basil's *Oratio ad adolescentes* (Venice, 1470/1), which exhorts young men to study Greek literature and thereby caught the latest intellectual fashion. Among the Latin Fathers, early printed editions included works by Lactantius (Subiaco, 1465), Cyprian (Rome, 1471), and Ambrose (Venice, 1495). On an altogether larger scale, editions of Augustine's and Jerome's works were published at Basel in 1506 and 1516 respectively, the latter by Erasmus, who went on to bring out a further edition of Augustine in 1528–9. That was a relatively straightforward task. The Bible itself presented far greater challenges, for the Fathers themselves despaired of its inelegant Latin, and Augustine remained dissatisfied with Jerome's version, though it went on to be the text of choice throughout Latin Christendom, albeit with minor variations in each of its innumerable manuscript copies.

Any Latin scholar seeking to iron out those variations and identify the translator's original meaning and intention required an understanding of Greek for the New Testament, Hebrew and Aramaic for the Old. Traversari's Florentine pupil Giannozzo

Manetti duly mastered Greek and Hebrew and, in the mid-1450s, translated the New Testament and the Psalms, 'improving' Jerome's text as he did so. Manetti's younger, Roman contemporary Lorenzo Valla examined the Vulgate as a translation from the Greek, making a sequence of notes rather than attempting a thorough edition. Valla broke new ground, suggesting more accurate translations from his readings of non-scriptural sources contemporary with the New Testament and concluding that Jerome had done no more than revise an existing text. Valla's work had no contemporary impact whatsoever. Instead, while his notes remained in manuscript, biblical studies were being taken in different directions, as the development of printing with movable type coincided with a trend for making vernacular translations of Scripture. Thus, although the first printed Bible was Gutenberg's 42-line Vulgate, it was followed by a German vernacular Bible, printed at Strasbourg in 1466, and then by Niccolò Malermi's Italian translation (Venice, 1471), a Dutch Old Testament (Delft, 1477), a Catalan translation of both testaments (Valencia, 1478), and a Czech translation of the same (Prague, 1488). For the most part, though, printers opted for the quickest returns and made them by means of devotional manuals, psalters, books of hours, or single-sheet indulgences, the last being documents issued by popes or bishops which granted remission of temporal punishment in purgatory upon the meeting of certain conditions.

In 1504 Erasmus discovered the second redaction of Valla's work on the New Testament, made in the 1450s, and published it as *Adnotationes* (1505). Thus was Valla's achievement finally made known, the discovery also launching Erasmus on his own career as a biblical editor, first concentrating on a Latin New Testament and later publishing his Greek edition of the same, *Novum instrumentum*, at Basel in 1516. There followed his *Paraphrases* of the Gospels, which proved popular with the laity, but it was the pioneering *Novum instrumentum* that particularly inspired other scholars, becoming the foundation for subsequent translations. Lefèvre's French New Testament was published in Paris in 1523 and William Tyndale's English translation appeared from 1525. Tyndale was already a religious exile in the Rhineland, where his work was printed, and in 1525 the French authorities declared all vernacular bibles to be tainted with heresy, in consequence of which Lefèvre's Old Testament was duly published in Antwerp. Luther's German New Testament was not completed until 1534. Scholarship was coming to serve the spiritual needs of the unlettered masses, but vernacular translations were a move in completely the wrong direction for anyone who so despaired of the Vulgate's Latin that no amount of editing, let alone translating, could raise it to a literary level worthy of its subject matter. Leo X therefore commissioned Marco Girolamo Vida to relate the life of Christ in a Latin epic. This *Christiad*, written in the style of Vergil, was finally published in 1535.

Elsewhere among the intellectual elite it was the study of Hebrew and its consequences for Old Testament scholarship that generated the greatest excitement. Earlier generations of Christian scholars had rarely, if ever, employed Hebrew texts, so the onset of Hebrew printing in Italy in the mid-1470s and the publication of the first complete Hebrew text of the Old Testament, at Soncino in 1488, was nothing short of revolutionary. There was enough interest for a sequence of Hebrew grammars to appear in quick succession: that published by Aldo Manuzio in Venice in 1500, another by the self-taught Hebraist Konrad Pellikan in 1503/4, and Johannes Reuchlin's *De rudimentis Hebraicis* in 1506. All the elements were therefore in place for scholars to undertake the most ambitious biblical edition of the Renaissance period: the Complutensian Polyglot Bible, which presented the Old Testament in parallel columns of Hebrew, Greek, and Latin text, together with the New Testament in Greek and Latin. The project was based at Alcalá (Latin: Complutum) in Castile, where a new university was established, all of it under the patronage of Cardinal Francisco Jiménez de Cisneros. The trilingual emphasis at Alcalá rapidly inspired a new college at Leuven and the library of Corpus Christi College, Oxford (both founded 1517) and Guillaume Budé's Parisian Collège Royal (from 1530), all of which were designed to further the

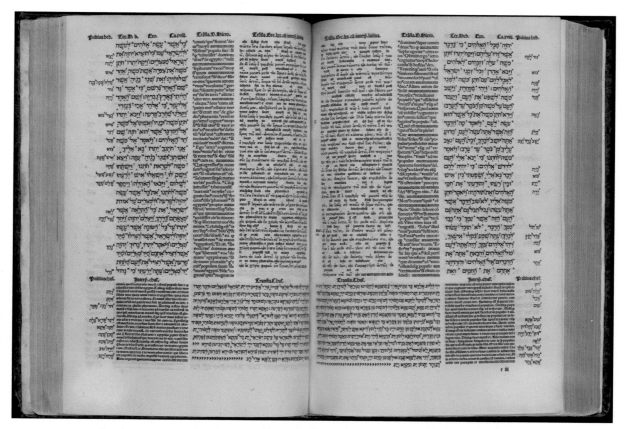

THE COMPLUTENSIAN POLYGLOT BIBLE WAS commissioned by Cardinal Francisco Jiménez de Cisneros, prepared by Spain's most notable linguistic scholars, and printed at Alcalá de Henares in 1514–17. The Old Testament (shown here) appears in parallel columns of Hebrew, Latin, and Greek, the New Testament in Greek and Latin.

study of Scripture. The first of the Polyglot Bible's six volumes was printed in 1514, but it was some years before the entire work was ready for publication.

The notional pilgrim at the opening of this chapter was left admiring the four Gospel books in manuscript form in Raphael's *Disputa*. It is time for him to turn round 180 degrees and face the more familiar *School of Athens*, by the same master. The positioning of these two works reflects the dilemma for educated men and women who sought to reconcile faith in Christ with appreciation of classical culture, which provided them with knowledge of the world and the cosmos, sciences and arts, history and legend, as the Bible simply did not. Must a Christian reject Cicero's prose or Vergil's poetry because those authors lived and wrote before the Incarnation? Yes, according to the message received by the young St Jerome in an exceptionally vivid dream. Appearing before Christ the Judge, he claimed to be a Christian, only to be told that his reading had made him a disciple of Cicero and no Christian at all. His resolution to devote himself exclusively to sacred texts provided a model for Renaissance luminaries, including Erasmus and Vittoria Colonna. Styling Jesus as Apollo and Mary as 'a true Diana', as some Renaissance figures permitted themselves to do, or comparing St Paul with the historian Suetonius, would not solve the problem.

In the *School of Athens* equal prominence is given to the figures of Plato and Aristotle. It was through Jewish scholars such as Moses Maimonides (d.1204) and Islamic ones led by Averroes (d.1198) that Western Christendom gained access to the works of Aristotle. Better translations from Greek to Latin were provided by William of Moerbeke in the thirteenth century and were rapidly employed by his fellow Dominican Thomas Aquinas. To give two of many possible examples, Aristotle's *Metaphysics* provided Thomas with inspiration for his early *Quaestiones disputate de veritate* and the *Nicomachean Ethics* loom large in the section on Christian moral thinking in his monumental *Summa theologiae*. Aristotle explained the realities of life by means of reason and Thomas sought to demonstrate that the truth of Christianity could also be proved rationally, even if divine revelation was nevertheless superior to reason. The prevalence of Thomism in the Renaissance period was itself a way to guarantee an abiding connection to Aristotle. More specifically, at the height of the Renaissance Lefèvre and his protégé Josse Clichthove wrote a commentary on the *Nicomachean Ethics*, while Lefèvre himself sought to live out the Aristotelian precept that contemplation is the highest goal of human existence.

Knowledge of Plato had never been entirely lost in Western Christendom, but it fell to Marsilio Ficino to provide translations of and commentaries on the Platonic dialogues. Alongside these, his *Theologica platonica* (1482) isolated Plato's teaching about the human soul, its divine origin, its desire to be reunited with God, and its immortality. Thereafter, Ficino worked on translations of Plotinus, the third-century Neoplatonic philosopher, and continued to argue for the essential compatibility of Christianity and the Platonic tradition, even though Porphyry and other Neoplatonists had been dismissive of Christian beliefs. One reason that Ficino's arguments gained currency was that Western Christendom already had its own pet Athenian, the

Christian convert Dionysius the Areopagite (Acts 17:34), who was thought to be one and the same as St Denys, the first bishop of Paris. The substantial degree of overlap between the works attributed to Dionysius and those of the Neoplatonists suggested that the latter drew on the erudition of St Paul's first-century convert. On the other hand, if Dionysius was able to quote from Proclus (d.485) and other Neoplatonists, that made him a pious fraud of the fifth or sixth century. Lorenzo Valla was the first scholar to doubt Dionysius' authenticity, with Erasmus and the sixteenth-century Protestants duly following suit. Lefèvre was a particularly high-profile victim, so it is little wonder that his older self chose to declare that 'to know nothing outside the Gospels is to know everything'. If one could not trust a Christian to be who he claimed to be, it boded ill for the reputation of Plato, who was regarded with suspicion by most Protestants, let alone for that of anyone else outside the Judaeo-Christian tradition.

Other dilemmas arose. If it was permissible for Christians to study the Old Testament because, as Jesus assured them, he had not come to abolish the Law of Moses or the writings of prophets such as (Second) Isaiah, but to fulfil them (Matt. 5:17), did that licence extend to non-Jewish texts that purported to pre-date Christianity and seemed to suggest that gentiles received their own revelation of the coming Saviour, parallel to that of the Jews? Such texts had previously attracted relatively little attention. Among the Fathers, Clement of Alexandria and Eusebius mentioned the Persian sage Zoroaster, the wonderful Egyptian Hermes Trismegistus, and the Thracian prophet Orpheus as precursors of Christianity, but there was no abiding interest in this *prisca theologia* ('ancient theology'). With regard to Zoroaster, interest was revived in the fifteenth century by the Greek scholar Gemistos Pletho, whose various enthusiasms were transmitted to Italians at the Council of Ferrara-Florence. The council was financed by the wealthy banker Cosimo de' Medici, who later commissioned his physician's son, Marsilio Ficino, to translate from Greek to Latin the corpus of texts attributed to Hermes Trismegistus. In reality, this *Corpus Hermeticum* probably dated from the third century CE and the *Oracula Chaldaica*, texts associated with Zoroaster, were not much more ancient, but what mattered for Pletho and Ficino was that these two supposedly venerable traditions were inherited by Greek philosophers, including Pythagoras, and culminated in the works of Plato. It was enough to merit Zoroaster's inclusion in the *School of Athens*, holding a globe towards the bottom right of the scene.

Inspired by Ficino, his younger contemporary Giovanni Pico argued for a line of religious descent from Zoroaster and the *Oracula Chaldaica* through Abraham and the Jewish tradition to Judaism's spiritual daughter, Christianity. This interest exposed Pico to the Zohar, an esoteric text purporting to date from early in the Christian era, together with its thirteenth- and fourteenth-century Jewish interpreters. Thus began a brief but intense flourishing of interest in Cabbala. Pico was a young man in a hurry and hardly had he employed a Jewish convert to Christianity to translate various cabbalistic texts into Latin than he declared himself ready to defend 900 *Conclusiones* in open debate. His syncretic thinking meshed so many religious traditions that some of his claims were rapidly denounced as heretical and, in due course, all 900 theses were condemned by Innocent VIII. Undaunted, Pico went on to compile a mystical interpretation of the opening chapters of Genesis. A more systematic approach to Cabbala was presented by Reuchlin, first in *De verbo mirifico* (*On the Wonder-Working Word*, 1494) and later in *De arte cabalistica* (1517). In both cases, Reuchlin's purpose was to use Cabbala to confirm Christ as the messiah and thereby encourage conversions from Judaism. Another enthusiast, Egidio da Viterbo, prior general of the Order of Augustinian Hermits, put his cabbalistic learning to an even more remarkable purpose when, in 1517, he urged Leo X to add at least two or three Hebrew letters to the Roman alphabet so that Christians—from the pope downwards—would be able to pronounce the name of Jesus correctly. Only then could they begin to unlock the mysteries of the sacred names, mysteries understood by Jews but stubbornly ignored by Christians. As an Augustinian hermit, Luther was under the obedience of this remarkable thinker, but did not share his interest in Cabbala. It was a minority interest dismissed by the sixteenth-century reformers as nothing more than magic.

While non-Christian texts might lead the faithful into idolatry and polytheism or tempt them into heresy regarding the Trinity or the nature of the soul, astrology suggested that God might be something less than omnipotent in the universe. In *De triplici vita* (1489) Ficino compounded the problem by explaining how both astrology and magic could be harnessed to promote health and prolong life. He knew about astrological magic and natural magic, but accepted that it was difficult to make a clear distinction between these 'white' occult sciences and 'black' sorcery—*maleficium*—which could similarly be traced back to antiquity. Interest in magic was not confined to Italy, for its practitioners and apologists included the learned bibliophile Johannes Trithemius, abbot of Sponheim and author of the notorious *Steganographia* (written *c.*1500, but not published until 1606), and the wandering scholar Cornelius Agrippa, who dedicated *De occulta philosophia* (1510) to Trithemius. Renaissance magi sought to communicate with the angels and demons that Christians of any background believed to exist, but beyond the educated elite there was also a rich world of popular beliefs about all sorts of malevolent spirits. Here were the practices that fifteenth-century clerics sought to eliminate by linking witchcraft with diabolism, most famously in the *Malleus maleficarum* (1486), a detailed guide to conducting a witch trial written by two German inquisitors. The campaign evidently worked: in 1516 Luther recalled that there had been many witches and sorcerers in his youth, but now they were rare indeed.

The spiritual beings in Raphael's *Disputa* are extremely orderly ranks of angels. This is not the heavenly host of Revelation 12:7, doing battle against the fallen angels under the leadership of the archangel Michael. Rather, it derives from a text known as the *Celestial Hierarchy* and attributed to Dionysius the Areopagite. This hierarchy was ninefold, ranging from seraphim and cherubim, who were closest to God, through to archangels and, at the lowest level, mere angels. In the first half of the fifteenth century the *Celestial Hierarchy* was translated into Latin by Ambrogio Traversari and championed by the great German philosopher Nicholas of Cusa. Towards the end of the century, Ficino made another translation and Traversari's translation was edited by

Lefèvre as part of the wider *Corpus Dionysiacum* (1499). In turn, Lefèvre's edition inspired a commentary on the *Celestial Hierarchy* by John Colet, dean of St Paul's Cathedral in London. Distinctively, Ficino claimed that each person has a guardian angel. It was a concept he developed from Plato's daimons, spirits existing somewhere between gods and men, and was therefore quite distinct from the Judaeo-Christian tradition. Earthly interventions by angelic messengers are rare in the earlier Jewish texts—Genesis 18:1–5 is an example—but feature prominently in the later books of Daniel, Tobit, and Enoch, where particular angels are identified by name. This Jewish inheritance can be seen in Filippino Lippi's Tobit-inspired painting of *Three Angels with Young Tobias* (1485, Galleria Sabauda, Turin), the angels being clearly identifiable as Michael the warrior, Raphael the healer, and Gabriel the herald. In Western Christendom the pictorial representation of angels soon passed its peak, as they did not lend themselves to more realistic styles of painting, though Orthodoxy remained loyal, as can be seen in the epically proportioned icon *Blessed be the Host of the King of Heaven* (Tretyakov Gallery, Moscow) in which the archangel Michael leads Russian troops after their victory at Kazan in 1552.

If angels could leave the heavenly realm and intervene in the affairs of men, the opposite journey was apparently made by mystics, who enjoyed direct experiences of God in the present life, without having to wait for death and the Beatific Vision in heaven. In the later sixteenth century Teresa of Ávila famously encountered an angel, who pierced her heart with an arrow, while she was in a state of mystical ecstasy. As with angels, Renaissance understanding of 'mystical theology' was rooted in the works attributed to Dionysius the Areopagite. In the fourteenth century mysticism flourished in the Rhineland, the Low Countries, and England, but one of the most characteristic and abiding features of mystical literature derives from the *Book of the Lover and the Beloved* by the Majorcan Ramon Llull. The Lover is the human soul, which seeks and achieves mystical union with God, the Beloved, as in: 'Deity and Humanity met, and joined together to make concord between Lover and Beloved.' In the fifteenth century Llull's copious works attracted the same scholarly minds that were interested in the *Corpus Dionysiacum*. Again, Nicholas of Cusa was at the forefront of this interest and Llullian inspiration can be discerned in his masterpiece, *De docta ignorantia* (c.1440), which argues—in a most learned fashion—that book-learning cannot lead a man to Truth. Llull wrote in the Catalan vernacular, which might suggest unlettered ignorance, though that could hardly have been further from the case. Still, his works required translation into Latin if they were to be more widely appreciated and it was a task to which Lefèvre, the editor of Dionysius, set some of his students. Lefèvre's own spiritual development was moulded by his studies, whether of Dionysius, Llull, or Cusanus, and is revealed in his *Liber de contemplatione* (1505), though he was no mystic himself.

The canonization of Catherine of Siena proved that the Church could formally accept mystics, providing they were unquestionably orthodox in their beliefs. Catherine's dependence on the sacraments was confirmed by that fact that her stomach could tolerate no food apart from the consecrated host, but the ecclesiastical authorities were generally suspicious of people who bypassed the priestly hierarchy by claiming to experience mystic union with God. The freedom from sacerdotal control offered by mysticism was particularly attractive to unlettered women, tempting them to venture beyond the bounds of orthodoxy. Among the best-known such cases are those of the lachrymose English visionary Margery Kempe, who was accused of being a Lollard, and the youthful French warrior Jeanne d'Arc, who claimed to hear the voices of SS Michael, Margaret of Antioch, and Catherine of Alexandria, was excommunicated as a relapsed heretic, and executed by the secular authorities. Jeanne's appearance in wartorn France appeared to fulfil popular prophecies about a Maid from Lorraine saving the nation. Like mystics, prophets defied control, but went beyond mystics by overtly challenging the authorities. As in other periods, they tended to foretell doom, few being as accurate as the wild man of Siena who, in 1527, warned Clement VII that Rome would be destroyed within a fortnight. His estimate of the imperialist onslaught was only a few days short of the reality.

Even the sack of Rome was but a rehearsal for the end of time. As in other respects, Renaissance men and women took their apocalypticism from the Nicene Creed: 'He will come again in glory to judge the living and the dead and his kingdom will have no end.' To see the deceased being sent to their fates, our pilgrim would have to walk from the Raphael Stanze to the Sistine Chapel and Michelangelo's fresco of the *Last Judgement* (1536–41), though the message is perhaps easier to read in Van der Weyden's altarpiece (*c.*1443–51) for the Hôtel-Dieu at Beaune, or Memling's (1460s, Muzeum Narodowe, Gdańsk) for the Medici agent in Bruges, both of which clearly depict St Michael carefully weighing souls to determine whether they are bound for heaven or hell. Precisely what sequence of events could be expected prior to this final judgement was a matter of dispute, but the opinion propounded by Joachim of Fiore and condemned by the Fourth Lateran Council (1215) had not been forgotten. Joachim divided history into three ages, those of the Father, the Son, and the Holy Spirit, corresponding to the period covered by the Old Testament, that ushered in by Christ, and a future thousand-year era of blessedness when all mankind would be converted to Christianity, thereby eliminating both Judaism and Islam. Joachim's predominantly Franciscan followers elaborated on this third age by predicting that the world would be united under the leadership of an 'angelic pope'. Bernardino of Siena sought to eradicate Joachimitism from among the Franciscans of fifteenth-century Italy, though a brief revival can be traced during the pontificate of Sixtus IV, whose Portuguese confessor João da Silva e Meneses is thought to have written a prophetic text called *Apocalypsis nova*. João—known in Italy as Amadeo—founded a new Franciscan congregation, which Sixtus installed at S. Pietro in Montorio, the patronage of which duly passed from Louis XI to Ferdinand of Aragon and Isabella of Castile, in whose realms Joachimite ideas were flourishing. Arnau of Vilanova (d.1311) had prophesied that an Aragonese king would conquer Jerusalem, create a worldwide Christian empire, and usher in the Last Days. The fall of Granada in 1492 was duly interpreted as the trigger for the fulfilment of Arnau's prophecy, not least in the opening discourse of that year's conclave, which was delivered by the Spanish monarchs' ambassador Bernardino López de Carvajal.

In 1495 Carvajal succeeded Mendoza as cardinal-priest of S. Croce. Although he shared Mendoza's devotion to the True Cross, a greater proportion of Carvajal's zeal was channelled into preparations for what he assumed would be the impending final defeat of Islam. This was never more apparent than in his sermon to the imperial court at Malines on the feast of the Exaltation of the Cross, 14 September 1508. Developing popular notions that Islam would survive for no more than a millennium, he confidently predicted its extirpation in the sixteenth century. The fall of Granada had been the beginning of its general geographical contraction, in addition to which the oceanic voyages of Portuguese and Spanish seafarers were hastening the process of unifying mankind under a single pastor, an angelic pope. With his eye on the young Charles of Ghent, heir to both Ferdinand of Aragon and Emperor Maximilian, the cardinal predicted that the union of Spain and Germany would complete the Christian conquest over this falsest of heresies. Such passion was not confined to Spaniards, though Lefèvre's lobbying of Christian princes to destroy Islam by violence was surely inspired by the Majorcan Ramon Llull. In his address to the Fifth Lateran Council Egidio da Viterbo urged Julius II to employ spiritual weapons against the Ottomans, but on other occasions he played an active part in preparing for war against them. By 1517 and the *Libellus de litteris Hebraicis* Jerusalem had fallen to the Ottomans, so Egidio's hope was that the city could be taken by Christian forces and that Leo X would be the pope of the millennium. When that was not realized Egidio directed his appeals elsewhere. His library was lost during the imperialist sack of Rome, but not even that cataclysmic episode prevented Egidio from hoping that Carvajal's sometime hero, now Emperor Charles V, would be able to control and redirect his military forces and deal Islam a knock-out blow.

From the perspective of a medievalist, the Renaissance has been described as 'the Middle Ages minus religion'. For the sake of a *bon mot* this conveniently overlooks the church-building, bead-fingering, prayer-book-reading piety conveyed by a range of physical remains, together with some dramatic developments in biblical scholarship, much of it disseminated in the revolutionary medium of print. There was no lack of religion in Renaissance Europe, whether among the overwhelmingly Christian majority or on the Jewish and Islamic fringes. Indeed, the imposition of Christianity on Granada's Muslims, like Ficino's attempts to mesh it with Neoplatonism, and Pico's to synthesize all known religions, suggests something of a religious surfeit. Neither Erasmus nor Luther complained about a lack of piety in the world around them. Rather, they regarded it as the wrong sort of piety: too physical and insufficiently spiritual, too legalistic and insufficiently scriptural. There are, however, pitfalls in mentioning those two individuals in the same breath, for it is all too easy to repeat the quip about Erasmus laying the egg that Luther hatched and to be tempted by alliteration into arguing that the Renaissance ushered in the Reformation, as if it served no other function. Erasmus was certainly at pains to distance himself from Luther and moved from the city of Basel when it turned Lutheran. Thus, Renaissance religion is in danger of being squeezed from both chronological ends. However, if it is appreciated in its own right, then it becomes a story of fervently imitating Christ and his saints, whether in the cloister of a recently reformed religious community or in a secular world imbued with mendicant teaching and spirituality.

CHAPTER 4

The Civilization of the Renaissance

FRANÇOIS QUIVIGER

Introduction: identity and individualism in Renaissance civilization

SINCE Plato stated that the goal of human life is to know oneself the concept of individuality has risen rather than decreased in the West. It has also changed across the centuries. Most scholars have now abandoned Jacob Burckhardt's assertion that the Renaissance invented individualism and instead understand this approach as an expression of nineteenth-century ideals. Indeed, concepts of individuality change with time. Since the emergence of the concept of the unconscious, and the spread of psychoanalytical ideas in the humanities, individuality has not been completely in the hands of the individual. It has increasingly become a polymorphous and dynamic concept, expressed in the late twentieth century through notions of self-fashioning, voiced among others by the literary historian Stephen Greenblatt, and of gender fluidity as developed by the gender theorist Judith Butler.

Burckhardt was not entirely wrong, neither was Freud: the Renaissance did not know the unconscious, but artists, writers, philosophers, and theologians were aware of the power of the mind to generate dangerous images threatening rational thinking. Self-fashioning consists in adapting one's physical and psychological appearances to suit the multiple situations and circumstances brought by life. Such patterns of behaviour apply particularly well to Renaissance courtiers and court artists, or to the penniless aristocrats satirized in Spanish picaresque novels; it is a useful angle from which to envisage Nicodemism, the attitude of religious dissimulation adopted by sympathizers of the Reformation living in Catholic countries. In this matter the rather distracting question of whether past scholars were right, wrong, or simply being anachronistic tends to overshadow the fact that historians always search the past for what is most relevant to their own time. Thus, keeping this universal purpose of history in mind, we should therefore focus on identifying defining features of the civilization of the Renaissance that are particularly relevant to the present.

ANDREA MANTEGNA, *Lodovico Gonzaga, Family, and Court*, 1452–75. Andrea Mantegna's *Camera picta* served as the audience chamber of the Gonzagas, the ruling family of Mantua. This scene of courtly life shows Ludovico Gonzaga and his wife, Barbara of Brandenburg, surrounded by their relatives and courtiers. At a time when the Italian peninsula was divided into competing city states, Renaissance courts formed a network sharing a similar ethical and aesthetic ideal shaped by humanism. Broadcast in works such as Castiglione's *Courtier*, this ideal eventually affected European elites.

The modern world has brought to the common man access to means of self-development—education, mobility, goods, and services—that were in the Renaissance exclusive privileges of the upper classes. The twenty-first-century Western self is not only a desiring and consuming entity but also one constantly amplified and extended by the electronic tools with which it interacts with others. Social media, and easy access to image-producing devices, have turned images into common means of self-presentation and communication thanks to which most people can aspire to at least fifteen minutes of fame.

The proliferation of images and texts brought by the invention of printing (*c.*1440) confirms that the Renaissance experienced a revolution comparable in magnitude to the recent emergence of the Internet. The word 'selfie' is recent but the Renaissance brought about and developed the self-portrait and the portrait. Similarly moving pictures were not unknown then. The Renaissance had a flourishing tradition of 'empathic visualizing', shaped by medieval religion and extended to secular literature, and, as we shall see, much fondness for animated images.

The historian John Jeffries Martin has suggested the existence of three categories of Renaissance self: the communal or civic self, the prudential or performative self, and the porous self. The civic self relates to social groups, family, and lineage; the prudential self handles relations between the inside and the outside world, and may roughly be characterized as self-fashioning. The porous self primarily expresses the difficulty of delimiting the self as an independent thinking entity—as will be the case from Descartes onwards. The porous self emerges from accounts of spirits, possessions, and planetary influences, but it can also apply to the broad assumption characteristic of early modern science and philosophy that man and the universe are composed of the same elements, on the balance of which health depends.

This sense of the self in the world suggests that the ways in which early modern humans may have experienced the world might also be closer to ours. Modern art, science, and philosophy articulate our experience of being in terms of a very close interdependence between the body, the mind, and the world. The Renaissance too understood the self as interconnected with the world, a historical phenomenon which scholars have expressed through the concept of the 'porous self'.

One faculty and two senses are particularly dominant in the Renaissance: imagination, sight, and hearing. Their characterization in medicine, philosophy, and late medieval religion had broad cultural consequences.

Civilization can be defined as the material, spiritual, and ideological productions of a society. If so, then artists are perhaps some of the best guides to approach Renaissance civilization. Since the works of E. H. Gombrich in particular, envisaging the arts as a reflection of the spirit of their time has been seen as unwelcome Hegelianism—an approach denying the individual by setting up an impersonal spirit as the core element of reality. But there is another reason why early modern arts are a reflection of their time: for the three centuries covered by the Renaissance artists and artisans served the church and the upper classes. Thus the arts of the Renaissance not only reflect the tastes, ideas, aspirations, and pleasures of the European religious and political elites, but also provided them with the means to fashion, display, and extend themselves into the world. Indeed, until well into the eighteenth century there is no such thing as 'titles' for works of art, there are only subjects. Artists always worked on commissions, or produced standard themes to answer the demands of the market. They can be considered individual authors only insofar as they produce works extending the will, aspirations, and individuality of their patrons. Artists were 'professional visualizers'. Their representation of the early modern worlds is therefore a representation of the way their audiences learned to see and imagine the world and themselves.

The world

In the pre-modern worldview humans are made of the same elements and elemental qualities as the universe surrounding them. The world of the Renaissance is therefore one of correspondences between nature and the self. To the four constituent elements of the world—earth, air, water, and fire—correspond two pairs of opposing qualities: hot and cold, moist and dry. Earth is linked to water by the common quality of coldness, water to air by the quality of moisture, air to fire by heat, and fire to earth by dryness. Following a doctrine that can be traced back to ancient Greek physiology, the correspondence extends to the four seasons of the year and the four humours of man—melancholic, sanguine, choleric, and phlegmatic—completing the pre-modern ideal of cosmic and individual harmony. The four humours are the biological foundations of pre-modern psychology; they control and regulate the whole existence of mankind, their combinations and balance constitute the basis of personality and determine mental and physical health.

This connection, at the core of the porous self, is put to practice in the most important Renaissance book produced on the care of the mind, Marsilio Ficino's *Three Books on Life* of 1489, the first part of which proposes recipes intended to readjust the elemental balance disturbed by intense intellectual activities. The main health issue faced by Renaissance intellectuals rested on their belief that contemplative work generates melancholy. They thought that in order to imagine and think we need to use a subtle and warm part of our blood, called spirit. Intense contemplative activities consume much spirit, leaving the blood cold and dry and the mind sluggish, thus generating the symptoms of the melancholic temperament. The remedies Ficino proposed range from moderate physical exercise, exposure to sunlight, walks in the open air, diets based on herbs and spices, to temperate alcohol consumption and head massaging with wine.

While Ficino's *Three Books on Life* often stands out as the first text addressed to those who work with their mind, his approach is far from isolated. It has medieval antecedents and a considerable following in the sixteenth and seventeenth centuries. Indeed, from the 1550s onwards the rise of Renaissance gastronomic literature unveils a nutritional science extending from dietetics and botany to zoology and medicine. Domenico Romoli's observations on chicken meat, in his *Singolare dottrina* of 1593, offer a typical sample of the genre: 'This meat expands the intellect and has a marvellous property to temper human complexion, and its broth is particularly beneficial to those suffering from leprosy. And it is said that the brain of the hen augments the substance of our brain and sharpens the mind, and increases sperm and blood, but it is important to select hens that are neither too old nor too fat.'

In this world where everything is composed of the same four elements and subject to planetary influences, nature has a fundamental attribute: variety and abundance. This twin concept features in texts praising the multiplicity of natural creation. It is central to Renaissance natural philosophy and also features quite literally in works of art.

PIETER AERTSEN, *MEAT STALL*, 1551. From the 1550s onwards a new genre emerged, displaying market food stalls. This new genre expresses both a delight for the variety and abundance of nature and a keen pleasure in its detailed study and observation.

The famous friezes of the Villa Farnesina in Rome executed by Giovanni da Udine under the direction of Raphael in 1510 provide the most spectacular example. The garlands of flowers and fruits surrounding painted episodes of the tales of Love and Psyche are also an encyclopedia of the flowers and fruits known to early modern humans. More broadly the idea that the visual arts can represent all things as well as all natural phenomena is a topos expressed by Leonardo da Vinci and repeated throughout sixteenth-century literature. In this spirit the Venetian painter Paolo Pino, in his *Dialogo di pittura* (1549), could describe painting as 'a poetry that makes us not only believe but see the sky ornate by the sun, the moon and the stars, rain, clouds caused by winds, waters and earth, and makes us delight in the variety of spring and the charm of summer, and contract in the representation of the cold and damp winter season'.

It is therefore no surprise that these attributes of nature should also be those of the mind of the artist. Indeed, at the end of the sixteenth century the painter and art theorist Federico Zuccaro (1542–1609) observed that a good artistic imagination should, like nature, express variety and abundance. Art and nature also feature in literature. In a very similar spirit the mid-sixteenth-century polymath Anton Francesco

VICENZO CAMPI, *FISH MARKET*, *c*.1580. The *Fish Market* is part of a series painted for the Fugger, a leading banking family based in Augsburg. Research has established a keen distinction between the variety of fish reserved for the table of the wealthy and the humble diet of the working class, composed of cheese and beans. The peasant couple is almost a caricature—a genre which also began in the sixteenth century. The man in particular, eating with his mouth wide open, is an example of the worse possible table manners, in sharp contrast to the elegant restraint of the guests of Veronese's *Marriage at Cana* (see p. 140).

Doni (1513–74) titled his collection of miscellaneous texts *La zucca* (The pumpkin) as a simile of his own fertile mind and named each section after a part of the pumpkin: the branches, the seeds, the flowers, the leaves, and the fruits.

We encounter these associations of the self with natural phenomena in many Renaissance academies. For example, on joining these early modern literary associations new members often left their civic name to adopt an academic nickname. This practice, sometimes compared to monasticism, was taken rather humorously. Doni belonged to the Piacentine Accademia degli Ortolani (of the Gardeners), which adopted a phallic emblem and academic nicknames related to vegetables evocative of male fertility. The members of the Florentine academy of the Umidi (the damp ones) took water-related nicknames such as Frothy, Cold and Damp, Dried (il Spumoso, il Gelido, l'Asciutto), the Intronati (Thunderstrucks) selected nicknames associated with a state of shock, while in Brescia the Occolti chose to name themselves after things hidden, dark, and obscure.

Variety and abundance were also stylistic qualities. In his treatise *On the Abundant Style* (*De copia*) of 1512 the Dutch humanist Erasmus of Rotterdam (1466–1536) teaches how to acquire the 'abundant style', and provides the practical examples of about 500 different ways of writing 'thank you for your letter'. Thus variety and abundance are criteria binding the appreciation of food, literature, music, and painting. The humanist Leon Battista Alberti (1404–72), in his *Della pittura* (1435), the first early modern treatise on painting, explains: 'In food as in music what is new and abundant always pleases as much as it is different from antiquated and usual things, and so the soul takes delights of every variety and abundance—and it is through this that variety and abundance pleases in painting.' Thus variety and abundance would be the founding principles of early modern notions of pleasure.

On the negative side, however, nature was considered imperfect and art was endowed with the mission of improving nature and even becoming its rival. The central concept is that of synthetic imitation and its biological model: the belief according to which bees select the best flowers in order to concoct the best possible honey. Plato already mentions this topos (*Ion*, 533e–544b)—a commonplace of pre-modern apiculture now entirely dismissed. In one of his letters the early Church Father, Basil the Great (330–79), allowed good Christians to read pagan texts, provided that they, like the bees, take the best parts and leave the rest. In the Renaissance the example of the bees serves as a simile for the acquisition of personal style. In the *Book of the Courtier* (1528) Baldassare Castiglione invokes it to explain how the ideal courtier should fashion himself not only by imitating his master but also by picking the best qualities of those surrounding him (I, xxvi). Thus the Renaissance approach to self-fashioning develops through discerning interaction. The Sienese writer Alessandro Piccolomini, in a dialogue of 1539 entitled *La Raffaella*, addresses similar advice to women and enjoins them to imitate the best of everything with discernment and without affectation.

The traditional apprenticeship of the visual arts involved a similar process: copying from live models as well as from ancient and modern masters. By selecting and synthesizing the best parts of the works they studied young artists would develop their personal style and improve or idealize the human figure. Not surprisingly such a topos features in the first biography of Michelangelo by his pupil Ascanio Condivi (1553). There the simile of the bees explains how Michelangelo, in a most Platonic way, infused his work with a more universal understanding of beauty by his constant observation and drawing of bodies. The outcome of this method of fashioning images, and of self-fashioning, is the Renaissance expression of ideal nature. It may be described as a certain graceful ease and elegance. Castiglione calls this quality *sprezzatura* and defines it as the contrary of affectation. *Sprezzatura* is a core attribute of Renaissance aesthetic and civic ideals: it is the art that conceals effort and that makes even the most difficult things look easy and natural. This approach stemmed in large part from the Renaissance definition of the mind and the senses, and its use in religion and love.

The mind and the senses

The history of the ideas and debate about the soul is complex but early modern popular psychology is straightforward. The brain holds three ventricles, or cells, housing the faculties of the sensitive soul—common sense, imagination, estimation, and memory. This mixture of late antique anatomy and Aristotelian psychology spans the period from the thirteenth to the seventeenth century, eventually collapsing under the philosophical assaults of Descartes and the observations of Thomas Willis's *Anatomy of the Brain* (1664).

The Renaissance mind thinks through multisensory images produced by the reception of sensory impressions. Aristotle designated this class of mental images 'common sensibles' and hypothesized the existence of the 'common sense' to handle them. Thus from multiple sensory impressions the common sense generates images corresponding to the categories of figure, size, number, movement, and rest. Once examined, inner images are stored in the memory, located in the third ventricle at the back of the head. Mental images of sense perception then are the means by which the higher faculties of the rational soul acquire knowledge of the world. They are the building material of early modern imagination and thought.

Medieval religion

Until well into the seventeenth century the church was the main patron of the arts; consequently its doctrinal views on images affected European ways of making, seeing, and imagining images. Pope Gregory the Great (540–604) founded the Christian doctrine of images with the assertion that images are the books of the illiterate. The Byzantine iconoclastic controversy of the eighth century, won by the partisans of images and crowned by the writings of John of Damascus (675–749) led to further developments. By then a cognitive theory of images had crystallized. It passed to the West and remained the standard doctrine of the church on art, stipulating that images had a tripartite function: to teach, to imprint the memory, and to inspire deeds of piety. In other words images, regardless of their style, must be didactic, mnemonic, and inspirational and activate the three faculties of intellect, memory, and will.

Another outcome of the Byzantine iconoclastic crisis was the assertion that by becoming human God made himself representable. In Western Christianity this doctrine eventually led to an empathic devotion developed, practised, and broadcast by monastic orders, the Franciscans and Dominicans in particular, and focused on the humanity of Christ. These developments prompted an entire literary tradition of retellings of the life of Christ, the so-called *Vita Christi* tradition, which bloomed in the age of the manuscript and continued well into the age of print. The Gospels are quite discreet regarding the last hours of Jesus, so these were imagined with a plethora of invented details to prompt empathy with his sufferings. The fountainhead of this tradition is undoubtedly the fourteenth-century *Meditations on the Life of Christ*, which survived through over 200 manuscripts and was regularly translated and reprinted until the seventeenth century. In this tradition the text frequently exhorts readers, or auditors, to imagine for themselves each scene of the Gospel as if they were present. They are invited to empathize with each character and given detailed and graphic descriptions to imagine the variety and abundance of pains Jesus suffered in his last hours—such as, for example, the 666 whiplashes allegedly administered during the flagellation. Far from fading away, this imagery and art of imagining was articulated in the early modern Catholic world via several channels. One of the most common is the devotion to the rosary, a spiritual exercise practised through the visualization of fifteen episodes from the life of Christ. Elaborated in northern monastic surroundings, the rosary was expelled by the Reformation but bloomed in Catholic lands in the private sphere of domestic devotion and in lay confraternities. Prayer beads frequently feature in portraits as a sign of the piety of the sitter. The practice of the rosary left in its trail an extensive material culture of prayer beads of different materials, sizes, shapes, and designs, from the humble to the princely, allowing the recitation of exactly 15 Pater Nosters and 150 Ave Marias while visualizing episodes of the life of Christ—as described in the *Vita Christi* tradition.

Another broad channel for the expression of the medieval multisensory imagination was the *Spiritual Exercises* (1541) of Ignatius of Loyola (1491–1556), the founder of the Jesuit order whose own vocation had been prompted by reading the *Vita Christi*. The *Spiritual Exercises* teaches a preparation to prayer called the composition of place. It consists in imagining scenes from the Gospels according to five layers corresponding to each of the five senses in order to achieve a feeling of presence which in turn lays the foundation of prayer and meditation. Loyola's successors advised those experiencing difficulties to use images in churches as the foundation for their own imagination.

The art of imagining features in representations of people praying. It is in fact one of the first means by which medieval and early modern donors made their effigy known to posterity. By the twelfth century portraits of donors in prayer began appearing alongside figures of saints. Up to the fifteenth century donors tend to be disproportionately smaller, but by the sixteenth century they are depicted with the same proportions as the main saintly figures with whom they frequently engage in tactile contact. Whether the donors pray next to their tutelary saints or merely witness a scene, these categories of image represent what the donor imagines. In this way this early portraiture served not only to represent and commemorate those who commissioned images decorating churches, but also to broadcast a model of devotion by producing literal representations of medieval imaginative prayer.

Thus religion had shaped and developed a particularly intense sensory imagination. In parallel with these practices artists learned to draw through the study of anatomy by conceiving their figures in terms of bones, muscles, and flesh, and also in terms of movement. From the fifteenth century onwards this culture of imagining took on new dimensions thanks to the revival of ancient art and the return of Neoplatonism.

Neoplatonism, gender, and imagination

Every civilization has its contradictions. Early modern men grew up in a society that simultaneously idealized women and considered them inferior to men. In the field of religion idealization took place via the image and model of the Virgin Mary and in the secular field through the Platonic doctrine of love. From the mid-fifteenth century Marsilio Ficino's translations and commentaries reintroduced the complete works of Plato to the West. Beyond the confines of philosophy Renaissance Neoplatonism had an important impact on the conception of love thanks to Ficino's vernacular commentary on Plato's *Symposium*. Platonic love is a spiritual ascension towards the divine triggered by the auditory or visual perception of beauty. It works within a sensory hierarchy dominated by sight and hearing, considered spiritual senses, insofar as they perceive an immaterial beauty that the lower senses of contact with matter—taste, touch, and smell—cannot apprehend. These incorporeal attributes of beauty perceptible by sight and hearing alone are for Ficino the first ascending steps towards the contemplation of the divine.

This aspect of Ficino's thought passed to mainstream vernacular literature thanks to influential works such as Pietro Bembo's *Asolani* (1505) and Baldassare Castiglione's *Il cortegiano* (1528), which are the fountainheads of Renaissance love literature. But Bembo did far more: the Italian vernacular tradition he inaugurated took Ficino's *De amore* as its philosophy and Petrarch and Boccaccio as its models for poetry and prose. It is principally through this channel that Neoplatonic ideas on love permeated vernacular literature and were broadcast throughout Europe. Petrarch's vernacular poetry, the *Canzoniere*, recounts his infatuation and amorous struggle with a certain Madonna Laura. The sonnets in particular were endlessly read, commented on, and imitated. The body of Laura reconstituted from head to toe through scattered allusions in the *Canzoniere* became a feminine ideal, blonde with pink cheeks and shining eyes, similar to the heroines of chivalric romances, to be loved in a Platonic key. By the seventeenth century even the shepherds of *L'Astrée* (1607–27), one of the best-selling French pastoral novel of all times, were preaching Platonic love.

This situation brought new dimensions to beauty, feminine beauty in particular, and gave rise to a stream of discourses idealizing women, and even courtesans. Writers like Cornelius Agrippa (1486–1535) or Alessandro Piccolomini (1508–79) composed orations on the superiority of women, while the lesser-known Antonio Brocardo (d.1531) left an oration in praise of courtesans as a ladder to the contemplation of the divine. In 1548 the Florentine cleric Agnolo Firenzuola completed his *Discorso delle bellezze delle donne* (Discourse on the beauties of women), enumerating the incorporeal qualities of *leggiadria, venustà, gratia, vaghezza, aria*, and *maestà* (roughly equivalent to 'gracefulness', 'loveliness', 'grace', 'vagueness', 'air', and 'majesty') as divine emanations shining through beautiful women. A few years earlier, in 1534–6, the Venetian writer Pietro Aretino published his *Ragionamenti* in which an experienced prostitute instructs her daughter on the appearance and behaviour to adopt in order to seduce men. Here, of course, the Platonic

AGNOLO BRONZINO, Portrait of Laura Battiferri, *c.*1560. Laura Battiferri, one of the few women poets of the Renaissance, is depicted both as a poet and a Muse. Her medal-like profile is evocative of Dante—the most important Italian poet of the late medieval and early modern era. In her hand she holds a copy of Petrarch's *Canzoniere*, a collection of love poetry which provided the model for sixteenth-century vernacular poetry. Her name, Laura, invites further association with Petrarch's Laura, to whom the poem shown in the picture is addressed. Her profile position is also one presenting her ear frontally, as if listening to the plea written in the poem.

aesthetic ideals of grace and beauty, so skilfully encapsulated by Castiglione in the word *sprezzatura*, serve to entice carnal desire rather than prompt a mystical ascent.

Women

Accounts of early modern male desire suggest a less than Platonic approach to women. Studies of the judicial handling of sex crimes in Venice from the fourteenth to the fifteenth century highlight lenient attitudes towards sexual violence towards women— men accused of rape would routinely be absolved if they agreed to marry their victim. In Venice as elsewhere marriage was expected to absorb and control male sexual drive, or rather overdrive. Prostitution was legal and controlled for the very same reason. In this respect the entrance of the Platonic doctrine of love on the stage of European cultural history is one further step towards the acquisition of self-control that charac- terizes the civilization process.

Platonic love, in its Renaissance incarnation, is a matter of male gaze and desirable female body. The beauty of the body may reflect that of the soul, Platonism might have brought more deference to women, but to be a step on a ladder, even a mystic ladder

SOFONISBA ANGUISSOLA, *Game of Chess with Three Sisters and Servant*, 1555. Sofonisba Anguissola, one of the rare Renaissance women painters, was born and raised in a higher social class than most male artists. She accessed these practices through her upper-class education, which provided her with proficiency in drawing and in music. This group portrait includes Sofonisba's sisters, Lucia, Minerva, and Europa. The idea of representing young women playing chess, a game considered intellectually demanding and mostly played by men, has been interpreted as an early example of feminine claim to parity with male minds.

leading to the divine, is to be a means to an end, rather than an equal. Thus twentieth-century critics have observed that the expansion of Platonism in matters of love contributed to the objectification of women. The shift from medieval courtly love to Platonic love can be envisaged as a transition from power play to idealization. While in courtly love women and men were interacting, in Renaissance Platonic love women are mere objects of male active idealization and passive bearers of a beauty allegedly reflecting the divine.

The Renaissance might have produced Giovanni Pico della Mirandola's *Discourse on the Dignity of Man* (1486), but it was not a particularly good time to be a woman. From the late Middle Ages onwards women's financial condition worsened while their access to education decreased. Diagnosed passive, cold, and moist by authorities such as Aristotle, Galen, and their commentators, women were considered inferior to men.

This lower status, as well as persistent medieval views on their social role, excluded them from higher education. Intelligent and talented women had fewer chances to expand in the early modern world than men. Aristocratic consorts became patrons of arts and letters like Isabella d'Este or Vittoria Colonna. Some courtesans, like Tullia of Aragon, Veronica Franco, Gaspara Stampa, wrote poetry and became the darlings of the literary societies of their time. It has been suggested that Renaissance courtesans answered the male elite demand for intelligent and educated sexual partners and interlocutors. On the whole, however, social constraints—a youth of seclusion followed by a domestic life as the mother of many children—considerably limited women's ability to contribute to the arts and sciences. Renaissance society produced very few women writers, and even fewer women painters. Religion was one of the rare fields that offered women space and structure to develop. Thus, very much in continuation with the Middle Ages, the Renaissance can boast many female mystics and saints who left written accounts of their meditations and visions.

Early pornography

Limiting love and desire to sight and sound, excluding the lower senses of contact with matter, may have endowed early modern men with more self-control than their predecessors, but it also perhaps loaded their imaginations with intense polysensory fantasies. Be that as it may, in parallel with the return of Plato and the expansion of Platonic love the Renaissance witnessed the first steps of a new genre of images exclusively addressing male sexuality.

Michelangelo's *Leda*, which illustrates the intercourse between a woman and the god Jupiter incarnated as a swan and flapping his feathers over her genital and anal zone, fits the current definition of pornography as a male-produced, gender-specific genre obsessively focused on the female figure. A great deal of modern literature on the subject is concerned with the undesirable values this genre broadcasts. Nevertheless its founders count among the best-known and most prestigious artists of the Renaissance: Michelangelo, Titian, and some of Raphael's most gifted collaborators such as Giulio Romano, Jacopo Caraglio, and Marcantonio Raimondi, who can be credited for the first notorious sets of erotic prints, *I modi* (1524) and the *Loves of the Gods* (1527). These sets display mythological couples, Venus and Mars, Jupiter and his multiple conquests, Nymphs and Satyrs, engaging in sexual intercourse in an abundant variety of positions. They reappear throughout the sixteenth century in mythological paintings and prints, as well as in the many illustrated editions and vernacular translations of Ovid's *Metamorphoses*, which almost invariably include illustrations of Jupiter's erotic adventures.

Titian's female nudes, such as the well-known *Venus of Urbino* (Florence, Uffizi), brought the genre of the reclining female nude to the domestic interior. Scholars have debated whether the *Venus of Urbino*, with her gesture inviting the viewer to compare her genitalia with roses, is a mere pin-up or a powerful evocation of the joys of

TITIAN, *VENUS OF URBINO*, 1538. In spite of its mythological title this painting was known as 'la bella' well until the seventeenth century. The roses she holds in her right hand, a traditional attribute of Venus, invite comparison and association with her genitalia, that she touches with her left. Whether intended to represent the joys of matrimonial sexuality, or merely addressed to masculine gratification, Titian's carnal reinterpretation of antique art set the model and the postures of erotic imagery up to the present.

matrimonial sexuality. Documents suggest that such images may have been placed in bedchambers, where they served as an aid to procreation. Be that as it may, Titian's variations on the reclining female nude, which are reinterpretations in flesh and blood of classical sculpture, have survived in some of the standard poses of Western pornography.

It all began with the human figure. Renaissance painters and their public considered the human figure to be not only the principal element of pictorial composition, but also the focal point for the expression and appreciation of artistic talent. The reintroduction of classical forms produced an imagery in which the bodily aspect of the figures became central and the narrative secondary. Very much in line with this approach the Venetian painter Paolo Pino, in his *Dialogo di pittura* (1549), advised his colleagues to include in their narrative composition 'at least one wholly mysterious figure, that is forced and difficult, in order to be recognized as a good painter by those who understand the perfection of this art'.

The birth and long rise of pornography, from Renaissance sub-genre to modern multimedia global industry, could be set against Michel Foucault's grand narrative of the history of sexuality, which asserts the rise of control and censorship of sexual matters from the Middle Ages to the birth of psychoanalysis and beyond. In parallel we can identify the rise of sensuousness in painting, the focus on its treatment of the human body, and the slow expansion of erotic imagery addressed to masculine private consumption. Thus, the Platonic doctrine of love, as well as its diffusion in vernacular literature which runs in parallel with the rise of erotic imagery, not only brought more respect and deference to women, but might also have contributed to shape and intensify men's erotic fantasies. Even if Platonism preached the dissociation of sight from the lower senses, in fact the very contrary happened as representations of the visual field brought the new body type revived from ancient art into the sensory imagination trained by religion.

The Renaissance artist and the new genres

By the end of the sixteenth century many things had changed in the art world. The convergence of the expectations of the church on images, the rise of imaginative piety, the revival of ancient art, and the scientific assumption that the mind is an image processor undoubtedly benefited the artistic profession. In an era which offered hardly any social mobility some artists began rising from the humble condition of artisans to that of celebrities and claimed the liberal status of their profession. In parallel their education system began migrating from the world of the workshops to that of the academies. This transition, initiated in the 1560s by the Florentine painter Giorgio Vasari and his entourage with the foundation of the Florentine Accademia del Disegno, would eventually transform art education in the following centuries. In the same years the publication of Vasari's *Lives of the Artists* (1550, 1568), the first extensive biographies of individual artists, complete with a full theoretical introduction, established a model followed in Italy and adopted in the rest of Europe.

Artists not only created new institutions, they also developed new genres. From the end of the sixteenth century onwards the still life, landscape, tavern, and domestic interiors emerged as independent genres and eventually became professional specializations. These new genres mostly stemmed from religious painting: still lifes stem from the symbolic objects featured in the foreground of sacred scenes, such as the fruits, vases, and flowers of Madonnas and Child; domestic interiors first appeared in evocations of the house of the holy family. Landscapes featuring as the background of Christian narrative eventually became self-standing subjects. Mythological imagery was also reborn through the commission of cycles for private and secular spaces—palaces, façades, town halls—and the many illustrated editions of Ovid's *Metamorphoses*. Anthologies of prints as well as casts and small-scale bronze reproductions ensured the international diffusion of classical art and classical bodily forms.

The portrait and the self-portrait expanded in unprecedented ways. In the Middle Ages most portraits were either of rulers, potential consorts, or donors in religious paintings. By the fifteenth century the secular portrait had developed and extended from the ruling classes to the upper middle classes. Not only patricians commissioned portraits, but also notaries, lawyers, merchants, physicians, writers. They are usually represented with idealized features, surrounded by objects emblematic of their occupation, learning, wealth, and taste.

A portrait by the Venetian artist Lorenzo Lotto (c.1480–1556/7) shows the Venetian patrician and collector Andrea Odoni rubbing a gold crucifix against the lining of his fur coat with the fingers of his left hand. His right hand firmly holds and presents a

LORENZO LOTTO, *Portrait of Andrea Odoni*, 1527. The objects surrounding the Venetian patrician Andrea Odoni, a collection of fragments of antique sculptures, coins, and a book, are signs of his wealth, education, taste, and devotion. His right hand holds a statuette of the Diana of Ephesus, a pagan symbol of fertility, while his left hand rubs a crucifix against the expensive fur lining of his coat. Thus the painter has combined the aristocratic taste of the sitter with signs of his religious devotion.

statuette of a Diana of Ephesus, an antique female bust covered with breasts generally interpreted as symbolic of fertility. On the table, an installation of coins, medals, one book, one inkwell, and some fragments of ancient sculptures all stand as evidence of Odoni's discerning aristocratic taste for the antique. The contrast between the gold crucifix rubbed against the soft fur and the marble statuette of Diana with its 100 spiky nipples highlights in a tactile way the blend of secular and sacred, antique and Christian, characteristic of the civilization of the Renaissance. We encounter this blend not only in objects but also in costume, as shown for instance in the 1544 portrait of Jean de Dinteville by Francesco Primaticcio (1504–70). Here Dinteville (1504–55), a French diplomat better known as one of Holbein's *Ambassadors*, poses as a Christian saint, St George, clad in a classical suit of armour.

One outcome of the revival of the classical world was the return, or rather the reinvention, of classical armour. After the introduction of gunpowder on the late medieval battlefield the suit of armour became mostly irrelevant as a protection but nevertheless survived as a fancy metal dress worn for display by the rich and famous. Its greatest exponent is the Negroli workshop, a Milanese armour-smith dynasty active throughout the sixteenth century which specialized in the production of modern suits of armour inspired by the antique and worn by European nobility.

Suits of armour could be seen shining at official events, pageants, and tournaments where participants would parade clad as antique heroes, with their horses, staff, and banners decorated with emblematic devices. Many rulers and members of the ruling class liked to wear a suit of armour in the portraits they commissioned, as a sign of their military dignity and skills. In contrast to the medieval armour, sober and built with a view to protection rather than display, the Renaissance version includes much ornament and features classical rather than Christian imagery.

Renaissance artists and armour smiths reinvented rather than copied antique armour, and included elements borrowed from the imaginary world of mythology and chivalric romances. In Dinteville's portrait, as in many other Renaissance versions, the lion-headed shoulder pads are a modern invention. Similarly, the helmet takes the Roman type as a starting point for countless variations. Accounts of Renaissance tournaments mention golden helmets with peacock feathers and emblematic animals: lions, dragons, salamanders on a bed of gilded flames, or hybrids with reptilian skin, bat wings, and eagle head... Sometimes helmets include images of mythological tutelary figures, such as Mars or Minerva, as in the portrait of Jean de Dinteville. Similarly, the muscled cuirass worn by Dinteville is another adaptation of Roman military costume for which the Renaissance had a particular fondness. This accessory, associated with imperial Rome, merged the body of the sitter with an antique athletic torso, both in portraiture and in reality, setting him in dialogue with ancient gods and heroes.

The expansion of self-portraiture follows that of portraiture. Medieval artists sometimes signed their work or inserted their effigy in larger compositions, a practice which continued well into modern times, but the art of self-portraiture really began expanding from the late fifteenth century. From this time onwards many artists left at least one

FRANCESCO PRIMATICCIO, Portrait of Jean de Dinteville as St George, 1544. This portrait by one of the Italian artists brought to France by King Francis I (1494–1547) embodies the blend of paganism and Christianity characteristic of the Renaissance. Jean de Dinteville, a French aristocrat, also known as one of Holbein's ambassadors, poses as a Christian saint in classical dress. The lion-headed shoulder pads as well as the helmet with mythological figures and hybrid creatures are Renaissance inventions after the antique, rather than reconstitutions. Such accessories feature prominently in Renaissance tournament culture, which offered the pretext for imaginative reinvention of the ancient world.

self-portrait. They usually stand half-length on their own, in urban costume, holding a pen or a small brush that could be mistaken for a pen. In other words, painters adopted or imitated the appearance of their wealthy patrons, concealing the manual and

FILIPPO NEGROLI, Parade helmet of Emperor Charles V, 1533. The introduction of gunpowder on the battlefield made the suit of armour irrelevant, yet it survived and bloomed during the early modern era as a metal ceremonial dress. Here the parade helmet of Charles V (1500–58), the most powerful man of his time, expresses imperial status through a head of golden locks evocative of the mythical figure of Alexander the Great.

collaborative side of their trade to focus on presenting the gentlemanly status to which they aspired. Albrecht Dürer's self-portrait of 1500 makes the point. Dürer gave himself symmetric features reminiscent of the image of Christ and he pinches the fur lining of his coat with his right hand. Fur coats were among the most expensive clothing items of the time, but fur also relates directly to the practice of painting since the best coats, as well as the best brushes, were made out of squirrel fur. In this way Dürer's gesture conveys the fame, wealth, and comfort his profession brought him.

An anthology of 122 artists' portraits published in London at the end of the seventeenth century, *The true effigies of the most eminent painters: and other famous artists that have flourished in Europe,* confirms that Dürer's gesture is far from unique. Many painters represented themselves with their fur coat and gloves, often with pen and paper rather than brushes and palette, thus concealing the hand-soiling tools of their manual trade.

The rise of the artist, as much as the substitution of a pen for a brush in self-portraiture, had theoretical underpinnings linking the visual arts to the tastes and modes of thinking of the elites. By the sixteenth century artists had theorized their profession thanks to the notion of *disegno,* an umbrella concept encompassing painting, sculpture, and architecture as well as the graphic arts. First expounded in the preface of Giorgio Vasari's *Lives of the Artists, disegno* conflates the Italian words for drawing, design, and thinking. From this theoretical standpoint *disegno* is a form of visualizing based on the Renaissance conception of imagination we have seen earlier. It theorizes a statement already asserted by Leonardo da Vinci (1452–1519), and repeated by most Renaissance art treatises, that painting is all in the mind of the artist. *Disegno* is a recognition of the conceptual character of artistic work, which involved not only conceiving paintings but also providing drawings for craftsmen with the relevant skills to produce, be this jewels, basins, ewers, knives, cups, salt cellars, tapestries, or theatrical costumes and stage sets.

Disegno as 'drawing' also points to a far less soiling practice than painting. As distinct from the teamwork and material necessary for painting, drawing only required the same minimal material as writing: pen and paper. Furthermore, according to Aristotle's *Politics* (book 8), drawing was part of the curriculum of the nobility, as it was believed to increase one's sense of observation, shape discernment in the acquisition of artworks, and help to plan fortifications. These views were part of a humanistic education, and we also know that the members of the first official art academy, the Florentine Accademia del Disegno, regularly taught the foundations of drawing and *disegno* to the Florentine elites.

Disegno is thus a window with a view onto the intimacy of early modern visual thinking. It was also through *disegno* that artists acquired their skills and their style. As we have seen, they learned to draw human figures from bones to muscles and flesh, and developed their style by copying, and synthesizing from nature, the antique and modern masters. In this way the classical image of the body entered the visual arts and eventually became the norm of body image and physical beauty. The image of Christ in particular changed its physical appearance from the fifteenth to the seventeenth century. The skinny, beaten, and bruised Christ typical of Flemish fifteenth-century painting was succeeded by an athletic god shaped by the study and absorption of ancient art.

By the mid-sixteenth century, north of the Alps, the leaders of the Reformation looked on the use of classical models in the depiction of religious scenes with disapproval, as they endeavoured to sort out issues of improper worship and idolatry. The Angel of the Annunciation, they wrote, looks like Mercury, the Virgin is a Venus, and Christ is Apollo. Images were eventually expelled from Reformed Protestant churches, but the copying and digesting of classical art remained the cornerstone of Western artistic education until well into the nineteenth century. By the seventeenth century classical sculpture had become the canon taught and studied in European art academies. Classical art not only changed representation, it also shaped expectations of beauty and self-image and even affected European representations of other cultures. This tendency increased throughout the seventeenth century and reached full bloom in the early eighteenth century, in the seven-volume *Cérémonies et coutumes religieuses de tous les peuples du monde* (1723–37). In these volumes the prints of Bernard Picart (1673–1733) depict the gods and priests of the religions of the world, from the Americas to East Asia, with the poses, anatomy, and body language of classical art.

Academies and *imprese*

Renaissance painters were managers of busy workshops rather than isolated thinkers. When depicting themselves, without their team, they were less presenting themselves as isolated individuals than as part of a higher group of individuals, such as writers, who primarily work with their mind rather than their hands. The decision of Renaissance painters to establish the first art academies in Florence (1563), Bologna (1580), and Rome (1590s) follows comparable initiatives in the field of letters and philosophy dating back to the fifteenth century. Academies are a distinctly early modern phenomenon: at least 377 academies were founded in the sixteenth century and 870 in the seventeenth century. Expanding from Italy to the rest of Europe, these institutions constituted one of the first scholarly networks.

An early modern academy is a society of learned men, linked by certain laws to which they subject themselves, who meet to dispute some learned question and produce works that they submit to the judgement of their colleagues. Thus the age of individualism also produced group identities in the world of letters. Academies mostly worked in the vernacular and did much for the advancement of learning.

BARTOLOMEO VENETO, *Portrait of a Man, c.*1520. Images, when affixed to clothes, took a personal meaning. We might never know the specific circumstances of this portrait, but the images the sitter wears offer clues to his state of mind. The medal featuring on the hat displays a boat about to shipwreck with the motto 'espérance me guide' (hope guides me). The labyrinth embroidered over the chest, the traditional seat of emotions, and surrounded by knots, serves as the background to the fist of the sitter, tightly clenched on the pommel of a large sword. All these silent signs of possible anxieties stand in sharp contrast to the sitter, whose slight squint conveys a dreamy expression.

They engaged with both the sciences and the humanities, they produced poetry and commentaries on poetry, literary theory, essays, dialogues, plays, and even the first dictionary of the Italian vernacular, the *Vocabolario degli Accademici della Crusca* (1612). From sixteenth-century literary clubs to seventeenth-century learned societies, early modern academies were elite societies where the local nobility mingled with scholars and writers. Keeping intellectuals under control, busy with literary and scientific matters away from religion and politics—two fields traditionally excluded from academic discussions—was only one of their important functions. Academies were also the means by which the European ruling classes acquired and practised vernacular eloquence and used writers and artists for their own benefit. A great deal, if not the whole, of Renaissance festive culture bloomed out of this collaboration. Two genres are particularly emblematic of this conjunction: the first, the *impresa*, displays the intimacy of personal thought, while the second, the princely banquet, is a multimedia performance in which the arts and letters both serve to represent the magnificence of the host.

An *impresa* is an interdependent compound of text and image, an image and a *motto* (i.e. a brief sentence) expressing the intention of the person wearing it. The word itself signifies *enterprise, project, aspiration*. A good *impresa* should be neither too obscure nor too obvious; it should look good and preferably avoid the human figure. Affixed on hats and helmets, *imprese* are comparable to windows on the soul. Emperor Charles V's *impresa*, for example, shows two columns against a seascape with the motto 'plus ultra' (further beyond). Here an educated early modern person would have recognized the columns of Hercules, which for the ancients marked the limits of the known world. The motto, associated with the most powerful man of his time, clearly expresses his colonial ambitions.

Renaissance academies produced an important body of theoretical literature discussing the origins, properties, function, and functioning of such devices since men of letters invented most of them for their masters. Many academies used this fashion as a playful yet didactic means of self-presentation. The Sienese academy of the *Intronati* took an *impresa* displaying a courgette with the motto 'Meliora latent' (The best is inside). *Imprese* of individual academicians also feature in the publications of the Brescian Academy of the *Occolti*, or of the *Gelati* (the frozen ones) of Bologna. Sources also confirm that *imprese* decorated the premises of the Florentine Accademia della Crusca and the Roman Accademia degli Umoristi.

The genre of the *impresa* had its antecedents in classical coins, medals, and Egyptian hieroglyphics. It also had medieval origins in tournament culture where the armoured participants would display signs, colours, and images expressive of their identity and intentions. In the fifteenth century *imprese* began appearing as hat jewels, or *enseignes*, and came to prominence in Italy, on the hats and helmets of the entourage of the French kings Charles VIII (1470–98) and Louis XII (1462–1515). The Italian nobility's adoption of the fashion for wearing an *impresa* is confirmed by many surviving portraits, hat jewels, plaquettes, and medals. In this last genre, inspired by the antique, one side features a portrait in profile and in relief while the other side carries an *impresa* which in this context serves as a portrait of the soul. The use of *imprese* seems to have been restricted to royalty, the nobility, upper classes, and liberal professions. As body decoration *imprese* feature as hat jewels, gilded, enamelled, framed with gems, shining on the head, and displaying the thoughts and character of their bearers. As hat decorations they replace images of tutelary saints, a practice going back to the more modest religious pewter badges intended to decorate and protect the hats and cloaks of medieval pilgrims.

Imprese did not replace coats of arms, but as a Renaissance development of heraldic types they seem to have been the first such symbolic device specifically expressing the individual rather than his dynastic identity. The emergence of the *impresa*, and the sheer intellectual energies it mobilized, certainly confirms individuality as an important component of the early modern worldview.

Paolo Giovio's *Dialogo dell'imprese militari e amorose* (Florence, 1555) inaugurates the literature on *imprese*. The main compilations, such as those of Ruscelli (1565), Camilli (1586), Cappaccio (1592), or Ferro (1623), are amongst the finest illustrated early books listing the *imprese* of the most famous names of their time. The analysis and commentary accompanying each *impresa* are usually in praise of their bearer, associating his emblematic device with his life and deeds. Writing on an *impresa* is essentially a way of composing a literary portrait of its bearer. Thus the Renaissance *impresa* and parade helmet are somehow the opposite of a mask: the mask hides but the helmet and *impresa* on the contrary display the intentions of the bearer.

The fashion of wearing *imprese* on hats faded towards the end of the sixteenth century with the advent of the Counter-Reformation. Nevertheless, *imprese* remained as a method of conveying ideas in an immediate and powerful way. They featured in pageants and festivals, on triumphal arches, and even on banqueting tables, where they conveyed striking messages to select audiences.

Banquets

Renaissance banquets encompass what European elites enjoyed most, from the variety and abundance of nature and the arts to the ideals of civility that were so dear to the age.

Renaissance banqueting was a multimedia genre of mostly secular character which took shape in the fifteenth century and bloomed in the sixteenth and seventeenth centuries. Banquets celebrated events such as births, marriages, anniversaries, or state visits. Very much like twentieth-century performance art, early modern banquets intended to engage the entire human machine, mind, body, and senses. They used the same iconographic tradition as the visual arts through a variety of media, from the edible to the metallic and mineral. Remaining sources include prints recording real banquets, paintings of ancient banquets from sacred and secular history, and above all the literature produced by banqueting professionals. To quote from one of them, Antonio Latini, author of the *Scalco alla moderna, overo l'arte di ben disporre i conviti* (*The Modern Steward, or the Art of Well-Organized Banquets*; 1694): 'The first prerequisite

PAOLO VERONESE, Marriage at Cana, 1562–3. Historical banquets were often presented in modern guise. This is the case of the wedding banquet where Christ transformed wine into water. In this highly theatrical display Veronese has contrasted the simplicity of Christ, dressed in plain clothes and placed in the centre, radiating, with the elaborate dresses and elegant attitudes of the other attendants expressive of mid-sixteenth-century sophistication.

of a banquet is to please the eyes with its variety, to feed the intellect with rich and sumptuous displays, and to give taste to the palate with the good apparatus of food. And a banquet cannot be called "reale" [royal/real: a pun in Italian], if it is not composed of all these parts.'

Renaissance banquets are also a useful standpoint from which to place Renaissance artists in context. If their claim to the liberal status of their profession was eventually successful in the following centuries, in the sixteenth century they belonged to the same class as other professionals involved in the service of the elites. At court their power came from the fact that they were among the *familiari* of the ruler. Those in charge of coordinating banquets, as well as looking after the diet of the prince, enjoyed very similar privileges. Apart from the good health of their master, their function, like artists, was to express his magnificence. It is then probably not a coincidence that from the mid-1550s, very much in tandem with the rise of Renaissance artistic literature and art theory, we see the expansion of a didactic literature on the art of banqueting written by professionals serving the ruling dynasties of the Italian peninsula: Cristoforo Messisbugo (1549), Bartolomeo Scappi (1570), Giovan Battista Rossetti (1584), Vicenzo Cervio (1593), Domenico Romoli (1594), Matthias Geiger (1629), Vittorio Lancilotti (1627), Antonio Frugoli (1631), and the already mentioned Antonio Latini (1694). This literature gives an overview of the skills, knowledge, and material necessary to orchestrate such complex events and provides detailed accounts of memorable banquets.

The arts of the banquet

Torches and candles generally lit banquets. Their flickering light accentuated the lustre of silverware, table decorations, and even food, frequently enhanced with gilding.

Silverware

Silverware usually featured on the dresser, a set of shelves with precious vases, ewers, and basins, some purely for display, some used between courses. The dresser was always well in sight of the guests. Sometimes, in order to multiply the visual pleasure of the glow, mirrors were placed in such a way as to make the dresser visible from every angle of the dining table.

Between courses some of the ewers and basins displayed on the dresser also served to pour perfumed water over the hands of guests. Many basins seem to have been designed with this function in mind. They frequently display aquatic themes with figures such as Neptune, Tritons, Nereids, and dolphins, but they sometimes also include images of fire and subjects such as naval battles. In other words these basins are representations on metal of water and fire designed to be set in optical movement by the random flow of scented waters poured over their glittering surface. They belong to a little explored class of Renaissance performing objects, that is objects decorated with images destined to change appearance through the optical illusions generated by the movement of fluids and shadows. Another good example of this is drinking cups, decorated with embossed images that would move as the drinker brought the wine to his lips.

The art of casting

Like suits of armour basins and ewers combined a large number of specialities: gilding, embossing, enamelling, as well as casting. The Renaissance delight in nature not only encouraged naturalism in the arts but also seems to explain developments in the art of casting, for one way of achieving naturalistic images is to take casts. In the sixteenth century this technique, uninterruptedly practised since antiquity, reached an unparalleled level of technical virtuosity. Amongst the objects produced by the workshop of the Basel master Wenzel Jamnitzer (1508–85) were basins superbly decorated with casts of insects and flowers—one of the most famous, the Jamnitzer bell, is kept at the British Museum. But the most interesting artist/artisan of the time is undoubtedly the Frenchman Bernard Palissy (c.1510–90). After trying his hand at painting and stained glass,

SCHOOL OF BERNARD PALISSY. Platter, probably Paris, 1575–1600, earthenware. The art of casting has been uninterruptedly practised since antiquity, in particular for funerary or votive effigies, and its techniques were familiar to most Renaissance sculptors. These techniques reached new heights in the sixteenth-century decorative arts, in the form of finely detailed casts of small and fragile animals, insects, and plants. The most important and innovative figure in this genre is French multimedia artist Bernard Palissy. Together with the rise of naturalism in painting and the emergence of the still life, Palissy's playful decorated plates testify to the interest in the observation of nature which fed the Scientific Revolution.

he specialized in ceramics and mastered the art of casting and baking small and delicate animals and plants, thanks to which he achieved some fame from the 1540s onwards. The dialogue he wrote in 1563 on a grotto he assembled using similar techniques highlights his interest in the art of casting. Palissy referred to his casts as 'sculptures'. In reference to the cast reptiles and amphibians decorating his grotto, and which he used extensively in his plates, Palissy assures his reader there is not a single wrinkle or scale which has not been observed, even the smallest nerves and arteries and little ribs, which are scattered on the leaves.

While casting reproduces natural forms, Renaissance casters nevertheless composed these in rather artificial ways. In particular the loop of the lizard tails and the 'S' shape of the snakes decorating Palissy's plates are not natural, but bring to mind early modern art theorists' fondness for 'S'-shaped figures, the so-called *figura serpentinata*. Thus the expansion of the art of casting, exemplified through Palissy's work, is emblematic of the dual aspect of the Renaissance: a delight in observing the variety and abundance of nature alongside a constant impulsion to reshape it.

The art of folding

An overview of the arts devoted to the pleasure of banqueting elites would not be complete without a brief mention of the little-known art of folding. By the end of the sixteenth century foldings are a common feature of most banquets and even the subject of a small treatise by Matthias Geiger (1629), a Bavarian cook settled in Italy. Two broad types of folding decorated princely tables: individual pieces and centre-pieces. Individual pieces displayed the coats of arms of the guests and the usual repertoire extended to peacocks, hens, dogs, bears, rabbits, salamanders, gryphons, dragons, as well as mountains, ships, and castles. As the banquet moved on these were removed from the table and placed on the dresser, next to the precious vases, basins, and ewers.

The second application of the art of folding extends to the centrepiece, an installation celebrating the main theme of the banquet. Some were in fact draped wooden structures, such as the column that stood to celebrate a Colonna wedding of 1589 or the allegory of Bologna surrounded by gryphons and river gods, all draped and gilded, to celebrate the retirement of a local senator, Francesco Ratta. in 1691.

The art of the fold has a double origin in fifteenth-century sartorial methods of folding fabric to create geometric patterns and above all in the study and treatment of drapery in artistic training and practice. Renaissance artists studied drapery from antique and modern art as well as from fabric dipped in plaster and left to dry on mannequins. They approached it as a particularly expressive mass of matter, light, and shade amplifying the presence and movement of the body. The placement of ephemeral masterpieces of starched and folded linen next to works of gold, silver, enamel, and gems is perhaps another manifestation of the Renaissance taste for artistic invention, for the value of human ingeniousness over that of precious and costly material.

The table

On the table itself, especially during the first course, guests would encounter a thematic mixture of sugar and marzipan sculptures. Cristoforo Messisbugo mentions, for example, the sugar figures of the twelve Labours of Hercules featuring at each of the twelve courses of a banquet given by Ercole d'Este. The 200-page anthology, *Trionfi da tavola*, compiled by Antonio Latini enumerates multiple examples of this tradition and confirms that just about all the figures of classical mythology graced the tables of European elites in visible and edible form at some time or another.

Variety and abundance were attributes of the table display as well as of each of the many dishes composing each course. Anthologies of recipes such as those of Latini or Frugoli are tongue-twisting gustatory polyphonies combining rarely less than ten flavours with preparations and sauces involving many more. Food is often given figurative appearance. Doughnuts in the shape of coats of arms or crowns and rabbit pâtés wittily shaped as golden lions are among the favourites.

The food served over four or five courses, sometimes more, encompassed the seasonal productions of nature to the point that printed anthologies of banquets, with their multilayered variety and abundance, are arranged month by month. Their authors promise to teach the best season for everything. They tell us much about the Renaissance rivalry with nature through the very common practice of re-feathering roasted birds in order to make them look alive. These were made the bearers of *imprese* addressed to the guests and frequently had incense sticks placed in their beak. The use of live animals seems to have been common in the fifteenth century. A banquet to honour the Medicis on the Campidoglio (1513) involved live birds and hares. Birds of various species would escape from under the napkins of the guests and play around the table for the duration of the banquet. Their colourful plumage would have further enhanced the table, usually decorated and scented with flower petals, or artificial silk flowers when out of season.

Music and sound are another standard feature of Renaissance banquets. In addition to bird tweets, the soundscape would have included musicians, sometimes placed on each corner of the banqueting hall, the frequent ring of crystal cups smashed after each toast, and of course the conversation of the guests.

Performing staff

This early modern festive shaping of nature was carried out and orchestrated by a particularly specialized staff with considerable knowledge and experience extending well beyond gastronomy and dietetics. The banqueting staff comprised at least ten different functions, including teams in charge of buying and storing, preparing food and other material, those in charge of the bread, of wine, of the dresser. Two figures are particularly important and revealing: the *Scalco*, the main orchestrator, and the *Trinciante* or carver.

The *Scalco* had to possess a broad knowledge extending not only to the taste of different meats, fruits, and vegetables, but also to their medical properties, more specifically the balance of the elements in their flesh and their seasonal variations, as well as the most appropriate time and methods to cook and present them. The literature transmitting their knowledge is extensive. Romoli's *Singolare dottrina* (1593) has 776 pages, Frugoli's *Prattica scalcaria* (1632) is 514 pages long, while Latini's *Scalco alla moderna* unfolds over 640 pages. These works reflect a world where the art of banqueting extends to dietetics, botany, zoology, and medicine.

The second most important office on a banqueting table was that of *Trinciante*, or carver. Sometimes the *Scalco* performed the art of carving in front of the guest, but this duty was often entrusted to specialized carving staff. Depending on the size of the banquet, several *Trincianti* were assigned to each table, one *Trinciante* for every ten guests. Carvers were the elite members of the banqueting staff. Their art was one of live performance, slicing all the food evenly with controlled grace and elegance, thanks to a combination of experience and a solid understanding of the anatomy of the animals, vegetables, fruits (and even pies) that they were slicing. Banqueting literature provided advice on cutting methods which were to be practised on loaves of bread or cauliflowers. Since the art of the *Trinciante* is a performance art, it was also subject to the central Renaissance preoccupation: the art of concealing art, of doing with ease and elegance what is difficult. And in the case of the *Trinciante* this had a very practical justification: meat carving could easily turn messy and ridiculous in inexperienced hands. As the member of the household closest to the guests, the carver had to adopt their manners. Indeed, he was sometimes himself a man of letters, as was the case for example with Cesare Ripa, author of the *Iconologia* (1593), the first modern dictionary of allegorical figures.

Civilities and the culture of wine

Much wine flowed at Renaissance banquets as servants were instructed to ensure that the cups of the guests would remained filled at all times. As with many modern art performances and installations, a banquet could only happen with the participation

PETER PAUL RUBENS AND ASSISTANTS, *Sleeping Silenus, c.*1612. Rubens set side by side the mythological figures of wine and the vessels of banqueting. These expensive objects made of precious reflective materials and intensely decorated with images and ornament would shine and move when filled with wine or water, under the flickering lights of a banqueting hall. These signs of civilization stand in sharp contrast to the mythological figures who embody the effect of wine. Bacchus here drinks new wine from a flat cup over the head of a satyr collapsed in drunken sleep while another satyr lustfully engages with a female figure.

and immersion of its audience. Drunken behaviour, however, was certainly not appropriate at a banquet, although, as we shall see, neither was sobriety.

Winemaking and consumption expanded from the end of the fourteenth century onwards. As the means of production, conservation, and transport improved, wine became more affordable and more accessible. Consumption increased. It seems to have trebled. The research of economic historians has established that from the early thirteenth century onwards we move from annual consumption figures of about 100 litres per capita to well over 300 litres from the fifteenth century onwards. Since these figures are usually calculated from tax records they are in fact most probably under-estimates of early modern alcohol consumption. They certainly seem modest in comparison to the five litres of wine a day consumed by the workforce of the Venetian Arsenal. Such high consumption stands in sharp contrast with present-day statistics for France and Italy, assessed at respectively 63.4 and 60.4 litres per person per year. Drinking was not only a festive affair. In the era of epidemics and low hygiene wine in the south and beer in the north were the safest ways to quench thirst. Indeed, the sixteenth century has been declared a 'drunken century'. The Renaissance and Baroque periods were Dionysian eras, the return of classical literature and philosophy occurring in a continent irrigated by wine. This phenomenon affected approaches to alcohol consumption and seems to have generated a proliferation of images of bacchanals and revived the concept of Bacchic inspiration.

Plato never particularly approved of states of frenzy. Marsilio Ficino is the main agent of the transformation of Plato's observations into a theory of inspiration. His commentaries on Plato's *Phaedrus, Ion,* and *Symposium* broadcast the concept of frenzies as states of enthusiasm experienced in ancient Greece by worshippers of the Muses, of Dionysus, of Apollo and Aphrodite. That wine should be associated with inspiration is not particularly new in the Renaissance, but Ficino's approach had a very tangible medical side, since wine was part of the diet of Renaissance intellectuals. In the first part of his *Three Books on Life*, written to help scholars preserve their health, Marsilio Ficino recommends drinking wine at least twice daily, a diet which Ficino admitted practising assiduously himself.

For Ficino, and the medical tradition he inherits—from Aristotle to Galen, Avicenna, Pietro d'Abano, and Arnaldo da Villanova—wine has the nature of fire and carries the properties of spices and medicinal herbs to the brain. The warm vapour of wine sustains and feeds the *spiritus* essential to the good functioning of the body and mind. Like most moralists of his time Ficino condemns drunkenness. Nevertheless he recommends absorbing wine in the same proportion as sunlight, abundantly, so long as neither sweat dehydration nor drunkenness occurs. Today sensible alcohol intake is quantified in terms of daily units, no more than two units per day. This approach is entirely irrelevant to Ficino and the tradition in which he was working, according to which you can drink as much as you need to keep your spirit warm—as long as you do not get drunk. Excessive consumption is damaging but prolonged moderate absorption was believed to be beneficial. Thus we have here a medical and philosophical justification for what we might today identify as a form of alcoholism: it amounts to cultivating an in-between state, neither drunk nor sober, just warmed up, light-hearted, and playful. This conception of health also coincides with a tone or a style, light and jolly, which Ficino himself associated with Bacchus. For assuredly, he writes, Apollo and Bacchus are brothers and inseparable companions; one is synonymous with music and light, the other with fire and wit.

This Dionysian rebirth in the heart of the new philosophical canon had one visible iconographic impact: the image of the winged Bacchus, which appears in Renaissance drinking bowls and emblem books from the 1560s onwards. The theme features in the works of Rabelais, who in turn borrowed from Erasmus, Pausanias, and Athenaeus. His *Gargantua* begins with a praise of Silenus, Bacchus' adoptive father and alcoholic teacher, followed by a praise of drinking. The wine to which Rabelais alludes is neither exclusively spiritual nor metaphorical. He explains that he wrote while drinking and exhorts the reader to do the same while reading. Wine is the means through which the reader can access the precious wisdom concealed under the mask of playfulness. As we shall now see, wine was considered particularly important not only to facilitate reading but also to facilitate communication.

Conversation

A standard practice of Renaissance academies and a central activity of Renaissance elite culture is the cultivation of vernacular eloquence through the art of conversation, a genre we might anticipate as particularly congenial to the Ficinian approach to drinking. Stefano Guazzo's *Civile conversatione* of 1574 confirms this impression. Book IV of this important text describes a banquet in which wine features as a subject of conversation. There we encounter advice very similar to that of Ficino, and indeed some emphasis on the property of wine to comfort melancholic spirits. Guazzo follows Ficino's ideal: avoid drunkenness and drink little but often. Too much drinking causes such discomfort as to impede breathing and thinking, he writes, but adds that if we administer wine often and in small glasses, not only will we not suffer drunkenness, but we will also feel reinvigorated and drawn to much joy by a certain pleasant eloquence.

This approach to wine supports the view of the Renaissance as a culture teaching and practising self-control. Castiglione's *Cortegiano* (1528), Erasmus' *De civilitate morum puerilium* (1530), Della Casa's *Galateo* (1558), and Stefano Guazzo's *Civile conversatione* (1574) have all been cited as milestones of the change that came to shape Western civilization. But there is an ironic misunderstanding here: when early modern authorities thought they were advising temperance rather than abstinence, they were in fact prescribing alcoholism. Drinking little but often (*bevere spesso ma poco*) means cultivating a delicate balance, remaining jolly without ever becoming drunk—more or less as prescribed 100 years earlier by Ficino. In this respect the Renaissance art of controlled drinking seems also at the heart of its ideals of wit and ingeniousness in conversation, literature, and the visual arts.

RUBENS, *LA KERMESSE*, 1635–8. The peasant feast is the opposite of the princely banquet. Wine is abundantly consumed in both, but while the overabundant universe of the banquet requires social grace and bodily control, the peasant feast is one of unrestrained release. In order to describe lower-class entertainment Rubens has adapted the ancient genre of the bacchanal, a list of the effects of excessive drinking: merriment, dancing, sexual harassment, brawls, vomiting, and collapse.

The rise of good manners occurs in parallel with the expansion of the bacchanal, a rather amoral form of tableau, derived and expanded from antique examples and featuring the effects of wine from the most pleasant to the least desirable: drinking, talking, dancing, excessive sexual appetite followed by staggering, urinating, vomiting, collapsing. Thus although much wine was consumed at a Renaissance princely table, bacchanals with their evocation of excessive inebriation could not be further from the ambience and values of Renaissance elites. Bacchanals nevertheless provided the main themes of another type of feast: the peasant kermis, a genre that displays the same progression from drinking to dancing, to sexual molestation, staggering, vomiting, and collapse.

For a high society upholding elegant, restrained, and controlled manners, peasant feasts provided a model of complete release and a burlesque catalogue of bad manners. Early modern elites associated peasants with ancient divinities of the woods. Like the companion of Bacchus, peasants are depicted dancing to the sound of the bagpipe. A particularly frequent tableau in the seventeenth century is that of the satyr and the peasant. The subject comes from the Greek fabulist Aesop recounting the bemusement of a satyr seeing a peasant blowing on his soup to cool it and on his hands to warm them. This theme sets the peasant and the satyr as familiar figures of the rustic world. We also encounter the figure of the peasant in market scenes. This genre, dating from the late sixteenth century, is another pretext for displaying the variety and abundance of nature. Early modern representations of the lowest classes range from caricature to idealization and tell us mostly about the perceptions of the elites while the world of the most modest layers of European society remains little known.

Conclusions

Three hundred years of cultural and political history defy characterization. The period 1350–1650 begins with the end of the Black Death, the epidemics that wiped out between one-third and one-half of Europe's population in the late 1340s. The Renaissance is the new world built by the survivors. These same years were also a time when the Aristotelian conception of the mind, attributing to images a primary role in thinking, held sway. The Renaissance is thus not only the golden age of vision but also above all that of imagination. Sight expanded through the introduction of the microscope, reading glasses, and the telescope, but the cultivation of the imagination expanded too, stimulated by the arts and letters, from the invention of pornography to the multimedia display of sacred and secular festive traditions.

The proliferation of images that distinguishes the Renaissance from previous periods seems to have facilitated and promoted a taste for self-display thanks to the collaborative work of artists, artisans, and men of letters. In this respect we could envisage the arts and letters as means by which the ruling classes represented themselves. But by setting some of the foundations of what would become Western pornography, Renaissance artists also inaugurated a long tradition of erotic imagery supporting solitary male fantasizing of the female body. More generally, the presence of Platonism in the vernacular world, the reception of classical forms, and the expansion of the arts and crafts opened a new era exploiting more than ever the potential of images as support for the imagination, representation of thought, and carriers of ideas.

The importance granted to the concepts of variety and abundance suggests an increasing awareness of the differences between things, brought to its climax by Montaigne's observation that there are more differences between two humans than between two animal species.

If mythology is a symptom of civilization, then there is a striking contrast between the way the Renaissance understood Apollo and Dionysus as inseparable loving brothers and their twentieth-century reception, following Nietzsche, as irreconcilable opposites. Indeed, Renaissance writers teach balance and control, in drinking as well as in manners, the so-called golden mean, or *mediocritas*, and hold an ideal of well-being with the world and with others mediated by elegant and sensitive courtesy. It is a culture of happily cohabiting contrasts, combining on the one hand intense delight in nature and on the other an irrepressible rivalry with nature, be it in engineering, painting, sculpture, or banqueting.

This sense of harmony between humans and nature seems at odd with other historical accounts of the Renaissance as a period of high mortality, low hygiene, and recurring epidemics; a time of gender inequality, strife, struggles, divisions, political and religious wars, ruthless repression, and violence. Renaissance audiences showed much thrill for life and its imitation in a time when death was a familiar neighbour, from high infant mortality to the spectacle of pain and agony regularly performed on public squares through brutal rituals of public execution. The Reformation brought in its wake countless deaths, martyrs, and the destruction, in France alone, of over 20,000 churches. In the south the Counter-Reformation runs in parallel with the rise of absolutism. It inaugurates a period of increased control and brutal repression exemplified by the rise of confraternities—lay associations supervised by religious authorities—and the bustling activities of the tribunal of the Inquisition.

Many scholars have observed that the ideals and values of the Renaissance are merely a sugar coating concealing the darker, violent, and ever present nature of men, driven by ambition and rivalry. Sugar coating is nevertheless a first step towards sweetening. This is simply a matter of not confusing a period with its ideals. The aspirations of Renaissance artists led to the creation of art academies, and eventually, in more recent times, to the affiliation of these academies with universities—but this was something unimaginable in their time. Similarly, the ideals of good manners and elegance voiced by Erasmus, Castiglione, Della Casa, Guazzo, and their followers may not have been the norms of their time but their European diffusion suggests that they did eventually have an impact upon the world.

CHAPTER 5

Art and Architecture in
Italy and Beyond

FRANCIS AMES-LEWIS

Introduction

THIS chapter is predicated on the notion that the Italian Renaissance was first and foremost a 'rebirth' of classical antiquity, revised in the light of the different religious, political, and social conditions of the fifteenth century. It therefore follows the guiding principle that underpins Giorgio Vasari's *Lives of the Artists* (1550 and 1568), that the central purpose of Italian Renaissance architects and artists was to reappraise and reuse classical forms and motifs—indeed to construct a wholly new 'classical' artistic language with which to create buildings and artworks that were appropriate in form and style to the changed circumstances of Italy in the middle of the second millennium after Christ. It need hardly be said that this is a narrow and restrictive outlook over the rich variety of art and architecture of the period embraced by the term 'Italian Renaissance'. But if by definition it causes the exclusion from discussion here of many works of art, some iconic, it offers a standpoint that has both internal coherence and the capacity to concentrate attention on what is arguably the major stimulus that guided art production in the period. And given the remarkable explosion in the production of buildings and artworks that was powered by the exceptionally propitious social and economic conditions in which patrons commissioned artworks and to which artists and architects responded, it is helpful, indeed necessary, to impose some limitations on the range of material and themes that can be productively pursued in one chapter of such a book as this.

The first two sections of this chapter therefore focus on ways in which architects and artists responded to and re-evaluated the heritage of classical antiquity, the reasons for reworkings of classical forms, and the meanings and messages that these revisions of classical exemplars might have carried. In the section on architecture, attention is paid in particular to the ways that Renaissance architects adapted classical Roman building types to suit new expectations, and how and why they redeployed the language of classical architecture. In the second section—the first of two that consider sculpture and painting in Renaissance Italy—discussion focuses on how the sculpture of classical antiquity was studied and reinterpreted, especially in artists' treatment of the human figure as a paradigm of artistic exploration. Here, Jacob Burckhardt's vision of the Renaissance as the first era in which Man (rather than the divine godhead) became the focus of intellectual and creative endeavour affects the choice of themes and artworks discussed. The expansion of secular art to complement the continuum of religious art production leads to the further exploration of human figures as actors in works with secular narrative subjects, especially those based in classical mythology and history. The notion of Man as individual also underlies the dramatic rise of portraiture, a relatively unexploited art genre in the medieval period, which becomes manifest in several forms during the period under review.

Prior to the discovery of Nero's Golden House in Rome in around 1480, virtually nothing was known of classical paintings. Anecdotes and comments by writers like Pliny the Elder in his *Natural History* were suggestive, but nothing survived of classical easel painting beyond references in texts like the letters of Pliny the Younger, so that few models were available to guide painters in the recreation of a classical style. The third section of this chapter explores an alternative view of Italian Renaissance painting, one based not on artists' reinterpretations of the visible survivals of the classical past but on the classical notion of mimesis, the 'imitation of nature'. This became an essential element in the art theory of Leon Battista Alberti, Leonardo da Vinci, and others. In pursuit of mimesis, Italian Renaissance painters of necessity turned to non-classical visual stimuli. Notable amongst these were works emanating from northern Europe, and in particular from centres associated with the court of the dukes of Burgundy, such as Bruges and Brussels. In recent decades it has become much clearer that Italian Renaissance painters owed profound debts to north European art, and especially to the painters of the Netherlands. These debts have not always been adequately acknowledged, perhaps because of the dominance in the historiographical tradition of Vasari's prejudices against northern European art and architecture and in favour of artistic achievement in Italy during the Renaissance period.

This chapter takes the opening of the fifteenth century as a convenient time to launch discussion of Italian Renaissance art. It is, of course, far too simple to see the 1401 competition for the second pair of bronze doors for the Florentine Baptistery as the start of the Renaissance, as has often been suggested. There are various masterworks, sometimes described as 'proto-Renaissance', such as the classicizing figures of Nicola Pisano's pulpit of 1258–60 in the Pisa Baptistery, or Giotto's majestically conceived narrative compositions in the Peruzzi Chapel of Santa Croce in Florence, which include elements that prefigure both formal and expressive qualities of fifteenth-century Renaissance art. Conversely, even in Florence, where motifs and styles that can be included under the banner 'Renaissance' appear earlier than elsewhere, the modellers of the two surviving 1401 competition reliefs, Lorenzo Ghiberti and Filippo Brunelleschi, continued into the 1430s and 1440s to produce works of sculpture and architecture that demonstrate at best a hybrid embracing of classical ideals. In other major Italian centres like Milan or Venice, Renaissance forms and language were not adopted before the mid-century at the earliest. Moreover, it can fairly be argued that the first truly Renaissance painting is Masaccio's *Trinity*, which dates probably from 1427, more than a quarter of a century after the Baptistery doors competition.

If it is difficult to distinguish for our purposes a starting point for Renaissance art and architecture in Italy, identifying when art production came no longer to conform with usefully limited definitions of 'Renaissance' is a yet greater problem, because this varies even more widely according to art form and location. In central Italy, notably Florence and Rome, the period between *c.*1500 and the deaths of Leonardo da Vinci in 1519, and more significantly of Raphael in 1520, is often termed the High Renaissance. But can the forms and styles of artworks dating from 1520 onwards rightly be considered still part of a late extrapolation of the Renaissance? If it is argued that not enough of the fifteenth-century classical rationale labelled 'Renaissance' survives in them, perhaps they should indeed be given a new category label, such as 'Mannerism'.

Michelangelo is a teasing figure in this regard: he was unequivocally a High Renaissance sculptor and painter during the first quarter of the sixteenth century, but his art production seems to have become less 'Renaissance' in spirit after the political upheavals around the Sack of Rome in 1527 and the religious backlash of the Counter-Reformation, to both of which he reacted strongly both in his beliefs and in his artistic output. For many it is difficult to categorize his *Last Judgement* fresco in the Sistine Chapel, completed in 1541, or his late *Pietà* groups in Florence and Milan as 'Renaissance' in the sense of the revival of the visual language of classical antiquity. On the other hand, his self-revealing 'presentation' drawings of subjects from classical mythology, such as *Ganymede* drawn in 1532 for his close friend Tommaso de' Cavalieri, are pervaded still with the visual and expressive qualities of Renaissance art.

Nevertheless, for the purposes of this chapter, the death of Raphael in 1520 will be considered as marking a defining change in central Italian art production. Architecture is a separate issue, however: the long history of the greatest single building of the Renaissance period, St Peter's in Rome (started by Bramante for Pope Julius II in 1506), demands to be seen through to the completion of the dome in 1590—more or less to Michelangelo's design, although over a quarter of a century after his death. On the other hand, in a work like the Palazzo Tè in Mantua, completed around 1534, Giulio Romano's playful subversiveness in his handling of ornament moves beyond the orthodox handling of classical architectural language during the Renaissance.

In the art and architecture of Venice and the Veneto 'Renaissance' values persisted for longer into the sixteenth century in the works of the two major figures, Titian and Palladio. Venetian painters did not experience to the same degree as their central Italian contemporaries the pressures exerted by the general cultural orientation towards the revival of classical motifs and styles. Nevertheless, Titian's handling of the human figure in both physical movement and psychological exploration is as expressive and affecting as Michelangelo's. His series of mythological *poesie* for Philip II of Spain, painted in the 1550s, can still be labelled 'Renaissance' in subject matter and in the treatment of form and narrative, despite his progressively loose handling of paint. The penetrating insights into the human condition that Titian shows in his portraiture stand comparison with Raphael's, and his abilities as a portraitist led to international renown and the dissemination of Italian Renaissance artistic values throughout the courts of Europe.

Based on a profound study of the buildings of ancient Rome, Palladio's architecture has a sober classical orthodoxy not maintained elsewhere in Italy in the later sixteenth century. Works like the Palazzo Chiericati and the Villa Rotonda, both under construction in the 1550s, match in built form the profoundly learned theory of his *Four Books of Architecture*. Palladio exerted powerful influence on later classicizing architecture throughout Europe and beyond: one thinks, for example, of Inigo Jones's Whitehall Banqueting House and Lord Burlington's villa at Chiswick. In this chapter occasional glances forward to non-Italian buildings as late even as these are indulged. The bulk of the discussion, however, reviews the evolution of artistic genres and stylistic tendencies on the Italian peninsula between 1400 and 1520.

The survival and revival of classical building types and architectural language

Introduction

The principal contribution of Italian Renaissance architects to the history of Western architecture was to revive and reuse classical Roman building types and architectural language. Medieval building types, such as the Latin cross, basilical church, retained their importance but were reinterpreted in the light of the proportions and vocabulary of classical architecture. Conversely, architects' adaptations of classical building types in the design of ecclesiastical buildings were of necessity guided by the needs of the Christian liturgy and ceremonial. Other building types, such as the centrally planned chapel or church, took on fresh importance in the new social and intellectual milieu; and the evolution during the Renaissance of the rural villa required the reworking of classical forms in the light of new patronal needs and vernacular conventions. One touchstone for what Vasari described as the 'rebirth' of the language of classical architecture is how the orders were used to articulate and enrich Renaissance buildings. The relationship of Renaissance buildings and building types to their classical ancestors, and the treatment of these structures using a revived language based especially on imperial Roman architecture, are the principal themes explored in this section.

Classical buildings survived in more or less good condition in large number on the peninsula. Through serious study of this heritage, and especially of the often ruinous buildings of imperial Rome, architects learned a great deal about the technology of classical construction, and about classical building types and architectural language. No classical treatises on painting or sculpture survived into the Renaissance period, but the *De architectura* of Vitruvius did (albeit corrupt and difficult in places to understand), and it stimulated the writing of many architectural treatises. Vitruvius dedicated his book to Augustus, the first Roman emperor, so his architectural theory and aesthetics pre-dated most of the surviving classical buildings on the peninsula, which were constructed later in the imperial period. Nevertheless, Renaissance architects learned much from Vitruvius, for example about the ideal ratios of height to diameter of Doric, Ionic, Corinthian, and Composite columns, the proportional relationships of these to their bases, capitals, and entablatures, and how this sequence of the orders should be applied. Vitruvius' treatise resonated throughout the Renaissance period, crucially informing architectural treatise writers from Alberti to Palladio. Its yet more extensive fame across the Western world and beyond is suggested by a dialogue written by Francisco Cervantes de Salazar in 1554 about the architectural language of the new palace in Hispanic Mexico City:

'...this is the façade of the royal palace...'
   '...it is easy to see it should be so, from the lofty arcades which boast so
many tall columns, that immediately lend it a regal splendour.'
   'The columns are rounded, since Vitruvius does not recommend square ones,
particularly when they are fluted...'
'How well the proportions of their height match their width!'
'And look how excellent the decoration on the architraves is!'

The survival of Vitruvius' treatise, and the renewed impetus given it by the discovery early in the fifteenth century of a hitherto unknown manuscript, also encouraged both humanists and architects to write their own theoretical manifestos. Like Vitruvius, Alberti's *De re aedificatoria*, presented to Pope Nicholas V in 1452, is divided into ten books and demonstrates a profound study and knowledge of the imperial architecture of Rome. Updating the classical prototype to provide for the different circumstances of the fifteenth century, Alberti developed a theory of the orders that derived, but also differed in details, from Vitruvius. This offered Renaissance architects a protocol by which the orders gained social and moral resonances, and this guided them and their patrons in the decorum of applying them. A later architectural treatise by Sebastiano Serlio, which was generously illustrated with woodcut diagrams, provided more detailed guidance. This was widely disseminated throughout Europe, and stimulated intriguing, if often rather sterile and academic, exercises in applying the orders, such as the Gate of Honour in Gonville and Caius College, Cambridge, completed in 1575, and the frontispiece—in the form of a bold triumphal arch—of the Chateau of Anet by Philibert Delorme in around 1550. Austere paired Doric columns and matching entablature here carry paired Ionic columns on high bases at *piano nobile* level; surmounting this are pairs of Corinthian columns bracketing rich sculptural decoration at attic level.

The centrally planned chapel and church

After losing the competition for the second pair of Baptistery doors in 1401, Filippo Brunelleschi appears to have spent time in Rome studying the building techniques and proportional systems of classical architecture. The first crucially informed the engineering achievement of the Florence Duomo cupola, which could scarcely have been constructed without an understanding of classical building technology. His knowledge of classical proportional systems underpins all his other buildings, although he worked essentially with a revived Tuscan Romanesque architectural language rather than that of imperial Rome.

The Old Sacristy of San Lorenzo was built as an independent structure before the Romanesque San Lorenzo was replaced by Brunelleschi's basilical church. It can therefore be seen as the first centrally planned chapel of the Renaissance. But it was not based on classical centrally planned buildings such as the Pantheon, but rather on the Byzantine formula of a cupola carried on pendentives over a square ground plan— the structural principle of buildings like the Baptistery in Padua, with which the Old Sacristy shares identical dimensions. This essentially non-classical system is enriched with fluted Corinthian pilasters, an architectural motif derived from the articulation of the Tuscan Romanesque Baptistery in Florence. Brunelleschi's study of classical architecture in Rome, however, inspired the quality of order and simple proportionality: the body of the chapel is a cube and the cupola is a pure hemisphere.

The structural system of the Old Sacristy was of crucial importance to the development of the Renaissance centrally planned church, paving the way for the more elaborately decorated Pazzi Chapel at Santa Croce, Florence, and later centrally planned pilgrimage churches like Santa Maria delle Carceri in Prato. One of the most remarkable descendants of the Old Sacristy is the ornately decorated Chapel of St Sigismund in Wawel Cathedral in Kraków, designed in 1517 by Bartolomeo Berrecci, who signed himself as Florentine but is otherwise unknown. Commissioned as a family funerary chapel by King Zygmunt I Stary, this is the most purely Italian Renaissance structure outside Italy. It shares with the Old Sacristy its square plan, its simple proportional system, and its hemispherical dome carried on pendentives and a high drum.

In none of Brunelleschi's completed buildings do his forms approach the grandeur of the paradigmatic classical buildings visible in Rome. Had the octagonal-plan Santa Maria degli Angeli, Florence, started in 1434, been completed, the pairs of attached pilasters that were to have carried the entrance arches to the niche-like chapels might have suggested a new monumentality. But Brunelleschi's debt to classical Rome begins to be evident only in the painted architecture of Masaccio's *Trinity*, which is different in temperament from the rather quotidian buildings of Masaccio's other works. It is generally accepted that Brunelleschi played a major part in the design of Masaccio's painted structure. Here an arch carried on unfluted attached Ionic columns is set within a pair of richly fluted pilasters with Composite capitals that support an elaborately detailed entablature. This arch opens into an apparently rectangular space covered by a deeply coffered barrel vault. The whole structure has the appearance of being based on a Roman triumphal arch, such as the Arch of Augustus at Rimini on which Alberti later drew for the façade of the Tempio Malatestiano. In the *Trinity*'s painted architecture Brunelleschi and Masaccio reinterpreted Tuscan Romanesque in the light of classical architectural language. The closeness of Masaccio's structure to imperial

FLORENCE, SAN LORENZO, OLD SACRISTY, interior to altar.

Roman architecture emphasizes by contrast the essentially Tuscan Romanesque inspiration behind Brunelleschi's churches.

Predictably, Leon Battista Alberti's Greek-cross San Sebastiano in Mantua is, unlike the Old Sacristy, assertively classicizing in its architectural vocabulary, although the plan is of early Christian rather than classical derivation. The much altered façade has a triangular pediment and high frieze carried on giant-order pilasters. The building appears to be essentially an intellectual exercise, whereby Alberti put theoretical

RIMINI, TEMPIO MALATESTIANO, façade and north-side exterior.

ideas into practice, rather than a functional ecclesiastical building. Centrally planned structures were favoured by Renaissance architects and architectural theorists because the square and the circle were regarded as perfect geometrical forms, reflecting the perfection of the Almighty. But churches built on central plans were less practical for liturgical or processional usage than Latin-cross or basilical planned churches. Central planning tended therefore to be most often used for cult churches like Santa Maria della Consolazione in Todi, which was built around a miracle-working image of the Madonna. In both plan and elevation this closely resembles one of Leonardo da Vinci's drawings of centrally planned churches. This suggests that it might have been designed in 1508 by Bramante, Leonardo's former contemporary in Milan, perhaps as a trial for ideas about the design of St Peter's in Rome, on which Bramante was working for Pope Julius II from 1506.

The prelude to Bramante's work on St Peter's, the most ambitious and monumental structure of the Renaissance, was his Tempietto constructed in 1502 adjacent to San Pietro in Montorio in Rome. This small structure is centrally planned because it was a

ROME, SAN PIETRO IN MONTORIO, TEMPIETTO, exterior.

commemorative monument built on the site of St Peter's martyrdom: the earliest Christian martyria were generally centrally planned. The circular peristyle has sixteen columns with capitals of the Tuscan form of the Doric order, which support a classically correct entablature with a frieze of triglyphs and metopes decorated with relief carvings of liturgical instruments. Within this peristyle rises the cella, which is as high as the peristyle is wide, and is surmounted by a hemispherical dome. The classical authenticity of the Tempietto, based as it is on the circular temple at Tivoli, led Palladio to include it as the only recent work amongst the classical temples illustrated in his *Four Books on Architecture*.

The St Peter's foundation medal struck in 1506 shows that Julius II and Bramante were, exceptionally, planning for a grandly articulated centralized space crowned by a vast dome on the scale of the Pantheon, and with two four-storey *campanili* at the corners of the western façade, an arrangement repeated in 1518 by Antonio da Sangallo the Elder for the miracle-working church of San Biagio, Montepulciano. Further evidence that St Peter's was to be centrally planned, appropriately for the church marking the site of the saint's tomb, is provided by Bramante's celebrated drawing of half of the plan. The central dome was to have been carried on massive piers articulated with niches and paired pilasters and surrounded by four smaller, domed spaces; and the arms of the cross terminated in semi-domed apses. Externally the façades were articulated with niches bracketed by paired pilasters and columns. This rich, plastic articulation is echoed in the applied Doric order used by Antonio da Sangallo throughout San Biagio, Montepulciano, and in the grandiose basilica of Raphael's *School of Athens*. On Bramante's death in 1514, Raphael and Baldassare Peruzzi were appointed jointly to supervise work, but their patron Pope Leo X required a setting for ceremonial and processional use. Raphael's plan, of which apparently nothing was put into practice, was a simplification of Bramante's central plan, extended on one side by a five-bay nave and aisles.

Work on the new St Peter's was considerably delayed during the politically unsettled decades after Raphael's death in 1520. The massive coffered arches carried on the principal piers of Bramante's unfinished building are recorded in drawings of the 1530s. A large-scale wooden model survives of a new proposal developed by Antonio da Sangallo in the early 1540s. Appointed as *capomaestro* on Sangallo's death in 1546, Michelangelo reverted to the principle of Bramante's plan while proposing a grand portico at one corner of a diamond-shaped structure. At the same time he simplified the interior articulation and massively strengthened Bramante's central piers so that they could support the great weight of his proposed dome. At his death in 1564 Michelangelo had established the exterior articulation of monumental, unfluted, giant-order Corinthian pilasters which continued upwards into the ribs of the dome. But the dome itself was completed only in 1590, long after Bramante's proposed centralized plan had given way to the liturgical requirement of a nave ending in a grand façade. The result is a hybrid between the Renaissance ideal of the Greek-cross plan and the basilical plan normal in Renaissance congregational churches.

The basilical church

The arches of San Lorenzo, Florence, planned by Brunelleschi from 1421 but not built until the 1440s, are turned on simple, unfluted Composite-order columns. Like the articulation in *pietra serena* against white stucco this again suggests the architect's desire to revive a Tuscan Romanesque architectural aesthetic. But due to Brunelleschi's preoccupation with simple proportions stimulated by study of classical Roman architecture, San Lorenzo has a calculated modular system of measurements. The strict application of this module meant that logically, if awkwardly, it became necessary to insert impost blocks over the nave arcade capitals. These correspond to the height of the entablature carried by the pilasters that separate the aisle chapels, which are raised on three steps. Despite this, however, the clarity and simplicity of the proportions and the architectural language generate a rare sense of spatial harmony.

Brunelleschi's Latin-cross buildings were parish or monastic churches. Since the simple proportions and articulation of their liturgically functional interiors was all-important, they needed no enriched façades. Alberti, by contrast, worked for the courtly nobility, and the exteriors of their buildings could productively express their power and authority. From around 1450 Alberti redesigned the western end of the Tempio Malatestiano, his re-cladding of the Gothic Franciscan church at Rimini, as a series of triumphal arch motifs, derived from the Riminese Arch of Augustus. This was to assert visually the commanding position of his patron, the ruthless and ambitious Sigismondo Malatesta, for whom this church became his family mausoleum. Along the sides, a series of monumental arches turned on heavy rectangular piers sheltered sarcophagi of Sigismondo's courtiers and humanists. On the façade shallow, round-arched niches bracketed by bold fluted, attached Corinthian columns were possibly intended to house the sarcophagi of Sigismondo himself and his mistress, Isotta degli Atti. The Tempio Malatestiano façade illustrates starkly the difficulties inherent in adapting classical building types to the demands of church buildings. San Francesco, Rimini, was characteristically constructed with a high nave between lower side aisles. For the lower level of the façade Alberti tripled the Arch of Augustus motif. Above, on either side, the aisle roofs were screened by plain triangular walls, and the higher nave was to have been covered by a further round arch carried on fluted attached pilasters. The result is richly classical in architectural vocabulary but inevitably unclassical in structure.

Commissioned by Ludovico Gonzaga, Marquis of Mantua, Sant'Andrea in Mantua was designed by Alberti in 1470. The triumphal-arch design system of the façade, articulated by giant-order Corinthian pilasters, is consciously matched in the nave wall treatment. Here high-arched openings onto rectangular chapels alternate with tabernacle-like openings leading into small, domed chapels reflecting the frames of the façade's side doors. Each opening is bracketed by giant-order pilasters; above the entablature extends a vast, richly coffered barrel vault. The pilaster order continues around the apse and transepts, and a brightly lit dome is carried on the crossing arches and pendentives. The grand architectural vocabulary and the rich decoration echo for the first time the monumentality of structures like the Basilica of Maxentius in Rome.

MANTUA, SANT'ANDREA, nave to east.

There could hardly be a sharper contrast in how the classical heritage was exploited than that between San Lorenzo in Florence and Sant'Andrea in Mantua. Compared with the growing interest in building small, novel, centrally planned churches, few ground-breaking basilical churches were built in the decades between Sant'Andrea and Palladio's great Venetian churches. In those that were, such as Francesco di Giorgio's Santa Maria in Calcinaio in Cortona, or Mauro Codussi's San Michele in Isola, Venice, architects failed to emulate Alberti's skill and confidence in reinterpreting the imperial Roman past. To trace further the increasing importance of classical buildings for the Italian Renaissance we must explore developments in secular architecture.

Palace façades

Renaissance forms and architectural vocabulary were first used in large-scale palace building in the Palazzo Medici in Florence, completed around 1460 by Michelozzo di

FLORENCE, PALAZZO MEDICI, façade.

Bartolommeo for the wealthy and politically ambitious Cosimo 'il Vecchio' de' Medici. The façade is an ostentatious display of Medici authority, reading as a modernization of the façade of the Palazzo della Signoria, the Florentine town hall, implying that the Palazzo Medici was a new centre of civic power. Michelozzo imitated the heavily rusticated ground level using even grander blocks of stone. On the *piano nobile* and the second floor he adopted the biforate window type hitherto used only for civic buildings and archbishops' palaces, updated using rounded arches decorated with Medicean emblems. At the top of the façade the Palazzo della Signoria's medieval system of machicolation is replaced by a beautifully designed classicizing cornice which proclaims the cultural self-consciousness, as well as the sociopolitical authority, of the Medici.

More elegant, and less domineering, is the façade designed by Alberti at much the same date for the new Florentine palace of the noble Rucellai family. This is the first Renaissance palace façade onto which the orders were applied, although not according to a strictly Vitruvian system: the attached pilasters on the ground floor have Doric capitals, those on the upper two storeys are Corinthian. The taller ground floor is enriched by a carved diamond pattern based on Roman *opus reticulatum*: this subtly adds to the *all'antica* sophistication of the whole façade, reaffirming Alberti as the early Renaissance architect best informed about the classical language of architecture.

The sharing of motifs by the Palazzo Rucellai façade and that of the Palazzo della Cancelleria, built for Cardinal Raffaelo Riario in 1486–96, has led to suggestions that Alberti participated in this Roman project; but Alberti died in 1472, well before the Cancelleria was commissioned. The architect has not been identified, but similarities in both façade and courtyard articulation with the Palazzo Ducale at Urbino, built for Duke Federigo da Montefeltro in the mid-1460s by Luciano Laurana, may suggest that Francesco di Giorgio Martini (who succeeded Laurana in 1472) and/or the Roman Baccio Pontelli, who trained in Urbino, were involved. As in the Palazzo Rucellai, the Cancelleria façade is articulated by modest, low-relief attached pilasters. On the *piano nobile* pairs of pilasters with Composite capitals bracket round-arched windows on unobtrusively decorated piers capped by light entablatures. The whole effect is of a delicately veneered surface broken mainly by the full-length cornice and principal entablatures. These emphasize the façade's horizontality, resolved by the slight forward stepping of the terminal bays.

The Palazzo della Cancelleria's early Renaissance façade is the most delicate in central Italy. Its Venetian equivalent is that of the Palazzo Vendramin-Calergi, designed by Mauro Codussi in around 1502 for the noble Andrea Loredan. This design brings under strict Renaissance control the standard elements of the Venetian palace façade, as required by the particular topographical conditions of Venice. It is of five bays, the middle three allowing light to be thrown into the central halls of the upper storeys. The end bays are emphatically bracketed by pairs of attached Corinthian pilasters along the water level with the main entrance from the Grand Canal, and attached columns on the upper storeys, fluted for emphasis on the *piano nobile*. This is a grand, classicizing

ROME, PALAZZO DELLA CANCELLERIA, façade.

statement of the power of the Venetian nobility that reached new heights at the start of the sixteenth century.

The classic High Renaissance palace façade is perhaps that of Bramante's Palazzo Caprini, the 'House of Raphael', since it was the painter's home from 1517 until his death. This was a relatively small, two-storeyed building with a rusticated *basamento* and—for its date, probably around 1512—a characteristically austere articulation of coupled Doric attached columns, and triangular-pedimented windows with balustered balconies. This façade was later reflected in Palladio's Palazzo Iseppo Porto, completed in 1552, although here the articulation is richer. Attached Ionic columns articulate the *piano nobile*, separating tall windows with alternating segmental and triangular pediments and balconies below; ornate decoration emphasizes the central bay's window. Classical architectural motifs are authentically applied in both façades, showing the sixteenth-century architects' confident handling of their ancient Roman heritage.

Unlike many of Palladio's palaces, the Palazzo Chiericati, designed around 1550, was built on open ground, which encouraged a tripartite division of the façade. The central

VICENZA, PALAZZO CHIERICATI, façade.

five bays are bracketed with coupled columns on both storeys: Doric on the ground floor, and Ionic on the *piano nobile*. Here windows with alternating pediments light the *gran salone*. Inigo Jones knew well the Palazzo Chiericati and the other Palladian palaces in Vicenza. By the turn of the century he already owned a copy of Palladio's *Four Books of Architecture*, and in this he made extensive marginal notes while studying in Italy in 1613–15. The Whitehall Banqueting House in London, designed by Jones in 1620–2, has an essentially Palladian street elevation. The central three bays of the seven-bay façade are emphasized with attached columns on both storeys, while the side bays are articulated by pilasters. The lower storey has windows with alternating segmental and triangular pediments, reflecting the window articulation of the *piano nobile* of Palladio's Palazzo Chiericati, or the rhythm of the Palazzo Iseppo Porto.

Palace courtyards

It is often claimed that the history of Italian Renaissance architecture opened with the canonical Loggia degli Innocenti, built by Brunelleschi between 1419 and 1424. This structure confirms that when in Rome Brunelleschi focused his attention on the system of rational proportions and order on which classical architecture is based, rather than on the vocabulary of imperial Roman architecture. The Loggia degli Innocenti shows little response to classical architectural language: its delicate arches and widely spaced columns deliberately reflect earlier Tuscan buildings, such as the nave arcades of the Romanesque SS Apostoli in Florence.

The paradigm established in the Loggia degli Innocenti dominated the design of palace courtyards for the rest of the fifteenth century, up to and including the Palazzo della Cancelleria courtyard. In the Palazzo Medici courtyard in Florence, by Michelozzo between 1444 and 1459, this Brunelleschian motif of round arches, here carried on columns with Composite capitals, is straightforwardly applied, as though a derivative of the Loggia degli Innocenti had been bent through 90 degrees at each corner. This arcade carries a high frieze with delicate *sgraffito* decoration and carved roundels of classicizing subjects. Light and elegant, this courtyard contrasts with the authoritative power of the façade: the architectural language here suits its domestic function, showing little concern to echo classical Rome.

By contrast, the unfinished courtyard of the Palazzo Venezia in Rome, built for the Venetian Pope Paul II in the later 1460s, powerfully reflects the monumentality of imperial Roman architecture. Here the arcade arches turn on rectangular piers, and the main entablature is carried on attached Tuscan columns raised on high plinths, emulating the nearby Theatre of Marcellus. It breathes something of Alberti's classicizing spirit, exemplified by the side arcades of the Tempio Malatestiano where deep arches turn on robust rectangular piers, although the courtyard's solid grandeur is more imperial in character. Its sobriety was later reflected in the Evangelists' courtyard of the royal Spanish Escorial palace, under construction not far from Madrid between 1563 and 1586. This has an entirely orthodox two-storey articulation crowned by a balustrade: the first storey has heavy arches turned on rectangular piers with attached Doric columns carrying a frieze of triglyphs and metopes, while above, lighter arches framed by attached Ionic columns carry an undecorated entablature.

No other Italian Renaissance courtyard displays forms so powerful and a mood so austere as that of the Palazzo Venezia. The contrasts provided by the Urbino palace courtyard or, in Rome itself, by the rather similar courtyard of the Palazzo della Cancelleria, suggest that later fifteenth-century architects and their patrons preferred the Brunelleschian to the imperial. In the two lower storeys of the Cancelleria courtyard the arches turn on delicate columns, as in the Loggia degli Innocenti, but the corners are strengthened by the introduction of coupled piers. The muted top storey has pairs of small, modestly framed windows set between undecorated pilasters, reflecting the treatment of the façade. The mood is restrained but graceful, although the alternation of columns and pilasters is indebted to the handling of the orders on the Colosseum.

If in its austere grandeur the Escorial's Evangelists' courtyard echoes the Palazzo Venezia, the Arcade Court in Wawel Castle, Kraków, reflects the Renaissance ideal as exemplified in the Cancelleria or at Urbino. In the two lower storeys round arches turn on elegant columns that are considerably more widely spaced than in the Cancelleria courtyard. The reinforcement of the corners with full-height coupled pilasters is

ROME, PALAZZO VENEZIA, courtyard.

reminiscent of the treatment in the Urbino palace courtyard. But the elegant early Renaissance effect is compromised by the thin, elongated double-order columns of the third storey, which is properly the *piano nobile*: although the vocabulary here is still Italianate, the proportions reflect a local, late Gothic temperament.

ROME, PALAZZO DELLA CANCELLERIA, courtyard.

Villas

Arguably, the new Italian Renaissance building type most important for the future of classicizing architecture in Europe and beyond was the country villa. Late medieval rural retreats, such as the villa of Cosimo 'il Vecchio' at Careggi outside Florence, were usually little more than grand farmhouses. Battlemented for defensive purposes, Careggi was given a Renaissance extension, including a classicizing portico that proclaims the patron's sophisticated taste. Later, with increasing prosperity and more settled sociopolitical conditions, purpose-built villas like Lorenzo 'il Magnifico' de' Medici's at Poggio a Caiano became popular. It was designed in the early 1480s by Lorenzo's architect Giuliano da Sangallo, but Lorenzo himself appears to have made significant contributions to the planning. It is the first villa designed on an H-plan with a symmetrical layout of rooms around the main axis. Its huge central *salone*, completed later but to Giuliano's design, has a terracotta coffered vault constructed using a classical Roman technique. An innovatory classical portico with a pediment carried on Ionic columns and a frieze decorated with glazed terracotta reliefs was applied to the façade. In several respects the design and planning reflect the patron's desire to emulate classical Roman villas: Poggio a Caiano stands at the head of a long tradition of classicizing villa architecture.

Started for Cardinal Giulio de' Medici (later Pope Clement VII) by 1518, Raphael's Villa Madama in Rome was never completed. Its plan and the functions of its various spaces are known, however, from a letter in which Raphael guides his patron through the villa. This shows that it was another villa consciously designed to reflect Pliny the Younger's descriptions of classical Roman villas. Regrettably, little was completed beyond a grand loggia that gave access to a garden with a fishpond below. After Raphael's death in 1520 his assistants ornately decorated this loggia's interior. Giulio Romano painted the series of scenes from Ovid, and Giovanni da Udine modelled the exquisitely delicate stucco panels based on the decorations of Nero's Golden House. If completed, this would perhaps have been the grandest villa of the High Renaissance. Although not directly a source for later sixteenth-century villas, it set a challenge met most successfully by Palladio in his series of villas built in the Veneto between about 1540 and 1570.

This series culminated in the centrally planned Villa Rotonda, built on a hilltop site on the outskirts of Vicenza in 1550–1. On each side a flight of steps leads up to an attached pedimented Ionic temple front giving access to the central domed hall. It has no associated farm buildings because it was intended as a *belvedere*, a pleasure dome for entertaining rather than a retreat from the pressures of city life. The most important

VICENZA, VILLA ROTONDA, exterior.

heritage of Palladio's villa architecture is found in the English early eighteenth-century Palladian movement. Designed around 1725 by Robert Boyle, 3rd Earl of Burlington (assisted by William Kent, with whom Burlington studied Palladio's buildings when in Italy in 1719), Chiswick Villa is an independent reworking of Palladio's Villa Rotonda. Large Diocletian windows in the drum of the flattened dome provide the increased lighting required in the English context, and the rich variety of room shapes reflects the planning of imperial bath architecture.

Conclusion

By the death of Raphael in 1520 Italian architects had acquired a profound knowledge of classical Roman architecture and its potential as a source for technical innovation, planning and design ideas, and architectural language. This is clearest in buildings like Bramante's Tempietto and Palazzo Caprini, and his centralized plan for St Peter's. Later, Palladio also intensively studied the buildings of ancient Rome, recording the outcomes in his *Antiquities of Rome*, published in 1554, which became the basis of his architectural theory published in 1570 in his highly influential *Four Books of Architecture*. A generation older than Palladio, Sebastiano Serlio was also important in disseminating the theory and practice of Italian Renaissance architecture, as observed earlier. Serlio spent the last decade of his life in France, publishing an eight-volume, illustrated treatise on architecture, soon reprinted in French as well as Italian, and rapidly translated into German, Spanish, Dutch, and finally English in 1611. The extensive plates in Serlio's treatise recorded otherwise unknown plans and elevations, for example of projects for St Peter's in Rome, and stimulated the design imaginations of architects outside Italy, especially in France and England.

Classical inspiration in early Renaissance sculpture and painting

Introduction

As noted, very few classical paintings were available for study before Nero's Golden House was excavated in around 1480, so, predictably, forms and motifs manifesting the early fifteenth-century revival of the classical tradition appear first in sculpture. Considerable quantities of classical marble carvings and small bronzes, and a few life-size bronzes, were known in the early Renaissance. Marble sculpture that Renaissance artists could study included life-size draped figures, youthful nude figures of Apollo or Antinous, or goddesses like Venus, reliefs on Roman triumphal arches, columns, and innumerable sarcophagi scattered across the peninsula, and a wealth of portrait busts.

Motifs derived from classical sculpture were already introduced into the two *Sacrifice of Isaac* reliefs cast by Lorenzo Ghiberti and Filippo Brunelleschi, then still a goldsmith/sculptor, for the 1401 competition for the Florentine Baptistery bronze doors—the first major Florentine artistic project of the new century. But the copy of the *Spinario* (the boy extracting a thorn from his foot) in Brunelleschi's relief, and the anatomically finely modelled torso of Isaac in Ghiberti's version are classicizing interpolations into reliefs that are still late Gothic in temperament. Brunelleschi's architectural language is indebted to Tuscan Romanesque rather than to imperial Rome: equally, his figural sculpture extrapolates late medieval styles into the fifteenth century. Similarly, however rational is his pictorial perspective in the 'Gates of Paradise' of the Florentine Baptistery, Ghiberti's figures retain fluid, curvilinear drapery folds and a decorative sense of movement that contrast with the gravitas of classical figure sculpture.

The draped figure

Identifying the precise classical sources that Donatello, the greatest sculptor of early Renaissance Italy, drew on is seldom possible. Nevertheless, his study of classical sculpture already shows in his early *St Mark*, carved in marble around 1408 for an external niche on the guild church of Orsanmichele in Florence. Classical inspiration underpins the ways that drapery expresses anatomical volume, the pensive facial type, and the figure's pose: here, the firmness of his weight-bearing right leg is emphasized by the drapery's visual likeness to a classical fluted column. By contrast, the late Gothic drapery of Ghiberti's bronze *St Matthew*, cast in around 1412 for another of the Orsanmichele niches, sways across the figure, undermining a sense of three-dimensional form and destabilizing the pose. But the figure's declamatory energy as he emerges from his niche, gesturing to capture the onlooker's attention, actively reflects the dynamics of gesture and expression in classical orator figures. This offers a visual parallel to the enthusiasm for the rhetoricians Cicero and Quintilian that pervaded the writings of Florentine humanists like Leonardo Bruni in these same years. Of all the Orsanmichele sculpture, however, Nanni di Banco's *Four Crowned Saints* (*c*.1410) most overtly imitates classical prototypes. Here the Roman dress that freely manifests the figures' forms and poses, the strongly classicizing facial types, and the statesmanlike interlinking of the figures through gesture and eye contact as they stoically face their martyrdoms, demonstrate a close study of classical statuary.

The sense of classical *gravitas* that runs through the early statuary of Orsanmichele was taken up by Masaccio in his treatment of the relationship between drapery fold patterns and anatomical form, and in his exploration of human feeling in his figures' facial expressions. This is so of many figures in his Brancacci Chapel frescos (Florence, Santa Maria del Carmine), especially those in the *Tribute Money* that dates from 1427–8, shortly before his visit to Rome, where he died in the same year. Perhaps the finest example, however, is the figure of the Virgin Mary in the Santa Maria Novella *Trinity*, already noted for Brunelleschi's probable collaboration in its classicizing painted architecture. The voluminous, richly articulated drapery folds of the thick fabric expressively emphasize the Virgin's pose and her gesture towards the onlooker, bringing to mind the dramatic drapery of Donatello's bronze *St Louis of Toulouse*, originally cast for Orsanmichele a few years earlier. Her foreshortened face, painted over vertical and horizontal incisions that demonstrate Masaccio's precocious transfer of the design from a squared drawing, powerfully expresses her poignantly self-possessed grief.

DONATELLO, *St Mark.*

Donatello's example guided many fifteenth-century painters in the treatment of drapery for both formal and expressive purposes. Also descended from his *St Louis* is, for example, the figure of St Zenobius in Domenico Veneziano's St Lucy Altarpiece, dating probably from the mid-1440s. Here too St Lucy's drapery was predicated on Donatello's last *Prophet* carved for the Florentine Campanile in the mid- to later 1420s, while her facial profile derives from female figures painted by the major north Italian late Gothic painter Antonio Pisanello. At much the same date Andrea del Castagno exploited simple but voluminous 'sculptural' draperies in his frescoed *Uomini famosi* in the Villa Carducci at Legnaia. Piero della Francesca was an assistant to Domenico

LORENZO GHIBERTI, *St Matthew.*

Veneziano in 1439–40: his experience of Donatello's Florentine sculpture can be traced in figures like the majestic frescoed *Mary Magdalen* in the Duomo of Arezzo, or the mysterious figures at the right of the Urbino *Flagellation*. By this time the function of drapery to manifest the underlying forms, and to suggest figural movement through complex fold patterns, is evident in paintings from Andrea del Verrocchio's workshop, such as the figures of the Virgin and Angel Gabriel in Leonardo da Vinci's early *Annunciation* (c.1475). Filippino Lippi developed a system of highly complex drapery-fold patterns, at some times sinuous and at others angular, although for consistency's sake when working on his Brancacci Chapel frescos he echoed Masaccio's practice of

MASACCIO, *Trinity*.

rendering the forms and volumes of the figures with a few simple folds. Domenico Ghirlandaio also closely emulated Masaccio's draperies; and while training in Ghirlandaio's workshop Michelangelo drew a detailed and precise copy of the St Peter in Masaccio's *Tribute Money*. By the turn of the century drapery-fold patterns that originated in

Donatello's adaptations of classical figures' drapery guided Michelangelo in achieving the grand, convincing monumentality of his Sistine Chapel ceiling figures. Likewise, the young Raphael learned gracefully to enliven the draperies of figures that have now an inherent, unselfconscious and anatomically articulate three-dimensionality.

Elsewhere in Italy also, the volumetric yet expressive draperies of classical statuary, often filtered through Donatello's reinterpretations in works like the Santo Altar in Padua, became part of a conscious revival of classical figural ideals. Leading this development was Andrea Mantegna, especially in his self-consciously archaeological paintings like the *Triumphs of Caesar*. In other works, however, he responded to the progressively more excited movements of Donatello's dramatic narrative figures. Here his figures' robes are made from less weighty fabrics that sometimes flutter around the anatomical forms to highlight moments of dramatic emphasis, or to reinforce expressive registers of gesture and physical movement. Mantegna's brother-in-law Giovanni Bellini, altogether calmer and more devout in temperament, exploited the ability of simple drapery-fold patterns to register pious tranquillity, especially in his monumental altarpieces such as the Pesaro *Coronation of the Virgin* and his greatest, the 1504 San Zaccharia Altarpiece.

Study of the nude figure

Early Renaissance artists' growing responsiveness to classical sculpture also led to increasingly frequent representations of the nude figure. With the growing use of secular, and especially mythological, subject matter later in the fifteenth century, the artist's figural subjects were more often properly without clothes. But earlier on artists took gratuitous advantage of opportunities to show nude figures. An early example is the overt genital display of Masolino and Masaccio's Adam and Eve in the *Temptation* and *Expulsion* frescos of the Brancacci Chapel. The *Expulsion* also provided Masaccio with the chance to reinterpret classical sculptures, such as the *Medici Venus*, with dramatic effect. Not long after this, in the *St John the Baptist in the Desert* predella panel for his St Lucy Altarpiece, Domenico Veneziano chose to represent a particular and unusual moment in St John's life story, when he had removed his clothes but had not yet dressed in his hair shirt, in order to study St John's nude figure in a pose recognizable as that of the Hercules of the Florentine civic seal.

As a plague saint, St Sebastian was a popular subject for devotional art, and this also provided painters with opportunities to study the male nude, often based on classical prototypes. The best example is perhaps Mantegna's *St Sebastian*, dating from the early 1480s: the observer is invited to draw an analogy between the saint's beautifully modelled classical torso and the monumentally precise fluted attached column to which he is bound. To reinforce the classical simile, his feet are directly compared with a fragmentary, classical sandalled foot in the lower left corner of the canvas. Hercules, the mythological parallel to the Christian St Sebastian, also offered artists chances to represent the human figure in all its muscular detail; and the group of *Hercules and Antaeus*, shown in engravings by Mantegna and iconically in Antonio

ANDREA MANTEGNA, *St Sebastian.*

Donatello, *David* (bronze).

Pollaiuolo's cast-bronze version, afforded perfect opportunities to explore the human form in dynamic movement.

In the Old Testament we read that David put aside the armour that Saul gave him, but not that he went naked into his duel with Goliath. Nonetheless, he provided sculptors with an ideal subject for their reinterpretation of nude classical figure sculpture. The cryptic, androgynous sensuality of Donatello's bronze version (Florence, Bargello) has given rise to many varied datings and interpretations. His gratuitous nakedness, empha-sized by his boots and shepherd-boy hat, is given an erotic charge through the caress of his inside thigh by a feather on the wing of Goliath's helmet. Moreover, the intricate torsion of the pose and the smooth, reflective texture of the adolescent flesh surfaces suggest that the sculptor intentionally sought for expressive ambiguity. Strikingly different in interpretation is Michelangelo's colossal, heroic *David* of 1504. Carved from a massive block of marble, this David has a fully mature and highly developed anatomical structure, and an air of self-confident expectation about the conflict to come. Michelangelo's sophisticated reinterpretation of the classical nude figure, generated at the peak moment of the High Renaissance in Florence, was originally intended to adorn the Duomo but was appropriated by the republican government to stand as a monumental civic icon at the entrance to the Palazzo della Signoria.

By deriving Eve's pose from a classical Venus, Masaccio set forth in his *Expulsion* an exemplar for the representation of the female nude. Life-size representations of Eve were rare, however, before the late fifteenth century, when for example Antonio Rizzo and Tullio Lombardo both carved figures of *Eve* in Venice, respectively in the later 1480s for the Arco Foscari and in 1493 for the Andrea Vendramin tomb. The latter is considerably more classicizing than the former. Very few other religious subjects offered artists the opportunity to study classical female figures. As mythological subjects grew in popularity, however, female nudes were more frequently depicted: Botticelli's *Birth of Venus* of around 1480 is an iconic example. Soon after 1500 Leonardo da Vinci painted a much admired (but sadly now lost) *Leda*, based on Ovid's story of Zeus taking the form of a swan in order to seduce the King of Aetolia's daughter. In early drawings Leonardo derived her pose from a classical *Crouching Venus*, but in the final painting (known through copies) Leda, based loosely on other classical Venus figures, stood embraced by the swan's wing, gracefully stroking his neck. Her languid pose, voluptuous forms, and sensuous facial expression suggest her arousal and sexual pleasure, which resulted in the two pairs of twins who emerge from broken eggs at her feet. A few years later, the Venetian Giorgione paraphrased a classical recumbent Venus in his naked but unforthcoming *Sleeping Venus*, a figure which in his *Venus of Urbino* Titian in turn adapted into a directly appealing, sensuously alert nude of considerable erotic force.

'Neo-classicism' in Renaissance sculpture and painting

One of the great classical figure-groups that survived into the fifteenth century, the bronze equestrian *Marcus Aurelius* had not been melted down for its precious material, as many classical bronzes had over earlier centuries, because it was thought to represent Constantine, the first Christian Roman emperor. Repositioned in 1538 to become later the centrepiece for Michelangelo's redesign of the Roman Capitol, the *Marcus Aurelius* stood in the fifteenth century next to the Lateran Palace. It served as a general inspiration for Donatello, when in Padua from 1443 he was commissioned to cast the life-size bronze equestrian monument of the *condottiere* Erasmo de Narni, known as Gattamelata. The notion of a mercenary soldier seeking commemoration in the style of a Roman emperor is a paradigm of the Renaissance celebration of

AFTER LEONARDO DA VINCI, *Leda and the Swan.*

individuality and revival of classical imagery. These ideas resonate later in the equestrian monument to Bartolomeo Colleoni by Andrea del Verrocchio (Venice, Campo di SS Giovanni e Paolo) and in the arrogant, although hubristically never completed, three-times life-size monument of the Milanese Duke Francesco Sforza, by Leonardo da Vinci. Characteristically, Donatello's *Gattamelata* does not directly reflect the *Marcus Aurelius*. Other Renaissance works, however, duplicate classical sculptural style so closely as to be almost plagiarisms. The *Marcus Aurelius* was literally copied in a precociously early small bronze cast probably around 1440. This was given to Piero 'the Gouty' de' Medici in 1465 by its maker, the eccentric Florentine sculptor-architect Antonio Averlino, who gave himself the pretentious nickname 'Filarete', which, transliterated from the Greek, means 'lover of virtues'.

Many classical small bronzes survived on the peninsula into the Renaissance period, and these provided inspiration for patrons and sculptors alike. Skills in bronze-casting technique gradually improved, and with an increasing range of secular subject matter figure-poses and movements grew in variety and versatility. The tensile strength of bronze allowed, and indeed encouraged, sculptors to explore complex, extruded poses that would be impossible to achieve in marble carvings: this development culminated in late Renaissance works like Giambologna's celebrated *Mercury*. With smooth three-dimensional forms and often gleaming, burnished surfaces, small bronzes invited both close scrutiny and also handling. This tactile intimacy led them to become collectors' items much sought after by Renaissance connoisseurs. In turn, this encouraged bronze sculptors to replicate both subjects and styles of classical sculpture. Pre-eminent in producing what might be termed 'neo-classical' bronzes was Pier Jacopo Alari-Bonacolsi, appropriately known as 'Antico', who cast small bronzes of classical figures like the *Spinario* for members of the Gonzaga family in Mantua, and for Isabella d'Este, the principal female patron of the Renaissance.

The Venetian marble-carver Tullio Lombardo, who spoke in defence of sculpture in the *paragone* debate (the comparison of the arts of painting and sculpture) in Baldassare Castiglione's *The Courtier*, exemplifies the strong if sometimes rather uncritical response of some Renaissance sculptors to classical sculpture. The pictorial compositions, architectural settings, and figure styles in Tullio's reliefs for the Arca di San Antonio in the Santo, Padua, show that he was deeply preoccupied with recreating an idealized classical style. This is also shown by his adaptations of the classical triumphal arch motif to the needs of grand Venetian funerary monuments, culminating in the heroic tomb of Doge Andrea Vendramin, probably completed by 1494 and now in SS Giovanni e Paolo in Venice. Here the central motif of a semicircular arch carried on richly decorated columns presses forward in front of the relatively low-relief side bays to frame the bier and effigy. Figures of virtues and soldiers are 'neo-classical' in dress and facial types, and most surfaces are richly covered with classical ornament and medallions with scenes from Greek mythology. With its gentle *contrapposto* pose, its understated muscular plasticity, and its smooth, softened surface textures, Tullio's *Adam* (New York, Metropolitan Museum of Art), which also originally adorned the

TULLIO LOMBARDO, *Adam.*

Vendramin tomb, is one of the most convincing Italian Renaissance reconsiderations of classical sculptural style. Perhaps his most idealizing work, however, is the compellingly exquisite *Bacchus and Ariadne* group in which the two bust-length figures, cut off diagonally just below the shoulders in the Roman manner, are blended through their classical features and expressions in a shared sentiment of cool 'neo-classical' purity.

At much the same date, Michelangelo sought to emulate classical exemplars in recreating a classical work—a plagiarism that was intended to deceive. After carving his (now lost) *Sleeping Cupid* in 1496, he aged it so that it would appear authentically classical. Taken in, Cardinal Raffaele Riario acquired the carving from Michelangelo's dealer as an antique, only to reject it once he discovered Michelangelo's authorship. It was subsequently acquired by Isabella d'Este who displayed it in her *studiolo* in the castle in Mantua for direct comparison with an authentic classical *Sleeping Cupid* in her collection.

Andrea Mantegna demands a special place amongst classicizing artists of the early Renaissance. Through his contacts during his apprenticeship years in Padua with intellectual antiquarians like Ciriaco d'Ancona, Mantegna developed a profound knowledge of classical sculpture and artefacts. One imperial Roman form that provided plenteous imagery for painters to study was the triumphal arch, which, as noted, also offered opportunities for adaptation by Leon Battista Alberti and by Tullio Lombardo. As monuments of architectural sculpture rather than functioning buildings, classical triumphal arches had tended to survive better than many building types, such as temples, which might have been demolished for building materials, built over, or converted for Christian worship. In one of his earliest works, the Ovetari Chapel fresco of *St James before Herod Agrippa* (lost in the Second World War), Mantegna recognized the form's resonances of power and prestige in victory by faithfully representing a Roman triumphal arch behind his figure group. Derived principally from the Arco dei Gavi in Verona, the arch is bracketed by pairs of fluted attached columns carrying a heavy entablature, and it is enriched by a sacrificial relief, a pair of emperor medallions, and an inscription copied from an ancient slab near Este. Later on, this inscription was copied also by Jacopo Bellini, Mantegna's father-in-law, onto a sheet in his Book of Drawings now in Paris.

These details, and the armour and dress of the Roman soldiers and other figures in the scene, are transcribed from classical prototypes with an archaeological accuracy that Mantegna developed further in later works such as the *Triumphs of Caesar*. In the fourth of these huge canvases, for example, he includes accurate representations of gold and polychrome marble vessels in the army's booty, trumpets with inscribed pennons, and ruined buildings in the landscape behind. Meanwhile, on the vault of the Camera Picta in the Gonzaga Castle in Mantua Mantegna had imitated classical images of Roman emperors, in grisaille, displayed frontally within roundels. He later developed this in sculptural form in his bronze self-portrait bust which is set against a porphyry slab within a marble roundel, at the entrance to his funerary chapel in Sant'Andrea, Mantua. This is a precociously self-conscious tribute to his artistic and creative prowess, and served as a source for the Roman emperor roundels commissioned by Cardinal Wolsey from Giuliano da Maiano at Hampton Court.

Mantegna's enthusiastic pursuit of classicism had two further outcomes: his grisaille painted reliefs, and his learned treatment of mythological subject matter. The grandest of his grisailles represents a Roman processional theme, the *Introduction of the Cult of Cybele at Rome*. Painted as though relief sculptures and set against panels of variegated coloured marbles, Mantegna's figures are invested with a boldly expressive narrative energy. This work hints at the painter's extraordinary ability to develop pictorial compositions based around complex and elaborate allegorical themes, like the

ANDREA MANTEGNA, *Triumphs of Caesar*, canvas 4.

Parnassus painted for Isabella d'Este's *studiolo* in 1497. This shows Venus and Mars with Cupid and Vulcan, Apollo and the Muses, and Mercury with Pegasus, ranged together on Mount Parnassus. With its cryptic allusions to Isabella's role in the cultural life of Gonzaga Mantua, this work finds its best parallels in Botticelli's *Primavera*, and in the terracotta frieze on the portico of Lorenzo 'il Magnifico' de' Medici's villa at Poggio a

Caiano. Like Mantegna's *Parnassus*, the *Primavera* is an assembly of figures from classical mythology which in its programmatic sophistication has also given rise to numerous interpretations. The highly complex programme of the Poggio a Caiano frieze, designed probably by Lorenzo's house sculptor, Bertoldo di Giovanni, has only recently been decoded: using a variety of classical figures, it deals with the passing of time from its origins, through the seasons and months to the passage from night into day.

In his drawing of Apelles' painting of *Calumny*, based on Lucian's description paraphrased by Alberti in his *On Painting*, Mantegna provided a more faithfully classicizing reconstruction of what Apelles' painting may have looked like than Botticelli did in the compelling but relatively fanciful figure group and setting in his painted version. In contrast with these complex, allegorical subjects, Raphael's *Parnassus* in the Stanza della Segnatura, originally Pope Julius II's private library, is a straightforward grouping together of Apollo and the Muses with major poets and letterati from classical and more recent times, with no underlying allegorical purposes. Painted in 1512, his *Galatea* is a rich response to a mythological story, showing a sinuous nude and much bravura depiction of figural forms and movement. His voluptuous female nudes in other frescos in the Villa Farnesina reflect Leonardo da Vinci's sensuous treatment of the Leda story. In turn these stimulated further renderings of erotic mythological themes by Giulio Romano (frescos for Duke Federigo Gonzaga in the Palazzo Tè, Mantua) and by Correggio, whose canvases of the *Loves of Jupiter* were also commissioned by Federigo Gonzaga, probably as gifts for Emperor Charles V.

Portraiture

The pictorial genre that perhaps most sharply encapsulated the personal aspirations of Renaissance men and women was the portrait. At the opening of the fifteenth century autonomous portraits, whether sculpted or painted, were still unusual; by the start of the sixteenth century portraiture was one of the principal activities of the High Renaissance artist. Until the 1450s painted portraits were almost always in profile, recording features but establishing no relationship with the beholder: this is generally true both of donor portraits, such as those commemorated in Masaccio's *Trinity*, and of easel portraits such as Antonio Pisanello's celebrated 1441 image of Leonello d'Este, Marquis of Ferrara.

Cast by Pisanello in 1438, the earliest Italian Renaissance medal, of Emperor John VIII Palaeologus, was inspired by the heritage of imperial Roman coinage. Around 1440 Pisanello started to cast portrait medals of courtly rulers such as Galeazzo Maria Visconti, Duke of Milan, or King Alfonso I of Naples. These uniformly showed the individual in pure profile on the obverse, emulating classical imperial images on Roman coins and medallions. But patrons and their sculptors had the opportunity to develop individual images, sometimes heraldic, sometimes with complex allegorical or cryptic personal meanings, on their medal reverses. Medals became vehicles of transmission of individual status and self-image, through courtly exchange or diplomatic gift. A classic example is Bertoldo di Giovanni's medal, cast in Florence in 1480,

BERTOLDO DI GIOVANNI, medal of Sultan Mehmed II, obverse and reverse.

of Sultan Mehmed II. The sultan's portrait on the obverse is closely based on a medal designed by the Venetian painter Gentile Bellini, who was loaned as a portraitist to the sultan for two years from 1479. The reverse, signed by the sculptor, celebrates Mehmed II as victor and emperor over Greece, Asia, and Trebizond. The medal was gifted to the sultan by Lorenzo 'the Magnificent' de' Medici, to be disseminated as a token of Mehmed's military triumphs.

Significant events were commemorated by medals, such as that cast (also by Bertoldo di Giovanni) in Florence in 1478 to mark the death of Giuliano de' Medici in the Pazzi Conspiracy that year, and the already-mentioned 1506 medal celebrating the laying of the foundation stone of St Peter's in Rome. By the start of the sixteenth century the commemorative use of the classicizing portrait medal had spread beyond the court environment into mercantile and humanistic circles. Medals were gifted as signs of friendship by intellectuals like Desiderius Erasmus of Rotterdam, who widely distributed his medal cast by Quentin Matsys in 1519; or they could be hung around the neck as tokens of affection or loyalty, as in the case of Nicholas Hilliard's gold medal of Queen Elizabeth I, cast in around 1580.

Another development in portraiture in the second half of the fifteenth century was the carved marble portrait bust. The earliest dated example is the 1453 bust by Mino da Fiesole of Piero 'the Gouty' de' Medici, who looks alertly and pugnaciously upwards to his left. He wears contemporary courtly dress, whereas his younger brother Giovanni is clothed in classicizing armour in his bust of 1456. The marble busts of the next decades follow the precedent of Roman imperial busts in carefully recording also the sitter's sometimes stridently expressed physiognomy and character. Unlike the forceful individuality of these male busts, female portrait busts routinely have an idealized

MINO DA FIESOLE, busts of Piero 'the Gouty' and Cosimo de' Medici.

impersonality, with undifferentiated facial surfaces and eyes decorously cast down-wards. The form of the early Renaissance bust, cut off horizontally above the elbows so as to stand on a flat surface rather than a plinth, marks a continuity with the late medieval tradition of the saint's head reliquary, most recently exemplified in Dona-tello's silver reliquary bust of *San Rossore* in Pisa. Not until Mantegna cut away the arms of his bronze self-portrait bust diagonally below the shoulders did a Renaissance sculptor closely follow classical precedent. This formula became standard in the mid-sixteenth century, in for example the monumental, idealizing bronze bust of *Cosimo I de' Medici* cast by Benvenuto Cellini in 1545. Earlier on Pietro Torrigiano, who was exiled from Florence after assaulting Michelangelo and breaking his nose, came to London where, still following the Florentine convention, he modelled portrait busts in terracotta of King Henry VII and members of his circle.

Painted portraits, a genre that became increasingly popular in the second half of the fifteenth century, show less response to the classical past than to contemporary developments in portraiture elsewhere in Europe, as will be explored later in this chapter. The sense that a painted portrait is the polychromed image of a contemporary sculpted portrait bust is conveyed in, for example, Giovanni Bellini's *Portrait of Doge Leonardo Loredan*. The strong individualization of physiognomies in portraits like Ghirlandaio's *Old Man and his Grandson* or Antonello da Messina's *Portrait of a Condottiere* may, however, owe as much to the sometimes hyper-real character of classical portrait busts as it does to Netherlandish art. This is an area in which the two principal sources of artistic inspiration during the early Renaissance—the classical and the contemporary—merge together in constructive fusion.

Drawing after the antique

Renaissance artists' growing interest in studying the classical past by making drawings after sculpture, and occasionally after other ancient Roman artefacts, offers a means of bringing together the themes treated in this section of Chapter 5. Seldom in the Italian Renaissance were drawings seen as finished artworks: Michelangelo's 'presentation' drawings for his friends Tommaso de' Cavalieri and Vittoria Colonna are the prime examples in this specialized category. Many drawings were made as preparatory studies as artists worked towards finished paintings or works in other media. Perhaps more often, though, drawings were made as records to be preserved in artists' workshops in portfolios; these could be consulted later and quarried for figures or other motifs to be included in finished works. Because artists were often concerned to achieve classical authenticity in their works, many portfolio drawings provided workshops with records of the classical past.

Thus the development of the Renaissance appreciation of classical objects may best be followed through drawings, even though the number that survives much before the mid-sixteenth century is not high. Classical Roman sculptures, both in relief and in the round, some of which are now lost, are recorded in portfolio drawings. But these also record other artefacts that were of special interest to learned antiquarians, such as carved Latin inscriptions, Roman coins and medals of concern to numismatists, and fragments of classical architecture. Travel eastwards in the Mediterranean into hostile, Ottoman-held territory was limited to all but the most intrepid, so it was through drawings made *in situ* by antiquarian travellers like Ciriaco d'Ancona that a few monuments of Greek architecture became known to intellectuals and artists in Italy.

The earliest surviving groups of drawings after classical sculpture were, ironically perhaps, made in the Roman workshops of the two greatest Italian late Gothic painters: Gentile da Fabriano and his successor, Antonio Pisanello. Figures like river gods, bacchanalian processions, and other motifs copied from classical relief sculpture were recorded in pen and ink, sometimes (to enhance longer-term preservation) on parchment rather than on paper. Although many of these figures derive from known or recognizable classical prototypes, the graphic style is essentially still late Gothic, and shows no visual engagement with the formal qualities of classical figure sculpture. In connection with his work as a medallist later in his career, Pisanello also made several carefully exact drawings of classical coins. Similar studies probably lay behind the profile heads derived from classical coins that enrich the illuminated borders of many Renaissance manuscripts, and major public works like the plinth of the Certosa of Pavia façade.

A group of drawings after the antique survives from sketchbooks used in the workshop of Benozzo Gozzoli, who owing to the decorative character of his Palazzo Medici Chapel frescos in Florence is often mistakenly considered essentially a late Gothic artist. These sheets include studies of classical Composite capitals and entablatures, and of workshop models posed as the *Spinario* or as one of the Quirinal *Horse-Tamers*.

In a study of a nude female marble torso (probably a *Venus*), the points of breakage of her limbs are recorded with archaeological precision. A similarly archaeological spirit rules over two sheets of record-drawings made probably in the 1450s of Latin inscriptions in Jacopo Bellini's Paris Book of Drawings. Bound in amongst numerous compositional drawings, these are reflections of north Italian antiquarian humanists' concern to collect, in books called 'sylloges', the texts of Latin inscriptions carved in classical times onto widely scattered marble slabs. Although his paintings appear essentially late Gothic in style, Jacopo Bellini had links with the Paduan antiquarian circle that also influenced Mantegna. Several other pages of his Paris Book of Drawings show groups including mythological figures brought together in subjects of obscure antiquarian meaning. These anticipate Mantegna's later paintings and finished, coloured drawings of quasi-classical reliefs and of allegorical or moralizing subjects. The archaeological quality of these and works like the *Triumphs of Caesar* imply that Mantegna also made, or collected, many copy-drawings after the antique.

By the turn of the century, formal volumes (as opposed to portfolios of loose sheets) of drawings after classical sculpture were standard materials in artists' workshops from which *all'antica* forms and motifs could be copied into paintings. A fine example is the so-called Codex Escurialensis, put together probably in the first decade of the sixteenth century by several draughtsmen associated with Domenico Ghirlandaio's workshop. Copies included in this volume are of celebrated classical sculptures such as the *Apollo Belvedere*, the *River God Nile*, then on the Quirinal, the *Marcus Aurelius*, and vignettes from reliefs on Trajan's Column. Several similar, largely academic, collections of drawings after the antique were put together during the first half of the sixteenth century. But by the turn of the century creative Italian painters increasingly sought original solutions to artistic problems, rather than relying on previously prepared motifs. Hardly any drawings by the great High Renaissance masters record classical objects. The principles of classical figure sculpture had by that time become part of Italian painters' instinctively understood vocabulary. Thus, for example, although classical resonances pervade Raphael's work, few motifs that are clearly indebted to classical figure sculpture survive in his oeuvre. Similarly, although Michelangelo gained considerably from his study of the classical past, very few of his carved or painted figures can be related directly to classical prototypes. The individual, monumental figure style of his Sistine Chapel ceiling frescos is a measure of his complete artistic independence.

Mimesis, or the imitation of nature

Introduction

Central to Italian Renaissance art theory was the concept of mimesis, the classical belief that nature must be the primary source for the artist's inspiration. Pliny tells several anecdotes about the mimetic skills of classical Greek painters. Of these, perhaps the most celebrated is the story of the competition between Zeuxis and Parrhasius. Zeuxis painted a bunch of grapes that was so accurate that birds flew to peck at the painted fruit, whereupon Parrhasius painted a curtain so realistically that Zeuxis asked that it be drawn aside to show his painting again. The brilliantly naturalistic swags of fruit, flowers, gourds, and insects sometimes ostentatiously placed in the foreground of paintings by north Italian artists like Carlo Crivelli or Mantegna were inspired by this and other Plinian anecdotes about pictorial naturalism. References to the primacy of nature in textual descriptions of classical paintings stimulated the emphasis on mimesis in Renaissance art theory. For Leon Battista Alberti, the art of painting 'arises from roots within Nature herself', and in his treatise *On Painting* he refers to what he himself has learned from nature, insisting on its central importance: 'The fundamental principle will be that all the steps of learning should be sought from Nature.' That great observer of natural forms and phenomena, Leonardo da Vinci, declared that 'painting...is the sole imitator of all the manifold works of nature'. To study natural forms, and to represent them faithfully in his paintings, became an essential aspect of the Renaissance artist's practice. Pisanello's acute observation of both structures and surface textures in his supremely naturalistic drawings of birds and animals shows that he gave primacy to the study of nature, just as Alberti recommended. Pisanello showed himself to be a master in mimesis, anticipating Leonardo's own nature studies by several decades.

Unfortunately, because of the almost total loss of classical paintings, Italian Renaissance artists could not experience how their classical forebears put the theory of mimesis into practice. They faced a serious challenge when early in the fifteenth century they strove to forge a new pictorial reality. Their search was for realism both in the natural forms represented and in the pictorial environment in which these forms were placed. The first issue confronting them was how to project behind the picture surface an illusionistic space that would nevertheless convince the onlooker of its three-dimensionality. This problem was first solved geometrically by Brunelleschi, who painted two (now lost) convincingly three-dimensional perspective townscapes of views in Florence. The geometrical construction of perspectively convincing pictorial space was first written up by Alberti in his *On Painting*, available to artists in his vernacular translation from the original Latin in 1436. This offered artists of Alberti's own generation, such as Donatello, in his San Lorenzo Old Sacristy reliefs, and Domenico Veneziano, in his St Lucy Altarpiece of *c*.1445, and of the next generations, such as Mantegna, Leonardo da Vinci, and notably Piero della Francesca, a blueprint for developing their own visually credible perspective constructions. The classic instance of geometrically exact pictorial perspective is Piero's *Flagellation*. As fine a mathematician as he was a painter, Piero wrote his own treatise on perspective, the *De prospectiva pingendi*, probably in the later 1460s. The perspective scheme of the left-hand side of the *Flagellation*, made up of an elaborately patterned chequerboard floor and the coffered vault of the Judgement Hall, has been proved to be mathematically correct: it may be seen as a self-conscious demonstration by Piero of his skills as both mathematician and painter. In Antonello da Messina's *St Jerome* the perspective layout of the tiled floor stretching back on either side of St Jerome's study similarly controls the recession deep into pictorial space.

PIERO DELLA FRANCESCA, *The Flagellation of Christ.*

Italy and the Netherlands

Once the problems of geometric perspective had been solved, and the methods of constructing pictorial spaces began to be applied in practice, artists next needed to populate their spaces with convincingly naturalistic forms. We have already explored how study of classical sculpture encouraged painters to represent the human figure with anatomical accuracy. But when approaching other aspects of pictorial realism, it is not surprising that, lacking classical paintings, early Renaissance painters and their patrons looked to another source of pictorial imitation of nature: the work of their Netherlandish contemporaries. The trickle of Netherlandish paintings that had reached princely collections by around the mid-fifteenth century increased to a flood by 1500. Moreover, many northern painters worked in Italy, notably Giovanni d'Alemagna from Ulm in Germany, who shared a workshop with Antonio Vivarini in Murano and Venice during the 1440s, and Justus of Ghent, who worked in Urbino for several years in the early 1470s. After the turn of the century many like Jan Gossaert, who worked in Rome in 1508–9, both introduced north European naturalism to Italian artists and exported Renaissance ideas to the Netherlands.

The *locus classicus* of Italians' aesthetic engagement with this body of work is a description of a triptych by Rogier van der Weyden that in 1449 belonged to Leonello d'Este, Marquis of Ferrara. The central panel of this triptych was a *Descent from the Cross* that may have looked quite like Rogier's Prado *Descent* discussed in Chapter 6, but with the figure-group set in front of a landscape. The description was written by Ciriaco d'Ancona, best known (as already noted) as an antiquarian humanist. Although an avid collector of drawings of classical architecture, artefacts, and inscriptions, Ciriaco was evidently deeply struck also by Rogier's mimetic skills:

> [The triptych] showed Adam and Eve, and Christ taken down from the Cross in a most pious image, with many men and women around him who wept with great grief; it is painted with admirable skill, one might say more divine than human. You seem to be seeing living faces breathing in those whom he wished to show as alive, and the semblance of death in the dead man and assuredly you might well say that so many draperies, so many cloaks of such various colours, so many dresses beautifully worked in crimson and gold, such living meadows, flowers, trees and leafy and shady hills ... such gold like unto gold, such pearls, gems and all the other things in the picture were not produced by the hand of a human artificer, but were born within it of nature herself, the universal parent.

From this description, four qualities of Rogier's triptych that particularly impressed Ciriaco d'Ancona can be picked out: realistic portraiture, naturalistic landscape, the representation of the lighting, colours, and surface textures of objects, and the emotionally affecting quality of this 'most pious' image.

The rise of oil-painting techniques

Before considering how Italian painters responded to these characteristics of Netherlandish painting, we need to recognize that their responses depended significantly on using a novel technique. The use of oil (usually linseed oil) as a binding medium was much refined and improved in the 1430s by Jan van Eyck, and exploited by Rogier van der Weyden and later painters in northern Europe for its colouristic and expressive potential. In mid-*quattrocento* Italy, on the other hand, egg tempera was still the standard medium for panel painting. Oil was used only occasionally, and then only for specialized purposes such as painting on walls, as in the bishop's chapel in Padua painted in 1437 by Giovanni d'Alemagna. Around 1440 Domenico Veneziano painted ornamental details in oil on the frescoed walls of the Portinari Chapel in Santa Maria Nuova, Florence, and as an assistant in Domenico's workshop, Piero della Francesca may have recognized the potential of the oil medium. Panel paintings by Piero of the early 1450s appear to be in a mixed tempera and oil technique, and some show surface wrinkling and craquelure that can be associated with an inexperienced oil painter. By the end of the century, however, oil was almost universally in use for easel painting by major painters like Leonardo da Vinci and Giovanni Bellini. Among the major exceptions were Botticelli, and Mantegna, who throughout his career painted in tempera on panel, although he did adopt the Netherlandish technique of painting on linen with an animal glue medium.

By 1460 the technique was taking firm hold in Italy: Cosmè Tura's *Calliope*, completed in about that year for Borso d'Este's *studiolo*, is thoroughly Rogierian in technique. From 1460 to 1463 the Duke of Milan's court painter, Zanetto Bugatto, trained in oil painting in Rogier van der Weyden's Brussels workshop, and it may have been through contact with him in Milan that Filarete, writing in his architectural treatise in 1464, knew to praise van Eyck and Rogier as having 'excelled in this colouring in oil'. Antonello da Messina's earliest works were in tempera, but by the later 1450s he was a proficient painter in oils, as were other painters in Naples perhaps as early as the 1440s. In 1466 the Pollaiuolo brothers painted the unusually Netherlandish altarpiece for the Cardinal of Portugal's chapel in San Miniato al Monte, Florence, in oils. In the next decade Leonardo da Vinci and others in Verrocchio's Florentine workshop were using oil: Leonardo's *Ginevra de'Benci* of 1474 is an early example. In his *Portrait of Jorg Fugger* of the same year, the Venetian Giovanni Bellini also adopted oil, which was the ideal medium for the particular aesthetic that he came to pursue.

Painted portraiture

In Rogier van der Weyden's lost *Descent from the Cross*, Ciriaco d'Ancona seemed 'to be seeing living faces breathing in those whom he wished to show as alive'. Although this well-used formula relates here to expressive physiognomies in general, as a principle of representation it can be applied in particular to portraiture. In this chapter we have examined the response of Italian sculptors to classical Roman portrait bust sculpture, and suggested that the treatment of facial features, skin surfaces, hairstyles, and other character-generating attributes was inspired by the realism of Roman practice. In Italian Renaissance painted portraits this source of visual stimulus was complemented by painters' experience of Netherlandish portraiture. A surprisingly large percentage of fifteenth-century Netherlandish portraits, from Jan van Eyck's *Arnolfini Marriage* to Hans Memling's *Man with a Coin of the Emperor Nero* (see Chapter 6) and beyond, were of Italian sitters—mostly diplomats, merchants, and bankers working at the Burgundian court or in the trading cities of Bruges and later Antwerp. The directness of gaze and strength of personality in many of these portraits may well have been a revelation to observers still accustomed to emotionally detached profile portraits, such as Pisanello's *Portrait of Leonello d'Este* dating from 1441. By mid-century, sitters from a wider social range were commissioning portraits, and this encouraged the development of new portrait types.

An early break with the idealized profile convention was Mantegna's robust rendering of Cardinal Ludovico Trevisan, who he portrayed at the Council of Mantua in 1459–60. Set against a very dark ground, Trevisan's powerfully modelled head resembles a portrait bust carved in the revived classical manner, and then polychromed with Netherlandish precision. His individualized curling hair and bristling eyebrows, his

ANDREA MANTEGNA, *Portrait of Cardinal Ludovico Trevisan.*

sharply cut features and facial markings, and his strongly expressive, unflinching eyes define Trevisan's character as forceful and uncompromising. Mantegna was later taken to task by Isabella d'Este for painting a portrait of her that 'has nothing of our likeness'—which probably meant that it was an unacceptably accurate and revealing record. By the date of Mantegna's Trevisan portrait, Antonello da Messina had adopted the treatment pioneered by Jan van Eyck in the 1430s: the three-quarter view lit from the side and set against a plain black background. Antonello imitated Jan's use of the finest of brushes to articulate each hair individually, and to define the morphology of the features and the glint of light in the eyes.

These developments in naturalistic portraiture, apparently honest in recording the finest details of the sitter's physiognomy, demonstrate the new desire to explore and

ANTONELLO DA MESSINA, *Portrait of a Man* ('il Condottiere').

distinguish prominent qualities of personality—a significant aspect of that concern to define individual character that was Burckhardt's hallmark for the Renaissance man. Botticelli and his youthful sitter in the Uffizi *Young Man Holding a Medal of Cosimo de' Medici* probably knew Memling's *Man with Coin of Emperor Nero* (see Chapter 6): dating from around 1470, Botticelli's sitter precociously poses frontally, makes eye contact with the beholder, and like Memling's sitter is set against a distant landscape. A few years later Leonardo da Vinci painted his innovatory female portrait of *Ginevra de'Benci*, who stares coldly and indecorously at the observer; and in his *Portrait of Cecilia Gallerani*, of around 1490, he explored the transitory movements of the sitter's pose and hands. In the *Mona Lisa* Leonardo created an iconic portrait formula that was immediately and productively taken up by the young Raphael, in his portraits of *Maddalena Strozzi* and, around 1515, of *Baldassare Castiglione*.

Landscape

Ciriaco d'Ancona's neat encapsulation of the character of the Rogierian landscape—'such living meadows, flowers, trees and leafy and shady hills'—recalls Alberti's discussion of

ANGELO MACCAGNINO DA SIENA (?), *Polyhymnia.*

pictorial variety, praiseworthy if it 'contained a properly arranged mixture of old men, youths, boys, horses, sheep, buildings and provinces'. This is one of a number of Alberti's comments and recommendations that suggest that he too had studied Netherlandish paintings, perhaps on a journey north in the early 1430s. Ciriaco is also echoed by Bartolomeo Fazio, who in 1456 wrote of a painting by Jan van Eyck that it included 'horses, minute figures of men, mountains, groves, hamlets, and castles, carried out with such skill you would believe one was fifty miles distant from another'. The receding landscape of Jan's *Virgin of Chancellor Rolin* (see Chapter 6) could be described almost in these terms; as could the expansive and minutely populated landscape of Domenico Veneziano's *Adoration of the Magi* tondo of around 1440. When Ciriaco admired Rogier's *Descent* triptych, the painter of the Muse *Polyhymnia*, the earliest of nine *Muses* for Leonello d'Este's *studiolo*, had just adopted a Netherlandish formula known as the 'plateau' composition for the landscape. The observer looks down and past the standing figure, and beyond three horsemen in the middle distance to a townscape and a meticulously rendered, rich green landscape of rolling hills and tilled fields.

As Jan van Eyck demonstrated, oil was the ideal medium for executing buildings, trees, and other microscopic landscape features set far back in pictorial space. Of Italian painters, Antonello da Messina came closest to his landscape style: the vignettes in his *St Jerome* are good examples of his detailed observation and miniaturist depiction. Piero della Francesca set his *Battista Sforza* and *Federigo da Montefeltro* portraits, of the early 1470s, against minutely transcribed, extensive topographical vistas. In his late *Nativity* Piero left unfinished a landscape vignette that is richly populated with Netherlandish landscape forms such as rocks and bushes. Less interested than contemporaries in naturalistic landscape depiction, Mantegna nonetheless painted a highly atmospheric view of the lakes and marshes visible from the Castello di San Giorgio in the Palazzo Ducale in Mantua, seen through the opening at the back of the architectural space of his Madrid *Death of the Virgin*. The tonality and colour of the lighting in Giovanni Bellini's *Crucifixion* of perhaps the mid-1450s, and the rounded bushes reflected on the surface of the river, are indebted to qualities of the landscapes in a triptych on linen by Dieric Bouts that, it seems, was accessible in Venice by around 1450. Similarly, the rocky surface of the summit of Mount Calvary reflects the Eyckian *Crucifixion* in the Ca' d'Oro which was almost certainly already in the Veneto by the same date. Bellini's response to nature in landscape representation reaches its climax in his great *Ecstasy of St Francis* of around 1480, in which a glowing light picks up the minute details of terrain, flora, and fauna that represent St Francis's own engagement with the natural world around him.

In Florence during the 1460s the Pollaiuolo brothers developed a minutely observed topographical treatment of landscape: small vignettes of the River Arno valley are seen in the 1466 Cardinal of Portugal's chapel altarpiece, and more expansively and atmospherically in their great *Martyrdom of St Sebastian* altarpiece of 1475. Concerned as ever with atmospheric perspective—the lightening of colours and tonality with recession into deep landscape space—Leonardo da Vinci generated for his early 1470s *Annunciation* a soft-focus view of a harbour with jagged mountains behind. From about this date, painters in Florence copied specific landscape motifs from paintings by Memling into their own works. The lines of rounded bushes in the landscape of a Memling male portrait in New York were reused verbatim in a *Madonna and Child* from

ANTONELLO DA MESSINA, *St Jerome.*

Verrocchio's workshop (Paris, Louvre); and the motif of a watermill in the central panel of the triptych painted by Memling in around 1480 for Bernardo Pagagnotti, the Florentine Archbishop of Vaison, was much imitated, by Filippino Lippi, Fra Bartolommeo, and others.

GIOVANNI BELLINI, *Crucifixion*.

ANTONIO AND PIERO POLLAIUOLO, Cardinal of Portugal's chapel altarpiece.

Colour, light, and texture

Ciriaco d'Ancona vividly expressed his admiration for the treatment of materials—minerals, for example, pearls and precious stones, and fabrics—that he observed in Rogier van der Weyden's *Descent from the Cross*: 'so many draperies, so many cloaks of such various colours, so many dresses beautifully worked in crimson and gold ... such gold like unto gold, such pearls, gems and all the other things in the picture'. When in Ferrara painting portraits for Leonello d'Este shortly before Ciriaco wrote his description, Mantegna too probably saw and admired Rogier's triptych. Although working in tempera, Mantegna achieved strikingly convincing representations of minerals: the multicoloured marble from which the huge vase carried by a soldier in the fourth canvas of the *Triumphs of Caesar* is carved, for example, or the veined and coloured marble backgrounds in his grisaille paintings. Antonello da Messina shows similar care in depicting inorganic materials in the stonework frame of his St Jerome and the lustrous gleam of the copper bowl placed on the step.

Gemstones and pearls were key indicators of wealth and status during the Renaissance period, and the accuracy of their depiction grew in importance. Commenting on the painting of the Muse *Clio* in Leonello d'Este's *studiolo*, Ciriaco d'Ancona wrote in 1449, 'what I had seen from one point as round, shining pearls and gleaming gems projecting from the base of the gold-coloured dais appear from another point as even, smooth panels of flat pigment; I am indeed bound to marvel exceedingly at this painter's talent.' It could well be that the painter of this panel, whom Ciriaco identifies as Angelo Maccagnino da Siena, the 'distinguished imitator of the celebrated art of Rogier [van der Weyden]', derived his skills in depicting the three-dimensionality and highlighting of pearls and gemstones from his knowledge of Rogier's work. Piero della Francesca also developed high skill in the precise placing of glinting highlights in pearls, for example in the necklace worn in her portrait by Battista Sforza.

PIERO DELLA FRANCESCA, *Portrait of Battista Sforza.*

Similar skills were shown by the Pollaiuolo brothers in St Vincent's bejewelled robes in the Cardinal of Portugal's chapel altarpiece. They also showed here a precocious sensitivity in the representation of fabric textures—the plush velvets of St Vincent's robe and St Eustace's doublet, with its white fur lining, the costly brocades worn by both St Eustace and St James, and the fashionable felt hat at St James's feet. Rich brocade fabrics had already been represented in a fully developed Netherlandish technique around 1460 by Cosmè Tura and others in the *Muses* for the d'Este *studiolo*; and in the 1502 *Portrait of Doge Leonardo Loredan* Giovanni Bellini anticipates the sumptuous textures of Venetian High Renaissance painted fabrics by clothing the doge in a rich brocade embroidered in thread of gold. Echoing Alberti's earlier advice in *On Painting*, the gold is depicted using pigment in the Rogierian manner that Ciriaco admired in his description of 'gold like unto gold', rather than by applying gold leaf or mordant gilding; indeed, already by the middle of the fifteenth century metallic gold was seldom used by Italian painters.

'Devout' painting

Ciriaco d'Ancona was also struck by the strength of expression of human feelings in Rogier's *Descent* triptych. It was 'a most pious image, with many men and women around [Christ] who wept with great grief'. This succinct description was echoed by Bartolomeo Fazio's praise for Rogier's achievement in the Ferrara triptych in showing 'Christ brought down from the cross, Mary his Mother, Mary Magdalen, and Joseph, their grief and tears so represented, you would not think them other than real'. In turn these comments reflect Alberti's advice in *On Painting* about observing the decorum of emotional expression: 'Nature provides . . .', he wrote, 'that we mourn with the mourners, laugh with those who laugh, and grieve with the grief-stricken.' As an example, he cited Giotto's *Navicella* in which the painter 'represented the eleven disciples struck with fear and wonder at the sight of their colleague walking on the water, each showing such clear signs of his agitation in his face and entire body that their individual emotions are discernible in every one of them'. A rich range of emotional response amongst Christ's apostles is the key to the expressive success of Leonardo's *Last Supper*. In parallel, Leonardo wrote extensively about variety and decorum in depicting human feelings. 'That figure', he wrote, 'is most praiseworthy which best expresses through its actions the passion of its mind . . . the motions and postures of figures should display the true mental state of the originator of these motions, in such a way that they could not signify anything else.' An early example of the Italian Renaissance painter's concern to explore and illustrate extreme human feelings is the contrast in Masaccio's *Expulsion* fresco between Adam and Eve's emotional responses to their ejection from Paradise. Similar expressions of raw emotion can be found in later dramatic works like Donatello's *Deposition* on the northern bronze pulpit in San Lorenzo, Florence, Botticelli's Munich *Pietà*, and Raphael's 1511 *Massacre of the Innocents* engraving that he circulated widely as an exemplar of his creative abilities.

But the notion of 'a most pious image' can apply also to intimate paintings made to stimulate personal religious devotion and contemplation. In 1460 the Florentine Alessandra Strozzi described a Netherlandish painting of the *Holy Face* as 'a devout figure, and beautiful'. Recognizing the special devotional strength of northern European art, Michelangelo famously commented that 'Flemish painting...will generally please the devout better than any painting of Italy, which will never cause him to shed a tear, whereas that of Flanders will cause him to shed many....' Michelangelo's single-minded preoccupation with the monumental human figure limited his opportunities for displays of pictorial verisimilitude. As first and foremost a sculptor of the human figure, he showed minimal interest in portraiture, in the painted landscape, or in hyperexpressive displays of religious feeling. Many Italian fifteenth-century painters, however, responded to the expressive mood of Netherlandish paintings, leading them to extrapolate beyond the sentiment of late medieval religious images to explore how to depict 'devout' or 'pious' feelings in the context of the new naturalism of Renaissance art.

The 'Madonna and Child' subject lends itself to the expression of emotions like tenderness, maternal love, or intimations of grief, and these were explored by Donatello from the 1440s through the close juxtaposition of his figures' faces in *Madonna and Child* reliefs. Interest grew in how physical interlinkings of the two figures could provide foundations for building their emotional bonds. As the figures in his *Benois Madonna* respond to each other's movements, Leonardo da Vinci considered the playful, fluid interweave of their poses and gestures, and how to convey pictorially a shared warmth of human feelings. Deeply influenced by paradigmatic works like this, Raphael produced a series of increasingly intimate and warm-hearted depictions of maternal love, culminating in the *Madonna della sedia* of around 1514. Following the curve of the tondo frame, the Virgin leans her head over to bring it into contact with Christ's face as she embraces him protectively in her arms. Stronger sentiments of dismay or grief were developed in fifteenth-century representations of the Pietà, an evolution that reached its touchingly distressing climax in Michelangelo's marble St Peter's *Pietà* of 1497. In the angular anatomy of the Christ's emaciated limbs, Cosmè Tura responded stridently once more in his small Venice *Pietà* of around 1460 to the emotionalism of Rogier van der Weyden's Passion scenes. The same source may explain Giovanni Bellini's expressive display of the pitiful sorrow felt by the Virgin and St John the Evangelist in the Brera *Pietà* of the 1460s as, set behind a parapet and against a chilly grey-blue sunrise, they hold between them Christ's pallid, slumped corpse. Numerous studies of the Virgin Mary's emotional life ranging from her early motherhood happiness to her grief after Christ's death demonstrate Italian Renaissance artists' wealth of responses to the mimetic realism of contemporary north European art. These responses were in turn encouraged by the public's growing desire for images in which human feelings with which they could identify are communicated by credible human figures.

RAFFAELLO SANZIO

N. AD URBINO 6 APRILE 1483
M. A ROMA 6 APRILE 1520

MADONNA della SEGGIOLA

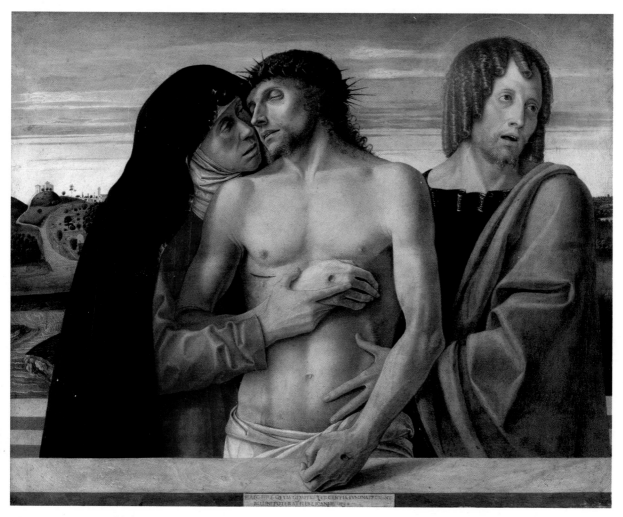

GIOVANNI BELLINI, *Pietà*.

Conclusion

By the turn of the century, Italian artists had learned from the study of the classical past how to depict convincingly three-dimensional human forms that were articulate in movement and expression. They had also effectively solved the problems presented by the new attention paid to the classical theory of mimesis. Few if any significant Renaissance painters experienced any difficulties in exploiting geometrical perspective to generate convincing pictorial spaces. Related issues, such as pictorial composition

Opposite: RAPHAEL, *Madonna della sedia.*

and the relationships in narrative art between the figures and their spatial environment, had generally been solved by the death of Raphael in 1520. Leonardo da Vinci, who died in 1519, undertook extraordinary investigations into human anatomy and physiology, although the outcomes of this detailed work were not available to painters and sculptors to inform their depictions of the human figure. Like Leonardo, Michelangelo studied human anatomy deeply, and he exploited his understanding of muscular function when showing the dynamic movements of the *Battle of Cascina* soldiers, or the monumentally grand figures of *Prophets and Sibyls* on the Sistine Chapel ceiling. Leonardo also extensively studied the natural world in writings on such subjects as landscape, geology, and flora and fauna, and in drawings and finished paintings. In his turn, Raphael learned crucially valuable lessons from studying the artistic practices of both Leonardo and Michelangelo when he worked in Florence between 1504 and 1508. Reinforced by study also of Michelangelo's Sistine Chapel frescos, Raphael painted in the following decade the *Madonna della sedia*, the *School of Athens*, the *Galatea*, and the *Portrait of Julius II*, to name only a few of his most original creations. In these he drew together the outcomes of a range of fifteenth-century artistic endeavours to generate works which stand at the zenith of Italian Renaissance artistic achievement.

CHAPTER 6

Art and Architecture in Flanders and Beyond

PAULA NUTTALL AND RICHARD WILLIAMS

Definitions and problems

AROUND 1420 a new pictorial language emerged in Flanders, based on the faithful observation of reality and the virtuosic application of oil paint. This visual revolution, associated primarily with Jan van Eyck (*fl.* 1422–41), was to have far-reaching artistic consequences as far afield as Italy, as discussed in Chapter 5. Chronologically, Van Eyck's innovations coincide with the equally momentous artistic developments that occurred in Florentine art around 1420. Yet although Van Eyck and his successors, notably Rogier van der Weyden (*fl.* 1427–64), shared many of the aims of their Italian peers, and exceeded their achievements in certain respects, to apply the term 'Renaissance', in the conventional sense of a classically inspired 'rebirth', to the visual arts in northern Europe is unhelpful for much of the period under discussion. The art of fifteenth-century Flanders was no less innovative and influential than that of Italy, but its creators and consumers were not, for the most part, aware of, or concerned with, the revival of a classically based culture. It was not until after 1500 that the cultural climate of Italian humanism, with its attendant influence on the visual arts, began to spread north of the Alps. Used as a convenient period label, the term 'northern Renaissance' suggests a parallel with 'Italian Renaissance', but is only valid, strictly speaking, for sixteenth-century art, and even then not universally—Jan Gossaert (*fl.* 1503–32), who painted Italianate nudes and architecture, and classical mythological subjects, might be termed a 'Renaissance' artist, but this is less helpful for Pieter Bruegel (*fl.* 1550–69), on whom Italian art made scant impact. Indeed, northern art of this period may be regarded as 'late Gothic' or 'late medieval' as much as 'Renaissance', as is evidenced by the title of the 2003 exhibition at the Victoria and Albert Museum, London—*Gothic: Art for England, 1400–1547*.

These problems of classification highlight the difficulty of accommodating northern art, particularly that of the fifteenth century, into the concept of the Renaissance as it is conventionally understood. This concept was defined by nineteenth-century historians, for whom the paradigm was the art of sixteenth-century Italy, and who perpetuated the polarization of 'medieval' and 'Renaissance' first signalled by Italian humanists, with its notion of the 'unenlightened' Middle Ages, to which north European art was perceived as belonging. The traditional view of 'progressive/ Renaissance' Italy versus 'backward/medieval' northern Europe is tellingly illustrated by the titles of two seminal cultural histories written in the mid-nineteenth and early twentieth centuries: Jacob Burckhardt's *The **Civilisation** of the Renaissance in Italy*, and Johannes Huizinga's *The **Autumn*** (or, in earlier translations, the ***Waning***) *of the Middle Ages*, which deals with France and the Netherlands in the same period (our emphases). The typecasting of fifteenth-century northern art as 'medieval', and therefore 'inferior' to that of Italy, has proved hard to shrug off. Although some early and mid-twentieth-century cultural and art historians drew attention to the innovativeness of fifteenth-century Flemish painting, and to its positive reception in Italy, it is only comparatively recently that the role played by northern art in Italian Renaissance visual culture has begun to be fully acknowledged. And even today, many more books are written, exhibitions staged, and courses taught on Italian Renaissance art than that of the north.

The relative value placed on Italian over northern art of this period owes much to the legacy of Giorgio Vasari's *Lives of the Artists* (1550, second edition 1568). Vasari was a Tuscan, trained as a painter in Florence, whose art and artists he knew well, and employed by its Medici ruler, to whom his book was dedicated; unsurprisingly, therefore, he extols the achievements of Florentine artists above all others. Northern artists, including Van Eyck, Rogier van der Weyden, and the great German engraver Martin Schongauer (*fl.* 1471–91), are dealt with summarily, in a single paragraph in the introductory section of the *Lives*, and although they are occasionally mentioned elsewhere in the book, it is usually to highlight the superiority of Italian art. For instance, Albrecht Dürer (1471–1528), peerless in the field of black-and-white design, was in Vasari's view disadvantaged by his northern style: he 'would have been the greatest artist of his age, had he been born an Italian'. By the time the first history of Netherlandish painting was written, Karel van Mander's *Het Schilderboek* (1604), Vasari's views on what constituted 'good' art were held by most cultivated Europeans; indeed, Van Mander's book was modelled on Vasari's *Lives*. Increasingly, in the centuries that followed, those northern artists—the majority of them, in fact—who did not conform to a Vasarian model of classically inspired figures, logically constructed spatial depth, and the pre-eminence of history painting, found scant favour with critics and collectors. Yet great artists such as Van Eyck, Schongauer, and Bruegel should not be judged by the alien standards of Renaissance Italy but by those of the rich artistic traditions of northern Europe.

This chapter is not, however, concerned with those traditions but with northern art in relation to the ideas of the Renaissance. It is divided into two parts, around the watershed of 1500, after which date the impact of the Italian Renaissance is increasingly evident in northern art, albeit mediated to a greater or lesser degree by local traditions. The first section, on the fifteenth century, concentrates not so much on the reception of Italian Renaissance art—although this will also be addressed—as on northern innovations which parallel or even anticipate developments in Italy. It will suggest that, while not fitting a classically inspired Renaissance paradigm, northern art of the fifteenth century *can* in some respects be considered 'Renaissance'.

It is, of course, impossible in a short account to cover artistic production across 'the north', by which is conventionally meant all of Europe outside Italy—not only the lands north of the Alps, but also the Iberian Peninsula—a vast geographical area over which Flanders, in the fifteenth century, exercised a hegemony in the visual arts comparable to that exercised by Italy in the sixteenth. It is therefore on Flanders that much of this chapter focuses, although 'Flanders' itself poses problems of terminology. It is often used to connote the geographical area encompassing modern-day Belgium, the Netherlands, Luxembourg, and parts of northern and eastern France ruled in the fifteenth century by the French dukes of Burgundy and subsequently by the Spanish Habsburgs. Flanders in reality, however, was only one (albeit the wealthiest, in the fourteenth and fifteenth centuries) of the provinces comprising this region, for which modern scholars prefer the more accurate 'Netherlands' or 'Low Countries'.

Nor is it possible to deal even-handedly with the wide range of media perfected by northern artists, including manuscript illumination, textiles, goldsmiths' work, and monumental sculpture. In the fifteenth century, the art form that arguably had the furthest reach in terms of innovation and renown, and which shared the most common ground with Italian Renaissance art, was Netherlandish panel painting, and the first section of this chapter focuses to a large extent on this. Central to the discussion is the new visual language developed by Jan van Eyck and Rogier van der Weyden, based on the close observation of reality, as exemplified by Van Eyck's *Virgin of Chancellor Rolin*, with its near miraculous evocation of material objects, lifelike figures, and distant panorama, made possible by the unprecedentedly skilful application of oil paint. These mimetic aspects of the Netherlandish *ars nova* (new art), a term adopted by the twentieth-century art historian Erwin Panofsky to suggest a correlation with, and at the same time a distinction from, the Italian Renaissance, are explored in the first subsection. Portraiture, which developed as a result of the new verisimilitude, and which embodies the archetypally 'Renaissance' concept of the discovery of the individual, fame, and posterity, is discussed in the second subsection, while a third focuses on the major technical innovation of printmaking in Germany. A final subsection considers fifteenth-century responses to the Italian Renaissance, including in the neglected area of architecture.

The second half of this chapter focuses on the sixteenth century, when the dominant direction of influence shifted from southwards to northwards, and Italian understandings of classical antiquity reshaped the artistic traditions of the north. Important humanist scholars emerged in the Netherlands, and their championing of classical texts

JAN VAN EYCK, *The Virgin of Chancellor Rolin, c.*1435. Nicolas Rolin, Chancellor of Burgundy, is shown at prayer before the Virgin and Child in this small image made for private devotion; the sumptuous setting suggests both Rolin's worldly status and that of the Queen of Heaven.

soon extended to a scholarly interest in the artistic and architectural legacy of the ancient world. In due course this knowledge was assimilated into the work of artists, sculptors, architects, and printmakers, and the creative imaginations of the north were increasingly informed by the classical ideals that had transformed the arts in Italy.

The fifteenth century

Jan van Eyck, Rogier van der Weyden, and the Netherlandish *ars nova*

Jan van Eyck and Rogier van der Weyden were regarded by fifteenth-century Italian humanists (such as Ciriaco of Ancona and Fazio, discussed in Chapter 5) not only as the greatest painters of their day, but as having surpassed the fabled painters of antiquity. Whilst recognizing that Netherlandish paintings were not classical in style (at this date not seen as a shortcoming), early Renaissance observers may well have considered such works as the modern equivalents of the lost masterpieces of antiquity, the hallmarks of which had been fidelity to nature and technical virtuosity. Certainly no painters since the classical era had succeeded in reproducing reality with quite such dazzling verisimilitude, and this ensured a warm reception for Netherlandish painting in Italian humanist circles. Yet the verisimilitude of Netherlandish painting itself belongs in a wider European artistic context, independent of the classical tradition, of growing interest in describing the visible world. This had already been developing in the fourteenth century, prompted by ideas that were arguably more 'late medieval' than 'Renaissance', notably the stress laid by theologians on the humanity of Christ and the Virgin, and the requirement for devotional images to prompt an empathetic response in the viewer.

The evolution of painting in Flanders cannot be charted with the same precision as in Italy, owing to the scarcity of surviving physical and documentary evidence; the Netherlands, unlike Italy, has suffered from the destructive effects of the Reformation, as well as of innumerable wars. It is generally agreed, however, that the first datable work painted in the new style is the Ghent Altarpiece, begun by Hubert van Eyck (d.1426) and completed by his brother Jan in 1432. At a date contemporary with Masaccio's ground-breaking Brancacci Chapel frescos and *Trinity*, therefore, the Netherlandish *ars nova* was fully fledged. The weighty figures of the Ghent Altarpiece are as persuasively lifelike as Masaccio's, their three-dimensionality similarly achieved through tonal modelling in light and shade. They occupy illusionistic, three-dimensional space (constructed, however, without the aid of mathematical perspective, unknown in the Netherlands before the late 1450s). One of the most virtuosic figures in this multi-panelled work is that of Adam, shown as if emerging from a shadowy niche beneath a fictive stone relief of the Sacrifice of Cain and Abel. One foreshortened foot protrudes into the viewer's space, while cast shadows reinforce the impression of his physical presence, as do the meticulously observed muscles, veins, and fine hairs on his body. Undoubtedly studied from life, this is as realistic a rendition of the human figure as that in Masaccio's Brancacci *Expulsion*.

JAN VAN EYCK, *Adam, c.1426–32*. Adam's pose, his arm across his chest and his genitals modestly covered, is based on the well-known antique statue of the *Venus Pudica* (Modest Venus).

The kinship between Masaccio and the Van Eycks, cornerstones of their respective schools of painting, has long been acknowledged, although it is not necessary to posit a journey to Italy for Jan, as some scholars have done, to account for this. Van Eyck possessed exceptional powers of observation, and could moreover build on a strong pre-existing tradition of naturalism, particularly evident in the work of Franco-Flemish artists employed at the French courts around 1400. An incipient interest in space, both interior and exterior, is found in the manuscript paintings of the Boucicaut Master and the Limbourg brothers, while the enamelled metalwork statuettes of the Parisian reliquary known as the Goldenes Rössl (Altötting, Schatzkammer), despite their extravagant materiality, are small masterpieces of naturalistic sculpture. Still more lifelike are the monumental sculptures of Claus Sluter (*fl.* 1379–1406), notably the *Well of Moses* at the Charterhouse of Champmol outside Dijon. Sluter's life-size figures of prophets were originally polychromed, enhancing their naturalistic appearance. Individualized and expressive, with their weighty draperies and scrolls, finely observed costume details, and facial features, they are as arrestingly realistic as the statues carved a generation later by Donatello and Nanni di Banco in Florence.

The catalyst in the emergence of Eyckian painting, however, was undoubtedly the oil technique. Far from being a new invention, as claimed by Vasari and successive writers until relatively recently, oil (usually linseed) was already well established as the medium for northern European panel painting by the thirteenth century, although it appears to have been temporarily displaced by a fashion for Italian egg tempera in the generation preceding Van Eyck. Its reintroduction needs to be seen in the context of increasing interest in naturalism, and the concomitant need for paint to be able to describe what the eye sees. In what seems to have been more a conceptual leap than a technical one, Van Eyck and his contemporaries, such as the Master of Flémalle—generally identified with Robert Campin (*c.*1379–1444), the master of Rogier van der Weyden—exploited the descriptive potential of the traditional oil medium to realize their vision of the material world.

Oil possesses an almost infinite variety of optical and handling properties. Many pigments mixed in oil appear translucent, enabling the layering of glazes of paint to create deep shadows, producing a tonal range which corresponds more closely to perceived reality than the bright colours and relatively light tonal spectrum produced by egg tempera and fresco. Oil dries slowly and can be blended while still wet, permitting imperceptible brushwork, but can also, depending on the pigment used, appear opaque, and the paint can be applied in varying thicknesses, to create highlights and a range of textural effects. One notable development facilitated by this was the depiction of gold using yellow and brown pigment, rather than gold leaf, a virtuoso technique introduced by Van Eyck's generation, at least a decade before Alberti wrote of similar effects in *On Painting*. Indeed, as noted in Chapter 5, Netherlandish approaches to light and colour chime with a number of Alberti's precepts, such as his advocacy of dark tonality and the sparing use of white.

CLAUS SLUTER, *The Well of Moses*, 1395–1404. Not in fact a well, but the base of the Great Cross (destroyed) in the cloister of the monastery founded by Philip the Bold, Duke of Burgundy, as a dynastic mausoleum. It shows Philip in the guise of the prophet Jeremiah, seen here reading a book.

The naturalism of early Netherlandish painting was not limited to describing the outward appearances of things, but also encompassed the depiction of emotion—what Alberti called 'the movements of the mind'. In Rogier van der Weyden's masterpiece *The Descent from the Cross*, minutely observed facial expressions and gestures convey a range of emotions from restrained pity to uncontrolled anguish; figures totter and fall, tears stream, garments become unlaced, and headgear unravels. At the same time, Rogier invites the viewer to share these emotions, through the poignant juxtaposition of the dead Christ and the death-like swooning Virgin. Passion imagery offered great scope for the depiction of grief, but other emotional registers were also explored. A painting by Rogier in Genoa, described by Fazio, showed a woman bathing with two youths peeping at her, 'remarkable for their grins'. Once again, parallels exist with Alberti's writings, notably his advice to painters on eliciting an emotional response by painting appropriate emotions, so that 'we mourn with the mourners, laugh with those who laugh, and grieve with the grief-stricken'.

ROGIER VAN DER WEYDEN, *The Descent from the Cross*, c.1436. This large altarpiece was made for the chapel of the Guild of Crossbowmen at Leuven. A sixteenth-century Italian viewer asserted that 'Michelangelo would not be ashamed to have painted it'.

Yet brilliantly though early Netherlandish painters represented both external and internal realities, they were also capable of manipulating reality for particular expressive, intellectual, or spiritual ends. On one level, the emotional impact of Rogier's *Descent* depends on the claustrophobic presentation of the figures close to the picture plane, and on the disconcerting perception that they are simultaneously contained in a shallow golden box, and standing outside on rocks and grass. On another level, the box itself suggests the gilded casing of a carved altarpiece, familiar to fifteenth-century audiences; the inference is of a polychromed altarpiece brought to life by the painter's skill. The seductively 'real' setting of the *Rolin Virgin* is challenged by the realization that the chamber and garden in the foreground are hovering impossibly over the city and river beyond; what we see is perhaps a heavenly vision evoked by the Chancellor's prayer. Adam's protruding foot in the Ghent Altarpiece, or the famous mirror in Van Eyck's *Arnolfini Portrait* (London, National Gallery), which reflects figures who are implicitly standing outside the picture, in the viewer's space, blur the boundaries of reality in other, equally sophisticated ways. These representational ambiguities recall the illusionistic games played in Masaccio's *Trinity*, which likewise invokes multiple realities with its *trompe l'œil* architecture and tomb, its lifelike figures and visionary subject matter.

Painted portraiture

In actuality, Chancellor Rolin, praying in front of the devotional image painted for him by Van Eyck, could see his action mirrored in his portrait, and thereby envision himself in the presence of the Virgin and Child. Concomitantly, the portrait served to record his likeness for future generations, perpetuating his memory. Philip the Bold, portrayed as the prophet Jeremiah on Sluter's *Well of Moses* in the great cloister of Champmol, knew that his likeness would have confronted the monks emerging into the cloister from the church in which he would be buried, keeping his memory alive and prompting prayers for his soul. Although this subsection will focus on the independent single-figure portrait, the above examples indicate not only the variety of media, formats, and contexts, but also the complexity of motives and representational choices available for portraiture in the Renaissance. Fundamental to all portraits, however, in the north as much as in Italy, was the desire to record an individual's appearance and preserve their memory. In Alberti's words, 'Painting...not only makes the absent present...but moreover makes the dead seem almost alive. Even after many centuries they are recognised with great pleasure and great admiration for the painter', while Albrecht Dürer remarked in 1508/9 that one of the prime functions of painting was 'preserving a person's appearance after his death'. This presupposes a sense of the self, and a desire for personal commemoration, concepts that have long been identified, like portraiture itself, with the Burckhardtian idea of the 'birth of the individual' in the Renaissance.

Lifelikeness was necessarily a prerequisite for portraiture, and Netherlandish artists, with their mimetic skills and their command of the oil medium, were not surprisingly in the vanguard of painted portraiture for most of the fifteenth century. In this regard they were building on a long-standing tradition of independent painted portraiture in northern Europe, judging from the earliest surviving examples, of *John II, King of France* (Paris, Louvre) and *Rudolf IV of Austria* (Vienna, Dom und Diozesanmuseum), of the 1360s. In the fourteenth century portraits were the preserve of the ruling elite, which may help to explain the prevalence of the profile view, perhaps derived from ruler imagery on antique coins (although *Rudolf IV* is notably in three-quarters view). By the 1430s, however, demand for independent portraits had burgeoned amongst the non-elite in prosperous Netherlandish towns, coinciding with the widespread adoption of the three-quarters view. This format is inherently more lifelike than the profile, since it reveals more of the face and hence of character, and creates a stronger impression of three-dimensional form.

Typical of this new type of highly naturalistic painted portrait is Van Eyck's *Man in a Red Turban* (see page 218). Unlike the profile view, which imposes a distance between the sitter and the viewer, the direct gaze produces an effect of immediacy and intimacy. Volume is suggested by the use of strong directional lighting (as in other works by Jan, such as the Ghent *Adam*), while the textures conveyed in the meticulously recorded details of stubble and fur, veins and wrinkles, reinforce the impression of physical presence. It is as though the sitter is physically present but just out of reach, an impression reinforced by the illusionistic inscriptions painted as though actually carved into the frame, which challenge our perception of what is painted and what is real.

By mid-century painters had begun to portray sitters in naturalistic settings. In place of the plain dark backgrounds favoured by Van Eyck and Van der Weyden, painters began to place the sitter in the corner of a room with a window, as in Petrus Christus' (*fl.* 1444–75) *Portrait of Edward Grimstone* or Dieric Bouts's (*c.*1400–75) *Portrait of a Man* (both London, National Gallery). The most enduringly successful innovation, however, was the landscape background, the hallmark of portraits by Hans Memling (*fl.* 1465–94), which were popular with expatriate Italian patrons in the Netherlands, and highly influential in Italy. Memling's *Portrait of a Man with a Coin of the Emperor Nero* (see page 219) probably represents Bernardo Bembo, a Venetian humanist and ambassador to the Burgundian court. He is shown close to the picture plane, his head silhouetted against an expanse of sky, and a distant landscape of rolling hills, trees and water, and minute figures extending behind him. Earlier portraitists, including Van Eyck, had often included hands, placed as if resting on the edge of the actual frame; here, the hand appears to protrude into the viewer's space, as if presenting the antique Roman coin to our scrutiny. Not only does this heighten the sense of the sitter's physical presence but, as a portrait within a portrait, the coin introduces a subtle play of genres—classical and contemporary, painted and sculptural—and, as an object from the distant past, invokes the role of portraiture itself, in relation to posterity and commemoration of the individual.

The Renaissance sense of self-consciousness provided fertile soil for the development of the self-portrait, both in Italy and in northern Europe, which produced the

JAN VAN EYCK, *Man in a Red Turban*, 1433. The frame is original; the inscriptions read, at the top (in Dutch, but written in Greek letters), 'As I can', and below, in Latin, 'Jan van Eyck made me, 1433, 21 October'. The 'turban' is a *chaperon*, a type of headgear worn by middle- and upper-class men.

earliest independent painted examples. Van Eyck's *Man in a Red Turban* is probably a self-portrait. This is suggested not only by the intent gaze, but by the inscription, '*Als ich can*' (As I can), at the top of the frame, which also appears on the portrait of the artist's wife, Margaret van Eyck (Bruges, Groeningemuseum). This may be a personal motto, punning on the artist's name ('*ich*'/'Eyck'), as well as a modest comment on his skill—'As well as I can'. The artist's signature at the bottom of the frame is written in

HANS MEMLING, *Portrait of a Man with a Coin of the Emperor Nero, c.1471–4*. The distinguished Venetian humanist and collector Bernardo Bembo, based in the Netherlands between 1471 and 1474, is identified here by virtue of the palm tree and laurel sprig (at bottom centre), his personal emblems.

the first person—'Jan van Eyck made me'. Both motto and signature proclaim the artist's self-awareness, his sense of his reputation and place in posterity, but also suggest the idea of a 'speaking' likeness, a paradigm often invoked by Renaissance commentators on portraiture.

Dürer, whose keen sense of self is well documented in his own writings, produced more self-portraits than any other Renaissance artist, beginning with a drawing aged 13

(Vienna, Albertina). His remarkably virtuosic *Self-Portrait* of 1500 (see opposite), so lifelike that reputedly his dog licked it, 'speaks' in the inscription placed beside the painter's eyes: 'I, Albrecht Dürer…painted myself thus.' Self-consciousness is also implicit in the prominently placed right hand, which would have wielded the brush, and the costly fur-lined coat, indicating social aspiration beyond that of a mere craftsman. The frontal pose is not unusual in German portraiture, but is here employed to evoke the well-known image of the Face of Christ, an impression underscored by Dürer's hair, beard, and the position of his hand. Dürer's self-fashioning as Christ has been interpreted as an allusion to the artist's God-given skill, and/or, in a more 'Renaissance' spirit, to his role as creator. What we see here is not simply a miraculous piece of mimesis in the depiction of hair, flesh, and fur, but visual testimony to the emerging view, itself a Renaissance construct, which can be paralleled in contemporary writings by Leonardo da Vinci, of the artist as creative genius, one who works not merely with his hands, but with his mind.

Printmaking

Skilled though he was in the deployment of oil paint, Dürer's fame, already widespread in his lifetime, was primarily due to his achievements in the medium of print. Like oil painting, which emerged around the same time, printmaking was a phenomenon that developed in northern Europe, with still greater consequences not only for the visual arts but the world of ideas.

The earliest technique used for printing images on paper is woodcut (long known in Asia), which is thought to have emerged in Germany around 1420, a generation before the invention of movable type, and to have gained momentum in the 1440s. Its origins are unclear—developments in paper production, growing demand for devotional images, and a relationship to the use of woodblocks in textile decoration have all been proposed. Woodcut is made using a relief-printing process: the design is drawn on a hardwood block (usually pearwood), and the lines isolated by cutting into the wood—a job undertaken by a specialist cutter rather than the designer—resulting in a network of raised lines, which are inked and transferred onto paper by pressure from a press. A woodblock is fairly durable and capable of yielding many impressions relatively inexpensively. Early woodcuts took the form of single-sheet religious images and playing cards. Images might include a few lines of simple text cut from the same block, belying the notion that their relative inexpensiveness and simple style predicates an unlettered audience. Before the invention of movable type around 1450 (discussed in Chapter 9), illustrated block-books, mostly of popular religious texts, were produced using this laborious process.

The technique of engraving emerged in about 1430, in the Rhineland. Engraving is made by an intaglio printing process, whereby the design is cut into a metal plate (usually copper, which is relatively soft), creating furrows with a needle-like burin; the ink is transferred to the paper not from the surface, as in relief-printing, but from the furrows, into which the paper is forced by the press. The incising of designs onto metal

ALBRECHT DÜRER, *Self-Portrait*, 1500. Dürer proudly signed this work twice, with his monogram and the date, and with Latin text, which reads, 'I Albrecht Dürer of Nuremberg painted myself thus, with undying colour, at the age of twenty-eight years'. These inscriptions suggest Dürer's expectation of enduring fame.

is closely related to goldsmiths' techniques, and intaglio printing probably evolved in this milieu. Significantly, many early engravers can be associated with metalworkers, including Schongauer and Dürer, respectively the brother and son of goldsmiths. Engraving has the advantage of producing much finer and more varied lines than woodcut, offering greater descriptive and aesthetic potential, although the plate wears out more quickly than a woodblock, affecting the quality of later impressions, and also restricting the number that can be taken.

For a number of reasons—its relatively exclusive nature, association with the high-status art of the goldsmith, and greater technical and aesthetic sophistication—engraving was a more elite form than woodcut. While woodcuts were often coloured, by hand or with stencils, engraving relied for its aesthetic effect on the artist's virtuosic command of black-and-white design. The subjects of engravings were more wide-ranging and experimental, including secular themes, and they were also produced as models for work in other media such as glass and goldsmiths' work. Unlike the anonymous designers of woodcuts, who tended to replicate other woodcuts, engraving attracted distinguished artists like Schongauer and Dürer (both trained as painters), or its first great Italian exponents, Andrea Mantegna and Antonio Pollaiuolo, all of whose engravings were original and beautiful inventions.

Dürer's *Adam and Eve* engraving exemplifies the virtuosic potential of the medium. Through infinitesimally nuanced hatching and stippling, Dürer creates tone and texture, suggesting spatial depth and the textures of flesh, bark, and fur, in a bravura display rivalling the mimetic effects of painting, but in black and white, masterfully balancing the demands of naturalism and graphic design. Dürer's signature on the tablet at top left proclaims his authorship, a form of self-advertisement, like the famous monogram with which he usually signed his prints, following the practice of earlier engravers.

Printmakers were conscious of the usefulness of the medium for disseminating their inventions and promoting their renown. Dürer himself made youthful journeys to visit Schongauer in Colmar and Mantegna in Mantua (abortively, as both died before he arrived) on the strength of having seen their engravings in Nuremberg. Part of the appeal of prints for their makers was the ease with which they could be distributed and sold. Schongauer, aware of their marketing potential, made a series of small engravings of the *Passion*, perfectly sized to be slipped into one of the new prayer books printed in movable type. Dürer took up this idea, building up a large stock of woodcuts and engravings, hiring an agent to sell them, and producing several print series, all in woodcut, which could yield many more impressions than engraving.

Opposite: ALBRECHT DÜRER, *Adam and Eve*, 1504. Dürer's engraving melds northern traditions of naturalism, technical virtuosity, and graphic design with elements inspired by Italy and the antique, notably the classical proportions and pose of Adam, based on the Roman statue of the Apollo Belvedere.

The first of Dürer's series, the *Apocalypse* of 1498, illustrating the *Revelation of John the Divine*, was a highly enterprising commercial venture, the first book to be illustrated and published by a major artist, capitalizing on interest in the approaching half-millennium of 1500. Novel in format, it is an album of fifteen full-page woodcuts, printed on large sheets, with text on the reverse of each sheet. The woodcuts are unprecedentedly virtuosic and complex in cutting and design, raising the status of the medium to rival engraving as black-and-white design.

Dürer's understanding of the potential of woodcut, aesthetic and commercial, undoubtedly came from his training with the Nuremberg painter and book illustrator Michael Wolgemut (c.1434–1519), and also through his godfather, Anton Koberger (c.1440–1513), the printer of the *Apocalypse* and the most important publisher in Germany, who had twenty-four presses in Nuremberg and an international distribution network. Illustrated printed books were a speciality of Nuremberg, and from 1484 Koberger enlisted Wolgemut to produce woodcuts for a number of lavishly illustrated projects. The most ambitious of these was the *World Chronicle* (generally called the *Nuremberg Chronicle*), published in 1493, which includes over 1,800 woodcut illustrations by Wolgemut and his stepson Wilhelm Pleydenwurff, the blocks for which were kept under lock and key to retain exclusivity (see page 226). Written by the Nuremberg physician and humanist scholar Hartmann Schedel (c.1440–1514), it presents an encyclopedic history of the world from the creation onwards, following the tradition of medieval universal chronicles. Yet in certain respects the book's modernity is striking. The illustrations are the most inventive before Dürer, and the page layouts are novel and varied in their integration of text and image. It is the first book to publish a large number of topographically accurate city views and maps, including a world map showing the Gulf of Guinea, recently discovered by the Portuguese, reflecting contemporary interest in geography and exploration. The sheer scale of its publishing enterprise was unprecedented. Instigated and financed by two Nuremberg humanist merchants, Sebald Schreyer and Sebastian Kammermeister, and published simultaneously in Latin and German editions targeting a diverse readership, it is characterized by an entrepreneurial initiative, appetite for knowledge, and artistic innovation that are thoroughly Renaissance in spirit.

Fifteenth-century northern artists and the Italian Renaissance

Nuremberg was an early outpost of humanist culture in northern Europe, as exemplified by individuals like Schedel, Schreyer, and Kammermeister, elite members of a mercantile society who experienced direct contact with Italy through study (Schedel had studied at Padua) and trade. Business took many Nuremberg merchants to Italy, notably Venice, which Dürer himself visited twice, in 1494–5, and 1505–7. It is likely that, even before his first visit, Dürer had seen engravings by Mantegna in Nuremberg, highlighting the role that prints would increasingly play in disseminating the visual culture of Italy. Dürer is notable as the first northern artist to cross the Alps motivated by interest in Italian art and 'improving' his style, a trend that would grow significantly

ALBRECHT DÜRER, *Four Horsemen of the Apocalypse*, 1498. Dürer's woodcut illustration follows the description of the four horsemen in Revelation 6:1–8, the first three respectively shown with a bow, a sword, and scales, and the fourth personifying Death.

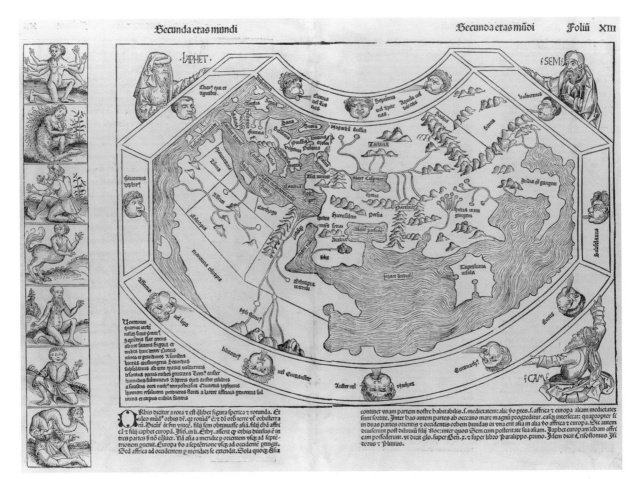

MICHAEL WOLGEMUT AND WILHELM PLEYDENWURFF (woodcuts) and Anton Koberger (printer), *Map of the World* from *The Nuremberg Chronicle*, fols XIIv and XIIIr, 1493. This map is based on the traditional Ptolemaic world map, but includes the Gulf of Guinea, discovered in 1470.

in the sixteenth century. Earlier northern artists who visited Italy, like the painter Justus of Ghent (see Chapter 5), or the numerous Netherlandish tapestry weavers and German printers documented there, did so because of Italian demand for their specialist skills, rather than for artistic experience.

Yet although the predominant flow of artistic traffic in the fifteenth century was from north to south, the mobility of artists, people, and objects meant that northern artists, at least in cosmopolitan centres, were aware of Italian ideas. Memling, for instance, had many Italian clients in the mercantile city of Bruges, offering opportunities for artistic exchange, as evidenced by his portrait of Bernardo Bembo holding a Roman coin; another of his patrons, Jan Crabbe, Abbot of the Dunes Abbey, was a collector of humanist texts, copied for him in Bruges by Italian scribes. Dieric Bouts may have learnt about one-point perspective, employed in his Altarpiece of the Sacrament

(Leuven, church of St Peter), from scholars at the University of Leuven who had visited Italy. Nevertheless, both in Flanders and beyond, responses to the Italian Renaissance were as yet sporadic. Even in the case of artists who had been to Italy, or who had contact with Italian artists elsewhere, Renaissance elements are used selectively and imaginatively, and do not signal the adoption of a new style.

The French painter Jean Fouquet (*c*.1440–1480) visited Florence and Rome in the 1440s, where he painted a famously lifelike portrait, described by early writers, of Pope Eugenius IV. Returning to France, he painted a number of works displaying knowledge of the latest Italian ideas, notably the spectacular miniature of *St Stephen presenting Étienne Chevalier to the Virgin and Child* from the *Hours of Étienne Chevalier*. Fouquet's familiarity with Renaissance architecture is evident in the fluted Corinthian pilasters, entablature, and frieze inscribed with Étienne's name in Roman capitals. He was also familiar with Italian perspective, although his application of it is only an approximation to the Albertian system: he was more interested in using it to block out areas of the design than to construct logical space. The putti with garlands atop the cornice are a Renaissance adaptation of the shield-bearing angels found in French art. In fact, hybrid elements abound in this image. The volumetric figure of St Stephen recalls Fra Angelico (whose paintings Fouquet undoubtedly knew), while the Virgin testifies to his familiarity with the Eyckian tradition. The arch behind her, sculpted like a Gothic church portal, frames a Renaissance shell niche modelled on Donatello's St Louis niche at Orsanmichele, Florence. This is not, however, an indiscriminate mélange of architectural styles, but an informed choice, enhancing meaning. As the current style for church architecture, Gothic was used from Van Eyck and Campin onwards to symbolize the New Covenant and the Church (for which Mary herself was a metaphor), while the shell, an ancient symbol of rebirth found on late Roman and early Christian sarcophagi, as Fouquet could have learnt in Italy, signifies resurrection through Christ. By using a different, Renaissance style of architecture behind the other figures, Fouquet establishes a distinction between their space and that of the Virgin, and between the visionary world inhabited by Chevalier in the image and the actuality of mid-fifteenth-century France, where such architecture did not exist.

Renaissance architectural elements first appear in actual buildings outside Italy at the end of the century in Buda, in the palace created by Italian architects and sculptors for the Italophile King of Hungary, Matthias Corvinus, in the 1480s. It was presumably here that the south German architect Benedikt Ried (*fl.* 1489–1534), employed at the court of Bohemia, learnt about Italian style. One of the most outstanding and innovative architects of his era, Ried was equally capable of working in the late Gothic and the Italian idiom, as exemplified in his early masterpiece, the Vladislav Hall at Prague Castle. The astonishing vault of this vast interior, a paradigm of the spatial experiments in Gothic architecture at the turn of the century, seems to flow organically from the wall piers into a complex network of looping and intersecting ribs, challenging traditional distinctions between structure and ornament. The exterior windows, however, dated 1493, are in the latest Italian style, with fluted pilasters and entablatures. Ried

JEAN FOUQUET, *St Stephen presenting Étienne Chevalier to the Virgin and Child*, from *The Hours of Étienne Chevalier*, *c*.1452–60. This lavish prayer book was made for Étienne Chevalier, Treasurer of France, whose name and initials appear on the frieze and shields in this double-page miniature, which combines traditional northern and modern Italian elements.

also used Italianate forms within the Vladislav Hall, in the doorway leading to the Parliamentary Hall, but in a far less orthodox fashion. Beneath the top-heavy portal with its chaste Italianate rounded arch and heavy entablature, the orders appear to twist and writhe; the columns supporting the lintel have spiral fluting, and the pilasters supporting the entablature are twisted into prismatic forms. This irreverent transposition of the classical orders into the dynamic idiom of late Gothic is a deconstruction of the canon as creative and witty as Michelangelo's at San Lorenzo, Florence, thirty years later.

Recent scholarship has suggested that late Gothic architecture, traditionally regarded as the decadent last gasp of High Gothic, should in fact be seen as a new architecture for a new age. Though using the language of pointed arches, ribs, and tracery rather than classically inspired round-headed arches and orders, its practitioners can be seen, like the architects of Renaissance Italy, as breaking with the past.

BENEDIKT RIED, Vladislav Hall, Portal to the Parliamentary Hall; Prague, Castle, 1493–1503. Ried's irreverently witty portal offers a late Gothic twist on Italian Renaissance architectural forms, anticipating the sophisticated games played by Italian Mannerist architects in the sixteenth century.

Late Gothic architecture is characterized by new structural techniques of dazzling boldness, geometric complexity, and novel spatial effects, together with perceptual games of immense sophistication, which often blur the boundaries between structure and ornament. Such games parallel the visual ambiguities of Van Eyck in painting, and likewise self-consciously draw attention to the artist's virtuosity. Like Van Eyck's paintings, or Dürer's prints, this architecture assumes a perceptually aware audience, capable of understanding the visual games being played, and of appreciating the artist's skill. In this respect, late Gothic architecture, though opposed to Renaissance architectural principles, shares in the novel 'Renaissance' characteristics of other works of art discussed here. It challenges the Burckhardtian model of a 'Renaissance' predicated on new developments taking place in Italy, inspired by the 'rebirth' of antiquity, and validates a more inflected view of parallel developments in fifteenth-century northern Europe.

The sixteenth century

Two major shifts characterize the transition from the fifteenth to the sixteenth centuries in northern European art. The first was a reversal in the predominant direction of artistic traffic so that now Italian art and its reinterpretation of the antique exerted a transforming influence on northern traditions. The second was that the notion of a classical revival can be applied more meaningfully to art in the north. However, this does not make the imposition of the Burckhardtian model of a 'Renaissance' on the north any less problematic. It is undoubtedly true that as humanist scholarship flourished, especially in the many newly founded universities and colleges, the valorization of classical texts broadened into a fascination with other aspects of Greek and Roman culture—from poetry to music, and so to the visual arts. Yet the fact that these art forms each began looking to the classical past in different regions at different times challenges the coherence of a 'Renaissance' in northern Europe if this is understood as the grand, universal movement as ascribed by Burckhardt and others to Italy. Nevertheless, limited to individual disciplines such as painting, sculpture, printmaking, and architecture, and localized to particular regions, the notion of a renaissance can usefully be employed to describe the assimilation of the Italianate classical ideal, even if this refused to follow the progressive, evolutionary trajectory defined by Vasari.

The transmission of Renaissance forms in the early sixteenth century

Prior to the sixteenth century northern European art had represented subjects from classical history or mythology in a wholly contemporary treatment. It was customary in the fifteenth century, for example, for tapestry weavers or manuscript illuminators to depict Hercules wearing medieval armour and set within a northern European landscape or market town. This disjunction of theme and motif (or subject matter and visual form) began to change in the sixteenth century, in some instances reflective of a more informed historical awareness but certainly indicative of the increasing exposure to motifs of classical art.

What had been isolated occurrences of classical motifs in Flemish painting of the fifteenth century, such as Hans Memling's use of putti and swags of fruit as framing devices, became a more general trend in the early years of the next century. This trend, labelled 'Antwerp Mannerism' by the early twentieth-century art historian Max Friedländer, flourished specifically for the first quarter of the sixteenth century. Alongside the putti, classical columns would make an occasional appearance in elaborate, hybrid architectural settings. Figures would be dressed in fantastical costume with helmets, breastplates, and drapery evoking a sense, if not the actuality, of an ancient past. Otherwise traditional religious subjects treated in this flamboyant manner, and heightened by exotically bright colour combinations, dominated the market for Flemish paintings centred on Antwerp. Applying the term 'mannerism' to this style can be somewhat confusing in that it is unrelated to Italian or later Flemish Mannerism. Rather, its particular mannerisms are better understood as developing from traits already present in late medieval art of the north.

The largely anonymous painters working in this style were, however, part of a much wider fashion for incorporating Italianate motifs which extended across northern Europe to inspire craftsmen working in virtually every medium. Whether used as a direct substitute for more traditional decoration or simply included alongside it, classical motifs were treated as exotic additions to the Gothic repertoire of ornament. They were more often applied like an eye-catching surface veneer to native, conventional forms. A case in point is the marble and limestone wall monument in Würzburg Cathedral that Prince-Bishop Lorenz von Bibra commissioned for himself. Carved by the celebrated German sculptor Tilman Riemenschneider between 1515 and 1522, the format essentially follows the funeral monument erected to the bishop's predecessor twenty years earlier, by the same artist in the same cathedral. However, supporting the inscription panel in Von Bibra's monument are the lively, rounded forms of naked putti rather than the Gothic angels with their typically heavy, angular drapery as found in the earlier monument. Rather than a canopy ornamented with Gothic tracery, the newer monument is surmounted by a rounded arch teeming with playful cherubs sitting astride classical swags. Supporting this arch are two columns which are clearly inspired by the classical tradition but not derived from it.

This approach to the classical orders is more widely characteristic of architecture in general across most of northern Europe during the first half of the sixteenth century. From the new French chateaux built in the Loire, to the country houses constructed by Henry VIII's courtiers on former English monastic lands, columns and other classically inspired elements were applied in a manner denoting a lack of awareness or at least a disregard for classical architecture's theoretical foundation of proportion, measurement, and decorum. Until the greater circulation of printed architectural treatises from the middle of the century, it is unsurprising that masons, painters, and other craftsmen might not have appreciated what was classically 'correct'. Their knowledge of classical architectural forms would more commonly have derived from representations on

TILMAN RIEMENSCHNEIDER,
monument to Lorenz von Bibra,
Würzburg Cathedral.

luxury goods imported from Italy, such as glassware, ceramics, and decorated fabrics. With the classical canon arriving as disjointed messages that had already been distorted for decorative means, it is understandable that its use in northern Europe can seem crude and unsophisticated compared with Italy.

Nevertheless, these early responses to the classical should not necessarily be dismissed as ignorant or haphazard. A theoretical rationale was certainly in operation but instead of one grounded in mathematics and measurement it embodied principles of social hierarchy. It is noticeable that the classical orders and other favourite motifs, such as busts of the Roman emperors in roundels, were used to mark the grand entrances and other high-status areas of great French and English houses. Cardinal Wolsey employed both, for example, in the inner, high-status courtyard at Hampton Court in the 1520s. This might well disrupt the aesthetic effects of symmetry and ignore systems of proportion, but as a means to separate and emphasize the high- and low-status ends of a house, the unbalanced disposition of ornament could make perfect sense.

A deeper engagement with antique forms gradually developed, in some quarters at least, through increasing exposure to contemporary Italian art. Prints became by far the most significant means of transmission. Engravings by Andrea Mantegna, including the *Drunken Silenus*, reached the young Albrecht Dürer in Nuremberg, most likely before he ever set foot in Italy. The drawings Dürer made in 1494 which copied and adapted Mantegna's work reveal how he absorbed new approaches to the nude, in terms of anatomical accuracy as well as the ability to animate figures with a sense of dramatic movement. Typically for Dürer at this date, he was engaging with the classical filtered through a contemporary Italian artist's response, in this case Mantegna's use of the conventions of a classical frieze in low relief.

Unlike Italy, northern Europe did not have abundant examples of original antique sculpture and architecture awaiting rediscovery. Nevertheless, the advent of reproductive prints brought this source material one step closer; for rather than being the printmaker's personal invention, these claimed to be a faithful record of celebrated works of art created in another medium. For example, the *Apollo Belvedere*, among the greatest classical marbles in the Vatican, was the subject of multiple reproductive prints issued throughout the sixteenth century. These, together with copies made in plaster, wax, bronze, and other materials, made the greatest antique pieces in Italian private collections accessible to artists even at the furthest reaches of Europe. The close resemblance between the *Apollo Belvedere* and Dürer's Adam in the 1504 engraving of *Adam and Eve* symbolizes the importance of copies for artists of every calibre. Moreover, the fact that Dürer's print in turn became one of the most copied images of the sixteenth century demonstrates how classical prototypes could arrive at more than one remove prior to their incorporation into northern works of art.

The 'Romanist' painters of the mid-sixteenth century

Although knowledge of classical learning and mythology was nothing new, a more informed and scholarly understanding reached a wider section of society in the sixteenth century. This extended to the highest ranks of society and further down to the burgeoning professional and merchant classes.

For the ruling elite, the role model for the ideal courtier had been redefined in Renaissance Italy, especially through the widely disseminated and translated book *Il cortegiano* by Baldassare Castiglione. According to this it was no longer sufficient for the nobility to have mastered the martial skills necessary to fulfil its principal duty of waging war, but an expectation arose that more intellectual and cultural accomplishments would be nurtured so as to produce a more educated and rounded individual. This is how the two Frenchmen in Hans Holbein's celebrated double portrait, *The Ambassadors* have clearly chosen to be represented by making books, instruments, and other objects associated with the liberal arts the centrepiece of the painting. Gradually an informed appreciation of painting and the visual arts became another mark of the ideal gentleman alongside knowledge of classical texts. These aspirations

HANS HOLBEIN THE YOUNGER, *Jean de Dinteville and Georges de Selve (The Ambassadors)*.

filtered down to the professional and merchant classes, for whom humanist study rapidly became critically important as a route to office and social advancement.

It was from these powerful social groups that the majority of patrons of the visual arts were drawn. It was their tastes and interest in the antique that pointed artists in new directions. By the second quarter of the sixteenth century a group of Netherlandish painters had emerged which shared and accommodated these tastes. Sometimes termed 'Romanists', these painters from both the Northern and Southern Netherlands demonstrated a more sophisticated understanding of classical prototypes combined with a direct engagement with the contemporary art of Renaissance Italy. This came about, for some at least, through making the journey to Italy, most especially to Rome. Use of the term 'Romanist' to describe these painters has somewhat fallen from favour for implying a coherence that fails to account for the independence and diversity of individual artists' responses. However, it can usefully serve to highlight an important trend in painting that was to last until the early seventeenth century, in which the formal language of Italian art became assimilated into the Netherlandish tradition.

A pioneering figure in this respect was the Antwerp-trained painter Jan Gossaert. When his patron, Philip of Burgundy (an illegitimate son of the Duke of Burgundy), set out on a diplomatic mission to Rome in 1508–9, Gossaert accompanied him. In line with his interests as a humanist scholar, Philip instructed Gossaert to make a visual record of the great monuments of antiquity. Four drawings from this enterprise survive, including one of the Colosseum. Another is a sheet comprising several studies after antique sculpture. The most immediately recognizable is Gossaert's sketch of the *Spinario*, the ancient bronze figure of a boy pulling a thorn from his foot, which can still be seen in Rome (Musei Capitolini). What are perhaps most striking are the departures Gossaert made from the original model, but equally significant are those features which seem most to have attracted his interest. The proportions of the limbs and neck in the drawing do not conform to those in the sculpture but owe more to the conventions of the late medieval northern representations of the nude. Classical idealism has been treated with a down-to-earth northern particularism. Similarly, the large sandalled foot sketched on the same sheet copies part of an ancient Roman statue called the *Genius populi Romani* (now in the Museo Archeologico Nazionale, Naples). Gossaert's focus on the highly ornamental sandal betrays the obsessive attention to minute detail that had characterized the Netherlandish tradition since Van Eyck. Whether he was acting self-consciously or subconsciously, this is classical sculpture subjectively viewed through the eyes of an artist conditioned by his native tradition.

In the years following his return from Rome Gossaert was able to draw on his studies of antique and contemporary Italian art. Philip of Burgundy provided the major opportunity to do this in commissioning a series of paintings of mythological themes for Souburg Castle, as part of his ambition to establish a humanist court culture to rival any found in Italy. Gossaert's *Hercules and Deianira*, although not definitively one of the works produced for Philip, is nonetheless entirely representative of those which were.

A contemporary setting has been eschewed for an evocation of the antique, with ancient Roman bucrania on the entablature, rich marble inlaid panels, and relief sculptures depicting some of the Labours of Hercules. The figures also dispense with clothing and other trappings of the contemporary world as Gossaert grapples with creating the classical nude. The muscled physique of Hercules is in marked contrast to the lean and unidealized body of Adam that Van Eyck painted for the Ghent Altarpiece. The poses and intertwined legs generate an unprecedented freedom of movement, which in this instance is charged with an erotic physicality. Several likely sources of inspiration have been proposed including paintings and prints by an Italian artist Gossaert would come to know in the north, Jacopo dei' Barbari. Moreover, the complex positions of the seated figures also bring to mind Michelangelo's *Ignudi* in the Sistine Chapel ceiling, which were painted in the year of Gossaert's visit to Rome. Judged according to the standards of his Italian prototypes, Gossaert's figures can appear awkward and ungainly. However, it ought to be recognized that he was not seeking to adopt an Italian manner in its entirety; his ongoing debt to the work of Dürer and other northern artists is testament to that. Rather he was attempting to introduce new conventions into the northern tradition that were quite alien. It is hardly surprising that such pioneering attempts might produce an often uncomfortable hybrid. Some might argue that it was not until Rubens 100 years later that a more harmonious synthesis of the Italian and northern traditions was reached, but without the first steps taken by Gossaert these later achievements would be unthinkable.

Gossaert had an immediate effect on Netherlandish painters of the next generation from whose ranks the key exemplars of Romanism were drawn. Jan van Scorel worked with him briefly in Utrecht around 1517 before travelling first to visit Dürer in Germany and then continuing south to Venice. By 1522 Van Scorel was in Rome, where he was appointed curator of antiquities at the Vatican. This extraordinary promotion of a foreign painter was surely facilitated by the new pope, Adrian VI, being a fellow Dutchman. The unprecedented access this gained to the great collection of classical sculpture was matched by exposure to the fresco cycles created for successive popes by Raphael and Michelangelo. Direct visual quotations from all three sources abound in the paintings Van Scorel produced after his return to Utrecht in 1524. He thus introduced new elements from Italian art not seen in Gossaert's works.

Van Scorel was able to pass on what he had learnt to younger painters, such as his pupil Maarten van Heemskerck. He did this so successfully that the attribution of several paintings to master or pupil remains highly contested. In 1532 Heemskerck followed in Van Scorel's footsteps to Rome, where he spent the next four or five years making a large number of drawings of antique sculpture from private as well as public collections, ancient buildings, and views of Rome. It is notable that his drawings of antique sculpture, such as the Belvedere torso, do not share the obvious distortions

---

Opposite: JAN GOSSAERT, sheet of drawings after the *Spinario* and other sculptures.

JAN GOSSAERT, *Hercules and Deianira.*

observed in Gossaert's work. Van Heemskerck's more far-reaching significance came from his relationship with printmakers. Not only did engravings after his Roman drawings disseminate source material for the antique, prints made after his own compositions provided a ready model for other Netherlandish artists seeking to incorporate the classical and contemporary Italian art into their work.

For the majority of Flemish painters who did not have the opportunity to travel to Italy there were increasing opportunities to gain direct exposure to Italian art in their own region. Italian prints made key works of contemporary art accessible, from Leonardo's fresco of the *Last Supper* in Milan to Michelangelo's Sistine Chapel ceiling. Pieter Coeck van Aelst's version of the *Last Supper* perhaps owed as much to the embellishments added by printmakers to Leonardo's composition as to the Flemish painter's own adaptations to local tastes through the inclusion of detailed landscape, still life, and ornamental elaboration.

Italian works in other media were also becoming accessible for study at first hand, such as Michelangelo's *Bruges Madonna*, a marble figure group of the Madonna and Child installed in the Church of Our Lady in Bruges in 1514. Michelangelo's rounded, cherubic form of the Christ child, with curled hair and standing in *contrapposto*, was adapted for inclusion in the religious paintings of several prominent figures such as Bernard van Orley, who was court painter to Margaret of Austria, regent of the Netherlands. In 1516, artists from across the Netherlands had the opportunity to examine monumental works by Raphael. Ten large cartoons painted by Raphael with depictions of the *Acts of the Apostles* arrived in Brussels to be woven into tapestries. The tapestries had been commissioned by Pope Leo X for the lower walls of the Sistine Chapel. Scenes such as *The Sacrifice at Lystra* acted as a sourcebook of classically inspired motifs, from sculpture and architecture to antique costume. Moreover, the cartoons were finished to such a degree as to give an experience almost equivalent to viewing one of Raphael's great fresco cycles in Rome. The monumental figures, vigorous movement, emotional expression of the narrative, and balanced harmonies of composition were nothing short of an object lesson in the Italian High Renaissance. The influence of the cartoons was immeasurable, not only for Flemish painting but even more so for tapestry. A major shift occurred in tapestry design in these years from a tendency to dispose figures and other elements decoratively across the surface to dynamic figures of Raphaelesque monumentality inhabiting an open expanse of illusionistic space.

The classical revival in the Netherlands and Germany

Rather than characterizing the introduction of classical elements as native traditions being displaced by foreign importations, northern artists increasingly rationalized the process as the recovery of an autonomous antiquity. An influential advocate of this position was Lambert Lombard, whose interests extended beyond the art and antiquities of Italy, which he studied in Rome, to a scholarly fascination with the history of art. He corresponded with Giorgio Vasari with enquiries after Italian artists reaching back

RAPHAEL, *The Sacrifice at Lystra*, from the series of cartoons depicting the Acts of the Apostles.

to fourteenth-century painters such as Giotto. Furthermore, he was able to share his own historical research on Netherlandish artists which Vasari incorporated in the second edition of *The Lives of the Most Eminent Painters, Sculptors, and Architects*. Looking even further back in time through archaeological investigation, Lombard concluded that the Roman invasion of the Low Countries had fostered an antique tradition of its own and it was this that was in the process of revival.

Essentially the same idea informed Karel van Mander's first published history of Netherlandish painting to follow Vasari's biographical model, *Het Schilderboek* (*The Book of Painters*), written between 1583 and 1604. According to this, European art had been plunged into darkness at the fall of the Roman Empire that had only recently begun to be illuminated by the rediscovery of antique sculpture and other works in Italy. Benefiting from this head start, contemporary Italian artists, wrote Van Mander, 'touched on the correct essence and the best appearance of figures earlier than we Netherlanders'. Netherlandish painters had continued to work in their 'habitual manner' which, according to Van Mander, largely comprised 'working from life', until enlightenment was brought from Italy by Jan van Scorel. The latter, Van Mander called 'the lantern bearer' based on the mistaken assumption that this was the first Nether-landish painter to have visited Italy.

Similar patterns emerged elsewhere in northern Europe in which artists, often aided by alliances formed with humanist scholars, sought a return to a native classical past. Albrecht Dürer's friend since childhood, Willibald Pirckheimer, was an internationally respected scholar. Tales of the years he spent in Italy as a student most likely encouraged Dürer's desire to journey across the Alps to Venice. In addition to Pirckheimer, Dürer forged friendships with Erasmus and other great men of letters who constituted an international network of humanist scholars. However, Dürer was far from exceptional in this as many other leading northern artists, from Cranach to Bruegel, developed similar working relationships with scholars that proved mutually beneficial. These connections could dramatically expand an artist's opportunities for patronage, as in the case of Hans Holbein, who initially gained employment in England at the court of Henry VIII on account of a letter of recommendation written by Erasmus to Sir Thomas More. Another result of these associations was a greater diversity in subject matter for art, whether through formal commission or informal encouragement. In the case of northern printmaking, for example, Dürer led the way in demonstrating that depictions of classical mythology need not be restricted to the most familiar stories but might represent more intellectually challenging themes that could allude to abstruse or obscure classical texts.

Parallel to this renewed interest in classical subject matter Dürer sought a revival of what he termed the 'principles and bases' of art in which the artists of ancient Greece and Rome had achieved perfection. In his *Treatise of Human Proportions*, published posthumously in 1525, Dürer defined these as 'the art of proportion, perspective and other similar things', declaring the weakness of artists from the Germanic countries in this respect. He subscribed to the idea that Italian artists of recent years had redis-covered this hidden knowledge and it was principally to their work more than to antique survivals that Dürer directed his attention. Through research and experiment Dürer sought to recover what he believed to be a secret formula of the ancients for representing the ideal proportions of the human body. Several drawings of the nude he made in Venice were inspired by Italian draughtsmanship and clearly taken from life. They demonstrate a new anatomical understanding, whether coherently articulated in movement or in repose. However, other drawings were experimental in nature and recorded detailed measurements of limbs and joints. Some sought to inscribe parts of the figure within a perfect circle or square so as to establish ideal proportions. This research, which preoccupied Dürer for much of the rest of his life, culminated in his treatise on the subject, and is exemplified in the precisely calculated proportions found in his print of Adam and Eve.

Although Dürer's prints provided the most accessible and digestible exemplar of the classical and Italianate for most artists working in northern Europe, more varied sources of artistic inspiration reached the Germanic region from Italy, and from Venice in particular. The trade route from Venice to Augsburg, Nuremberg, and other great

German commercial centres had built strong connections over many centuries. By the sixteenth century the Germans were by far the largest and most economically important group of foreign merchants established in Venice. This importance was reflected in the prestige of their headquarters, the so-called Fondaco dei Tedeschi, which was not only centrally situated on the Grand Canal adjoining the Rialto Bridge, its exterior walls were painted in fresco by the best artists the Republic had to offer—Giorgione and Titian. Being immersed in the visual and material culture of Venice resulted in some German merchants acquiring a taste for Italian Renaissance art. The wealthiest of them all, the Fugger family, constructed a family sepulchral chapel which led this trend. Built in 1510–12 as an extension to St Anna's Church in Augsburg, the Fugger Chapel was directly modelled on the richly ornamented interiors of Venetian Renaissance churches. Most explicitly, Santa Maria dei Miracoli, built by Pietro Lombardo between 1481 and 1489, provided the model for the marble pilasters, full entablature, rounded arches, balustrade with sculpted putti, circular motifs of inlaid coloured marble, and other elements that make the Fugger Chapel one of the earliest large-scale architectural responses to Italian Renaissance style in Germany. The marble epitaph slabs on the rear walls follow the Venetian architectural tradition of low relief stone carving in illusionistic perspective, although their specific designs seem to have been created by Dürer in a series of drawings which survive.

This new taste for the classical and Italianate, which the Fugger Chapel exemplified, was referenced explicitly in contemporary German culture. The word widely used to identify it in artworks was 'Welsch'. According to art historian Michael Baxandall, 'Welsch' generally meant exotic or foreign, yet in the early sixteenth century it became most especially associated with trends from Italy. Its usage was pejorative, as the negative antithesis to the native Germanic tradition, described simply as 'Deutsch'. It encompassed all the newest fashions from Italy whether in clothes, haircuts, dance, or the visual arts, which more conservative voices roundly dismissed as faddish and trivial.

The 'Deutsch' in art could be no more than a generic term to encapsulate the dominant strains in German artistic production of the late fifteenth and early sixteenth centuries. This would later be labelled 'late Gothic'. In sculpture this was characterized as an emphasis on the decorative use of line. An example is the figural group of Tobias and the Angel carved by Veit Stoss in 1516. Stoss was a great exponent of the German tradition of limewood sculpture which used line to create cascading, sinuous shapes. The crisp edges that typify Stoss's drapery were later described by Vasari as paper-thin. They produce flamboyant, swirling patters that are unrelated to any sense of a body beneath or to the natural behaviour of fabric, but create a joyously abstract flourish. Sculptors working within this tradition faced a fundamental challenge in creating the solid and fully rounded forms of the classical nude, for which their training and experience had not prepared them. Even well-connected court sculptors shared these problems, such as Conrad Meit, a German who worked from 1514 to 1530 at the court of the Archduchess Margaret of Austria, regent of the Netherlands. For the

THE FUGGER CHAPEL in St Anna's church, Augsburg.

anatomy of his nude figures he resorted, like so many of his contemporaries, to Dürer's prints as his model even though his medium was wood, stone, and metal.

The few German sculptors who borrowed directly from Italian sources had mostly encountered them at first hand in Italy. Brothers Hermann and Peter Vischer visited Siena and Rome in the 1510s and after their return to Nuremberg began to incorporate elements from Italian models into works such as the shrine to St Sebald and secular

VEIT STOSS, *Tobias and the Angel.*

statues, medals, and plaquettes in brass and bronze. Peter Flötner, from the same workshop, gave a radically Italianate treatment to the Apollo Fountain of 1532 commissioned by a Nuremberg archery club. The classicizing bronze Apollo stood on a pedestal ornamented with the types of classical motifs he would have encountered on the trip he made to Padua.

This taste for the Italianate in Germany remained distinctly avant-garde and associated with a wealthy and international elite. Beyond the rich commercial centres of Nuremberg, to which the Vischer workshop catered, and Augsburg, site of the Fugger Chapel, direct Italian influence on German sculpture was limited. Even in examples where this is discernible the finished result resembles a hybrid amalgamation with native traditions. The same characterization can be applied to German art in other media, including the work of Cranach, Holbein, and Dürer. Yet, what might appear anachronistic in these works, such as the stags and fir trees which provide the backdrop to many of the classical mythological works of Cranach, Dürer, and others, could conceivably be a self-conscious attempt to establish a Germanic classicism that was not dependent on Italian models. Tacitus' *Germania* had described the native Germanic peoples of the ancient past as forest dwellers, and so for some the forest became emblematic of Germany's classical past. It is possible that this was connected with the native, dormant classicism that Dürer and others sought to reawaken. Dürer's sense of regional pride is most clearly expressed in his *Adam and Eve* engraving in which his signature, set against the forest background, reads 'Albertus Dürerus Noricus', meaning 'of Nuremberg'. Similarly, the signature included on some of his painted works styles him 'Germanus'.

Mannerism and the princely courts of northern Europe

From the mid-sixteenth century onwards the influence exerted by Italian Renaissance art continued to develop in northern Europe, in multiple directions. The most significant new trend was Mannerism. The traditional definition of this art historical term is a stylistic phase in European art which first emerged in Rome during the 1520s and endured for the remainder of the sixteenth century, until it was superseded by the Baroque. In contrast or even in reaction to the measured and harmonious classicism of Raphael, early Michelangelo, and other artists of the High Renaissance, Mannerism struck a dramatically discordant note of instability, distortion, and exaggeration. It can be recognized from a variety of characteristics. These include representing the human body with distortedly elongated proportions, often in complex poses, and with a sense of restless movement. In paintings, the setting might lead the eye from a compressed space in the foreground to an abrupt plunge into a distant background. The palette might juxtapose lurid colours in clashing combinations. The overall effect of these visually startling and dynamic features seems designed to evoke a heightened emotional response in the viewer.

Netherlandish painters from the generation after Gossaert, such as Jan van Scorel and Maarten van Heemskerck, encountered and absorbed many of these Mannerist traits during their stay in Rome. By the time the Antwerp painter Frans Floris arrived in 1541, art in Rome was entering the height of its Mannerist phase. This was the year in which Michelangelo painted the *Last Judgement* on the east wall of the Sistine Chapel. Perhaps Michelangelo's design, with its sheer density of twisting figures, was one of Floris's sources for his *Fall of the Rebel Angels*. Commissioned as an altarpiece for Antwerp Cathedral in 1554, the central section of the triptych features St Michael expelling Satan and his demonic cohorts from heaven down to hell. The violent maelstrom of writhing, muscular bodies might owe a debt to Italian Mannerism and yet the formation of the demons from disparate body parts of birds, animals, and other creatures looks back to the northern artistic inheritance associated with Hieronymus Bosch.

From the mid-sixteenth century Mannerism was to achieve a pervasive presence in painting and the visual arts as a whole, especially on account of its prestigious association with the princely courts of Europe. Prior to this, Italianate classicism had already become established as an international visual language of power and cultural prestige. From the early years of the century, artists versed in the latest classicizing trends from Italy were in high demand, and Italian artists who made the journey north could even benefit from high-level competition for their services. Pietro Torrigiano, one of Michelangelo's early contemporaries in Florence, was among several Italian sculptors given prestigious royal commissions in England, the Netherlands, Spain, and elsewhere. His funerary monuments in Westminster Abbey and his portrait busts, dating between approximately 1510 and 1525, introduced new styles and also the use of terracotta into Tudor England.

The King of France, Francis I, not only employed itinerant Italian artists but actively sought to recruit the very best permanently into his service. His overture to Michelangelo might have been declined but Leonardo da Vinci accepted the invitation, spending the last years of his life at Amboise from 1516 to 1519. The French court had cultivated a specific taste for the art and architecture of northern Italy, stimulated by France's invasion and occupation of that region. This had begun in 1494 and was to last, in some areas, for nearly thirty years. As a result, architectural borrowings, including the use of coloured marble inlay from the Certosa di Pavia near to Milan, came to embellish the chateaux of the Loire, such as the Chateau de Chambord (begun in 1519). Italian art, including important works by Michelangelo, Raphael, and others entered French collections at an early date.

Thus Francis was following an established pattern when he entrusted the interior design of his new gallery at the Chateau de Fontainebleau to two leading Italian artists. The Galerie François I, created at the heart of the chateau between 1534 and 1539, drew the admiration of Europe for the dazzling originality of its decorative scheme. It not only set the standard for displays of princely magnificence in the palaces of northern Europe, it was also instrumental in establishing the appeal and prestige of Mannerism. The artists responsible were Rosso Fiorentino (Giovanni Battista Rosso), a Florentine painter previously based in Rome, and Francesco Primaticcio, who had come from

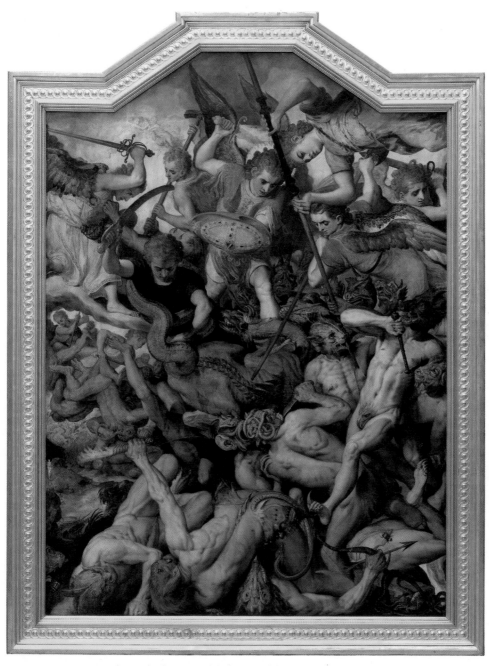

FRANS FLORIS, central panel of a triptych, *The Fall of the Rebel Angels*.

the workshop of Giulio Romano at the Palazzo Te in Mantua. Together they created a series of decorative compartments between the windows along the gallery. Each of these was centred on a fresco painting of classical inspiration by Rosso, surrounded by a frame and flanked by either additional frescos or else classical nudes fashioned by Primaticcio in stucco. The high relief and white colouring of these stucco figures made them resemble marble. The frames gave the impression of overlapping one another, with a fictive mosaic beneath giving the illusion of a multilayered display. Along the lower register of the gallery walnut panelling had been intricately carved and gilded by the Italian carpenter Scibec da Carpi, who also created the richly ornamented ceiling. The overall effect was of an overwhelming opulence.

Fontainebleau's distinctive version of Mannerism was disseminated across Europe in the form of prints, paintings, sculptures, tapestries, and objects in most other media. The elongated proportions and complex poses of Primaticcio's stucco figures, which included examples in other rooms of the chateau, were emulated throughout Europe. For example, Lucas Cranach the Elder's later female nudes painted at the court of Saxony are indebted to Fontainebleau. Although not a direct source owing to their

ROSSO FIORENTINO, FRANCESCO PRIMATICCIO, and others, the Galerie François I in the Chateau de Fontainebleau.

PRIMATICCIO, *Four Nymphs*, in the bedchamber of Madame d'Étampes, Chateau de Fontainebleau.

later date, the *Four Nymphs* in the bedchamber of Madame d'Étampes (1541–4) share common sources with the figures of Venus which Cranach painted repeatedly during the 1530s.

In the last two decades of the sixteenth century artists working at the royal and noble courts of the north elaborated these figure types to mounting extremes of refinement. With regard to painting, late Flemish Mannerism marked a culmination of this trend. It was the creation of celebrated court painters such as Bartholomeus Spranger. Originally from Antwerp, Spranger became influential largely on account of the cachet from working for such patrons as the pope in Rome and Rudolf II, the Holy Roman Emperor in Prague. Spranger's mythological nudes are noted for their pin heads and grossly extended limbs which contort and seem to twist out of control in an overtly sensual ballet. Even religious subjects treated by Spranger, or contemporaries such as Joachim Wtewael, feature similar distortions, with unbalanced figures which often appear to be teetering on their toes.

Mannerist sculpture was equally centred on precariously poised figures animated by dynamic movement. Giambologna's bronze Mercury epitomizes the wider trend. Its sense of restless motion is heightened by being freed from a single, fixed viewpoint within a niche or other framing device. This compels the viewer to observe the figure fully in the round. Giambologna was a very rare instance of a northern artist wholly adopting the Italian manner. Giovanni Bologna was the Italian version of this Flemish sculptor's real name, Jean Boulogne. So successful was he in this that, once established in Florence, he became acknowledged as the pre-eminent sculptor in Renaissance Italy following the death of Michelangelo. However, his direct impact on sculpture in the north was limited, at least until the early seventeenth century.

Non-figural Mannerist ornament was also propagated as a Europe-wide standard. The example of Fontainebleau popularized particular decorative motifs, most notably strapwork. This was a form of scrolling flourish resembling curled straps of leather. These motifs, in turn, were further elaborated by artists in the Netherlands, Germany, and elsewhere into designs that combined multiple patterns with human figures, animals, monsters, fruits, plants, and other natural forms. Surfaces of two and three dimensions were densely packed with such features in often bizarre but playful confections. In the second half of the sixteenth century examples could be found printed into books and maps, carved into funerary monuments and fireplaces, adorning architectural interiors and exteriors, and seemingly incorporated into every other conceivable surface receptive to decoration.

Even the centuries-old interior of a medieval church was ripe for Mannerist treatment. Such was the case at Tournai Cathedral in the 1570s when Cornelis Floris erected a new rood screen. Not only does its surface ornament of Flemish Mannerism strike the modern observer as an odd juxtaposition against the Gothic ecclesiastic interior, its architectural form also marks a turn to the classical tradition. Architecturally it owes a debt to Jacopo Sansovino's Loggetta in the Piazza San Marco in Venice. More generally,

---

Opposite: LUCAS CRANACH THE ELDER, *Venus and Cupid.*

GIAMBOLOGNA, *MERCURY.*

it resembles a Roman triumphal arch. Arches in that tradition appeared in the streets of many European capital cities during the sixteenth century, to honour the entry of a ruler. Although only usually constructed in wood and painted canvas, temporary structures such as these contributed to the assimilation of classical architectural elements in the public sphere. Thus when the burgers of Antwerp commissioned a new town hall (1561–5), they chose the architectural idiom of the classical orders and the triumphal arch. This building, for which Cornelis Floris was also largely responsible,

CORNELIS FLORIS, *rood screen,* Tournai Cathedral.

became, in turn, one of the most important and influential Renaissance public buildings in northern Europe.

Despite his association with this prestigious building, Cornelis Floris represented a
new breed of artist whose renown rested on published designs more than completed
works. The Antwerp presses printed large numbers of designs by Floris, Jan Vredeman
de Vries, and others covering a wide range of subjects, from funerary monuments to
architectural elements and abstract ornamental schemes. Similarly, the influence
exerted by Sebastiano Serlio, the Italian architect who settled in France, rested in his
profusely illustrated treatise on architecture rather than the few buildings he constructed. Serlio's publications combined modern Mannerist designs with a visual
record of the celebrated edifices of ancient Rome. Publications such as these disseminated an academically informed understanding of the classical tradition throughout
northern Europe.

Even those craftsmen who lacked the education or curiosity to engage at the highest
intellectual level nonetheless used the printed illustrations in architectural treatises as a
pattern book to meet the increasing demands of patrons for work in a classicizing
style. It was through this means that Wollaton Hall, a country house built between
1580 and 1588 in Nottinghamshire, came to have an exterior covered in unrestrained

WOLLATON HALL, NOTTINGHAMSHIRE.

Flemish Mannerist ornament. Its fanciful gables with their scrolling strapwork and most other elements of its design are directly traceable to the publications of Vredeman de Vries and others. Busts of the philosophers and other great men from antiquity appear in roundels on the walls. However, the shape, or more specifically the silhouette, of the building gives the air of a medieval castle, which is reinforced by the turrets at the corners of its raised central structure. This appropriation of classical elements to create a hybrid with native traditions remained characteristic of architecture throughout the sixteenth century in northern Europe.

The Reformation and the rise of 'art'

In the sixteenth century, ideas coming from Italy coincided with forces unleashed by the Protestant Reformation which together caused a fundamental re-evaluation of the visual image. Traditional religious functions of images came under attack but, aided by emerging notions of art and collecting, the visual arts began to attract a different cultural and social status.

LUCAS CRANACH THE ELDER, *The Law and the Gospel.*

From its inception, the call for reform initiated by Martin Luther challenged the traditional religious functions of images. He argued that, in practice, images used in these ways had inevitably been put in the place of God, which was idolatry. Nevertheless, in line with his relatively moderate view, Luther still believed images were capable of reform, even for use in church. Only the didactic function remained valid, as a means to spread the gospel message. Working in collaboration with Lucas Cranach the Elder, he developed *The Law and the Gospel* as a visual representation of Luther's theology of salvation. This was painted onto numerous panels and adapted for a range of media. This image's function as an instructional tool is reflected in its diagrammatic form. A central division separates judgement under Mosaic law on the left from salvation through the grace of Christ on the right. The figures, even the crucified Christ, are abstracted from any narrative context and so excite no emotional or devotional response but act as mere symbols to illustrate the biblical texts beneath. In this way, image became entirely subservient to text, which exemplifies an essential tenet of Protestant culture.

However, many of Luther's followers and most of his successors, from Zwingli to Calvin, adopted an entirely uncompromising stance on the issue of images in churches. Their fundamentalist reading of the Bible, and the Ten Commandments in particular, convinced them that God had expressly demanded the destruction of images. The resulting devastation is unquantifiable. Religious images that had accumulated for centuries in the churches and cathedrals of northern Europe were swept away in multiple waves of destruction.

Iconoclasm and the image controversy were primarily concerned with religious images in churches and other places of worship. In houses and other secular settings even Calvin could sanction pictures provided they were in no danger of serving a religious function. This stimulated painters, sculptors, and other craftsmen to greater diversification and experimentation. New markets developed in the sixteenth century for landscapes, still lifes, and other types of genre imagery. It would be wrong to posit a crude causal link connecting the Reformation and the flourishing of these subjects, not least because the latter were equally significant in Catholic areas as in Protestant. Whether their appearance signals a fundamental cultural shift in northern art or merely a reordered emphasis of pre-existing elements remains a highly contested question concerning the interrelationship between the Renaissance and Reformation in the north.

Landscape backgrounds in Flemish paintings continued to provide models for many Italian artists, as they had in the fifteenth century. Especially popular were Joachim Patinir's panoramic bird's-eye views with dramatic rock formations that all but overwhelmed the narrative figures. Pieter Bruegel the Elder took an even more expansive view of the natural world, as illustrated by his *Hunters in the Snow*, which was originally part of a series of six paintings of the changing seasons. Bruegel represented climatic conditions and human activities that broke from the traditional divisions of the labours of the months. A further break with the past was made in Germany by Albrecht Altdorfer in creating landscape views in prints, drawings, and even a painting with a complete absence of figures and any reference to narrative, which are therefore accounted the earliest independent landscapes.

A similar pattern emerged in the tradition of still-life painting. What had previously been incidental details came to dominate the foreground of works by Pieter Aertsen, Joachim Bueckelaer, and others. Although narrative scenes from the life of Christ might have retreated to the background, this by no means indicates an undermining of the religious message of such paintings. The foreground objects might have been intended to strike a symbolic resonance with the scene behind, whether to a religious, moral, or political effect. Such interpretations continue to be disputed, and none more so than the peasant scenes with which Bruegel is most associated. Bruegel was part of a trend in the Netherlands and Germany in which these marginal figures took centre stage but, as with earlier works by Hieronymus Bosch, opinions divide whether this was from a moralizing, celebratory, or comic perspective.

PIETER BRUEGEL THE ELDER, *Hunters in the Snow.*

Portraiture in the sixteenth century developed in closer parallel between Italy and the north. Painted portraits became larger, with full-length formats enjoying great popularity at court in both regions. A humanist interest in the importance of the individual seems also to have affected the genre. Rather than a timeless delineation of the facial features, recording little more than an individual's position in society, some portraits created the illusion of capturing a fleeting moment. The expression on the face could even give an apparent glimpse into the realm of experience, or what Leonardo called 'the motions of the mind'. Specific thoughts or ideas were sometimes represented through symbolic visual conceit, such as the flames surrounding the love-sick Elizabethan gallant in one of Nicholas Hilliard's portrait miniatures. The portrait miniature was a northern innovation of the 1520s, but a possible inspiration was the classical medal whose revival flourished in Italy and northern Europe.

Although new treatments of established subjects could affect the function of pictures and sculpture, a more profound re-evaluation of visual images was stimulated by the new fashion for collecting. A collection differed from earlier accumulations of precious objects, such as those in medieval treasuries, by implying a selective pro-gramme of acquisition guided by a system of categorization. Rare and exotic objects

NICHOLAS HILLIARD, *Unknown Man against a Background of Flames.*

displayed in a *Wunderkammer*, or 'cabinet of curiosities', for instance, would often be ordered into categories, defined by their origins or materials. The ultimate aim was an encyclopedic representativeness. Antique coins and medals could be formed into a collection following a chronological sequence to create a microcosm of ancient history. Even a controversial object could acquire a new legitimacy by being placed in relation to other objects. This was how a Lutheran embroiderer in Saxony could keep Martin Schongauer's *Death of the Virgin* engraving in his collection of prints and drawings, despite its Catholic iconography. In an inscription of 1550 he insisted that he kept the print owing to its status as one of the 'finest works of art to have come out of Germany' and 'not because of the story'.

Thus collecting was an activity that cut across the boundaries of religious ideology, enabling it to spread from Italy to both Catholic and Protestant regions of northern Europe. The visual arts were initially collected within the context of a cabinet of curiosities but their rising prestige was reflected in the appearance of the distinct 'art room' or *Kunstkammer*, by the end of the sixteenth century. An early example of the latter was the Antiquarium begun in 1569 for the Duke of Bavaria at his palace in Munich. It was designed by the duke's Italian artistic adviser, Jacopo Strada, who based it on a room at the ducal palace in Mantua. Its ordered display of antique busts and

BERNARD AND SIMON ZWITEL AND JACOPO STRADA, Antiquarium, Residenz, Munich.

other sculpture had precedents in ancient Rome and this, combined with the *all'antica* decoration of the room, situated both collection and collector within the intellectual and cultural inheritance of the classical world.

Sculptures and paintings displayed in this way functioned as what would later be termed 'works of art'. Redefining their purpose as stimulating aesthetic and intellectual admiration rather than any practical or religious utility was legitimized by an attempt to reclassify painting and sculpture as liberal arts. This would mark an important elevation in status since the intellectual foundation of the liberal arts made them an appropriate interest for the educated gentleman. It would redeem painting and sculpture from their traditional categorization as mechanical arts, which stigmatized them as craft skills of the uneducated workman. Not only would this shift permit the visual arts to be valued beyond their material cost, as bearers of cultural capital, it would also greatly enhance the status of the artists who created them. Dürer followed the Italian lead in arguing for this through relentless self-promotion. This took numerous forms including writing academic treatises, signing his works, sometimes with Latin inscriptions, and painting self-portraits in which he appears ostentatiously dressed in the rich

JAN VAN CROES AFTER CORNELIS FLORIS, *House of Frans Floris in Antwerp.*

furs and leather gloves of a gentleman. Nevertheless, these ideas were slow to extend beyond educated circles. Dürer noted the contrast with Italy, observing that while in Venice he was respected as a 'gentleman', whereas back home he was looked upon as a 'parasite'.

Similar pretensions were expressed by painters in the northern and southern Netherlands. A later drawing records how the external façade of Frans Floris's house in Antwerp acted as a visual manifesto of the claim of painting and sculpture to be liberal arts. Personifications painted to resemble bronze statues together with Apollo and other figures formed an allegory which proclaimed that art was essential to a civilized society. The visual language of its argument, together with its classical architecture of the orders, masks, and garlands, underlined that the authority for this claim rested on antique precedent. The texts of Pliny the Elder and others provided examples of the high esteem in which great painters were once held in ancient Greece. Furthermore, accounts of the close personal relationship between Alexander the Great and his painter, Apelles, helped legitimize the beginnings of a gradual shift in the hierarchical relationship between patron and artist. These stories achieved such common currency that most of the celebrated artists of northern Europe came to be praised at some point as the new Apelles or the new Praxiteles.

For many northern European artists of the sixteenth century, a 'renaissance' or rebirth of classical culture offered little more than a source of ornamental motifs or of subject matter unburdened by religious controversy. For some the art of the ancient world and its contemporary Italian revival left little discernible influence, even for an artist such as Bruegel who managed to travel to Italy. Northern art did not follow a steady progression to greater classicism but assimilated new ideas on its own terms. The Dürer who promoted the classical nude was the same Dürer who engraved the German forest and painted the *Great Piece of Turf*. However, classical culture as made apparent through its authoritative texts provided the grounds for northern artists to challenge and redefine the status of their profession and even to re-evaluate the very nature of art.

CHAPTER 7

The Performing Arts: Festival, Music, Drama, Dance

MARGARET M. McGOWAN

In the Renaissance, the performing arts flourished most conspicuously in festival. Across Europe, in churches, cities, and courts, actors, musicians, and dancers, poets, artists, and composers, supported by a vast army of craftsmen, developed and practised their art in the service of spectacle. Forms of performance were fluid, evolving and progressing as artistic skills became more sophisticated, as princes invested more and more in shows that were politically motivated, as royal courts became less peripatetic, and as knowledge of the ancient world increased and provided a stimulus for ambitious creators of festival.

Festivals depended on collaboration: between the poet charged with an overall design, the artist responsible for the architectural structures, machinery, and symbols, the composer whose music was essential for creating an atmosphere of celebration and accompanying the many voices who sang praises or who spoke holy words to the populace, and the choreographer whose job was to coordinate the steps of both amateur and professional dancers. Their joint activity not only blended the arts in impressive ways but also helped artists to realize the benefits of harmonizing their skills. Such blending allowed them, in the second half of the sixteenth century, to create: in the theatre, illusory worlds; and in the streets, the transformation of a real city into an imaginary landscape. These worlds were ephemeral, lasting for a day or a night, until the crowd demolished the temporary structures in the marketplace, or the guilds put away their painted wagons for another year. It is not possible to reconstruct these performances in their wholeness but, from the many printed accounts of them and from financial records (dating from the early sixteenth century), we can assess their nature, their significance for Renaissance culture, and discover the forms which inspired princes as remote as Matthias Corvinus (1443–90) in Hungary or Rudolf II (1550–1612) in Prague. It is a strange coincidence that, on the continent of Europe, festival performances multiplied and flourished when wars afflicted almost every country. Was spectacle perhaps a way of coping with times of uncertainty and disruption?

The nature of festival

Musicians, dancers, tumblers, and theatre groups travelled across Europe from court to court, employed by princes to enliven special occasions. Moresque dancers, impersonating exotic, bizarre, or comic characters, were hired in Toulon in 1447, for instance, to welcome Jeanne de Laval (1433–98), wife of René, King of Naples. Although such hirings were common, courtiers were well equipped to provide their own entertainment, for a sign of courtly status was the ability to play a musical instrument well (most often, the lute) and to execute a great range of dance types including the skill to improvise. When, after his defeat at Pavia, Francis I (1494–1547) was welcomed in Valencia by ladies of the Spanish court, dressed in their richest attire, they came to dance with him. The experience roused mixed emotions in the king: his delight to be dancing yet his sorrow as his steps brought a vision of entertainment at home. In Italy too, Lorenzo the Magnificent's (1449–92) light-hearted inventions, *Canzoni a Ballo* (songs for dancing), were published and sung at many Florentine festivals, while in Ferrara, notable for its choreographers whose rules for dancing formed the foundation of that art (Domenico, d.1476/7, and Guglielmo Ebreo, *c.*1420–*c.*1483), the court in 1502 enjoyed five comedies by Plautus on successive nights, enlivened by danced interludes. Evening balls were a regular occurrence: they were organized throughout the year-long journey of the future Philip II to the Netherlands (1548–9) in every town he visited; and towards the end of the sixteenth century, Henri III, King of France (1555–89), ordered that dancing should take place after supper at least three days a week.

In order that such entertainment was instantly available, musicians were sought from all over Europe. The papal college, unique in its structure, employed many singers from Flanders whose Burgundian musical style exerted great influence on the choral music which formed the central part of papal ceremonial. A mixed choir of Italian, French, and Flemish musicians performed under the direction of Guillaume Dufay (*c.*1397–1474)—whose hymns continued to be played long after his death—and later of Palestrina (*c.*1525–1594), who gloried in polyphonic harmonies. Tudor monarchs, too, were keen patrons of music and appointed a Master of the Revels to take charge of their entertainments. Henry VIII (1491–1547), no mean musician himself, supplied his court with a lavish selection of instruments, and recruited the finest organists and singers from Italy, Flanders, and Spain so that, by the end of his reign, The King's Musick was sixty strong. Palestrina's motets and madrigals were regularly performed, and Henry's daughter Elizabeth I maintained a remarkable conservatoire of musical talent: Thomas Tallis (1505–85), William Byrd (1540/3–1623), and John Bull (1562/3–1628). Over the Channel, Francis I doubled his French and Italian musical establishment from sixteen to thirty-two, and increased the size of his court so that unprejudiced observers remarked, 'Anyone who has not seen the court of France does not know true grandeur.' Yet Philip II of Spain outdid the French monarch by keeping 150 musicians at his court. Northern Italian states competed with each other in the size and quality of the performing artists they employed. Ludovico Sforza, Duke of Milan, known as Il Moro (1452–1508), exploited the resources of the brilliant chapel, founded in the 1470s by Josquin des Prez (c.1440/55–1521) and marked every occasion with great display, dramas, interludes, and feasts. Similarly, for twenty-five years, the Gonzaga court in Mantua had benefited from that theatrical animateur Leone Ebreo di'Sommi (c.1526–1591/2) who, with the composer Giaches de Wert (1535–96) ensured that the renown of the court's spectacles spread all over Italy. Further afield, in Munich, Albert V (r.1550–79), recognizing the propaganda power of magnificence, revolutionized the performing arts. Orlando Lassus resided there from 1557 to 1594, and developed musical forms, adding to the number of performers, and attracting many Italian masters to the city. Similarly, in Prague, Rudolf II, who had spent his childhood in Spain, on succeeding to the dukedom (1564), built a castle which became an inspirational environment for creative work. When Philip Sidney visited in 1575, he found the palace filled with gifted scholars (Tycho Brahe, 1546–1601, and Johannes Kepler, 1571–1630), and painters like Giuseppe Archimboldo (1527–93), chief organizer of festivals whose allegorical programmes were printed alongside music for pavanes, galliards, and courantes.

The festivals put on by these resourceful musical establishments were very varied. There were dramas performed with elaborate machinery mounted in the nave of cathedrals; in Messina (1535), the city of Constantinople, 'very well made', hung in the air until the fireworks inside the structure exploded to the delight of the devout Christians below. Lorenzo the Magnificent's many *sacre rappresentazione* (sacred shows) were performed in San Lorenzo where Filippo Brunelleschi (1377–1446) had earlier made great strides in solving the mechanics required for staging mobile effects, creating a star-spangled heaven whence Gabriel appeared in a blaze of artificial fire stretching the length of the nave. In Mantua, sacred dramas were even more elaborate as distinguished composers (de Wert and Palestrina) wrote masses for Santa Barbara where (as in St Mark's in Venice) alternating chant and polyphony could be heard from different parts of the building, projecting power, authority, and status for both the prince and the church.

Later, as funerals became increasingly theatrical—with processions of mourners and vast ornate catafalques erected in the centre of the nave—the church itself became more than ever the spectacle of Catholic belief, of achievement and of commemoration, recalling in detail the virtuous deeds of the dead. It suffices to remember the massive structures built for monarchs in the Spanish church in Rome, the great ship of Charles V in Brussels (1559), or the huge friezes that decorated the Church of St John in Florence for the funerals of Philip II of Spain (d.1589), or of Henri IV of France (assassinated, 1610). This recollection of military achievement mirrored the lessons of kingship that had accompanied their entries into cities of their realm on their accession when, since the fourteenth century, they had been greeted with processions, exchange of gifts, and popular demonstrations of joy. Such cross-fertilization was a constant feature in festivals throughout the Renaissance.

Banquets were naturally a traditional mode of celebration, and their elaboration particularly engaged the performing arts. The dukes of Burgundy, for instance, indulged in extravagant chivalric displays and sumptuous feasts such as the Feast of the Pheasant (1454), organized to mark the anniversary of the Order of the Golden Fleece. The courses of the feast were lavish and given a continuity through the theatrical scenes recited, mimed, and danced. In 1454, the climax came with a re-enactment of the adventures of Jason and the Argonauts—a theme which was to recur again and again in Renaissance spectacle. Emperor Charles V, knowing the benefits of shows for princes, was an avid reader of the Burgundian courtier, chronicler, and poet Olivier de la Marche, who cherished all the details of the Feast of the Pheasant which he had masterminded, recording them in his *Mémoires*. The Burgundian splendour would, however, be surpassed by the banquet arranged at Pesaro in 1475 to celebrate the nuptials of Costanzo Sforza and Camilla Marzano d'Aragona. A detailed manuscript narrative from the Vatican Library (now translated into English by Jane Bridgeman) with thirty-two colour illuminations evokes the delicious dishes, paints the messengers of the gods who provided the food and sugar sculptures, the planets who brought the gifts, all carried in on mobile floats decorated with symbols. The twelve courses of the banquet took twelve hours to consume, as each relay of food came in to music: concerts, songs, and dances. The dancing, probably choreographed by Guglielmo, was as varied as the music played for the feats of acrobats and for the ambitious pantomimic figures performed by twelve young men who simulated the growing and harvesting of crops. Synchronizing the figures of another complex entry of 120 dancing youths was a major achievement, since nothing on this scale appears to have been attempted before.

Moving from the great hall of a palace to the marketplace in Florence, the same large-scale spectacle is in evidence. For instance, when the pope and Galeazzo Maria Sforza visited Florence in 1469, a ball was given in the New Market decorated with tapestries. The perimeter was closed in by a fence provided with padded benches arranged in three tiers. A small dais was provided for His Holiness and the count, with a raised platform built for the shawm, trombone, and trumpet players. Every rooftop was crammed with crowds. On the dancing area, sixty young people, wonderfully dressed and bejewelled, waited to dance and, as soon as the music started, lords and ladies performed, including the count who 'in dancing did not make mistakes'. The three-hour long spectacle was twice interrupted by the arrival of welcome baskets of food and wine. What is remarkable here is not only the duration of the dancing but the scale and control of the crowds; and such staging and overall management were characteristic of the celebrations which marked important dynastic unions.

A typically grand sequence of well-prepared magnificences was contrived in Mantua (1608) where three weeks of pomp and splendour marked the marriage of Francesco IV Gonzaga (1586–1612) to Margherita di Savoia (1589–1655). Every evening, balls and banquets were held, preceded by plays with extravagant interludes and followed by fireworks. Every day, there were chivalric displays—tournaments, jousts and barriers, naval sea battles on the lake, or assaults on castles. The events were notable for the variety and innovative quality of their festival forms: the impressive learning that was

ENTRY OF MARS AND JUPITER TO THE BANQUET, *A Renaissance Wedding*, 1475.

displayed on the triumphal arches which welcomed Margherita with citations from Vergil's *Eclogues* and the *Aeneid*; and the beginnings of new forms—ballet and opera. Claudio Monteverdi's *Il ballo delle ingrate*, danced by sixteen ladies, aroused the passions, an artistic aim that had long been an ambition of Renaissance artists. Early traces of opera are present in the two dramas performed in 1608: Guarini's *Idropica*, staged with many choral and danced interludes composed by Gabriel Chiabrera (1552–1638).

Antonio Maria Vianini's (*fl.* 1582–1632/5) machines transformed the scene. Seascapes became gardens, Pluto's region changed into caves inhabited by the winds, fierce mountains turned into palaces and towers. Concerts of music played by violins with polyphonic choruses accompanied all these changes, while dialogues and solos characterized the personages. Ballets were diverse in their figurations; morescos were followed by full-blown choreographic military displays, where two teams of twelve dancers confronted each other performing steps of great intricacy, and joining battle with a ferocity of blows from naked blades which never seemed to break the rhythm of the dance. Monteverdi's *Arianna*, composed to verses by Ottavio Rinuccini (1562–1621) introduced entirely new active and dramatic effects from the soaring sound of the choruses interwoven with ballets announcing the descent of gods to the appealing solos given to these divine beings which built up to Arianna's final lament—suppliant prayers which are famous to this day.

Spaces for the performing arts

The nave of churches played an important role in drama production throughout this period. Earlier, miniature dramas based on stories from Jesus' life had, by the beginning of the fifteenth century, blossomed into vast musical events which relied on the services of composers and architects of genius. Often the action spilled over outside the building; in Bologna, for example, in 1470, the cathedral doors became the backcloth for a tournament. The marketplace or public square offered a desirable location to satisfy the needs for entertainment by all levels of society. Although the focus on dance in the New Market in Florence (1459) was unusual, the fact that it took place in a market square was not. In Bruges (1468), the market square was the venue for a great tournament, *Le pas de l'arbre d'or*, to celebrate the marriage of Margaret of York (1446–1503) to Charles the Bold (1433–77). St Mark's Square in Venice, under the inspiration of Jacopo Sansovino (1486–1570), had developed into an important ceremonial space, with the basilica, the Piazza itself, and the Piazzetta unifying the whole. Its setting, with the fine façades of the square, seemed like the walls of a rich theatre. City streets were also filled with people at carnival time; for the entries of princes into towns of their realm; or during Lent and on special feast days for the performances of mystery plays which could last several days. Stage installations varied from place to place. In Spain, two-tiered chariots carried the actors, who were supported by music and dancing as they went along. In England, mystery plays were performed at well-established stations (platforms) along the route and were reliant for their success as much on the vagaries of the weather as on the planning and ingenuity of the guilds.

For the elite, the great courtyards of palaces were transformed for entertainment. Although that of the Pitti Palace in Florence became famous for the ambitious shows enacted there, the sea battle fought in 1589 seemed to stretch resources beyond their limit. The entire space was flooded and engravings suggest that room for manoeuvre was very tight. A much less cluttered space in the open air was the Vatican's Belvedere courtyard, where spectators had a clear view of the action from all parts for the tournament performed there in 1565. A little earlier, Ferrara had offered an example of the ingenuity with which such space could be used when, in March 1561, structures modelled on a real theatre were built in the great court, capable of holding the 10,000 spectators crammed in to see *Il castello di Gorgoferusa*. Waterways were an indispensable mode of communication, and they too provided attractive space for festival. When Henri III visited Venice in 1574, he travelled from Murano to the centre of the city in the doge's bucentore (ceremonial barge), arriving at the Foscari Palace, his residence. Music-making on the canals was a noted pastime, and thus his journey was accompanied by choral music composed by Gioseffo Zarlino (1517–90). Such performances astonished visitors, as Thomas Coryate recorded (1608): 'I saw Venice…which yieldeth the most glorious and heavenly show upon the water that ever any mortal eye beheld.' He might have made a similar observation had he been present at the naumachia on the Thames in 1613 when Frederick V, Count Palatine (1596–1632), came to marry James I's daughter,

NAUMACHIA IN THE COURTYARD OF THE PITTI PALACE, Florence, 11 May 1589. Engraving by Orazio Scarabelli.

Elizabeth Stuart (1596–1662). Such water shows were much appreciated by Londoners, who regularly processed down the Thames with boats and bunting to inaugurate the annual installation of a new Lord Mayor.

Great halls were the most common location for early court entertainments. Tudor interludes saw performers coming in through screens at the end of the hall with few props to help interpret their actions. On the continent of Europe, such scenes had evolved into more ambitious performances as mobile cars brought in among the guests, gods, and goddesses suitably dressed and equipped. The most glorious space created solely for splendid entertainment were the rooms painted by Giulio Romano (1492/9–1546) in the Palazzo del Te (1530). The hall of Psyche depicted a wedding banquet with Cupid, crowds of nude figures, tables loaded with gold and silver projecting the very essence of theatrical splendour. The hall of the giants represented on the walls the whole universe tumbling about as the rocks of the giants and the thunder of the gods brought down temples. Emperor Charles V was very impressed, thinking, as he stood at the centre of this theatre set, that it had been designed to congratulate him (Jupiter) on his victories at Tunis (1535).

Permanent public theatres sprang up in England from 1576 and, thereafter, multiplied such that, by 1590, it has been calculated, 10,000 spectators a week could enjoy dramatic performances. Similarly, in Spain, inn yards had been transformed into theatres to meet demand. Small private theatres had grown up in Venice as each nobleman sought regular entertainment; and, alongside these, were the many public establishments. These may have been fairly modest as, according to Coryate, they were not much to boast about: 'their Playhouses [are] very beggarly and base in comparison of our stately Playhouses in England'. Indeed, when both the Globe and the Fortune theatres burnt down in 1613 and 1621 respectively, they were immediately replaced by almost exact replicas, suggesting that managers, poets, and performers alike were satisfied with their arrangements. Permanent private theatres had earlier been provided in northern Italian courts—Ferrara 1528, and Milan 1549—and after many delays, the Teatro Olimpico (Verona) opened its doors in March 1585 with an adaptation of Aeschylus' *Edipus tyrannus*. Inspired by the work of the architect Andrea Palladio (1508–90), whose study of ancient theatres from the *De architectura* (1511) of Vitruvius and from the *De re aedificatoria* (1485) of Leon Battista Alberti was profound, the theatre was sumptuous in design, the stage opening onto three street perspectives, with classical statues gracing the proscenium arch and every gallery in the auditorium. In Florence, Buontalenti constructed the Medici theatre in the Uffizi in 1589. The creation of these large-scale, purpose-built theatres (many more were to follow) had a significant impact on the quality and effect of dramatic performances: celestial machinery, now distanced from the spectator, could be manipulated successfully; words were more audible; musicians could be installed in diverse parts of the building. Monteverdi himself stressed the interdependence of music and architecture. From now on, stage and auditorium formed a single unit.

Feast days

All over Europe, cities had celebrated Corpus Christi and other important religious festivals with processions and dramatic spectacle performed on mobile wagons. Such performances persisted in England until the sixteenth century and, in Spain and other Catholic countries, even to this day. Declared a feast day by papal bull in 1264, Corpus Christi processions occurred first in Toledo before spreading to every major city. Church authorities initiated the process, calling on the town's guilds to contribute cars destined to carry an effigy representing their patron saint or an elaborately decorated structure on which drama might be mounted. Examples from Spain illustrate the nature and extent of the festival. In Seville (1513), three chariots processed through the city, each one divided into two sections: the first presented on one side David with the Virgin, St Joseph, and the child Jesus, and on the other St Matthew with an angel; the second depicted the pains of hell and then the spectacle of the last supper; while the third showed the throne of Justice and Death, with Elijah seated in a fiery chariot. Gradually, the show became more ambitious and the number of cars multiplied. In 1594, for example, the Seville guilds created a universe worthy to welcome Christ when all the citizens participated in erecting biblical statues on the façade of the cathedral, altars, and arches along the processional route, all diverse forms serving the same ideology. Every year, on Good Friday and Easter Sunday, a passion play was performed in Vienne on the marketplace, with four scaffolds built for musicians and actors. In Bruges (1536), eyewitnesses thought the Acts of the Apostles represented real-life stories.

The strong presence of mystery plays in England, especially in the north and east (York, Chester, Coventry, and Norwich), came to an abrupt end in the 1570s when prohibition from the Ecclesiastical Commission forbade depiction of God, Jesus, and the Holy Ghost. Great was the loss of verbal complexities telling the stories of salvation and of familiar visual traditions. Teaching through spectacle and speaking pictures gave way to more secular concerns. A similar pattern can be recorded for France, where mystery plays flourished everywhere until, in Paris in 1549, spectacular dramatization of religious stories by the Confraternity of the Passion was abolished. The second half of the sixteenth century saw the abandonment or transformation of sacred dramas in northern Italy too.

The Feast of St John the Baptist (24 June), patron saint of Florence, regularly featured a blend of religious and profane symbolism. Traditionally, a series of triumphal cars, designed and painted by foremost artists of the day—Andrea del Sarto (1486–1530), Jacopo Pontormo (1494–1557), and Giorgio Vasari (1511–74)—paraded through the streets to the cathedral to the sound of music. In 1454, there were twenty-one cars depicting the story of Adam, the fall of Lucifer, and God giving the laws to Moses. Under Lorenzo the Magnificent, however, all that was changed. In 1491, abandoning the traditional religious themes, he commissioned fifteen cars illustrating the triumphs of

The Performing Arts   271

Paulus Aemilius, introducing for the first time historical figures from ancient Rome. By this means, he was unashamedly declaring the glorification of the Medici rule; Florence was to be a new Rome with a powerful dynasty at the helm. A mixture of profane and biblical symbolism dominated the procession in succeeding years. In June 1513, offering both instruction and praise, ten *edifizi* (cars) showed biblical topics, pictures of faith, and moral edification, followed by four cars, each carrying a Roman emperor—Caesar, Pompey, Octavian, and Trajan. Thus, from a uniquely religious celebration, the Feast of St John became a showy vehicle for political statement and persuasion.

Carnival

Carnival engaged the whole community. It was the time between Christmas and Lent when subversive dramas were enacted through the streets, releasing tension, turning the world upside down, satirizing the establishment and its norms, and defusing violent elements in society by re-enacting them in processions and plays. The most vivid impressions of carnival-like festivities are found in the paintings of Bruegel the Elder (*c*.1525–69), although his inspiration came as much from Sebald Beham's (1500–50) prints depicting peasant feasts and weddings as from his own observations. There is a sense of freedom and vigour in the crowd evidently overjoyed to be released from the grim routine of daily toil; their gestures are unconstrained, their dancing extravagant to the music of shawms and pipes. In France, students, called Basochiens in Paris or Conards in Rouen, through farces and outlandish dress sought to upset the patterns of order and to comment on contemporary matters, guying the customs of universities and, in their verbal debates, even ridiculing the church. In so vast a country, there were regional variations. In Brittany, for instance, where communities were passionate about dance, they explored all available forms, often performing to their own singing, while, in Provence, the bold and vigorous *volta* was born. In Berne, any excuse provoked dancing and the activity intensified at carnival time when music and dance were always linked to satire.

Nuremberg has been called the capital of carnival-making, for between 1550 and 1560, Hans Sachs (1494–1576) devised eighty-five playlets for carnival. Ruse, guile, and knavery were the standard features of his work, designed to provoke laughter implicating the spectator in the action. By contrast, in Rome, Florence, and the Low Countries, carnival took on a much more serious tone. It was in 1460 that Pope Paul II first permitted extensive festivities to celebrate carnival time with allegorical and historical triumphal chariots. Supervised by a council, each district of Rome contributed a car every year, the theme being determined in advance. Some reflected political affairs such as the car (1492) supporting figures of the Spanish king and queen, signalling their victory over Granada. Other inventions brought gods and planets, designed to demonstrate heavenly influences on the formation of human character. Whereas in many countries (especially France) joy often spilled over into violence and disruption, the Florentines were very controlled. Under Cosimo I's rule (1541–50), the city enjoyed many days of celebration, including chivalric displays, buffalo fights, and comedies. The principal show was the traditional procession through the streets. In 1546, the theme was Universal Folly, with cars filled with fools and cripples; 300 torches followed the parade and every performer sang, since music was an essential component, as it emphasized the moral themes that were present in the visual material. The same moral concerns can be found in the *Ommegang* (processions) devised by the chambers of rhetoric in the Low Countries. Created in the fourteenth century to express religious fervour, these long processions of decorated cars exhibited, by the seventeenth century, profane subjects. Illustrated programmes, engraved by artists such as Maarten van Heemskerck (1498–1574), still survive. In 1559, the burghers of Antwerp celebrated the return of tranquillity and prosperity to Europe, after the Peace of Cateau-Cambrésis, with ten triumphal cars whose decoration emphasized the benefits of peace for the secure exchange of goods, for the return of virtues, brotherly love, justice, and good fellowship. No one could be misled as to the meaning of the figures which stood on the cars, as each was clearly labelled with a placard.

Venice celebrated carnival with music which accompanied the *mascherate* (costumed processions). Some were didactic and political with virtues carried on *soleri* (platforms), processing to Giovanni Gabrieli's (*c.*1554/7–1612) compositions; others reflected traditions elsewhere as masked performers crowded the streets playing and singing ballads in dialect. The most prolonged celebrations came with the victory at Lepanto (1571). Days of festival continued into the New Year, culminating in a *mascherata* on Carnival Sunday when 340 people followed the thirteen chariots carrying 100 Turkish slaves.

Travelling theatre companies of professional actors often came at carnival time when their spontaneity and improvisation were especially appreciated. Gil Vicente (*c.*1460–1536), who organized royal pageants and festivals for the Portuguese monarch Manuel I (1469–1521), travelled the country far and wide with his company, well provided with costumes and musical instruments; but, for the forty-nine plays which survive (comedies, farces, and religious works), he needed few other props. Constantly experimenting, he appealed to a wide audience, dancing in short costumes equipped with bells (and sometimes swords), he satirized affairs of the day, giving exaggerated imitations of well-known characters. But it was the qualities of improvisation perfected by the *commedia dell'arte* which were most esteemed. Such troupes emerged in Italy in the second half of the sixteenth century, and when Henri III saw the company I Gelosi, in Venice (1574), he was infatuated and invited them to France. Two important pictorial sources have recorded their antics: the castle at Trausnitz (Bavaria) where, in 1575, the staircase was (and still is) decorated with figures from the *commedia dell'arte*; and the engravings produced by Jacques Callot (*c.*1592–1635). Their athletic dancing, with exaggerated and grotesque movements, contrasted starkly with the decorous and elegant steps of contemporary social and court performers.

COMMEDIA DELL'ARTE: RAZULLO AND CUCURUCU, etching by Jacques Callot, *Balli di Sfessania* (Paris, *c*.1621).

Princely parades

A traditional and persistent obligation for the performing arts was to collaborate in making the presence of princes spectacularly visible to the crowds when they made their formal entries into cities or were disguised on their way to display their chivalric skills on the marketplace. As a Spanish visitor to London remarked, commenting on Elizabeth I's progresses, 'in pompous ceremonies a secret of government doth much consist'. Princely entries in the Renaissance were ubiquitous: a monarch entering his capital after his coronation; an emperor riding in a great cavalcade into a conquered city; a prince being received by a friendly power; a pope taking possession of his charge or celebrating his jubilee; or an emperor introducing his son to his heritage. Each event required close collaboration from the designer/poet, the artist, the composer, and the expert in inscriptions. The interplay of their skills emerges from specific examples. Forms of royal entries evolved from simple structures peopled with live actors singing and reciting verses in praise of the city and the prince, to become elaborate arches, covered with learned mottoes and symbols, their overall form inspired from buildings in Rome and from books of architecture and prints. There was an evolution too in the focus of such events. In the early entries, corporations expressed sincere welcome to a prince whom they exalted; affection, gifts, and a renewal of the city's privileges were the dominant features. By the time Charles IX entered Paris in 1571, the king was no longer depicted as a dispenser of justice; that virtue had been absorbed into a display of majesty. With this evolution came a shift in the imagery used; simple biblical and allegorical themes gave way to complex symbolism derived from history and mythology.

Princely entries tended to be highly personalized. When Pope Leo X made his triumphal entry into Florence in 1515, the city had thoroughly absorbed the lessons of Lorenzo the Magnificent. He saw arches depicting the four cardinal virtues, human and divine felicity, while mingled in were structures that imitated monuments in Rome: the Castello Sant'Angelo, the Vatican obelisk, and a stately column—a copy of one in Rome. After all, the Medici pope was at home in both cities. The Emperor Charles V, too, was accorded numerous triumphal entries in Italy. In Bologna (1529/30), where the pope crowned Charles as emperor, a vast procession paraded through the streets demonstrating the emperor's military might: cannons mounted on chariots;

CORTÈGE FOR THE ENTRY OF HENRI IV INTO LYON (1595), drawing attributed to Jacques Perrissin.

and an army which accompanied Charles V in full armour, his helmet topped with the imperial golden eagle. His followers reminded the crowd of the vast territories over which he ruled, yet the decorations on the arches argued for peace. His entry into Rome (February 1536) was equally spectacular. Here, many buildings were destroyed to create unhindered vistas onto surviving triumphal monuments of the ancient city to which were added structures forming a replay of the victories of Paulus Aemilius. The parallels with the emperor could not have been more potent, and their personal application was explained to him as he stopped to study each arch.

Elizabeth I's entry into London (1559) was also notable for the role the queen played. Her journey through the city in her gilded coach was performed to 'a noyse of instruments'; and she was an integral part of the action, voicing her pleasure at the sight of her ancestors, noting the references to good governance, and acknowledging the parallel between herself and Deborah's achievements. During her reign, the Lord Mayor's annual procession copied many of these elements. As the newly elected mayor travelled through the streets and listened to praises of the city and of the queen, he saw his future duties performed by actors on scaffolds which depicted, over time, more and more historical and even mythological characters.

In the theatrical ducal processions in Venice, position was everything. Order and place, established by tradition and known from books of ceremonies, were the watchwords so that musical performances erupted just when they were expected and crowds could anticipate the ritual from past experience. Processions were as much a method of social control as of stimulating wonder and in no other city could the approach for the arriving prince be more inspiring: first, a procession by water, and then the journey across the ceremonial space of the piazza to St Mark's, and the splendour of alternating choirs of music. The experience provided a kind of visual discourse on the order of this state, an image of the city itself. In distant Kraków, on the other hand, numbers were the important thing. For the entry of Sigismund III (1592), the multitude was extraordinary: 2,900 knights on horseback; 2,700 soldiers on foot; and 162 coaches and carriages filled with aristocratic ladies. Moreover, by this time engravers had found a more accurate way of recording such profusion. Instead of a series of images depicting the detail of each theatrical structure with its musicians, actors, and symbols, they engraved the whole assembly, the cortège snaking around the page and processing beneath the arches.

Royal entries in France were particularly frequent. Indeed, Henri II made forty-eight entries into cities of his realm during his short reign (1547–59). Outstanding for the collaborative effort between all the arts were those undertaken in three successive years to major towns: Lyon (1548), Paris (1549), and Rouen (1550). All exhibited their debt to classical forms, and the contribution of significant scholars, poets, and artists: Maurice Scève (c.1501–1564) designed the Lyon entry; Jean Martin with the help of Jean Cousin (1500–c.1593) and the sculptor Jean Goujon (c.1510–1565) masterminded the Paris entry; while Claude Chappuys (c.1500–1575) was responsible for Rouen. Here, the king witnessed a Roman triumph (October 1550) with three triumphal cars and a replica

& fama peragrato Jam Jam redit œyus orbe'
Henricum cunctis auribz Jntonuit

CHARIOT OF FAME FROM *HENRI II'S ENTRY INTO ROUEN*, 1550, miniature.

of Andrea Mantegna's (*c.*1431–1506) *Triumphs of Caesar* with touches of Petrarch's (1304–74) *Triumphs* thrown in. The record makes explicit that the planner and his colleagues deliberately sought to reproduce a Roman spectacle: 'in direct imitation of Roman triumphant generals, similar to that custom used by Roman knights of old'. There were musicians with trumpets; soldiers in Roman garb carrying trophies, images and models of conquered cities; elephants bearing castle, chapel, and ship—recalling the king's recent victories at Boulogne. The principal figure on each car was seated on a throne—the winged figure of Renown, for example, holding a model of the church on the car of Religion, demonstrating the king's support for the Catholic faith. Other spectacles confronted this knowledgeable display of monuments from the past with visions of the New World—chief among which was the depiction of ceremonies of native Brazilians, of whom fifty genuinely came from South America. They were shown naked engaging in their customary duties: building, making war, fighting, putting out fires, boating, dancing, hunting, and making love.

This attempt to harness the new with the old was novel and not to be found in the great city of Antwerp—where successive entries were recorded in print with engravings showing the care in preparation, the visually ambitious projects, and the political messages spelt out plainly. The 1549 entry is important since Antwerp was still an opulent metropolis of trade, and it was in this year that Charles V chose to present his son as successor. The event was recorded by Cornelius Grapheus (1482–1558), in a book printed by Plantin Moretus in three languages, and illustrated by Pieter Coecke van Aelst (1502–50) who, having spent time in Rome, was addicted to classical forms. The city had employed 1,726 artists and artisans, including a large number of actors, actresses, and musicians for the *tableaux vivants*, and merchants and bankers were prominent in the proceedings, anxious to affirm their role in the city's prosperity and determined to extol their own histories and artistic achievements. Thus, the Florentine arch promoted its modern poets and artists—Petrarch and Dante, Giotto and Michelangelo: 'Let Zeuxis give way to them and the thrice-great Apelles too'. The Genoese arch depicted a familiar theme, painted by Frans Floris (1517–70), and one which Charles V would have particularly appreciated for it showed the defeat of the giants by Jupiter. By 1594, when the city was controlled by a Spanish nominee, Antwerp, having withstood the Spanish sack in 1576, was dying; yet the governor, Archduke Ernst (1553–95) was received with untold splendour. This time, however, the structures told a sad story of decline. Songs and verses pleaded for the seas to be opened so that the city could attain its former glory. This was not to be, and when Peter Paul Rubens (1577–1640) came to design, in 1635, the magnificent reception for the new governor, Cardinal Infante Ferdinand (1609–41), the situation was beyond repair.

In the matter of princely parades, popes were not to be outdone. For the Jubilee (1500), a triumph of Julius Caesar, with eleven cars, swept through the streets of Rome. After his recovery of Bologna in 1507, Pope Julius II staged his return to Rome as a Roman *imperator*; and again in 1513, he celebrated carnival with twelve cars whose symbolism set forth the power of Italy—one car carrying *Italia Liberata*, another the Apennine mountains with, at their peak, a colossus. All the districts of the papal state paid him homage; and the crowning moment of the parade was the final structure, with an effigy of Julius himself, brandishing a sword in his right hand and the sphere of the world in his left. Papal pomp had thus completely absorbed pagan traditions of the ancient triumph.

Knightly encounters and chivalric display flourished everywhere in Europe from the eleventh century. By the Renaissance, they had virtually lost their principal function—training for war; yet the early competitive spirit, and the demonstration of military skills and social status, remained fundamental, although they came to be overladen with exorbitant display. The procession to the lists, theatrical setting, and mini-musical dramas counted for more than the knightly deeds themselves. It was the disguises, the cortège, and the machines to which witnesses gave most attention, for knights had become actors and musicians. With names from Boiardo or Ariosto, from *Amadis of Gaul* or from the Spanish romances of Perez de Hita (*c.*1544–*c.*1619), they brought their literary past with them. The crowds were well versed in the ritual, the rules, and themes of tournament. In the Low Countries, after all, hardly a year passed without such an event, often organized by the burghers themselves. In Lille, they put on such annual

FIELD OF CLOTH OF GOLD, 1520. Painter unknown.

spectacles partly because the citizens wanted a regular show and partly to ape their social betters, who were very willing to participate.

An event which provoked international interest was the meeting of Francis I with Henry VIII at the Field of Cloth of Gold in 1520. As a diplomatic venture it achieved very little; as the greatest show yet seen, it aroused great enthusiasm. Henry had come with 5,172 followers; he had Richard Gibson and a team of artists and artisans build a palace which contemporaries compared to those found in romances, while the tents and pavilions were likened to Egyptian pyramids and Roman amphitheatres. Diplomacy required that chivalric success in the tournaments should be equally balanced between the two monarchs. Honours had to be even, whether in the lists or in the dancing and music which the courts exchanged on successive evenings. The weather was mixed throughout the days of entertainment, but not as bad as in Kraków (1543) when tournaments, races, and tilting had to be abandoned.

Other festivities on the scale of those in 1520 were conceived by Mary of Burgundy (1505–58) at Binche in 1549. Chivalric displays, banquets, mascarades, concerts, and ballets were planned, illustrating the interrelation of all festival forms for, here, themes interlocked and different stages of the entertainment were announced at one festive meeting for the next. So it was that arriving at Binche in the middle of a masked ball, Charles V received a letter from Belgian knights seeking his protection against the magician Novabroch, who inhabited a tenebrous castle on the island. We are in the realm of Arthurian legend since the enchanter can only be overcome by the knight who succeeds in pulling a jewelled sword out of a pillar, and, unsurprisingly, the future Philip II (Beltenebros) was successful. The feats of arms lasted three days and, despite the make-believe, some knights were wounded and could not take part in the tournament which accompanied the entry into Antwerp.

Venice, as always, had its own idiosyncratic interpretation of chivalric display. In 1562, to greet Anne de Foix, the new Queen of Hungary (1549–80), a joust was performed on the Grand Canal, where each movement was made in time to the music. However, despite the fact that almost every city in the Italian peninsula prided itself on the quality of its chivalric displays, Ferrara was the place where knightly festivals most successfully blended music, dance, drama, and chivalric skills. For the marriage of Alfonso II (1533–97) to Barbara of Austria (1539–72) in 1565, Torquato Tasso (1544–95) created *The Temple of Love*, a work of superb poetry, varied musical forms, and decors which transformed every scene. Banks of seats lined up against the rear of the palace looked onto a mountain landscape with a temple; at each side successive scene changes brought into view grottoes and pyramids; and the bell on the temple tower rang each time combatants came into the lists. The whole occasion began with a prologue by magicians who denied access to the temple; combats followed, interrupted by fanfares of instrumental music alternating with sweet, harmonious madrigals and choruses. The confusion and chaos wrought by magic is eventually overcome, when the audience is entertained by a literary tournament on the theme of love, and the duke—bringer of harmony and joy—is regaled with instrumental dances. For this event,

KNIGHT'S HEADDRESS (1608), drawing by Giulio Parigi.

chivalric skills were integrated into drama, music, and dance, but although the gorgeous procession through the streets to the lists had lost none of its splendour, it was not the focal point it was to become in the annual celebrations of Liberty enjoyed for many years in Bologna. In this city, during the night, the nobility amused itself with music, ballets, and banquets; in daylight, it was the turn of the admiring citizens to participate. One of the most notable occasions was in 1628 when local academicians devised thirteen triumphal cars with elaborate costumes, intricate machines, and learned devices on the theme of *Love prisoner in Delos* for a tournament. The sole preoccupation here was splendour, detailed in the realistic designs for triumphal cars inhabited by gods. Venus, drawn by peacocks amid clouds, heralded the procession: then came Mars, Apollo on Parnassus with the Muses drawn by four stallions, and Hercules dominating a huge hydra. The interest is all in the dazzle and magnificence, and in wonder at the preposterous headdresses worn by knights whose exploits were drawn from romance.

Such undiluted attention to outward show (the actual performance of the knights received little attention) underwent political manipulations in the north. The celebrations for the coronation of Christian IV of Denmark in 1596, while assuming traditional forms—running at the ring, dancing, and fireworks—were unusual. For his chivalric display, Christian (vehemently anti-Catholic) disguised himself as a pope, wearing a heavy triple crown (quite unsuitable for running at the ring). The setting was a square building with an open gallery at the top where royal singers and instrumentalists performed, dressed as monks, hermits, and clerics. On the building were painted frescos of the Vatican: papal palace, the Belvedere courtyard, the Castello Sant'Angelo, and the church of Santa Maria Rotonda. The king rode up and down ridiculing the pope and all his works. Similarly, politics played a significant role also in the entertainments at Protestant courts in Germany. Between 1605 and 1618, a variety of martial exercises were enjoyed—tilts, running at the ring, foot combats, carousels, and (unusually) comic jousts—all stressing True Religion and making important statements about peace, national identity, and the strength of Germania: an earlier tournament prepared for Landgrave Moritz von Hessen-Kassel in 1589 had already appropriated many of the themes and structures which had marked entertainments in other parts of Europe. Here, the parade was longer, incorporating the five planets, the four elements, and the four continents; America with cannibals, Africa's chariot led by negroes, Asia with followers in turbans, Europe crowned by an angel, with her emblems announcing Greek wisdom and Roman justice. Musicians were threaded through the procession, but here fighting was not just show. The conflicts were serious and reflected increased links between spectacle and politics.

Performance and politics

Display and magnificence were the tools of princes, and drama offered distinctive and satisfactory symbolic representations of power which, at the same time, inspired extraordinary creative impulses in artists, poets, and musicians. As princes embarked

TOURNAMENT IN THE BELVEDERE COURT, Vatican, Rome, 1565. Engraving attributed to Étienne du Pérac.

on organizing festivals worthy of their lofty notions of themselves, they found that they were in competition with others both in the conception of forms of celebration and in the need to attract the best artists. For musicians, Ferrara competed with Mantua, Milan, the Vatican, Cambrai, and Fontainebleau, or Hampton Court and Prague. Artists were in demand in all Italian courts. Some were attracted to France (Leonardo, Andrea del Sarto, Rosso, and Primaticcio) or to Nonsuch and Hampton Court (Torrigiano and Niccolò da Modena). Dancing masters also travelled: weddings and christenings took Guglielmo from Pesaro to Urbino, to Ferrara, Milan, and Naples, while Cesare Negri (c.1535–c.1605) sent dancing masters to France, the Low Countries, Bavaria, and Germany. Some years later, French dancing masters were in the ascendant, supplying expertise for the English court and for the German courts of the Protestant Union. This internationalism encouraged cross-fertilization, and the closeness of the arts in the minds of the designers of theatrical events is reflected in the language used to describe their elements: dance movements (for instance) described as decorous, diverse, and graceful were terms borrowed from painting, whose norms were also adopted by poets to argue for the qualities of their own craft. This collaborative agenda was encouraged by the discussions of humanists in the academies of Florence, Paris, and elsewhere, and by their conviction that powerful effects derived from the fusion of poetry and music. Ancient authority did, indeed, lie at the origins of such thinking. After all, Homeric poetry was structured on music and dance rhythms, and Plato had shown that choral singing embraced both dance and song. Efforts at harmonizing the arts were intended to make the word more audible, and therefore more effective, so that it might arouse and then control the passions, initiate and maintain virtue, and in specific instances, when fully orchestrated and extended, establish order and stability in the state.

These mixed forms acquired different emphases. Pastoral plays had incorporated song and danced elements from their inception with Jacopo Sannazaro's *Arcadia* (1484–6), a genre which remained popular and was exploited by Pierre de Ronsard (1524–85), for example, in the *Bergerie* (1564) which focused both on creativity and on the lessons that young kings might learn from ancestral example. In Portugal, Gil Vicente (1465/70–1536/40) incorporated dances and singing in his plays while, in the next generation, Lope de Rueda (1505–65) entertained Spanish crowds both in churches and on the streets, separating the acts of his comedies with sung and danced interludes. Musical drama developed particularly in Italy where attempts to bring all the arts together were most marked and where the scale of the operation was extraordinary. A cognate form, the *ballet de cour* (court ballet), evolved at the French court when verse, song, and choral displays provided the framework in which dance took on the major role. Another mixed genre, the masque, was largely the creation of the English court, although many of its features derived from French ballet and from Italian musical drama. Despite their diversity of form, these genres had a family resemblance. Whatever the play (tragedy or comedy), the sung and danced interludes had a unity of theme, supported by scenery whose content became almost mandatory—forest, grotto, seascape, vision of hell, or spectacle of heaven—all giving a satisfying cohesion to the performance. The themes themselves recurred in productions across Europe: Apollo and the Muses acknowledging the princes' qualities which bring harmony to the world; Hercules and his labours which mirrored princely achievements; Jupiter and the gods, a representation of the earthly court; Jason and his Argonauts signifying the work and dedication of the prince, leading ultimately to triumph; or Orpheus and Arion, masters of harmony, who celebrate the return of peace and the establishment of prosperity.

Because of the expense involved, interludes were often performed more than once, incorporated between the acts of new plays, or transported in their entirety to a different place. In this way, travelling theatre companies introduced new drama and brought new ideas and new ways of performing, such as the improvisatory character and singing gifts of I Gelosi (Italian strolling players). In Lyon (1548), for example, the

Florentine company La Cazzuola performed *La Calandria* as part of the festivities for the entry of Henri II into the city. It had been performed in Urbino (1513) with four interludes and a postlude, but in Lyon it was augmented by eight fresh interludes devised by Luigi Alamanni (1495–1556) who used, for his inspiration, the 1539 interludes written by G. B. Strozzi (1504–71) for the wedding festivities of Cosimo I (1519–74).

The Lyon performance lasted four hours and such stamina on the part of the audience was common. The most celebrated theatrical event of these times, the performance of *La pellegrina* with six interludes (Florence, May 1589) for the marriage of Ferdinand I (1549–1609) to Christine of Lorraine (1565–1637), is reported to have taken seven hours. This show was the centrepiece of several weeks of celebrations, planned for over a year, and designed to aggrandize the Medici dynasty. Ferdinand and Christine, seated on a dais at the centre of the auditorium in the Medici theatre, were the recipients of praise and a focus of attention in their own right. Christine would have had some insight into the unprecedented scale of the arrangements through her earlier visit to the Duomo. While the archbishop delivered his oration, a huge white cloud descended full of angels whose singing was so magnificent 'that it seemed like paradise itself'. The overall theme of the interludes to *La pellegrina* was the power of musical harmony to influence gods and men. It also implied an obvious but important political message: just as heavenly bodies revolve around the earth, so individuals, courtiers, and other social classes revolve around the prince. Moreover, just as Harmony overcame the ills of the world, so men learn, through experiencing its influences, how to bring peace and make it endure. A fixed view of Pisa formed the backcloth on the stage and was revealed for each act of the comedy. Each interlude required a new scene beginning and ending with heaven, while in between, in succession, came a forest, a grove, a rocky cave, hell, and a seascape. These varied prospects appeared and disappeared smoothly and at speed. The interludes explained musical harmony, its operation, and its benefits, achieved by the interlocking of the arts, and fusing instrumental music, song, and dance into a coherent whole. The action of the interludes began with the descent of Harmony, whose prologue announces blessings directly addressed to the new Minerva (Christine) and Mighty Hercules (Ferdinand). The goddess is accompanied by the three Fates, eight gods and goddesses, and a choir of sirens. A contest between the Muses and Pierides follows with the expected triumph of Apollo's charges; the god himself then appears and, to martial music and dance, kills the python. A prophecy of the return of the Golden Age in the next interlude contrasts with a vision of hell reminiscent of Canto 3 from Dante's *Inferno*. Another contest ensues, this time between some sailors and Arion, whose songs compel the dolphin to rescue him. For the finale, gods send Rhythm and Harmony to earth as a golden sunburst and golden rain burst over all. A chorus of shepherds, extended dancing, and expansive music close the performance with a lengthy Epithalamium.

Bernardo Buontalenti's (1531–1608) control over all the elements of this production was remarkable. The movement of the clouds required 82 men; 286 costumes had to be tailored carefully; hundreds of lamps had to be installed and kept from smoking; 82

DESCENT OF HARMONY AND RHYTHM (*La Pellegrina*, 1589), engraving by Epifanio d'Alfiano.

craftsmen were needed to build the sets; and numerous rehearsals were organized to ensure that vision and sound blended perfectly. These were significant achievements for the future of theatrical shows and their usefulness to princes. For opera and ballet, in particular, the variety of musical and choreographic forms opened up new dramatic possibilities: the alternating vocal contest between the Muses and the Pierides; the five-part military dance which precedes Apollo's triumph and his own daring display afterwards; the songs of Arion; and the finale, composed by the chief organizer, Emilio de' Cavalieri (1550–1602), with the massive chorus that accompanies Harmony (sung by the celebrated Vittoria Acchilei, *c.*1560–1620) and the elaborate danced spectacle with all kinds of permutations on a single two-part arrangement exploring a set of variations on two simple passages of music which alternated with each other. For this grand finale, we have the convergence of humanist ideals for music with the practice and repertory of courtly dance, involving 25 instrumentalists, 60 singers, and 27 dancers. A visitor to Florence, Giuseppe Pavoni, noted in his diary: 'the great expenditures and the magnificence and splendour deployed by the Grand Duke in these nuptials…have shown the world the power and grandeur of the House of Medici.' That was certainly the intention.

The complex choreography, well rehearsed and expert, of the 1589 finale owed much to the traditions of court ballet which had developed in France from the 1560s,

BALL AND MASQUERADE, Munich, 1568, engraving by Frans Floris.

where dance became the central feature of many court festivals and where the harmonious effects interpreted from the figures danced on the floor were believed to have political significance. In France, dancing in all its forms had always been very popular, as can be seen from the abundance of dance music published there by Pierre d'Attaignant, royal printer of music (1494–1551/2). Dance tunes were both the accompaniment to social dancing and music to which verses were sung. Its popularity can be explained partly because a dance such as the stately pavane was eminently suited to court ceremonial all over Europe, from the nightly entertainments in France and Italy to the activities enjoyed after banquets in Germany where, for instance, Nikolaus Solis (*c*.1542–1584) recorded a ball given in the palace at Munich (1568). The popularity and status of the dance is also related to the fact that gentlemen and ladies were all taught to dance from an early age. Most notable among the attempts to stabilize what was often an inherently explosive political atmosphere at court was the ballet *Paradise of Love* (1572) performed in Paris two days after the wedding of the future Henri IV (1553–1610) and Marguerite de Valois (1553–1615) when spectacular display took on two contrasting forms. First, there was an assault on Paradise when the king, his brothers, and the groom dramatized their religious difference by fighting with each other, displaying their martial skills, until the vanquished Protestant warriors were sent to hell. At this point the second form of celebration came with the descent of Cupid (sung by the famous castrato Estienne le Roy), who explained that the king and his troupe had conquered all comers since, equipped with special weapons, he was supported by heavenly forces. After this song, twelve nymphs began their dance of love, with figures of complex design lasting over one hour.

During the reign of Henri III, his passion for the dance ensured that performances were frequent at his court. The most influential spectacle was *Le Balet comique de la reyne* (1581), created by the choreographer Balthasar de Beaujoyeulx (*fl.* 1540–*c*.1587) as part of the two weeks of magnificences which Henri III gave to his favourite Anne, duc de Joyeuse (1560–87), on his marriage to his wife's half-sister Marguerite. This work has become famous not only for its fusion of verse, music, dance, and mobile decors, but also because an illustrated account, complete with music and the names of both creators and performers, together with four explanations of its meaning, has survived. The ballet tells the story of the struggles encountered by the virtuous who sought to release Ulysses and his companions from the power of the enchantress Circe. Their release is finally effected by the combined efforts of music and dance: dialogues, choruses, and heavenly music, and a succession of complex dance figurations. At last, Circe is subdued, brought forward before Henri III, and forced to acknowledge his superior powers. Beaujoyeulx, in his dedication to Henri III, sees his work as a demonstration of that monarch's ability to bring peace and prosperity to a land being destroyed by strife.

Although the political realities of the religious wars were, in fact, untouched by the aspirations of Beaujoyeulx, the form he had perfected was taken up with enthusiasm in other countries—in Italy, and especially in Savoy; and in Scotland, whose close

BALET COMIQUE DE LA REYNE, 1581, anonymous engraving of the opening scene.

connections with France meant that French verse and dance models were all-important. Scottish poets, musicians, and choreographers imitated La Grotte's (1530–1600) settings of Ronsard's poems; enjoyed Jannequin's (c.1485–1558) music; and adopted the galliard, 'brant new frae France'. Embassies, especially that of Esmé Stuart, sire d'Aubigny (1542–83) brought back French court styles and taste, while Mary, Queen of Scots' (1542–87) return to her homeland ensured that ballet was frequently performed there. By the early years of the seventeenth century, court ballet had crossed the Rhine and, along with chivalric shows, became the most common mode of entertainment. In Württenberg and in Stuttgart, court ballet was copied from French examples, composed by writers, musicians, and choreographers who were either French or much travelled in France, and promoted an idealized image of the court. Stately dances (which had come to be called *Grand Ballet* in France, where knights performed complex figures to demonstrate their skill) ended each performance, and accounts dwell on the skill, graceful speed, the amazing leaps, twists, and turns, and the overall ingenuity of the performers. In 1614, for instance, a *Ballet des nations* (Heidelberg) ended with a 'perfect and ingenious ballet lasting almost half an hour' in which the dancers gradually revealed in their steps the letters which formed the names of Frederick V, Count Palatine, and his wife, Elizabeth. This international style extended into Denmark by 1634. Its influence, however, was most strongly felt in England, where French musicians and dancing masters were employed by the court and where Ben Jonson (1572–1637), in particular, sought to outdo his Continental rivals. The French influence naturally intensified when Henrietta Maria, daughter of Henri IV (1609–69), became Charles I's (1600–49) wife in 1625.

Cultural exchange was an essential accompaniment to diplomatic negotiations. English ambassadors at the French court, like Sir Henry Cobham (1537–92), witnessed and commented upon the entertainments there, and Elizabeth I was eager to have their accounts. In addition, English gentlemen increasingly travelled abroad and were exposed to the spectacle of magnificence much greater than that experienced at home: Nicholas Lanier (1588–1666) and Inigo Jones (1573–1652), for instance, accompanied Lord Cranborne (1591–1668) on his European tour (from 1609), where they encountered impressive classical ruins at Nîmes and Orange and theatrical marvels at Paris, Venice, and Padua. Jones had first-hand knowledge of the work of Giorgio Parigi (1571–1635), who had succeeded Buontalenti at the Medici theatre; and he owned essential books such as those of Vitruvius and Sebastiano Serlio (1475–c.1554), and of architects Andrea Palladio and Androuet du Cerceau (1510–84), which he assiduously annotated. And, true to the Aristotelian concept of imitation, he copied his mentors. Likewise Jonson, steeped as deeply as Continental designers in the mythological compendia of the time, explained the allusions of his learned masques with painstaking care. Jones and Jonson, unlike George Chapman (c.1559–1634) in *The Lords' Masque*, 1613, had only a passing interest in music and, while little music survives, masque musicians were characterized as priests or poets of more than ordinary authority whose songs elucidated the mysteries of the work. Jonson's texts and some of Jones's designs survive, showing many characteristics of court ballet in that dance was taken very seriously. In the principal masque and in the lively anti-masques, dance was the main thread joining all parts together. King James I (1566–1625) did not dance, though he enjoyed watching and absorbing the adulation that was often very explicit—although the political resonances of each masque varied greatly as performances echoed and commented upon current individual and institutional concerns.

The *Masque of Augurs*, presented on Twelfth Night (1621) on the very day that Parliament had been dissolved, offers a good instance of how, after the Master of the Revels had produced two anti-masques, the high tone of the work is then established with dance and song dominating the proceedings. Amid a sunburst, Apollo descends from heaven and is swiftly joined by his four sons. His song immediately draws attention to the king;

> Behold the love and care of all the Gods
> [King] of the Ocean, and the Happie Isles.

This divine appearance is made at the behest of Jove himself to discover the king's wishes and to pronounce joyful auguries. Augurs and torchbearers sing and dance out their prophecies until Apollo and his sons, one by one, interpret the meaning in song for the king. The main dance is then performed by all the masquers, and after the revels, Apollo and the chorus proclaim the 'Glories' of peace—a prelude to the finale when the heavens open and Jupiter and all the gods are discovered to welcome back the sun god into their midst. This masque has a special interest in that Jonson, in a note on his text (printed early in 1622), acknowledges the contribution of others: 'The invention was divided betwixt Mr Jones and me…the music was composed by Alfonso Ferrabosco [1543–88] and Nicholas Lanier', artists regularly involved in the production of masques.

As the masque grew in complexity and became more spectacularly ambitious, so the power of illusion increased, to the extent that Charles I came to believe in his piety and virtue as displayed on stage, and even thought that—through such gifts—he could easily implant and sustain order in his kingdom. Typical of such illusion was the final scene for *Salmacida spolia* (1640) which was covered with clouds and deities representing the spheres filled with apparitions generating harmony. The spectators were, in fact, seeing a rerun of the finale to *La pellegrina* (1589).

The growing importance of machines is evident. The vast space of churches had, on feast days, been filled with extraordinary contraptions bringing down heavenly hosts to fill the space with music and wonder. These engineering triumphs were soon transported into the secular theatre where purpose-built structures could accommodate the quantity of scenes, traps, and cloud machines required for sudden apparitions and disappearances: mountains grew visibly on stage; villains disappeared into hell; gods gracefully descended from the heavens; ships crossed the stage in stately progress and waves seemed to move; rival vessels fought amid the clang of thunder and visible rain; or, even more ambitious, hell was revealed with apparitions of demons caught up in cascades of fire. Other technical feats were dragons spitting fire, a hydra, or sea monsters ready to devour the virtuous—all made of cardboard but realistic enough to scare.

Such engineering exploits transformed the structure of drama, ballet, or masque, and demanded formidable organizational powers from their promoters. A striking instance of this was *La Festa del Paradiso* (1490), performed in Milan and devised by Leonardo da Vinci (1452–1519). Before the play, several sets of masques and dances of diverse nations (Spanish, Hungarian, Turkish, and French) entertained the company. Between the duke's dais and the stage, tiers of seats on each side provided space for ladies; and a bench at the foot of the stage was reserved for the masked dancers. The area between the rows of seats and in front of the dais was set aside for dancing. The stage, raised above the hall, was filled with the shining machine of paradise, shaped like an egg, in front of which planets, virtues, and graces paraded. By the end of the sixteenth century, technical development made the most ambitious stage sets mandatory. They had become essential ingredients in the creation of the kind of illusion that carried spectators into a world of make-believe, a world ardently desired where gods and princes triumphed and brought the vision of harmony to an often dislocated reality. It was a counterblast to the grim realities that often threatened.

In order to ensure that the scale, expense, and the messages of such extravagant theatrical enterprises reached a wider public, accounts of these events quickly found their way into print. A privileged few received illuminated manuscripts, yet something more was needed. Printed versions not only put the reader on a par with the prince insofar as text and image assured close proximity to the actual intentions of the designers, they also furnished a source of inspiration and of imitation to countless creators of theatrical shows. Emperor Maximilian I (1459–1519), in particular, recognized the opportunities; print was an excellent way of promoting himself, his reign, and his empire. He devised his series of make-believe festival books, dictating the detail to his secretary Marx Treitzauerwein (1450–1527) between 1508 and 1512. Over twenty artists and writers were involved when the *Theuerdank* (Maximilian's adventures and courtship) appeared in 1517. Significant names were connected with this enterprise: Albrecht Dürer (1471–1528) designed the Great Triumphal car which survives in Vienna in the great frieze of 59 sheets (originally more than 100 metres long) painted by Albrecht Altdorfer (1480–1538). Hans Burgkmair (1471–1531) published the entire triumphal procession with 135 woodcuts by command of Ferdinand II in 1526. Sadly, the emperor's 255 mascarades and tournaments, beautifully illuminated (*Freydal*), never reached a publisher until the nineteenth century.

Maximilian's example was swiftly followed. French royal entries from the 1540s onwards were recorded and published in full at the expense of the city councils. Emperor Charles V also made sure that his glorious peregrinations, and those of his son Philip II, were properly recorded. Courts rivalled each other in their anxiety to tell the world about the magnificence and originality of their shows, and of their taste and good judgement in the artists they employed. An unparalleled propaganda effort recorded the Florentine magnificences (1589). Indeed, some accounts were printed in

MOMMERIE AT THE COURT OF MAXIMILIAN I, miniature.

advance: Raffaele Gualterotti's (15?–1638) description of Christine de Lorraine's entry into the city with all its *apparati*; Bastiano de' Rossi's (*fl.* 1585–1605) narrative on *La pellegrina*; and Cavalieri's publication of the music in a limited edition of 116 copies. Although such records (along with municipal and royal archives) are indispensable for any reconstruction of these dramas from the past, they must be treated with caution. The distance between what actually happened and what is recorded can be very large. A text (even with illustrations) does not perform the play, sing the aria, or dance the complex figurations required. Praise was mandatory, and hyperbole was the style of discourse used to project the partisan intentions of prince and artists alike. Many shows were mounted at short notice and were incomplete on the day. Narrators rarely tell us that the rain spoiled everything (an exception was Antwerp 1549), or that the machinery failed to deliver. Moreover, descriptions could be deceptive. We know, for instance, that Maurice Scève (Lyon, 1548) deliberately manipulated his text to enhance the antiquarian character of the triumph in order to give higher status to the city's achievement. Yet publication offered some guarantee of success and approval at a time when change and insecurity were the day-to-day experience of so many. This age of intense theatrical activity, of advance and innovation in the arts, came about when political unrest in Europe was widespread. Religious controversy divided the Empire; wars erupted in Italy throughout the first half of the sixteenth century, while Spain's problems with the rest of Europe continued well beyond. France had its own troubles from 1560, its wars of religion extending into the reign of Henri IV (1589–1610); and even the performance of court ballet was interlaced with mortal duelling. The cultural significance of the sword was not diluted by decorous manners and civility. At one and the same time, Ronsard wrote poems extolling the engraved armour of the duc de Guise (1550–88) while praising the creative qualities of his lyre. How is it that court festivals and violence flourished together? The turbulent context in which courts thrived perhaps helped to develop them. The exaggerated idealism of many theatrical performances which sought to identify the prince with well-established heroes from the past or to liken him and his court to the gods of Olympus contrasted with grim reality. Such showy retrospection served at once as a relief and a temporary cure.

Learned drama

Italian princes shared a taste for Greek and Latin culture, illustrated in the number of plays performed by the end of the fifteenth century: comedies for Lorenzo the Magnificent based on those of Plautus and Terence, with similar performances at Ferrara and Mantua. The urge to bring these discoveries from the past to other courts is evident in the programme of plays put on at the imperial court by Conrad Celtis (1459–1508) after his return there from Italy in 1497. The genre soon flourished everywhere; in Spain, Juan de la Cueva (1550–1610) turned learned classical sources into the vernacular. In England, Elizabeth I was entertained by Latin plays in the University of Cambridge, Plautus' *Aulularia*, 1564; and in Oxford (1566) Sophocles' *Ajax flagellifer* and with a Latin adaptation of Dido and Aeneas. These plays were characterized by sustained verbal debate, and by rhetorical virtuosity calculated to please a cultured elite audience who tended to admire translations into the vernacular as original works to be read for their style, and for their imitation of classical rules of structure, time, and place.

The declamatory content of these plays was admirably suited to the pedagogic needs of burgeoning colleges for which many plays were created. George Buchanan

(1506–82), for example, wrote tragedies for annual performances at the collège de Guyenne, translating *Medea* (1543) and composing his most influential play, *Jephté* (1545, ed. 1554), where the problem of vows was transferred from divine power and external agency to human predicament, thereby greatly developing the complexity of character. Estienne Jodelle's (1532–73) *Cléopâtre captive* was considered to be the 'purest' classical tragedy in the vernacular. First played before the king, Henri II, at the Hôtel de Reims on 9 February 1553, and repeated at the collège de Boncourt a few days later, it aroused tremendous enthusiasm from the packed audience, who applauded Jodelle's ability to delve into the power of passions (love or pride) and to have given the chorus true lyrical qualities. Its traditional role of universalizing the moral impact of the dramatic struggle was supplemented by the chorus's interruptions within the evolving conflict in order to clarify Cléopâtre's tragic resolution. This attention to character portrayal was also present in the tragedies of Robert Garnier (1544–90); yet his chief concern was to use his depiction of civil wars in Rome to highlight the horrors of contemporary strife in France. He was obsessed with the parallel, arguing that his tragedies were 'all too appropriate to our ills'. His representation of the ruin of Rome in *Cornélie* (1574) and in *Marc Antoine* (1578) was graphic and explicit, thanks to his reading of Seneca's plays and the knowledge he had gleaned from the *Histories* of Plutarch and others. He thoroughly understood the grandeur that was Rome and the extent of its loss, and he rendered the calamity of these times by conjuring up the very presence of Rome just as Jacques Grévin (*c.*1537–1570) had done when he powerfully evoked the ruins of that city in *César* (1561). For his last play, *Les Juives* (1583), Garnier turned again to Seneca and to the Bible to bring to life characters who really engage in contesting the moral power of princes. The intensity of the prophet's imprecations against the monster/king's revenge and the explicit nature of Sédécie's witnessing his children's death impressed those who expected a Christian interpretation of Nebuchadnezzar's ruthlessness. As Garnier sang of the sorrows of Israel, he always had in mind those dreadful happenings around him as civil war continued without restraint in France. His drama sought to redress the inflation which characterized the representation of princes in court performances by underlining the way God chastises their excesses.

As far as is known, *Les Juives* was never performed in the sixteenth century, but it attained a significant reputation. The emphasis on reading (as for the famous early dialogue/play, *La Celestina*, 1499) rather than on performance was an important factor in Protestant exploitation of learned dramas. Théodore de Bèze (1519–1605) (*Abraham*, 1550) and Jean de la Taille (*c.*1540–*c.*1607) (*Saul le Furieux*, 1572) emphasized the ancient origins of their work (especially Seneca) and assumed close reading of their texts so that the heroic figures they created, tested by faith, could be thoroughly understood. Their works, and those of the many Protestant authors who used plays to promote religious propaganda, were polemical, violent, partisan, contentious, and expressly designed to spread the belief of their authors. However, by the mid-sixteenth century, another religious strain became prominent turning declamation into theatre and education into performance. The Society of Jesus, founded by St Ignatius Loyola

(1491–1556), started schools in every major city in Catholic Europe. For reasons of good moral instruction and effective preparation for the professions, they, too, produced plays; and as their theatre expanded so their dramas became more grandiose. In Rome, in Spanish cities, in France at the collège de la Trinité in Lyon, for example, their theatre flourished; and in Munich, too, where Andreas Fabricius (1520–81) extended the scholarly plays, fashioning them so that they explored themes to do with kingship. And thus they became suitably extravagant for the entertainment of princes. His Latin play *Samson* was put on by Jesuits with choral interludes composed by Lassus during the wedding celebrations for the marriage of the duke's son to Renée de Lorraine (1544–1602) in 1568. Ultimately, Jesuit theatre helped to internationalize spectacle.

The elements of spectacle

To recall the imperial splendour of ancient Rome, whether in the streets, on the theatre stage, or as inspiration for other forms of spectacle, several elements were essential: the triumphal arch, the triumphal car, and the presence of ruins. The triumphal arch, still visible in the imperial city and in other parts of the Roman Empire, became a standard mode of welcome. Erected at traditional venues, a series of such arches imposed an imaginary space on the everyday reality of the city. Pictures painted on canvas adorned its surface, as did statues of heroes or of allegories made out of wood (yet covered to resemble marble). Decorations such as these recounted Philip II's deeds and showed his Habsburg forebears, for his entry into Milan (1549). Sometimes, the scenes mounted on arches were activated, like the play depicting the giants' attack on Jupiter, designed to delight Emperor Charles V on his visit to Naples (1535). Because of its imposing nature, its size and air of permanence, with its surfaces capable of promoting political messages to the world, the arch would endure into modern times, whereas the triumphal chariot gradually faded from view. The survival of the arch is also due to the quality of design by major artists; Leonardo for Louis XII's entry into Milan (1509); Baldassare Peruzzi (1481–1536) for the pope's entry into Rome (1513); and Giulio Romano (1499–1546) for the entry into Florence (1541).

Nonetheless, the chariot was a familiar sight at festival times. The triumphal car—inspired by the *Triumphs* of Petrarch with their strong moral implications and their potential for visual enactment or copied from *The Triumphs of Caesar*, created by Mantegna for festive decorations—was (initially) a paradigm for good behaviour and a pattern for princes. The Roman emperors were born again in the cavalcades at Florence; and these soon became transformed from lessons from history to legend and allegory. Such modifications are amply displayed in the cars conceived by Francesco Cini for the spectacle on the Arno (1608) of Jason's seizure of the Golden Fleece. The cars here became sixteen ships, designed by Giulio Parigi, who commissioned Remigio Cantagallina (c.1582–1656) to etch each vessel. These mobile conveyances owed much to earlier floats which had dominated the religious dramas in the streets of Europe. On these floats were built platforms carrying actors and musicians; and they paused along the route for speeches and performances. The Chester cycle of mystery plays, for instance, was performed on such wagons where plays such as the creation of the world, or pageants telling the Christmas story, involved mechanical wonders. On the other hand, static virtues or allegories provided the principal spectacle for the Lord Major's show, each figure with 'a story painted about him' (1561).

It is not always possible to determine the nature and fabric of these cars. In Spain, the mobile floats (often with two storeys) provided the place for the action. In Venice, the platforms were carried on men's shoulders around St Mark's square. In the Low Countries, the mobile wagons carried silent figures bedecked with symbols and devices. In Italy, and increasingly elsewhere, stories drawn from mythology and classical themes were painted on the wooden structures which were normally pulled along by men or animals. The cars moved very slowly unless propelled by some secret mechanism or technique. In Spain, for example, the wheels were greased with lard to make them roll along more smoothly.

The depiction of ruins attracted many designers since, although the concept of antiquity was a highly unstable one, ruins seemed to evoke faithfully the actual state of the imperial city. Inigo Jones, for example, chose and transformed decorative elements from available prints to suit his purpose. He used ruins on the backcloth of the Fallen House of Chivalry in Prince Henry's *Barriers* (1610), inserting a representation of Cestius' tomb which had survived intact through the centuries, in order to give a sense of verisimilitude to the spectacle's setting. Again, for *Albion's Triumph* (1632), he attempted a scholarly reconstruction of antiquity to drive home its propaganda purpose. On the stage, increasing sophistication was a feature in the mastery of visual effects. The early mechanical contrivances in churches had led the way in conquering the expectancy of dedicated spectators. They became accustomed, on the theatre stage, to the play of complex cloud formations, moving effortlessly in the skies, managing descents to earth and disappearances heavenwards. They admired the ebb and flow of waves engineered by flats that could slide in and out across the stage. They applauded the sudden appearance of figures, caves, mountains, or grottoes that surged up from the trapdoors skilfully controlled. Lights were abundant, creating a visibility between actor and spectator dramatically different from present-day experience. Such feats were often transferred to the open air, erected in gardens and courtyards, such as the large mountain that figured in the *Temple of Love* (Ferrara, 1565), or that of Circe dominating the lists in Bologna (1600).

During this period, outward show was considered essential evidence of good manners and appearances impacted immediately. For dramatic performances, most attention was given to the preparation of costumes which had to reflect the divine or daemonic character of the actor and had to demonstrate extravagance. Garments were woven in rich materials, threaded with gold and silver, and covered in jewels. Despite—perhaps because of—the conscious ostentation, there developed in time an air of sameness about many of these spectacular wonders, partly because each court reproduced the same forms of entertainment and used the same set of scenes—seascape, forest, city view, hell, and heaven; and, in part, because graphic conventions were limited, tending to depict similar sorts of triumphal chariots and illusionist scenery. Such set pieces became increasingly familiar to artists and audiences alike, who then yearned for even greater ingenuity and more outrageous inventions.

Audiences

Any consideration of the audiences for Renaissance drama must take account of the variety of places where plays were performed, their size, their location, and the amenities provided. Indoors, the privacy of one's own armchair creates a different experience from that of a great hall, or theatres specially built for princes; or again, in the paying theatres which exploded on the scene in the late sixteenth century, especially in London. Another audience waited in the streets for entries and processions, for knightly parades, mystery plays, and civic shows; or in market squares where the collective and integral nature of Renaissance culture was most apparent. Audiences' tastes changed, too, with the nature of their expectation. Technological development brought enhanced visual appetite; greater expertise in the playing of instruments and in the ability to dance demanded higher standards; virtuoso singing in church was matched by parallel feats on the stage. The intended purposes of drama multiplied and diversified: plays offered a fruitful terrain for religious controversy; a vehicle for tricky diplomacy; a way of controlling the court. They provided competition between artists and princes; offered modes of devotion and celebration, or moments of seasonal festivity. Diverse, fluid, and responsive dramatic forms, because of their popularity, were ever open to new approaches increasingly adopted as a consequence of audience or patron pressure. The knowledge of audiences should not be underestimated. The recipients of drama were connoisseurs; humanists fully acquainted with classical sources looked for the same qualities in modern versions; spectators danced and sang expertly and were appreciative of performances that were planned and of those moments when performers shifted to improvise a step or weave variations around a pre-existent melody.

Some audiences were merely readers, and playwrights like Jacques Grévin explicitly ignored the general public, catering only for like-minded Protestants able to engage in the minutiae of his verbal attacks upon the church. Readers of the accounts of festivities recognized that their authors were aware of their presence and of their expectations as every detail of an event was recaptured, enhanced, and commended. Private theatres, especially in their early temporary state, provided for an elite audience. In the great halls, performers—often on the same level as the spectators—came close to their audience, for whom it was an easy matter to recognize the actor beneath his role. As permanent private theatres came into being, relationships between spectator and actor changed, distancing viewers from the stage; duke or king were carefully placed on a dais with direct view of the perspective of the scene. This privileged position was not shared by all spectators seated on tiered benches in a rectangular hall, along the sides and back of the hall, or in a U-shaped auditorium, on steps rising to the rear, above which boxes and galleries were located. Spectators, having recognized a familiar city on the backcloth—Pisa, Florence, or Rome—were expected to admire the transformations on the stage. They were carried into another world of divine activity and heavenly music. In the Medici theatre at the Uffizi, despite the fact that (in 1589) Harmony and Rhythm descended to earth, and that the glories of the newly-weds were directly addressed, the celestial singing and the figured choreography which had filled the final scene kept spectators remote. A greater intimacy was established in the Hôtel de Bourbon in Paris for the *Balet Comique de la Reyne* (1581), where performers were on the same level ground as the king. Performers came up directly to address the king and offer him homage through ballet and song. His silent assent to their triumph over Circe was an integral part of the performance. A more physical intermingling of spectator and performer was a regular occurrence in the new Banqueting Hall in Whitehall where again the king's dais occupied the centre of the auditorium. Masquers interacted with the audience, first by addressing the king directly at their first appearance, and then interrupting the spectacle as they descended onto the floor of the hall to engage in social dancing (called the Revels) with members of the audience, before returning to the stage to perform their main dance and then take their departure.

Whole populations were actively present for the religious dramas whose impact was tightly controlled by the authorities (ecclesiastical and political) of each parish or district. In this way, spectators were participants, sometimes chosen as actors, and at others (especially in Spain) contributing dances and music-making. There was little space between the wagons, where the action was displayed, and the standing room around the platforms, so that spectators could join in, believing in the truths enacted. If rain fell, it drenched spectacle and audience alike. In some cities, like Romans-sur-Isère (*Histoire des trois doms*, 1509), where detailed accounts have been preserved, extensive arrangements to accommodate spectators were made in advance and the scale of the operation seems to have been exceptional. Tiers of scaffolds were constructed from the foot of the stage plateau to the loggias at the back. These loggias held between 500 and 600 persons, and for the three days of performance the total numbers recorded were: for day 1, 1,840; for day 2, 1,360; and for day 3, 3,847. No explanation is given for the doubling of numbers on the final day, but these records point to crowds responding as a mass, although there is no indication of the noise or movement of such numbers. Similar dense groupings accompanied the performance of impromptu plays and processions put on for carnival time when crowds surged forward to participate and interrupt the verbal exchanges, for example, of the *commedia dell'arte* who deliberately encouraged dialogue with the audience—or pressed forward to the stories on the floats that trundled along the streets. Din, noisy music, and uncontrolled revelling characterized these audiences. Such crowds were also still present at the knightly parades, civic cavalcades, and princely entries into cities. At these times, strident music from drums and trumpets and the noise of artillery helped to regulate the rhythm of processions, while street discipline was enforced by the municipality or through barriers guarded by the prince's military escort. Roofs and windows allowed the common people to glimpse the proceedings, as was typically reported from Orléans (1576): 'the windows full and the roofs covered with all kinds of people trembling with joy and desire to see their king' (Henri III). The more formal processions in St Mark's square (Venice), founded in traditional ritual, similarly provided entertainment and wonder for the noble spectators who looked down from the palace balconies or the undifferentiated public standing below and looking upwards. The same kind of segregation was enforced in the market square where scaffolding was erected behind barriers for spectators of all ranks. In fifteenth-century Lille, the burghers built such structures for their townspeople who came eagerly to scrutinize and admire not only the deeds of the knights but also their fictional role.

Moving indoors, into the paying theatres, spectator experience and understanding varied enormously. The tiny theatres of Venice offered an intimate atmosphere in contrast to that found in the yards of inns in Spain or in England, where galleries on three sides were open to the skies, and many theatregoers stood in the yard. Even permanent theatres in London tended to be small and friendly (one of the largest at Shoreditch held about 3,000 people), despite physical conditions which were not of the best—crowding, importunate hats and ruffs, pickpockets, tobacco, and other smells—but did nothing to put off the ladies who were there as a spectacle in themselves. In this setting, playwrights sought to direct and manipulate the audience (as Hamlet does). Christopher Marlowe's (1564–93) mighty lines worked on the emotions of the spectator who began to identify himself with the hero. Ben Jonson knew how to encourage specific behaviour and response, realizing that there were many ways of looking. He used his prologues (as did other writers) to explain and direct where sympathy should go on those issues of the day which concerned him; and he also encouraged spectators to share in his dramas, deriding them or railing at them to provoke their reaction. The matter of audience response becomes even more complex when the language of writers brought the spectators' imagination into play. In paying theatres, with minimal scenery, inducing spectators to think beyond the words and to be in touch with a world that they help to make, became the craft that created works that still speak today.

Paying theatres and drama

In Spain, following the impetus from Lope de Rueda, drama flourished everywhere. During the 1570s and 1580s, permanent paying theatres were established when yards (*corrales*) were hired and transformed into theatres. These venues, managed by charitable brotherhoods or municipal authorities, were so popular that hundreds of dramatists emerged to meet demand. From such enthusiasm, the Golden Age of Spanish theatre was born with Lope de Vega's (1562–1635) mixed dramas, expertly constructed, full of wit, and remarkable for the subtleties of female characterization. A similar intensity of performance developed in London during these years (1570–1642) when, as the population expanded to some 200,000 by 1600, twenty-three playhouses became active, creating unprecedented competition and turning playwrights into professionals as each theatre management sought to attract paying customers. Theatre companies came and went, marked by fluidity and volatility, as noble lords (taking their lead from the Earl of Leicester, 1532/3–88) tried to promote their own image through the agency of drama. Lord Strange's Men were forever on the move; and the Queen's Men (1583) boasted leading players drafted in from other companies. Gradually, the Admiral's Men, led by their star performer, Edward Alleyn (1566–1626), and the Lord Chamberlain's Men founded in the same year (1592) (and with whom Shakespeare was associated from 1595/6) became the dominant companies. They played in theatre space that was remarkably varied. All were, by modern standards, quite small and intimate, with a stage projecting into the auditorium and, usually, three tiers of galleries rising from the pit. The Fortune was planned as a square; the Globe, made with timber from the ruined Theatre at Shoreditch, with its ceiling decorated as the heavens, formed a polygon; and the Cockpit was rounded with room for the audience on all sides of the stage. Alongside these public venues, private theatres flourished, like St Paul's where John Lyly's (c.1553/4–1606) romantic comedies were performed. Late medieval stagecraft merged into the practice of drama in these theatres, as elsewhere in Europe; they mostly housed a descent machine, had three doors at the back of the stage—one very large to allow 'discoveries'—and actors could point to the ceiling to evoke the heavens.

Although performances at court often required more elaborate scenery (from 1605, Serlio's unified perspective setting became the norm), there was continuous interaction with public paying theatres. Ten new plays from the professional theatre were put on at court in 1601–2; and, in the period 1603–13, 138 performances by the King's Men were given before James I. Plays had to continue to attract paying customers, so writers borrowed from each other—themes, ideas, and even characters—or they collaborated when the pressure to produce new works became overwhelming. They reflected topics of the day: satirizing current affairs; exploring in depth major human weaknesses such as intellectual pride, as in Christopher Marlowe's *Dr Faustus* (1583); and filling their dramas with the uncertainties and multiple, conflicting values of daily life. They even depicted the theatre as holiday (Thomas Dekker's *A Shoemaker's Holiday*, 1599/1600). On the one hand, magic haunts the ground of both the great and the humble in Robert Greene's *Friar Bacon and Friar Bungay* (c.1588–92) where he achieves a fine balance between court and country, the urban and the rural; on the other, a pestilent atmosphere of foul and destructive vitality reigns over John Webster's *The Duchess of Malfi* (c. 1612), where a relentless rhythm supports characters whose turbulent natures operate by instinct, indulging in bribery and in the revenge that made the play famous—a theme which had already been successfully explored by Thomas Kyd (*The Spanish Tragedy*, 1587), where madness and revenge extend beyond the grave.

Abundant themes and structures prevent any straightforward evolutionary account of drama in London at this time. The works of Ben Jonson illustrate the difficulty. He was a different writer when he conceived masques for the court from when he produced plays for the Globe or Blackfriars. He showed a keen awareness of the theatre space in which he was creating drama and of those who paid to listen to him. He speaks directly to the audience, and is familiar with them: in the prologue of *Bartholomew Fair* (1614), for instance, where the stage keeper warns those who watch that a play is 'as full of noise…as sport'. Amidst the satire, he displayed lofty notions for dramatic poetry as a means of exposing life. He prided himself as an insightful judge of human behaviour, forcing Overdo to recognize: 'remember you are but Adam, flesh and blood.' His dramas are characterized by their structural cleverness; the controlled yet frenetic pace of the action; characters vividly conceived, named, and depicted to satirize elements in society of which Jonson deeply disapproved. Thus he ridicules credulity (*The Alchemist*, 1610); the inadequacies of judges who see only with other men's eyes; or greed and avarice (*Volpone*, 1605). Contemporary figures are identified, chastised, and picked to pieces.

Shakespeare went one step further. His dramas serve as a kind of summation of all the forms and influences that flowed in at this time from history, spectacle, and contemporary theatre activity. His plays are strikingly aware of themselves as theatre. Shows and festivities are drawn in to entertain, marking the incredible speed of events and offering a conclusion compatible with an imagination indulged and allowed to run riot as in *A Midsummer Night's Dream* (1595/6); or they are given a more poignant role in the revels of drama and of life which fade 'like an insubstantial pageant' at the end of *The Tempest* (1611–12), performed as part of the festivities at court in 1613. It has often been remarked that Jaques's famous speech from Act II of *As You Like It* (*c.*1599), beginning 'All the world's a stage', epitomizes the universality, breadth, and depth of Shakespeare's dramas in which he incorporated all forms of spectacle—songs, dances, disguisings, puppet shows, processions, and the rituals of magic and display associated with court policy and patronage. In *Hamlet* (1601–2), such intrusions taught actors their craft; in *A Midsummer Night's Dream* (1595/6), they celebrated both elite and popular forms of festival with the tragedy of Pyramus and Thisbe so ironically presented as to underline the sheer entertainment value of the whole performance. In the long unfolding of *The Winter's Tale* (1610–11), dances are used to mark the passage of years.

Often, in these dramas, the outward show engineered by machinists is transferred inwards as the language of the play calls on the imagination to conceive the spectacle: through narrative, in the presentation of Cleopatra's barge; or through fear, as the queen visualizes her own presence in Caesar's triumph in Rome, a fear made all the more potent by the emperor himself, who sees her future life as uniquely defined, being 'eternal in our triumph'. The most powerful impact of such incorporation comes when the show is integrated into the characterization: dreams and apparitions, the working of the witches on Macbeth who, as a consequence, sees himself as a walking shadow, a poor player. Shakespeare's ability to put himself in others' minds and situations enhances the terror. In this dark play (*Macbeth*, 1605–6), Shakespeare does not neglect contemporary concerns: James I's authoritative preoccupation with witchcraft, for instance; or, in *Cymbeline* (1609–10), his sombre view of the court, ridden with intrigue;

or again, in *The Tempest* (1611–12), hints about discovery, newly found lands to enjoy and exploit. In *Hamlet* (1600–1), he had gone beyond the terror he was to engender in Macbeth. In an atmosphere chill with apprehension, the fragility of the human condition is displayed. The joins between madness and sanity are explored through hesitations, through a sense of guilt rampantly present in every moment of intense self-examination. These sensations are extended and universalized to expose the ineffectual nature of man. The same opening-out through self-probing occurs in *King Lear* (1605–6), where the adulation of the prince so common in court spectacle is replaced by an exploration of the ethics of kingship. The issues that concerned Shakespeare are those which still exercise us today: reflections on the human condition; the probing of passions (desire, ambition, ingratitude, and forgiveness); concerns about governance and about the insidious nature of human behaviour in war—ambition, greed, or the soulless search for fame. Such preoccupations, shared by so many contemporaries, demand that Renaissance drama be revisited, even reinvented and adapted for our use. In many ways, England was on the edge of Europe in these years. Its drama, however, brought it right into the centre of Renaissance culture and performance.

CHAPTER 8

Vernacular Literature

WARREN BOUTCHER

THE Renaissance in vernacular literature is principally the rediscovery and reuse in vernacular contexts of classical Latin words, phrases, commonplaces, and works. But what kind of rediscovery and reuse? Consider two vernacular writers who give a single line of verse by the Roman poet Vergil a new lease of life. In book VI of Vergil's Latin epic, the *Aeneid*, Aeneas and his band of Trojans, exiled after the sacking of Troy, land at Cumae, on the shore of Italia. Aeneas asks the Sibyl to help him descend down through the forest of Avernus into the cave that gives entrance to the underworld, so that he can see his deceased father once again. She then exhorts him—in a perfectly balanced, steadying line of verse—to be courageous as they plunge down together:

> nunc animis opus, Aenea, nunc pectore firmo
> ('now is there need of courage, Aeneas, now is there need of a firm heart').

Once below, they find the road to the river Acheron, where the shades of the unburied dead beg passage across to their resting place. When the ferryman Charon sees Aeneas, a living, armed stranger, moving through the silent wood towards the shore, he becomes very angry and accosts him, refusing him transit. But the Sibyl speaks on his behalf and presents Aeneas as a famous warrior and as a living image or *imago* of *pietas*. She then pulls out the golden bough, which is sacred to the goddess of the underworld Proserpina, from beneath her robe. Charon's angry breast is calmed and he grants the Trojan safe passage across. Aeneas and his guide then explore the underworld together.

In canto III of the *Inferno*, completed *c.*1314, Dante rewrites the Vergilian narrative within a Christian framework, using the new poetic style of the Tuscan vernacular. He gives 'Virgil', as a character in the poem, the Sibyl's role of guide on the journey. As Boccaccio would point out sixty years later (1373–4) in his public lectures on Dante in Florence, Dante's character Virgil echoes the Sibyl's words about the need for courage when addressing the terrified Dante before the gates of hell. The two verses translate the balance of Vergil's single line through means of repetition ('si'/'sia'; 'convien'/

'convien'; 'ogni'/'ogni'), and replace the adverbials of time ('nunc'/'nunc') with adverbials of place ('Qui'/'qui');:

> Qui si convien lasciare ogni sospetto;
> Ogni viltà convien che qui sia morta.
> ('Here must all distrust be left behind, here must all cowardice be ended.')

In the rest of the canto that follows, Dante turns Vergil's pagan god Charon into a demon, and has the souls initially dropping behind to avoid the crossing to hell. This time the angry Charon is calmed not by the golden bough but by the all-powerful will of the Christian God, as invoked in words by Dante's character Virgil.

Nearly three centuries after Dante, in a different part of Europe, Vergil's poem remains a resource for any educated person thinking or writing in the vernacular about the securing of safe passage on a dangerous journey. Some time after 1588 and before 1592, in south-west France, Michel de Montaigne was reading through the printed version of his vernacular essay on physiognomy (*Essais* III 12). For the next edition, he decided to insert the same verse from Vergil, *Aeneid* VI, into the middle of a novelistic anecdote about a dangerous journey on which he escaped death. The context is the efficacy of Montaigne's presence and manner in gaining trust from strangers, and his own willingness to trust in nature and fortune or 'heaven'.

During a truce, Montaigne had been attacked and taken prisoner by a group of horsemen, then dragged into a neighbouring forest. On this occasion the Vergilian verse is inserted in Latin amidst Montaigne's recollections of the incident, written in French. But Montaigne changes one word of the original Latin text—'nunc' or 'now' to 'tunc' or 'then'—in order to fit the verse into his own train of thought reflecting back on a past incident:

> In truth, there were many threatening circumstances that showed the danger I was in.
> Tunc animis opus, Ænea, tunc pectore firmo.
> ('Then was there need of courage, Aeneas, then was there need of a firm heart.')
> I kept standing on my rights under the truce...

Montaigne goes on to relate that the leader of his captors undergoes a sudden change of heart—somewhat like Vergil's Charon—and unexpectedly grants him safe passage. Another inserted Latin verse, from Catullus 68, implicitly compares this man to Catullus's 'auxilium' or 'aid' Allius, who is like the gentle breeze for which storm-beaten sailors pray to Castor and Pollux. So Montaigne was saved neither by the Sibyl and the golden bough, nor by a companion invoking God's omnipotence. What was the cause of his deliverance? 'I truly do not even now well know,' he says. Was it divine goodness at work through the efficacy of his face and manner?

The nature of Montaigne's use of Vergil's text, and of classical poetry more generally, is very different from Dante's. He cites both Vergil's and Catullus' verses in Latin, rather than absorb them by translation into his own text. He is not concerned to transpose the pagan poets' words into a more explicitly Christian context. Indeed, it would have been striking to Montaigne's contemporary reader that, writing about a moment of mortal danger, he brings in the words of the Sibyl and the sailors' prayer to Castor and Pollux rather than a Christian prayer or a line from a psalm. He is interested in the allusive interplay between his own vernacular voice and experience and the poetry and narratives offered by the great Latin poets. He raises questions about the role of ethos, fortune, and divine goodness in the risk-laden lives of his contemporaries by implicitly measuring the distance between his own and classical narratives of deliverance. But he has no definitive answers; he remains uncertain.

One way of describing and evaluating the difference would be to say that Dante's vernacular use of Vergil is more 'medieval' in manner, Montaigne's more 'Renaissance'. The purpose of the description might be to argue that Montaigne's use of Vergil's text is more secular and sceptical, more sensitive to its original context and meanings—though with a twist that adapts the verse to its new context ('tunc' for 'nunc'). From this point of view, it might be imagined that Vergil's episode was in his mind from the start, shaping the way he told his story. The premise would be that in order to produce authoritative literature, whether in the vernacular or in neo-Latin, one has to be seen to be imitating and alluding to a certain canon of classical authors in a particular intellectual style: a literarily and historically sensitive style that eschews Christianization of pagan texts and draws on a cycle of renewed and allied disciplines in the humanities (grammar, rhetoric, logic, history, moral philosophy). So where Dante incorporates Vergil into a universal Christian frame-work, Montaigne uses classical poetry to enquire philosophically into his own experiences and their causes, without imposing dogma.

This type of engagement with classical writing on Montaigne's part is sometimes labelled 'humanist', and associated with the fact that he received his early education in Latin from a German humanist who spoke no French. His literary culture also included relationships with many Italian vernacular authors, but not with Dante, whom he does not mention in his journal of his voyage to Italy. Even though he does quote a few verses from the *Commedia* in the *Essais*, he possessed no copy, and his contemporaries in Renaissance France largely ignored the poem (there was no printed translation until after Montaigne's death). In this respect Montaigne falls into the tradition deriving from Petrarch, who dissociated Dante and the *Commedia* from the reborn literary culture he sought to create and embody.

But these descriptions of our two authors, and the divide placed between them, can be contested. They could be said, instead, to have participated in the same broad European process of laicization and vernacularization of literature. Montaigne did not write in the learned Parisian vernacular used by professional lawyers and humanists of the time. He used colloquial and visceral language, along with idioms of his region (Gascony), just as Dante used those of Florence and Tuscany. He might in this respect be placed in the vanguard of a vernacular counter Renaissance, a fightback against new humanistic learning and scholastic Latinity in the name of nature and inherited customs. He himself might have said that all he took from Vergil was a bit of ornamental Latin to give his vernacular text some classical lustre, not a model for his experience and writing.

GIORGIO VASARI'S *PORTRAIT OF SIX TUSCAN POETS* was commissioned by Luca Martini of the Accademia Fiorentina and produced in 1544 as an intervention in contemporary debates about the Italian vernacular tradition and the place of Dante within it. In Vasari's scene Dante is the central figure, holding a copy of Vergil, with Cavalcanti to his left. To Dante's immediate right are Boccaccio in the background and Petrarch in the foreground with a copy of his *Rime*.

Conversely, Petrarch's close literary associate Boccaccio did at various moments see Dante as the origin of a vernacular Renaissance, of a new conception of literary culture and the writer's role. After all, Dante made Vergil talk again in the vulgar tongue; he successfully fashioned himself as the first vernacular author to achieve the status and *auctoritas* of a classical writer, paving the way for later authors such as Montaigne, who became known as the French Plutarch. At the height of the sixteenth-century vernacular Renaissance, Dante's conversation with Vergil, in the company of Tuscan writers including Petrarch, Cavalcanti, and Boccaccio, was a central theme of Vasari's painting of the Italian Renaissance canon of vernacular writers.

The subject of this chapter lies at the intersection of two broader histories first constructed by the Western European nation-states in the nineteenth century: the rise of the national European vernaculars, and the Renaissance. The first of these traditional histories traces the emergence between the twelfth and the eighteenth centuries of a particular group of vernacular Western European literatures, including some that in the modern period have spread across the globe. It centres on two interacting groups: the main Romance languages and literatures (Italian, French, Spanish, Portuguese) that evolved from medieval Latin, and that overcame rival regional dialects, then Latin itself, to acquire national and international status; and the major west Germanic vernacular literatures (English, German, Dutch-Flemish) that evolved through literary interaction with the whole Latin-Romance group and—more than the Latin-Romance group— through vernacularization of the Bible and of religious discourse (which is not to say that there was not a strong tradition of biblical literature in Italian and French).

This first history begins with vernacular writings in the *langues d'oïl* (Old French, Anglo-Norman), the Italian dialects, and Occitan. They were certainly not the first significant vernacular literatures produced in Europe; these were produced in vulgar or medieval Latin, and in the Celtic, Germanic, and Semitic languages. But in deriving from a common Latin heritage and in sharing themes and forms they can claim to constitute the first properly pan-European movement in vernacular literature. They were produced and circulated in the courts and towns of the territories now known as France, Italy (including Sicily), Spain, Portugal, and England—territories that would remain the epicentre of European vernacular literary production for centuries. Between 1150 and 1250 there emerged written traditions of vernacular romance, courtly love lyric, allegory, and dream-vision, as well as what would now be designated non-fictional or historical modes of writing, that connected the vernacular literatures of the Continent for the first time.

It was the spread and growing popularity of these literatures amongst urban and courtly elites that provided the setting for what are normally identified as the beginnings of the literary Renaissance: Dante's, Petrarch's, and Boccaccio's heterogeneous projects for new or 'reborn' styles of vernacular and Latin literature. The vernacular literary culture of chivalric romance had already claimed the classical heritage and associated itself with clerical learning and the elite arts; it began with translations of Latin epics into *romanz* or French which gave lay audiences access to the matter of antiquity. It provided ethical and emotional codes for a courtly, then (from the thirteenth century) urban elite keen to distinguish itself from the non-gentle. So one way of describing vernacular Renaissance literature is to say that it sought to do the same things, for the same audience, but in new and distinct ways that related to a reboot of philosophy, theology, and the arts. Going back to classical, especially Latin, authors, in what was claimed to be a more historically and literarily sensitive style, was a way of competing for the attention and investments of the same elites.

This first history draws to a close in the late eighteenth century, with the beginnings of the dominance of each national vernacular or set of vernaculars in the literary cultures of each Western European country and of the final decline of Latin letters as a living medium of European scholarly and literary communication and composition, if not as a primary goal of elite secondary education (in which role it continued into the twentieth century). Literature, understood as the writing of imaginative poems, prose, and drama in the relevant 'national' vernacular, was now distinct from the activity of doing philosophy, oratory, scholarship, and science in several languages; it would soon be a separate subject for study at school and university ('English literature', 'French literature' etc.). Thus ends the long story (medieval, Renaissance, early modern) of the fluctuating complementarities and rivalries between formal Latinate learning and vernacular literatures. The written vernaculars' uses in civic and communal life, bureaucratic state-making and record-keeping, and private religious devotion prepared the ground for the emergence of lay publics of merchants, professionals, courtiers (including women) who sought the freedom to read and write beyond scholastic institutions and forms of language and knowledge (*grammatica* or formally taught Latin as the basis for further study).

The second, intersecting history—already mentioned—is that of the period of change and renewal in the arts and culture, *c.*1300–*c.*1650, designated since the late nineteenth century as the Renaissance, which was held by Burckhardt to have begun in *trecento* Italy and to have spread north by the sixteenth century. The notion of the Renaissance as a period in general history has lost credibility and has largely been replaced by the concept of an 'early modern' era beginning not *c.*1300 but *c.*1450. The social and cultural changes occurring across the world between the mid-fifteenth and mid-sixteenth centuries are now held to be more fundamental than those occurring in the fourteenth century on the Italian peninsula.

The notion of a Renaissance originating in *trecento* Italy retains force, however, as the term for a self-conscious cultural movement—or set of connected movements—in the realm of arts and letters. As we shall see, this movement was traced back in the period itself to figures such as Petrarch and Boccaccio, who—amongst other things—raised up the Italian vernacular, and founded European traditions of love poetry and prose fiction. And in modern literary and intellectual history the transition to 'Western' modernity via new forms of selfhood and self-fashioning, of vernacular realism and historicist critique, of statehood and political language, continues to be located in the early and late Renaissance vernacular writings of authors such as Petrarch and Boccaccio, Shakespeare and Cervantes, Montaigne and Hobbes.

Many modern literary historians identify the literary Renaissance closely with humanism and the heyday of humanist literary studies, pedagogy, and neo-Latin writing—from which 'illustrated' or more artful and prestigious vernacular literatures rooted in particular nations are said to have flowed. The first 'national' vernacular Renaissance, in this traditional account, is that of the *tre corone* (Dante, Petrarch, Boccaccio), which, after a *quattrocento* hiatus, is continued by writers from Ariosto through Machiavelli to Tasso in the long sixteenth century. The vernacular writings of these three *trecento* masters constitute for the first time the very idea of a canon of imaginative literature, worthy of study, in a language other than Latin.

The rebirth of French vernacular letters under Francis I takes us from Rabelais through Du Bellay and Ronsard to Montaigne. The Spanish Golden Age of vernacular literature coincides with the unification of Spain and the rise of the Empire, taking us from Fernando de Rojas's *La Celestina* through Juan Boscán or Joan Boscà (in Catalan) and Garcilaso de la Vega, *Lazarillo de Tormes*, Cervantes, to Lope de Vega and Calderón. The Portuguese Renaissance offers Gil Vicente (who also wrote in Spanish) and Camões. The English Renaissance takes us from Wyatt and Surrey to Sidney, Spenser, Shakespeare, then to Jonson, Donne, and the early Milton. This gives us at least eight authors that remain icons of world literature in the present day (Dante, Petrarch, Boccaccio, Machiavelli, Rabelais, Montaigne, Cervantes, Shakespeare) and a body of work to match that of classical Greece and Rome.

However, as we saw in relation to Dante and Montaigne, 'medieval' and 'Renaissance' or 'medieval' and 'humanist' are complementary pairs of terms. They denote a tradition of contingent and often polemical descriptions and evaluations of continuity and change in the history of Western European culture between c.1100 and c.1650. They can mean many different things in different contexts and are constantly being redefined. Other modern literary historians have not identified the Renaissance or the emergence of the literary vernaculars so closely with humanism. The most important of these is the German literary scholar Erich Auerbach. Auerbach made the realistic expression of lived, everyday experience—ultimately derived from the humble, mixed style of the Bible—his criterion of authenticity in vernacular literature, rather than humanistic imitation of classical texts, styles, and personae. He identified both Dante and Montaigne with breakthrough moments in the achievement of this style, rather than with imitation of classical writers.

But it remains the case that the humanists succeeded in making their style of analysis and composition of what was then called 'poetry' (fictive or imaginative writing) central to all elite European culture and knowledge in several languages, including a run of vernaculars, by the mid-sixteenth century. Auerbach's whole enterprise as a scholar of vernacular realism is shaped by their legacy. And he tended, from a post-romantic perspective, to identify humanism with arid neo-classicism. Humanism was on the one hand about a philological scholarship oriented towards the recovery of a pure classical Latin and the knowledge needed to gloss, translate, and imitate its texts. But it was also a pragmatic movement that aimed to reorient philosophy and the arts, even theology, more towards social and performative life, less towards scholarly and contemplative life. This kind of life included women and non-Latin literate men, even the lower classes. Described in this way, humanism can claim back many of the authors that Auerbach took from its grasp, including Montaigne.

How was the literary Renaissance described at the time? The learned humanist commentators who in the fourteenth and fifteenth centuries used metaphors of restoration and reawakening in relation to literature normally applied them to the revival of Latin letters and learning, often alongside Greek and Hebrew, and only tangentially or secondarily to vernacular writings. The powerful notion that proper classical Latin retreated into dusty books in monasteries for 800 years, understood by no one, until revived by Petrarch and his successors, could not be applied to either the Romance vernaculars, which derived from the corruption of classical Latin, or the Germanic vernaculars, which were never lost in dusty books. And early commentators never specified fictional vernacular poetry, prose, and drama to be the spearhead of the whole Renaissance movement, in the way that various modern critics have implicitly or explicitly done.

But if the vernaculars could not be directly revived in their lost ancient forms from dusty books, they could be renewed by imitation or translation of Hebrew, Greek, and Latin texts, authors, and genres, as our opening example showed. Petrarch, in *Epistolae familiares* ('Personal letters') 1.1.6, described how the kinds of lyric poetry practised in ancient Greece and Rome were reborn in the Sicilian vernacular. Guido da Pisa described the Dante of the vernacular *Commedia* as a writer who revived the art of poetry and made the ancient poets live again in our minds. Later, Sannazaro would claim to have reawakened the classical pastoral woods and to have taught the shepherds to sing forgotten songs, in his vernacular *Arcadia*, and Du Bellay would describe Rabelais as he who made Aristophanes to be born again.

Alongside this there was the specifically Italian question first authoritatively raised by Dante in works such as the *Convivio* ('Banquet') and the *De vulgari eloquentia* ('On eloquence in the vernacular'): how to authorize literary writing in the vernacular. Could or should a normatively eloquent Italian, not derived from a single place, be fashioned to displace the regional Italian dialects, even Latin? Could it become the shared, transregional language of letters for the peninsula's curial and courtly elite, for a newly restored Holy Roman Empire? Could modern authors in the vernacular rival the ancients for eloquence and fame, even outdo them?

Dante described the 'illustrious vernacular' in *De vulgari eloquentia* 2.1 in terms that placed it in relation to status and gender hierarchies. He made it analogous to other qualities, ornaments, and instruments of the male mercantile, military, and governmental elite, from magnificence to robes and horses. The illustrious vernacular called to itself similarly illustrious men, whether as authors or patrons. It was, that is, a possession that demanded the right kind of male owner. Just as magnificence—as a virtue—demands great people, just as regal purple robes demand noblemen, so the illustrious vernacular seeks those who are excellent in intellect and learning, and disdains others. It is not suitable for mountain folk discussing rustic matters, but for individuals who show their worth in trading, fighting, and ruling. It is for the *optimi*, the best classes of men; it is 'cardinal, courtly, and curial'—courtly in the sense of dwelling in the (imagined) imperial court of all the Italians, rather than in one region (1.18).

This was a potent idea, but it was only really picked up across the Italian peninsula and Europe in the first decades of the sixteenth century. Dante's treatise on vernacular eloquence and its concept of an 'illustrious vernacular' superior to regional dialects first entered a wider debate in the 1520s, when it was printed in Italian, and when parallel debates opened up in other countries. By the later sixteenth century, more general narratives of the age had developed that incorporate the notion of 'illustrated vernacular' languages and literatures into versions of the Renaissance that identify it with nexuses of place, power, and culture.

The French professor of Greek studies Louis Le Roy offers the most comprehensive account in his 1576 work of vernacular historiography, *De la vicissitude ou variéte des choses*, the full title of which was given in the 1594 English translation as: 'Of the interchangeable course, or variety of things in the whole world; and the concurrence of armes and learning, thorough [through]…from the beginning of civility, and memory of man, to this present.…: And that we ought by our own Inventions to augment the doctrine of the Aunciens; not contenting our selves with translations, expositions, corrections, and abridgements of their writings.' Le Roy's title makes it clear that not only learning and arms but the exposition of the writings of the ancients and the invention of new things go together.

The premise of Le Roy's history of civilization is that power or arms, and mastery of the arts and philosophy, rise and fall together. Wisdom is transmitted by means of the learned languages capable of conveying the arts and sciences. So the concurrence of arms and learning first arose in ancient Egypt, Assyria, Persia, and Asia Minor; then later again in Greece, Italy (Rome), and 'Sarrasmesnie' (probably the lands of the Saracens or Arab Muslims); then finally in 'this age' when all the arts are restored with languages, after having been lost for 1,200 years, and others newly invented.

Like all other human artefacts languages change incessantly, affirms Le Roy. Yet within each country and language 'there are some that speake finer, and purer than the rest'. Examples of this are the Athenians in Greece, the Romans in Italy, and the Tuscans there at this day, the Castilians in Spain, the Saxons in Germany, the Persians in Asia, the nobles and courtiers in France. These are the 'illustrated' versions of each country's language, explicitly associated in the case of France not with a particular region but with the country's social elite, the nobles and courtiers.

Further on in the same passage we gather the outlines of Le Roy's understanding of the vernacular Renaissance. When the fine and pure version of Latin was corrupted, it gave birth to Italian, French, and Spanish. But Italian remained for a long time unpolished, because no one took care of it, or applied such polish—until Dante, Petrarch, and Boccaccio, who embellished it with ingeniously expressed conceptions, elegantly styled in prose and verse. Others followed to enrich the language further with fair works and translations. Then the same thing happened to Spanish and French, which in the last fifty years, says Le Roy (writing c.1575), has been rendered more elegant than ever before by excellent personages. They have translated a great many Greek and Latin books, as well as books in Italian, Spanish, and other languages, thereby showing that all sciences could be treated in the French tongue.

Le Roy at this point develops a discourse and history of translation and its role in the communication of arts and sciences to each nation. He does dwell for a moment on the servility of the translator, relative to the inventor of new things. But translation remains a core literary exercise for fashioning one's style and settling one's judgement on the best authors. To translate Greek authors into French is to bring the schoolmasters of mankind into use, where before they had been hidden in schools, or buried in libraries—thus aligning vernacular translation with the revival of letters from disuse. It is by handling good matters—philosophy, public government, deeds of arms, sciences—in the vernaculars that they will come to perfection like Greek and Latin, not by writing fabulous romances or amorous sonnets, the trivial stuff with which the vernaculars in question are all 'pestered'.

With one fell stroke Le Roy here excludes the broad European traditions of vernacular narrative and lyric from Boccaccio and Petrarch to Cervantes and Shakespeare—traditions of the novel and love poetry that for most moderns would now be identified with the literary Renaissance. His Renaissance is very different. He himself had translated a series of political and historical works from classical Greek

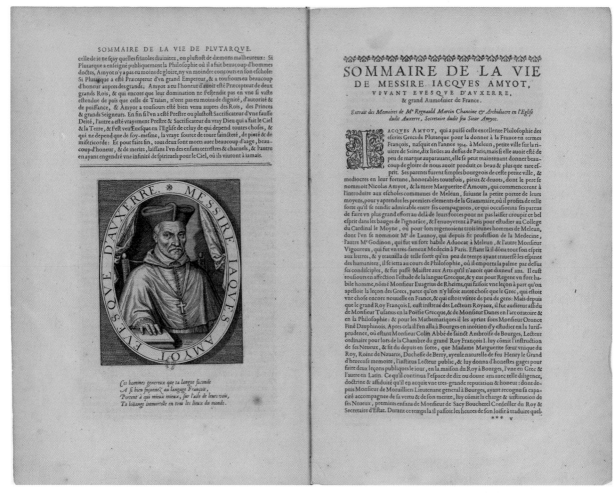

IN THE PARIS 1619 EDITION of Jacques Amyot's translation of Plutarch's parallel lives of various Greek and Roman heroes, the lives and images of Plutarch and of his translator, Amyot, are presented in the preliminary matter one after the other and compared as equals.

into French, before inventing a new historical work in the vernacular—the *Vicissitude*. The greatest figure of the French vernacular Renaissance from this perspective would not be Du Bellay or Ronsard but the most illustrious of all sixteenth-century vernacular translators from the Greek classics: Jacques Amyot, Bishop of Auxerre. In one publication of the time we can see the status that Amyot was afforded in sixteenth-century literary culture: the 1619 edition of his translation of Plutarch's *Lives* affords him, via a portrait and a biography, the same kind of status as one of the classical heroes described by the Greek author in the main text.

In the tenth book, Le Roy outlines the whole Eurasian revival of arms and letters, then moves on to the invention of new things including the printing press, the compass, ordinance, or artillery. But he follows up with bad things newly invented since antiquity, including new diseases such as the 'French disease' or syphilis, and new sects such as the Lutheran and Qizilbash movements in the German and Persian territories respectively. Though Le Roy continues to describe it as 'excellent', it has become an age of revolution, war, and heresy in Europe, Asia, Africa, and the New World.

Le Roy, then, serves as a late Renaissance expression of professional intellectuals' changing and evolving understanding of an age of 'renewed' or newly invented forms of knowledge and artefacts. These range from the printing press to virulent forms of disease, from the rediscovered and reinterpreted works of Lucretius and Aristotle, to the illustrated vernaculars which are our focus in the current chapter. The geography of this self-conscious Renaissance was Eurasian, if not global, and in Le Roy's case included awareness of languages or language groups such as Slavonian. He does group illustrious men of letters and inventors by nations, but these groupings do not correspond to the territorialized, institutionalized literatures of the kind put in place in the long nineteenth century by some Western European nation-states.

The core of Le Roy's narrative, with respect to the vernacular Renaissance, is the progression from the moment when Petrarch and Boccaccio revive classical Latin and polish the Tuscan vernacular in the mid-fourteenth century, to the moment when illustrated forms of French and Spanish are added to the Latin–Italian axis. This progression begins in the earlier sixteenth century and continues after Le Roy's lifetime, when illustrated English literature self-consciously adds itself to the roster. How can we best explore and interrogate this narrative?

One productive current approach to the Renaissance identifies it with a new material and discursive world of objects, commodities, and inventions that were made, consumed, visited, promoted, and circulated by learned and social elites across Europe, and across territories connected with Europe through colonialism, conflict, or trade. Even if they did not amount to a clean philosophical break with a whole middle age, and defined an elite rather than a general culture, they contributed to changes in society that were commented upon at the time, both positively and negatively.

The approach can be extended to literature. We can ground our understanding of the vernacular Renaissance in consideration of: the ways in which vernacular literary language came to be considered a marker of distinction for the elite; the forms of books and other verbal and discursive artefacts that were prized and promoted; the geography not just of the production but of the circulation and use of these artefacts; the places, institutions, and bookshops that people visited in order to acquire literature or understand its context; the roles not only of writers but of teachers, scholars, editors, collectors, and publishers in mediating, in describing, and in evaluating such artefacts in ways that associated them with literary renewals and reformations of various kinds.

Consider the example of university scholar Isaac Wake's 1607 Latin description of the English poet Samuel Daniel's work *The Queenes Arcadia*, which had been performed during a royal progress to Oxford in 1605, then printed in 1606. Daniel pursued what might be described as a vernacular humanist career in Elizabethan and Jacobean England, as he ranged across poetry, moral philosophy, and history. He left no works in Latin. But in his English works he triangulated classical with modern French and Italian sources in order to introduce, by imitation, new literary forms into English. One of these was the genre of *The Queenes Arcadia*: a pastoral tragicomedy, on the model of Guarini and Tasso, about the classical topos of Arcadia and the golden age. As a historian interested in the same issues as Le Roy, Daniel uses the theme to describe an innocent world threatened by some of the less desirable commodities and inventions brought by the new age: new customs and arts from tobacco-smoking and puritanical piety to innovations in professional law and medicine, and seductively lyrical 'love'.

Wake's point is that this elegant court drama has now joined the intellectually respectable canon of 'Renaissance' English vernacular literature, though he does not of course use that term. He describes in Latin the original occasion, at which he was present: how the king and his courtiers separated from the queen's court to visit the Bodleian Library. This was judged an opportune moment to offer 'something also for the ears of the less learned men, and, above all, of the noblewomen' ('etiam hominum minùs eruditorum, & inprimis illustrium fœminarum auriculis'). For it was no doubt the case that some were more assiduous in 'the writings of our Sidney and Chaucer than in those of Plautus or Aristotle'.

Wake is here talking about the writings of the two most authoritative English authors of his time, the only authors (together with Daniel himself, in 1601) whose collected works had been published in large-volume formats. He describes them as vernacular equivalents for two classical authors, Plautus and Aristotle, who featured on grammar-school and university curricula respectively. He goes on to praise Daniel's adoption of the pastoral pan pipe in the vernacular, citing a line from Vergil's *Eclogues* concerning Thalia, the Greek muse of lyrical and comic poetry. Daniel's play taught actors in our native tongue … 'how great a difference there is between the commercial and the learned stage' ('quantùm intersit inter scenam mercenarium, & eruditam'). And he describes how the play is now in everyone's hands in book form as a model for other writers of what can be achieved in the vernacular.

Such descriptions and evaluations of what is new and authoritative in the vernacular field, made against a background of writings identified as popular or less authoritative (the 'mercenary' or popular stage of Shakespeare and his ilk), began, then, in the period itself. They have a richly varied and disputatious history down through Burckhardt, who based much of his argument on pre-1500 literary sources, to the present. But in the period associated with the Renaissance they had a very different context. For imaginative literature in the vernacular did not have at the turn of the seventeenth century what it achieved during the nineteenth century in some major Western European nation-states: a fully institutionalized, monolingual, and demarcated space in each national culture.

There were monolingual audiences for imaginative vernacular literature, catered for by particular booksellers. And there are other statements and actions that can look like the beginnings of the nineteenth-entury development of national literatures. Samuel Daniel is being endorsed by an Oxford University intellectual, and his works were later included in the Bodleian library. But this endorsement was in Latin, partly to demonstrate to an international audience that the English 'nation' of writers could produce significant works in their vernacular (even if most people internationally could not understand it). And Daniel's status in this respect was fleeting. It did not make him a nationally recognized poet whose works were read, taught, and studied throughout the land by all people with any education. Later in the seventeenth century he was known principally as a historian.

Wake's example shows that to legitimize vernacular literature was inevitably to justify it in relation to the cultural capital held by Latin, by the institutions, roles, forms, and claims to truth associated with Latin literature and grammar (including the Latin Aristotle), even if the legitimization in question was oppositional in its stance. But apologies for vernacular literature were not only produced by critics and historians; they did not always take the form of critical commentary or treatises in poetics. They could be implicit in the books themselves.

Let us now take the concrete examples of two books dating from the two principal moments of the vernacular Renaissance identified by Le Roy, and which are connected respectively with the worlds of the two writers with whom this chapter started, Dante and Montaigne. They are compilations rather than single works. The first is a manuscript anthology of texts gathered by and written out in the hand of Boccaccio *c.*1363–6 (Vatican Library, MS Chigi L.V. 176). Let us consider a double page from this manuscript. On the left is the end of Dante's work 'La vita nuova' ('The new life'); on the right is the beginning of Cavalcanti's 'Donna mi prega' ('A lady asks me'). Both authors are described by Boccaccio as 'of Florence', for he wishes to establish the tradition of vernacular writing he is gathering in that city.

'La vita nuova' consists of sonnets accompanied by narrative contexts and analytical divisions—all composed by Dante. Cavalcanti's single *canzone* of seventy-five lines stretches out over eight pages. The rest of the manuscript contains Boccaccio's life of Dante (before these two texts), Boccaccio's Latin poem dedicating the collection to

THE VATICAN LIBRARY'S MANUSCRIPT CHIGI L.V.176 is an autograph of Boccaccio's that gathers a tradition of lyric poetry in the vernacular by offering texts of works by Dante, Petrarch, Cavalcanti, and Boccaccio himself. Dante's 'La Vita Nuova' concludes on the left, and Cavalcanti's poem 'Donna mi prega' begins on the right, both with glosses of the kind associated at the time with classical and scholastic texts.

Chomincia la cancone di guido di axti
cavalcante de cavalcanti di firençe;

Donna mi priega, ch'eo voglio di
re d'uno accidente, che sovente
è fero, e si altier, ch'è chiamato amore:
si chi lo nega, possa il ver sentire, e al
presente conoscente chero, perch'io non
spero, ch'om di basso core, ad tal ragione
porti conoscença, ch'e senza natural dimo
stramento, non ò talento di voler pro
vare, là ove posa, e chi lo fa creare, e
qual è sua vertute e sua potença, l'esse
ça, e poi ciascun suo movimento; E 'l pia
cimento, che 'l fa dire amore, e s'omo
per vedere il pò mostrare;

Petrarch (after these two texts), fifteen of Dante's longer *canzoni*, and an early version of Petrarch's collection of vernacular lyrics now known as *Rerum vulgarium fragmenta* ('Fragments of vernacular matters'). But this represents the final form of a manuscript that had evolved through two prior stages. In the first stage, it had been an edition of works by Dante, including at that stage the *Commedia*. Then, in a second stage, Petrarch's lyrics were added. In a third stage (the manuscript as we now have it), the *Commedia* was taken out, to form a separate manuscript, and Cavalcanti's lyric was put in.

The first feature to notice is the authoritative look of the texts. In fact, Boccaccio is using the format of scholastic books of the time. Both texts appear with marginal glosses. On the left, they appear both in the side and bottom margin. In Dante's original text, these comments, which consisted of analytical divisions of the sonnets, were incorporated in the main text. But Boccaccio has separated them out, in order to give the work the visual aspect of a glossed and therefore authoritative text. On the right, Cavalcanti's lyric appears in the middle, surrounded by the voluminous Latin commentary of Dino del Garbi (hence the extension over eight pages), who discusses the *canzone* as a rational analysis of love. Before Cavalcanti's lyric was inserted, the *Commedia* appeared here with an apparatus similar to that of a glossed manuscript edition of Vergil or Statius.

These vernacular texts, the visual format says, are worthy of grammatical and philosophical study. It would not be until the sixteenth century that a whole range of vernacular authors—Garcilaso, Du Bartas, Spenser, Colonna—were provided with learned commentaries and presented in analogous ways in print.

The same messages appear in a different form in the first text in Boccaccio's manuscript, his life of Dante (*c*.1351–5), which is modelled on Donatus' life of Vergil. Boccaccio's little treatise represents the first vernacular biography of a modern (i.e. late medieval) vernacular poet, and the inception of the idea that the reputation of a great vernacular poet could be integral to the international reputation of a city-state or nation-state. The version in the Chigi manuscript is a second, shorter redaction of a treatise that in its first version is still more heavily oriented towards a Florentine audience.

The purpose of the biography is threefold. First, it aims to bring Dante, his works, and his literary reputation back to Florence, to have them honoured there, to let them foster a public revival in the liberal arts there, and to do so in the Florentine idiom. It is claimed throughout that Dante yearned during the latter part of his life to return to his home city, as long as his honour was preserved. Florence had exiled Dante in 1302, and in so doing (in Boccaccio's eyes) lost her title to be a just city that rewarded the virtuous and punished the vicious. Boccaccio also made attempts to bring Petrarch, while alive, back to Florence, without success—one of these attempts is part of the context of the Chigi manuscript.

Second, it would authorize and elevate, through the example of the way of life of Dante as a poet-theologian, the composition of learned poetry in the vernacular for a broad, vulgar audience. Boccaccio claims that Dante began his poem in Latin, in the style of Vergil. But he stopped and restarted in the vernacular tongue in a style more fitted for modern ears ('in istile atto a' moderni sensi'). His point is that Dante could have composed it in Vergilian Latin, but for civic reasons decided to compose it in the vernacular, which made it a different work, with a different voice, for a different audience. Third, it is designed to serve as the entrance to manuscript compilations of Dante's works on the part of Boccaccio—literally bringing the works back in writing to Florence for a Florentine audience.

Boccaccio describes, then, a Dantean Renaissance in Florence. The great poet opened the way for the return to Italy of the banished muses; he made the splendour ('chiarezza') of the Florentine idiom manifest; the beauties of common speech were set to numbers; by him dead poetry was brought back to life. However, this passage and several others of the kind were not retained in the version of the text copied into the Chigi manuscript. This may be because Boccaccio had a specific addressee in mind for that manuscript: Petrarch. As we heard earlier, Petrarch did not share Boccaccio's views about Dante as the originator of the Florentine literary Renaissance, or about the vernacular. It may be that in trying to persuade him to modify these views, and to join a common literary movement with himself, Dante, and Cavalcanti, he toned down the praise of the author of the *Commedia* and his and the vernacular's role in the literary Renaissance—leaving space for Petrarchan humanist Latin to step in more authoritatively. The description of the literary Renaissance can change between two versions of the same manuscript by the same scribe, for rhetorical reasons.

If the Chigi manuscript gathers a tradition of lyric poetry in the vernacular, we can briefly consider another by Boccaccio that gathers a tradition of narrative prose in the vernacular. In a sense it is still a compilation, but a compilation authored by him: the *Decameron*, as transcribed by Boccaccio a few years later in MS Hamilton 90 (Berlin), *c*.1370–2. Once again this manuscript uses the format of a scholastic book, this time to raise a collection of short vernacular fictions to the level of dignity of the ruling model of learned book production of the time, and to task it with a revival of Florence's civic culture—torn apart by the 1348 plague described in the work's introduction. For what is being revived in the *Decameron* is not intimacy with classical Latin letters—even if the prose does mimic Latinate syntactical structures with considerable elegance, and even if some of the sources of the tales are of antique provenance. It is very much an oral, social world that is revived and reinvigorated; there is little or no mention of writing, books, and classical 'letters'.

Boccaccio takes a whole gamut of existing forms of narrative ('stories or fables or parables or histories or whatever you choose to call them', he says)—from the French chivalric romance through saints' lives and *exempla* to collections of mottoes and sayings—and makes them 'new', makes them *novelle*. The novelty lies not in the plots of the stories, which are often derivative, but in the vernacular display of narrative and improvisatory ability, in the realization of credible fictions and incisive repartee, on the part both of the narrators of the stories and of the social narrators and actors within the stories—from the high tragic discourse of Ghismonda in the first story of the fourth day (4.1) to the scandalous personification of the Angel Gabriel by Frate Alberto in the following story, 4.2.

Corresponding to this ability to make or perform fictions is the capacity to read or judge speech-acts and behaviours that claim verisimilitude, to interrogate and examine them if necessary—sometimes on the part of actual magistrates seeking to test witnesses' testimony. When such narrations, sayings, and fictions are used and received to good ends—and there are, of course, many counter-examples of their use and reception to bad ends—they serve to recreate the civic fabric of the community. The happy resolution to the seventh story of the second day, a Mediterranean aristocratic romance, hinges on the way in which Antigono instructs Alatiel to narrate her long adventures in exile to her father, so that he believes (falsely) she is still a virgin. But in other *novelle* the truth itself can be received as an implausible fiction: when Andreucci ends up destitute in the street in Naples, tricked out of all his belongings, he cannot convince the people of the neighbourhood that he is telling anything but 'ridiculous tall stories' (2.5).

If Petrarch's vernacular poems offer a body of erotic liturgy to rival religious services of Christian love, Boccaccio's collection of tales offers a corpus of secular sermons as an answer to contemporary friars' 'loud harangues and specious parables', which strike terror into people's hearts and embroil them in almsgiving and mass-offerings (3.7). Instead of poetry-as-theology, as in the case of his account of the *Commedia*, we have poetry as a secular alternative to the friars' specious use of rhetoric and stories. The rationale of vernacular 'fiction' here is verbal and pragmatic inventiveness—including lying, pretending, performing—in everyday life, and especially in that sphere of life which the masters of 'literature', theologians and preachers, would replace with monastic and Hermetic solitude: the life of profane, extramarital love.

Boccaccio captures this point with the incomplete *novella* he offers in the prologue to day four: the story of a boy who, brought up as an apprentice hermit by his father, and taken on his first day trip to Florence, immediately turns without hesitation from adoration of the painted angels in churches to courtship of the live angels (beautiful women) he sees there for the first time—the inverse of Miranda's brave new world of men like Ferdinand in Shakespeare's *The Tempest*. In this 'Renaissance', what is being brought out of the monk-like cell is not a dusty copy of a classical text but a living, breathing person who needs to find ways of narrating and enacting his or her new-found passion in the vernacular. In the same way, in the collection's introduction, the company of ladies leave the church of Santa Maria Novella in Florence, where they are saying their paternosters, to tell worldly stories—*novellare*—in various countryside villas. This does mean that in Boccaccio's milieu the new style of vernacular literature is still very much associated, as in chivalric culture, with the art of love, whether slanted towards spiritual or towards physical fulfilment.

Let us now move forward nearly 250 years to Daniel's and Montaigne's era, to another book with a scholastic format, but of a very different kind. The rise of humanist education in the interim—not really widespread in Italy and Europe until the late fifteenth, early sixteenth centuries—put classical and foreign language-learning, and literary (as opposed to logical) analysis and recomposition of texts at the heart of the general culture of a broad, educated elite, through to adulthood, in a way it had not been before. They studied secular poetry, philosophy, oratory, history, and, in some confessional cultures, biblical texts. Most educated adult men, and some elite women, were trained in humanist-style grammar and rhetoric.

This meant that the study and meditation of texts in non-native languages became the fundamental pedagogical and literary activity for lay people with access to advanced education. For those people, to read and to write was to translate and to imitate foreign texts; to speak their own vernacular was to cultivate an illustrated, eloquent, or 'translated' form of ordinary language, equivalent to the sumptuous apparel that set apart the higher gentry and nobility. Literary and linguistic training gave them access to a multilingual, Europe-wide culture of knowledge and power, whether through books or through travel and political service, that was denied to the vast majority of the people. This literary culture was increasingly dominated by the triangular relationship between the three most prestigious, pan-European languages: humanistic neo-Latin, French, and Italian. The consolidating nation-states of Iberia and England in turn promoted their own elite literary vernaculars—in Iberia's case across the Habsburg territories and the New World—in ways shaped by that triad's domination of the literary scene.

Consider these developments through the prism of a humanistic teacher of modern languages, Cathérin Le Doux or Catharinus Dulcis. In the early seventeenth century he published a textbook (*Schola italica*, or 'Italian school') to gather various materials that had begun to go into print in various separate parts in 1593. It contains an anthology of texts which largely use Latin to teach Italian. In its fullest form, there is, first, an Italian grammar, written in Latin, consisting of a grammatical treatise, and sections on pronunciation, the alphabet, the parts of speech, articles, pronouns, verbs, all the way through to participles and prepositions. There follow various texts: a parallel Latin–Italian text of the sacred dialogues of Sébastien Châteillon, though not attributed to him (the translation is by Dulcis); a set of secular dialogues in the vernacular largely taken from John Florio's *Second Frutes*, but edited, and with prayers interspersed at the beginning and end that are not in the original; a list of Italian *sententiae* or proverbs; vernacular *apophthegmata* ('maxims'); examples of vernacular letters; a text of Tasso's *Aminta*; Dulcis's own vernacular comedy, *La mora*, in imitation of Terence's *Eunuchus*; vernacular lives of Alexander, Caesar, and Scipio; vernacular orations, each with a little note describing the 'Effetto' or outcome of the speech; and an Italian–Latin dictionary.

In this book we find Florentine Tuscan, augmented with words and idioms from other Italian dialects, as a standardized literary language taught through grammar in the manner of Latin, using Latin. It has a canon of imaginative literary texts and can be taught and used across Europe by humanists and their pupils with no cultural roots in Italy. Dulcis was born in 1540 in Cruseilles, between Annecy and Geneva, in what is now France, but was then the Duchy of Savoy. At the time of his birth, Savoy was occupied by Francis I of France, but it was liberated by a treaty of 1559. Vanished now, Savoy was then as typical of the territories of Europe as emergent nation-states such as France and England. It was on the crossroads between France, the other northern Italian states, and the Swiss confederation of cities and cantons to the north, and was divided into Calvinist and Roman Catholic areas. It had no one language; the local vernacular was Francoprovençal or Arpitan, which today is on UNESCO's definitely endangered list; the other languages of the region were French, Italian, and Latin.

Dulcis's life was divided into two halves, one half spent on the move, one half spent rooted in one place, one court. After his early education in humanism and Protestantism, he began an extraordinary itinerary across Europe and the Near East. Along the way he encountered Sultan Süleiman, was enslaved on an Ottoman galley, and stripped of his horse, money, and clothes in Hungary (an experience similar to the one recounted by Montaigne in his chapter on physiognomy). He served and resided with various princes and aristocrats as he went, especially as a tutor to the young nobility. We know about this from the curriculum vitae he published in print in Latin in 1622. By then he had settled down; he was professor of exotic or foreign languages—which meant French and Italian—at the Protestant University of Marburg, which made him one of the first university professors of modern languages in Europe. It is interesting in this respect that it was at the request of German students that a chair in Tuscan had been instituted at the University of Siena in 1588 by Ferdinando I de' Medici—the first university chair for study of a modern vernacular language in the history of Europe.

At one point in his journey (February 1596), after a spell teaching in England, an inventory of his books was made that complements and enlarges the picture we get from his *Schola italica*. It is divided into four sections by language (Latin, Italian, French, Spanish), with monetary values added, possibly so that the books could be cashed in or used as security against a debt.

These were the texts Dulcis was using to teach languages and literature to elite English clients in one of the households that also employed John Florio, around the time he began his translation of Montaigne. Both Florio and Dulcis belonged to a broad category of itinerant teachers and intellectuals who were criss-crossing Europe due to the religious troubles, and who combined modern-language teaching with intelligence work. They had an important role in the European dissemination of Renaissance culture due to their ability to work—despite their Protestant affiliations—across confessional borders and across Latin and modern languages (though Florio had no Latin).

Dulcis's library of teaching books had been published in cities all over Europe, including Basel, Venice, Frankfurt, Paris. There are at least five published in England, though only one of them was entirely in the English language: an unidentified English Bible. From one perspective, the list does seem to correspond to the multinational European literary tradition recovered by scholars such as Auerbach and Ernst Robert Curtius in the twentieth century: a European tradition consisting of international

THE CATALOGUE OF THE BOOKS of Cathérin Le Doux or Catharinus Dulcis is found in the papers of Francis Bacon's brother Anthony, held at Lambeth Palace, and is divided into four sections by language. This page shows his Latin and Italian books and the monetary value attributed to them in pounds and shillings. The Italian section includes several works by Tasso and is the most valuable in the catalogue.

Latin literature and the separate national literatures. It has both classical literature and the Bible, and literature in the three main modern Romance languages. Each Romance language is developing a literature and a canon of its own, including a translated Bible and translated classics. This is particularly clear in the case of Italian.

But from another perspective, despite the division by language, this document does not point to a multinational literary Europe—a Europe, that is, already consisting of distinct national literary traditions. It points instead to a single, multilingual, transnational, mobile literary culture in demand across the north-western Eurasian peninsula. Dulcis is, after all, a Savoyard teaching Italian, French, and probably

Hispanicorꝰ

- Historia Imperial — 10
- Cronica del principe Castricto — 7
- Auenturas de Antonio Perez — 2.6
- Las epistolas de Guevara — 6
- Vocabulario de las dos lenguas Tos. y Castellana — 3.6
- Historia Ethiopica — 3
- Euangelios y actos de los Apostoles cō coment. — 2.6
- Psalmos de David — 1.6
- Reglas Grammaticales — 1.

1#.17

- ✝ fioretti della lingua volgare e latina — 1/8
- the french Alphabet — 1
- Dos tratados del papa y de la missa — 2.6
- Bible dorée en Anglois — 6.
- Terence en petit volume — 1

Summa Summarꝰ 14# 9-/8.

Gallicorꝰ   186

- La deliurance de Hierusalem in 4° — 8
- Hierusalem en rime francoise — 3.6
- Cornelius Tacitus — 4
- Les harangues militaires — 13
- Essays de Montaigne — 6
- Les sepmaines du Bartas — 6.
- Les fables d'Esope en taille doulce — 3.
- Sleidan des 4 empires — 2 Henry l'a

2 #s./8 6 s

Somma Summarꝰ 11 # 1/8.

- Il nuouo testamento latino e volgare — 3.
- Le coffre de bonne esperance — 12
- Mons'. petit vn meelot — 10   Some 12 # 6/8
- Onomasticon 7. linguarꝰ Junij — 4
- Sallustio volgare — 2.6
- Commentarij Cæsaris — 2 6
- Sallustius latine — 2
- Terentius latine & Italice in 4° — 6
- Hercolano del varchi — 2.6
- Giambulari della lingua fiorentina — 3
- Commentaires de Cæsar de Vigenere in 4° — 5
- Comedie di plauto — 2
- Nomenclator quatrilinguis — 2 ✝

THE CATALOGUE OF THE BOOKS of Cathérin Le Doux or Catharinus Dulcis continues here with the Spanish, then French, sections, including the 'Essays de Montaigne'. The cataloguer adds up the total value as eleven pounds and a shilling before adding three further items and a revised total, followed by another fourteen books listed across two pages and a final total of fourteen pounds and nine shillings.

Spanish in England and the German states. The list has several polyglot reference works including two editions of the *Nomenclator* (a lexicon published in various combinations of languages) and one of the *Onomasticon* (another lexicon with seven languages) of Junius, as well as a bilingual Tuscan–Castilian vocabulary and a French–Italian dictionary.

The end of the sixteenth century and the beginning of the seventeenth century saw a plethora of multilingual publications which offered the same texts in all the literary languages of the day. One noteworthy example is the Frankfurt 1619 edition of Georgette de Montenay, *A Booke of armes, or remembrance*. Montenay's book of Christian

SAPIENS MVLIER ÆDIFICAT DOMV

Vera effigies Regina Nauarræ.

I. GALLICE.

Voyez comment ceste Reine s'efforce
De cœur non feinct d'auancer l'edifice
Du temple fainct, pour de toute fa force
Loger vertu, & dechaffer tout vice.
Notons que Dieu la rend ainfi propice,
Afin qu'il foit glorifié en elle:
Et qu'onfoit prompt (ainfi qu'elle) au feruice,
Dont le loyer eft la vie eternelle.

I. LA-

Eur, age, fic inftas operi, fanctumq́, laborem
Ipfa tua celeras, Dux generofa, manu?
Sollicitat pietatis amor rediuiuus, & alma
Relligio, cultu confpicienda facro.

ALITER.

Id virtutis iter vafto fub gurgite mundi,
Quod Regina fciens relligione terit.
Illa patrocinio cœlebs, & moribus aras
Ædificat fuperis: pauperibufq́, domum.

I. HISPANICE.

Quan bien auenturado.
Quien muger fabia tiene.
Paz y profperidad de aqui viene:
Y el mando fe huelga defcanfado.
Mos tal de Deos es dada
Al los que la han bufcado
Con piedad vera y pofada.

I. ITALICE.

Vedi quefta Reina effempio di virtu,
E vera pietà, come da giouentu.
In quella da parenti e ftata cleuata,
Cofi in matura ità ne fu anchor parata,
Mantenandolsi in cafe per tutt il fuo regno,
Ond in fua lode fi mette quel diffegno
Da femina prudente la cafe edificata.

G 2   I. GER.

THE FRANKFURT 1619 EDITION of Georgette de Montenay's book of Christian emblems gives French, two Latin, Spanish, Italian, English, German, and Dutch texts of the poem that accompanies each picture and motto. Here the motto is from Proverbs 14 ('The wise woman builds her house') and the picture is of Jeanne d'Albret, Queen of Navarre, at whose court Montenay was raised. The poems in the various languages are not literal translations of one another but independent versions of the same ideas.

emblems was first published in French at Lyon in 1567, dedicated to the Queen of Navarre. But it saw several Latin editions before this polyglot edition appeared with parallel texts in Latin, Italian, French, Spanish, Dutch, German, and English (the other languages are over the page). It was also separately translated into Dutch and English in manuscript by female writers Anna Visscher and Esther Inglis, creating a transnational community of female Calvinist voices. This is a very different image of literature from the one offered by Vasari's painting, which gathers a male, monolingual canon of Italian literature in the setting of Florence. And there was a secular equivalent too; from the 1530s and 1540s there was a renaissance of secular vernacular writing by elite women in Italy and Europe.

Dulcis's booklist points to another transnational aspect of literary culture: cross-border Calvinist affiliations similar to those forged by Montenay's text. These were the books of someone who was connected with Protestant intellectuals and movements across the Continent, who possessed prohibited vernacular editions of the Bible in Spanish and Italian, and works by the Spanish reformer Cyprian de Valera, but who at the same time was open to a broad literary culture, including quite militant Catholics like Tasso.

So instead of saying that the list comprised the distinct, newly emergent national literatures of France, Spain, and the Italian peninsula, plus international Latin literature, we could say it comprised transnational authors and texts, current across Europe in many different languages and editions. Besides the Bible these of course include classical authors such as Terence, Caesar, and Sallust. A particularly good example rooted in the late Renaissance period is Heliodorus. He appears only in Spanish on Dulcis's booklist but the Savoyard describes at length in his *Schola italica* how Heliodorus in Italian is one of his authors of choice, alongside Boccaccio, Tasso, and the other modern Italian classics, when teaching his noble pupils. The *editio princeps* of Heliodorus appeared at Basel in 1534. The inaugural vernacular translation was Jacques Amyot's into French in 1547. Within a twenty-year period there followed translations into Italian, Spanish, English, and German. The Spanish translation was done from French then compared with the Greek.

But many of the more recent authors on the list were also pan-European phenomena. This applied obviously enough to some of the neo-Latin works Dulcis owned, including Lipsius, Lewenclavius, Sleidanus. In the case of the Italian copy of Sleidanus published at Geneva with a dedication to the Duke of Saxony by Sleidanus himself, we might again ask whether it was being acquired by an emergent Italian literature or by an international Calvinist community. It was also published in French from Geneva.

The same thing applied, however, to many of the vernacular authors on the list: Tasso, Mexia, Guevara, Du Bartas. And the point here is not just that this document shows there to have been many pan-European texts and authors in the teaching library of a humanist employed by English clients. It is rather that these books and authors were integral to the literary Renaissance of the place—England—where Dulcis had been using them to teach. They were the books and authors imported from the Continent by English readers, and translated and imitated by English authors such as Samuel Daniel. Many of them, including Lipsius and Tasso, were being translated into English at the very moment the inventory was made. Heliodorus had been fundamental to Phillip Sidney's revised *Arcadia*, left unfinished a few years before.

Montaigne must also be counted as one of these transnational vernacular authors and it is worth pausing on his example once again. Here he is, a Roman Catholic author, in French, in England, in the hands of an itinerant, multilingual Protestant humanist using his text to teach French to aristocratic clients in the same household as John Florio, who would begin translating him into English about 1598. Copies of

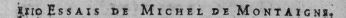

L'vne suit l'autre, & l'vne l'autre fuit.
Par cette cy, celle-là est poussee
Et cette cy par l'autre est deuancee:
Tousiours l'eau va dans l'eau, & tousiours est-ce
Mesme ruisseau, & tousiours eau diuerse.

Il y a plus affaire à interpreter les interpretations, qu'à interpreter les choses; & plus de liures sur les liures, que sur autre subiect. Nous ne faisons que nous entregloser. Tout fourmille de commentaires: d'autheurs, il en est grãd' cherté, Le principal & plus fameux sçauoir de nos siecles, est-ce pas sçauoir entendre les sçauans? Est-ce pas la fin commune & derniere de tous estudes? Nos opiniõs s'antét les vnes sur les autres. La premiere sert de tige à la seconde: la seconde à la tierce. Nous eschellons ainsi de degré en degré. Et aduient de là, que le plus haut monté, a souuent plus d'honneur, que de merite. Car il n'est môté que d'vn grain, sur les espaules du penultiéme. Combien souuent, & sottement à l'aduenture, ay-ie esté du mon liure à parler de soy? Sottement, quand ce ne seroit que pour cette raison: Qu'il me deuoit souuenir, de ce que ie dy des autres, qui en font de mesmes. Que ces œillades si frequentes à leurs ouurages, tesmoignent que le cœur leur frissonne de son amour, & les rudoyemens mesmes, desdaigneux, dequoy ils les battent, que ce ne sont que mignardises, & affetteries, d'vne faueur maternelle. Suyuant Aristote, à qui, & se priser & se mespriser, naissent souuent de pareil air d'arrogance. Car mon excuse: Que ie doy auoir en cela plus de liberté que les autres, dautát qu'à poinct nommé, i'escry de moy, & de mes escrits, comme de mes autres actions: que mon theme se renuerse en soy: ie ne sçay, si chacun la prendra. I'ay veu en Allemagne, que Luther a laissé autant de diuisions & d'altercations, sur le doubte de ses opinions, & plus, qu'il n'en esmeut sur les escritures sainctes. Noustre contestation n'est verbale. Ie demáde que c'est que nature, volupté, cercle, & substitution. La question est de paroles, & se paye de mesme. Vne pierre c'est vn corps: mais

suum cuiq pulcrum

quot sont tot sententiæ.

THE DUTCH LAWYER PIETER VAN VEEN, brother of the painter Otto van Veen, filled his copy of the Paris 1602 edition of Montaigne's *Essais* with drawings and annotations that turned it into a personalized emblem book. Here Van Veen pictures Luther with a book generating more doubts about his own opinions amongst his followers than he himself raised about the meaning of the scriptures. The two Latin adages ('what is one's own is beautiful'; 'so many men, so many opinions') had already been applied by Van Veen's countryman Erasmus to religious strife.

ANDREAS BRETSCHNEIDER'S ENGRAVING appeared in a 1614 festival book that commemorated the 1613 baptism of Eva Katherine of the principality of Anhalt-Dessau in the Holy Roman Empire. The mock procession is led by a dwarf, followed by characters from *Don Quijote* part one (1605), with objects alluding to some of its episodes: the curate, holding a windmill; the barber, with a basin on his head and a barrel in his arms; Dulcinea dressed up as a princess; Don Quijote and his lance.

Montaigne's work were travelling in this way all over Europe at the time. In another case we find him transmitted via the teachings of the humanist Justus Lipsius to the personal library of Pieter van Veen, a Dutch lawyer of The Hague in the early seventeenth century. Van Veen annotated and illustrated his copy of the *Essais* to create a kind of personalized emblem book, with a memoir at the back, that he could hand on as a family heirloom to his son. Instead of his maternal tongue, he used the French language in the annotations and memoir.

Boccaccio's and Dulcis's books of the late fourteenth and early seventeenth centuries trace a historical trajectory of continuity and change, and suggest a number of themes for any treatment of vernacular Renaissance literature. One important theme we have not mentioned so far is that of the relations of vernacular literature with other media— oral, performative, festive, visual, musical. We heard earlier how Boccaccio's collection of *novelle* is immersed in the performative and oral medium of contemporary social life. This is just as true of Cervantes's *Don Quijote*, though literary and printed texts feature much more frequently and self-consciously as properties in his fictional world. The festive aspects of Cervantes's creation were so obvious and pronounced in his contemporaries' minds that the figures of Don Quijote and his companions quickly assumed a life of their own, independently of the name of Cervantes, in contemporary festivals.

The teaching of modern languages in the latter part of the period, and therefore the uses of modern-language literature, also had an inherently oral and performative dimension. Ariosto was sung in the streets and countryside in sixteenth-century Italy. This performative dimension can even be seen in Dulcis's highly Latinate and literary textbook: he inserts some of the dialogues Florio composed to socialize English people in Italianate conversational culture, and vice versa. The relationship between text and image was also fundamental to the production and consumption of vernacular literature: from the symbiosis between epic painting and writing in Renaissance France, to the illustrations that accompanied Spenser's *Shepheardes Calendar* and, as we have just seen, the transformation of Montaigne's *Essais* into a personal emblem book by Pieter van Veen.

There is also the question of the perceived stasis or mobility of vernacular works; equal and opposite forces fixed texts in particular places, with defined groups, and moved them on from city to city, hand to hand. We saw that Boccaccio was concerned very much to tie the persons and vernacular oeuvres of Dante and Petrarch to the city of Florence and its reputation, even though—or partly because—both writers were, in different circumstances, itinerant individuals with ambivalent relationships to the city. Later, the vernacular writings of other Italian authors including Castiglione, Boiardo, Ariosto, and Tasso became associated with other Italian city-states such as Urbino and Ferrara. What other city-states across Europe produced themselves on the international stage through vernacular literature to the same extent as Florence? As we have seen, one candidate in the sixteenth century is Geneva, but this was in relation to the production of a Calvinist vernacular corpus. More generally, the Florentine model was transferred via writers including Du Bellay to emergent nation-states such as France.

However, it was also the case that other regions and sovereign entities such as the Duchy of Savoy did not territorialize particular languages and literatures, remaining multilingual. And as we saw through the example of Dulcis, writers, languages, and books associated by some with particular city- or nation-states were highly mobile across borders. At one and the same time, or at different times, writers and their works could be associated with different places or entities, seen as local or universal, static or mobile. Dante could be seen as the author of Renaissance Florence or as the poet of universal European *Christianitas* and the Holy Roman Empire; Montaigne's *Essais* were the product of a Gascon, a French, a European or 'Roman' writer, of someone at home in his library or abroad on his travels across Europe. Though it is not so apparent in Dulcis's life, or on his booklist, this period saw the first consolidated moves towards the globalization of literature, through colonialism, mercantilism, and evangelism. European texts were circulated and produced on other continents, and Asian and American texts reached Europe. Of the great writers only Camões, however, directly depicted the enterprise and experience of discovery and conquest in an extended work of imaginative literature.

We started with a view of the vernacular literary Renaissance that emphasized the role of authors who still have a place in the canon of world literature. But we have seen that other actors, or authors exercising other kinds of agency, were also involved in the making of that Renaissance. This is not only a matter of translators such as Amyot and Le Roy, and the less illustrious individuals who vulgarized the classics into Italian languages, outside of the purview of institutions and noble patrons, between 1250 and

1350, or the jobbing translators who worked with printers in the late Renaissance period. We must also consider editors, patrons, readers, publishers, teachers, ambassadors, collectors, institutions, even, as we have seen, cities.

We heard how Boccaccio wrote for a powerful intellectual patron, Petrarch, whose support he was seeking for the inclusion of Dante in the Florentine canon. We have also seen him identify the audience for *novelle* with courtly female readers. Daniel's work, likewise, was published as the Queen's *Arcadia*: it was addressed to his royal patroness and her ladies both in performance and in print. Such ladies could also become published writers, as we saw in the case of Georgette de Montenay, who was brought up at the court of Jeanne d'Albret, the Protestant Queen of Navarre, and as is also clear in the case of the greatest sixteenth-century imitator of Boccaccio, and another Queen of Navarre, Marguerite d'Angoulême. Perhaps the most powerful 'patron', though, was not the aristocrat or monarch but the figure of the lay reader-writer—male or female—who emerged between *c.*1100 and *c.*1650 to provide the audience, the motive, and the scribe of Renaissance vernacular literature. By the end of the period this figure was omnipresent in the composition of that literature, whether in the form of authors such as Montaigne, or fictional characters such as Don Quijote.

Boccaccio also featured as an editor and mediator of other authors' works: he is consciously shaping a Florentine tradition of lyrical and novelistic literature by means of his production of manuscripts and of biographies of illustrious writers. Pietro Bembo would later take up a related role in the context of print culture. His editions of Boccaccio and Petrarch, along with his critical writings, were perhaps more important than any other individual's in shaping the sixteenth century's understanding of 'Italian Renaissance literature'. Booksellers such as Montaigne's editor, Abel L'Angelier, and his publisher in England, Edward Blount, began to specialize in imaginative vernacular literature and to form a clientele for it.

Institutions such as the Dante lectures established in *trecento* Florence, the monarchical courts, and the Dutch chambers of rhetoric, were also instrumental in the production and legitimization of vernacular literature. Many of the court-like academies of late Renaissance Italy played a conscious role in the composition, performance, promotion, and publication of vernacular literary texts. In 1595, the Accademia della Crusca collectively attempted to take control of the text and understanding of the 'noble Florentine' Dante's *Commedia* by publishing a new edition in Florence. This did not necessarily mean that academies were organs of open vulgarization: the Accademia Fiorentina's reforms of 1547 sought to enforce a stricter divide between popular orality and elite vernacular speech.

Dulcis has been included as a representative of the broad range of humanist teachers and other humanistically educated intellectuals, including the modern-language teacher Florio at one end and the scholar-diplomat Isaac Wake at the other. These intermediaries played a fundamental role in disseminating vernacular Renaissance literature and the demand for it across Europe. But at the same time it is interesting to note that, after the era of Rabelais and Bembo, professional textual scholars, humanists, and clerics were hardly involved in the production of great works of imaginative vernacular literature. All Dulcis produced, in terms of his own imaginative work, was a dull and derivative court play based on the Geneva Bible's version of the story of Tobias (with many borrowings from Montaigne), and a stilted imitation of Terence. He and other professional humanists such as Le Roy did continue, of course, to produce important vernacular translations. Conversely, the writers of works we now recognize as the great literature of the age were less involved in professional learning. Camões, Sidney, Montaigne, Shakespeare, and Cervantes all specialized in imaginative, secular vernacular literature; none of them wrote formally learned treatises in Latin.

Was this because imaginative literature had become even less respectable for professional intellectuals, or because it had begun to carve out its own domain? Vernacular plays could be seen as diabolical invasions of the senses; chivalric romances as causes of insanity. Arguably, in literary cultures from post-Reformation England to Counter-Reformation Spain, it was the attacks on fictional writing—as idle romances, lascivious poetry, false histories—that first began to constitute the category we now in anglophone cultures call vernacular 'literature', meaning imaginative works of poetry, prose, and drama. Such works came to be defended directly or indirectly by the likes of Sidney and Cervantes because they had been attacked as a matter of harmful lies by the religiously correct clerisy. It nevertheless remains the case that the period did not see the establishment of clear distinctions between fictional and non-fictional writing, between imaginative and learned literature—these were to come much later.

Between the two moments of Boccaccio and Dulcis there was a vast expansion in the domain of vernacular literature, with respect to the range of both imaginative and learned literary genres, though it is important to make differentiations between the situations of particular languages in particular sub-periods and places. Dante's great poem undoubtedly contributed to the enfranchisement of a lay readership of vernacular literature in Florence and other Italian city-states. But his literary achievement (as described by Boccaccio) in appropriating the domain of all knowledge for the vernacular, from theology down, was a one-off. His poem did not achieve a European dissemination or dimension of influence during the period of the Renaissance. Boccaccio's and Petrarch's vernacular oeuvres did, but they were largely confined to the imaginative genres of the *novella* and the lyric. Both authors produced their learned works in Latin.

During the fifteenth century, however, a number of Italian humanists began to produce philosophical works and translations in the vernacular, and during the sixteenth century there was a very important movement of vernacular Aristotelianism in Italian, matched to a degree by French, German, and Spanish, but not by English. Dulcis's booklist contains no vernacular Aristotle but it ranges across history, secular and divine poetry (Du Bartas's versification of Genesis), philosophy, dialogues (Castiglione), letters, and reference literature (encyclopedias). There were many other new or renewed genres of vernacular writing by the sixteenth and early seventeenth centuries: the epigram, the essay, the emblem book, the oration, the sermon, the rhetorical and conduct manual, the pastoral romance, the masque, the epic.

But perhaps the most important difference between Boccaccio's era and Dulcis's era in this respect is the widespread availability of vernacular bibles, sermons, and devotional literatures. Boccaccio presented the *Decameron* as an alternative to the oral and literary culture of the friars. Dulcis was a Calvinist who integrated religious and secular material in his teaching and literary work.

But how typical was he, and what was the balance of religious and secular elements in vernacular Renaissance literature? Can they even be disentangled? Most nineteenth-century and modern histories of literature—until quite recently—have not only nationalized and de-Latinized the textual past, they have secularized it in the name of a Western modernity defined by emancipation from religion. While it is true that drama and prose fiction, more than lyric and epic, gravitated away from biblical and devotional topics, they were still shaped by religious cultures and literacies. Shakespeare may have been prohibited by law from staging biblical stories but his plays recall late medieval religious drama and are informed by both Protestant and Catholic beliefs and practices. Similarly, religious writing by the likes of Luis de Granada and John Donne was shaped by Renaissance and classical traditions such as rhetoric, and by humanist educators such as Erasmus. By *c.*1660 Protestant states such as Britain and many of the German territories had produced a much more significant body of vernacular devotional and religious literature than they had of imaginative literature. This suggests we should attend to the Renaissance of secular vernacular letters in its context in the broader social and religious process of vernacularization.

The lay study, translation, and vernacular imitation of classical authors beyond Aristotle enabled many forms of vernacular writing that were self-consciously 'new'. We have seen that Amyot's translations of Plutarch and Heliodorus facilitated the development of the vernacular humanist essay and romance. Machiavelli translated Terence and wrote Terentian drama in Tuscan. Shakespeare's oeuvre is unthinkable without his uses of Ovid, Vergil, and Seneca, and his attempts to rival others' vernacular translations and imitations of the same poets in ways that show his work in both poetry and drama as new and authentic. Rabelais imported Lucian's satirical mode into the vernacular.

But some languages confined their efforts more to the production of vernacular translations, without producing much original Renaissance writing. This was the case with 'new' high German, which originated *c.*1400, but which did not produce a 'national' canon of imaginative writers in the Renaissance mode, in the manner of English. Dulcis was teaching in Germany but does not mention German texts. The German tradition is normally thought to have occupied itself almost exclusively with various forms of popular and religious literature (Luther). But the German language did participate in the vernacular Renaissance through translation of classical literature, and the German states, as we have seen, were important learners and consumers not only of Latin but of the Romance languages and literatures.

The same is true to a certain extent of west Slavic literary cultures such as the Polish and Czech, as well as of Hungarian literature, though these cultures relied more on the mediation of German and Latin than on the Romance vernaculars. Translation of neo-Latin literature into the vernaculars was an important Renaissance phenomenon in its own right: from the vulgarizations of John Barclay's highly popular neo-Latin novel (*Argenis*) to the translations of the Polish poet Sarbiewski's neo-Latin work, and the Latin versions of authors such as Guevara that gave rise to further vernacular translations in Eastern Europe.

This takes us to the varying relations between languages, and between Latin and the vernaculars, in different locations. We should not assume that the relationship between Latin and the vernacular in Florence and Tuscany was reproduced all over the Italian peninsula and Europe. Petrarchan orthodoxy about the supremacy of neo-Latin led Boccaccio to paint a picture of Dante's literary context that was exclusively bilingual, Latin and Italian. He left out the role of Provençal, despite the episode in the *Commedia* in which Arnaut Daniel speaks in that tongue. Later, the southern Italian states, including Naples, added Catalan and Spanish along with their Aragonese and Habsburg masters. French language and literature was more important in Ferrara and Venice than elsewhere in the peninsula. French intellectuals, meanwhile, would claim a closer relationship of their language with ancient Greek than with Latin. As we heard above, the example of Dulcis may suggest that in the later Renaissance European literature was more markedly multilingual, and increasingly distinct from monolingual forms of popular oral and literary culture.

This raises in turn the question of register. Between c.1350 and c.1600, most European cultures developed three literary and linguistic registers: learned and Latinate, learned or cosmopolitan vernacular, and popular vernacular. The relations and boundaries between these registers and literatures were being constantly negotiated, enforced, described, staged, whether in terms of social status, religion, gender, national/supra-national affiliation, or of the material forms of texts. We have already encountered many examples of this, such as the reform of the Accademia Fiorentina. If in many cases vernacular texts imitated the forms of learned Latin literature (Boccaccio's manuscripts), they were in others shaped by more popular forms, or both at once. Some of the greatest Renaissance writing derives from complex negotiations between low and high cultures and between popular and classical literary forms. We have already seen how true this is of Boccaccio's *Decameron*; it is true also of Rabelais's *Gargantua*, of Spenser's *Shepheardes Calendar*, and of the whole dramatic oeuvre of Shakespeare.

In many Reformation and post-Reformation contexts, such as the famous dispute between Sir Thomas More and William Tyndale, antagonism developed along confessional lines between the transnational Latin culture associated with Roman Catholicism and Christian humanism, and the vernacular cultures associated with new translations of the Bible such as Tyndale's. In Wake's case, Daniel's play is identified as appropriate not for the Latin-literate male scholars who accompany the king to the

Bodleian, but for an audience of educated court women, only one or two of whom have studied any Latin, and non-scholarly men. It is distinguished from the vulgar, mercenary works performed in the public playhouses.

Distinctions between learned and cosmopolitan, on the one hand, and popular forms of speech and writing, on the other, did not necessarily correspond to the Latin–vernacular dichotomy—as, arguably, they do not in Wake's case (he is bringing news of an elegant vernacular work to an international Latin-literate audience). By the later Renaissance, a pan-European elite educated by humanists such as Dulcis were fashioning cosmopolitan identities from civil conversation, travel, and reading, identities designed to secure them influential friends across borders and faiths. Crucial to these identities was mastery not only of Latin—and in some contexts, not principally of Latin—but of the cosmopolitan vernaculars. These comprised French, Italian, Spanish, and, in the case of the English elite, the elegant literary and court English of authors like Daniel, shaped in the environment of Latin and Romance languages and literatures.

This gave a new cultural dimension to existing social divides between the gentle and the vulgar. Whereas the literate elite could potentially participate in three overlapping literary cultures—learned Latinate, 'illustrated' vernacular, and popular oral cultures—the uneducated were alienated from two of the three, or from what they perceived as a single literate sphere. The cultural divide in question was policed from above. But it could also be policed in rebellious political terms, from below. Consider the case of a 'mercenary' play in which a cosmopolitan nobleman is captured by hostile parties—another episode similar to the one recounted by Montaigne at the beginning of this chapter.

When Jack Cade's illiterate rebels capture the highly educated Lord Saye in the second part of Shakespeare's *Henry VI*, they expose the hostility to which an elite, cosmopolitan identity based in the run of learned, cosmopolitan languages from Latin to courtly English could give rise—in a manner that has great resonance in our contemporary world. A populist, nationalist rebellion seeks to purge a liberally educated class convicted of selling out to foreign nations and cultures. The language or 'tongue' of the gentle, literate elite—whether they are speaking Latin or illustrated and eloquent versions of vernacular languages—is considered to be a sign of corruption. The ringleaders blame Saye for signing away the French lands won by true English warrior-noblemen, and for bringing in grammar schools, printed books, and the rule of Latin-literate state power.

In one scene, Cade brands Saye a traitor for speaking the tongue of the enemy: French. Saye then confronts his captors and speaks openly and confidently like Montaigne confronting his captors in the forest: 'Hear me but speak, and bear me where you will.' But he makes a terrible mistake in addressing the rebellious men of Kent who have captured him. Where Montaigne throws a Latin tag into his text in 'Of Physiognomy', Saye throws a Latin tag into his actual conversation. And it is one which brands Kent a good land full of bad people ('bona terra, mala gens').

In the first-quarto text of the scene, the rebels know only that this is a suspiciously foreign and continental tongue—maybe 'French', or 'Dutch', or 'Out-Italian', which is their garbled term for Italian. Saye compounds his error by citing and translating Caesar's Latin commentaries in an elevated English idiom. He also emphasizes how his multilingual tongue had 'parlayed unto foreign kings', which once again compounds his error by means of a Gallicism ('parley') that signifies how much political and cultural territory he has conceded to the French.

Unsurprisingly, in this context, no miraculous reversal of fortune is caused by Saye's cosmopolitan persona. The multilingual tongue in question, along with Saye's head, is immediately cut off by the rebels. As far as they are concerned, Saye is speaking a foreign language in every respect; whether that language is Latin, French, Italian, or a form of English that apes those prestigious languages, it is not their native language, and its speaker does not have their nation's interests at heart. Here we have a popular vernacular revolution against Latin-and-vernacular Renaissance cosmopolitanism, though Cade's claim to be speaking on behalf of an authentic Englishness localized in Kent is undermined by the play. A few scenes later, his head is in turn presented to the king by an honest esquire of Kent.

Vernacular medieval and Renaissance literature from the generation of Arnaut Daniel and Chrétien de Troyes to that of Shakespeare and Cervantes is characterized by an extraordinarily rich but conflicting range of creative and critical approaches to a broad social process of literate vernacularization. This process transcends the boundaries between literature and real life, and between authors and the other agents involved in literary and oral culture. It consists of two closely related acts: the sourcing of materials, whether 'classical' or 'medieval' and 'popular'; the social making from those materials of new fictions and discourses for uses and in places other than those of scholastic and professional study and practice. One could cite myriad examples, in relation to many different places and kinds of social actor, both from within texts (Lord Saye) and from without, in the history of their making (Montaigne's transformation of Amyot's Plutarch as the *Essais*). There were readers like the miller of Friuli, Menocchio, who accessed various diverse popular and elite sources, including a *novella* by Boccaccio he read in a borrowed copy of the (by then) prohibited *Decameron*, to build and communicate his own theology of the universe. We know about this because he fell foul of the Inquisition in his area.

We have seen that there was continuity and change between the beginning and the end of the period traditionally associated with the Renaissance. On the one hand, by the end of the period, more materials were undoubtedly available to more lay people, and to clerics and professionals in their lay or private identities, and they could make more oral and literary artefacts and do more things with them. On the other hand, there were more intensive attempts at both practical and intellectual regulation of the process whereby literary materials became new works, ideas, actions in the vernacular, everyday world. These attempts were made on the part of institutions from royal courts and established churches to literary academies and publishing houses; on the part of humanists and writers such as Le Roy and Wake; on the part of aristocratic patrons from the Duke of Urbino to King James I and VI of England and Scotland.

This is one of the themes of Cervantes's *Don Quijote*. Cervantes's most famous literary creation is an old knight dedicated to the reading and enacting of passé chivalric romances. A whole community of clerics and patrons seek to censor or control this self-evidently 'mad' dedication and either put him on a morally more balanced and productive course of study and action or turn him into safe entertainment for the aristocratic elite. The story of their failure results in a new work that both is and is not a revival of popular chivalric literature. There could be no better example of the social and literary process of reinvention that drove the vernacular Renaissance from the era of Boccaccio to the era of Cervantes.

Cervantes's work has in recent years been reinterpreted in relation to the interactions between Christian and Muslim peoples and traditions in the Iberian peninsula. In our globalized, connected world, shaken as it is by resurgent forms of populist nationalism and religion, there are important questions to be raised about the cultural and social geography of the vernacular literary Renaissance. In the period between the late eighteenth century and the First World War, literature was 'nationalized', and this nationalization was projected into the past.

Burckhardt insisted that the Renaissance derived primarily from the character—revealed most clearly in literary sources—of the Italian people, who were about to come together in a nation-state, and only secondarily from the humanists' rediscovery of classical antiquity. At the same time, other Western European nations and peoples projected distinct national stories back into the past, each discovering separate vernacular rebirths of their own. The emancipation of each national vernacular literature and its lay readership from medieval religion, and from the dominance of scholarly Latinity, increasingly provided the foundations of the Renaissance as the birth of a distinctively Western modernity in particular European nation-states. Cervantes played a key part in building such a story for the nation-state of Spain.

But those living in the shadow of the colonial powers were for various reasons not able to build similar histories. The newly founded modern nation-state of Greece did not, for example, recover its Cretan Renaissance vernacular heritage, perhaps because it was neither a political nor a literary player in nineteenth-century European cultural politics. Many Balkan and east and central European states formed national literatures in the nineteenth century, but did not lay claim to a distinctive body of Renaissance writing they could call their own, with the exception of Poland, and the partial exception of Ragusa, modern Dubrovnik, which produced Croatian writers such as Marin Držić, as well as many translations from Latin and Italian.

Where the image of a common European literature was constructed by the dominant Western European powers, it had to be in terms of a unity such as Latin Christianity or 'Western civilization' rather than as a changing field of literary alliances and emulations, conflicts and rivalries between cities, regions, and states. But should we continue to consider Renaissance literature as a uniquely authoritative and modern heritage, located in Western Europe and in its Latin-Romance and Germanic languages and literatures? Or should we begin to class it as a European variant of a more global and variable process of neo-classical vernacularization and anti-classical vernacular counter-revolution, in a number of cultures once dominated by cosmopolitan, transregional literary languages (Latin, Sanskrit, classical Chinese), across the Eurasian world?

Was it even, just from an intra-European perspective, an intrinsically national and international matter? Tuscan was the shared literary language of many city-states in the Italian peninsula by the sixteenth century, and was the language of the Italian 'nation' understood as a group of people from the Italian city-states coming together for study or worship in a foreign country, but it was not the language of a nation-state until the later nineteenth century. French was from the late medieval period a literary language used in many regions outside the territories now contained within the nation-state of France, as we saw in the case of Pieter van Veen. And what do we do with Occitan, an early example of a successful and transregional literary language that survives today, but corresponds to no nation or nation-state?

In the decades to come, scholars will have to undo the work done by the literary nation-builders of the nineteenth century. We need a connected history of medieval and Renaissance north-western Eurasian literature, conceived as a common body of vernacular and neo-Latin, literary and learned writings composed and circulated in many languages across a polycentric area stretching from Danish Iceland to Hungarian Transylvania, from Portugal to Poland-Lithuania.

CHAPTER 9

Craft and Technology in Renaissance Europe

PAMELA O. LONG AND ANDREW MORRALL

THE profound changes that took place in the two centuries between 1400 and 1600 both included and, in part, were caused by technological and craft developments. This is not to say that technology determined historical changes or that social or economic changes determined technology. Technological determinism, popular as it sometimes is among the general public, has long been rejected by historians of technology as a fiction or oversimplification. Instead, in this transitional age, innovations often appeared within the context of established crafts and technologies, and developed alongside them. Or they came out of them in complex ways. To give just one example, the printing press emerged from a variety of traditional skills and products such as papermaking, the manufacture of inks, goldsmithing, and minting. Printing initially developed alongside manuscript book production.

Whether traditional or innovative, crafts and technological production were carried out by individuals and groups of people in particular locales and following their own specific traditions. Craft refers to the skilled making of things within specific domains, such as pottery, leatherworking, or goldsmithing. Technology suggests larger systems of material production such as mining and metallurgy, artillery and fortification, navigation, building construction, or the technologies of agriculture or household production. Neither crafts nor technologies can be separated from artisans and other workers who worked with their hands or manipulated tools and machines, or participated in larger systems of production. Nor can such activities and practices be separated from economic, social, political, and cultural developments.

Craft production from ancient times was called by the Latin word *ars*, which could refer to anything from harness making to fine embroidery, to goldsmithing, or to the many processes required for making leather gloves or shoes. The Greek word *techne* referred to a similar range of productive practices. The term 'mechanical arts' was coined in the ninth century, and acquired further substance and meaning in subsequent centuries. Mechanical arts were contrasted with the higher-status liberal arts—rhetoric, grammar, dialectic, geometry, arithmetic, music, and astronomy—that were taught in the universities and other institutions of higher learning such as cathedral schools, or the new colleges that developed from the sixteenth century.

Guilds and apprenticeship

The worlds of artisan craft production and the worlds of learning in the medieval period were usually quite separate, both physically and socially. Craft production was carried out in workshops and transmitted by apprenticeship through one or other of the vernacular languages and by hands-on practice. Learned culture, transmitted in universities and in other teaching establishments, was based on traditional texts, as well as discourse and commentaries upon those texts. The language of learning was almost exclusively Latin. It was characteristic of the transitional age between 1400 and 1600 that the status of 'the mechanical arts' rose and that the two realms moved closer together, and at times became interchangeable.

Training in a craft almost always involved an apprenticeship, either formal or informal, in which a skilled person or master taught an apprentice in a workshop and provided him or her with hands-on experience, while demanding gradually more complex tasks. Formal apprenticeships were usually arranged by contract between a master and a young person's parents, often when he or she was 12 or 13 years old. Informal apprenticeships also occurred frequently—for example, mothers often taught their daughters how to spin wool. Indeed, craft skill often was transmitted through families, in which case formal contracts were unnecessary.

Many crafts were organized into guilds, which varied in their powers and functions from one locality to another, and from craft to craft. The craft guild often regulated training and the system of apprenticeship. It also usually maintained a monopoly in its locale for making its own products, and it maintained quality control. Finally, the guild, or a confraternity associated with the guild, provided a safety net, for example providing for the burial of deceased members and assisting widows. After some years, usually four to seven depending on the craft, the apprentice became a journeyman. In many crafts it was usual for the journeyman to travel, sometimes called tramping, in search of work elsewhere, for one or more years. Countering the traditional view that the structure of the guilds and their practices operated against innovation, recent scholarship suggests that travelling journeymen transmitted their own knowledge and skills to other localities, and learned new skills and techniques as well—exchanges that led to innovations. They were significant conveyers in the circulation of technical and craft knowledge, particularly in the sixteenth century. To become a master, the journeyman needed to acquire a workshop; consequently, and increasingly in the late Renaissance, many journeymen never became masters.

Women as well as men were extensively involved in craftwork and were members of guilds, often as wives and daughters of masters, or as widows carrying on the crafts of their deceased husbands, and, in addition, as masters and guild members in their own right. However, the situation of craftswomen worsened in the sixteenth century. Journeymen, realizing that they would never become masters, began to organize themselves into their own guilds and, in so doing, they excluded women and actively worked to prevent them from working in the crafts. Their views, gradually accepted by urban councils and other legal bodies, made it increasingly difficult for women to practise their crafts.

Artisans outside the guilds

New arenas for craftwork also developed. Perhaps the most important of these comprised the patronage of wealthy individuals and the opportunities provided by the aristocratic courts. In numerous areas of Europe, popes, princes, and wealthy aristocrats attracted numerous artisans and other craftworkers to their cities and households as they also welcomed humanists and other learned men, thereby creating important nodes of interchange between learned and artisanal culture.

In these transitional centuries between 1400 and 1600, the artisanal world became far more fluid than it had been. Whereas in the earlier centuries male children usually took up the craft of their fathers, increasingly they could choose alternative paths. New or newly conceived crafts and practices developed that did not fall under traditional guild control—engineering, architecture, printing, engraving, and gunpowder artillery, among others. Certain crafts, while developing new techniques, such as linear perspective, and new stylistic criteria, such as the classical, enjoyed rising status. From the early fifteenth century, both practitioners and learned men wrote tracts and treatises focused on particular arts and crafts—from painting to glassmaking, to mining and fortification. Such writings enhanced the status of the crafts.

Artisans and the culture of learning

Artisanal and learned cultures began to draw closer together. An early thesis concerning artisanal influence is referred to as the 'Zilsel thesis', after Edgar Zilsel (1891–1944), who argued that craftsmen influenced the new development of the 'Scientific Revolution' in the seventeenth century. Zilsel, an Austrian Marxist and a positivist, suggested that characteristics of artisanal work—such as the value of hands-on experience, empirical approaches, including measurement, the value of individual making, and observation—influenced the development of empirical and experimental methodologies of the late sixteenth and seventeenth centuries. More recently, the influence of artisanal culture on learned culture and vice versa has been investigated in various ways. Some have suggested the growing importance in the sixteenth century of 'trading zones', that is, arenas in which there has been substantive communication between artisanal practitioners of various kinds and university-educated men. Others, from another angle, have explored the development of 'artisanal epistemologies' —the ways in which apprenticeship-trained artisans understood and even theorized the natural world, and the profound influence that they exerted on the larger culture.

Agriculture and food production

Although most histories of Renaissance crafts and technologies focus on urban centres and the artisanal production of goods, the underlying importance of techniques of agriculture provided essential support for both rural and urban populations and must not be overlooked. Scholars have shown, in fascinating detail, the ways in which agricultural practices changed and developed during the centuries of the Renaissance, as a result both of experimentation and the study of ancient agricultural practices and texts. Developments often involved gradual changes, some of which became highly significant. One example entails crop rotation—a standard technique for avoiding soil depletion. As is well known, many areas of medieval Europe increased crop production by changing from a two-field to a three-field rotation system. In this system, in a single year, one-third of the land lay fallow, one-third was planted in spring crops, and a third in autumnal crops. Yet rotation practices differed widely from one region to the next, and increasingly intricate systems were developed through the fifteenth century. In Italy complicated rotation systems, including the rotation of flax and beans, grain and hemp, and grain and millet, were developed, sometimes in association with irrigation.

Another change in the direction of commercial agriculture is known as the 'enclosure movement', and was important both in England and on the Continent. In England, for example, landlords, responding to high prices, first of wool and then of grain, fenced off land previously used in common by villagers, and they used this newly enclosed land to graze sheep, or to cultivate grain. Enclosure was a highly disruptive process that ended the traditional practices of village cooperative strip farming and the common land use among peasants that accompanied strip farming.

In England, another significant change entailed a shift to convertible husbandry in which the traditional distinction between permanent arable (i.e. cultivated) and permanent pasture was abolished. Instead, farmers alternated the same land between both functions, increasing the productivity of both crops and livestock. An added advantage of the new system was that the need for fallow fields ended. Another innovation was the practice of marling, that is, fertilizing the fields with marl, a mixture that included clays and shells—helpful in lime-deficient soils.

Irrigation became ever more significant in agricultural production. A sixteenth-century innovation in England entailed 'floating meadows', a new system of irrigation in which entire fields were covered with water for certain parts of the year. Flooding provided silt, protected against frost, and also allowed adequate water in the summer, increasing productivity. In other areas, entirely new systems of agricultural production came out of new irrigation practices. For example, in Italy's Po Valley, the development of irrigation systems permitted a large increase in the production of hay and fodder, which allowed the development of cattle breeding. In irrigated areas, grain and hay, and then clover and alfalfa (sometimes called lucerne), replaced the traditional grain and vine crops, as farmers gradually replaced sheep with cattle, and used them as beasts of burden and for milk and meat.

Textiles

The fifteenth and sixteenth centuries saw an expanded demand for textiles of all kinds—for furnishings and tapestries as well as for dress. In addition, textiles became increasingly important in signalling differences in social status. The two most important fabrics used for clothing in fifteenth- and sixteenth-century Europe consisted of wool, derived from sheep, and linen, derived from the flax plant. Silk, a cloth manufactured from the durable thread produced by domesticated silkworms, became Europe's most important luxury cloth. Cottons, imported from India, would come to be of major importance only in the seventeenth century and after.

Wool production

Wool production in the medieval period and into the fifteenth century entailed the manufacture of three main kinds of wool cloth. The first, called "woollens" in England and "greased" wools on the Continent, consisted of a heavy, dense, and highly valued cloth that was a commodity in long-distance trade. These fine woollens were made from short-stapled wools (a staple being a cluster of wool fibres). The wool was cleaned and carded (rather than combed), and then woven on a horizontal loom. The woven cloth was subjected to extensive finishing, including fulling (hammering or stamping in water, urine, and other substances to strengthen the fabric), drying on a tentering frame, stretching, napping (raising the fibres with teasels), and shearing (cutting away excess fibres).

A second type of cloth, called "worsted" wool in England and dry or light draperies on the Continent, consisted of cheap fabrics for local use. They were made from long-fibred, coarse, and straight wools that were combed rather than carded, and were ready for use after they had been woven and without elaborate finishing. A third type of wool cloth, sometimes called serge, was made with a combination of long-stapled and short-stapled (and greased) wool.

Wool-making in this period cannot be discussed coherently without reference to the whole series of technological innovations that were made in the previous medieval centuries and came to full fruition in the fifteenth century. Most important was the horizontal treadle loom, both the narrow version and, later, the broad loom that was able to produce wider cloths. Carding was introduced as a substitution for the traditional comb—using the newly invented card, a leather-covered board with hundreds of short wire hooks. The spinning wheel and its radically improved version, the Saxon wheel, greatly increased the speed and productivity of spinning wool into yarn. The fulling mill, which slowly replaced foot fulling, was powered by a waterwheel which drove hammers that were released by rotating cams. In the fifteenth century the water-powered gig mill was invented. It contained a rapidly rotating metal cylinder into which had been inserted teasels that raised the nap of the cloth as it moved along a revolving belt. All of these innovations were introduced slowly and at different rates in different geographic areas. All were met with some protest and occasionally with laws

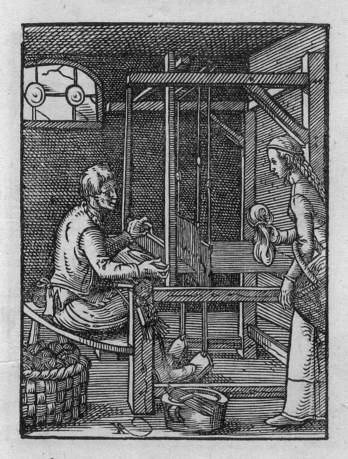

Der Weber.

Ich bin ein Weber zu Leinen Wat/
Kan wircken Barchent vnd Sponat/
Tischthücher/Handzwehl/Facilet/
Vnd wer luſt zu Bettziechen hett/
Gewürffelt oder Kamaca/
Allerley gmödelt Thücher da/
Auch Flechſen vnd wircken Haußthuch/
Die Kunſt ich bey Aragnes ſuch.

Der

'THE WEAVER'. The horizontal treadle loom from Jost Amman and Hans Sachs, *The Book of Trades* (*Ständebuch*), originally published as *Eygentliche Beschreibung aller Stände* ('Exact Description of All Ranks on Earth') (Frankfurt am Main: Sigmund Feyerabend, 1568).

against their use, the main reason being the fear (sometimes realistic) that they would degrade the quality of fine woollens.

During the fifteenth century, *nouvelles draperies*, cheaper imitations of luxury woollens, and manufactured first in small towns and villages of Flanders, found increasingly large markets, particularly in Italy and the Mediterranean basin. Later, northern Italian towns also established thriving wool industries based on these new draperies. In the sixteenth century, the best English and continental woollens were gradually replaced by the superior product derived from Spanish Merino sheep. These sheep, which grew uniformly short-stapled wool, may have developed from a mixing of traditional Spanish and North African breeds.

Highly successful wool-making centres shifted from one region to another depending on a complicated mix of political, economic, and technological circumstances. During the sixteenth century the Habsburg-Valois Wars and an expanding English market decimated Italian production, with the exception of Venice, which then only gradually recovered from mid-century onward. In Spain, the production of heavy, felted woollens flourished, especially in Segovia and especially for home markets, but also as exports to the New World. The sixteenth century saw a huge resurgence in popularity of serges or (as they were also called) 'says'—the cloth made by combining long- and short-stapled wool. They were now woven on upright, rather than horizontal, looms. Along with serges came the creation of new light fabrics made by mixing wool with other textile yarns—cotton, linen, and silk.

Linen and hemp production

The production of linen and hemp cloth and other materials such as rope may have been as extensive as the production of wool cloth, but it is much less well documented. Such items were made from plant fibres—either flax or hemp. The resulting cloth was used in all kinds of items—underwear, shirts, breeches, gowns, collars and cuffs, layettes for babies, sailcloth, canvas (undyed linen in plain weave), sacking, and sails. The plants were harvested by pulling the entire stalk from the ground. Then they were dried and subjected to extensive processes to remove the fibres and render them suitable for spinning. After weaving on a loom, the resulting cloth was often bleached, either by the cloth-makers or by specialists.

Silk production

Silk, the luxury cloth of Europe, represented wealth, status, and power. Although silks in Europe originally came from the Byzantine and Islamic silk industries, several cities of Italy—Genoa, Venice, Bologna, and Lucca—had developed their own industries by the thirteenth century. In the sixteenth century, Italy and Spain were the main producers of silk cloth for Europe. It was used in various kinds of luxurious clothing, including ecclesiastical vestments, and for elaborate embroideries, made with silk floss often combined with metal elements, and tapestries. Silk production entailed intricate specialized processes, including the exacting and fraught task of raising silkworms and the mulberry trees that provided their sustenance in the form of mulberry leaves. Yarn production required vat tenders who boiled the cocoons and reelers who unwound the silk threads. Warp (foundation) threads had to be twisted further. The silk was dyed and then woven. Innovations in equipment for diverse stages of silk production in the fifteenth and sixteenth centuries were notable.

Other kinds of textile production

In the fifteenth century the craft of knitting arose, beginning with the popularity of knitted caps. In the sixteenth, a great expansion of knitted hosiery production was given a huge boost by the invention of the stocking frame in the 1580s. Lace-making developed at around the same time. Carpet-making initially brought from Islamic lands through Spain, became an expanding industry in the sixteenth century.

Tapestry

In a culture where wealth often depended upon the textile trade, tapestry was the most prestigious elite decorative medium throughout the period. The principal centres of manufacture were located at Paris, Tournai, Arras, and, from the later fifteenth century onwards, Brussels. Monumental in scale, the most splendid examples were fashioned in silk and gold and silver thread; indeed, their representational value lay as much in their material opulence as in their imagery. Fundamentally public in character, tapestry was used as a backdrop to most occasions at court. Accounts of royal entries record how the routes through which monarchs and dignitaries progressed were regularly lined with tapestries hung from the façades of urban homes; and the spectacles of state—whether dynastic ritual or wedding banquet—were invariably enacted before the most lavish examples.

Material opulence was accompanied by appropriate historical or mythological themes, chosen to embody the ideals of the owner or as appropriate to the occasion of state. A tapestry series displaying the Twelve Labours of Hercules (of which six survive in the Royal Palace in Madrid), for instance, acted as a pointed backdrop to the Feast of the Pheasant, organized in 1454 by Philip the Good, the Duke of Burgundy, at which the noble guests swore an oath committing each to participation in a crusade to the Holy Land, as well as to the promise of individual heroic deeds in proof of their valour.

By the later fifteenth century, the Brussels tapestry factories had emerged as one of the most prominent groups of high- and low-warp tapestry looms in Europe. Their high technical quality led Pope Leo X to commission Pieter van Aelst (*c.*1495–*c.*1560) to weave the Acts of the Apostles after Raphael's cartoons (1516–19) as a set of hangings for the Sistine Chapel. The success of this commission established Brussels as the leading tapestry centre in Europe, a success compounded by the designs of outstanding painter-practitioners such as Bernard van Orley (*c.*1488–1541) and his pupil Pieter Coecke van Aelst (1502–50), who developed a monumental style that combined a traditionally Flemish realism of detail with an Italianate sense of classicizing form in tapestry sets that were exported to all the major courts of Europe.

Embroidery

Throughout the high and later Middle Ages, elaborate embroidered or embroidered appliqué panels had been used to adorn both secular and religious textiles, from wall hangings to devotional and processional banners, copes, dalmatics, and altar frontals. Manufacture of such objects varied from city to city according to local regulations, or to whether textile work was dominated by (male) guilds or companies, such as the Broderers' Company in London, or other kinds of craft community, such as convents. In the course of the sixteenth century, embroidery became an increasingly prevalent

ENGLISH, ANON, *The Garden of Eden*, embroidered panel, velvet worked with silk and metal thread, last quarter of the sixteenth century.

feature of domestic life. Markers of growing prosperity, taste, and social prestige among the landed and professional classes, embroideries were applied to a whole range of household furnishings that included valances, cushion covers, table carpets, the surfaces of caskets, book covers, and items of clothing, so as literally to underpin social life, bringing adornment to clothing and comfort into the home.

At the same time, it spoke to more than material comforts. In Protestant communities in particular—and this was especially true of England—the medium was imbued with the religious and ethical values, centred around notions of the well-ordered household. Many of the embroideries of this period were made by non-professional female householders and their daughters, for whom embroidering formed a principal part of their education. An active sign of female virtue, it kept women in the home, away from idle pursuits and focused on pious devotions. Embroidered images of biblical heroes and heroines—of Susanna, of David and Abigail, Esther and Ahasuerus, and so forth—served as models in the education of young girls of the professional and propertied classes, the moral example literally inured into their being through the act of making. Once completed and put to use, they became part of the habitus of the household in which embroidery and religious devotion were integral and related parts of a daily routine.

Mining and metallurgy

By the mid-fifteenth century, with a rising population and a growing need for metals, especially for coins and guns, the available supply of metals failed to meet demand. This scarcity led to a European mine boom between about 1460 and 1550, during which the production of copper, silver, and other metals increased as much as fivefold. Greater productivity was a result of the high prices of scarce metals, which in turn motivated the excavation of deep mines. Such costly enterprises required capital investments, and were carried out by wage labour. They also required new, large-scale equipment for deep excavation, water removal (the perennial problem of deep mines), and extensive ore and metallurgical processing.

Ironmaking

Technical developments in metallurgy occurred relative to specific metals. In the medieval centuries, iron was worked with a hammer and forge, and blacksmiths created a myriad of iron objects from pots and pans to horseshoes. In this process, they roasted iron ore with green timber and quenched it with water. They mixed the ore with charcoal in a furnace, covered it with fuel, and flamed the fire with bellows directed at the centre of the hearth. The blacksmith worked the remaining product, called bloom, by hammering, reheating, and rehammering to remove the slag. In the fifteenth century, some furnace bellows were powered by waterwheels, allowing the size of the bloom to increase to over 100 kilograms. Wrought-iron products continued to be made through the Renaissance and well beyond, indeed to this day.

In the early fifteenth century, the blast furnace developed from the wrought-iron furnace—but with the height raised and the bellows improved. The new furnaces were able to reach higher temperatures so that the iron liquefied and could then flow out to be cast as molten pigs. Blast furnaces required large capital outlays and had to be operated continuously for effective productivity. Cast iron was used for, among other things, cannonballs, pots and pans, and, after the mid-fifteenth century, cannon, although wrought-iron cannon dominated until a century later.

Silver, copper, and other metals

Capitalist transformations of mining with regard to copper, silver, and lead were most pronounced in several regions of central Germany—the Harz Mountains near Goslar, the Erzgebirge Mountains in Saxony and Bohemia, and the Tyrolean Alps to the south. Gold was discovered in Hungary and a variety of other locations. Gold and silver were used in numerous luxury artisanal craft products, while silver was a major component of many coins that were produced in mints. Around 1460 a new way of processing silver-bearing copper ores was discovered (the *Seigerhüttenprozess*), wherein the separation of silver from copper was made with the help of lead.

Large-scale ore-processing and smelting plants were constructed in central Germany, plants that included many hearths, furnaces, bellows, hammers, stamping machinery driven by waterwheels, crucibles, and many other kinds of tools along with hundreds of workers. At the same time, more powerful drainage pumps and other drainage engines, often powered by great waterwheels or by animals, were developed along with more skilfully constructed drainage trenches or adits, and better methods of ventilation.

Such large-scale operations required capital, and rulers and other mine owners were successful in attracting capital from shareholders. A large group of people developed who were not actually miners or ore processors, but who had a great interest in these operations because of their investments. This is the basis of the flourishing literature on mining and metallurgy that appeared in the sixteenth century. These books, in Italian, German, and Latin, included the famous Latin treatise *De re metallica* by Georg Agricola, the woodcut illustrations of which displayed technical processes in meticulous and intriguing detail.

Metalwork

Much of the wealth that accrued from the central European silver and copper mines in the sixteenth century came to be controlled by merchants such as the Augsburg banking firm of the Fugger, who secured extensive monopolies on the mines from emperors and princes such as Sigismund of Tyrol, Maximilian I, and Charles V, in return for extensive credit loans. In this way, the merchants came to control a very large stake in the trade in metals and other raw materials. It was access to this that gave particular stimulus to local Augsburg and Nuremberg artisans in high-end areas of production and allowed these cities to become centres of luxury goldsmithing,

Etfi uerò in reliquis tribus uenarum excoquendarum rationibus quædã
eft fimilitudo, quod ora fornacum femper pateant, ut metalla liquefacta cõ-
tinenter effluere poffint, tamen multum inter fe differunt: nam os primæ al-
D   tius in

'SMELTING FURNACES'; from Georg Agricola, *De Re Metallica* (1556). An illustration showing
the complex process of smelting silver ores to extract the silver, which is also explained in the
Latin text.

gradually overtaking in importance other traditional centres such as Paris or Cologne. By the second half of the sixteenth century, a new class of professional dealer had emerged, largely from the ranks of the goldsmiths themselves, who both supplied the raw materials, precious metals, and stones to goldsmiths and arranged large-scale commissions. The result, by the end of the period, was a highly organized, specialized workforce that could complete large-scale orders speedily and to a high standard.

Goldsmiths traditionally enjoyed a higher status and income relative to other artisans, in part by virtue of the high financial value of their medium, in part because of a theoretical propensity peculiar to their craft, which, involving expertise in ornamentation and mathematical proportion, was closely allied to architecture. Filippo Brunelleschi and, later, Albrecht Dürer are but two of the numerous Renaissance artist-theoreticians to have received their initial training as goldsmiths. While the Nuremberg goldsmith Wenzel Jamnitzer (1507/8–85), discussed below, was famously versed in mathematics and geometry, the Spanish goldsmith Juan de Arfe y Villafañe (1535–1603), whose monumental *custodia* (monstrance), made for Seville Cathedral between 1580 and 1587, is an architectonic exercise in Vitruvian classicism, left a series of treatises on geometry and gnomonics (the art of making sundials), the proportions of architecture, and on human anatomy.

Throughout the late Middle Ages and the early modern period, the collection and display of precious metalwork and its use at ceremonial banquets were among the traditional ways by which the elite classes maintained and demonstrated their wealth. Before any established systems of credit, such plate constituted a family's or individual's readily realizable financial assets, to be melted down as need arose. Opulent display at banquets and grand ceremonial occasions was an index of status, grounded in a theory of 'magnificence' drawn ultimately from Aristotle, by which it was incumbent upon the ruler, lord, civic institution, or wealthy householder—at whatever level of society—to express the authority of his position through large-scale expenditure. The continuation of this late medieval tradition of sumptuous dining into the Renaissance period is exemplified by the famous *Salt Cellar* by Benvenuto Cellini, now in the Kunsthistorisches Museum in Vienna, one of the supreme examples of sixteenth-century goldsmith's work. Designed as a container for salt and pepper and executed in gold and enamel, the *Salt Cellar* is conceived as an elaborate allegory of the riches of the earth and sea. Neptune, god of the sea, presides over a ship containing salt, while Ceres, goddess of the earth, gathers up the bounties of the earth with her right hand. Beside her a triumphal arch contains the pepper. Their sensuously entwined legs suggest their mutual interdependence, a cosmic principle, reinforced by the Michelangelesque figures of the Times of the Day and the Four Winds arranged around the base. Destined originally for the table of King Francis I of France, it subsequently served as a wedding gift from King Charles IX to Archduke Ferdinand of Tyrol, finding its way into the latter's *Kunstkammer*.

In Germany, the *Pokal*, or ceremonial drinking cup, became a pre-eminent art form. As the apprentice goldsmith's 'masterpiece'—the test piece via which he became a fully fledged master—it was an especial site of technical skill and ornamental inventiveness. Its social function as a ceremonial drinking cup, moreover, reflects the centrality of drinking during this period in habits of social discourse, when the communal or shared drink played a part in nearly every public and private ceremony. Such cups also served as corporate gifts—to guilds, confraternities, or city councils. (In England the large ewer and basin tended to have this role.) They owe their high survival rate to their representative and commemorative functions. Whereas other kinds of metalwork, candelabra, salts, plates, spoons, all fell victim to subsequent melting down for reasons of financial need or fashion, the *Pokal*, in its capacity as a prestige public gift or as a privately commissioned family or civic memorial, was displayed as much as used, and valued down through the ages.

At the highest levels of creation, the drinking cup and its variants became vehicles for the expression of virtuoso workmanship, aesthetic sophistication, and intellectual ambition. The conceptual and technical virtuosity of the Cellini *Salt Cellar* was echoed in the manifold creations of the Nuremberg goldsmith Wenzel Jamnitzer. Jamnitzer served as court goldsmith to four successive Holy Roman Emperors and other noble patrons and was famous in equal measure for his studies in perspective and geometry as for his supremely skilled goldsmith work. His so-called *Merckel Tablepiece* of 1549, probably made as a gift for the emperor, was conceived as a receptacle for fruit. Its stem is in the form of a Venus-like figure, who stands upon a mound of natural grasses and flowers and small animals, all cast meticulously from life, a technique that Jamnitzer pioneered and for which he was famous in his own day. The Venus figure supports a basket-like basin, surmounted by an elaborately enamelled vase, containing a bouquet of equally naturalistic, cast flowers. A Latin poem, running from the base to the rim of the basin, has her proclaim: 'Sum terra, mater omnium' ('I am earth, mother of all things'). This generative principle is evoked not only in the expressive fecundity of the figure herself, but also in the implied transformation of the natural from a primal, untamed state at her feet, rising through her, to the ripe pendant fruits held in the basin: raw nature, tamed, as the accompanying poem makes clear, by agriculture.

Ceramics and glass

The fifteenth and sixteenth centuries witnessed an unprecedented development in ceramics and glasswares both in variety and scale of production. The chief innovations were in the manufacture of tin-glaze earthenwares, known in Italy as *maiolica*, and elsewhere in Europe as *faience* or *delftware*; of stonewares, chiefly in the German-speaking territories; and of *cristallo* glass, initially in Venice, spreading to other parts of Europe in the later sixteenth and seventeenth centuries. Each medium owed its economic success and concomitant rise in social capital to increasingly refined ideas of decorum among the educated elite classes, especially in regard to habits of dining. Indeed these wares, imbued with the aesthetics and values of humanism, were themselves central in shaping new norms of taste and behaviour.

The technique of tin glaze in Western Europe originated in the Islamic world, where, sometime in the eighth century, potters in present-day Iraq and Syria discovered that by adding tin oxide to a transparent glaze they could create an opaque, white, and even surface. This provided a stable ground for colourfully painted ornamentation, achieved with a range of metal oxide pigments such as manganese purple or copper green. A further category of lustre wares was produced by the addition of silver or copper oxides to the already glazed surface of a pot, which was then refired at a lower temperature (about 800° C) in a kiln from which the oxygen was removed. The result was an iridescent metallic surface. Tin-glazing techniques had reached Muslim Spain by 1000 CE, lustre-making by the thirteenth century, notably in Málaga, the main port of the Nasrid dynasty, centred in Granada. The brilliant 'golden wares' of Málaga were exported in considerable numbers throughout the Mediterranean and northern Europe. In the fourteenth century, the centre of gravity of the ceramic industry moved northwards to areas outside the Islamic sphere, especially to Manises in Christian Valencia, where an extensive export market to Italy and the north developed. The Italian term *maiolica* owes its origins either as a corruption of *obra de malica* (Málaga ware), the Spanish term for these wares, or 'Majorca', the Spanish island which served as an entrepôt for ships carrying lustre wares from Valencia to Italy.

In the course of the fourteenth and fifteenth centuries the tin-glaze technique gradually spread throughout Italy. By about 1450, potters in Tuscany, Umbria, and the Romagna had developed a wide colour palette for the decoration of their pots, that included, in addition to manganese purple and copper green, a cobalt blue, an antimony yellow, and a range of ferrous oranges. By 1460, the Umbrian centres of Gubbio and Deruta had also mastered ruby- and silver-lustred techniques respectively. The early Italian products were influenced by the ornamental vocabulary and forms of imported Iberian and Middle Eastern wares, as characterized, for instance, by the fifteenth-century waisted storage jars, or *albarelli*, spouted jars and long-necked bottles produced in Florence for pharmacies and hospitals. Their decoration in rough cobalt blue brushstrokes against the white ground emulated Islamic vine and leaf patterns. Gradually, however, polychromed wares became the norm, and the decorative vocabulary and the shapes of maiolica wares expanded to include the classical motifs of the Renaissance style. Characteristic types from Deruta included large chargers (*piatti di pompa*), decorated with bands of fashionable *all'antica* grotesque and arabesque designs, often surrounding a central family armorial; or platters with the profile heads of idealized female beauties with amatory inscriptions. The Della Robbia family workshop in Florence produced a range of glazed terracotta figural pieces and reliefs of religious subjects, notably of the Madonna and Child, as substitutes for polychromed stone or wood sculpture.

By the sixteenth century, commercial competition of local pottery-producing towns had effectively finished off the Spanish trade. The quintessential 'Renaissance' maiolica type that developed from the 1520s onwards, associated with the pottery-producing towns of Umbria, the Marches, and the Romagna, Casteldurante, Urbino, and Faenza, was so-called *istoriato* (history-painted) ware: plates and dishes, vases, whole dining sets completely covered with highly coloured narrative scenes, drawn from classical history or myth and aimed at an educated and discriminating audience. Their appeal lay in bringing together a new technical finesse with subjects drawn from classical antiquity, executed in the classicizing style of contemporary painting. Often dependent for their designs upon contemporary prints that were liberally plundered for figurative poses and classical motifs, such works acted as fitting props to humanist interest and discourse. The more prominent maiolica painters, such as Francesco Durantino (*fl.* 1543–54) or Francesco Xanto Avelli (*c.*1487–1582) of Urbino, often signed their works. Xanto Avelli's works often included inscriptions, sometimes his own poems, on the back.

Though these wares were never more than a small fraction of the total output of ceramic production, their much greater relative survival speaks to their cultural and aesthetic importance within elite Renaissance society. The humanist interest they inspired is attested by surviving encomia by discerning patrons, like Lorenzo de' Medici, who praised their artistry over their material worth. In November 1524 Elea-nora Gonzaga, Duchess of Urbino, ordered a set of *istoriato* plates from Nicola da Urbino, one of the most gifted of the contemporary maiolica painters, as a gift for her mother, Isabella d'Este, which she described expressly as suitable for use in her villa ('*per essere cosa da villa*'). The twenty-two surviving pieces mostly illustrate scenes from the *Metamorphoses* of Ovid, set in landscapes bathed in sunset. The air of nostalgic pastoral that suffuses Nicola's compositions together with the classical references clearly lent themselves to the sophisticated informality of villa life of the d'Este court.

At and below these elite social levels, the types of ceramic forms produced became ever more varied and specialized, ranging from luxury sets of stacked bowls and dishes intended for women in their lying-in period following a birth, to increasingly elaborate dining sets. The marked success of the maiolica trade has been characterized as a symptom of an emerging 'consumerist society', in which an interplay of technological possibilities and social practices led to increased production and the elaboration of new types of wares, stimulated by the desire of a cultural and social elite to differentiate themselves from their social inferiors. It also had the effect of sharpening and refining aesthetic sensitivity among users.

Evidence for the techniques of manufacture is provided by an illustrated treatise written in *c.*1557 by Cipriano Piccolpasso, *Tre libri dell arte del vasaio* (*The Three Books of the Potter's Art*), commissioned by the French Cardinal de Tournon as a practical design source for French potters. Piccolpasso claimed his intention was 'to show forth all the secrets of the potter' so that the art of maiolica 'will pass to courts among elevated spirits and speculative minds', thus claiming for the medium a dignity and status normally accorded to painting and sculpture.

Though Piccolpasso's manuscript appears not to have left Italy, maiolica took root in France. In 1535, Anne de Montmorency, the Constable of France, had received an *istoriato* service made in the workshop of Guido Durantino in Urbino, perhaps as a

NICOLA DA URBINO, Armorial Plate (*tondino*), with The Story of King Midas, tin-glaze ceramic (maiolica), Urbino, *c*.1520–5.

diplomatic gift. Montmorency was later to patronize the native maiolica production of the potter Masseot Abaquesne of Rouen, as well as two other highly original forms of French Renaissance pottery, that known as Saint-Porchaire and the work of Bernard Palissy.

The beautiful and fragile productions of 'Saint-Porchaire' pottery reflect the qualities of French courtly design. Little is known of this manufactory, not even its precise location. Archeological and textual references link this class of ceramics to the area of Poitou, as well as Paris. Active before 1542 (when its products were mentioned in an inventory), the workshop's output appears to have been small and made for an elite clientele, including King Henri II and his queen, Catherine de' Medici, and Anne de Montmorency. The works themselves are invariably small-scale, fragile showpieces, of

CANDLESTICK, *c.* 1547/1559, lead-glazed fine earthenware, 29.5 cm × 16.6 cm. probably
Saint-Porchaire (Deux-Sevres), or Paris region.

little practical utility; the body is made from a white clay, applied with complex surface
decoration derived from a variety of influences, including Paduan metalwork and the
foliated arabesques and intricate knotwork of Hispano-Moresque metalwork, probably
transmitted via prints, book bindings, and textiles. The knotwork decoration also
exemplifies one of the technical marvels of this class of ceramics: uniquely, it has
been achieved by stamping the pattern into thin, still-damp strips of white clay using
an embossing iron—akin to those used in contemporary leather book bindings—and
filling the cavities thus created with a brown or reddish clay slip or paste. These strips

would then be applied to the underlying white clay form, and glazed with an overall clear lead glaze before firing.

The greatest French potter of the period was Bernard Palissy (c.1510–c.1590), whose work stands out in its technical originality and in its opposition to the sophistications of the Fontainebleau style. A lifelong autodidact and experimentalist, with a profound interest in natural philosophy, he developed highly idiosyncratic theories about the origins of rocks and of the generation of matter, based on his own empirical studies of nature, which he wrote up in one of two published treatises, the *Discours admirable de la nature des eaux et fontaines*, of c.1576. As a ceramicist, he is significant as the inventor of a class of lead-glazed earthenwares which he termed *rustiques figulines*, a series of dishes and platters which recreated pond environments, using casts of actual plants and animals—particularly frogs, snakes, and lizards, comparable with the silver casts of Wenzel Jamnitzer. In the light of his writings, it is possible to regard Palissy's clay creations as scientific demonstrations of natural forms and processes, and eminently suited to the collecting interests of the elite classes. His use of muddy colours floated in a clear *faience* (lead) glaze on earthenware spawned many imitators. He was commissioned by both the Constable de Montmorency (1555) and Catherine de' Medici (1566) to build ceramic grottoes, the latter at the Palace of the Tuileries in Paris, though neither survives. A lifelong and vocal Protestant, he was arrested in 1586 for heresy and died in the Bastille.

German stoneware

While tin-glazed earthenware became the dominant type of ceramic in Italy, in northern Europe the production of salt-glazed stoneware underwent a similar, almost proto-industrial expansion. Stoneware is a very hard, non-porous pottery made from a mixture of clay and a fusible stone, usually feldspar, fired at a temperature high enough to vitrify the stone but not the clay. The centre for production since the Middle Ages had been the Rhineland area of Germany. From the early sixteenth century onwards, the manufactories in Cologne, Frechen, Raeren, and Siegburg achieved a measure of artistic distinction, producing jugs and drinking vessels decorated with moulded relief designs of a steadily increasing variety and sophistication. The coming together of the print revolution and improved methods of mass-producing moulded relief decoration significantly raised the status and social desirability of the stoneware medium. Sophisticated Renaissance designs, mediated through prints, transformed the nature and appeal of these wares and created new markets among the higher social classes, traditionally unaccustomed to drinking from ceramic vessels.

In contrast to the Italian taste for classical subject matter, the predominant themes of decoration on stoneware jugs and drinking vessels were drawn from the Bible. The emphasis on the religious within the domestic sphere to which such imagery contributed was a consequence of the Protestant Reformation, whose leaders, from 1517 onwards, either banned or discouraged imagery in churches in their attempts to eradicate what they considered superstitious cultic practices, while yet encouraging its use within the home for purposes of moral example and teaching. Such views were also in keeping with a broader, humanist ethos, espoused by Catholic reformers like Erasmus of Rotterdam, who regarded the home as an important locus of spiritual and moral instruction. They too regarded the stories of the Bible as *exempla*, from which men and women could learn how to conduct their lives. In this way, across the social and confessional divides, on painted glass, woodwork, textiles, plasterwork, as well as on ceramics, biblical subjects became a normative part of the aesthetic experience of domestic life in northern Europe. The stoneware potters of the Rhineland responded to this ethos by decorating their pots with a wide variety of Old Testament stories set in fields of Renaissance leaf-work and grotesque ornament.

A similar humanist ethos informed the decoration of another form of ceramic art, the tiled stove, which had been in use in southern Germany and the Alpine regions since the thirteenth century. By the mid-sixteenth century, due largely to maiolica techniques of tile decoration imported from Italy, it had developed also into a significant art form. The more elaborate examples, such as those by the Pfau family dynasty of tile makers from Winterthur in Switzerland, show the influence of printed picture bibles and emblem books that made the stove a kind of picture gallery and a natural locus for communal family bible reading or other forms of homiletic education.

Glass

Like maiolica, Italian glassmaking witnessed a comparable increase in production and product differentiation during the Renaissance, due in large part to important techno-logical advances that allowed glassmakers to both respond to and help create the conditions of a luxury market. The centre of glassmaking was the Venetian island of Murano, where glass had been made for centuries (the first written regulations for glassmakers were codified in 1271). In the fifteenth century, its glass-blowers, the *fiolari*, succeeded in making significant technical refinements to both the glass frit and the available colourants. Angelo Barovier (d.1461) is credited with perfecting a clear soda glass that was light and of great surface brilliance, known as *cristallo*, because it emulated rock crystal. Its lightness was due to the low lead content of the frit, allowing it to be blown and manipulated into thin membranes of ever more fantastical shapes. An accompanying innovation was *vetro a fili*, a filigree glass made by embedding thin canes of white glass in a clear glass matrix. On heating and blowing out the glass into the required shape, the canes could be extended and twisted into spirals, *a retorti*, to wonderful effects of airy thinness.

These inventions were accompanied in the second half of the fifteenth century by a new range of blues, greens, and purples, which achieved effects of coloured transpar-ency on clear glass. The glass workers also successfully revived gold sandwich glass and *millefiori*, techniques both known to the ancient Romans. The first involves a floating layer of granulated gold embedded within the transparent *cristallo* body of a bowl; the second involves cross sections of thin, multicoloured canes of glass embedded within a glass vessel. A technique for imitating veined hardstones was known as *vetro calcedonio*, chalcedony glass. Antonio Neri, whose *L'arte vetraria* published in 1612 was the first detailed account of glassmaking, praised *calcedonio* as an art whose colours and 'jokes' (*scherzi*) surpassed the effects of nature. These virtuoso types of Venetian glass were valued by collectors for many of the same reasons as natural curiosities. Isabella d'Este was a passionate collector of Murano glass. The Florentine Filippo Strozzi bought eleven chalcedony vases in 1479; the Spanish King Philip II possessed sixty-five examples of ice-glass or *vetro a ghiaccio* in his palace El Pardo, a kind of glass created by plunging a vessel into cold water before it had cooled or annealed, so as to create a splintered and roughened surface, akin to ice or unworked crystal.

These manifold techniques also gave rise to a new range of luxury dining products that were in great demand in the Italian courts and beyond. These luxury products perfectly matched contemporary aristocratic ideals of civility, of *sprezzatura*, of a desired grace and a courtly ease of comportment. The lightness and fragility of the Venetian *cristallo* wine glass, for instance, demanded a complementary delicacy in its use that called attention to the social grace of the drinker. Beyond its own intrinsic beauty,

VASE, GOBLET, AND SPRINKLER, *cristallo, vetro a retorti* technique with frieze of lions and eagles; mould blown; Venice (Murano), second half of the sixteenth century.

therefore, Murano glass, like *istoriato* maiolica, helped inculcate an aesthetic of social differentiation in the user that met the aspirations of a refined elite.

Despite the attempts by the Venetian government to safeguard the secrets of Venetian glass—glass workers were prohibited on pain of death from working elsewhere, just as foreign imported glass was prohibited—eventually the art of making crystal glass spread throughout northern Europe. Giacomo Verzelini (1522–1606) introduced the technique to Elizabethan London, where he obtained a twenty-one-year monopoly of glassmaking in the Venetian fashion in 1575. In Germany a hard crystal glass was developed that provided a suitable medium for engraved decorations by such masters as Caspar Lehmann (c.1565–1622), though it was in the Netherlands that the art of engraving on glass was brought to one of its highest points in the seventeenth century. Here too, a form of filigree wine glass was developed in harder clear glass of higher lead content, known appropriately as *façon de venise*, in close imitation of the Venetian prototypes.

Leatherwork

Leather was an important material made from the hides of animals such as oxen, cows, and horses; or from the skins of smaller animals such as sheep, deer, and pigs. Tanners and other leatherworkers obtained such materials from butchers. Leather provided a large variety of products, both everyday and luxury: shoes, boots, belts, gloves, cloaks, armour; the material for harnessing and handling animals, including saddles; and sacks and bottles for the storage and transport of liquids. Leather was also used for making parchment (from sheepskins) and vellum (from cowskins). Leatherworkers were divided into many specialities, the most basic division being between those who prepared the raw materials and the great variety of specialized artisans who made particular products, such as saddles or shoes or gloves.

Tanning hides to make leather was a stench-producing and water-polluting process, often relegated to the outskirts of the towns and cities. Tanners acquired hides from butchers and first trimmed and cleaned them. They treated the hides in two stages. First they placed them in a pit with weak tanning material such as oak bark and moved them around continuously. Second, they put them in deep pits with various materials and left them for up to a year. Oak bark, a prime tanning material, was often ground with millstones at tanning mills. After the skins had acquired a uniform colour, the tanners rinsed them, smoothed them with specialized tools, and hung them to dry. The tanner then gave the material to a currier who further treated it. Different specialists prepared leather variously for different purposes—saddles and harnesses required far less preparation than did such luxury items as fine gloves or purses.

Leather artisans usually specialized in one kind of product, whether gloves, saddles, parchment and vellum for books, shoes, purses, or buckets. For luxury products, the leather could be decorated by stamping, or it was modelled in a way that left an image in low relief, or embossed, using a special embossing tool. Leather could also be decorated with coloured dyes and it could be gilded. Decorated leathers were first developed in Spain at centres such as Córdoba, Granada, Seville, and Valencia. Such ornamented leathers were used for upholstery, cushions, floor coverings, and wall hangings. Decorated leathers soon spread to centres of production throughout Europe.

Machinery and power

The most important power machinery of the medieval period, the mill, remained basically important in the fifteenth and sixteenth centuries. Mills could be powered by animals, especially if the locale lacked sufficient water resources. The watermill could be designed in several different ways depending on local conditions and resources. The horizontal mill, the easiest to build and repair, was most often used by individuals and small groups without large resources. It was built with a horizontal paddle wheel that was immersed in and turned by moving water. The horizontal wheel was attached to a vertical shaft that turned a horizontally placed grinding stone, the whole a simple apparatus that required no gears. Vertical waterwheels were more complex. They were mounted on axles and required gearing to transfer their vertical motion to the horizontal grinding stone. The undershot wheel was turned by water moving under the wheel, while the more powerful overshot wheel was constructed so that the water fell over the top of the wheel. Waterwheel power was used for many tasks such as grinding grain and powering piston pumps used in mine drainage.

Additions to the basic waterwheel-powered machine provided new sources of power. One of the most important was the addition of the camshaft. A camshaft activating a trip hammer turns the rotary motion of the waterwheel into linear motion, and then with the help of gravity into reciprocating motion. Fulling mills were made by adding trip hammers operated by camshafts in which short extensions such as blocks of wood (the cams) were added to rotating axles. On its downward motion the machine released trip hammers. Such trip hammers soon found many uses—for example in hemp mills, which pounded the woody fibres of the hemp plant into a form suitable for making rope, sails, and cloth; and in paper mills in which the rags that formed the material basis of papermaking were pounded into pulp. Ironwork could now be mechanized so that camshafts and trip hammers could hammer the semi-molten blooms. Trip hammers rotating upwards could open powerful bellows which were weighted to shut after the camshaft mechanism had lifted them open. Such mechanized bellows led to improvements in firing furnaces, and made blast furnaces possible. Other industries that required the pounding of particular materials put the mechanisms to use as well: brewers used them to pound mash for beer, while tanners used them to crush the bark they used for tanning.

A further elaboration of machinery involved the application of the crank to the mill, resulting in machines such as crankshaft-operated sawmills. The crankshaft found many other uses in the fifteenth and sixteenth centuries, such as in blade-sharpening machines, organ grinding, and lifting devices.

Craft and Technology   361

GRAIN MILL POWERED BY AN OVERSHOT WATERWHEEL; piston pumps force the waste
water up pipe R for discharge into the pool above for reuse; Agostino Ramelli, *Le Diverse
et Artificiose Machine* (Paris: in Casa del autore, 1588), plate 116 (cxvi).

The windmill found increasing use during the Renaissance centuries. Windmills were used in earlier Asian and Islamic societies, but a new variety developed that was adapted to conditions of England and northern Europe where the winds come from variable directions. The post mill allowed a miller to turn the machine to face the direction from which the wind blew, but was limited to a size that could be turned by one man. The tower mill, built with an immovable tower with a top that could be turned to face the wind, could be larger, since only the top had to be turned to the wind, rather than the entire machine. Windmills were used for a variety of tasks such as grinding grain and, in the Low Countries, pumping water as an essential part of that region's extensive drainage system.

What is significant about these machines and modalities of power in the Renaissance centuries is not when or where each machine or component was invented (in the past a primary focus of historians of technology), but how they were employed and understood within diverse economies and cultures. Especially from the fifteenth century, machines exerted a powerful cultural interest and fascination. The lure of the machine, as it might be called, resulted not only in the widespread development and creative use of diverse machines and machine components, but also in the emergence of writings about machines, which often displayed images. For example, in the late fifteenth century the Sienese architect/engineer Francesco di Giorgio Martini (1439–1501) and his contemporary, Leonardo da Vinci (1452–1519), each wrote treatises on engineering and machines accompanied by drawings that displayed numerous variations and alternative designs (all of which remained in manuscript form until modern times). By the late sixteenth century, so-called 'Theatres of Machines', beautiful printed books that dramatically displayed diverse machines and machine parts, had become the rage.

Building and ship construction

The development of classical architecture, the importance of Vitruvianism, and the making of innovative structures, such as Brunelleschi's double-shelled dome in Florence, are treated elsewhere in this volume in the chapters on art and architecture. Here it remains to note that urban construction included not only the renovation and new construction of great palaces and magnificent churches, but also the construction of new streets, the straightening and paving of existing ones, and the construction of sewers. If a city was bisected by a river, as were many including London, Paris, and Rome, bridge construction was centrally important, as were attempts to deal with the problem of flood control. Some cities, such as Rome in the late sixteenth century, were supplied with much needed water by the repair of ancient Roman aqueducts, and other cities received an augmented water supply by the construction of new aqueducts and water conduits.

The sixteenth-century boom in building construction fuelled the trades that provided building materials, such as stone, lime for mortar, timber, and bricks.

Brickmaking was an important industry that entailed digging the appropriate kind of clay, packing it into moulds, and firing it in kilns. Kilns were also used to produce lime from limestone (sometimes from found marble taken from ancient ruins). Lime was an essential ingredient of mortar. Masonry construction required many skilled and unskilled tasks, such as quarrying and roughly finishing the stone and hauling it to the building site for finishing and placement. Timber was felled and cut for roofing and flooring, for scaffolding, and for the centring of arches and vaults. Renaissance architects and engineers studied ancient Roman methods of building construction, and began to use the material invented by them—concrete—more extensively. Hauling and heavy lifting equipment, such as cranes of various types, was essential. Innovations in construction machinery appeared. In England and on the Continent, mathematical practices were increasingly important to the identity and work of architects and to building construction from the fifteenth century. Such practices impinged upon the processes of design, and were crucial to such tasks as surveying, making estimates of cost, and the keeping of accounts.

Ship construction

Ship construction was a complex, large-scale, and specialized activity that adopted numerous innovations in an age that undertook oceanic voyages, which called for new kinds of ships (and new navigation techniques), but which also continued large-scale shipping and naval expeditions in the Mediterranean and the waterways of northern Europe. One basic ship-type used primarily for Mediterranean and North Sea trade was the galley, an oared ship of various specialized designs (depending on its use) that was also powered by sails. In the early fifteenth century, the Venetian Senate, which governed a huge arsenal where both guns and ships were manufactured, encouraged experimentation (and competition) in galley design. Shipwrights created new versions of great merchant galleys, a new round ship (called the *barza*) for fighting pirates in the Mediterranean, and light galleys. Innovative ideas required the presentation of models and arguments in favour, often made against the objections of detractors. A humanist scholar and public lecturer in Greek eloquence in Venice, Vettor Fausto (after 1480–*c.*1546), carried out one project to design and then improve on the quinquereme, a galley with five rows of oars that had been used by the ancient Greeks. Fausto had studied literature and mathematics and had produced a text and translation of the pseudo-Aristotelian *Mechanics*. After much debate, the Venetian Senate provided him with the personnel, materials, and space at the arsenal to build it. It was launched in 1529 with great fanfare.

In the Baltic and the North seas, a flat-bottomed ship called the cog that had a single large square sail was the cargo ship most utilized, its box-like hold suited for carrying bulky items such as grain and lumber. It was developed around the seaborne trade of the Hanseatic towns but was used for warfare as well. In the Renaissance its range extended to the Mediterranean, but it was gradually replaced by the hulk, which differed from the cog in many ways, most importantly in having a rounded hull (the body of the ship), making it more seaworthy. Such cargo ships in the Mediterranean were called round ships to distinguish them from the 'long ships' or galleys. The combination of Mediterranean and northern shipbuilding traditions led to the three-masted full-rigged ship, called the carrack or *nao*, the combined features of which included the use of both square-rigged and lateen (triangular) rigged sails. In addition to such large ships, a characteristic of fifteenth- and sixteenth-century shipbuilding was the development of a great variety of innovative and specialized smaller vessels.

As Spain and Portugal turned toward the Atlantic, oceanic conditions—high-velocity tidal currents, violent gales, and huge waves—called for a new kind of ship. The galleon, which might be described as a modified carrack, was a large three-masted (and eventually four-masted) sailing ship that came into use between 1520 and 1540. Spain's northern coast became a centre for building the new ocean-going vessels, the design of which was the focus of ongoing debate and experimentation. The galleon was a well-armed, fast sailing ship that was well suited for carrying cargos such as silver across the Atlantic. It came to be used by many nations, including England.

Arts of communication

The Renaissance centuries can be thought of as a great age of books and prints. In the fourteenth and fifteenth centuries those books consisted of manuscripts, handwritten or copied. These books could be constructed out of vellum (cowhide) or parchment (sheepskin), each the product of specialized leatherworkers. Increasingly in the fifteenth century, a cheaper material—paper—was used instead. Paper had arrived in Europe from China via the Islamic states in the twelfth century and was widely used by the late fourteenth. Although more fragile than parchment, it was far cheaper and easier to produce in large quantities. From the fourteenth to the eighteenth centuries, paper in Europe was made entirely out of old linen and cotton rags. Rag shortages were a continuing problem, which was only solved in the nineteenth century when a commercial method for making paper from wood pulp was perfected.

The printing press was a composite invention that consisted of three separate elements—movable type cast in metal, an oil-based ink, and the press itself. Goldsmiths and minters, who were familiar with using punches to make designs in metal, developed methods for making movable type. Between 1430 and 1450 experiments in several places aimed to make a commercial printing press using movable type. The first successful printing business emerged in Mainz, Germany, around 1450. It was brought to fruition by three men, Johann Fust (*c.*1400–1466), a rich citizen who provided the capital, Peter Schoeffer (*c.*1425–1503), probably a scribe before becoming a printer, and Johannes Gutenberg (1397/1400–1468), who is generally accepted as the inventor of lead-based movable type. Although the expenses of the project drove Gutenberg into bankruptcy, as we know from Fust's lawsuit against him in 1455, printed books soon spread throughout Europe, first finding a market alongside manuscript books and then gradually superseding them.

IMPRESSIO LIBRORVM.

Poteſt vt vna vox capi aure plurima: *Linunt ita vna ſcripta mille paginas.*

'IMPRESSIO LIBRORUM' (Book Printing). Plate 4 of *Nova Reperta* by Jan van der Straet, called Johannes Stradanus. Engraved by Philip Galle.

The development of the printing press led to a multiplicity of kinds of books and readers—from learned books to the thousands of inexpensive, small books intended for the larger public throughout Europe—'cheap print'. Concerning the latter, small religious tracts, collections of recipes and home remedies, or 'books of secrets', and other kinds of inexpensive printed material for general consumption became ubiquitous, especially in the urban centres of Europe. In northern Europe, Protestant Reformation ideas were rapidly disseminated through pamphlets. At the same time, lavish and large books on subjects such as machines, navigation, and natural history began to populate the shelves of the well-to-do.

It seems likely that printing also helped to stimulate the growing importance of the visual in the fifteenth and sixteenth century. Carved woodblocks could be inserted into the press along with the type to create an illustrated page. Both used a method of surface relief printing, that is, the letters and lines that were printed on the page were made by the raised part of the type and the woodblock. Another means of printing pictures emerged in the fifteenth century—using copper plates. In engraving, a design was cut into a polished copper plate with a burin. In etching, the plate was waxed, a design incised in the wax, and then corrosive acid applied to the incised lines, burning the image into the plate. In both cases, the plates would be inked. Ink was wiped from the surface but remained in the grooves. Copperplate engraving and etching required its own special press. Many such copperplates were printed as stand-alone images. They could be title-pages, but also single sheet images—copies of famous paintings, religious images, maps, and images of monuments. And increasingly they could be used to illustrate plants, birds, animals, insects, and human anatomies—as a way of validating observational and empirical methodologies that were gaining importance in anatomy and natural history.

Military technologies

Warfare changed between the fourteenth and the seventeenth centuries, but for the most part it changed gradually. New weapon technologies were often developed and used along with traditional weapons. The best known and ultimately the most import-ant of the new technologies was gunpowder artillery. Gunpowder weapons appeared in Europe from the 1320s, but they became central to the conduct of war only in the sixteenth century. In the fourteenth century the standard missile-shooting weapons were the longbow, the crossbow, and the trebuchet. The longbow was a powerful weapon that was drawn to the ear instead of the chest, shot a long arrow that went much further than the traditional arrow, and had great penetrating power at close range. It was an English weapon that required training from childhood. The intense training period was consonant with English values and the raising of male children in the fourteenth and early fifteenth century. However, gradually, as longbow skills came to be less valued, fewer children were trained and less well. The long training period was the Achilles heel of the longbow. As skill declined, the weapons' effectiveness declined as well.

The crossbow had a mechanical loading mechanism and thus could deliver far more power than the human arm. The trebuchet was a large artillery machine that dis-charged lead or stone balls through a counterweight mechanism. It was a highly effective weapon against fortification and was used until the end of the fifteenth century. As a complement or alternative to missiles, armies of pikesmen could be used. Pikesmen were tightly massed and disciplined soldiers holding elongated spears called pikes. They moved together in formation and were trained to stop the charges of cavalry without breaking. The Swiss came to be renowned practitioners of pike warfare in the fifteenth century.

As can be seen, not all societies could produce all weapons. Longbows were the product of a particularly English set of circumstances and longbow proficiency was not developed in, say, Italy or Spain. Pikesmen came from small countries with cohesive populations such as the Flemish and the Swiss. They could not easily be created by the Italians, the Germans, or the French. Especially fifteenth-century wars were fought with a great variety and mixture of traditional and new weaponry and the tactics that went along with them.

Into this complex mix of weaponry and its accompanying mix of strategies came gunpowder artillery. During the first century of its development, such artillery was notoriously inaccurate, had a slow rate of fire, and required immensely heavy and difficult-to-move cannon or bombards. Gunpowder, which is made from saltpetre, sulphur, and charcoal, underwent a development in the fifteenth century which increased its reliability. An improvement in terms of more rapid burning and easier transport was the development of 'corning', which was done by making the gunpowder into a paste and then drying it, ready to be crumbled before loading it into a gun.

In the fifteenth century, after a century of experimentation, handheld firearms came into their own. The first matchlock arquebuses began to appear around 1450—guns with a long barrel and a small bore. Locks were designed variably, and early ones resembled household locks. Small guns included the arquebus and the musket for infantry and, later, the handheld pistol. Other developments include the change from stone to iron cannonballs. Bronze cannon and guns became forged iron weapons, and then cast iron.

Around 1500 and consequent to the French invasions of Italy of the 1490s, gunpowder artillery began to change fortification. In the 1490s, French forces rapidly and decisively defeated key Italian states with an army armed with cannon that shot

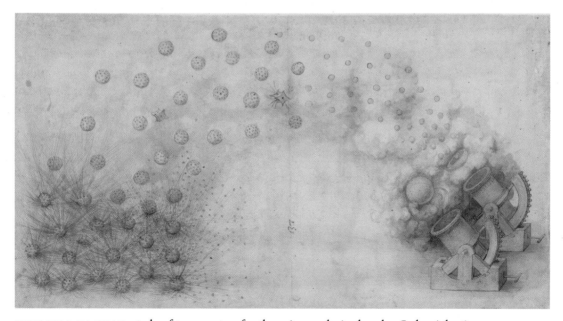

LEONARDO DA VINCI, study of two mortars for throwing explosive bombs; Codex Atlanticus, fol. 33 recto.

iron cannonballs. This brought the realization, in all too vivid form, that traditional medieval fortifications and city walls were inadequate against the new weapons. The tall, flat surfaces and round towers of traditional wall fortification turned out to be perfect targets for the new gunpowder weapons. Polygonal bastion fortifications soon appeared in numerous locations. Their triangulated surfaces, raised gun plat-forms, ditches, ravelins (detached forts), and artificial slopes created far more effective defences. Not only did the siege artillery have greater difficulty hitting the walls, the defensive guns positioned on the triangulated bastions could provide far more effective coverage for the defenders. The new bastion fortification required geometric planning to create the most useful angles for each particular site, and encouraged the association of mathematics with artillery and fortification.

Measuring time and place

Accurate measurement of time and of place became a growing interest in the Renais-sance centuries. First, there was a great development of timekeeping in the form of new kinds of clocks. The earliest mechanical clocks, invented in the late thirteenth century, were weight-driven, and regulated by a verge and foliot escapement that allowed the slow descent of the weight and the regular motion of the clock. By the late fourteenth century numerous cities contained clocks—large iron mechanisms installed in towers—often including bells that struck the hours and moving figures, such as Magi, roosters, and celestial bodies. A source of pride to many cities, they symbolized orderly rule and began to regulate urban life. For example, textile workers in Flanders began work at the sound of a mechanical clock.

The large, heavy, weight-driven clocks could not be carried around! But by the beginning of the fifteenth century, spring mechanisms were developed for the regula-tion of clocks. Since the force of the spring on its own diminishes as it unwinds, a method was needed to equalize that force over time. The problem was solved with a conical *fusee* shaped like a top, which the mainspring turned around by means of a cord. Spring-driven clocks allowed not only greater accuracy, but smaller clocks. In the sixteenth century these smaller clocks were gradually made even smaller and eventu-ally became entirely portable—that is, they became watches.

Timekeeping instruments constitute only one example of the many kinds of measuring or mathematical instruments that were developed and used in this period. The astrolabe, which came to Europe from Islamic lands in the eleventh and twelfth centuries, could demonstrate the circumpolar movements of the sun and stars, could measure the altitude of a star or other celestial body, and could find time and place. Other instruments were developed from the astrolabe, including the astrolabe-quadrant. Another observational instrument was the cross-staff—a graduated rod over which slid a cross-piece. Different versions were developed for different tasks. Dimensions of distant objects could be measured with versions of this instrument, and it was used as a surveying instrument, and to measure the altitude of celestial bodies.

BRASS ASTROLABE
MANUFACTURED BY THE
WORKSHOP of Georg
Hartmann in Nuremberg
in 1537.

Oceanic voyages in the fifteenth century posed serious problems of navigation. These difficulties were ameliorated with the (prior) development of the magnetic compass. Navigators added to the traditional toolkit of position-finding instruments with astronomer's instruments that were developed for navigation, including the cross-staff, the mariner's astrolabe, and the mariner's quadrant. Thus a navigator could find his latitude by measuring the altitude of the North Star or the sun from the location of the ship, and then using a table, such as one showing the sun's declination through the year. Finding longitude at sea, also necessary for accurate positioning, was not achieved until the eighteenth century.

Magnetic variations were discovered in the mid-fifteenth century, leading to a variety of instruments and techniques to measure that variation at sea. Sea charts remained inaccurate because they were made by transferring geometric projections onto a flat surface, failing to take account of the curvature of the earth. The problem was solved first by the mathematical work of Pedro Nunes (1502–78) of Spain, who demonstrated that on a sphere a rhumb line (a line of constant compass heading) is not straight as it is on a plane. Rather, it is a spiral ending at the pole. Rhumb lines cut all meridians (imaginary north–south lines on the earth's surface that connect the geographic poles) at a constant angle. The Flemish cartographer Gerhard Mercator (1512–94) drew such lines for the first time on the gores of a terrestrial globe, and in 1569 published the first sea chart in which directions were true.

Historians have increasingly investigated the ways in which monarchies such as Spain encouraged and directed research into cosmography and navigation, motivated by their fundamental interests in oceanic navigation and the exploitation of the New World. Recent research has demonstrated, for example, the Spanish crown's emphasis on the collection of empirical data as well as its interest in keeping secret this growing body of navigational and cosmographical knowledge from outside competitors.

Beyond navigation, numerous instruments were developed or adopted for military use. Perhaps the most important was the gunner's quadrant, an instrument consisting of a 90-degree arch with one long leg and a plumb line. The gunner inserted the leg into the gun barrel and could read off the elevation of the gun—an important piece of information, as it determined the trajectory of the fired shot. Other gunnery instruments included calibrated rules for converting bore diameters into shot weights in different materials, calipers for measuring the external diameters of shot and internal diameters of bores, and graduated sights with screw adjustments for adjusting cannon elevations and for levelling of the carriage.

Measuring instruments were also important for surveying, an increasingly significant activity and one related to the development of cartography. Cartography in the fifteenth century was initially inspired by the discovery and diffusion of the *Geographia* by the ancient author Ptolemy (c.90–168 CE). During the sixteenth century, hundreds of maps and globes were made. The earliest extant ichnographic map (that is, a map in which every structure is viewed from directly above and as fully measured) is the map of Imola by Leonardo da Vinci of 1502.

Makers of mathematical instruments enjoyed growing status. Especially in London, the shops of instrument makers became the focus of gatherings for demonstrations of how to use the instruments and discussions of natural philosophy and the world. They became, in other words, arenas of communication, or trading zones, between the practitioners who made and used the instruments and the learned men who also used them.

Craft and Renaissance culture

The classicizing tendencies in the design and content of many of the objects discussed thus far, in the themes of *istoriato* maiolica plates, in the gods on Cellini's salt cellar, in the Vitruvian and Euclidian ideals of Jamnitzer, and so forth, point to the variety of the ways in which crafted objects were informed by humanist taste. To follow the adoption of a new stylistic and thematic language in the applied arts across different parts of Europe is to follow the gradual integration of a movement of cultural renewal into the structures of everyday life: it is to witness the translation of the new, humanist ideals into a design for living.

The revival and reintegration of the forms and ideals of classical antiquity into the applied and decorative arts began in Italy in the fifteenth century, as taste followed the architectural projects of wealthy, educated patrons like the Strozzi and the Medici in

Florence or the d'Este family of Ferrara, who consciously remodelled their urban *palazzi* and country villas in line with ancient Roman precedent. Across the period, architects from Alberti to Filarete to Serlio and Palladio revived Vitruvian architectural theory and applied its precepts to modern building designs, while the visible remains of the ancient past, its ruins, sarcophagi, statues, and coins, provided a vocabulary of classical ornament which was adopted in interior architecture and furnishings. The contemporary taste for 'grotesque' designs, derived from the fanciful masks and monstrous hybrid creatures discovered on the walls of Nero's palace, the *Domus Aurea*, during its excavation in Rome in the late fifteenth century, is one prominent example. Named after the 'grottoes' where they were found, these motifs were richly adapted by artists who regarded them as a fertile source for their own inventions. Produced as ornament prints, they were widely disseminated across Europe and adapted into a wide variety of decorative schemes.

Just as the façades of modern palaces were organized according to the rules of classical proportion, so the interiors were designed with classical columns and cornices, their fireplaces, doorways, and other fixed elements adorned with antique ornament. The furnishings that complemented this new architectural style followed in kind. Among the characteristic pieces of furniture of the fifteenth-century Florentine town palace was the *cassone* or marriage chest, in which the bride kept her trousseau. Used to symbolize the transfer of property between families at the occasion of a betrothal, *cassoni* were carried through the streets in ritual procession when the bride moved from her father's to her groom's house. Once installed, the *cassoni* were associated with the bedchamber. The grandest examples were of gilded poplar wood,

APOLLONIO DI GIOVANNI AND MARCO DEL BUONO (WORKSHOP), Wedding chest (*cassone*), with *The Conquest of Trebizond*; tempera on poplar and gilded fruit wood. Florence, after 1461.

carved with classical ornament and decorated with narrative scenes drawn from Roman history or literature: famous battles or scenes from the lives of famous women such as Lucretia, Helen of Troy, Dido, or Griselda. The use of such exemplary ancient figures, whose stories often underscored civic as well as personal virtues, demonstrates how far the themes of literary humanism had entered the sphere of domestic life.

The fullest expression of such humanist values was the *studiolo*, a room or small space dedicated to private study and contemplation, which housed private papers or precious collectibles. Its decoration tended to reflect these functions. The philosophers Ficino and Montaigne each inscribed Greek and Latin aphorisms on the walls of their respective studies. Isabella d'Este adorned her *studiolo* with her collection of antiquities and contemporary works of art. The *studioli* of Federigo da Montefeltro, Duke of Urbino, made for his palaces at Urbino and Gubbio (the latter today in the Metropolitan Museum of Art, New York), were decorated across their walled surfaces with designs in inlaid woods, or *intarsia*, depicting in *trompe l'œil* a series of wall cabinets, whose half-opened doors reveal the accoutrements of the ideal humanist study. These include books, astrolabes, compasses, and musical instruments, all meticulously drawn in one-point perspective in astonishing illusionistic detail.

These wall panels were also virtuoso demonstrations of intarsia technique, the intricate patterning of differently figured, grained, and textured woods. It was a singular art form that literally 'constructed' representation by assembling geometrically regular shapes, an art in which, as the art historian André Chastel put it, 'mathematical form creates its [own] object'. As such it was closely linked to the development of perspective, and its practitioners revelled in difficult perspectival viewpoints and in the rendition of light and space.

The art of intarsia was closely associated with another specialized type of furniture connected with the study: the writing desk and small collector's cabinet. In Spain, the *escritorio* emerged as a form of portable cabinet that contained many small drawers and a drop-down writing surface. Its characteristic surface decoration was made up of complex geometric and foliate inlays in wood, bone, or ivory in the *mudéjar* style, an idiom based on Islamic decorative traditions that incorporated Jewish and Christian elements. In sixteenth-century Germany, intarsia workers produced similar types of multi-drawered *Schreibtische* and *Kunstkabinette*, decorating their surfaces with geometrical solids and architectural vistas inspired by the mathematical and perspectival interests of the Italians.

The collecting and display of objects associated with classical antiquity that these rooms and cabinets encouraged was another practice by which Renaissance values entered everyday life. Indeed, the accumulation and display of luxury objects, designed for aesthetic discernment and enjoyment rather than use, became an increasingly important means of self-representation. This practice too had classical roots. In his treatise *De splendore*, of 1498, the Naples-based humanist Giovanni Pontano explained the category of 'ornamental' objects as those things acquired 'not so much for use as for embellishment and polish'. Such things as 'seals, paintings, tapestries,…ivory seats, cloth woven with gems, cases variously painted in the Arabic manner, little vases of crystal', he wrote, 'bring prestige to the owner of the house', when seen by visitors, each 'arranged in its own place…one fitting for the hall, another for the women's apartments'. Crafted objects, made for their aesthetic and representational value rather than use, thus assumed an importance in the cultural economy of the elite home.

In northern Europe, the Gothic style prevailed in both the secular and ecclesiastical spheres well into the sixteenth century, even developing a late 'flamboyant style' in the Netherlands and Spain. Yet from the early years of the sixteenth century, Italianate elements increasingly intermingled with and eventually absorbed the Gothic. Their introduction was sporadic and local and their application at first ungrounded in theory. In Augsburg, for example, a flourishing mercantile city on the north–south trade route, a classicizing style was initially associated with wealthy merchant families like the Fugger, whose extensive commercial contacts in the Italian peninsula gave them a lively interest in Italian fashions, architecture, and art. Given its historical associations with ancient Rome, the style was also adopted by the Emperor Maximilian I for his propagandist projects in the first two decades of the sixteenth century. The Italianate was thus understood on some level in social terms, its initial reception coloured by political and ideological factors, of high finance, imperial power, and international prestige. These developments were aided by the spread of imported Italian ornament prints into the north and their emulation by local printmakers in a process of creative adaptation of classical forms to existing cultural and social contexts.

In France, the greatest impetus for the development of an Italianate style came from the court of Francis I, who recognized the importance of artistic patronage for the prestige of the monarchy. After his exposure to Italian art during his military campaigns, he began actively to recruit Italian artists, architects, and artisans into his service. The rebuilding and decorating of Francis's palace at Fontainebleau between 1528 and 1540 by the Italians Rosso Fiorentino and Francesco Primaticcio, especially the long ceremonial hall, now known as the Gallery of Francis I, became the touchstone for subsequent French art and design. Most notable was their use of bold stucco decorations consisting of pronouncedly elongated figures, set among heavy, scrolled strapwork, a form of decorative banding evocative of square-sectioned cut leather that enclosed central pictorial fields. The tendency to allow the decorative language of the frame to dominate the elements of the central field was to become a key characteristic of French Mannerist design. It was widely disseminated through prints made by Rosso's and Primaticcio's assistants and followers and applied to a variety of forms, both monumental and miniature, from the lintels of doorways to title-pages of books, and further elaborated by influential designers such as Jacques Androuet Du Cerceau (1510/12–after 1584) and Hugues Sambin (c.1520–1601/2).

Netherlandish designers followed a similar path. Antwerp, a thriving centre of craft production and book publishing, produced a school of ornamental printmakers who also created a distinctive and influential ornamental vocabulary. Designers such as

Cornelis Bos, Cornelis Matsys, and Hans Collaert developed inventive and fantastical variations of the grotesque style that found their way into a great many settings. The most influential was Hans Vredeman de Vries (1527–1604). His designs, published in twenty-seven volumes between 1557 and 1587, covered objects ranging from architecture to furniture, silverware, and perspective designs for intarsia makers. Based on the architectural principles of Vitruvius, which he encountered via Sebastiano Serlio's simplified digest, the *Regole generali di architettura sopra le cinque maniere de gli edifici* (*The General Rules of Architecture Concerning the Five Styles of Building*) of 1537, his essentially ornamental attitude to architecture (in contrast to the more strictly structural approach of the Italians), with its emphasis on meaningful surface ornament, on term figures, caryatids, and niche statues, dominated architectural and ornamental practice throughout northern Europe. The same principles were applied to the writing cabinets and *Kunstschränke* produced in Nuremberg, Augsburg, and Antwerp, whose iconographic programmes often spoke to the virtues of the patron and of good rulership.

By the second half of the sixteenth century, therefore, a 'Renaissance' decorative vocabulary, with all its local variants, had come to express a broad homogeneity of cultural reference and response across northern European society. In this sense, decoration acted as a unifying factor across geographical and political boundaries, establishing through the movement of designers and artisans, and the easy transportability of printed designs and patterns, a common set of aesthetic and associative criteria that proclaimed adherence to a universally understood, pan-European set of humanist values based on those of antiquity.

Craft and the *Kunstkammer*

A second important unifying factor of style and taste lay in aristocratic patronage. The central European courts emerged as important centres of artistic patronage and collecting, attracting artists and their works from all different parts of northern Europe and Italy. Already well established in the fifteenth century, from the 1550s onwards habits of courtly collecting coalesced around the concept of the *Kunst- und Wunderkammer*, the cabinet of art and wonder. Among the earliest were the *Kunstkammer* of Emperor Ferdinand I, begun in *c*.1553, and of the Elector August of Saxony and Archduke Ferdinand of Tyrol in Schloss Ambras, both begun in the 1560s; Duke Albrecht V of Bavaria housed his collection in a purpose-built structure, erected in Munich between 1564 and 1567. The greatest collection of all was that of the Habsburg emperors, extended by Maximilian II (emperor 1564–76) in Vienna and transferred to Prague, where it was enlarged on a massive scale by his son Rudolf II (emperor 1576–1612). These collections were organized around an encyclopedic principle that saw in the multitude of things collected a microcosm of the larger world. Samuel Quiccheberg, Flemish adviser to Duke Albrecht of Bavaria and author of a treatise on the *Kunstkammer*, called the Bavarian collection a 'theatrum sapientiae' (a theatre of wisdom), by which he meant a system for organizing knowledge about the universe. The objects within these collections generally conformed to two broad categories:

natural objects (*naturalia*) and man-made objects (*artificialia*). Natural objects, drawn in large part from the explorations of new worlds, were chosen for their rarity, their exotic provenance, or their aberration from nature's norm. Man-made objects were collected for their ingenuity, intricate skill, and the beauty or value of their raw materials.

The effect of these new categories of collecting upon the applied arts was profound, for, at this highest level of patronage, it brought the inventions of artisans directly into registration not only with the highest expectations of luxury, inventiveness, and technical expertise, but also—and this was new—with natural philosophy and contemporary science that the *Kunst- und Wunderkammer* fostered. A letter from a prominent Augsburg instrument maker, Christoph Schißler, to the Elector August of Saxony in 1572 testifies to the mixture of aristocratic entertainment and scientific interest that resulted. In a direct sales pitch, he offered a range of specialized goods, including terrestrial and astronomical globes, astrolabes, 'planispheres', 'unusual and wonderful' clocks, sundials, and compasses. But beyond practical instruments, he also offered collectable luxury items such as a 'clock of Achaz', drawn from the biblical narrative (2 Kings 20:11), which could cause the shadows to retreat a full ten hours backwards in time. In addition, Schißler had already offered, in 1570, a 'Motus planetarum', a form of cosmic clock, made up of a large disc, on which the planets moved in synchronic order, as well as an automatic, self-playing musical instrument.

On another level, the dual categories of art and nature encouraged an implicit rivalry between the powers of nature and of human ingenuity. Philosophers and artisans came to believe that they could improve upon nature's raw material and learn something of nature's laws in the process. The natural philosopher Francis Bacon viewed the *Kunstkammer* not only as an ideal place in which to study nature 'free and at large' but also a place where 'by art and the hand of man she [Nature] is forced out of her natural state, and squeezed and moulded…seeing that the nature of things betrays itself more readily under the vexations of art than in its natural freedom' (*Advancement of Learning*, 1605). Artisans manipulated exotic natural materials such as nautilus shells, coral, and hard stones, matching nature's powers of creation with fantastically wrought mounts of their own that often blurred the distinction between the natural and the man-made; or they might work to bring out the material's intrinsic, inner virtues. A piece of unworked agate might be formed into a dish, carved and polished to bring out dazzling bands of polychrome, the better to reveal its 'true', ideal nature, that was obscured in its dull, natural state. Such lessons in the transformative hand of craft were also applied to exotic natural objects such as bezoar stones or rhinoceros horns, materials of great rarity to which early modern medicine accorded special powers.

All these virtuoso works of craft reflect the aspirations of talented artisans, who were stimulated to explore new areas of activity and to raise themselves socially and professionally by associating themselves and their inventions with the tastes and interests of the courts. The process went both ways. The close involvement of rulers such as the Elector of Saxony and the Emperor Rudolf II with their artisans, and with

the processes of making, demonstrates a commonality of intellectual and practical interests that allowed the practical, artisanal knowledge of the workshop together with the artisan's own humanist aspirations to enter the province of court culture. An important consequence of this process was a gradual re-evaluation of the status of craft from an index of luxury or status to one of knowledge and learning.

Above all was the sense that implicit in these works was the idea that human ingenuity could challenge the existing order of nature. The rivalries between human and natural energies that were explored in the workshops and collections of the later sixteenth century were ultimately to give rise to the experimental culture of the following century. In this respect, the *Kunstkammer* stood at the cusp of two eras, a place where one could glimpse, at the junctures of practical and theoretical knowledge, of the wondrous and the empirical, of credulity and curiosity, the gradual emergence of a new order amid the slow passing of the old.

Opposite: Wenzel Jamnitzer, drinking vessel in the form of Daphne, *c.*1550; silver, parcel gilt, coral, semi-precious stones, height 66.5 cm.

CHAPTER 10

The Renaissance of Science

PAULA FINDLEN

IN an interesting twist of fate, two of the most famous paintings to depict the philosophical and scientific preoccupations of the Renaissance reached their completion within a year of each other. In his *Three Philosophers* (1508–9) the Venetian painter Giorgione depicted the history of knowledge as an allegory of three ages. A bearded sage holding a sheet of paper containing scientific drawings and notes, possibly lunar observations, looks dreamily across a diffuse landscape. A lightly bearded man wearing a turban, at the prime of life, seems to look away from nature while firmly gripping his corded belt from which a pouch hangs, though we can only guess what it contains. Finally, a beardless youth, dressed in the sandals and robes of a novitiate, sits on the rocky outcrop, intently observing nature with a surveyor's compass in hand, a sheet of paper ready to record what he sees, replicating effectively what the wise sage once did. This philosophical trinity makes knowledge a product of the dialectic of time, creating a dialogue between ancient wisdom and its fifteenth-century rebirth to the virtual exclusion of what lay in between. In this painting Giorgione effectively captured the allegory of science that lay at the heart of the Renaissance—namely, its certainty that the distant past was the most powerful source of inspiration to guide the present, if one could only recover the most authentic and complete version.

The complex recovery of ancient philosophy lies at the heart of Raphael of Urbino's masterpiece in the Stanza della Segnatura in the Vatican known as *The School of Athens* (1509–10). In this famous fresco generations of Greek philosophers, mathematicians, astronomers assemble before us at the feet of the two central figures—Plato carrying his *Timaeus* points upward to the heavens and Aristotle with his *Ethics* gestures outward, as if to touch those looking at him beyond the plane of the painting. Together, they orchestrate another Renaissance allegory of philosophy. At the bottom left, Pythagoras furiously inscribes his mathematical harmonies and proportions in a book, with Aristotle's greatest medieval Islamic commentator Averroes looking over his shoulder. To the right, a figure who evokes Euclid or possibly Archimedes draws mathematical diagrams. Ptolemy stands majestically tall just above this ancient mathematician; the terrestrial globe he holds evokes the impact of the rediscovery of the ancient Greek

GIORGIONE'S *THREE PHILOSOPHERS*, 1508–9.

astronomer's *Geography* rather than his *Almagest*. They are but a few of the many ancient minds represented in Raphael's famous philosophical painting. While Giorgione chose to represent the transmission and transformation of knowledge abstractly, Raphael instead revelled in the idea that he could bring an entire section of the Renaissance library to life by creating a collective portrait of knowledge in a single panoramic image.

The changing status of natural philosophy, mathematics, and medicine mattered a great deal at the height of the Renaissance. The efforts of leading painters to capture the expanding horizon of ancient science evoke the excitement of intellectual rediscovery and the ensuing debates about which approach to knowledge best explained the nature of the universe and the place of humanity within it. Long before Nicolaus Copernicus (1473–1543) thought to reconfigure the heavens, Leonhart Fuchs (1501–66) wondered how best to describe a plant, and Andreas Vesalius (1514–64) contemplated how regular and systematic dissection might change the understanding of the human body, the renaissance of science had begun. Rather than starting in a world *circa* 1543, as many traditional narratives of the Scientific Revolution often do, a study of Renaissance science explores how the evolution of scientific knowledge in the fourteenth and fifteenth centuries laid the foundation for the landmark accomplishments of the mid-sixteenth century.

What's the matter with Aristotle?

By the mid-fourteenth century natural philosophy had been firmly installed in the university curriculum for at least a century and the struggles to legitimize this new form of knowledge in the twelfth and thirteenth centuries seemed long past. No longer viewed as a profoundly pagan enterprise created by medieval Islamic commentators who interpreted the writings of ancient Greek philosophers and physicians, its Christian status had been carefully and authoritatively brokered by Dominicans such as Albertus Magnus and his pupil Thomas Aquinas; they laid to rest the moral concerns of the Paris theologians that natural philosophy might imperil the soul. Aristotle's *libri naturales* became the foundation of thirteenth-century natural philosophy. Thus, at the beginning of the Renaissance natural philosophy was neither a marginal nor dubious enterprise, but an essential component of the intellectual edifice of learning across Western Europe.

What kind of portrait of nature did scholastic knowledge offer? The arts curriculum that emerged in the late medieval and Renaissance universities focused on Aristotelian logic, metaphysics, moral and natural philosophy, understood primarily through Latin scholastic commentaries and translations of the important twelfth-century Arabic commentaries by Averroes (Ibn Rushd, 1126–98). Generations of students learned about a geocentric cosmos in which celestial and terrestrial nature were absolutely distinct, the former eternal and unchanging, the latter dynamic and enmeshed in cycles of birth and death. They parsed a world composed of Aristotle's four elements (earth, water, air, and fire) and classified natural phenomena based on tangible qualities (hot, dry, cold, and wet). Finally, they subjected everything they observed to intensive philosophical scrutiny and debate, guided by an Aristotelian understanding of the importance of making each particular observation a building block for a much larger theoretical understanding of knowledge. Thus, Aristotelian natural philosophy had structure and purpose; it bristled with specific insights into the natural world, and allowed room for interpretation, debate, and commentary in the quest to understand the formal properties and final causes of things. Fundamentally, it rendered the world intelligible, disciplining the mind to ask and answer a wide variety of questions. No other component of scientific learning was as thoroughly institutionalized, save for Avicenna's (Ibn Sina, 980–1037) *Canon of Medicine*, a tenth-century Arabic encyclopedia that masterfully synthesized centuries of Galenic medicine and Aristotelian natural philosophy. Both Aristotle and Avicenna remained an essential part of the Western European university curriculum to at least the mid-seventeenth century, structuring the mental habits and outlook of Renaissance scholars.

Despite the importance of Aristotle as the most authoritative philosophical source of knowledge of the natural world, there were rumblings in various corners about the limits of an Aristotelian worldview. The quest for alternatives became an essential feature of Renaissance intellectual life. In the 1350s Petrarch, one of the most eloquent and thoughtful spokesmen for a new kind of humanistic learning, revealed his own dissatisfaction with scholasticism when he confessed: 'I do not adore Aristotle.' He poked fun at the alleged omniscience of scholastic natural philosophers who obsessed about 'how many hairs there are on a lion's mane, how many feathers in the hawk's tail', turning knowledge into a trivial pursuit. In making these statements, Petrarch was not rejecting Aristotelian explanations of how nature operated, a subject in which he expressed virtually no interest. Instead, he resisted the habit of proclaiming Aristotle the most important ancient philosopher, perhaps even critiquing the idea that an ancient Greek could tell him more about God, nature, and humankind than his beloved Augustine. To follow Aristotle or to take a different path—this was truly one of the great questions of Renaissance science. How to follow Aristotle—and which version of Aristotle to read and learn from—became equally important.

Petrarch's desire to topple Aristotle from his pedestal certainly raised an important question about whether any one person, living or dead, should be an authoritative source of knowledge. He indirectly encouraged renewed interest in the surviving corpus of ancient scientific writings by demonstrating why seeing the medieval library with fresh eyes mattered for a more comprehensive and historical understanding of antiquity. His highly publicized discoveries of forgotten codices, filled with the precious words of Cicero, Vergil, Livy, and many other Latin authors, inspired other manuscript hunters to imagine what treasures of antiquity awaited them in their quest to learn more from the past. Poggio Bracciolini's famous rediscovery of Lucretius' *On the Nature of Things*, a philosophical poem whose atomistic philosophy offered a radically different account of matter theory from the elemental building blocks of Aristotelian physics, in a monastic library near Lake Constance in 1417 is the best-known example of how these impulses genuinely expanded the Renaissance understanding of ancient science. The result was a new kind of library filled with tantalizingly understudied texts containing many different, even conflicting, and at times controversial explanations of the natural world.

Petrarch's unfulfilled desire to read Greek in order to access this other important intellectual legacy that he knew only indirectly was equally prescient. Already in Petrarch's lifetime Niccolò da Reggio was busy translating the minor works of the great Roman physician Galen from Greek into Latin to increase the stock of medical learning. An unillustrated Greek manuscript of Ptolemy's *Geography* had been found in a monastery in Constantinople as early as 1295, though it would not be translated into Latin until 1406. In Florence Manuel Chrysoloras, who became one of the most famous Greek teachers of this era after arriving in the city in 1397, encouraged his disciples to read Plato in the original. He began but never finished a translation of Ptolemy's *Geography*; the Greek original had been brought to Florence, the same city to which

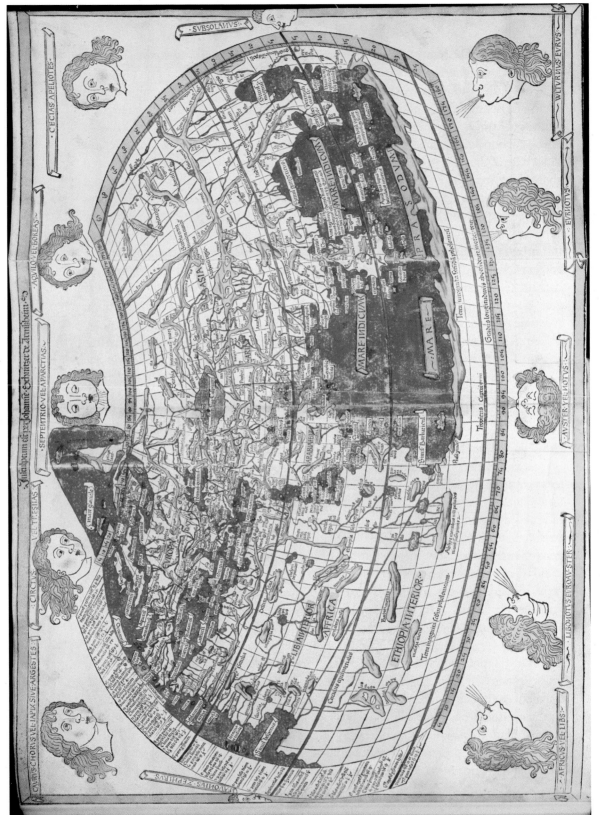

RENAISSANCE EDITION OF PTOLEMY'S *Geography*, 1482.

Poggio returned bearing a codex of Lucretius. Jacopo d'Angelo instead completed this project in 1406, realizing Ptolemy's lost maps from his calculations.

These early successes encouraged scholars to expand the search for scientific manuscripts. Around 1405, Giovanni Aurispa returned from Constantinople bearing codices containing the most important botanical works of antiquity by Aristotle's disciple Theophrastus; his philosophical interrogation of the nature of plants and rules of taxonomic classification, inspired by Aristotle's influential works on animals, stimulated new interest in botany as a scientific pursuit rather than its practical role as an important branch of pharmacy. Even the Latin writings of antiquity occasionally survived to a greater degree in the Eastern seat of the ancient Roman Empire than in Rome itself. In 1426 Guarino of Verona discovered the Roman Celsus' surgical work during a trip to Constantinople where he also found a copy of Strabo's *Geography*, which he later translated. By the 1440s early humanist geographers were correcting Strabo's understanding of the known world. Pappus on mathematics, Manilius on astronomy, Vitruvius on architecture and engineering, Frontinus on aqueducts and hydraulics are but a few examples of authors who emerged into view. Petrarch's dream of accessing a much broader range of ancient learning in their original languages was on the verge of becoming a reality.

The central role of the Italian city-states in these developments encouraged northern European scholars to travel south to be at the epicentre of this intellectual movement. In 1417, the year in which Poggio rediscovered Lucretius' influential account of ancient atomism, a learned German cleric, Nicholas of Cusa (c.1401–64), left Heidelberg to complete his studies in Padua; he would later become a cardinal, papal legate to Germany, and Bishop of Brixen. Profoundly attracted to Platonic philosophy, Euclidean geometry, Ptolemaic astronomy, and eventually Archimedean physics, Nicholas hoped to soak up the new kind of learning he associated with northern and central Italy. He wanted to learn Greek. Padua was another early centre for Greek studies. As the principal university of the Venetian Republic, whose commercial empire stretched throughout the Greek-speaking eastern Mediterranean, Padua attracted scholars such as Nicholas who considered it a cosmopolitan centre of learning. Unlike Florence, Padua also maintained a strong scholastic tradition. Paduan philosophers pioneered new approaches to Aristotelian thought that emerged from reading the original Aristotle and his late antique commentators, coupled with a decided (and not uncontroversial) preference for the medieval commentaries of Averroes. They emphasized the importance of separating philosophy from theology as two distinctly different ways of apprehending the world over the power of the Thomist synthesis of the two.

Nicholas, however, did not follow this path. He participated in one of the most important Renaissance critiques of Aristotelianism by exploring the possibilities of a Platonic worldview. The Greek science that Nicholas imbibed with great fervour was mathematical. He began with Plato and Euclid, and enriched his understanding of Greek mathematics, physics, and astronomy as the list of authors he read grew. Later in life, dedicating one of his mathematical works to Nicholas V in 1453, Nicholas could not contain his excitement at seeing the recent Latin translation of Archimedes commissioned by the pope. Becoming a Neoplatonist was certainly a reason to reject Aristotle's complete disregard for the power of mathematical reasoning. Let us keep in mind that Raphael's *School of Athens* gave Plato the understanding of the divine while limiting Aristotle's significance to the realm of human reason. Plato's *Timaeus* was already well known in the Middle Ages, but access to the full range of Plato's writings was a product of the Renaissance. Nicholas knew far less of Plato than the Florentine physician and philosopher Marsilio Ficino (1433–99), who translated Plato under Cosimo de' Medici's patronage in the 1460s and completed the project of fully harmonizing Platonic thought with Christianity in his *Platonic Theology* (1473). Yet his generation was the first to experiment with the possibilities of a Platonic worldview.

Fundamentally, Nicholas wished to understand nature according to a new logic. This act of intellectual iconoclasm inspired him to write *On Learned Ignorance* (1440). Composed during his return from Constantinople, as part of the papal embassy accompanying the Byzantine emperor, Greek patriarch, and their numerous delegates in the wake of a temporarily successful campaign to reunify Eastern and Western Christianity at the Council of Florence (1439), Nicholas's *On Learned Ignorance* was a manifesto for a new age. It invited readers to acknowledge the limits of the human mind while contemplating the vastness of infinity; for Nicholas, professing ignorance was the first step in achieving wisdom. Nicholas's cosmology was deeply theological, mathematical, and philosophical. He rejected a finite, qualitative universe in the belief that God, in allowing mankind to imagine something as unbounded as infinity, created an expansive world with far greater subtlety and complexity than Aristotle ever imagined. Almost as an aside, Nicholas suggested but offered no definitive proof, mathematical or otherwise, of the possibility of a heliocentric universe. Copernicus would take up this theme in the early sixteenth century.

Cardinal Nicholas's willingness to rethink absolutely everything inspired his dialogue on *The Layman* (1450)—literally an *idiota* in Greek—in which an ordinary man shows an orator and a philosopher how to think about the universe in new ways. Despite the fact that he was the younger contemporary of a highly literate and enquiring physician's daughter, Christine de Pizan (c.1364–c.1430), whose *Book of the City of Ladies* (1405) celebrated women's learning and accomplishments, it did not occur to him to include women among the participants in his dialogue. This was a theoretical exercise in the nature of knowledge with an explicit purpose. Nicholas sought to break the boundaries of traditional scholastic learning, by contrasting this approach to the lessons of experience. He proposed a mechanics no longer derived solely from the pages of Aristotle and his commentators but found in the daily pull of the lever and turning of the Archimedean screw. Surely Nicholas agreed with the early fourteenth-century Florentine preacher who proclaimed that in his age—the era of the compass, portolan, eyeglasses, and mechanical clock—'the finding of arts will never come to an end'. What might the craftsman who worked closely, even intimately, with nature understand that the scholar did not?

It is tempting to see this development in Nicholas's natural philosophy as a product of his experience of Florence more than Padua. The role of artisans—the 'man without letters', to invoke Leonardo da Vinci's (1452–1519) famous self-description—in shaping new approaches to science was an important development in Renaissance science, strongly connecting making with knowing. Thus, by the middle of the fifteenth century two different strands of Renaissance thought began to intertwine. On the one hand, the writings of the ancients were an important source of ideas about how to interpret nature, inspiring new levels of scholarship and translation. On the other hand, there was a growing respect for the kind of experiential knowledge of nature possessed by artisans. The challenges to the Aristotelian worldview began to multiply.

How to experience the world

By the time Nicholas of Cusa wrote about the value of experience, the artisanal culture of the prosperous commercial cities in Italy and northern Europe had begun to produce new kinds of craftsmen—articulate, literate, and increasingly conscious of their status. Just before 1400, a Paduan painter named Cennino d'Andrea Cennini wrote a handbook called *The Book of Art*, filled with instructions about how to extract colour from plants and minerals to produce the most desirable pigments, how to make ink from charred animal bones, how to affix colour to a freshly plastered wall so that its brilliant hues might never fade or blur, and numerous other details of the painter's craft. Cennini presented painting as a 'science' made by hand, an alchemy of materials in which experience was the basis for knowledge. This was hardly Aristotle's definition of *scientia*—certain and universal knowledge—but instead advocated an emerging concept of science as *technique* (what the Greeks called *techne*), generated by making things from nature. The shops of numerous Renaissance cities were teaming with artisans who knew how to produce paper and ink, work with glass, metal, and marble, transform animal by-products into wool and leather, cultivate silkworms, process cotton, refine sugar, and combine the most exotic ingredients that nature could offer into apothecaries' confections. They knew a lot about nature and they began to record their knowledge to transmit it beyond the workshop. In an age in which practical literacy became more common in the most prosperous commercial cities, the 'how-to' book was born. The intersection between the humanistic quest for a scientific antiquity and the ambitions of learned craftsmen shaped key elements of Renaissance science: most importantly, the desire to make knowledge through a fruitful combination of a theoretical and practical knowledge. Perhaps Nicholas even knew of this otherwise obscure painter who composed *The Book of Art*?

In the early fifteenth century an ambitious Florentine humanist named Leon Battista Alberti (1404–72) boldly transformed the painter's practice of linear perspective which emerged in Tuscany around the beginning of the century into the science of perspective (*perspectiva*). Alberti's *On Painting*—published initially in Latin for learned patrons and humanists in 1435 and then in Italian to appeal to less educated readers in

1436—exemplified the new kind of thinking about science that Nicholas had in mind when he expressed the hope that natural philosophy might matter not only in the classroom but to society at large. Alberti's treatise on painting was a product of an intense dialogue between theory and practice. It also was a blueprint for a generation that no longer felt simply dissatisfied with Aristotle but revelled in their ability to create something new with the ingredients of the past. While lamenting the loss of many things known in antiquity, including a full understanding of ancient geometry at least in Western Europe, Alberti celebrated his own age for overcoming this deficit by giving birth to 'new arts and sciences'. He was no longer thinking of late medieval inventions but emphasized the knowledge that arose from the rebirth of ancient science. One of these subjects was perspective. Skilfully combining elements of art and science, it exemplified the kind of novelty that Alberti had in mind when he imagined his own age surpassing antiquity.

If Aristotle belonged primarily to the schools, Euclidean geometry and its way of perceiving the world as a combination of points, lines, and surfaces emerged in multiple contexts. A number of Renaissance paintings depict Euclidean diagrams but

JACOPO DE' BARBARI, attributed, *Portrait of Luca Pacioli*, 1495.

none is more famous than the portrait of the Franciscan mathematician Luca Pacioli (c.1447–1517), whose *Divine Proportion* (1509) was illustrated with engravings 'drawn by the divine left hand of my friend Leonardo of Florence'. This portrait captures Pacioli's reputation immediately after the publication of his *Summa of Arithmetic, Geometry, Proportions, and Proportionality* (1494). Pacioli is celebrated as the new Euclid, demonstrating a problem in the *Elements of Geometry* (book 12) for an aristocratic pupil. A polyhedron hangs from the ceiling. Pacioli's left hand directs viewers to exactly the right page in Euclid, but his *Summa* is in the foreground, challenging Euclid's authority. This iconic portrait of a Renaissance mathematician is not only a tribute to the power and prestige of his subject, but also an artistic demonstration of the application of geometry to perspective. When we look at Pacioli, we see the importance of geometry to grasping the world.

Pacioli's portrait belongs to the mature phase of the renaissance of mathematics but we should begin by considering how we got here. Giovanni Campani's thirteenth-century translation of the Arabic version of Euclid arose in the context of the commercial success of the Italian city-states and their discovery of the sophisticated mathematical practices of the medieval Islamic world that they encountered throughout the Mediterranean. The growth of commercial arithmetic in the late Middle Ages stimulated an investment in mathematical education, encouraging merchants to absorb and master the best practices of Arabic mathematicians in order to do business. Inevitably, this interest transcended purely practical concerns about calculation to encompass the full range of mathematical traditions in the medieval Islamic world, including Euclidean geometry.

Before Pacioli became the most famous mathematician of the fifteenth century, a Pisan merchant's son, Leonardo Fibonacci (c.1170–c.1250), recorded all that he had learned for the benefit of his society in his *Book of the Abacus* (1202). His lengthy residence in North Africa exposed him to the *modus Indianus*—the Hindu-Arabic numbering system and its use of decimals and algebraic functions to facilitate large, quick, and complex calculations in contrast to the more cumbersome Roman numeral system. Fibonacci's textbook complemented a new pedagogical interest in the quadrivium (geometry, arithmetic, astronomy, and music) in relation to the trivium (grammar, rhetoric, and logic). During the next two centuries northern and central Italian cities employed 'masters of the abacus' (*maestri d'abbaco*) in the belief that numeracy was essential to their prosperity. By the fifteenth century Hindu-Arabic numerals had become the norm, and mathematical notations such as +, −, and × were in the process of being introduced. The humanist enthusiasm for the rediscovery of the Greek mathematical tradition should not blind us to the fact that the Renaissance revival of mathematics began, first and foremost, with a pragmatic appreciation of the transformation of Greek mathematics in the medieval Islamic world and their invention of algebra.

One of the most important lessons of commercial mathematics involved how to calculate the relative value of things in proportion to each other, otherwise known as the Rule of Three. Merchant account books of this era are filled with these calculations and numerous abacus treatises survive to impart these skills, including one by the great painter Piero della Francesca (c.1412–92). Young men aspiring to take their place in the trading houses, commercial partnerships, and banks, and on the ships that made long-distance trade possible, learned how to handle different currencies, weights, and measures since there were no universal standards of measurement. Observing numerical differences, converting, and resolving them were daily habits in a society that invented marine insurance, bills of exchange, and double-entry bookkeeping (a crucial element of Pacioli's textbook, for which he is still celebrated today as the father of modern accounting). Mathematics was also embedded in a new technology that began to proliferate in the fourteenth century—the public clocks that emerged in many European cities marking the hours in regularly spaced intervals. Comparing a clock to a compass, the Vatican librarian Giovanni Tortelli observed in 1449 that both contained twenty-four points along a circle. This was truly a calculating society, preoccupied with questions of time, space, and number.

What role did this mathematical mentality play in facilitating, perhaps even encouraging, a new kind of perspective in painting? The geometric sensibilities of Renaissance artists such as Giotto, Masaccio, Brunelleschi, Donatello, Ghiberti, Paolo Uccello, and of course Piero della Francesca are well-known expressions of a highly numerate society that valued what one could do with numbers and proportions. Pacioli considered proportion to be essential for every art and science. Representing the world as a picture intersecting a geometric plane that ended at its vanishing point was one of the creative outcomes of the growing appreciation for Arabic mathematics, Euclidean geometry, and Roman architecture. In order to fully understand the fusion of these different ingredients, we need to see what each contributed to the idea of *perspectiva*.

Zero did not exist in European mathematics before the fourteenth century. Once introduced as a result of increased exposure to Arabic mathematics, it proved useful to anyone who wished to balance accounts, indicate place value, or more abstractly contemplate how to express nothing in number. Much like Nicholas of Cusa's concept of infinity, zero did not easily conform to the Aristotelian image of the universe as a plenum, but mathematics is both a science of the tangibly real and the impossibly ideal; its relationship to natural philosophy was not yet a pressing question for all but a handful of mathematical Neoplatonists. Did the idea of zero need to be in place in order to envision a vanishing point? In the end, we will probably never know, but we can nonetheless contemplate the emergence of a new mathematical culture and a new artistic culture as products of a shared moment that would indeed proclaim the artist to be a new kind of scientist—not only an alchemist of colour in Cennini's formulation but eventually a practising mathematician in the case of Piero della Francesca, whose theoretical engagement with mathematics transcended its utility for his painting, just as Leonardo's anatomical, mechanical, and natural historical investigations went well beyond anything he might need for the handful of paintings he completed.

Before we get to this stage, however, we need to consider the preoccupations of Alberti's generation. Looking at buildings was a great exercise in practical geometry. Florentine artists like Brunelleschi who made the pilgrimage to the Eternal City, much as Petrarch had done in an earlier era, were inspired by Roman ruins to see buildings differently. They built new structures with the principles of Roman architecture in mind and considered the effect to be a radical break with Romanesque and Gothic architecture. This new style found its theoretical expression with Poggio Bracciolini's rediscovery of Vitruvius' *Ten Books on Architecture* in the monastery of St Gall in 1414. Vitruvius made clear how important geometry was to building and surveying, including exercises in geometric projection. Imagining ground zero, where two straight lines reach their point of convergence, was not simply a theoretical possibility but reflected new urban realities inspired by the cultural aesthetics of antiquity. Alberti's fame derived not only from his treatise on painting but his work on architecture, mathematics, and, of course, his humanistic literary writings; his building projects as well as his efforts to present himself as the new Vitruvius made him the necessary complement of the learned artisan, namely, the scholar who did not consider it beneath his dignity to practise a craft, thereby assuring its elevation.

Seeing also was a matter of how theory inspired practice. During the 1380s Biagio Pelacani of Parma gave a series of lectures in Florence on *Questions of Perspective*. The 'perspective' that Biagio taught did not concern artistic representation but focused on the mathematical optics and physics of Alhazen (Ibn al-Haythan, 965–1040), based on a twelfth-century Latin translation of his work. Alhazen's efforts to understand how light worked on the eye, how the eye captured retinal images, and how light might be measured inspired several generations of Renaissance mathematicians, astronomers, and anatomists, including Leonardo who carefully explored Alhazen's findings to develop his own ideas about optics. Alhazen's famous experiments with mirrors offered a concrete example of how to explore a scientific problem through observation. What Alhazen did not do, however, was suggest that his theories might lead to new ideas about vision and new practices of representation. This was a uniquely Renaissance development.

Early fifteenth-century Florentines experimented with Ptolemy's method of placing objects in a theoretically empty space. They abstracted their city to perform this experiment. Combining insights from medieval mathematics and optics with a practical understanding of the value of ancient geometry became a virtuoso demonstration of how to represent the world. It also indicates the ambitions of learned painters even before Leonardo, who called the hand 'the instrument of instruments', to make art scientific. If Euclid established the terms and postulates of geometry and Vitruvius demonstrated the utility of Greek mathematics for building, Ptolemy contributed one final ingredient by making geometric projection essential to the revitalized science of cartography. Leonardo would later compare his anatomy of the body to Ptolemy's ancient map of the world, considering it a parallel investigation to his version of Piero della Francesca's intensive exploration of the body's proportions that culminated

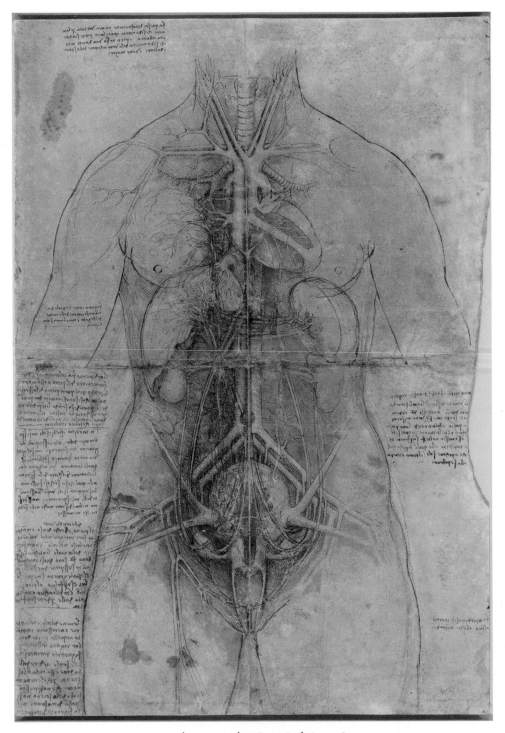

LEONARDO'S FEMALE ANATOMY known as the 'Great Lady,' *c.*1508.

in his Vitruvian man. Thus, a variety of ancient and medieval scientific theories were skilfully converted into new practices shaped by experience, including the rationalization of sight.

More than fifty manuscript copies of Ptolemy's *Geography* survive from the fifteenth century. The city of Florence played no small role in its early diffusion. Nicholas of Cusa discussed Ptolemy with his Paduan classmate Paolo Toscanelli (1397–1482) when he came for the Council of Florence. Toscanelli embodied the new ethos of the scholarly merchant whose fascination with the mathematical sciences was intimately connected with knowledge of the world in which he did business. The Portuguese enquired about Toscanelli's maps in 1474, searching for further information on African routes as they travelled down the west African coast in the early stages of establishing their overseas trading empire. In the following decade, Columbus wrote to the ageing Toscanelli from Seville about the size of the Atlantic to assure himself that the Florentine mathematician's calculations would encourage the Spanish monarchs, Ferdinand of Aragon and Isabella of Castile, to finance his first voyage. If Pacioli challenged Euclid with a mathematics born of the fusion of art and science, Toscanelli convinced many contemporaries that his instruments, maps, and knowledge of mathematics and astronomy made him a worthy heir to Ptolemy.

Less than a decade after Ptolemy's *Geography* was translated into Latin in Florence, roughly between 1413 and 1420, Filippo Brunelleschi (1377–1446) performed his famous experiments with a mirror and a pinhole, using some of the most important public buildings in Florence—the Duomo (to which Toscanelli affixed his gnomon around 1468 to measure the sun's shadow), the Baptistery, and the Palazzo Vecchio—to create two painted panels demonstrating the illusion of reality. Brunelleschi left behind no record of his public demonstration of the power of linear perspective but his biographers immortalized this moment in celebrating his accomplishment as the most ingenious mind of their age. Instead, Alberti explained the implications and transformed it into a Renaissance discipline. Grasping reality with the tools of science and art did indeed bring about a rebirth of knowledge and produce something new. Leonardo would famously declare painting to be a science born of experience, insisting with Alberti that the painter must learn from nature. These lessons were not lost on subsequent generations of Renaissance scholars and artisans.

Creating the scientific library

In the middle of the fifteenth century Greek science seemed to be flourishing everywhere, including Rome. In a sign of how much ground the Eternal City ceded during the prolonged absence of the papacy in Avignon (1309–77) and the unsettled era of the papal schism (1378–1417), the papal library of the early fifteenth century compared unfavourably to its counterparts in Florence, Venice, and many other locations where humanistic learning thrived. When Eugenius IV died in 1443, his library contained precisely two Greek manuscripts.

The years between the conclusion of the Council of Florence, with great hopes for relations between Eastern and Western Christianity, and the Ottoman conquest of Constantinople in 1453, which increased the migration of Greek scholars and their materials to the Italian peninsula, transformed the papal library. In 1455 Nicholas V bequeathed to his successors a papal library of 1160 books; the best-established room in the nascent Vatican Library was the *Bibliotheca Graeca* with 353 Greek manuscripts, a substantial portion of them dealing with philosophical, mathematical, and medical subjects, including the manuscript that inspired the Latin edition of Archimedes praised by Nicholas of Cusa. Nicholas subsequently loaned the Vatican Archimedes to his learned Greek friend Cardinal Bessarion, whose personal library was one of the scholarly marvels of the age.

Bessarion played an important role in encouraging Nicholas V to invest in Greek learning, including its science, since he believed that the world from which he came could no longer maintain these traditions. He ultimately donated his impressive library—almost as large as the papal library and containing over 600 Greek manuscripts—to Venice in 1468, but for the final period of his life he participated in the intellectual rejuvenation of Rome. Wherever Bessarion went, he stimulated the growing appetite for Greek science. In 1460 Bessarion's appointment as the papal legate to Vienna led him to encourage a talented young German mathematics professor and astronomer known as Regiomontanus (Johann Müller, 1436–76) to return to Rome as a member of his household. Regiomontanus had been working closely with his colleague Georg Peurbach (1423–61) to create a better version of Ptolemy's *Almagest*, indeed a new and improved astronomy that more accurately described planetary orbits, but neither of them had access to the Greek original. Bessarion promised Regiomontanus instruction in Greek and invited him to use his scientific manuscripts.

One year later, immersed in the cardinal's library, Regiomontanus encountered the sophisticated mathematics of Euclid and Apollonius, and Archimedean physics in the manuscript that had by now changed hands several times; he copied Jacopo of Cremona's translation praised by Nicholas of Cusa. The two Germans met and agreed on many things, making Regiomontanus one of Nicholas's important collaborators in mounting efforts to reform the Julian calendar whose year (365 days precisely) made the dating of Easter notoriously imprecise. While completing the *Epitome of the Almagest* begun in Vienna with Peurbach after the death of his colleague shortly before the trip to Italy, Regiomontanus deepened his knowledge of Ptolemaic astronomy. By 1464 Regiomontanus' mastery of Greek science was so widely admired that the University of Padua invited him to give an oration in praise of mathematics. On this occasion, Regiomontanus declared with great conviction, 'The theorems of Euclid have the same certainty today as a thousand years ago.' His posthumously published *Five Books on Every Different Kind of Triangle* (1533) helped to establish the science of trigonometry as a Renaissance discipline. Regiomontanus mastered these lessons in Bessarion's household during the era in which Greek studies finally arrived in the Eternal City, along with men of learning in search of opportunities that came with the Renaissance papacy's investment in knowledge as an expression of the power of faith, and the growing recognition that a more precise astronomy could solve an important liturgical problem. The accumulation of manuscripts to support the scholarly work of the curia and custodians to safeguard and shape the business of creating a major library became a significant papal investment. Under Sixtus IV (1471–84), the Vatican Library grew threefold.

The exponential growth of Renaissance libraries provided the impetus for new knowledge to be made from them. During Nicholas V's papacy (1447–55) an ambitious project to create definitive translations of virtually every important Greek scientific authority from the most authentic original versions of these ancient texts, *ad fontes*, began in earnest. No longer satisfied with the thirteenth-century Latin editions of Aristotle's zoological works, Nicholas V commissioned George of Trebizond to retranslate Aristotle in 1449–50. Declaring himself to be dissatisfied with the behaviour of his translator and possibly the result, he asked Theodore Gaza to translate Aristotle anew. By contrast, the disgraced Trebizond's 1451 translation of Ptolemy's *Almagest* from yet another Greek manuscript in the papal library seemed to please his papal sponsor. The application of the humanistic skills of grammar, philology, and rhetoric to new scientific translations by the most passionately humanist mathematicians, natural philosophers, and physicians played an important role in encouraging scholars to believe that they could contribute something new to the shape of knowledge by remaking the old. While Nicholas of Cusa provocatively suggested that ignorance was the first step in knowing anything, he knew that a good library was the key to knowing more.

Back in Florence, other projects were under way to rival the ambitions of papal Rome. Under the patronage of Cosimo de' Medici, Florence had become a city of great libraries in the 1440s and 1450s. Housed in the important monasteries of San Marco and San Lorenzo as well as in the private homes of leading humanists and, of course, the savvy banker who lived in Palazzo Medici, they attracted considerable attention and admiration. Cosimo kept the leading Florentine bookseller Vespasiano da Bisticci busy churning out manuscript copies to please his patron; rulers such as the Duke of Urbino, whose library had one of the best collections of Greek mathematical texts outside Venice, and of course Nicholas V, did business with Vespasiano, in part because he earned Cosimo's approval. The result was a truly manuscript-rich culture filled with sophisticated and knowledgeable readers in search of important texts that would further test their skills and potentially answer their questions.

Assembling the complete corpus of Platonic writings to produce a new translation was Cosimo's most spectacular project of intellectual patronage. Throughout the 1460s Ficino carefully rendered Plato into Latin for the Medici as the signature accomplishment of a group of scholars who considered themselves members of a new Platonic Academy. In 1463, however, Ficino interrupted this task to translate an enigmatic text of great antiquity, attributed to an Egyptian priest named Hermes Trismegistus who was believed to have prophesied the coming of Christ. In reality, the *Corpus Hermeticum* was a late antique example of Christian mystical Neoplatonism, though this fact was not widely known before Isaac Casaubon debunked its greater antiquity in 1614. The discovery of the 'Thrice-Great Hermes' gave credence to the idea that magic, astrology, and alchemy were crucial sciences that belonged to the origins of the quest to understand man's relationship with the cosmos. Knowledge was no longer a matter of rational epistemology but an ecstatic journey into the esoteric wisdom of Egypt that pre-dated even Plato yet seemed compatible with Christian doctrine. The idea of the Renaissance magus—a quasi-divine figure with absolute dominion over nature bridging the celestial and terrestrial worlds with his powers—was born.

Inspired by these developments, a young Pico della Mirandola (1463–94) resolved to probe ever deeper into the ancient past, complementing his knowledge of Greek with the study of Hebrew to learn the secrets of the Jewish Cabbala, followed by some Arabic. His quest for original wisdom (*prisca sapientia*) boldly attempted to unify different strands of knowledge by searching for universal truths hidden in numbers, signs, and characters. Pico believed that the most powerful insights of natural philosophy lay in these arcana. The task of the Renaissance magus was to crack the code. In his *Oration on the Dignity of Man* (1486) Pico ecstatically proclaimed the freedom of the human intellect. The exuberant paganism of his philosophy, in contrast to the more measured and systematic exploration of the relationship between the natural and the supernatural in Ficino's Neoplatonic philosophy, represented a worrisome development for the Roman Catholic Church. In 1487 Innocent VIII roundly condemned the most controversial of the 900 theses which the 23-year-old Pico brashly presented in Rome in his *Conclusions* (1486). This was one of the unanticipated offshoots of Renaissance Neoplatonism that made natural magic one of the important scientific disciplines of the sixteenth century. Henry Cornelius Agrippa's *Three Books on Occult Philosophy* (1531–3) brought together these esoteric traditions under the broad category of 'occult philosophy', while the Neapolitan magus Giambattista della Porta composed a *Natural Magic* (1558) filled with experiments demonstrating the variety of ways in which nature was transformed by human ingenuity.

During the period in which the magical, mystical, and occult sections of the Renaissance library expanded, scholars and patrons began to consider new ways to distribute ancient scientific texts and disseminate their own work. In 1471 a partially printed edition of the Hermetic Corpus appeared. The thirst for knowledge in the century before the invention of the printing press encouraged late medieval innovations in paper—far more affordable if less durable than costly vellum made of animal skin—followed by the development of a new technology to distribute words and images. Transforming the Renaissance scientific library into a printed corpus became a collective project of European scholars and printers between roughly the 1460s and the 1530s.

Printing scientific books

Contemplating the effects of printing on the production of knowledge around 1466, Alberti praised 'the German inventor who in these times has made it possible, by certain pressings down of characters, to have more than two hundred volumes written out in a hundred days from an original, with the labor of no more than three men; for with only one downwards pressure a large sheet is written out'. The German goldsmith and engraver Johannes Gutenberg (*c.*1397/1400–1468) and his partners in this new enterprise began to print books around 1450, after a decade of experiments with movable type and a screw press between Strasbourg and Mainz. By 1470 nineteen German and Italian cities had printing presses; this number grew to more than 250 European cities and towns by 1500, when anywhere between six and fifteen million printed books were already in circulation. The quantity multiplied more than tenfold by 1600 to over 150 million, with growing numbers of books appearing in different vernacular languages to reach larger audiences who did not have the full benefit of a humanist education but were eager to read and learn.

To this list we should also add a variety of other kinds of printed materials, from inexpensively produced woodcuts and broadsheets to the elaborate copperplate engravings innovated especially by the Nuremberg artist Albrecht Dürer (1471–1528), and ultimately a wide variety of paper instruments, including astrolabes, sundials, quadrants, compasses, maps, globes, geometric shapes, and paper bodies whose

HANS HOLBEIN, *Portrait of Nicolaus Kratzer*, 1528.

parts could be assembled by cutting them out and gluing them together. In 1520, for example, Nicolaus Kratzer (c.1487–1530), court astronomer to Henry VIII and professor of astronomy and geography at Oxford, asked Dürer to send all of his engravings as well as anything related to instrument-making, for which this son of a Bavarian sawsmith was renowned. Hans Holbein's 1528 portrait depicts Kratzer holding a pair of dividers and an unfinished polyhedral sundial in his study, which is a room filled with mathematical instruments, perhaps even the distance-measuring device Kratzer asked Dürer to design for him in 1524. This is also a place for making books. Dürer hoped to see Kratzer's German translation of Euclid reach completion so that he might learn from it, being unable to read the Latin. Needless to say, Nuremberg was an important Renaissance centre for printing as well as art and instrument-making. Printing made the scientific book a more artisanal project, even as it captured mechanically the humanist preoccupations of Renaissance scholars.

The rapid diffusion of the printing press by no means signalled the end of manuscript culture. Reflecting on the results of several decades of printing, the learned Abbot of Sponheim Johannes Trithemius (1462–1516), known for his work on cryptography and other arcane secrets of knowledge, completed a treatise *In Praise of Scribes* (1494). He considered the printed book ephemeral in comparison with the enduring products of the scriptorium, declaring, 'The printed book is made of paper and, like paper, will quickly disappear.' Trithemius reflected a conservative view of an emerging technology, but he also highlights the ongoing appreciation for manuscript culture. Many works were never printed; some were simply too arcane, technical, or controversial to circulate widely. The considerable investment involved in printing a book also limited production. Scholars continued to copy and excerpt printed works and personalized their reading of the printed page by filling it with marginalia. The Renaissance library evolved with these developments, becoming a repository of different kinds of books— scribally produced texts, the mechanical products of 'artificial writing', and hybrid artefacts combining script, print, and hand-coloured illustrations.

Printing increased the size and scope of the Renaissance library. The question of which books to print reflected the commercial value of different kinds of knowledge. The Aristotelian corpus was printed over and over again. More Latin commentaries on Aristotle were written—and printed—after 1500 than in the millennium before. Let us return to the moment when Gaza completed his state-of-the-art translation of Aristotle's books on animals in 1473–4. By then it was possible to consider two different outcomes—a splendidly illuminated and rubricated manuscript for Sixtus IV and a printed version, designed to rival the recent Paduan edition of the medieval Latin Aristotle (1472–4) with Averroes' commentary. Gaza's 1476 version published in Venice, based on his impeccable Greek philology, was considered more authoritative, but both competed in the new marketplace for printed books. Similarly, Gaza's translation of Theophrastus' botanical writings in 1453–4 enjoyed a second life with its publication in Venice in 1483. Ficino's translations of Plato appeared in 1484.

Publishing the corpus of ancient science and medicine was one of the great intellectual and commercial projects of the late fifteenth and early sixteenth centuries. Johannes Speier, the first German printer to set up shop in Venice, printed Pliny the Elder's *Natural History* in 1469. As a sign of its importance to a variety of readers compared with more specialized scientific books, an Italian translation appeared in 1476; within two decades there were twenty-two printings of this Roman encyclopedia. Approximately 200 medieval manuscripts of Pliny's *Natural History* survive, making it a medieval bestseller, but this pales in comparison with the number of printed copies in circulation by 1500, let alone by 1600 when fifty-five editions were in print. Printing put this book and the knowledge it contained in the hands of many people; by the 1490s physicians and humanists furiously debated why Pliny's encyclopedia contained numerous errors, attributing them to scribal error, Pliny's poor knowledge of Greek, and ultimately his preference for synthesizing what was known and described by others rather than observing things for himself. This was the kind of Renaissance reading that inspired the creation of new books about the natural world.

Renaissance readers also wanted greater access to newly rediscovered texts. The first printed version of Lucretius' *On the Nature of Things* appeared in 1473; by 1600 there were thirty different editions competing with numerous manuscript copies in circulation. Lucretius was not as widely read as Pliny, but he was nonetheless well read. Ficino supposedly found reading Lucretius liberating, but then regretted and allegedly destroyed his writings inspired by it. Machiavelli annotated a copy around 1500, drawing the following conclusion from his encounter with the ancient doctrine of atomism: 'motion is variable, and from this we have free will.' We can only wonder what Pico might have done with this theory of random colliding bits of matter, had he lived longer. A Florentine church council attempted to ban reading Lucretius in 1517, but there was no stopping the flow of manuscript and print copies.

The importance of geometry encouraged a Venetian printer to publish Giovanni Campani's thirteenth-century translation of the Arabic Euclid in 1482. Two hundred and fourteen mathematics books were printed in Italy alone by 1500. The 1482 edition of Euclid was the first mathematics book to overcome the technical difficulties of printing diagrams since images were essential to geometry. This is surely the copy in Pacioli's 1495 portrait, since a new Latin translation from the Greek wasn't printed until 1505. Here we are reminded of another important fact about the Renaissance library— it was filled with medieval manuscripts, some of which became printed books. The traditional image of Renaissance science rejecting outright its medieval precedents is unsustainable when we pay attention to how many medieval scientific and medical works appeared in print. The Aristotelian commentaries of Albertus Magnus (not to mention a popular scholastic sex manual on *The Secrets of Women* attributed to the learned thirteenth-century Dominican), the medical and alchemical writings of Arnau of Villanova and Ramon Llull, the natural and experimental philosophy of Roger Bacon, and the *Sphere* of Sacrobosco (John of Holywood), which instructed students in mathematical astronomy for four centuries, were among the well-read medieval books on the Renaissance shelf.

Of all the ancient works of science rediscovered in the fifteenth century, Ptolemy's *Geography* best exemplifies how printing an ancient work of science became the foundation for new kinds of knowledge. In Istanbul the disgraced George of Trebizond composed a preface to an updated Arabic version dedicated to Sultan Mehmet II in 1465, leading Paul II to briefly imprison him when he returned to Rome the following year, since a fifteenth-century map was a truly precious commodity not to be shared with other rulers who might use it to advance their own interests. At the same time, Ptolemy's *Geography* was simply too important to circulate only in manuscript once printing became a possibility. In 1475 printers in Cologne and Vicenza published the Latin translation but did not rise to the challenge of including maps; a Bolognese printer corrected this deficiency in 1477, printing a version with twenty-six engravings. The next two centuries saw over fifty editions of this book, accompanying the explosion of printed maps and descriptions of different lands by Renaissance cosmographers, geographers, and cartographers. Instead, the technical details of Ptolemy's astronomy and astrology were primarily for specialists. Gerard of Cremona's twelfth-century Latin translation from an Arabic version of Ptolemy's *Almagest* was published in 1515. A new translation from Greek did not appear until 1528, making it clear which Ptolemy the majority of Renaissance readers were most eager to read.

With the exception of Pliny's encyclopedia of nature and Aristotle's zoological writings, the earliest works of natural history revealed an overwhelming concern with the medicinal uses of nature. They were the ultimate how-to guides, works of reference for patients as much as practitioners. The first printed Latin edition of the Greek physician Dioscorides' *On Medical Materials*, the most important guide to the medical uses of Mediterranean plants and, to a lesser degree, animals and minerals, appeared in 1478. That same year a popular German book on distillation rolled off the presses. While Dioscorides initially was unillustrated—fulfilling Pliny's view that illustrating nature was a dubious and uncertain enterprise that rarely translated well from one copy to another, relative to written description—popular herbals, beginning with the German *Herbarius* (1485) and the influential *Garden of Health* (1491), began to experiment with woodcuts of plants. These rough-hewn images paled in comparison with the sophisticated techniques in painting and watercolour, refined especially by Leonardo and Dürer, to depict the fine-grained detail of the natural world, rendering even a lowly blade of grass seemingly animate. Early printed images of animals— including Dürer's iconic 1515 engraving of the rhinoceros brought by the Portuguese from India to Lisbon, which famously depicts an exotic animal he never saw—also lacked the subtlety and complexity of efforts to paint living examples from nature. The question of how to replicate nature became one of the technological challenges of the Renaissance. Leonardo was famously sceptical about printing as the best way to convey visual knowledge. Instead, he and his disciples experimented with nature

ALBRECHT DÜRER, *Great Piece of Turf*, 1503.

ALBRECHT DÜRER, *Hare*, 1502.

printing, pressing inked leaves on the page, but they never attempted to make the results mechanically reproducible.

By the end of the fifteenth century many well-known scientific and medical texts were in print. In 1490 the medieval translation of Galen's known medical works appeared. A year later, a Venetian publisher created a medical compendium of useful medieval and early Renaissance books of the body known as the *Fasciculus medicinae* (1491), edited by Johan de Ketham. It included Mondino de' Liuzzi's *Anatomy* (1316), whose anatomical textbook shaped the institutional understanding of what one could learn from dissection for two centuries. The *Fasciculus* found its way into numerous Renaissance libraries, both in the Latin original and in Italian translation. One woodcut in the 1494 edition entitled 'Figure of the uterus of a woman from nature'—the first printed image of any internal organ based on personal observation—famously inspired Leonardo's reworking this image around 1508.

This Renaissance medical compendium was one of the books in Leonardo's library, which grew from 37 books around 1495–7 to a total of 116 books by the end of 1503. Leonardo possessed many staples of the late medieval library, including an abacus treatise, a lapidary, books by the surgeon Rhazes (al-Razi, 854–925) and Albertus Magnus, Isidore of Seville's *Etymologies*, Goro Dati's *On the Sphere*, and Roberto Valturio's *On Warfare*. He had popular ancient works of science, including Pliny's *Natural History* and Ptolemy's *Geography*, and more recent works such as the fifteenth-century physician Ugo Benzi's *On the Preservation of Health*, and a book on one of the most controversial topics of the Renaissance, *On the Immortality of the Soul*. This list of books hardly explains how Leonardo transcended his professional apprenticeship as a painter to become a curious, enquiring, if erratically educated scientific mind by 1500, nor does it fully encompass all the subjects he investigated with pen in hand. Instead, exploring Leonardo's library helps us to understand how the early decades of printing expanded access to knowledge.

Leonardo absorbed a great deal of the Renaissance library that took shape across the fifteenth century. The same can also be said of the handful of women humanists who belonged to this generation. Laura Cereta (1469–99) of Brescia and Cassandra Fedele (1465–1558) of Venice were celebrated for their ability to read ancient languages and their knowledge of astronomy and natural philosophy. They left behind a scant record of what knowing science did for them, though Cereta repackaged a number of medical and cosmetic recipes lifted from Pliny in her *Collected Letters* (1488). Fundamentally, they demonstrated that women, if educated, were capable of understanding science. Knowing something of natural philosophy was part of a humanist education, even for those who had no desire to contribute to scientific knowledge. The significance of this potential audience of consumers of scientific knowledge was not lost on scientific practitioners and their publishers. They began to consider which kinds of books bridged the gap between the classical library of science and the interests of Renaissance readers, both male and female.

Another contemporary of Leonardo—Caterina Sforza (1463–1509)—sheds greater light on the active roles that Renaissance women played in the practical dimensions of scientific knowledge. In the late fifteenth century Sforza established a laboratory and a herb garden in the small town of Imola that she ruled, as regent of Forlì and Imola, after the assassination of her husband, Girolamo Riario, in 1488. Corresponding with her apothecary, her confessor, a Roman cosmetics maker known as 'Anna the Jewess', the abbess of the Florentine convent of Le Murate famed for its nun-apothecaries, and contacts at various Renaissance courts, she embarked on an energetic programme of experimentation that resulted in her manuscript book of *Experiments*; bequeathed to her son, it eventually became the possession of her grandson, the future Grand Duke of Florence, Cosimo I de' Medici, and the women in this family. Sforza recorded many secrets in a mixture of Latin and Italian, including remedies for a wide variety of ailments such as plague, epilepsy, gout, catarrhs, and syphilis; how to make poisons, antidotes, unguents, beauty secrets, vivid colours, elixirs to prolong life, alchemical transmutations of metals; and two perennial favourites of Renaissance rulers—how to counterfeit coins and mix good gunpowder. She invited anyone who consulted her over 500-page manuscript to add to it if they discovered anything worthy of inclusion.

Sforza's long forgotten *Experiments* reminds us of the limits of the Renaissance library in telling us everything we want to know about the evolution of science in the fifteenth century. Where did she get her ideas for these experiments? Late medieval and Renaissance recipe books and 'books of secrets' had no especially ancient pedigree since they were inspired more by artisanal and alchemical forms of writing. They circulated primarily in manuscript among courts, households, monasteries, and pharmacies. Printed versions would be attributed to an eclectic variety of authors from Albertus Magnus (who never wrote but became famous for his *Book of Secrets*, a popular work of mineralogy and gemology) to the mysterious Alessio Piemontese, whose *Secrets* (1555) became a late sixteenth-century bestseller (seventy editions by 1599) and the probably fictitious Isabella Cortese, whose gender lent greater authority to the medical and beauty secrets published under her name in Venice in 1561. Sforza's *Experiments* offers an interesting example of a new genre of scientific writing that was further transformed by its encounter with the marketplace for print. Like the fourteenth- and fifteenth-century physicians who recorded their most interesting case histories by writing them down so that medical practitioners and families of the deceased might benefit from this knowledge, she did not rush into print, initially envisioning a select audience for her experiments.

The profusion of printed materials encouraged the writing of new works of natural philosophy, mathematics, astronomy, medicine, natural history, natural magic, astrology, and alchemy, fundamentally changing the nature of scientific knowledge. As people increasingly saw the advantages of publishing what they knew, especially when that knowledge transcended the portrait of nature etched in the writings of long-dead authors, they began to think of the printed book as a medium in which to present fresh observations and new ideas, to repackage old concepts for new audiences, and to establish a public reputation as a new kind of scientific authority. Scientific and medical books would change dramatically by the late sixteenth century, including growing numbers of books published in vernacular languages and vernacular translations of ancient and medieval authors so that Latin was no longer a barrier to knowledge. The starting point, however, was the rebirth of the medieval codex, filled with the most cherished ideas of antiquity and the labour of medieval translators and commentators, as a Renaissance printed book.

The languages of science

In his forties Leonardo famously composed Latin word lists to shore up his shaky vocabulary in an ancient language he was trying to learn. No similar vocabularies exist in the approximately 6,000 surviving pages of his notebooks in Greek or any other scholarly language. As the limits of Leonardo's learning suggest, there were many different renaissances of science at work in the same moment. Leonardo's scientific renaissance rested on a strong foundation of medieval learning brought into print, combined with access to aspects of ancient science, medicine, and engineering considered especially valuable by his society, such as Euclidean geometry, Vitruvian architecture, Pliny's natural history and Ptolemy's cartography, and the new kind of vernacular scientific literacy that inspired artisans to write more. Perhaps he learned some Ptolemaic astronomy. The printed version of Peurbach and Regiomontanus' *Epitome of the Almagest*, a textbook essential for Copernicus' intellectual development, appeared in 1496. Leonardo claimed not to value 'abbreviators of works', however, revealing a humanistic preference for the original. Yet there were limits to how far Leonardo could pursue this project, which is why he read Ketham's medical compendium in translation. He could not participate in the culminating episode of publishing the fifteenth-century library, which saw the printing of many scientific books in the original Greek.

In the late fifteenth century the Bolognese medical professor Alessandro Benedetti (*c.*1450–1512) proclaimed anatomy to be a profoundly Greek subject. He decried numerous errors in medieval anatomy and deplored the use of 'barbarous terms' to describe the human body. Benedetti belonged to a generation of humanist physicians who envisioned anatomy as a revived Greek science performed in a Vitruvian theatre purged of any trace of Arabic influence. The Latinized Arabic vocabulary in Mondino's *Anatomy*, translations of Islamic medical authorities such as Rhazes and Avicenna, and other medieval medical works seemed as appalling to him as Pliny's imperfect knowledge of Greek. Such sentiments were widely shared by physicians and natural philosophers of his generation who came of age during the expansion of the Ottoman Empire and the rise of Greek studies in Western Europe. The most classically minded scholars believed that definitive Greek editions were essential to a true renaissance of knowledge because they would facilitate a new language of science. They wanted to speak of body, nature, and cosmos in Greek.

Scholars who travelled in the eastern Mediterranean or otherwise had contact with the Levant recognized that Greek learning was a shared legacy. They found Renaissance Greeks woefully ignorant of their ancient heritage—unable to identify a single medical plant named by Galen or Dioscorides, as the French apothecary Pierre Belon tartly observed in 1553, returning from Egypt via Crete—in contrast with the scholarly communities in Cairo, Damascus, Aleppo, and Istanbul or the learned Jewish scholars throughout Iberia and the Mediterranean who often brokered knowledge between cultures. The irony of adapting Latinized Arabic mathematical terms—algebra, algorithm, zenith, and zero, to name only a few—to advance European mathematical learning, while dismissing the value of Islamic medicine and natural philosophy, did not escape them; certainly, it complicates the rhetoric of a long scientific 'Dark Age' perpetuated by the most fervent scientific and medical humanists invested in the glory of their own renaissance.

In 1494 Aldus Manutius (1449–1519) established a printing shop in Venice with the explicit goal of creating a new standard for the humanistic book, including Greek editions of the most important scientific and medical works of antiquity. The Aldine edition of Aristotle appeared between 1495 and 1498, accompanied by Theophrastus' botanical works (1497) and Dioscorides' medical botany (1499). Two of Galen's works followed in 1500, suggesting the degree to which medical professors and their students encouraged these publications. One of Aldus' collaborators was Niccolò Leoniceno (1428–1524), then teaching medicine and philosophy at the University of Padua, where he insisted that his students read Aristotle in Greek. Leoniceno's library was not as large as Cardinal Bessarion's, but it was a considerable and well-chosen collection for a professor of medicine: 345 volumes, 117 of them in Greek. The Florentine physician Antonio Benivieni (1443–1502) had a very respectable library of 175 volumes, yet only six were in Greek, putting Leoniceno at the intellectual avant-garde of his generation. Leoniceno's *On the Errors in Medicine of Pliny and Many Other Medical Practitioners* (1492) demonstrated why reading Theophrastus, Galen, and Dioscorides in the original mattered to the advancement of knowledge.

Reflecting the gradual transition from manuscript to print, 167 of Leoniceno's books were codices, including Greek manuscripts of Euclid, Proclus, Theon, Ptolemy (his astronomy, astrology, and geography), Aristotle, Theophrastus, Dioscorides, and Galen. Virtually every significant scientific manuscript was in Leoniceno's library and Aldus understood the value of this collection. Leoniceno's Aristotelian manuscripts helped him establish the definitive version of Aristotle in print, just as the Ferrarese physician's copy of Galen's *On the Usefulness of the Parts of the Body* became the basis for the printed text in the 1525 edition of Galen's works published by Aldus' heirs. The next year the Aldine Hippocrates (1526) appeared.

In the following decade the humanist presses of northern Europe began to compete with the Aldine publishing project. As a young medical student in Montpellier, the French writer Rabelais edited Hippocrates' *Aphorisms*, published in Lyon in 1537. Greek editions of Euclid and Ptolemy's *Geography* (with an introduction by the renowned Dutch humanist Desiderius Erasmus) were published by Johannes Froben in Basel in 1533, followed by Ptolemy's *Almagest*, a second edition of Galen's works which included his *On Anatomical Procedures* in 1538, and Archimedes in 1544. Both Copernicus and Vesalius consigned their most important works to Basel printers in this period, knowing that they were capable of printing complex, polyglot scientific and medical works with ambitious programmes of illustration, based on the printed books they had seen and read during the 1530s.

In practice, Islamic science and medicine continued to be a source of fresh ideas and perspectives on ancient scientific traditions and an essential part of scientific and medical education, identifying a crucial fault line in the Renaissance project of rethinking the relationship to antiquity. More than thirty editions of Avicenna's *Canon of Medicine* appeared by 1550, including the 1527 translation by Andrea Alpago (d.1522), who learned Arabic in Damascus with the goal of producing an improved Latin edition of Avicenna, while also studying the original works of other well-known Islamic medical authorities such as Rhazes and Ibn al-Nafis. Christian converts such as the

Arabic scholar Leo Africanus (al-Hasan ibn Muhammad al-Wazzan al-Fasi, 1494–1554), who after leaving Rome briefly taught Arabic in Bologna where he also composed an Arabic–Hebrew–Latin medical vocabulary in addition to writing his famous geographic *Description of Africa* published in 1550, ensured a place for this language in the Renaissance universities. Commercial and diplomatic relations between European states and the Ottoman Empire facilitated this parallel investment in the most important language of medieval science and medicine that was also the written language of Ottoman scholarship, allowing a small group of European scholars to use these skills to deepen their understanding of Islamic science and medicine. Heirs to Pico's dream of universal knowledge such as Guillaume Postel (1510–81), who after several years in Istanbul did not understand how one could access the secrets of nature without learning Arabic, provide crucial evidence of an alternative vision of humanism, which considered every language associated with a distinguished intellectual tradition to be essential to the pursuit of knowledge.

Jewish scholarship of this era also reveals ongoing efforts to convey the most important insights of Arabic scholarship in fields such as astronomy, mathematics, medicine, and philosophy. After the expulsion of the Jews from Spain in 1492, the migration of many Sephardic Jews to Italy increased the vitality of Hebrew scholarship in centres of learning such as Padua, which graduated its first Jewish medical student in 1409 but considerably more throughout the sixteenth and seventeenth centuries. Its proximity to the important Jewish community in Venice, where many Hebrew books were published, made this a meeting point for many different intellectual traditions, though it was not the only centre for Hebrew scholarship. As an example of the complex circulation of scientific knowledge across cultures, we should consider Elijah Mizra'hi (d.1526), whose *Compendium of Mathematics* was published in Basel, home to a number of important humanist printers, in 1546. The Christian Hebraists Oswald Schreckenfuchs and the cosmographer Sebastian Münster annotated the Hebrew text in Latin to create a bilingual edition of a book written in Istanbul where Mizra'hi was Chief Rabbi. In the end, the renaissance of Greek science competed with a range of projects to bring all-important knowledge into print.

At the end of the sixteenth century Giovanni Battista Raimondi began to print scientific and medical works in Arabic under the auspices of the Medici Press (*Tipografia Medicea*), founded in 1584. An Arabic version of Avicenna appeared in 1593 and al-Idrisi's geography in 1592. Raimondi ambitiously printed 3,000 copies of the thirteenth-century astronomer al-Tūsī's edition of Euclid in 1594, intended primarily for a readership within the Ottoman Empire where there were no printing presses. Much like Matteo Ricci's Chinese translation of Euclid in 1607, this was a political and religious project of knowledge generated in Europe but intended to facilitate relations between Europeans and the people they encountered elsewhere who also valued scientific and medical learning and prided themselves on the distinction and antiquity of their own traditions. The printed book was a powerful cultural artefact and language was its tool. Presenting scientific knowledge in print became a way to broker relations between different societies of differing faiths, who nonetheless shared many scientific interests and were genuinely curious about each other's knowledge.

Within Europe, efforts to create vernacular languages of science also reveal an emerging politics of knowledge that rejected the entire premise of Greek studies. The most powerful example concerns the writings of the Swiss physician, alchemist, and prophet Philippus Aureolus Theophrastus Bombastus von Hohenheim, more commonly known as Paracelsus (1493–1541). Paracelsus, a contemporary of Martin Luther though he remained Catholic in his unorthodox fashion, insisted on writing in his native German though he sprinkled it liberally with key Latin phrases when it suited him. He studied with Abbot Trithemius, learned practical medicine and alchemy from his father, and after a great deal of travel and study in the European universities finally purchased a medical degree in Leoniceno's Ferrara, well known as a Renaissance degree mill.

Paracelsus railed against learned physicians who believed that everything worth knowing must have an ancient pedigree and that every cure could be found in books written by long-dead authors in foreign languages who knew nothing of the local environment in which he lived. He had a great deal of practical medical knowledge from his experience as an army surgeon, where he saw the effects of syphilis at first hand and developed a mercury ointment to treat it. Working for the wealthy Fugger merchants, he observed and described the occupational diseases of German miners. Appointed town physician in Basel in 1527, Paracelsus provoked the ire of other physicians when he publicly burned the books that were the staple of the Renaissance medical curriculum, loudly declaring, 'my shoebuckles are more learned than your Galen and Avicenna'. Paracelsus felt that there was a great deal of vernacular wisdom contained in folk knowledge, advising his learned colleagues to talk with peasants and wise women to truly understand nature from experience. The inhabitants of this city in which many Greek scientific editions appeared did not take kindly to his polemics, and he soon moved on.

Despite the fact that Paracelsus' new philosophy of nature emerged from a vast amount of ancient and medieval learning, he did not feel that Latin, let alone Greek or Arabic, was the preferred language for his ideas. He aspired to convey his radical rethinking of the nature of the universe—no longer defined primarily by the Aristotelian elements but by a chemical philosophy of creation that declared that every substance could be distilled into three essences, or *tria prima* (salt, sulphur, and mercury)—in an everyday vocabulary as accessible as Luther's translation of the New Testament. Fundamentally, Paracelsus' decision to write in German represented an effort to capture the language of experience, just as Sienese military engineer Vannoccio Biringuccio would write his *Pirotechnia* (1540) in Italian to share his practical knowledge of metallurgy and munitions with the broadest possible audience. His writings on chemical medicine were controversial and few were printed during his lifetime. Yet by the end of the century, Paracelsus would be renowned as a legendary healer and inspire many followers between the 1570s and 1610s, with his promise that anyone could speak the language of science and learn from experience. His radical Christian philosophy of nature, infused with his reading of alchemy, astrology, and magic, explicitly rejected the legacy of antiquity.

Seeing a New World

Paracelsus remained utterly sceptical of the other important development in Renaissance science occasioned by an age of European exploration, discovery, and conquest: the importance of the Americas in stimulating new approaches to knowledge and ultimately a new understanding of the natural world. In *The French Disease* (1529) he informed readers that guaiacum, an aromatic American wood considered by many to be the most efficacious cure for syphilis, which appeared with great virulence in Europe in 1494, was an example of everything that was wrong with the Renaissance understanding of nature and disease. From his perspective, every disease had a local cause and therefore a local cure—in this instance, his much vaunted mercury ointment. Rumours that syphilis was a venereal disease brought by Spanish soldiers from the Americas were nothing more than an advertising ploy by the Fuggers, who monopolized the sale of guaiacum. Having already critiqued the exotic and costly medical ingredients of the medieval spice trade, Paracelsus was reluctant to believe that anything from the New World could address a European medical problem.

During the period in which Renaissance scholars rediscovered ancient science and reassessed medieval learning, they also began to see the world in new and different ways. The rediscovery of Ptolemy's *Geography* was no accident but the outcome of the search for knowledge that allowed late medieval trading nations to maintain their commercial advantage by increasing their understanding of the world. This was also valuable knowledge for new competitors—the Ottomans, Portuguese, and Spanish—with geographic ambitions. The result was a renaissance of science and empire that produced a great deal of new knowledge and inspired the development of new kinds of expertise, instruments, and institutions to meet the needs of overseas empires.

In 1428 Prince Pedro, brother-in-law to Prince Henry the Navigator (1394–1460), enquired about obtaining maps from Venice and Florence to accompany the Arabic maps he also acquired for the recently established Royal Observatory at Sagres. Founded by Henry the Navigator in 1420, this Portuguese scientific institution emerged to meet the needs of an empire in the making; around 1450 the Portuguese began to establish their presence along the west African coast. The maps Prince Pedro requested were portolans—sea charts that established lines between known points using a compass rose to indicate the most direct route for relatively short distances. They were a product of the late medieval Mediterranean that made the transition to the Atlantic. The Sagres Observatory was a facility with the latest maps and instruments for establishing direction, measuring and calculating angles, surveying distances, and observing the heavens. It drew upon different scientific traditions to create a bureau of experts whose knowledge would support the state.

By the time Bartolomeu Dias rounded the Cape of Good Hope in 1488, Vasco da Gama returned triumphantly to Lisbon from Calicut in 1499, and Pedro Alvares Cabral skirted the Brazilian coast in 1500, the Sagres Observatory was but a distant memory since it did not survive the death of its founder in 1460. Instead, the Storehouse of Guinea and India (*Almazén de Guiné e India*) in Lisbon, the commercial hub connecting Portugal to Africa, India, and America, became the repository of accumulated knowledge and expertise needed to maintain a long-distance empire, especially knowledge of coasts and waters. By the end of the century the Portuguese no longer asked the Italians for maps, considering their own to be jealously guarded state secrets; instead, Italian navigators and entrepreneurs guided Iberian and English ships across the Atlantic. The cumulative product of this initial phase of exploration was the Nuremberg cloth merchant Martin Behaim's 1492 globe, created after he travelled down the west African coast in search of profit. Scientific knowledge now became entangled with an emerging political economy in which knowledge of nature was an affair of state and a commercial investment.

European perceptions of nature changed significantly between the fifteenth and sixteenth centuries, especially after the Spanish voyages of exploration inaugurated by Christopher Columbus (c.1451–1506) in 1492. In many respects, the Genoese weaver's son Columbus bears comparison with Leonardo, who never once expressed any interest in the fact of the New World, despite his much vaunted curiosity. They read many of the same books, including Pliny, Ptolemy, and that fantastic medieval travelogue, Mandeville's *Travels*. They both knew Toscanelli. They dabbled in astronomy and cosmology, though in the case of Columbus there were professional reasons to take an interest in the science of the heavens, as King Ferdinand and Queen Isabella reminded him in September 1493 when they suggested that he might want to take a 'good astrologer' along on his second voyage.

Columbus participated in the emergence of a new understanding of cosmology at the end of the fifteenth century. He read the fifteenth-century astrologer Pierre d'Ailly's *Image of the World* to assist him in understanding the nature of the globe; he carried Regiomontanus' *Ephemerides* (1490) with him on his fourth voyage, using its up-to-date tables of planetary motions to terrify the native inhabitants of Jamaica with the accuracy of Western science by successfully predicting a lunar eclipse on 29 February 1504. Nonetheless, Columbus did not cross the Atlantic because of the state of scientific knowledge in 1492, though he promised to record everything he learned in a new portolan and dreamed of writing a book in imitation of Ptolemy's *Geography*. Neither materialized. Columbus was a brilliant, experienced navigator who used dead reckoning to overcome Toscanelli's miscalculation about the size of the Atlantic and the mistaken presupposition that he would swiftly reach Asia by sailing west. He found science intriguing but not essential to his enterprise.

At the same time, Columbus sailed on a ship full of instruments—a sand-clock, magnetic compass, quadrant, and mariner's astrolabe. It is not clear that he used them very much or particularly well. Having mistaken a far more ordinary star for Polaris, his quadrant readings were disastrously off. No one examining his logbooks would have mistaken Columbus for a celestial navigator, though he did note the problem of magnetic declination from compass readings taken in different locations. Perhaps this was why the Spanish king and queen suggested that he be accompanied by an astrologer, an expert in reading the stars, to complement the presence of a ship's physician, Dr Chanca, on the second voyage. They wanted scientifically trained observers on board.

With his knowledge of *materia medica*, Dr Chanca turned out to be a far more careful observer of nature than Columbus ever was. In 1492 Columbus informed his patrons that the only plant he recognized among the thousand plants in bloom on Hispaniola was aloe. He described the uses of tobacco but failed to recognize its commercial potential. Several years later, sailing on ships provisioned with livestock and sugar cane that inaugurated the European transformation of American nature and catastrophic devastation of its human population, Chanca corrected Columbus' impression that Caribbean aloe was the same as Spanish aloe; he found the cinnamon there less aromatic than the spice from the East. Columbus was neither an astronomer and mathematician, nor a physician and naturalist, but he grasped the essential fact that these sciences would matter to the enterprise of the Indies. His published letter of 1493—printed nine times alone the year it appeared and many more times thereafter—made descriptions of a distant nature some of the most exciting news of the late fifteenth century.

A Medici agent in Seville named Amerigo Vespucci (1451–1512), observing the fanfare surrounding Columbus' initial two voyages, decided to join the first ship not commanded by Columbus bound for the Americas. Vespucci claimed to make four voyages for the Spanish and the Portuguese between 1497 and 1504, but in reality seems to have sailed only twice, in 1499–1500 and 1501–2. It was Vespucci who definitively called this region a 'New World' in his first published account of his experience in 1503. Capturing the spirit of the times, Vespucci boldly presented himself as a scientific explorer who knew more and travelled further than Columbus. 'I have discovered a continent in those southern regions that is inhabited by more numerous peoples and animals than in our Europe, or Asia or Africa,' he declared after seeing the Brazilian coast, repudiating ancient wisdom that no living being could inhabit the Torrid Zone. Recognizing the need for men knowledgeable in navigational sciences, he developed an interest in astronomy and cartography, and embarked on a quest for a star that became known as the Southern Cross to guide celestial navigators below the equator. Vespucci prominently advertised his facility with a mariner's astrolabe, presenting himself as a brilliant pilot and cosmographer, even though he never commanded a ship or made a map.

In 1507 the German mapmaker Martin Waldseemüller, working in the town of Saint-Dié for the Duke of Lorraine, decided to include a Latin translation of Vespucci's four voyages in his new *Introduction to Cosmography*. Waldseemüller drew and engraved a map containing Vespucci's portrait as the new Ptolemy, inscribing the name 'America' on the part of Brazil described by Vespucci as a new world. One year later, the Spanish monarchs appointed Vespucci the first chief navigator (*piloto mayor*, 1508–12) in the House of Trade (*Casa de Contratación*) in Seville, founded in 1503 to coordinate the commercial and colonial activities of the Spanish empire. They expected Vespucci to ensure that pilots were proficient in celestial and cartographic navigation, and knew how to use instruments such as the quadrant and the astrolabe in which he claimed great expertise. They asked Vespucci to update the *Padrón real*, the official map of Spanish discoveries containing a comprehensive record of all the information pertaining to an emergent empire. Vespucci never completed this task. In 1513 Waldseemüller removed his praise of Amerigo from his bestselling map, crediting Columbus for discovering a land he now called *terra incognita*. Yet the first decision stuck. When the Flemish cartographer Gerard Mercator (1512–94) divided the new continent into two parts on his 1538 cordiform map of the world, he labelled them North and South America. Perhaps Vespucci's uncle, Giorgio Antonio, who participated in Toscanelli's informal geographic academy in Florence, provided his nephew with just enough exposure to this subject to facilitate Vespucci's brash reinvention as a scientific expert for a new age.

By the 1520s the scientific consequences of the Americas were evident in multiple projects designed to demonstrate the utility of science for empire. The discovery of the New World reminded Renaissance readers of Pliny that his original dream of a comprehensive natural history was a Roman imperial project; if cataloguing and understanding nature were essential to Rome's prosperity, they seemed all the more important to Renaissance states scrambling to acquire new territories. Natural history became a science of description to comprehend a distant nature. Identifying foreign animals, plants, and minerals, comparing them to their European counterparts, and appraising their economic value were a pragmatic enterprise with both intellectual and empirical consequences.

In 1526 the Spanish notary Gonzalo Fernández de Oviedo (1478–1557) published *On the Natural History of the Indies*. Oviedo subsequently expanded the scope of his project into a *General and Natural History of the West Indies* (1535–49), based on his considerable experience of the Spanish Americas where he worked as a gold-mine inspector before using his pen to earn renown as the official chronicler of the early Spanish Americas and the Pliny of the New World. The Americas became a testing ground for writing a new kind of natural history. Oviedo strongly emphasized the importance of first-hand experience as he described iguanas, guaiacum, tobacco plants, rubber trees, Nicaragua's volcanic hills, and many other marvels of American nature. While Columbus searched for what looked familiar, Oviedo defined America by the scale and grandeur of its difference. He lamented not having a famous painter like Leonardo at his side to illustrate everything he saw.

Oviedo's desire to write the natural history of the Indies inaugurated a new genre of natural history that was increasingly outward-looking, ultimately stimulating the writing of more universal natural histories that ambitiously sifted through centuries

JACOPO LIGOZZI'S WATERCOLOUR OF A PARROT, *c*.1577–91.

of facts, opinions, and misinformation to come to a better understanding of the natural world. In 1534 the Portuguese physician Garcia d'Orta (1501–68) left Lisbon, bound for Goa. Almost thirty years passed before he reported on how his experience of Portuguese India had changed his understanding of medicine in his *Colloquies on the Simples and Drugs of India* (1563), raising numerous questions about the validity of Galenic medicine and the limits of the ancient pharmacopoeia. The publications of Iberian naturalists challenged European naturalists to incorporate new information into their natural histories. They did not rush to meet the challenge. In 1551 the Swiss naturalist Conrad Gessner (1516–65) managed to insert a description of a single American animal—the opossum—in the first volume of his *History of Animals* (1551–8), though he was already growing tobacco, tomatoes, and possibly corn in his Zurich garden. In the end, as the famous example of Dürer's 1515 rhinoceros reveals, seeing live exotic animals was very difficult if one did not travel far.

For a previous generation, observation had been a means of resolving textual problems that arose from reading the ancient naturalists. While these practices continued throughout the sixteenth century, they competed with a new image of natural history as a repository of the most important, useful, and curious facts of nature that emerged from global encounters. Even naturalists who had not travelled as far as Portuguese India or the Spanish Americas insisted on their authority and expertise, as

THE APOTHECARY FERRANTE IMPERATO'S NATURAL HISTORY MUSEUM IN NAPLES, 1599.

direct observers of nature. Travel, collecting, preserving, and illustrating specimens—practices first celebrated in the 1530s—became the norm later in the century. As Europe's first botanical gardens in Pisa (1543) and Padua (1545) began to cultivate indigenous and exotic plants to demonstrate properly empirical botany to medical students, and as natural history collections emerged, filled with specimens, images, and descriptions from all over the world, the idea of natural history as a truly global enterprise gradually took shape. Oviedo indeed helped to inaugurate a new kind of empiricism which made natural history one of the quintessential sciences of empire.

If the world could be contained in a garden or a cabinet of curiosities, it seemed even more important to fit it on a map. The growing demand for navigational expertise increased the value of astronomy and mathematics. Cartography, geography, and hydrography—all of them initially encompassed within the science of cosmography—gradually became distinctive kinds of knowledge. The ability to make and use new instruments inspired intensive collaborations between scholars, artisans, and navigators, as we have already seen in Dürer's relationship with the English court astronomer Kratzer. As early as 1507 a German broadsheet instructed readers in how to make and use Jacob's cross, a fourteenth-century sighting device that assisted celestial navigation. By 1527 the Nuremberg mathematician Georg Hartmann (1489–1564) embarked on an ambitious project of printing every instrument useful for the new cosmography. Paper instruments were not only blueprints to make more durable copies but inexpensive and highly transportable devices that put mathematical instruments in the hands of many people who could not afford the bejewelled versions made for princes. The result was a genuinely new way of seeing and depicting the world.

In Leuven the Flemish mathematician Gemma Frisius (1508–55) began to instruct students in mathematical techniques of mapping and surveying, devising new instruments capable of more precise measurement, inspired partly by his reading of Regiomontanus' mathematical astronomy and trigonometry. In the fifteenth century portolans, terrestrial maps, and celestial maps were three distinct ways of seeing the world. Frisius, who became an early advocate of Copernican astronomy, instead envisioned a unified field of knowledge. He first articulated his vision of a new cosmography in the late 1520s while updating Apianus' recent *Cosmography* (1524) to reflect his vision of what cosmography might become. Frisius was simply bursting with new ideas to conquer the world with science. He invented a *planimetrum* to improve triangulating the relative positions of different locations and considered how two reliable clocks might accurately measure longitude, which remained one of the great navigational problems of the next two centuries until John Harrison invented a marine chronometer whose mechanisms could withstand weather and motion. Frisius completed *On the Principles of Astronomy and Cosmography* (1530), the same year in which a young Mercator arrived in Leuven to study with Frisius.

A cobbler's son with a basic grammar-school education and some exposure to Ptolemy and Pliny, Mercator hastily absorbed Euclidean geometry as the basic prerequisite for entering Frisius' classroom. By 1532 he was Frisius' assistant in a new enterprise, making globes, maps, and instruments with an Antwerp goldsmith. Printed globe gores were first invented by the mathematician and astronomer Johann Schöner in 1517, but Mercator's 1541 globe went yet another step further. He introduced loxodromes (curved lines that maintained a constant compass bearing, first envisioned by the Portuguese royal cosmographer Pedro Nunes) on his globe gores, creating a portable globe whose accuracy made it useful to navigators. Spherical geometry was now an eminently practical science. As Mercator emerged from the shadow of his mentor, he became widely admired as the man who made cartography a fully mathematical science. In 1569 Mercator accomplished the Herculean task of straightening out rhumb lines to project the curvature of the earth on eighteen flat sheets of paper; he created a new way of representing the entire world on a map, filled with up-to-date geographic and hydrological information yet prudently resisting the temptation to resolve ongoing puzzles such as the problem of magnetic declination. Little wonder that Mercator's contemporaries thought he had actually squared the circle! Mercator rightfully earned the epithet of the new Ptolemy that Vespucci rushed to claim, and proved his mettle by recalculating the size of Ptolemy's Mediterranean to reduce it by four degrees.

In the half-century after 1492, physicians, naturalists, astronomers, and mathematicians all began to come to terms with how knowledge of the New World and the urgency of the projects of knowledge it engendered altered their understanding of science itself. It would be an exaggeration to say that any dramatic revolutions in knowledge had taken place in this initial period, since even Mercator's projection did not emerge until 1569. The full impact of European ambitions to expand their commercial interests, political goals, and missionary enterprises in different parts of the world would not become apparent until the seventeenth century, when virtually every major European power staked a claim to territory at a distance. Nonetheless, a crucial question had been raised: could new worlds be understood by reading ancient texts? The French essayist Michel de Montaigne thoughtfully observed in 1580 that the insights of Aristotle and Plato 'cannot apply to these new lands'. The Portuguese sceptic Francisco Sanches put it far more baldly in a philosophical polemic titled *That Nothing is Known* (1581). 'A new world has been discovered—new realities—in New Spain or in the West and East Indies,' he declared. 'Construct another "science", then, for your first is now false.' This was the view from the late sixteenth century, however, which was a perspective with hindsight. It was also the product of the final episode of Renaissance science, which crystallized in a series of bold new publications that defined, once and for all, what it meant for science to be reborn.

Circa 1543

While historians generally shy away from ascribing too much significance to the serendipity of a particular moment, 1543 was nonetheless an important year for the development of a new understanding of nature. That year two landmark publications—Nicolaus Copernicus' *On the Revolutions of the Heavenly Spheres* and

Andreas Vesalius' *On the Fabric of the Human Body*—appeared in print, in the prosperous northern European cities of Nuremberg and Basel respectively. Filled with cosmological diagrams, astronomical tables, and detailed depictions of every aspect of human anatomy, they represented the emergence of a new kind of scientific book almost a century after Gutenberg's invention of the printing press. In both instances, the visual message of the woodcuts buttressed the rhetorical power of the ideas and information contained in the text. Copernicus and Vesalius demonstrated how a new appreciation of ancient learning—a rebirth or, as we would now say, a 'renaissance'— could indeed change the fundamental shape of knowledge.

In his *On the Revolutions of the Heavenly Spheres* the Polish church canon and astronomer Copernicus offered a bold heliocentric cosmology, hoping to resolve several centuries of 'confusion in the astronomical traditions'. Offering an aesthetic appraisal of the portrait of the universe created by the intricate combination of Ptolemaic epicycles and equants that made a moving earth appear motionless, Copernicus expressed an almost Vitruvian distaste for this cosmological monstrosity, explaining his desire to simplify and order a system that had become unwieldy and overly complex. He also advertised his Platonism and full absorption of the Euclidean renaissance by reproducing a Greek phrase that famously greeted visitors to Plato's Academy on the title-page of his book: 'Let no one untrained in geometry enter here.' Citing the work of Aristarchus of Samos, Copernicus proposed a wholesale revision of the traditional understanding of planetary motion that negated the premises of Ptolemaic astronomy and Aristotelian physics by setting the earth in motion as one of the planets orbiting the sun. Part of Copernicus' inspiration was philological and textual. Unlike his medieval predecessors, Copernicus read Ptolemy's *Almagest* in its original Greek (published in 1538) as well as new Latin editions, and absorbed the recent revisions to Ptolemaic astronomy by Peurbach, Regiomontanus, and others. He found references in Cicero and Plutarch to ancient theories of a moving earth. In short, Copernicus was the full beneficiary of the Renaissance scientific library in print.

Copernicus was also a patient and persistent calculator. Even before Galileo's invention of the telescope as a scientific instrument in 1609, late medieval and early Renaissance instruments began to yield fresh observations of the heavens. Copernicus understood the problem of planetary motion to be essential to the reform of the church calendar, which did not occur until the completion of the Gregorian calendar in 1582. He combined the data of ancient and medieval astronomers with some of his own observations in a home-grown observatory in Frombork, to see whether this information might accommodate alternatives to a geocentric universe. In some way that we have yet to fully understand, though it probably occurred during his studies in Padua in 1501–3, Copernicus seems to have had access to some of the sophisticated critiques of Ptolemaic astronomy produced by late medieval Islamic astronomers such as Nasīr al-Dīn al-Tūsī (1201–74) and his successors. His encounter with Ptolemy was mediated by reappraisals of Ptolemaic astronomy culminating in the work of Regiomontanus and the astronomers he encountered in the Renaissance universities.

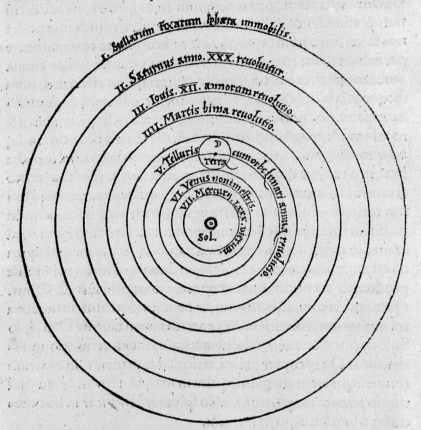

net, in quo terram cum orbe lunari tanquam epicyclo contineri
diximus. Quinto loco Venus nono menſe reducitur. Sextum
deniĉ locum Mercurius tenet, octuaginta dierum ſpacio circũ
currens. In medio uero omnium reſidet Sol. Quis enim in hoc

pulcherrimo templo lampadem hanc in alio uel meliori loco po
neret, quàm unde totum ſimul poſsit illuminare? Siquidem non
inepte quidam lucernam mundi, alij mentem, alij rectorem uo-
cant. Trimegiſtus uiſibilem Deum, Sophoclis Electra intuentẽ
omnia. Ita profecto tanquam in ſolio re gali Sol reſidens circum
agentem gubernat Aſtrorum familiam. Tellus quoĉ minime
fraudatur lunari miniſterio, ſed ut Ariſtoteles de animalibus
ait, maximã Luna cũ terra cognationẽ habet. Concipit interea à
Sole terra, & impregnatur annuo partu. Inuenimus igitur ſub
hac

COPERNICUS' heliocentric universe, 1543.

By demonstrating the mathematical possibility of a heliocentric universe, Copernicus cast real doubt on the inevitability of the Aristotelian–Ptolemaic cosmos, though he did not offer definitive proof in favour of his argument. He assured his readers that the ideas he proposed were not his alone but had ancient precedents that had remained obscure until his rediscovery of these exciting possibilities. What seemed radically new was actually a revival of something very old. Disciples eager to see his work in print presented him with a copy of his book as he lay dying, inserting a second preface by the Lutheran Andreas Osiander, who completed the final editing of the book that to some degree anticipated its potentially controversial implications for biblical cosmology by insisting on the entirely hypothetical nature of Copernicus' theory and attempting to restrict its implications to the realm of mathematical astronomy.

Halfway across Europe, delighting medical students at Pisa, Bologna, and especially Padua with iconoclastic lectures on everything that was wrong with traditional academic medicine and challenging senior faculty to public anatomical debates, the young Flemish physician and anatomist Vesalius argued eloquently for the revival of Galenic anatomy. He was a product of Leuven and Paris, and the touchstone of his medical education was his *Paraphrase of the Ninth Book of Rhazes's Almansorem* (1537); he described Rhazes as a 'most famous Arabic physician', reminding us again that inside every Renaissance scholar was a careful reader of medieval texts. After absorbing Galen's entire corpus, which grew to an eleven-volume Latin edition by the Giunti press in Florence in 1541–2 based on the Aldine Greek, but especially *On Anatomical Procedures*, the 28-year-old Vesalius found himself contemplating the consequences of the decline of anatomy, which he blamed on the Goths, Arabs, and even the Romans for not adequately preserving Galen's legacy.

Reflecting on the growth of medical humanism, Vesalius celebrated his century for reviving this ancient art which he considered an important branch of natural philosophy. Vesalius insisted on the power of observation and philology. He lampooned the ignorance of scholastic physicians who 'squawk like jackdaws from their lofty professorial chairs' about things they had only read and never seen. Even reading Galen carefully in a pristine copy was not enough without adequate experience. Citing more than 500 errors he had so far found in Galen's account of the human body, which combined observations of animals with far less frequent inspection of human parts, Vesalius announced his re-establishment of the ancient science of anatomy, inviting a new generation to learn with him and 'apply their hands like the Greeks'.

Vesalius was certain that true knowledge of the body came from repeated dissection and a more careful understanding of the structural differences that made humans a particular kind of animal, male and female. He advocated for the importance of 'ocular belief'. Lest anyone miss the artisanal dimensions of his new science, he included a detailed illustration of the tools of dissection as well as copious images of the bones, muscles, organs, arteries, veins, and nerves of the human body 'according to nature', described with the Greek-inflected vocabulary that Benedetti and Leoniceno advocated at the beginning of the century. Vesalius' goal was to create a canonical body, an

ANDREAS VESALIUS dissecting in an imaginary and highly allegorical anatomical theatre, 1543.

THE WELL-KNOWN PHYSICIAN
Girolamo Mercuriale with
Vesalius' *On the Fabric of the
Human Body*, 1589.

anatomical norm against which to explore the nature of human difference. The physician and astrologer Girolamo Cardano (1501–76), who cast Vesalius' horoscope in 1547, praised him for the seriousness of his intellect but faulted him for his excessive ambition. Yet he nonetheless appreciated the magnitude of Vesalius' accomplishment in creating an illustrated anatomy. By comparison, he found Leonardo's anatomical drawings which he had seen in Milan 'very beautiful … but indeed worthless'. This kind of discerning eye was precisely what Vesalius hoped to encourage by insisting that anatomy was still a science in its infancy despite its ancient pedigree. Prominent Renaissance physicians like Girolamo Mercuriale had themselves portrayed with Vesalius' *On the Fabric of the Human Body* to demonstrate the role of this book in their own intellectual authority.

Copernicus and Vesalius placed their books in the hands of experienced and accomplished printers. Copernicus' Nuremberg printer Johannes Petreius studied in Basel, where he was apprenticed in the printing house of his uncle before becoming one of the most prolific scholarly publishers of his age. When the German mathematician and astronomer Georg Joachim Rheticus visited Copernicus in Frombork in 1539, in order to learn first-hand what he had heard at a distance about the Polish church canon's wholesale revision of astronomy, Petreius gave him several books of astronomy and mathematics to encourage Copernicus to trust him as a printer capable of handling a book with complex diagrams, astronomical tables, and trigonometry. This issue did not entirely go away even for later generations. The German astronomer Johannes Kepler (1571–1630) possessed his own type for printing numbers and symbols, since he did not expect most publishers to meet his standard of technical production.

Vesalius' publisher Johannes Oporinus was the learned son of a painter who attended Paracelsus' lectures and served as his alchemical assistant while also working as a proofreader in the most important humanist printing shop in Basel. Ancient languages were his specialty. In 1543 he had only recently resigned his university professorship in Greek to devote himself full-time to the business of making books. Vesalius' *On the Fabric of the Human Body* posed multiple technical challenges to a Renaissance publisher, including the complex layout of more than 250 elaborate, beautifully rendered woodcuts created by Jan Stephan Calcar and other artists in Titian's workshop, many of them intricately labelled to ensure that the readers could correlate anatomical description with depictions of different parts of the body. Arguing in the spirit of Leonardo that pictures 'place a subject before the eyes more precisely than the most explicit language', Vesalius invoked geometry and botany as two other scientific disciplines where images were essential for full comprehension. He had been examining Renaissance scientific books to inspire his own thinking about the look and feel of his new anatomy.

Describing the effect he wished to achieve in presenting anatomy as visual knowledge, Vesalius praised 'the most detailed imaginable illustrations ... of plants' as a point of comparison to his desire to illustrate all the 'parts of the human body'. The books he had in mind were the work of German naturalists, beginning with Otto Brunfels's *Living Images of Plants* (1530–1) and culminating in the Tübingen physician Leonhart Fuchs's *Notable Commentaries on the History of Plants* (1542) which appeared as Vesalius put the finishing touches to his preface. Depicting plants from nature (*ad vivum*) had been a preoccupation of prominent Renaissance painters such as Leonardo and Dürer, including their roots, imperfections, and actual state at the moment of observation, but no one succeeded in creating printed images that could be used to identify specific plants before the important work of the German naturalists. It seems almost certain that Vesalius knew these botanies, since Fuchs published with Oporinus in Basel. Fuchs fulsomely praised the two painters who made his images, arguing that a skilfully executed picture contained more certain knowledge than the 'bare words of the text', though without words details such as colour could not be added into the black-and-white woodcuts. Unlike Vesalius, Fuchs thanked his collaborators by including their portraits and mentioning them by name.

Fuchs saw himself as a restorer of botany, which he believed to be the oldest branch of medicine. He praised the Latin editors and translators of Dioscorides for rescuing this science from oblivion, insisting strongly on botany's Greek pedigree, including

THE GERMAN PAINTERS Albrecht Meyer and Heinrich Füllmaurer respectively draw and create woodcuts of plants for Leonhart Fuchs, *De Historia Stirpium*, 1542.

Dioscorides' important discussion of *autopsia*, or seeing through things, which also was central to Vesalian anatomy. Demonstrating a distinct aversion to Paracelsus' folksy homilies about the value of ordinary experience, the Lutheran Fuchs blamed 'monks and old wives' for corrupting Greek names for plants through their ignorance, and enumerated the errors of medieval Islamic physicians and those influenced by them. While appreciating the role of the European-wide republic of letters in making the botanical renaissance possible through the exchange of specimens, descriptions, and images, Fuchs proudly reserved his greatest praise for the sixteenth-century German naturalists. In this respect, he shared Paracelsus' view (also the perspective of the Saxon physician and mine inspector Georg Agricola in the midst of writing an important work of metallurgy), that the Italian peninsula was not necessarily the source of every innovation in science in the past century, especially when one considered the significance of German universities, instrument-makers, and artists in shaping Renaissance scientific and medical culture.

Fuchs seemed only marginally aware of the innovative work of Iberian naturalists in globalizing the study of nature. Later generations remedied this omission, especially the Dutch naturalist Carolus Clusius (Charles de l'Écluse, 1526–1609), who translated the most important Portuguese and Spanish works of natural history and *materia medica* into Latin to reach a broader audience, summarizing his most interesting findings in *Ten Books of Exotic Things* (1605). In 1542, however, Fuchs was rightfully convinced that Western Europe was a botanical *terra incognita* filled with plants Theophrastus, Dioscorides, and Galen had never seen. The profusion of information at his disposal, which increasingly included American nature, and his exacting standards in establishing a definitive description are among the reasons he failed to complete the second edition he planned but never published since the empirical study of nature was a project without end.

The publication of these three books by Copernicus, Vesalius, and Fuchs within the space of just over one year was hardly a coincidence. Humanist scholarship and the technology of printing had matured greatly together in the course of a century, and both the Portuguese and Spanish empires were now well established and beginning to integrate a new vision of nature as well as encourage innovation in the sciences and instruments that addressed the most pressing needs of knowing nature at vast distances. These developments made the scientific renaissance possible. The question around 1543 is what it would become next. While arguing for the importance of reviving ancient science, Copernicus, Vesalius, and Fuchs did not consider the knowledge of antiquity to be sufficient to meet the needs of the present. They were increasingly aware of the limits of knowledge, past or present. Aristotle did not know the iguana or the opossum; Theophrastus had never seen a sunflower; Dioscorides had never experienced the marvellous effects of cacao. What had Ptolemy observed beyond the Mediterranean? What did they know of their own world? And how was one to know?

Looking beyond these three important Renaissance books, even a cursory glance at scientific activity *circa* 1543 offers a revealing portrait of the state of knowledge. In 1543 Niccolò Tartaglia (1500–57), the mathematically gifted son of a post rider, published the first vernacular translations of Euclid and Archimedes, as a complement to his *New Science* (1537) which explained the value of mechanics for understanding ballistics, an important subject in an age of incessant warfare. In England, the physician Robert Recorde completed his *Ground of Artes*, a popular mathematics textbook in which he modestly proposed the introduction of the equals sign (=) to continue the project of standardizing mathematical notation. The Spanish programme to train pilots in the science and instruments of navigation was long established but the crown wanted the House of Trade to play a more visible institutional role in ensuring the quality of the results. In the mid-1540s the Council of the Indies was forced to intervene in debates among competing cosmographers about which kind of map should become the standard from which all pilots navigated. There was a crying need for the work that Frisius and his disciple Mercator had begun in the Low Countries, including Mercator's study of magnetic declination which appeared in 1546, to sort out the numerous technical problems of making science a reliable foundation for empire. The Spanish established the first professorship in cosmography at the House of Trade in 1552.

In Paris in 1543, three printers competed to produce unauthorized reprints of Fuchs's botany to meet the demands of medical students and professors eager to read about plants and compare his descriptions with living and dried specimens in the botanical gardens that had just begun to emerge. The apothecary Belon had only recently returned to Paris from his travels throughout Europe and the Levant. By 1553 Belon was inspired not only by what he had seen and learned, but by all the new books that had recently appeared, to declare that knowledge of nature was undergoing what he called a *renaissance*. What might he have been reading? Candidates include the Sienese physician Pietro Andrea Mattioli's 1544 commentary on Dioscorides, which competed successfully with the work of the German naturalists as a repository of empirical discovery and intellectual debate since it went into many more editions than Fuchs's botany; Sebastian Münster's lavishly illustrated *Cosmography* (1544); and the second edition of Oviedo's natural history of the Indies of 1547.

This scientific renaissance took on many different forms. At the Collège de Presles, Petrus Ramus (Pierre de la Ramée, 1515–72), the talented son of a Picardy peasant, lectured on Euclid and developed a non-Aristotelian logic in support of his new approach to philosophy and pedagogy. In 1536, Ramus brashly defended a thesis titled *Everything Aristotle Said is Wrong*, declaring his three and a half years of university education to be a colossal waste of his mind. Like Paracelsus, he gave up the habit of lecturing in Latin to present knowledge in his native French. After Ramus published his *Remarks against Aristotle* (1543), the famously conservative Sorbonne temporarily convinced the French king to ban him from teaching philosophy. By 1551, Ramus had been appointed to a royal chair in philosophy. Eventually Catholic Paris became fatally dangerous for the Huguenot Ramus, but not before he revolutionized the most traditional subject in the university curriculum by envisioning a new Ramist logic that did away with the hierarchical formality and causality of Aristotelian logic. Paracelsus was surely smiling from his grave, as his disciples began to edit and publish his works. A self-educated Huguenot potter named Bernard Palissy (c.1510–90) was just beginning to create magnificent life castings of animals that would eventually lead him to publish books and lecture to Parisian audiences on everything he learned about nature, transforming it into a new kind of art that seemed to perfectly replicate nature in its three-dimensional form, something no painter could claim to do. Aristotle was dead, they declared, down with Aristotle.

Or was he? Contemplating the state of knowledge in Padua as he completed his studies in 1542, Alessandro Piccolomini (1508–79) was not so sure. The 1540s was also a decade in which Aristotelian natural philosophy underwent an important revival. Efforts to establish the methodological principles of science based on a careful reading of Aristotle's logic culminated in the work of Paduan professors such as Jacopo Zabarella (1533–89) as well as the highly empirical Aristotelian programme of animal dissection enacted by William Harvey's mentor, Girolamo Fabrici (1533–1619), in Padua's new permanent anatomy theatre, finally completed in 1594–5 to institutionalize the reforms in anatomy begun by Vesalius. Some Paduan professors and their students decided to fully embrace the idea that Aristotle was a pagan philosopher whose ideas need not conform to Christian ethics and beliefs. Becoming a radical, unorthodox Aristotelian was also a possibility around 1543, and surely inspired the radical Platonism later in the century that produced works such as Francesco Patrizi's *New Philosophy of Everything* (1591). Throughout the sixteenth century Aristotle's views on the mortality of the soul and the eternity of the universe became touchstones for renewed debates about the autonomy of philosophy from theology, despite the condemnation of Pietro Pomponazzi's philosophy in 1518, foreshadowing in important ways the problems Galileo Galilei (1564–1642) faced in attempting to convince the Roman Catholic Church to accept the truth of Copernican astronomy.

Like Ramus, Piccolomini found himself enmeshed in debates about the politics of knowledge. He attended lectures in a Paduan academy in which radical humanists declared the absurdity of learning in antiquated languages when Aristotle and Plato had written and taught in their native tongue. Why shouldn't they do the same? During the 1540s Aristotelian logic, natural philosophy, and cosmology became more widely accessible in the vernacular. Piccolomini began to publish vernacular works of Aristotelian science and philosophy, often filled with unorthodox readings of Aristotle, combining his understanding of Aristotelian philosophy with subjects of current scientific and philosophical interest such as the revival of Lucretius and new developments in astronomy and cosmology. His first book, *On the Sphere of the World* (1540), was printed fourteen times by 1600, and his *On the Fixed Stars* (1540) was almost as popular. Italian translations of Aristotle's works began to appear in 1545, encouraging new audiences to discover what an encounter with this important ancient philosopher might do for their understanding of the world. Piccolomini complemented this work with his comprehensive guide to Aristotelian natural philosophy in 1551.

There was a hunger for scientific knowledge *circa* 1543 that many people sought to meet with very different agendas in mind. Women were one of the audiences that Piccolomini explicitly addressed. His Aristotle was as potentially subversive as Ramus' efforts to wipe Aristotle off the intellectual map. In 1584 Camilla Greghetta Erculiani, apothecary at the Three Stars in Padua, published her *Letters on Natural Philosophy* in Kraków, dedicating them to the Queen of Poland, Anna Jagellona. Like Piccolomini, she saw Aristotelian natural philosophy as a place to discuss many new and controversial ideas about nature and cosmos, including the perennially controversial issue of whether the soul was mortal or immortal. The Paduan inquisition questioned her about the potential heterodoxy of her ideas. Erculiani assured them that she spoke only philosophically, and not theologically. In the late sixteenth century this response was still possible.

The scientific renaissance emerged in several distinct phases between the mid-fourteenth and mid-sixteenth centuries. It began with dissatisfaction with the present state of knowledge and commercial ambition. The response was to create a new standard for what it meant to learn from the ancients and to develop a better understanding of the role of experience in making knowledge. Both of these projects developed and matured in the course of these two centuries. By then, the world had changed dramatically, laying the groundwork for the intellectual, religious, and political developments after 1543 that shaped an era commonly known as the Scientific Revolution. When the English Lord Chancellor Francis Bacon (1561–1626), who pursued natural philosophy with a politician's vision of knowledge as power, declared in his *New Organon* (1620) that printing, gunpowder, and the magnet were the three most important inventions to have changed the course of the world, he acknowledged the great debts of his own age to the Renaissance. Bacon dreamed of a utopia he called the *New Atlantis* (1627), where he transformed everything he observed about science and all the changes that knowledge had undergone into an allegorical vision of an omniscient scientific society, invisible to the world yet capable of knowing everything about it and working collectively to make knowledge from a plethora of facts and experiments. Bacon's New Atlantis combined the best aspects of every project to reform knowledge and make it useful to society during the sixteenth century, creating a blueprint for something that did not yet exist until the founding of the Royal Society in 1660. The Scientific Revolution has often been perceived as the starting point for understanding the origins of modern science. Today, in a more consciously global environment, we are far more inclined to consider this seventeenth-century history in the context of a much broader history of how different systems of knowledge emerged in light of changing political regimes, empires, institutions, and technologies of communication. The European Renaissance played an essential role in all of these developments.

CHAPTER 11

The Global Renaissance

FELIPE FERNÁNDEZ-ARMESTO AND PETER BURKE

Introduction

ON the flyleaf of his copy of Vitruvius' work on architecture, Antonio de Mendoza, first viceroy of New Spain, recorded that he 'read this book in the city of Mexico' in April 1548. At the time, Franciscan professors in the nearby College of Santa Cruz de Tlatelolco were teaching young Aztec nobles to write like Cicero. Later in the same century, Jesuits presented Akbar the Great with prints by Dürer for Mughal court artists to copy. Within little more than a generation's span, the Italian missionary Matteo Ricci introduced Chinese mandarins to Renaissance rhetoric, philosophy, astronomy, geography, and the art of memory as well as to the Christian message. The Renaissance—so a headline-writer might say—'went global'.

Nowadays, we are used to cultural globalization. Fashion, food, games, images, thoughts, and even gestures cross frontiers with the speed of the World Wide Web. At the time, however, the success of the Renaissance—by which we mean the collective movement attempting to revive the culture of classical antiquity, especially in art, literature, and ideas—in penetrating remote parts of the world was strictly without precedent.

Previous intellectual and artistic movements had spanned Eurasia, in, for instance, the first millennium BCE and the Song and Mongol eras, but the way they began and spread differed from the Renaissance in two important respects. First, in the earlier cases, the ideas and images originated outside Europe and ended up there, rather than the other way round. Secondly, their reach was limited by the isolation of the New World and of much of Africa from existing long-range routes of communication. The Renaissance, on the other hand, could be borne—like the life forms swapped across continents by transoceanic voyages in the so-called 'Columbian Exchange'—to new destinations. In the sixteenth century, for the first time, much of the world beyond the oceans and the Sahara became accessible to Eurasian peoples, and had an unprecedented opportunity to influence them in turn.

IN 1521 THE MILANESE ARCHITECT Cesare Cesariano published an edition of Vitruvius'
De Architectura, purporting to show how great buildings of the era since the ancient architect's
work reflected Vitruvian principles. This engraving fits the cathedral of Milan, albeit built 'in
the German manner' or, as we should now say, 'Gothic' style, into a geometrical and symmetrical
framework.

From then onwards, explorers, conquerors, traders, craftsmen, missionaries, pilgrims, settlers, and colonial administrators carried objects and texts from Latin Christendom to the extremities of Asia, Africa, and the Americas. In consequence, though Australasia and much of the Pacific island world remained beyond reach, the Renaissance can fairly be called the first genuinely global movement in the history of ideas: the first, that is, to resonate effects on both hemispheres and to penetrate deep into continental interiors on both sides of the equator. Ways, derived from the study of or the desire to imitate classical antiquity, of understanding language, representing reality, or modelling life accompanied the humanist curriculum around the world. Ancient Greek and Roman values and aesthetics became more widely available than any previously devised repertoire of texts, objects, and images.

In some ways, the Renaissance is best understood as an acceleration of long-standing or intermittent interest in reviving the supposed glories of antiquity in the medieval West, but for present purposes we treat it as a single, continuous episode, first clearly detectable towards the middle of the fourteenth century, fully discernible in Italy in the *quattrocento*, and generalized and, in some fields, dominant in much of Europe in the sixteenth century. We propose to take account of the specificity of the Renaissance, in this sense, like that of other movements of cultural revival. We should not assume that all revivals are equally important, but treat their relative importance as a matter for empirical investigation. The map opposite summarizes the case for seeing the Renaissance spread from Italian cities across Europe in the fifteenth and sixteenth centuries. The rest of this chapter concerns the positioning of the Renaissance in the contexts of other, further-flung cultures, discussing the problems of where it came from, where it went, how it got there, and what happened to it on arrival.

Origins and development of the Renaissance

One major problem is that of how the diffusion of the Renaissance occurred. More urgent, perhaps, is that of how it started. While the Renaissance was global in its effects, room remains for debate on how and how far influences from outside Christendom affected its origins. The movement developed in the sixteenth century under the influence of widening intercultural contacts, but did it originate in isolation? The question is important for the history of the world, because, despite many attempts to recontextualize the Renaissance as one among many comparable events, the movement's exceptional resonance remains intact for most readers and students.

Renaissances in the plural

The first really influential attempt to view the movement in a global perspective was launched in 1954, when Arnold Toynbee, the scholar who, perhaps, did most to encourage historians in the comparative study of civilizations, denied that the Italian Renaissance of the *quattrocento* was 'a unique occurrence'. According to him, it was 'no more than one particular instance of a recurrent historical phenomenon'. Subsequent

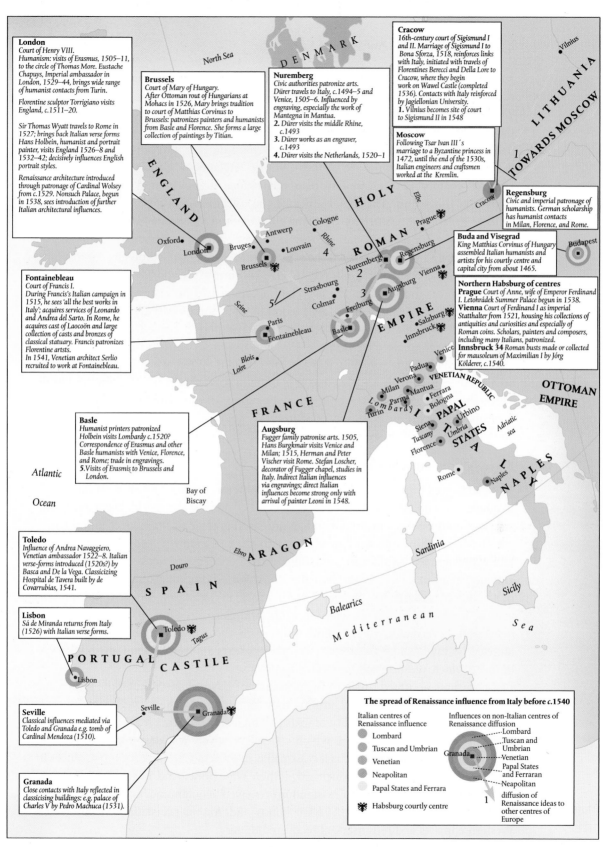

London
*Court of Henry VIII.
Humanism: visits of Erasmus, 1505–11,
to the circle of Thomas More. Eustache
Chapuys, Imperial ambassador in
London, 1529–44, brings wide range
of humanist contacts from Turin.*

*Florentine sculptor Torrigiano visits
England, c.1511–20.*

*Sir Thomas Wyatt travels to Rome in
1527; brings back Italian verse forms
Hans Holbein, humanist and portrait
painter, visits England 1526–8 and
1532–42; decisively influences English
portrait styles.*

*Renaissance architecture introduced
through patronage of Cardinal Wolsey
from c.1529. Nonsuch Palace, begun
in 1538, sees introduction of further
Italian architectural influences.*

Brussels
*Court of Mary of Hungary.
After Ottoman rout of Hungarians at
Mohacs in 1526, Mary brings tradition
to court of Matthias Corvinus to
Brussels: patronizes painters and humanists
from Basle and Florence. She forms a large
collection of paintings by Titian.*

Nuremberg
*Civic authorities patronize arts.
Dürer travels to Italy, c.1494–5 and
Venice, 1505–6. Influenced by
engraving, especially the work of
Mantegna in Mantua.*
2. *Dürer visits the middle Rhine,
c.1493*
3. *Dürer works as an engraver,
c.1493*
4. *Dürer visits the Netherlands, 1520–1*

Cracow
*16th-century court of Sigismund I
and II. Marriage of Sigismund I to
Bona Sforza, 1518, reinforces links
with Italy, initiated with travels of
Florentines Berecci and Della Lore to
Cracow, where they begin
work on Wawel Castle (completed
1536). Contacts with Italy reinforced
by Jagiellonian University.*
1. *Vilnius becomes site of court
to Sigismund II in 1548*

Moscow
*Following Tsar Ivan III´s
marriage to a Byzantine princess in
1472, until the end of the 1530s,
Italian engineers and craftsmen
worked at the Kremlin.*

Regensburg
*Civic and imperial patronage of
humanists. German scholarship
has humanist contacts
in Milan, Florence, and Rome.*

Buda and Visegrad
*King Matthias Corvinus of Hungary
assembled Italian humanists and
artists for his courtly centre and
capital city from about 1465.*

Northern Habsburg of centres
Prague *Court of Anne, wife of Emperor Ferdinand
I. Letohrádek Summer Palace begun in 1538.*
Vienna *Court of Ferdinand I as imperial
Statthalter from 1521, housing his collections of
antiquities and curiosities and especially of
Roman coins. Scholars, painters and composers,
including many Italians, patronized.*
Innsbruck 34 *Roman busts made or collected
for mausoleum of Maximilian I by Jörg
Kölderer, c.1540.*

Fontainebleau
*Court of Francis I.
During Francis's Italian campaign in
1515, he sees 'all the best works in
Italy'; acquires services of Leonardo
and Andrea del Sarto. In Rome, he
acquires cast of Laocoön and large
collection of casts and bronzes of
classical statuary. Francis patronizes
Florentine artsts.
In 1541, Venetian architect Serlio
recruited to work at Fontainebleau.*

Basle
*Humanist printers patronized
Holbein visits Lombardy c.1520?
Correspondence of Erasmus and other
Basle humanists with Venice, Florence,
and Rome; trade in engravings.*
5. *Visits of Erasmus to Brussels and
London.*

Augsburg
*Fugger family patronise arts. 1505,
Hans Burgkmair visits Venice and
Milan; 1515, Herman and Peter
Vischer visit Rome. Stefan Loscher,
decorator of Fugger chapel, studies in
Italy. Indirect Italian influences
via engravings; direct Italian
influences become strong only with
arrival of painter Leoni in 1548.*

Toledo
*Influence of Andrea Navaggiero,
Venetian ambassador 1522–8. Italian
verse-forms introduced (1520s?) by
Basca and De la Vega. Classicizing
Hospital de Tavera built by de
Covarrubias, 1541.*

Lisbon
*Sá de Miranda returns from Italy
(1526) with Italian verse forms.*

Seville
*Classical influences mediated via
Toledo and Granada e.g. tomb of
Cardinal Mendoza (1510).*

Granada
*Close contacts with Italy reflected in
classicising buildings: e.g. palace of
Charles V by Pedro Machuca (1531).*

The spread of Renaissance influence from Italy before c.1540

Italian centres of
Renaissance influence
- Lombard
- Tuscan and Umbrian
- Venetian
- Neapolitan
- Papal States and Ferrara
- ✸ Habsburg courtly centre

Influences on non-Italian centres of
Renaissance diffusion
- Lombard
- Tuscan and Umbrian
- Venetian
- Papal States and Ferraran
- Neapolitan
- **1** diffusion of Renaissance ideas to other centres of Europe

THE SPREAD OF THE RENAISSANCE FROM ITALY, The map shows how travelling artists and humanists spread
Renaissance conventions from Italian cities to courtly centres across Europe in the late fifteenth and early
sixteenth centuries.

researchers discovered or asserted revivals of classical ideas, style, and imagery in just about every century from the fifth to the fifteenth, referring, for instance, to a 'renaissance' of classical architecture among basilica-builders in Rome even before the last Western Roman Emperor died.

Historians often speak of a Visigothic renaissance in seventh-century Spain, a Northumbrian renaissance in eighth-century England, a Carolingian renaissance in ninth-century France, an Ottonian renaissance in tenth- and eleventh-century Germany, and so on. The 'renaissance of the twelfth century' is recognized in the routine lexicon of historians of Latin Christendom. In some ways, the classical tradition never needed revival: writers and artists almost always exploited classical texts and models where and when they could get them. Consular diptychs, for instance, inspired the decorator of a church in eighth-century Oviedo. In eleventh-century Frómista, in northern Spain, the carver of a capital had no example of the famous ancient Greek representation of the Laocoön to hand, but he based his work on Pliny's description of it. Florentine builders of the same period copied a Roman temple sufficiently well to deceive Brunelleschi. A sculptor in thirteenth-century Orvieto made a credible imitation of a Roman sarcophagus. What we usually call 'Gothic' architecture of the high Middle Ages was often decorated with classicizing sculpture. Throughout the period these examples cover, writers of moral and natural philosophy continued to echo such works of Plato and Aristotle as they could get hold of, and prose stylists often sought the most nearly classical models they could find.

Renaissances outside Europe

As renaissances multiply in the literature in the West, so they appear with increasing frequency in scholars' accounts of culture in other parts of the world. Jack Goody, the doyen of anthropology in Britain and an unremitting critic of Western ethnocentrism, who has made fundamental contributions to the comparative study of cultures, has recently examined similarities and differences between episodes of the revival of antique values in China, Islam, and the West. For Goody, the Renaissance was part of a family of renascences, paralleled, for instance, in the Islamic world in the 'humanism' of a series of scholars, starting with Abdullah Ibn Qutayba, who called for beneficent government in the ninth century in the course of philological studies targeted on establishing the accuracy of ancient texts and reminiscent, in some ways, of those which Western scholars came to practise.

As Muslims occupied much of the heartland of classical antiquity in the Hellenistic world and the former Roman Empire, they had access to the same legacy as Latin Christians: indeed, the availability of texts and intact monuments from Graeco-Roman antiquity was superior in Islam, which covered relatively less despoiled and ravaged parts of the region. So not only is it reasonable, in principle, to look for renaissances in the Islamic world: it would be surprising if there were none. And, as we shall see, some of the texts with which Latin Christendom renewed acquaintance in the Renaissance had formerly passed through Muslim hands and Arabic translations, from which Western copyists and retranslators recovered them.

Other transmissions of classical models came from Eastern Christendom, especially through Syriac translations of classical texts and via Byzantine art and scholarship, from regions around the eastern Mediterranean where the classical tradition was easier to sustain than in the West. Unsurprisingly, renaissances have become part of the vocabulary of historians of Byzantium, too, especially in the context of the revival of humanist scholarship and retrospective arts in Constantinople in the late tenth century. Byzantine workers in bone and ivory, who usually avoided pagan and lubricious subjects, were able in a brief dawn in and around the reign of Constantine VIII to make such delicate confections as the Veroli casket, where the themes are all of savagery tamed by art, love, and beauty. Hercules settles to play the lyre, attended by cavorting putti. Centaurs play for the Maenads' dance. Europa poses prettily on her bull's back, pouting at pursuers and archly waving her flimsy stole.

Historians of civilizations far from the classical, Hellenistic, and Roman frontiers have now appropriated 'renaissance' as a term for analogous revivals. All cultures have their own 'classics' and retrospective values become fashionable or popular or influential almost everywhere from time to time. In China, neo-Confucian revivals happened at intervals during what we think of as the Middle Ages and the early modern period in the West. One might without much more contrivance also cite the retrospective scholarship of the Buddhist priest Keichu in seventeenth-century Edō (now Tokyo), reconstructing classic texts, rediscovering forgotten values, and searching for authentic versions of Shinto poems, half a millennium old, which became the basis of a born-again Shintoism, stripped of the accretions of the intervening centuries.

The problem of influence

Analogies are one thing, influence another. Similar episodes in the history of different cultures may arise independently, or be traceable to common causes rather than to the diffusion of influence from place to place. If we agree to assign to the Renaissance, for the range and durability of its influence, exceptional prominence in the history of the world, and grant that it arose independently within Western tradition without decisive influence from elsewhere, the potential implications are arresting: the claim that the Renaissance was an entirely home-grown movement, without debts to extra-European influences, then becomes inseparable from the case for what is commonly called Eurocentrism—the assertion of uniqueness of Western achievements and their unparalleled impact on the rest of the world. The Renaissance, in such circumstances, would have to be seen as one of the West's gifts to the rest. But would that be a valid or useful vision? Would it be consistent with the evidence?

The doctrine of the 'uniqueness of the West' has long been in retreat. Today, the rise of global history on one side and of local history or micro-history on the other diminishes the Renaissance. The former 'provincializes Europe', as some scholars like to say, by locating it in a larger conceptual whole. The latter atomizes what formerly looked like a single movement, by drawing attention to local anomalies and peculiarities. Historians have tried to 'reframe' or 'decentre' the movement, to detach it from the Grand Narrative. All the same, the importance of the Renaissance in the 'rise of the West', the origins of 'modernity', or the vanguard of cultural 'globalization' (more precisely, in the conquest of much of the world by values and practices of Western origin) still has powerful academic advocates and tenacious popular appeal. It is hard to find a global history textbook for students or popular consumption or televised history on an appropriate scale that does not give the Renaissance privileged space and ascribe to it decisive influence. It is time to put the doctrine of the centrality of the Renaissance in global history to the test of conformity or variance with the facts.

A further, comparative problem arises: how to fit the Renaissance not only into the context of other, similar episodes in other cultures, but also to locate it in the history of such events across time. Great cultural movements do not usually happen by parthenogenesis. Cross-fertilization nearly always helps and is usually vital. Western initiatives have usually been inexplicable or unintelligible without the context of trans-Eurasian transmissions of influence. In classical antiquity, for instance, Helicon had an 'east face': ancient Greeks shared much of their lore with, and got some of their learning from, cultures on the eastern shore of the Aegean, or in Egypt or Mesopotamia. Logic, philosophy, science, art, and religious thought in the first millennium BCE exhibited, from East Asia to Mediterranean Europe, continuities so strong as to suggest that some content, at least, must have been transmitted along the trade routes that spanned or looped the land mass.

In the case of the high Middle Ages, it is hard to accept that the florescence of ideas and technologies in Western Europe was unstimulated by influences that flowed with the 'Mongol Peace'. The period of acceleration in science in early modern Europe owed some of its urging to the discoveries explorers, scholars, and specimen-hunters made in the Americas, Asia, and Africa. The Enlightenment of the eighteenth century, we increasingly acknowledge, borrowed aesthetic and political models from China, India, and Japan, and relied on contacts with remoter cultures, in the Americas and the Pacific, for such influential notions as those of the noble savage and what has been called 'green imperialism'. If the Renaissance were to have happened in Europe without comparable external influences the anomaly would be startling.

The rupture of contacts

Nonetheless, the case for seeing the Renaissance as an event severed from extra-European sources of influence is, on the face of it, strong. Previous and subsequent intellectual and artistic movements of long reach owed a lot to 'interculturation' along the Silk Roads and across the Indian Ocean. But from the mid-fourteenth to the late fifteenth centuries, in the very period when the Renaissance, as we define it, took shape, Latin Christendom was experiencing an age of intense cold and plague—conditions apparently hostile to, and very different from, those of, say, the high Middle Ages and the eighteenth century. 'The West' was largely isolated during the formative period of the Renaissance in the fifteenth century, with few or none of the enriching contacts with China, central Asia, and India that had inseminated earlier movements with exotic notions and representations or equipped them with useful knowledge and technology or inspiring ideas. We often speak of America as 'unknown', except to its own inhabitants, in the Middle Ages. But so, in a sense, was Europe, which hardly figured on the maps and in the calculations of the immensely richer, more populous, and technologically more advanced civilizations of maritime Asia.

The rupture of trans-Eurasian contacts occurred just as the Renaissance was becoming discernible in the work of Petrarch and Boccaccio and in the art of Sienese and Florentine successors of Giotto and Duccio. In the 1340s, Ambrogio Lorenzetti painted a scene of Franciscan martyrdom, surveyed by Mongol and Chinese onlookers. At about the same time Francesco Balducci Pegolotti wrote his guidebook for Italian merchants along the Silk Roads. An Italian miniature of the same period in the British Library shows a plausible Mongol khan banqueting while musicians play and dogs beg. Less than a generation later, Andrea da Ferrara depicted the Dominican Order spreading the gospel over what Westerners then knew of the world— somewhat in the fashion of what later became triumphalist Jesuit images of universal evangelization—with what seem to have been intended for Chinese and Indian participants in the scene.

Then, however, trans-Eurasian travel was severely curtailed. The collapse of the Yüan dynasty in 1368 ended the Mongol Peace, or at least shortened the routes it policed. Rome lost touch with the Franciscan mission in China, which seems to have withered by the 1390s as its existing staff died out, and faced the hostility of the Ming. No further individual cases of European travellers crossing Eurasia are known before the sixteenth century. The West in which the Renaissance matured and flourished was more isolated from remote Asian centres of art and learning than classical Greece, or high medieval Latin Christendom, or Enlightenment Europe. When Columbus set out for China in 1492, his royal masters' information about that country was so out of date that they furnished him with diplomatic credentials addressed to the Great Khan.

The discovery of the world

In the interim, not much happened to repair the broken links between Latin Christendom and other civilizations. Jules Michelet, the historian who launched the concept of the Renaissance in the mid-nineteenth century, summarized it as 'The Discovery of the World and of Man'. His successors have assumed a link between what they often call 'outreach' or even 'out-thrust' from parts of Europe and new humanist scholarship, learning, and ways of looking at the world; implicitly, the effect is to make Europeans active makers of the Renaissance, and the rest of the world the passive recipients of its echoes and benefits. Yet, although in the sixteenth century European explorers, colonists, *conquistadores*, merchants, missionaries, artefacts, and printed books and engravings did carry elements of the culture of Latin Christendom to faraway regions, long-range contact in what we usually think of as the formative period of the Renaissance in the fourteenth and fifteenth centuries was conspicuous by its absence.

It owed, in any case, less, at first, to new learning than to traditional lore: tales of knight-errantry and derring-do, in which protagonists, frustrated by the limitations of an unnavigable acceptance world at home, sought wealth, fame, and power by setting out on long-distance adventures, usually by sea, discovering new lands, contending with monsters, and typically achieving a fade-out involving marriage with a native princess and elevation to rulership.

In real life, from the fourteenth century to the early seventeenth, explorers from Europe's Atlantic edge emulated these heroes, seeking and, surprisingly, realizing similar trajectories of their own. Increasingly, in the late fourteenth and fifteenth centuries, some communities along Europe's western edge—mainly in Portugal and Spain, but also, to a lesser extent, in France, England, the Netherlands, and Denmark—turned to exploration of the Atlantic in a search for resources, rather like 'Third World' countries today, desperately drilling offshore. But the prevailing westerly winds seemed to pinion them inside the area east of the Azores. The intensification of efforts in the early and mid-fifteenth century, from ports in Iberia and France, to get further into the ocean and further around the African coast occurred in conditions of, at best, only modest recovery, as did attempts in the same period to penetrate the Sahara from starting points mainly in Italy. Much the same can be said of Russian voyages in the White Sea in the same period, which are ill documented, but which seem to have displayed, as far as the sources go, some of the features of Western European seaborne exploration at the same time: purportedly religious inspiration, mercantile finance and activity, monkish colonization of remote islands, painful adjustment to new environments, and the expulsion or extinction of indigenous inhabitants.

Gradually, however, the intellectual context of the Renaissance began to have an effect on the ambitions and outlook of explorers. Humanists wanted to know whether the golden age of primitive innocence, of which antique poets sang, was instantiated in remote regions of the world. Philologists wondered whether the languages of apparently primitive peoples could cast light on the problem of identifying the language of Eden or the relationship between the tongues of the world after Babel. What we have come to call 'early anthropology' pondered whether phases of development characterized universal history and how humans were related to apes. The hunt was on for the monstrous beings with whom Pliny peopled the fringes of the earth.

More directly influential for explorers' trajectories, however, were the strictly geographical problems classical texts raised. Although debate invoked many texts, two were dominant. Ptolemy, whose *Geography*, compiled in second-century Alexandria, dwarfed all other authorities on the subject in the fifteenth-century West, not only raised the question of the accessibility of the Indian Ocean, but also helped to reignite old enquiries about the size of the globe. Debate intensified about the extent of the eastward prolongation of Asia, the size and navigability of the ocean, and the importance of establishing coordinates of longitude and latitude for the accurate mapping of the world. Strabo's *Geography*, which first became available in Italy in Greek texts in the 1420s, helped focus interest on the problem of the existence and, if they existed, the location of the Antipodes—a speculative continent or continents that invited discovery. While geographical discourse became fashionable among European savants, the quest for the Antipodes, in which at one time Columbus proposed to take part, became one of the most consistent objectives of European explorers.

Among participants in the conversations and related activities—and a collector of ancient geographical lore—was Prince Pedro of Portugal, whose brother, Henrique, is known traditionally but misleadingly as 'the Navigator'. Henrique never made more than a couple of short trips by sea, but became a promoter of exploration in the African Atlantic. His project combined the conquest of the Canary Islands (in which the prince made little progress), the colonization of the Madeira group and the Azores, the acquisition of west African slaves (itself perhaps influenced by what people at the time thought of as a classical way of life), and the search for the sources in west Africa of the Saharan gold trade. By the time of his death in 1460, Henrique's ships had groped as far as the lee shores that obstructed their route beyond the latitude of the Cape Verde Islands. In 1469 a commercial sponsor, Fernão Gomes, took over the concessions Henrique had obtained from the crown and the papacy, and, until the crown revoked his rights in 1475, pursued the work of exploration as far as Cape St Catherine, two degrees north of the equator. Thereafter, under royal patronage, exploration, trade, and evangelization increased, especially after the inauguration of relations with the kingdom of Kongo in the 1480s and the arrival there in the following decade of permanent Portuguese missions. In 1488, Bartolomeu Dias rounded the Cape of Good Hope, albeit with difficulty that deterred followers. By about that time charts—coordinated by Duarte Pacheco and the originally Moravian compiler known as Valentim Fernandes in a work of 1508—recognizably showed every feature of the west African coast, despite considerable errors in longitude and some small ones in latitude.

Coastwise exploration, however, against the current, was too slow and painful to yield a route to the Indian Ocean—even had Dias not found the Cape to be dangerous and hostile to navigation. Portuguese cabotage contributed little or nothing to knowledge of the high Atlantic. The fifteenth century was nearly over, and 'the discovery of the world' had got stymied without getting very far. There was still no direct contact with south or east Asia. The Americas were still unknown and unsuspected.

Yet with extraordinary suddenness, after such a long period of gestation, preparation, and frustration, explorers went on to crack the code of the Atlantic wind system within the space of a single decade. In 1490, Pedro Covilhão and Afonso de Paiva made overland journeys to the Indian Ocean to report on whether it was genuinely landlocked. In 1492–3 Columbus discovered viable, exploitable routes to and fro across the Atlantic, which, although they proved disappointingly useless as ways to maritime Asia, opened up alluring possibilities of other kinds. Voyages in Columbus' wake revealed the south Atlantic wind system, which, in 1497, Vasco da Gama could use to break through into the Indian Ocean, and which led Cabral to Brazil in 1500. Once the sea-route to the Indian Ocean was open, the monsoons ensured relatively fast and easy navigation to south-east Asia and China, where Portuguese emissaries arrived in 1512.

Private capital paid for the breakthrough and explains its suddenness. In the 1480s Atlantic exploration, after a long unremunerative period, began to yield dividends. The revenues of Madeira, by dint of a long, cumulative process, started to make a conspicuous contribution to the finances of the Portuguese crown. In the north Atlantic, turnover increased in valuable commodities, such as narwhal and walrus ivory, whaling products, and perhaps (though the evidence is equivocal) salt cod. Sugar production began in the Canary Islands—where most of the future financiers of Columbus already had heavy commitments—in 1484. Two years earlier, the Portuguese trading post of São Jorge (now Elmina) on the underside of west Africa's bulge, began to yield significant amounts of gold. There is nothing like profit to stimulate investment. Backers were willing to take risks with explorers—even those, like Columbus, Cabot, and Vasco, whose projects were implausible—only when the ocean had proved itself as an investment opportunity.

In any case, the achievements in question were not so much those of Europe in general as of a few communities dispersed along Europe's Atlantic edge. For world-ranging explorers, maritime tradition and access to Atlantic winds were of more importance than any feature of European culture generally. Indeed, the discoveries of the 1490s were not, strictly speaking, discoveries of unknown lands—which of course were already well known to their inhabitants—but of unexploited winds. The history of the world, as traditionally written, contains too much hot air and not enough wind.

Encounters with Byzantine culture

More important than any cultural contacts explorers opened in the fifteenth century were links between contiguous regions in Europe and the Near East. Some scholars have stressed exchanges across the Alps between Italy and the sites of a 'northern Renaissance' that had some distinctive features. But these instances of interpenetration serve only to make the Renaissance seem more variously European, not to identify sources of influence from the wider world. The mutual influence of Western and Eastern Christendom was also a vital part of the context. The impact of encounters between Latin and Byzantine scholars at the Council of Florence, for instance, is uncontested. The Council was a meeting place for delegates of astonishingly wide provenance, demonstrating that Renaissance Europe, though relatively isolated, was by no means sealed. The Byzantine emperor brought 700 people in his train. Copts from Egypt and Ethiopia sent delegations. Niccolò Conti, a trader who had been as far as Java, came to the Council seeking absolution for having saved his life, at one point in his travels, by abjuring Christianity. His report, recorded by the humanist Poggio Bracciolini, who already had an excellent reputation as an editor of classical texts, helped enlarge the world-picture of his Western contemporaries. The *Mappa Mundi* that Fra' Mauro made in Venice in the 1440s assembled—as appears from internal evidence—data contributed by some of these visitors, as well as traditional literary and cartographic sources.

The impact of Byzantine culture on Western Europe, especially Italy, was not only the effect of the Council. It used to be claimed that the fall of Constantinople to

Ottoman forces in 1453 led to a flight of Greek scholars to Italy and so to the revival of Greek studies. Greek studies were indeed revived, and refugee scholars from Byzantium played an important part in this process. However, they had already begun to flee westwards earlier in the fifteenth century as the Ottomans drew nearer and nearer to the Byzantine capital. In any case, some Italian humanists such as Francesco Filelfo spent years in Constantinople and brought back manuscripts of the classics.

Islam and the Renaissance

The culture from which the Christian world appropriated most in the centuries preceding the Renaissance was Islam. The best-known examples concern cultural borrowings from Arabic and Persian traditions, from 'Moorish' Spain and from the Ottoman Empire. Scholars concerned with the classical tradition in the Middle Ages have long been aware of the importance of the Islamic world, especially of the Muslims of southern Italy and Spain, in the transmission of Greek learning to the West. Research on Arab translations of Greek thinkers continues, even though the importance of the role of Muslims (which included interpretation, adaptation, and elaboration as well as translation) has not always received the recognition that it deserves.

In the visual arts, the striped churches of medieval Siena and elsewhere imitated the decoration of mosques in Cairo, Damascus, and elsewhere, while the famous hospitals of Florence and Milan in the fifteenth century followed precedents in Damascus and Cairo. The ogee arches framing the windows of late medieval Venetian palaces were an 'orientalizing' touch, while the *fondachi* in which foreigners (such as Germans and Turks) were segregated are similar to, and copied from, the *funduqs* familiar to Venetian merchants who resided in Aleppo and elsewhere. The design of the Doge's Palace (it has recently been argued) alluded to the architecture of Mamluk Cairo, while Piazza San Marco was inspired by the courtyard of the Great Mosque at Damascus.

COSTANZO DA FERRARA, who was one of the Italian artists who went to Constantinople to paint Mehmed II in the 1470s, also produced this medal of the same subject as 'Emperor of Byzantium'. Especially after conquering the city in 1453, Mehmed took a great interest in his potential role as the inheritor of the authority of ancient Roman emperors and became a lavish patron of Renaissance artists and craftsmen.

In Spain, Toledo was a favoured destination for students from twelfth-century Latin Christendom if they wanted to be at the cutting edge of learning. Daniel de Morlay went there to learn Arabic. Gerbert of Aurillac, who became Pope Sylvester II, went there to learn mathematics. Gerard of Cremona went there to translate Ptolemy's *Almagest* and the medical encyclopedia of the eleventh-century Persian sage known as Avicenna, which became one of the most influential texts in the history of Western medicine.

In some ways it may be helpful to think of the western Mediterranean in the Middle Ages not as a zone severed by Muslim conquests into two mutually uncommunicative zones, but as a region where some elements of cultural unity, or at least some habits of cultural exchange, survived, and where literary themes, conventions of behaviour, and decorative features in architecture and the arts could cross the sea and look similar or identical on either shore. Time, however, and growing religious antagonisms, fears, and hatreds would erode contacts and accentuate differences.

In contrast to studies of the Middle Ages, which discuss the topic in detail, accounts of the Renaissance have had a relatively modest (though growing) amount to say about contributions from the world of Islam. In the second half of the fifteenth century, scholars and artists rattled back and forth across the eastern Mediterranean between the Ottoman and Italian courts. Mehmed II, 'the Conqueror', saw his acquisition of Constantinople by conquest in 1453 as conferring on him the status of continuator of the Roman Empire. George of Trebizond, who taught Greek in Rome after coming west for the Council of Florence, returned to Constantinople in 1465 in the hope of achieving Ottoman patronage. Meanwhile, in 1461, the ruler of Rimini, in pursuit of an alliance, sent his court painter to depict Mehmed; the Doge of Venice did the same in 1479. Mehmed was the dedicatee of a translation of Ptolemy's *Geography* by the Florentine scholar, Francesco Berlinghieri. The artist Costanzo da Ferrara, during his time in Constantinople in the 1470s, where he made a famous medal depicting Mehmed, both absorbed and transmitted influences. After the sultan's death, Western artists continued to hope for patronage from his successor, Bayezid II, who issued invitations to both Leonardo and Michelangelo.

Renaissance painting would have looked very different without objects and pigments imported from Islamic countries: the turquoise and Turkish red that coloured canvases in unprecedented hues; the textiles and carpets that added texture to the scenes; the Kufic and pseudo-Kufic inscriptions painters added to lend an illusory air of authenticity to their depictions of the Holy Land in portrayals of sacred history. These influences are all present and occasionally prominent in *quattrocento* art. Demand for exotic types and settings in sacred painting drove artists to Islam as a source of inspiration and of models. Tatar slaves were the only alternative. Pisanello added their images in pursuit of what he presumably thought was local colour when he depicted the Trebizond of St George. Some of these captives reached European markets via the hands of Muslim middlemen and may have been converted to Islam en route. Others were the gleanings of Russian and Polish raids and ended up for sale in

Bruges, where, according to a Spanish visitor in 1432, their rarity value and supposed docility made them command three times the average price of other slaves.

In architecture, it is clear that influences from Islam were at least as important as in painting. The renewal of direct contact with India at the end of the fifteenth century extended the range of available models, mediated to the Portuguese via the Muslim courts with which they traded. Indian culture made an impact on Renaissance architecture in Portugal (the so-called 'Manueline style'), before the Jesuits and others brought Renaissance art in their baggage, as it were, to India. In Venice, the palace of Ca' Zen, built between *c.*1533 and 1553, has oriental arches on the façade, continuing a local tradition but also making an allusion to the economic and political involvement in the affairs of the Middle East of the palace's owners, the Zen family.

In the age of the *uomo universale*, when a number of outstanding individuals, not only Leonardo, mastered a number of arts and sciences, what happened in painting and architecture had inescapable parallels in what we would think of as mathematics, science, and technology. Piero della Francesca's understanding of perspective derived in part from his reading of Euclid in a translation from Arabic. The Franciscan mathematician Fra Luca Pacioli, who is credited with the first complete expositions in the West of double-entry bookkeeping and of triangulation, and who collaborated with Leonardo, relied heavily on Arabic treatises in composing his works. Copernicus was only one of the Western mathematicians and astronomers of the sixteenth century who drew on work compiled in Persia in the thirteenth century: the exact means of transmission is unclear but the echoes are unmistakable.

In the case of literature, Boccaccio and Chaucer were representative examples of Western writers who had access to many tales of oriental origin. There is a remarkable parallel between the lyrics of Petrarch and his followers and the *ghazals* of the Islamic world, evoking the sweet pain of love, the cruelty of the beloved, and so on. In any case, Petrarch was familiar with the poetry of the troubadours, who were in turn familiar with the poetry of Al-Andalus (the very name 'troubadour' is derived from the Arabic *taraba*, 'to sing').

A major contribution to the Spanish Renaissance is the picaresque romance, such as *Lazarillo de Tormes* (1554), in which a rogue (*pícaro*) is the hero, or rather the anti-hero. However, the picaresque tradition is a continuation of an earlier Arab tradition, that of the *maqamat*, going back to the tenth and eleventh centuries. In similar fashion, Western accounts of the tricks of beggars and thieves, going back to the fourteenth century and reaching their climax in the sixteenth, follow Arab accounts of the urban underworld, the *Banu Sasan*, from the ninth century onwards. This should not surprise us, since the growth of large cities in the Middle East, such as Cairo, Baghdad, and Damascus, also preceded the growth of cities in Western Europe.

In the domain of intellectual history, we have only fragments of information, fascinating as they are. We know, for example, that the commentary on Aristotle's *Poetics* by Averroes (Ibn Rushd) was published in Latin translation in Venice in 1481; that Regiomontanus transcribed the *Algebra* of al-Khowarizmi; that Peurbach and

Copernicus knew the work of the ninth-century Arab astronomer al-Battani; and that Avicenna (Ibn Sina) was studied in the Renaissance as he had been in the later Middle Ages. The humanist polymath Giovanni Pico della Mirandola was particularly open to ideas from different cultures. In his famous oration on the dignity of humanity, Pico quoted a remark by 'Abdala the Saracen', as he called him (more exactly Ibn Qutayba, who, as we have seen, anticipated features of what we think of as Renaissance humanism in tenth-century Iran), to the effect that 'nothing is more wonderful than man'.

The debt to Islam that we now see in the architecture of the Renaissance, from Portugal to Lithuania, Ukraine, and Moscow, where Italian engineers contributed to the building programme that Ivan III launched in 1472, was virtually invisible to previous generations. One reason for this invisibility is the fact that Renaissance artists learned most from the so-called 'minor', 'applied', or 'decorative' arts, the study of which used to be relatively neglected; or they absorbed techniques and technologies of Islamic origin, with little obvious effect on subject matter or style; or they introduced orientalizing touches which added exotic appeal to their work without seriously modifying its content. Renaissance maiolica, for instance, developed from the Hispano-Moresque tradition of ceramics, introduced to Italy by Catalan merchants from Majorca (hence the name 'maiolica').

Perhaps the biggest debt of Renaissance artists to Islamic culture was to the repertoire of decorative motifs, floral, calligraphic, and geometrical, that we still describe as 'arabesques'. In the fifteenth and sixteenth centuries, carpets and metalwork in this style (ewers, dishes, and so on) were fashionable items in Venice. It used to be thought that these forms of metalwork were made in Venice, and the style of decoration was labelled 'Veneto-Saracenic'. It is now believed, however, that these objects were made in Damascus and other places in the Middle East, often to order, complete with the coat of arms of the future owner. From the later fifteenth century onwards, Italian artists drew on this decorative repertoire. Benvenuto Cellini, for instance, attempted to emulate the decoration on Turkish daggers, while some artisans used arabesques to ornament books, both the leather covers and the texts themselves. Knowledge of these ornaments spread through Europe via printed pattern books such as Peter Flötner's *Maureskenbuch* (1549) or Jacques Androuet du Cerceau's *Grandes Arabesques* (1582).

South and east Asia

Still, in sum, the input from the Islamic world seems too limited, selective, and, in some cases, late to compromise the case in favour of the home-grown Renaissance. The most problematic provenance of possible influences in the making of the Renaissance lay beyond the Near and Middle Eastern heartlands of Islam—in India and China, which had contributed so much to Western arts and thought in antiquity and the Middle Ages and would do so again in the Enlightenment.

Early in the twentieth century scholars searched indefatigably for such origins, but with only very modest success. In 1910 the critic Oskar Münsterberg noticed the

A PAGE FROM PETER FLÖTNER'S *Maureskenbuch* of 1549—one of many pattern books of 'Moorish' inspiration at the time—illustrates the Renaissance fashion for arabesques. Flötner was also important in introducing Italian patterns to German designers.

SO-CALLED VENETO-SARACENIC METALWORK illustrates the European vogue for 'oriental' models in the arts. Though usually exported via Venice, ewers such as this, which is now in the Victoria and Albert Museum and probably came from Damascus, were typically of Syrian or Egyptian manufacture.

similarities between Leonardo's landscape style and Chinese precedents, arguing that the correspondences were too exact to be coincidental. Two years later Aby Warburg, the great cultural theorist who founded the Warburg Institute, discovered an Indian astrological image in the frescos in Palazzo Schifanoia in Ferrara (transmitted to Italy via the Arab astrologer Abu Ma'shar or Albumazar).

In 1922–5 Gustave Soulier, who had made a reputation as an expert on Cimabue, published *Les influences orientales dans la peinture toscane*, claiming that much that was innovative in Western painting of the late Middle Ages and Renaissance resembled Buddhist models from China and India; the similarities, he argued, in themes, gestures, the rendition of flesh, the etiolated complexions, the diaphanous textures, the delicate hands, the long fingers were so marked as to make it unthinkable that Westerners could have developed them by coincidence. The year 1925 was also the date of a monograph on Botticelli by Yukio Yashiro, a scholar who was drawn to that artist because, he said, he perceived an affinity—not, however, alleging any connection—between the work of Botticelli and Japanese traditions, from picture scrolls to the woodcuts of Utamaro.

In *La Chine, l´Italie et les débûts de la Renaissance* (1935), I. V. Pouzyna, a Russian expert on Renaissance philosophy, wove the evidence into a general theory: the Renaissance, at least in painting, was the result of Chinese influence. Under the scrutiny of Leonardo Olschki, however, towards the end of the Second World War, the sum of these early enquiries did not seem to amount to much. Most of the alleged Asiatic exoticism, he averred, was of Italian origin, both technically and stylistically: 'There is no trace of East Asiatic influence.' Since then, scholars rationally interested in the similarities between Chinese and Western art in the fifteenth century have focused on the development theories of common or universal sensibility, rather than on arguments for cultural transmission.

Technology, as far as we know at present, was the field in which medieval Europeans were keenest to appropriate Chinese influence. Many of the key technologies that we now associate with 'the rise of the West' to global hegemony originated in China and seem to have reached Europe in the course of the cultural transmissions of the high Middle Ages: nautical technologies, such as the separable bulkhead, the rudder, and direction-finding devices; key ingredients of early capitalism and industrialization, such as paper money and the blast furnace; and gunpowder, the key element in military firepower.

The temptation to seek continuations of Chinese influence in the fifteenth century is therefore strong. There are suggestive similarities between the engineering devices depicted in a section on implements in the early fourteenth-century Chinese treatise on agricultural improvements, the *Nong Shu*—gears, for instance, and devices for pumping, bridging, scaling, boring, and grinding—and drawings in *quattrocento* Italian designers' notebooks, from Mariano di Jacopo il Taccola, 'the Sienese Archimedes', and his fellow citizen Francesco di Giorgio Martini to Leonardo. No text of the *Nong Shu*, however, or anything similar, is known to have existed in Europe, and there are equally convincing precedents in fourteenth-century European works.

Printing continues to provoke speculations. Was Gutenberg's famous printing press a Western innovation, or a case of the transfer of technology from east Asia? There is no doubt that printing was invented in China, in the seventh century CE or soon after. However, printing in China usually took the form of 'block printing', of a whole page of text at a time, rather than of movable type, as in Europe. Block printing was better suited to the Chinese form of writing, with tens of thousands of ideograms in place of Western alphabets. All the same, the Chinese did experiment with movable type from the eleventh century onwards, while in Korea founts of movable type were cast and a twenty-four-letter alphabet was devised by order of two successive rulers in the first half of the fifteenth century, leading to a system of book production with what the French scholar Henri-Jean Martin has called 'an almost hallucinatory similarity to Gutenberg's'. Could Gutenberg have heard rumours about these innovations?

It is tempting to suggest that the news from Korea was sufficient to stimulate Gutenberg into creating his own press, just as news of the invention of a telescope in the Netherlands was apparently sufficient to stimulate Galileo into inventing his own one. However, for news from Korea to reach Gutenberg's ears it would have had to travel through the Islamic world, where printing was largely resisted until the end of the eighteenth century, so that there was little incentive to transmit the information. The evidence is inconclusive. Printing looks like one of those technologies, like farming, writing, and metallurgy, that arose independently in different places.

To explain the Renaissance, it is not necessary, therefore, to indulge in sensationalist fantasies about unrecorded Chinese fleets and embassies in fifteenth-century Europe. In any case, despite the interruption of former trans-Eurasian contacts, some transmissions did happen across Eurasia, or substantial parts of it, in the fifteenth century by credible, documented means, via Islam. The Muslim world filled and to some degree bridged the gap between Europe and south and east Asia. Chinese and Indian artefacts, which became models for European imitators, arrived in European courts as diplomatic gifts with embassies from Muslim potentates. Porcelain is recorded in gifts from Egyptian rulers to European counterparts from 1442 onwards. It is impossible to say how much of this material was either genuine porcelain or genuinely Chinese: factories in Samarkand and other centres produced imitations good enough to impress European clients. One way or another, however, porcelain or pseudo-porcelain objects, conveyed in embassies, could transmit images of Chinese origin to Europe. The effect on Western artists and their patrons did not take long to register. Lorenzo de' Medici accumulated fifty pieces, which he kept locked in his bedchamber.

The fifteenth-century Mamluk sultan of Egypt, Qa'it Bey, was perhaps the most important middleman between China and the West. Leonardo sought his patronage in the 1480s and was well placed to know the Chinese artefacts that had arrived among the sultan's diplomatic gifts. The embassy the Egyptian ruler sent to Florence in 1487 brought gifts that featured in paintings by other artists. Mantegna showed an interest in imitating Chinese porcelain from the 1450s, when he worked at the ducal court of Mantua, where some porcelain vessels were among the treasures of the Gonzaga dynasty. The Veronese painter Francesco Benaglio included what might have been intended for a representation of a lotus-form Ming pot in a painting of the next decade. In what is commonly said to be the first depiction of a porcelain object in Western art, one of the magi in Mantegna's version of the epiphany of about 1499 holds a Ming wine cup, painted with blue flowers. By the time Giovanni Bellini painted his *Feast of the Gods* in Ferrara in 1514, more porcelain had arrived in Venice with further Egyptian embassies in 1498 and 1508. He could include a copious set of blue-and-white china, in casual use among the revellers—but perhaps the vessels in question were modelled on relatively inexpensive European or Islamic imitations of Chinese ware: if so, early Ming designs inspired them.

The porcelain items that Qa'it Bey and his like sent to Europe introduced Westerners to Chinese painting, albeit of a specialized and limited kind. Muslim taste favoured stylized floral motifs, and these are apparent in the samples that appear in Western paintings. Chinese porcelain-painters of the period included many other subjects, especially dragons, phoenixes, lions, birds, fish, and winter gardenscapes, which, while appealing to established taste in Persia, were treated by artists in ways unfamiliar to Muslim customers. Figures in landscapes became increasingly common in the course of the fifteenth century. No inventory, as far as we know, describes the materials in sufficient detail for us to know how wide a range of images was available to Western artists; and most European ceramicists imitated the widely available wares from the Islamic world. To judge, however, from the way European potters decorated their attempts to imitate porcelain in the fifteenth century, they had a wide range of examples at their disposal; the fairly frequent occurrence of Chinese motifs, especially dragons, in other arts suggests the same inference. A Florentine chest or *cassone* of 1448 has many Chinese motifs, including a cloud-dragon. If there was any direct Chinese impression on Renaissance artists' imagination, porcelain is the most likely medium for it. By the sixteenth century, Genoese craftsmen were producing good imitations of Ming porcelain, though by then direct contact with China had reopened by way of the Cape Route across the Indian Ocean.

The Americas

If influences from Asia, beyond the frontiers of Islam, were slight or oblique, those from Africa and the Americas were—inevitably, because of the chronology of exploration—too late to play a part in the inception of the Renaissance. They were, however, copious and conspicuous in their day. Before Columbus crossed the Atlantic, cartographers and geographers speckled the ocean with allusions to the Antipodes and the Hesperides, but although this evidence shows that European minds were predisposed to fit the Americas into a classically inspired panorama of the world, they do not, of course, constitute real American influences on the Renaissance.

In one respect, America's impact on the Renaissance was fairly rapid: almost as soon as Columbus encountered it, the New World made an impact on the understanding of classical texts. Encounters with naked islanders turned Columbus' thoughts, perhaps, and those of Peter Martyr of Anghiera, certainly, to the classical Golden Age. Waldsee-müller and Ringmann revised their projected edition of Ptolemy to reflect the work of the new Ptolemy, Amerigo Vespucci. If readings of Pliny made explorers seek monsters and Amazons in the Americas, their disappointed quests led slowly to re-evaluations of the text.

In general, exploration of parts of the Americas brought revelatory amplifications of real experience of the world, which liberated minds from texts and stimulated empir-ical epistemologies. Columbus, who exulted in disproving Ptolemy, started a trend that became characteristic of early modern critical scholarship. New World ethnography contributed to departures from the classical frameworks of political and social thought. Thomas More's *Utopia* returned to its place of inspiration by 1531. 'Aristotle and the American Indians' proved an explosive combination. Contemplation of the evidence of Native American societies inspired Las Casas and the Jesuit José de Acosta with schemes, unprecedented in antiquity, of how to narrate the history of social and cultural change.

As European knowledge of the material culture of the New World grew, occasional American motifs can be found in Renaissance art and architecture, from Rome to Liège, where finials inspired by Aztec featherwork, sent from Cortés to Charles V, surmounted the bishop's palace. In Viseu Cathedral in Portugal, in a painting by Vasco Fernandes, a Brazilian native took on the role of one of the three kings of the Epiphany in an almost instant effect of the circulation of the first images of Brazil in maps and woodcuts illustrative of or inspired by Vespucci's voyages. Other Brazilians danced in court masques. In a woodcut representing the triumphs of the Emperor Maximilian in about 1517 or 1518, Hans Burgkmair included sheaves of maize—though he placed them, oddly, in the hands of inhabitants of Calicut. In most respects, America was slow to change European minds. Knowledge seeped through. Most recipients assimilated it without adapting their own ideas, save gradually or grudgingly. Still, it is hard to imagine early modern European science, literature, or art without the ultimately transforming effect of specimens, images, and reports from across the Atlantic.

Meanwhile, a few individuals with prominent roles in the Renaissance, from Albrecht Dürer to Grand Duke Cosimo de' Medici, collected early examples of art made for export: objects from Africa in what is now known as an 'Afro-Portuguese' style. An inventory of Cosimo's possessions made in 1553 mentions two Afro-Portuguese ivory horns, while in 1560 his wife, Eleonora di Toledo, owned five Afro-Portuguese ivory spoons. Local artisans adapted their tradition to what Europeans wanted: ivory tableware, including forks and spoons, beaded and braided in imitation of the embellish-ments of Manueline architecture, and adorned with carvings in which European subjects such as centaurs or coats of arms appear alongside elephants and crocodiles. These hybrid products may be viewed equally well as African contributions to the Renaissance or as witnesses to the spread of the Renaissance to Africa.

THIS EARLY SIXTEENTH-CENTURY PORTUGUESE *EPIPHANY*, often but insecurely attributed to Vasco Fernandes, is the first such work to draw on a Native American model for one of the magi. By convention, one magus was typically black, but here a Brazilian native, as depicted in maps and engravings to travellers' tales, takes his place.

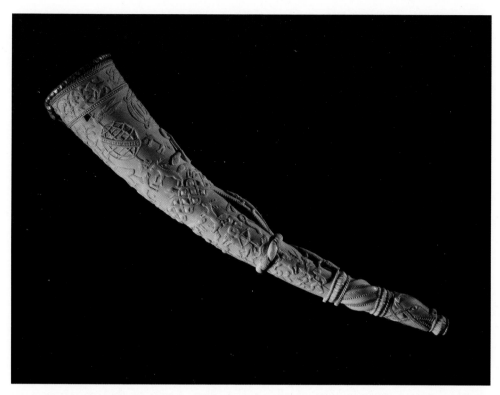

AFRO-PORTUGUESE IVORY HORN, sixteenth century, now in the British Museum, illustrating the hybrid style adopted by African artisans working for the Portuguese market. A globe surmounts scenes of warfare and hunting in which African and European people and animals take part.

Dissemination and reception of the Renaissance

Innovation is usually the result of either social change or encounters with other cultures. In the case of the Renaissance, the urbanization of Europe was making the example of urban cultures such as Rome and Athens more relevant to Europeans than it had been. We have already seen what Renaissance art, literature, and ideas owed to other cultures, especially the world of Islam. It is time to examine the extent to which and the ways in which the Renaissance and its products spread beyond Europe.

Both people and things played important parts in the process of dissemination. Travellers, missionaries, conquerors, settlers, works of art, and other objects of material culture transmitted ideas and images. By a remarkable coincidence, the ocean-spanning reach of European navigations, which, as we have seen, began with amazing suddenness in the 1490s, came just at the moment when the printing industry was beginning to boom in the voyagers' homelands. Books bore explicit ideas; engravings could transmit thinking implicitly and acquaint people who had never met a European with the themes, techniques, and content of Western art, which captured attention and imagination in regions it had never previously reached and among peoples whom it had never previously touched.

When Mehmed the Conqueror began construction of the Topkapı Sarayı—his dauntingly big palace-complex—he tried to get leading Italian architects onto his payroll, including Filarete, who advocated ancient Roman models as the means of building an ideal city, and Michelozzo, who designed the Medici palace in Florence.

The effects of the New World on the Renaissance were more modest than those of the Renaissance on the New World, where classical learning shaped Europeans' perceptions of what they encountered and the way they behaved in response. Gonzalo Fernández Oviedo and Acosta both followed the model of Pliny in their natural histories of the Indies. Pietro Martire and João de Barros both entitled their histories 'Decades' in homage to Livy, implicitly comparing the rising Spanish and Portuguese empires with that of Rome. Knowledge of Greek and Roman paganism occluded missionaries' understanding of indigenous religions, few, if any, of which were best understood as enshrining pantheons of personal deities, each with responsibility for his or her own department of nature. The grammars of non-European languages—Nahuatl, Quechua, or Tupí—produced by missionaries with a humanist training, followed the model of Latin grammars, despite the structural differences between those languages and Latin.

Humanism was quickly introduced to the New World and especially to New Spain. After the Spanish conquest of Mexico, Latin schools were established in Mexico City, in Michoacán, and most famous of all, in Tlatelolco. Some of the masterpieces of Renaissance literature, notably *Utopia* and *Don Quijote*, were well known in the New World. Some humanists arrived from Spain, among them Francisco Cervantes de Salazar, who taught at the newly founded university in Mexico City in the middle of the sixteenth century. Humanist academies were founded on the European model, notably the Academia Antártica in Lima in the 1590s.

Contributions to Renaissance literature were also made in the New World. Petrarch's lyrics were translated into Spanish in Peru, and a member of the Academia Antártica, Diego Davalos y Figueroa, published poems in a Petrarchan style. The Spanish poet Alonso de Ercilla wrote his famous epic the *Araucana* in South America, describing the resistance to the Spaniards by the indigenous people of Chile (then a remote part of the viceroyalty of Peru) and presenting this resistance in a heroic style inspired by both classical epic and Ariosto. Gaspar de Villagrá began his epic on the conquest of New Mexico with the words 'Arms and the heroic man I sing'.

Translation, hybridity

Much of what was transmitted changed in the course of transmission, whether consciously adapted or misunderstood. Hence scholars have come to speak of the spread and 'reception' of the Renaissance in terms of domestication, syncretism, hybridity, cultural translation, and creolization. These concepts have cast so much light on the problems of how cultural (or, more specifically, intellectual and artistic) movements happen that it seems possible in principle that they may illuminate the origins of the Renaissance.

Students of the origins of religions, languages, fashions, artistic movements, technologies, cuisines, and ideas have successfully applied similar models of how diverse influences from mutually distinct cultures converge creatively. The idea of cultural hybridity or *métissage, mestizaje,* or *mestiçagem* is one of the rare successes of what is sometimes called 'Southern Theory', produced on the cultural periphery, in Havana, for instance, or Recife, and later adopted by the centre, in Paris and New York. The systematic study of this domain goes back to scholars working on Afro-American cultures in the Caribbean and Brazil, from the 1930s onwards, among them Gilberto Freyre, Fernando Ortiz, and Alejo Carpentier, the author of an important study of music in Cuba that discusses the interaction of musical cultures on the island as early as the sixteenth century. Carpentier noted the survival, after the Spanish conquest, and even the employment in church music, of indigenous instruments such as the *maraca* (a rattle made from gourds containing seeds) and the *güiro* (a ribbed gourd that is scraped with a stick).

In the last generation, the older language of hybridity has been increasingly replaced by a linguistic model, and cultural historians, like anthropologists, now speak of 'cultural translation', when what is adopted from one culture is also adapted to suit the needs of the other. One advantage of this model is that it offers more space for human agency, for the work and the skills involved in the process of translation.

In an incisive account of the consequences of cultural encounters, the American anthropologist Marshall Sahlins distinguished between two stages of the process. In the first stage, the cultural order absorbs new elements in fragmentary form, so that we might speak of localization, or 'indigenization'. In a second stage, after a critical threshold is passed, the cultural order is itself transformed. It is at this point that some scholars speak about creolization, in other words the emergence of a new grammar for a new order. In this context another term from linguistics may be useful. Students of language contact speak of 'convergence', at the level both of individual words and of entire languages. In the case of lexical development, two similar words become one, combining the meanings of the original two. Whole languages also come to resemble each other more closely after contact. In the case of other forms of culture too, we might speak of perceived affinities leading to convergence.

A remarkable case of intellectual hybridity in the Renaissance is that of the 'Inca humanist' Garcilaso de la Vega, whose mother was an Inca princess, while his father was a Spanish *conquistador*. Garcilaso grew up in Peru but emigrated to Spain. He absorbed much of the culture of the Italian Renaissance and his library included books by Ficino and Bembo as well as Ariosto's *Orlando Furioso* and Castiglione's *Courtier*. His history of Peru before the coming of the Spaniards expressed his nostalgia for the lost empire of the Incas. He used the language or languages of Western humanism, from philology to Neoplatonism, to refute the Spanish claims that the Amerindians were barbarians and idolaters. He claimed that the inhabitants of Peru already believed in one God before the arrival of the Spaniards. His history implied that

Peruvian culture fitted the pattern of the ancient theology discussed by Ficino and others. Neoplatonists had a cult of the sun but the sun was also worshipped in Peru. In this way one form of syncretism, between pagan and Christian cultures in the first centuries after Christ, was used to justify another.

Spaniards wanted to bring the look of the Renaissance to the New World following the designs of Serlio, for instance, or decorating façades with medallions and grotesques. Vitruvian town planning and architectural precepts stamped the hemisphere with urban grids and speckled it with stoai and pediments. Indeed, it has been argued that the classical style of architecture played a political role in Spanish America because it both represented and reinforced the European sense of cultural superiority. The many new cities in the Americas often followed the regular grid plan recommended in Renaissance treatises on architecture but difficult to achieve in the old cities of Europe.

However, regular city plans were also part of local traditions, as in the case of Tenochtitlan, over which Mexico City was built, and military camps—also, perhaps, influential models in the minds of founders of early colonial towns—were generally laid out on a grid pattern. Conversely, so it has been argued, Albrecht Dürer's plan for a symmetrical ideal city was influenced by what he knew about Tenochtitlan.

Plans were extemporized by *conquistadores* or—in his capacity as the least uneducated person present—a priest; they were not usually, in the sixteenth and seventeenth centuries, the work of professionals. The grid pattern, though from the 1570s the crown repeatedly issued ordinances endorsing it, seems to have come almost unreflectingly to untutored minds. Pizarro, who could barely read, designed Lima himself, as a grid of 137 symmetrically arrayed blocks. Cuzco was exceptional in retaining its pre-conquest street plan, but the image of the colonial grid was so powerful that when the engravers of *Civitates Orbis Terrarum* depicted the city, they stamped it, erroneously, with the common pattern. To Brazil in 1549 with Tomé de Sousa, governor of Salvador de Bahia, came numerous artisans who developed the city, confined by the surrounding topography, in a triangular but grid-like layout. In 1554, barely a generation after the conquest, a guidebook to Mexico City, written in impeccably Ciceronian Latin, praised the main square as the 'forum' and the nascent university as the 'House of Apollo, Minerva, and the Muses'.

Distinctions naturally need to be drawn between the impact or influence of the Renaissance in Africa, Asia, and America. For example, the relative importance of the Renaissance in Spanish America owed a good deal to the Spanish expatriates who were trying to reproduce their home culture in their new home, whereas in most of Asia, outside the Philippines and a few relatively defensible enclaves, Europeans were present on sufferance and more or less at the mercy of indigenous states, with only selective opportunities to change the prevailing programmes in aesthetics or education.

Until quite recently it was assumed that there was nothing to say about the Renaissance in Africa, except perhaps for the ill-documented work that Portuguese craftsmen put into the building of a new palace for the ruler of Kongo in the early sixteenth century. But, as we have seen, 'Afro-Portuguese' ivories echoed themes

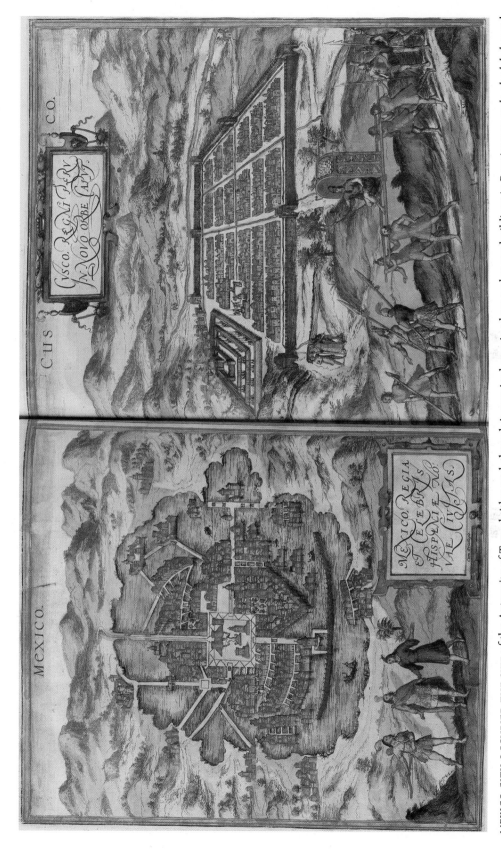

MEXICO CITY OCCUPIED THE SITE of the Aztec city of Tenochtitlan and, though it acquired a main plaza and many buildings in Renaissance style, the lakebound location ensured some continuity in appearance with the indigenous past. When Georg Braun and Franz Hogenberg placed a map of it alongside one of the former Inca courtly centre, in their great collection of engravings of *Civitates Orbis Terrarum* in 1572, they misrepresented Cuzco, which retained the pre-conquest street plan, as a typical colonial city, built on the grid plan familiar from ancient Roman ideals of urban planning.

EMISSIO SPIRITVS.   130

Matth. xxvij. Marc. xv. Luc. xxiij. Ioan. xix.   ciij

A. Excepit clamorem Christi emissio spiritus.
B. Tenebræ hactenus perseuerantes à sexta hora, incipiunt euanescere.
C. Velum templi ad Sancta sanctorum scissum in duas partes à summo, &c.
D. Contremiscit terra.
E. Petræ scinduntur, &c.
F. Monumenta multa aperiuntur.
G. Centurio videns, quod sic clamans expirasset, glorificat Deum.
H. Omnis turba videns, quæ fiebant, percutientes pectora sua reuertebantur.
I. Capiunt sæuum consilium Iudæi, vt crucifixis crura frangantur.
K. Mittunt ad Pilatum qui peterent, vt crucifixi fractis cruribus tollerentur.
L. Franguntur alijs crura.
M. Vnus militum lancea latus IESV aperuit.
N. Stabant longe omnes cognati, & mulieres.

A TYPICALLY PERSPECTIVE-RICH SCENE of the Crucifixion from *Evangelicae Historiae Imagines* of Jerónimo Nadal of 1593. The work, intended as an aid to meditation, reflects the Jesuits' importance as disseminators of such products and shows how exchanges of influence helped to produce Renaissance work: Nadal collected models of northern European artists' work as sources of inspiration.

A SEVENTEENTH-CENTURY CHINESE DRAWING of the Crucifixion shows Christ, the two Marys, the Roman soldiers, and other bystanders with Chinese features. Only the Jewish priests, skulking away in the bottom right, are depicted as foreigners.

454 *Felipe Fernández-Armesto and Peter Burke*

prominent in Europeans' minds. Hence African craftsmen might be said to have participated in the Renaissance without knowing that they were doing so. In east Asia, Jesuits brought the Renaissance along with the Counter-Reformation (in Europe, from England to Switzerland, Italian Protestants brought the Renaissance along with the Reformation!). The many studies of the Italian missionary Matteo Ricci make it abundantly clear that he introduced Chinese mandarins to Renaissance rhetoric, astronomy, geography, and the art of memory as well as to ancient philosophy. As in Mexico and Peru, the Jesuits imported religious prints into China, and as art historians have pointed out, these prints made a considerable impact on Chinese art, on landscape painting in particular. Chinese landscape painters did not imitate Western models, but awareness of an alternative to their own tradition helped them to innovate.

In Japan, the penetration of both Christianity and Renaissance culture was deeper than in China. Francis Xavier arrived with religious images and noted that they helped awaken interest in Christianity. Another Jesuit, the Italian Antonio Valignano, founded colleges at Arima (now part of Minabi Shinamara) and Azuchi. As in Mexico, Ciceronian Latin was taught in these colleges, using local editions of classical texts. Painting and engraving were also taught there. Some secular as well as religious paintings followed the models provided by European prints, including a screen with a battle scene based on a print of Lepanto. The Japanese 'embassy' of young samurai to Lisbon, Rome, and elsewhere in Europe (1582–90) brought paintings—and possibly a copy of Castiglione's *Courtier* as well—when they returned from their long visit.

The New World registered so much of the impact of the Renaissance because it was easy to reach from Europe, and because many or most indigenous cultures were hospitable to strangers and their ideas. East Asia, remote and less accessible, was harder to permeate owing to indigenous contempt for Western barbarians. But unless and until their European guests offended them by excesses of zeal or arrogance, Chinese and Japanese elites were disposed to welcome such useful knowledge and ideas as the Westerners were able to display. The missionaries believed that they had converted these elites to Christianity, but scholars who have studied the indigenous sources for this cultural encounter suggest that for both Chinese and Japanese 'converts', the new ideas were added to Buddhist and Confucian traditions rather than replacing them. Hence they speak of 'Confucian–Christian syncretism', for instance, and point out that the late Ming period, in the course of which the Jesuits founded their mission, was 'the heyday of syncretism in China' in which Judaism and Islam as well as Christianity were viewed through Confucian spectacles. Something similar occurred in art, where Western forms were assimilated into the traditional order of painting, whether consciously or as a result of the 'habitus', the embodied knowledge of the artists, a knowledge that was so much part of them as to have become unconscious.

The Islamic world

The world of Islam was different, influencing European culture but responding only very selectively to its allure. In the case of the Ottoman Empire, half in and half out of

Europe, the evidence is particularly rich and it has been studied intensively. As we have seen, Sultan Mehmed II shared the Renaissance interest in ancient Roman models of government. We now know that the sultan was not only the conqueror of Constantinople but also a patron of Italian artists such as Costanzo da Ferrara, who made a portrait medal of the sultan, and Gentile Bellini, who painted his portrait in oils. The Greek humanist George of Trebizond and the Florentine humanist Francesco Berlinghieri were among those who dedicated books to Mehmed, who showed interest in some classical texts, among them Ptolemy's geography and the histories written by Herodotus, Livy, and Quintus Curtius, the biographer of another conqueror, Alexander the Great. It was Ottoman rather than European expansion that led to cultural encounters and exchanges, although the examples cited in this paragraph show the Turks as receiving Renaissance culture rather than contributing to it.

Mehmed's successors were less oriented towards Italy, but Bayezid (to whom Leonardo once offered his services) invited Michelangelo to Istanbul, while in the earlier part of his reign, in the 1530s, Suleiman the Magnificent, encouraged by his grand vizier, Ibrahim Pasha, was a patron of Renaissance art, including a crowned helmet that he commissioned from a workshop in Venice and tapestries made by Flemish weavers who came to Istanbul for the purpose.

Much less is known about Safavid Persia, but we learn from recent research that the artist Kamāl ud-Dīn Behzād Bihzad copied Costanzo da Ferrara's drawing of a seated scribe, turning him into an artist in the process. The traveller Pietro Della Valle recorded seeing Italian paintings for sale in the city of Isfahan. The seventeenth-century painter Muhammad-Zaman ibn Haji Yusuf of Qom made use of Renaissance prints.

Mughal India was the furthest from Europe of the three gunpowder empires, but it was also the one with the most intensive cultural contacts with the West, especially in the time of the Emperor Akbar. Jesuits gave Akbar paintings and engravings, and Akbar ordered his artists to copy them. They coloured the prints and employed elements from them in their own work. For example, the miniature painter Basawan, Akbar's favourite, adapted prints by Dürer. The Jesuits introduced Renaissance architecture into India, where Serlio enjoyed an 'afterlife', like Vitruvius in Mexico.

There are even traces of humanism to be found there. In 1586, for instance, a Florentine merchant in Cochin found a copy of Castiglione's *Courtier* for sale there. The Jesuit press—starting in Goa, where operations began in 1556, and spreading beyond India with similar initiatives in Macau in 1581, Nagasaki in 1592, and the Philippines from 1593—concentrated on devotional books and translations of Christian materials in native languages but also produced contributions to the humanist curriculum, including a digest of philosophy attributed to St Francis Xavier and a Japanese version of Aesop's *Fables*.

On the fringes of the Mughal Empire and beyond it to the east, scattered Portuguese dwellers from Cambay to Melaka and Macao built homes and churches that echoed classicizing features of the architecture of home. In the Philippines, in the relatively small enclaves Spaniards settled, a world more like that of Spanish America took

TUMAMBA KHAN, with his wife and sons, from a manuscript, attributed in a note in red ink at bottom right to Basawan and his colourist, Bhim Gujarati, showing the legendary descent of the Mughal Emperor, Akbar, via Genghis Khan. Attendants bring perfumes, refreshments, and a classical-style architectural model to the scene. Though Basawan never allowed Western influence to predominate in his work, except when executing the emperor's orders to copy Western engravings, his handling of space was influenced by Western notions of perspective.

shape. Spaniards could found their own institutions of humanistic education and impose European-style townscapes on the land. Along with Catholicism, they introduced church music in Renaissance style. However, as often happens, what was intended by the Spaniards to be cultural transfer turned out in practice to be more like cultural exchange. The conversion of the Filipinos was accompanied by the 'philippinization' of Christianity, while in the case of music, according to a recent study, the Jesuit strategy of accommodation 'ensured the incorporation . . . into church music' of song in local languages. Indigenous musicians learned Western music from Spaniards and then passed on what they had learned, probably adapting it without knowing that they were doing so, while some indigenous genres were retained 'under the guise of hispanization'.

The main theme that emerges from our attempt at a bird's-eye view of the process is the importance of hybridization. In the case of painting and sculpture, a by-product of missionary endeavours to convert the Indians and to sustain their devotion was what has been described as an 'invasion of European images'. It began with the import of European religious prints and was followed by the arrival of European painters, and finally the rise of local artists working in a hybrid style and creating their own local forms (such as the Peruvian paintings of angels carrying guns). At the Mughal court, for instance, images of Christian saints and angels were used 'to proclaim a message based on Islamic Sufi and Hindu symbolism and linked with Persian poetic metaphor'.

Examples of Western art arrived in Japan before they arrived in China. Early in the 1560s, the Queen of Portugal sent a painting of the Virgin Mary to a Japanese nobleman (*daimyō*). In the 1580s, an Italian missionary, Giovanni Niccolò, established an academy in Nagasaki to train Japanese Christians to paint in the Western style. He also taught the art of engraving. Painted screens that represented the Europeans, known as 'Southern Barbarians' (*Nanban*), became fashionable in Japan around the year 1600, paying particular attention to details of their costume and their ships.

In China, examples of Western art were introduced by the missionaries. Ricci brought paintings in the Western style to Beijing, but a greater impact was made by Western engravings including illustrations of the Gospels, the famous atlas of Ortelius, and the views of cities collected in the *Civitates Orbis Terrarum*. The subsequent changes in Chinese landscape paintings have been described as 'a convergence of old Chinese practice and response to foreign stimuli'. The European engravings impressed the Chinese because, as one Jesuit wrote in a letter to Rome, they were 'considered very artistic and subtle because they make use of shadows, which do not exist in Chinese painting'. With their strong *chiaroscuro*, the engravings reminded some Chinese artists of landscapes painted during the Northern Song dynasty. These affinities led to a revival of the Northern Song style—with a difference, due to the new awareness of alternatives to Chinese traditions. Both Chinese and Japanese artists resisted Western perspective until the eighteenth century, remaining faithful to their traditional, non-geometrical forms of representing space.

PART OF A LANDSCAPE PAINTED in 1601 by the prolific Wu Bin, now in the Honolulu Museum of Art. Wu, born in Fujian, perhaps owed part of his reputation for originality to Western influence. His work shows a sense of perspective and an interest in depicting depth of space reminiscent of Renaissance landscapes.

In New Spain, Ovid's *Metamorphoses* were themselves metamorphosed. Mural paintings, for instance, might refer both to classical and local traditions, as in the case of the house of the Dean of Puebla, decorated with mural paintings of monkeys and female centaurs. In the case of architecture, the Spaniards made few concessions to local tradition. Indeed, it has been argued that the revived classical style both represented and reinforced the Spanish belief that their culture was superior to that of the Aztecs and Incas. All the same, some churches were built on the site of earlier temples and even used the same stones, as in the case of the cathedral of Cuzco, built from 1559 onwards on the ruins of the temple known as Kiswarkancha, or in Diego de Landa's great friary-church at Izamal, where the glyphs on recycled stones can still be seen in the cloister.

In both Mexico and Peru, the masons and sculptors were mainly indigenous. They probably had their own traditions, their own habitus (although we cannot be sure that they had worked as masons and sculptors before they were trained by the colonizers). As a result, the sculpture on church façades of the sixteenth and seventeenth centuries in the New World, especially Peru, may have been classical in its syntax but it was partly indigenous in its lexicon, in other words the converse of the *media lengua* of Ecuador. In the sixteenth century the combination of local and imported motifs is already visible. However, it was in the seventeenth century that a distinctive Peruvian style or ecotype emerged, which some art historians have named the *estilo mestizo*, and others 'hybrid baroque'. This hybrid style includes local items such as pumas on church façades as well as a tendency to decorate surfaces more fully and in a flatter manner than in the European architecture of the time, as if the artisans had translated designs from indigenous textiles into stone. A famous example of the style is the Jesuit church in Arequipa known as *La Compañía*.

The emergence of this *estilo mestizo* may have been encouraged by the Jesuits, whose missionary strategy in different parts of the world, from China to Peru, was that of 'accommodating' Christianity to local tradition. Hybridity is often the result of accommodation, a term that has recently come into use in linguistics, or more exactly come back into use, since ancient Roman rhetoricians already used the term.

The hybrid style of Peru may also have been encouraged by the interpenetration of Christian and Muslim cultures in medieval Spain, divided as it was into Christian and Muslim kingdoms. In Spain during the Middle Ages and the Renaissance, in Toledo for instance, in Alcalá and elsewhere, some Christian churches were decorated by Arab artisans in the so-called *mudéjar* style, with geometrical and calligraphic motifs of the kind to be found in mosques. It might therefore be suggested that Spanish colonial patrons of architecture were prepared by their experience in the peninsula to favour or at least to accept a mixture of European with indigenous artistic traditions. Bailey favours the idea of hybridization, Kaufmann is more suspicious.

It remains an open question whether decorations such as these, like the façades of churches from Arequipa to Goa, represent conscious artistic syncretism, or whether they are the unintended consequence of asking local craftsmen to follow European models that were unfamiliar to them. However, similar points may be made about European artefacts, from statues to texts, many of which combined elements from medieval and classical or from Christian and pagan traditions.

Conclusion

Several important general themes emerge from this survey. One is the role of missionaries in introducing the Renaissance as well as Christianity to the world beyond Europe. They brought religious images because of their content, but these images provoked interest on account of their style. The medium was part of the message. Missionaries are 'cultural interpreters', though they vary in their methods: for example,

THANKS TO THE EMPLOYMENT OF INDIGENOUS CRAFTSMEN, the Church of San Francisco, Quito—an unusually rich example of the colonial style of church architecture, of European inspiration in structure but local in detail—exhibits the distinctive Peruvian style which some art historians have named the *estilo mestizo*, and others 'hybrid baroque'.

the Jesuit policy of 'accommodation' to local cultures was criticized by rival orders such as the Dominicans, who were hostile to the idea of meeting potential converts halfway and translating the Christian message into terms that were at least semi-familiar to them.

Another recurrent theme is the important role of prints, which were easy to export in large numbers, in spreading the knowledge of Renaissance art. Vital, of course, were the contexts that made possible the long-range reception of culture of European origin: exploration, unprecedentedly far-flung empires, widening circles of trade, the increasing mobility of travellers, migrants, sojourners, and armies, and the technologies that made non-Europeans respect Western wisdom. It is hard, for example, to imagine China or Japan or some south-east Asian states evincing enthusiasm for ignorant, poor, smelly barbarians without the attractions of Jesuit cartography and astronomy.

But whether carried by war or wares, imperialism or example, and however modified by hybridity, the Renaissance was an unprecedentedly far-reaching movement. The impact of the Renaissance on much of the rest of the world was abundant: thin, of course, in most of the places it touched, but, in some areas, transforming.

If the Renaissance was global in its effects, the question of how far afield to trace its origins is harder to answer. The Renaissance did not start by conspicuous consumption. It was anomalous by the standards of comparable earlier and later movements, because it occurred at a time of attenuated trans-Eurasian contacts, with little or no input from east and south Asia. It is not possible to discern in the making of the Renaissance, on a similar scale, the obvious input from far afield that helped to stimulate innovations in the first millennium BCE, for example, or the high Middle Ages, or the Enlightenment.

Nevertheless, the Renaissance was a hybrid of European initiatives with transplantations of extra-European culture that originated in or passed through the Islamic world. Further impact—albeit slow and modest in effect—from the Americas and Africa helped shape the development of the movement in the sixteenth century. In the period of the making of the Renaissance, Europe was not conquered by a host of influences from outside. Rather, a threadbare series of stragglers penetrated the heartland, mostly from not very far afield, and made important but hardly decisive contributions.

In the case of the visual arts, at least, a provisional conclusion might be that Western culture had actually been more open to exotic influences in the Middle Ages than it was in the Renaissance, both during the period of Europe's relative isolation between the collapse of the Mongol Peace and the voyage of Vasco da Gama, and even during the 'high' Renaissance of the early sixteenth century, when the ideal of classicism (the 'grammar' of architecture, for instance) increased the obstacles to hybridization, which smacked of impurity. For instance, an analysis of possible cases of Mexican influence on the decoration of the loggia at the Vatican by Raphael and his workshop concluded that Aztec art was too alien to assimilate. All the same, not the least advantage of viewing the Renaissance from a global perspective is to make more visible processes of hybridization that were important at home as well, but have only come to be recognized quite recently.

FURTHER READING

Chapter 1: Humanism and the Classical Tradition

M. Baxandall, *Giotto and the Orators* (Oxford, 1971)

R. Black, ed., *The Renaissance; Critical Concepts in Historical Studies*, 20 vols (London, 2006)

R. Black, *Machiavelli* (London, 2013)

A. Brown, *The Renaissance*, 2nd edn (London, 1999)

J. Burckhardt, *The Civilization of the Renaissance in Italy* (first pub. in German in 1860; numerous reprs of the English tr.)

G. Ernst, *Tommaso Campanella: The Book and the Body of Nature* (Dordrecht, 2010)

P. Ford et al., eds, *Brill's Encyclopedia of the Neo-Latin World*, 2 vols (Leiden, 2014)

F. Gilbert, *Machiavelli and Guicciardini* (Princeton, 1965)

A. Grafton, *Joseph Scaliger: A Study in the History of Classical Scholarship*, 2 vols (Oxford, 1983–93)

A. Grafton, *Commerce with the Classics: Ancient Books and Renaissance Readers* (Ann Arbor, 1997)

A. Grafton et al., ed., *The Classical Tradition* (Cambridge, Mass, 2010)

L. D. Green and J. J. Murphy, eds, *Renaissance Rhetoric Short-Title Catalogue 1460–1700* (Aldershot, 2006)

J. Hale, *The Civilization of Europe in the Renaissance* (London, 1993)

J. Hankins, ed., *The Cambridge Companion to Renaissance Philosophy* (Cambridge, 2007)

C. Kallendorf, ed., *Humanist Educational Treatises* (Cambridge, Mass., 2002)

J. Kraye, ed., *The Cambridge Companion to Renaissance Humanism* (Cambridge, 1996)

P. Kristeller, *Renaissance Thought and its Sources* (New York, 1979)

P. Mack, *Renaissance Argument: Valla and Agricola in the Traditions of Rhetoric and Dialectic* (Leiden, 1993)

P. Mack, *A History of Renaissance Rhetoric 1380–1620* (Oxford, 2011)

A. Mazzocco, ed., *Interpretations of Renaissance Humanism* (Leiden, 2006)

A. Pettegree, *The Book in the Renaissance* (New Haven, 2010)

A. Rabil Jr, ed., *Renaissance Humanism: Foundations, Forms and Legacy*, 3 vols (Philadelphia, 1988)

L. D. Reynolds, ed., *Texts and Transmission: A Survey of the Latin Classics* (Oxford, 1983)

L. D. Reynolds and N. G. Wilson, *Scribes and Scholars: A Guide to the Transmission of Greek and Latin Literature*, 4th edn (Oxford, 2013)

E. F. Rice and A. Grafton, *The Foundations of Early Modern Europe, 1460–1559* (New York, 1994)

C. B. Schmitt et al., eds, *The Cambridge History of Renaissance Philosophy* (Cambridge, 1988)

Q. Skinner, *The Foundations of Modern Political Thought*, 2 vols (Cambridge, 1978)

R. G. Witt, 'In the Footsteps of the Ancients'. *The Origins of Humanism from Lovati to Bruni* (Leiden, 2000)

J. Woolfson, ed., *Palgrave Advances in Renaissance Historiography* (Basingstoke, 2005)

Chapter 2: War and the State, *c.*1400–*c.*1650

GENERAL

M. S. Anderson, *War and Society in Europe of the Old Regime, 1618–1789* (London, 1988)

J. Black, *European Warfare, 1494–1660* (London, 2002)

J. Black, *War in the World. A Comparative History, 1450–1600* (London, 2011)

P. Contamine, *War in the Middle Ages* (Oxford, 1984)

J. R. Hale, *War and Society in Renaissance Europe, 1450–1620* (London, 1985)

L. Martines, *Furies: War in Europe, 1450–1700* (London, 2013)

F. Tallett, *War and Society in Early Modern Europe, 1494–1715* (London, 1992)

F. Tallett and D. Trim, eds, *European Warfare, 1350–1750* (Cambridge, 2010)

PRIMARY SOURCES

J. de Gheyn, *The Exercise of Arms*, ed. D. Blackmore (London, 1986)

F. de Vitoria, 'On the Laws of War', in *Vitoria: Political Writings*, ed. A. Pagden (Cambridge, 1991)

D. Erasmus, *Praise of Folly*, trans. B. Radice (London, 1993)

D. Erasmus, *The Complaint of Peace*, trans. T. Paynell (Philadelphia, 2014)

H. Grotius, *The Law of War and Peace*, ed. S. Neff (Cambridge, 2012)

J. Lipsius, *Six Bookes of Politickes or Civil Doctrine* (London, 1594; facsimile edn, Amsterdam and New York, 1970)

N. Machiavelli, *The Art of War*, trans. E. Farneworth (New York, 1965)

N. Machiavelli, *The Prince*, ed. Q. Skinner (Cambridge, 1988)

T. More, *Utopia*, ed. G. Logan (3rd edn, Cambridge, 2016)

R. Williams, *A Briefe Discourse of Warre* (London 1590; repr. in J. X. Evans, ed., *The Works of Sir Roger Williams* (Oxford, 1972)

EUROPEAN POLITIES, ARMIES, AND WAR

C. T. Allmand, *The Hundred Years War: England and France at War c.1300–c.1450* (Cambridge, 1989)

C. Allmand, ed., *War, Government and Power in Late Medieval France* (Liverpool, 2000)

J. M. Bak and B. K. Király, *From Hunyadi to Rakocki; War and Society in Late-Medieval and Early-Modern Hungary* (Brooklyn, NY, 1982)

K. Barkey, *Empire of Difference: The Ottomans in Comparative Perspective* (Cambridge, 2008)

R. Bartlett and A. MacKay, *Medieval Frontier Societies* (Oxford, 1989).

M. C. Bartusis, *The Late Byzantine Army 1204–1453* (Philadelphia, 1997)

M. Burleigh, *Prussian Society and the German Order: An Aristocratic Corporation in Crisis, 1410–1466* (Cambridge, 1985)

F. W. Carter, *Dubrovnik (Ragusa): A Classic City State* (London, 1972)

D. Chambers, *The Imperial Age of Venice, 1380–1580* (London, 1970)

D. Chambers, *Popes, Cardinals and War: The Military Church in Renaissance and Early Modern Europe* (London, 2006)

J. Glete, *War and the State in Early Modern Europe: Spain, the Dutch Republic and Sweden as Fiscal-Military States, 1500–1660* (London, 2002)

D. Goffmann, *The Ottoman Empire and Early Modern Europe* (Cambridge, 2002)

M. C. 't Hart, *The Making of a Bourgeois State: War, Politics and Finance during the Dutch Revolt* (Manchester, 1993).

J. Israel, *The Dutch Republic and the Hispanic World, 1606–1661* (Oxford, 1982)

H. Kaminsky, *A History of the Hussite Revolution* (Eugene, Ore., 2004).

J. L. Keep, *Soldiers of the Tsar: Army and Society in Russia 1462–1875* (Oxford, 1985)

T. A. Kirk, *Genoa and the Sea: Policy and Power in an Early Modern Maritime Republic, 1559–1684* (Baltimore and London, 2005)

M. E. Mallett and J. R. Hale, *The Military Organization of a Renaissance State: Venice c.1400 to 1617* (Cambridge, 1984)

R. Murphey, *Ottoman Warfare, 1500–1700* (London, 1999)

J. M. Najemy, *A History of Florence, 1200–1575* (Oxford, 2006)

M. Newitt, *A History of Portuguese Overseas Expansion, 1400–1668* (London, 2008)

D. M. Nicol, *The Last Centuries of Byzantium, 1261–1453* (Cambridge, 1993)

C. Parker, *Global Interactions in the Early Modern Age, 1400–1800* (Cambridge, 2010)

G. Parker, *The Grand Strategy of Philip II* (New Haven and London, 1998)

G. Parker, *The Army of Flanders and the Spanish Road, 1567–1659: The Logistics of Spanish Victory and Defeat in the Low Countries* (2nd edn, Cambridge, 2004)

J. H. Parry, *The Spanish Seaborne Empire* (London, 1966)

D. Potter, *Renaissance France at War: Armies, Culture and Society, c.1480–1560* (Woodbridge, 2008)

J. D. Tracy, *Emperor Charles V, Impresario of War: Campaign Strategy, International Finance and Domestic Politics* (Cambridge, 2010)

O. van Nimwegen, *The Dutch Army and the Military Revolutions, 1588–1688* (Woodbridge, 2010)

R. Vaughan, *Valois Burgundy* (London, 1975)

WAR, CAMPAIGNS, AND BATTLE

D. Abulafia, ed., *The French Descent into Renaissance Italy, 1494–95* (Aldershot, 1995)

N. Capponi, *Victory of the West: The Story of the Battle of Lepanto* (London, 2006)

A. Curry, *The Hundred Years War* (Basingstoke, 2003)

R. I. Frost, *The Northern Wars: War, State and Society in Northeastern Europe, 1558–1721* (London, 2000)

R. Knecht, *The French Civil Wars* (London, 2000)

M. Mallett and C. Shaw, *The Italian Wars, 1494–1559* (Harlow, 2012).

G. Parker, *Spain and the Netherlands, 1559–1659: Ten Studies* (London, 1979)

G. Parker, *The Dutch Revolt* (London, 1985)

R. Vaughan, *Charles the Bold* (Woodbridge, 2002)

P. Wilson, *Europe's Tragedy: The Thirty Years' War* (London, 2009)

THE CHANGING CHARACTER OF WAR?

J. Black, *A Military Revolution? Military Change and European Society, 1550–1800* (London, 1991)

W. Caferro, *John Hawkwood: An English Mercenary in Fourteenth-Century Italy* (Baltimore, 2006)

J. Glete, *Warfare at Sea, 1500–1650: Maritime Conflicts and the Transformation of Europe* (London, 2000)

J. F. Guilmartin, *Gunpowder and Galleys: Changing Technology and Mediterranean Warfare at Sea in the Sixteenth Century* (Cambridge, 1974)

J. R. Hale, *Renaissance War Studies* (London, 1983)

S. Hall, *Weapons and Warfare in Renaissance Europe. Gunpowder, Technology and Tactics* (Baltimore and London, 1997)

G. Hanlon, *Italy 1636: Cemetery of Armies* (Oxford, 2016)

M. Mallett, *Mercenaries and their Masters: Warfare in Renaissance Italy* (Barnsley, 2009)

G. Parker, *The Military Revolution: Military Innovation and the Rise of the West* (Cambridge, 2nd edn 1996)

D. Parrott, *The Business of War: Military Enterprise and Military Revolution in Early Modern Europe* (Cambridge, 2012)

S. Pepper and N. Adams, *Firearms and Fortifications: Military Architecture and Siege Warfare in Sixteenth-Century Siena* (Chicago, 1986)

M. D. Pollack, *Cities at War in Early Modern Europe* (Cambridge, 2010)

M. Roberts, 'The Military Revolution' and 'Gustav Adolf and the Art of War', both in M. Roberts, *Essays in Swedish History* (London, 1967)

C. J. Rogers, ed., *The Military Revolution Debate: Readings on the Military Transformation of Early Modern Europe* (Boulder, Colo., 1995)

I. A. A. Thompson, *War and Government in Habsburg Spain, 1560–1620* (London, 1976)

P. Williams, *Empire and Holy War in the Mediterranean: The Galley and Maritime Conflict between the Habsburgs and the Ottomans* (London, 2014)

VIOLENCE AND FEUD

S. Anglo, *Chivalry in the Renaissance* (Woodbridge, 1990)

S. Anglo, *The Martial Arts of Renaissance Europe* (New Haven and London, 2000)

S. Carroll, *Blood and Violence in Early Modern France* (Oxford, 2006)

M. Keen, *Chivalry* (New Haven and London, 1984)

J. R. Ruff, *Violence in Early Modern Europe* (Cambridge, 2001)

M. Vale, *War and Chivalry* (London, 1981)

H. Zmora, *State and Nobility: The Knightly Feud in Franconia, 1440–1567* (Cambridge, 1997)

MOTIVATIONS FOR WAR, PEACEMAKING, AND LIMITS ON WAR

J. Bireley, *The Counter-Reformation Prince: Anti-Machiavellianism or Catholic Statecraft in Early Modern Europe* (Chapel Hill, NC, and London, 1990)

D. Croxton, *Westphalia: The Last Christian Peace* (London, 2013)

J. Duindam, *Dynasties: A Global History of Power, 1300–1800* (Cambridge, 2016)

J. H. Elliott, 'A Europe of Composite Monarchies', in J. H. Elliott, *Spain, Europe and the Wider World, 1500–1800* (New Haven and London, 2009)

A. Gotthard, 'The Settlement of 1648 for the German Empire', in O. Asbach and P. Schröder, eds, *The Ashgate Research Companion to the Thirty Years' War* (Farnham, 2014)

N. Housley, *The Later Crusades: From Lyons to Alcazar, 1274–1580* (Oxford, 1992)

N. Housley, *Religious Warfare in Europe, 1400–1536* (Oxford, 2008)

M. H. Keen, *The Laws of War in the Later Middle Ages* (Oxford, 1968)

D. H. Nexon, *The Struggle for Power in Early Modern Europe; Religious Conflict, Dynastic Empires and International Change* (Princeton, 2009)

G. Oestreich, *Neostoicism and the Early Modern State* (Cambridge, 1982)

H. Rowan, *The King's State: Proprietary Dynasticism in Early Modern France* (New Brunswick, NJ, 1980)

J. Russell, *Peacemaking in the Renaissance* (London, 1986)

Chapter 3: Religion

GENERAL

J. Bossy, *Christianity in the West, 1400–1700* (Oxford, 1985)

J. McManners, ed., *The Oxford History of Christianity* (Oxford, 2002)

J. Pelikan, *The Christian Tradition: A History of the Development of Doctrine*, vol. 4: *Reformation of Church and Dogma (1300–1700)* (Chicago and London, 1984)

J. Pelikan, *Jesus through the Centuries: His Place in the History of Culture* (New Haven and London, 1985)

R. Po-chia Hsia, ed., *The Cambridge History of Christianity*, vol. 6: *Reform and Expansion, 1500–1660* (Cambridge, 2014)

M. Rubin and S. Walter, eds, *The Cambridge History of Christianity*, vol. 4: *Christianity in Western Europe, c.1100–c.1500* (Cambridge, 2014)

C. Trinkaus and H. A. Oberman, eds, *The Pursuit of Holiness in Late Medieval and Renaissance Religion* (Leiden, 1974)

PRIMARY SOURCES

B. Collett, *A Long and Troubled Pilgrimage: The Correspondence of Marguerite d'Angoulême and Vittoria Colonna, 1540–1545* (Princeton, 2000)

D. Erasmus, *Praise of Folly*, trans. B. Radice (London, 1993)

M. Ficino, *Book of Life*, trans. C. Boer (Woodstock, Conn., 1980)

M. Ficino, *On Dionysius the Areopagite*, 2 vols, ed. M. J. B. Allen (Cambridge, Mass., 2015)

M. Ficino, *Platonic Theology*, 6 vols, ed. M. J. B. Allen and J. Hankins (Cambridge, Mass., 2001–6)

M. Kempe, *The Book of Margery Kempe*, trans. B. Windeatt (London, 1985)

C. S. Mackay, *The Hammer of the Witches: A Complete Translation of the* Malleus Maleficarum (Cambridge, 2006)

Pius II, *Commentaries*, 2 vols, ed. M. Meserve and M. Simonetta (Cambridge, Mass., 2004, 2007)

C. Salutati, *On the World and Religious Life*, ed. T. Marshall (Cambridge, Mass., 2014)

Thomas à Kempis, *The Imitation of Christ*, trans. R. Jeffery (London, 2013)

Vespasiano da Bisticci, *The Vespasiano Memoirs: Lives of Illustrious Men of the XVth Century*, trans. W. George and E. Waters (Toronto, 1997)

M. G. Vida, *Christiad*, ed. J. Gardner (Cambridge, Mass., 2009)

MATERIAL CULTURE

P. F. Brown, *Venetian Narrative Painting in the Age of Carpaccio* (New Haven and London, 1988)

E. Duffy, *Marking the Hours: English People and their Prayers 1240–1570* (New Haven and London, 2006)

N. A. Eckstein, *Painted Glories: The Brancacci Chapel in Renaissance Florence* (New Haven and London, 2014)

L. D. Ettlinger, *The Sistine Chapel before Michelangelo: Religious Imagery and Papal Primacy* (Oxford, 1965)

J. Freiberg, *Bramante's Tempietto, the Roman Renaissance, and the Spanish Crown* (Cambridge, 2015)

R. Goffen, *Piety and Patronage in Renaissance Venice: Bellini, Titian and the Franciscans* (New Haven and London, 1986)

G. L. Hersey, *High Renaissance Art in St Peter's and the Vatican: An Interpretive Guide* (Chicago and London, 1993)

P. Humfrey and M. Kemp, eds, *The Altarpiece in the Renaissance* (Cambridge, 1990)

D. Kent, *Cosimo de' Medici and the Florentine Renaissance* (New Haven and London, 2000)

C. D. Muir, *Saintly Brides and Bridegrooms: The Mystic Marriage in Northern Renaissance Art* (London, 2012)

S. Nash, *Northern Renaissance Art* (Oxford, 2008)

V. Reinburg, *French Books of Hours: Making an Archive of Prayer, c.1400–1600* (Cambridge, 2014)

C. P. Thiede and M. d'Ancona, *The Quest for the True Cross* (London, 2000)

T. Verdon and J. Henderson, eds, *Christianity and the Renaissance: Image and Religious Imagination in the Quattrocento* (Syracuse, NY, 1990)

R. Viladesau, *Triumph of the Cross: The Passion of Christ in Theology and the Arts from the Renaissance to the Counter Reformation* (New York and Oxford, 2008)

A. J. Wharton, *Selling Jerusalem: Relics, Replicas, Theme Parks* (Chicago and London, 2006)

LITERARY CULTURE

J. H. Bentley, *Humanists and Holy Writ: New Testament Scholarship in the Renaissance* (Princeton, 1983)

J. F. D'Amico, *Renaissance Humanism in Papal Rome: Humanists and Churchmen on the Eve of the Reformation* (Baltimore and London, 1983)

A. Edelheit, *Ficino, Pico and Savonarola: The Evolution of Humanist Theology 1461/2–1498* (Leiden and Boston, 2008)

M. Firpo, *Juan de Valdés and the Italian Reformation* (Farnham, 2015)

E. G. Gleason, *Gasparo Contarini: Venice, Rome, and Reform* (Berkeley and Oxford, 1993)

L. A. Homza, *Religious Authority in the Spanish Renaissance* (Baltimore, 2004)

A. Levi, *Renaissance and Reformation: The Intellectual Genesis* (New Haven and London, 2002)

J. McConica, *Erasmus* (Oxford, 1991)

R. Marius, *Thomas More: A Biography* (London, 1985)

C. L. Stinger, *Humanism and the Church Fathers: Ambrogio Traversari (1386–1439) and Christian Antiquity in the Italian Renaissance* (Albany, NY, 1977)

C. L. Stinger, *The Renaissance in Rome* (Bloomington, Ind., 1985)

J. B. Trapp, *Erasmus, Colet and More: The Early Tudor Humanists and their Books* (London, 1991)

C. Trinkaus, *In our Image and Likeness: Humanity and Divinity in Italian Religious Thought*, 2 vols (Chicago, 1970)

SAINTS AND THEIR CULTS

S. J. Boss, ed., *Mary: The Complete Resource* (Oxford, 2007)

D. S. Ellington, *From Sacred Body to Angelic Soul: Understanding Mary in Late Medieval and Early Modern Europe* (Washington, DC, 2001)

M. J. Gill, *Augustine in the Italian Renaissance: Art and Philosophy from Petrarch to Michelangelo* (New York, 2004)

S. Haskins, *Mary Magdalen: Myth and Metaphor* (London, 1993)

J. Jenkins and K. J. Lewis, eds, *St Katherine of Alexandria: Texts and Contexts in Western Medieval Europe* (Turnhout, 2003)

R. Maniura, *Pilgrimage to Images in the Fifteenth Century: The Origins of the Cult of Our Lady of Częstochowa* (Woodbridge, 2004)

J. Pelikan, *Mary through the Centuries: Her Place in the History of Culture* (New Haven and London, 1996)

E. F. Rice, *Saint Jerome in the Renaissance* (Baltimore, 1985)

D. Webb, *Patrons and Defenders: The Saints in the Italian City-States* (London, 1996)

D. Weinstein and R. M. Bell, *Saints and Society: The Two Worlds of Western Christendom, 1000–1700* (Chicago and London, 1982)

C. C. Wilson, *St. Joseph in Italian Renaissance Society and Art: New Directions and Interpretations* (Philadelphia, 2001)

RELIGIOUS ORDERS

S. D. Bowd, *Reform before the Reformation: Vincenzo Querini and the Religious Renaissance in Italy* (Leiden, 2002)

B. Collett, *Italian Benedictine Scholars and the Reformation: The Congregation of Santa Giustina of Padua* (Oxford, 1985)

S. Evangelisti, *Nuns: A History of Convent Life 1450–1700* (Oxford, 2008)

J. R. H. Moorman, *A History of the Franciscan Order: From its Origins to the Year 1517* (Oxford, 1968)

F. Mormando, *The Preacher's Demons: Bernardino of Siena and the Social Underworld of Early Renaissance Italy* (Chicago and London, 1999)

J. W. O'Malley, *The First Jesuits* (Cambridge, Mass., 1993)

S.T. Strocchia, *Nuns and Nunneries in Renaissance Florence* (Baltimore, 2010)

M. Tavuzzi, *Prierias: The Life and Works of Silvestro Mazzolini da Prierio, 1456–1527* (Durham, NC, and London, 1997)

P. Temple, *Survey of London: The Charterhouse* (New Haven and London, 2010)

FAITH IN PRACTICE, FAITH IN ACTION

G. Alfani, *Fathers and Godfathers: Spiritual Kinship in Early-Modern Italy* (Farnham, 2009)

D. Bornstein and R. Rusconi, eds, *Women and Religion in Medieval and Renaissance Italy* (Chicago and London, 1996)

C. W. Bynum, *Holy Feast and Holy Fast: The Religious Significance of Food to Medieval Women* (Berkeley, 1987)

N. Z. Davis, *Society and Culture in Early Modern France* (London, 1975)

E. Duffy, *The Stripping of the Altars: Traditional Religion in England 1400–1580* (New Haven and London, 1992)

J. Henderson, *Piety and Charity in Late Medieval Florence* (Chicago and London, 1994)

H. Parish, *Clerical Celibacy in the West: c.1100–1700* (Farnham and Burlington, 2010)

L. Polizzotto, *Children of the Promise: The Confraternity of the Purification and the Socialization of Youths in Florence 1427–1785* (Oxford, 2004)

B. Pullan, *Rich and Poor in Renaissance Venice: The Social Institutions of a Catholic State, to 1620* (Oxford, 1971)

M. Rubin, *Corpus Christi: The Eucharist in Late Medieval Culture* (Cambridge, 1991)

T. N. Tentler, *Sin and Confession on the Eve of the Reformation* (Princeton, 1977)

N. Terpstra, ed., *The Politics of Ritual Kinship: Confraternities and Social Order in Early Modern Italy* (Cambridge, 2000)

R. Trexler, *Public Life in Renaissance Florence* (New York, 1980)

ANGELS, SPIRITS, PROPHETS

W. Christian, *Apparitions in Late Medieval and Renaissance Spain* (Princeton, 1981)

C. Copeland and J. Machielsen, *Angels of Light: Sanctity and the Discernment of Spirits in the Early Modern Period* (Leiden and Boston, 2013)

M. J. Gill, *Angels and the Order of Heaven in Medieval and Renaissance Italy* (Cambridge, 2014)

T. Herzig, *Savonarola's Women: Visions and Reform in Renaissance Italy* (Chicago and London, 2007)

D. Keck, *Angels and Angelology in the Middle Ages* (Oxford, 1998)

P. Marshall and A. Walsham, eds, *Angels in the Early Modern World* (Cambridge, 2006)

O. Niccoli, *Prophecy and People in Renaissance Italy* (Princeton, 1990)

L. Polizzotto, *The Elect Nation: The Savonarolan Movement in Florence 1494–1545* (Oxford, 1994)

M. Reeves, *The Influence of Prophecy in the Later Middle Ages: A Study in Joachimism* (Oxford, 1969)

M. Reeves, ed., *Prophetic Rome in the High Renaissance Period* (Oxford, 1992)

D. Weinstein, *Savonarola and Florence: Prophecy and Patriotism in the Renaissance* (Princeton, 1970)

RELIGIOUS MINORITIES

R. Bonfil, *Jewish Life in Renaissance Italy* (Berkeley and London, 1994)

C. Burnett and A. Contadini, eds, *Islam and the Italian Renaissance* (London, 1999)

P. Díaz-Mas, *Sephardim: the Jews from Spain* (Chicago and London, 1992)

J. Edwards, *The Spanish Inquisition* (Stroud, 1999)

L. P. Harvey, *Islamic Spain, 1250–1500* (Chicago and London, 1992)

L. P. Harvey, *Muslims in Spain, 1500–1614* (Chicago and London, 2005)

D. E. Katz, *The Jew in the Art of the Italian Renaissance* (Philadelphia, 2008)

Chapter 4: The Civilization of the Renaissance

P. P. Bober, *Renaissance Artists & Antique Sculpture: A Handbook of Sources* (2nd edn, updated, London, 2010)

F. Braudel, *The Structures of Everyday Life: The Limits of the Possible* (new edn, London, 1981)

C. Classen et al., eds, *A Cultural History of the Senses* (London, 2014)

Ecclesiastical History Society and D. Wood, eds, *The Church and the Arts* (Oxford, 1992)

N. Elias, *The Civilizing Process* (Oxford, 1978)

C. J. Farago, *Leonardo Da Vinci's Paragone: A Critical Interpretation with a New Edition of the Text in the Codex Urbinas* (Leiden, 1991)

M. Foucault, *The History of Sexuality,* (London, 1998)

R. Goffen, *Titian's Women* (New Haven, 1997)

J. Kelly-Gadol, 'Did Women Have a Renaissance?', in *Women, History and Theory: The Essays* (Chicago, 1984)

J. J. Martin, *Myths of Renaissance Individualism* (Basingstoke, 2004)

F. Quiviger, *The Sensory World of Italian Renaissance Art* (London, 2010)

G. Ruggiero. *The Boundaries of Eros: Sex Crime and Sexuality in Renaissance Venice* (Oxford, 1985)

P. H. Smith, *The Body of the Artisan: Art and Experience in the Scientific Revolution* (Chicago and London, 2004)

B. Talvacchia, *Taking Positions: On the Erotic in Renaissance Culture* (Princeton, NJ, 1999)

B. A. Tlusty, *Bacchus and Civic Order: The Culture of Drink in Early Modern Germany* (Charlottesville, Va., and London, 2001)

M. Warnke, *The Court Artist: On the Ancestry of the Modern Artist* (Cambridge and New York, 1993)

R. Williams, *Art, Theory, and Culture in Sixteenth-Century Italy: From Techne to Metatechne* (Cambridge and New York, 1997)

Chapter 5: Art and Architecture in Italy and Beyond

PRIMARY SOURCES

L. B. Alberti, *On Painting and On Sculpture*, trans. and ed. C. Grayson (London, 1972)

L. B. Alberti, *On the Art of Building in Ten Books* (Cambridge, Mass., 1988)

D. S. Chambers, *Patrons and Artists in the Italian Renaissance* (London, 1970)

Leonardo da Vinci, *Leonardo On Painting*, trans. and ed. M. Kemp and M. Walker (New Haven and London, 1989)

C. E. Gilbert, *Italian Art 1400–1500: Sources and Documents* (Englewood Cliffs, NJ, 1980)

A. Palladio, *The Four Books on Architecture*, ed. R. Tavenor and R. Schofield (Cambridge, Mass., 2002)

P. L. Rubin, *Giorgio Vasari: Art and History* (New Haven and London, 1995)

G. Vasari, *Lives of the Artists*, trans. G. Bull, 2 vols (Harmondsworth, 1965 and 1987)

ARCHITECTURE

C. Anderson, *Renaissance Architecture* (Oxford, 2013)

D. R. Coffin, *The Villa in the Life of Renaissance Rome* (Princeton, 1979)

C. L. Frommel, *The Architecture of the Italian Renaissance* (London, 2007)

R. J. Goy, *Building Renaissance Venice* (New Haven and London, 2006)

L. H. Heydenreich, *Architecture in Italy 1400–1500*, rev. P. Davies (New Haven and London, 1996)

R. Lieberman, *Renaissance Architecture in Venice* (London, 1982)

A. Lillie, *Florentine Villas in the Fifteenth Century: An Architectural and Social History* (Cambridge, 2005)

J. R. Lindow, *The Renaissance Palace in Florence* (Aldershot, 2007)

W. Lotz, *Architecture in Italy 1500–1600*, rev. D. Howard (New Haven and London, 1995)

A. Payne, *The Architectural Treatise in the Renaissance* (New York and Cambridge, 1999)

D. Thompson, *Renaissance Architecture: Patrons, Critics and Luxury* (Manchester, 1993)

SCULPTURE AND PAINTING: GENERAL

M. Baxandall, *Painting and Experience in Fifteenth Century Italy* (Oxford, 1972)

S. J. Campbell and M. W. Cole, *A New History of Italian Renaissance Art* (London, 2012)

R. Goldthwaite, *Wealth and the Demand for Art in Italy 1300–1600* (Baltimore, 1993)

J. Paoletti and G. Radke, *Art in Renaissance Italy* (4th edn, London, 2011)

J. Pope-Hennessy, *Italian High Renaissance and Baroque Sculpture* (London, 1963)

J. Pope-Hennessy, *Italian Renaissance Sculpture* (2nd edn, London, 1971)

C. Seymour, *Sculpture in Italy 1400–1500* (Harmondsworth, 1966)

E. Welch, *Art in Renaissance Italy 1350–1500* (Oxford, 1997)

SCULPTURE AND PAINTING: SPECIALIST STUDIES

B. A. Bennett and D. G. Wilkins, *Donatello* (Oxford, 1984)

P. P. Bober and R. Rubinstein, *Renaissance Artists and Antique Sculpture* (London, 1986)

A. Cole, *Art of the Renaissance Courts* (London, 1995)

P. Fortini Brown, *Venice and Antiquity: The Venetian Sense of the Past* (New Haven and London, 1996)

L. Freedman, *Classical Myths in Italian Renaissance Painting* (Cambridge, 2011)

P. Humfrey, *Painting in Renaissance Venice* (New Haven and London, 1995)

N. Huse and W. Wolters, *The Art of Renaissance Venice 1460–1590* (Chicago and London, 1990)

R. Jones and N. Penny, *Raphael* (New Haven and London, 1983)

M. Kemp, *Leonardo da Vinci: The Marvellous Works of Nature and Man* (2nd edn, Oxford, 2006)

R. Lightbown, *Andrea Mantegna* (Oxford, 1986)

R. Lightbown, *Sandro Botticelli. Life and Work* (London, 1989)

P. Nuttall, *From Flanders to Florence* (New Haven and London, 2004)

W. E. Wallace, *Michelangelo: The Artist, the Man, and his Times* (Cambridge, 2009)

R. Weiss, *The Renaissance Discovery of Classical Antiquity* (Oxford, 1969)

F. Zöllner, *Leonardo da Vinci 1452–1519: The Complete Paintings and Drawings* (Cologne, 2015)

F. Zöllner, C. Thoenes, and T. Pöpper, *Michelangelo: The Complete Works* (Cologne, 2014)

Chapter 6: Art and Architecture in Flanders and Beyond

GENERAL (FIFTEENTH- AND SIXTEENTH-CENTURY ART)

M. Baxandall, *The Limewood Sculptors of Renaissance Germany* (New Haven and London, 1980)

L. Campbell, *Renaissance Portraits: European Portrait-Painting in the 14th, 15th and 16th Centuries* (London and New Haven, 1990).

L. Campbell, S. Foister, and A. Roy, eds, 'The Methods and Materials of Northern European Painting 1400–1550', *National Gallery Technical Bulletin*, 18 (1997), 6–55

J. Chipps Smith, *The Northern Renaissance* (London, 2004)

C. Cuttler, *Northern Painting from Pucelle to Bruegel* (New York, 1968)

Gothic and Renaissance Art in Nuremberg, 1300–1550, exhibition catalogue, New York, Metropolitan Museum of Art, and Nuremberg, Germanisches Nationalmuseum (Munich, 1986)

J. L. Koerner, *The Moment of Self-Portraiture in German Renaissance Art* (Chicago and London, 1993)

D. Landau and P. Parshall, *The Renaissance Print, 1470–1550* (New Haven and London, 1994)

S. Porras, *Art of the Northern Renaissance: Courts, Commerce and Devotion* (London, 2018)

J. Snyder, *Northern Renaissance Art: Painting, Sculpture, the Graphic Arts from 1350 to 1575* (2nd edn, New York, 2004)

FIFTEENTH-CENTURY ART: GENERAL

L. Campbell, *The Fifteenth-Century Netherlandish Schools*, National Gallery Catalogues (London, 1998)

M. E. Kavaler, *Renaissance Gothic: Architecture and the Arts in Northern Europe, 1470–1540* (New Haven and London, 2012)

S. Nash, *Northern Renaissance Art* (Oxford, 2008)

P. Nuttall, *From Flanders to Florence: The Impact of Netherlandish Painting 1400–1500* (New Haven and London, 2004)

E. Panofsky, *Early Netherlandish Painting: Its Origins and Character*, 2 vols (Cambridge, Mass., 1953)

P. Parshall and R. Schoch, *Origins of European Printmaking: Fifteenth-Century Woodcuts and their Public*, exhibition catalogue, Washington, National Gallery of Art, and Nuremberg, Germanisches Nationalmuseum (New Haven and London, 2005)

B. Ridderbos, A. Van Buren, and H. Van Veen, eds, *Early Netherlandish Paintings. Rediscovery, Reception and Research* (Amsterdam, 2005)

G. Ring, *A Century of French Painting, 1400–1500* (London, 1949)

FIFTEENTH-CENTURY ARTISTS

T. H. Borchert, *Van Eyck* (Cologne, 2008)

L. Campbell and J. Van der Stock, eds, *Rogier van der Weyden, Master of Passions*, exhibition catalogue, Leuven, Museum M (Leuven, 2009)

J. Campbell Hutchison, *Albrecht Dürer: A Biography* (Princeton, 1990)

M. Evans, 'Jean Fouquet and Italy', in M. P. Brown and S. McKendrick, eds, *Illuminating the Book: Makers and Interpreters. Essays in Honour of Janet Backhouse* (London, 1998)

S. Kemperdick and J. Sander, eds, *The Master of Flémalle and Rogier van der Weyden*, exhibition catalogue, Frankfurt am Main, Städel Museum, and Berlin, Gemäldegalerie (Ostfildern, 2008)

B. Lane, *Hans Memling. Master Painter in Fifteenth-Century Bruges* (Turnhout, 2009)

S. Nash, 'Claus Sluter's "Well of Moses" for the Chartreuse de Champmol Reconsidered: Part I', *Burlington Magazine*, 147 (2005), 798–809; 'Part II', 148 (2006), 456–67; 'Part III', 150 (2008), 724–41

NORTHERN RENAISSANCE ART OF THE SIXTEENTH CENTURY

B. Aikema and B. Brown, eds, *Renaissance Venice and the North: Crosscurrents in the Time of Bellini, Dürer and Titian* (London, 1999)

M. Belozerskaya, *Rethinking the Renaissance: Burgundian Arts across Europe* (Cambridge, 2002)

A. Blunt, *Art and Architecture in France, 1500–1700* (2nd rev. edn, New Haven and London, 1999)

C. Christensen, *Art and the Reformation in Germany* (Athens, Oh., 1972)

E. Eichberger and C. Zika, eds, *Dürer and his Culture* (Cambridge, 1998)

W. K. Ferguson, *The Renaissance in Historical Thought: Five Centuries of Interpretation* (Boston, 1948)

T. Kaufmann, *Court, Cloister and City: The Art and Culture of Central Europe, 1450–1800* (London, 1995)

J. Koerner, *The Reformation of the Image* (London, 2004)

E. Panofsky, *The Life and Art of Albrecht Dürer* (Princeton, 1955)

P. van den Brink et al., *ExtravagAnt!: A Forgotten Chapter of Antwerp Painting 1500–1530* (Antwerp, 2005)

C. S. Wood, *Albrecht Altdorfer and the Origins of Landscape* (London, 1993)

Chapter 7: The Performing Arts: Festival, Music, Drama, Dance

GENERAL WORKS

S. Anglo, *Spectacle, Pageantry and Early Tudor Policy* (Oxford, 1969; repr. 1997)

J. Bate and D. Thornton, *Shakespeare, Staging the World* (London, 2012)

P. Butterworth and K. Normington, *European Theatre Performance Practice, 1400–1580* (Aldershot, 2014)

T. Da Costa Kaufmann, *Court, Cloister and City: The Art and Culture of Central Europe, 1450–1800* (London and Chicago, 1995)

J. Dillon, *The Language of Space in Court Performance, 1400–1635* (Cambridge, 2010)

I. Fenlon, *Music and Patronage in Sixteenth-Century Mantua*, 2 vols (Cambridge, 1980)

I. Fenlon, *The Ceremonial City: History, Memory and Myth in Renaissance Venice* (New Haven and London, 2007)

A. Gurr, *Playgoing in Shakespeare's London* (Cambridge, 1987; 3rd edn 2004)

A. Low and N. Myhill, eds, *Imagining the Audience in Early Modern Drama, 1558–1642* (New York, 2011)

M. M. McGowan, *Dance in the Renaissance. European Fashion. French Obsession* (New Haven and London, 2008)

L. Manley and S.-B. Maclean, *Lord Strange's Men and their Plays* (New Haven and London, 2014)

B. Mitchell, *The Majesty of State: Triumphal Progresses of Foreign Sovereigns in Renaissance Italy* (Florence, 1986)

J. R. Mulryne and E. Goldring, eds, *Court Festivals of the European Renaissance: Art, Politics and Performance* (Aldershot, 2002)

J. Peacock, *The Stage Designs of Inigo Jones: The European Context* (Cambridge, 1995)

N. Pirrotta and E. Povoledo, *Music and Theatre from Poliziano to Monteverdi*, trans. K. Eldes (Cambridge, 1982)

N. Russell and H. Visentin, *French Ceremonial Entries in the Sixteenth Century: Event, Image, Text* (Toronto, 2007)

N. D. Shergold, *A History of the Spanish Stage from Medieval Times until the End of the Seventeenth Century* (Oxford, 1967)

M. Shewring, ed., *Waterborne Pageants and Festivities in the Renaissance* (Aldershot, 2013)

K. van Orden, *Music, Discipline and Arms in Early Modern France* (Chicago, 2005)

M. Wade, *German Court Culture and Denmark: The Great Wedding of 1634* (Wiesbaden, 1996)

G. Wickham, *Early English Stages, 1300–1660*, 4 vols (London, 1959–2002)

STUDIES OF SPECIAL THEMES

J. H. Astington, *English Court Theatre, 1558–1642* (Cambridge, 1999)

D. Bevington, *Shakespeare: The Seven Ages of Human Experience* (Oxford, 2005)

L. M. Bryant, *French Ceremonial Entries: The King and the City in the Parisian Royal Entry* (Geneva, 1986)

M. Butler, *The Stuart Masque and Political Culture* (Cambridge, 2008)

H. L. Chrétien, *The Festival of San Giovanni: Imagery and Political Power in Renaissance Florence* (New York, 1994)

J. Clare, *Shakespeare's Stage Traffic: Imitation, Borrowing and Competition in Renaissance Theatre* (Cambridge, 2014)

M. A. Katritsky, *The Art of Commedia: A Study of the Commedia dell'Arte, 1560–1620, with Special Reference to the Visual Records* (Amsterdam and New York, 2006)

A. Kernan, *Shakespeare, the King's Playwright: Theater in the Stuart Court, 1603–13* (New Haven and London, 1995)

A. M. Nagler, *Theatre Festivals of the Medici, 1539–1637* (New Haven and London, 1964)

J. Nevile, *The Eloquent Body: Dance and Humanist Culture in Fifteenth-Century Italy* (Bloomington, Ind., 2004)

J. Orrell, *The Human Stage: English Theatre Design, 1567–1640* (Cambridge, 1988)

M. Plaisance, *Florence in the Time of the Medici: Public Celebrations, Politics and Literature in the Fifteenth and Sixteenth Centuries*, trans. and ed. N. Carew-Reid (Toronto, 2008)

J. M. Saslow, *The Medici Wedding of 1589: Florentine Festival as Theatrum Mundi* (New Haven and London, 1996)

R. Sherr, *Papal Music and Musicians in Medieval and Renaissance Rome* (Cambridge, 1998)

N. Treadwell, *Music and Wonder at the Medici Court: The 1589 Interludes for 'La pellegrina'* (Bloomington, Ind., 2008)

P. Walls, *Music and the English Court Masque* (Oxford, 1996)

DOCUMENTS AND MODERN EDITIONS

J. E. Archer, E. Goldring, and S. M. Knight, eds, *The Progresses, Pageants and Entertainment of Queen Elizabeth I* (Aldershot, 2007)

D. Bevington, M. Butler, and I. Donaldson, *The Cambridge Edition of the Works of Ben Jonson*, 7 vols (Cambridge, 2012)

J. Bridgeman, trans. and ed., *A Renaissance Wedding: The Celebrations at Pesaro for the Marriage of Costanza Sforza and Camilla Marzano d'Aragona, 26–30 May, 1475* (London and Turnhout, 2013)

B. Mitchell, ed., *A Renaissance Entertainment for the Marriage of Cosimo I dume of Florence, in 1539* (Columbia, Mo., 1968)

R. J. Mulryne, M. Shewring, and H. Watanabe O'Kelly, eds, *Europa Triumphans: Court and Civic Festivities in Early Modern Europe*, 2 vols (Aldershot, 2004)

Chapter 8: Vernacular Literature

GENERAL WORKS

E. Auerbach, *Literary Language & its Public in Late Latin Antiquity and in the Middle Ages*, trans. R. Manheim (London, 1965)

E. Auerbach, *Mimesis: The Representation of Reality in Western Literature*, trans. W. R. Trask (2nd edn, Princeton, 2003)

P. Benson and V. Kirkham, eds, *Strong Voices, Weak History: Early Women Writers and Canons in England, France, and Italy* (Ann Arbor, Mich., 2005)

P. Burke, *Languages and Communities in Early Modern Europe* (Cambridge, 2004)

P. Burke, *Popular Culture in Early Modern Europe* (3rd edn, Farnham, 2009)

T. Cave, *The Cornucopian Text: Problems of Writing in the French Renaissance* (Oxford, 1979)

W. Cohen, *A History of European Literature: The West and the World from Antiquity to the Present* (Oxford, 2017)

V. Cox, *Women's Writing in Italy, 1400–1650* (Baltimore, 2008)

B. Cummings, *The Literary Culture of the Reformation: Grammar and Grace* (Oxford, 2002)

B. Cummings and J. Simpson, eds, *Cultural Reformations: Medieval and Renaissance in Literary History* (Oxford, 2010)

E. R. Curtius, *European Literature and the Latin Middle Ages*, trans. W. R. Trask (London and Henley, 1953)

M. W. Ferguson, *Trials of Desire: Renaissance Defenses of Poetry* (New Haven, 1983)

M. W. Ferguson, *Dido's Daughters: Literacy, Gender, and Empire in Early Modern England and France* (Chicago, 2003)

S. Greenblatt, *Renaissance Self-Fashioning: From More to Shakespeare* (Chicago, 1980)

T. M. Greene, *The Light in Troy: Imitation and Discovery in Renaissance Poetry* (New Haven, 1982)

L. Hutson, ed., *Feminism and Renaissance Studies* (Oxford, 1999)

A. J. Krailsheimer et al., eds, *The Continental Renaissance, 1500–1600* (Harmondsworth, 1971)

J. Kraye, ed., *The Cambridge Companion to Renaissance Humanism* (Cambridge, 1996)

G. P. Norton, ed., *The Cambridge History of Literary Criticism*, vol. 3: *The Renaissance* (Cambridge, 1999)

A. Petrucci, *Writers and Readers in Medieval Italy: Studies in the History of Written Culture*, trans. C. Radding (New Haven, 1995)

S. Pollock, *The Language of the Gods in the World of Men: Sanskrit, Culture, and Power in Premodern India* (Berkeley, 2006)

H. L. Sanson, 'The Romance Languages in the Renaissance and After', in M. Maiden, J. C. Smith, and A. Ledgeway, eds, *The Cambridge History of the Romance Languages*: vol. 2: *Contexts* (Cambridge, 2013), 237–82

J. G. Turner, 'Literature', in G. Ruggiero, ed., *A Companion to the Worlds of the Renaissance* (Oxford, 2007), 366–83

D. Wallace, ed., *Europe: A Literary History, 1348–1418*, 2 vols (Oxford, 2016)

STUDIES OF AUTHORS AND SPECIAL THEMES

G. Armstrong, R. Daniels, and S. J. Milner, eds, *The Cambridge Companion to Boccaccio* (Cambridge, 2015)

G. Braden, *Petrarchan Love and the Continental Renaissance* (New Haven, 1999)

C. Burrow, *Shakespeare and Classical Antiquity* (Oxford, 2013)

D. Clarke, *The Politics of Early Modern Women's Writing* (Harlow, 2001)

A. Cornish, *Vernacular Translation in Dante's Italy: Illiterate Literature* (Cambridge, 2011)

M. Eisner, *Boccaccio and the Invention of Italian Literature: Dante, Petrarch, Cavalcanti, and the Authority of the Vernacular* (Cambridge, 2013)

S. A. Gilson, *Dante and Renaissance Florence* (Cambridge, 2005)

R. Greene, *Unrequited Conquests: Love and Empire in the Colonial Americas* (Chicago, 1999)

R. L. Krueger, ed., *The Cambridge Companion to Medieval Romance* (Cambridge, 2000)

M. L. McLaughlin, 'Humanist Concepts of Renaissance and Middle Ages in the Tre- and Quattrocento', *Renaissance Studies*, 2 (1988), 131–42

M. L. McLaughlin, *Literary Imitation in the Italian Renaissance: The Theory and Practice of Literary Imitation in Italy from Dante to Bembo* (Oxford, 1995)

A. Stewart, 'The Trouble with English Humanism: Tyndale, More and Darling Erasmus', in J. Woolfson, ed., *Reassessing Tudor Humanism* (Basingstoke, 2002), 78–98

Chapter 9: Craft and Technology in Renaissance Europe

PRIMARY SOURCES

G. Agricola, *De re metallica*, trans. H. C. Hoover and L. H. Hoover, repr. edn (New York, 1950)

B. Cellini, *Autobiography*, trans. G. Bull (Harmondsworth, 1956)

Leonardo da Vinci, *The Madrid Codices*, 5 vols, ed. and trans. L. Retti (New York, 1974)

C. Piccolpasso, *The Three Books of the Potters Art*, trans. and introd. R. Lightbown and A. Caiger-Smith, 2 vols (London, 1980)

A. Ramelli, *The Various and Ingenious Machines of Agostino Ramelli (1588)*, trans. M. T. Gnudi, notes by E. S. Ferguson (Baltimore, 1976)

The First Treatise on Museums: Samuel Quiccheberg's Inscriptiones 1565, trans. M. A. Meadow and B. Robertson, introd. M. A. Meadow (Los Angeles, 2014)

GENERAL STUDIES

J. Blair and N. Ramsay, eds, *English Medieval Industries: Craftsmen, Techniques, Products* (London, 1991)

C. Singer, E. J. Holmyard, A. R. Hall, and T. I Williams, *A History of Technology*, vol. 3: *From the Renaissance to the Industrial Revolution* (London, 1957)

AGRICULTURE

M. Ambrosoli, *The Wild and the Sown: Botany and Agriculture in Western Europe: 1350–1850*, trans. M. MacCann Salvatorelli (Cambridge, 1997)

ARTISANS AND THE CULTURE OF KNOWLEDGE

P. O. Long, *Artisan/Practitioners and the Rise of the New Sciences, 1400–1600* (Corvallis, Ore., 2011)

P. H. Smith, *The Body of the Artisan: Art and Experience in the Scientific Revolution* (Chicago, 2004)

CRAFT PRACTICES, GUILDS, AND MARKETS

S. A. Epstein, *Wage Labor and Guilds in Medieval Europe* (Chapel Hill, NC, 1991)

S. R. Epstein, *Freedom and Growth: The Rise of States and Markets in Europe, 1300–1750* (Abingdon, 2006)

CERAMICS AND GLASS

L. N. Amico, *Bernard Palissy: In Search of Earthly Paradise* (Paris and New York, 1996)

D. Gaimster, *German Stoneware 1200–1900: Archaeology and Cultural History* (London, 1997)

R. A. Goldthwaite, 'The Economic and Social World of Italian Renaissance Maiolica', *Renaissance Quarterly*, 42, no. 1 (1989), 1–32

P. Hills, *Venetian Colour: Marble, Mosaic, Painting and Glass, 1250–1550* (New Haven, 1999)

D. Thornton and T. Wilson, *Italian Renaissance Ceramics: A Catalogue of the British Museum Collection*, 2 vols (London, 2009)

ARTS OF COMMUNICATION

S. Dackerman, *Prints and the Pursuit of Knowledge in Early Modern Europe* (Cambridge, Mass., 2011)

L. Febvre and H.-J. Martin, *The Coming of the Book: The Impact of Printing, 1450–1800*, trans. D. Gerard (London, 1976)

S. Kusukawa, *Picturing the Book of Nature: Image, Text, and Argument in Sixteenth-Century Human Anatomy and Medical Botany* (Chicago, 2012)

D. Landau and P. Parshall, *The Renaissance Print, 1470–1550* (New Haven, 1994)

BUILDING AND SHIP CONSTRUCTION

A. Gerbino, and S. Johnston, *Compass and Rule: Architecture as Mathematical Practice in England* (Oxford, 2009)

R. A. Goldthwaite, *The Building of Renaissance Florence: An Economic and Social History* (Baltimore, 1980)

ENGINEERING AND MACHINES

P. Galluzzi, *Renaissance Engineers from Brunelleschi to Leonardo da Vinci* (Florence, 1996)

J. Sawday, *Engines of the Imagination: Renaissance Culture and the Rise of the Machine* (London, 2007)

MEASURING TIME AND PLACE

J. A. Bennett, 'Shopping for Instruments in Paris and London', in Pamela H. Smith and Paula Findlen, eds, *Merchants and Marvels: Commerce, Science, and Art in Early Modern Europe* (New York, 2002), 370–95

G. Dohrn-Van Rossum, *History of the Hour: Clocks and Modern Temporal Orders*, trans. T. Dunlap (Chicago, 1996)

M. M. Portuondo, *Secret Science: Spanish Cosmography and the New World* (Chicago, 2009)

D. Woodward, ed., *Cartography in the European Renaissance*, 2 vols, *The History of Cartography*, vol. 3, pts 1 and 2 (Chicago, 2007)

MILITARY TECHNOLOGIES

B. S. Hall, *Weapons and Warfare in Renaissance Europe* (Baltimore, 1997)

MINING, METALLURGY, AND METALWORK

J. F. Hayward, *Virtuoso Goldsmiths and the Triumph of Mannerism, 1540–1620* (London, 1976)

J. U. Nef, 'Mining and Metallurgy in Medieval Civilisation', in M. M. Postan and E. Miller assisted by C. Postan, eds, *The Cambridge Economic History of Europe*, vol. 2: *Trade and Industry in the Middle Ages*, 2nd edn (Cambridge, 1987), 691–761

D. Thornton, *A Rothschild Renaissance: The Waddesdon Bequest* (London, 2015)

TEXTILES

T. P. Campbell, *Tapestry in the Renaissance: Art and Magnificence* (New York, 2002)

D. Jenkins, ed., *The Cambridge History of Western Textiles*, 2 vols (Cambridge, 2003), vol. 1: 177–714

A. Morrall and M. Watt, eds, *English Embroidery from the Metropolitan Museum of Art, 1580–1700: 'Twixt Art and Nature* (New Haven, 2008)

GENERAL STUDIES OF EUROPEAN CRAFT, DECORATIVE ARTS, DESIGN, AND COLLECTING

O. Impey and A. MacGregor, eds, *The Origins of Museums: The Cabinet of Curiosities in Sixteenth and Seventeenth-Century Europe* (London, 2001)

L. Syson and D. Thornton, *Objects of Virtue: Art in Renaissance Italy* (Los Angeles, 2001)

M. Trusted, *The Arts of Spain: Iberia and Latin America 1450–1700* (University Park, Pa., and London, 2007)

Chapter 10: The Renaissance of Science

PRIMARY SOURCES

Francis Bacon, *New Atlantis and the Great Instauration*, ed. J. Weinberger (Wheeling, Ill., 1980)

Giordano Bruno, *The Ash Wednesday Supper*, ed. and trans. E. A. Gosselin and L. S. Lerner (2nd edn, Toronto, 1995)

Nicolaus Copernicus, *Three Copernican Treatises*, ed. E. Rosen (2nd edn, New York, 1959)

Nicolaus Copernicus, *On the Revolutions*, ed. and trans. E. Rosen (2nd edn, Baltimore, 1992)

Leonardo da Vinci, *The Notebooks of Leonardo da Vinci*, ed. and trans. I. A. Richter (Oxford, 1952)

Camilla Erculiani, *Letters on Natural Philosophy*, ed. E. Carinci, trans. H. Marcus (Toronto, forthcoming)

Marsilio Ficino, *Three Books on Life*, ed. and trans. C. V Klaske and J. R. Clark (Binghampton, NY, 1989)

Leonhart Fuchs, *The Great Herbal of Leonhart Fuchs*, ed. F. G. Meyer, E. Emmart Trueblood, and J. L. Heller, 2 vols (Stanford, Calif., 1999)

William Gilbert, *De magnete*, trans. Father F. Mottelay (New York, 1958)

Bernard Palissy, *Admirable Discourses*, trans. A. La Rocque (Urbana, Ill., 1957)

Paracelsus, *Four Treatises of Theophrastus von Hohenheim called Paracelsus*, ed. and trans. H. Sigerist (Baltimore, 1941)

Andreas Vesalius, *On the Fabric of the Human Body*, ed. and trans. D. Garrison and M. Hast, accessed online: <http://vesalius.northwestern.edu>

Amerigo Vespucci, *Letters from the New World*, ed. L. Formisano, trans. D. Jacobson (New York, 1992)

Jacopo Zabarella, *On Methods*, ed. and trans. J. McCaskey, 2 vols (Cambridge, Mass., 2013)

GENERAL STUDIES

M. Boas, *The Scientific Renaissance 1450–1630* (New York, 1962)

B. P. Copernhaver, 'Did Science Have a Renaissance?' *Isis*, 83 (1992), 387–407

A. G. Debus, *Man and Nature in the Renaissance* (Cambridge, 1978)

S. Gaukroger, *The Emergence of a Scientific Culture: Science and the Shaping of Modernity 1210–1685* (Oxford, 2006)

A. Grafton, *New Worlds, Ancient Texts: The Power of Tradition and the Shock of Discovery* (Cambridge, Mass., 1993)

G. Huppert, *The Style of Paris: Renaissance Origins of the French Enlightenment* (Bloomington, Ind., 1999)

K. Park and L. Daston, *Wonders and the Order of Nature, 1150–1750* (New York, 1998)

K. Park and L. Daston, eds, *The Cambridge History of Science*, vol. 3: *Early Modern Science* (Cambridge, 2006)

G. Saliba, *Islamic Science and the Making of the European Renaissance* (Cambridge, Mass., 2007)

G. Sarton, *Appreciation of Ancient and Medieval Science during the Renaissance (1450–1600)* (Philadelphia, 1955)

W. P. D. Wrightman, *Science in a Renaissance Society* (London, 1972)

HUMANISM AND SCIENCE

A. Blair, *Too Much to Know* (New Haven, 2011)

E. Cassirer, *The Individual and the Cosmos in Renaissance Philosophy*, trans. M. Domandi (New York, 1963)

E. Cochrane, 'Science and Humanism in the Italian Renaissance', *American Historical Review*, 81 (1976), 1039–57

A. Grafton, *Defenders of the Text: The Traditions of Scholarship in an Age of Science, 1450–1800* (Cambridge, Mass., 1991)

A. Grafton, ed., *Rome Reborn: The Vatican Library and Renaissance Culture* (Washington, DC, 1993)

V. Nutton, 'Greek Science in the Sixteenth-Century Renaissance', in *Renaissance and Revolution: Humanists, Scholars, Craftsmen and Natural Philosophers in Early Modern Europe* (Cambridge, 1993), 15–28

A. Palmer, *Reading Lucretius in the Renaissance* (Cambridge, Mass., 2014).

J. H. Randall, *The School of Padua and the Emergence of Modern Science* (Padua, 1961)

D. B. Ruderman, *Jewish Thought and Scientific Discovery in Early Modern Europe* (New Haven, 1995)

C. B. Schmitt, *Aristotle and the Renaissance* (Cambridge, Mass., 1983)

M. Sgarbi, *The Italian Mind: Vernacular Logic in Renaissance Italy (1540–1551)* (Leiden, 2014)

ART AND SCIENCE

M. Baxandall, *Painting and Experience in Fifteenth-Century Italy* (Oxford, 1988)

H. Belting, *Florence and Baghdad: Renaissance Art and Arabic Science*, trans. D. L. Schneider (Cambridge, Mass., 2011)

S. Y. Edgerton, Jr, *The Heritage of Giotto's Geometry: Art and Science on the Eve of the Scientific Revolution* (Ithaca, NY, 1991)

J. V. Field, *Piero della Francesca: A Mathematician's Art* (New Haven, 2005)

T. DaCosta Kaufmann, *The Mastery of Nature: Aspects of Art, Science and Humanism in the Renaissance* (Princeton, 1993)

M. Kemp, *Leonardo* (Oxford, 2004)

S. Kusukawa, *Picturing the Book of Nature: Image, Text, and Argument in Sixteenth-Century Human Anatomy and Medical Botany* (Chicago, 2012)

P. H. Smith, *The Body of the Artisan: Art and Experience in the Scientific Revolution* (Chicago, 2004)

PRINTING AND SCIENCE

S. Dackerman, ed., *Prints and the Pursuit of Knowledge in Early Modern Europe* (Cambridge, Mass., and New Haven, 2011)

E. Eisenstein, *The Printing Press as An Agent of Change: Communication and Cultural Transformation in Early Modern Europe*, 2 vols (Cambridge, 1979)

A. Johns, *The Nature of the Book: Print and Knowledge in the Making* (Chicago, 2000)

P. H. Smith, 'Why Write a Book? From Lived Experience to the Written Word in Early Modern Europe', *Bulletin of the German Historical Institute*, 47 (2010), 25–50.

ASTRONOMY, ASTROLOGY, AND MATHEMATICS

A. W. Crosby, *The Measure of Reality: Quantification and Western Society, 1250–1600* (Cambridge, 1997)

A. Grafton, *Cardano's Cosmos* (Cambridge, Mass., 1999)

T. Kuhn, *The Copernican Revolution* (Cambridge, Mass., 1957)

A. Marr, *Between Raphael and Galileo* (Chicago, 2011)

P. L. Rose, *The Italian Renaissance of Mathematics* (Geneva, 1975)

R. Westman, *The Copernican Question* (Berkeley, 2011)

COSMOGRAPHY AND CARTOGRAPHY

M. Monmonier, *Rhumb Lines and Map Wars: A Social History of the Mercator Projection* (Chicago, 2004)

J. R. Short, *Making Space: Revisioning the World, 1475–1600* (Syracuse, NY, 2004)

A. Taylor, *The World of Gerard Mercator: The Mapmaker Who Revolutionized Geography* (New York, 2004)

N. Wey-Gómez, *The Tropics of Empire: Why Columbus Sailed South to the Indies* (Cambridge, Mass., 2008)

ALCHEMY, MAGIC, AND HERMETICISM

W. Eamon, *Science and the Secrets of Nature: Books of Secrets in Medieval and Early Modern Culture* (Princeton, 1994)

W. R. Newman, *Promethean Ambitions: Alchemy and the Quest to Perfect Nature* (Chicago, 2004)

T. Nummedal, *Alchemy and Authority in the Holy Roman Empire* (Chicago, 2007)

M. Ray, *Daughters of Alchemy: Women, Scientific Culture and Literary Discourse in Early Modern Italy* (Cambridge, Mass., 2015)

C. Webster, *From Paracelsus to Newton: Magic and the Making of Modern Science* (Cambridge, 1984)

F. Yates, *Giordano Bruno and the Hermetic Tradition* (Chicago, 1964)

PARACELSUS AND PARACELSIANISM

A. G. Debus, *The Chemical Philosophy: Paracelsian Science and Medicine in the Sixteenth and Seventeenth Centuries*, 2 vols (New York, 1977)

W. Pagel, *Paracelsus: An Introduction to Philosophical Medicine in the Era of the Renaissance* (2nd edn, Basel, 1982)

C. Webster, *Paracelsus: Medicine, Magic and Mission at the End of Time* (New Haven, 2008)

A. Weeks, *Paracelsus: Speculative Theory and the Crisis of the Early Reformation* (Albany, NY, 1997)

ANATOMY AND MEDICINE

A. Carlino, *Books of the Body: Anatomical Ritual and Renaissance Learning*, trans. J. and A. C. Tedeschi (Chicago, 1999)

A. Cunningham, *The Anatomical Renaissance: The Resurrection of the Anatomical Projects of the Ancients* (Brookfield, Vt., and Aldershot, 1997)

C. Klestinec, *Theaters of Anatomy: Students, Teachers, and Traditions of Dissection in Renaissance Venice* (Baltimore, 2011)

C. D. O'Malley, *Andreas Vesalius of Brussels 1514–1564* (Berkeley, 1964)

K. Park, *Secrets of Women: Gender, Generation and the Origins of Dissection* (New York, 2006)

N. G. Siraisi, *Medieval and Early Renaissance Medicine: An Introduction to Knowledge and Practice* (Chicago, 1990)

N. G. Siraisi. *The Clock and the Mirror: Girolamo Cardano and Renaissance Medicine* (Princeton, 1997)

NATURAL HISTORY

P. Findlen, *Possessing Nature: Museums, Collecting, and Scientific Culture in Early Modern Europe* (Berkeley, 1994)

B. Ogilvie, *The Science of Describing: Natural History in Renaissance Europe* (Chicago, 2005)

K. Reeds, *Botany in the Medieval and Renaissance Universities* (New York, 1991)

IBERIAN SCIENCE AND EMPIRE

A. Barrera-Osorio, *Experiencing Nature: The Spanish American Empire and the Early Scientific Revolution* (Austin, Tex., 2006)

D. Bleichmar, P. De Vos, K. Huffine, and K. Sheehan, eds, *Science in the Spanish and Portuguese Empires* (Stanford, Calif., 2009)

A. Crosby, *The Columbian Exchange: Biological and Cultural Consequences of 1492* (Westport, Conn., 1972)

D. Goodman, *Power and Penury: Government, Technology and Science in Philip II's Spain* (Cambridge, 2002)

Chapter 11: The Global Renaissance

GENERAL ASPECTS

J. Brotton, 'A Global Renaissance', in *The Renaissance Bazaar* (Oxford, 2002), 33–61

P. Burke, *The European Renaissance: Centres and Peripheries* (Oxford, 1998)

P. Burke, *Cultural Hybridity* (Cambridge, 2009)

P. Burke, 'Jack Goody and the Comparative History of Renaissances', *Theory, Culture and Society*, 26 (2009), 1–17

C. Farago, ed., *Reframing the Renaissance* (New Haven, 1995)

J. Goody, *Renaissances: The One and the Many* (Cambridge, 2009)

S. Gruzinski, 'Vers une histoire globale de la Renaissance', in *L'Aigle et le dragon* (Paris, 2012), 405–15

A. J. Toynbee, *A Study of History*, vol. 9 (Oxford, 1954)

BYZANTIUM

D. J. Geanokoplos, *Interaction of the Sibling Byzantine and Western Cultures* (New Haven, 1976)

K. Setton, 'The Byzantine Background to the Italian Renaissance', *Proceedings of the American Philosophical Society*, 100 (1956), 1–56

ISLAMIC WORLD

H. Belting, *Florence and Baghdad: Renaissance Art and Arab Science* (English trans., Cambridge, Mass., 2011)

L. Darling, 'The Renaissance and the Middle East', in G. Ruggiero, ed., *A Companion to the Worlds of the Renaissance* (Oxford, 2002)

D. Gutas, *Greek Thought in Arabic Translation* (London, 1998)

D. Howard, *Venice and the East* (New Haven, 2000)

R. E. Mack, *From Bazaar to Piazza: Islamic Trade and Italian Art, 1300–1600* (Berkeley, 2002)

G. Makdisi, *The Rise of Humanism in Classical Islam and the Christian West* (Edinburgh, 1990)

J. Raby, *Venice, Dürer and the Oriental Mode* (London, 1982)

G. Saliba, *Islamic Science and the Making of the European Renaissance* (Cambridge, Mass., 2007)

N. G. Siraisi, *Avicenna in Renaissance Italy* (Princeton, 1987)

SOUTH AND EAST ASIA

G. Bailey, *The Jesuits and the Great Mogul: Renaissance Art at the Imperial Court of India, 1580–1630* (Washington, DC, 1998)

M. Beach, *Mughal and Rajput Painting* (Cambridge, 1992)

J. Cahill, *The Compelling Image: Nature and Style in Seventeenth-Century Chinese Painting* (Cambridge, Mass., 1982)

S. Pierson, *From Object to Concept: Global Consumption and the Transformation of Ming Porcelain* (Hong Kong, 2013)

J.-P. Rubiés, *Travel and Ethnology in the Renaissance* (Cambridge, 2000)

J. Spence, *The Memory Palace of Matteo Ricci* (London, 1984)

M. Sullivan, *The Meeting of Eastern and Western Art* (Berkeley, 1989)

THE AMERICAS AND THE PHILIPPINES

G. Bailey, *The Andean Hybrid Baroque* (Notre Dame, Ind., 2010)

D. Brading, 'The Incas and the Renaissance: The Royal Commentaries of Inca Garcilaso de la Vega', *Journal of Latin American Studies*, 18 (1985), 1–23

A. Carpentier, *Music in Cuba* (English trans., Minneapolis, 2001)

J. H. Elliott, *The Old World and the New* (Cambridge, 1970)

V. Fraser, 'Architecture and Imperialism in Sixteenth-Century Spanish America', *Art History*, 9 (1986), 325–35

V. Fraser, *The Art of Conquest* (Cambridge, 1990)

S. Gruzinski, *Painting the Conquest* (Paris, 1992)

D. R. M. Irving, *Colonial Counterpoint: Music in Early Modern Manila* (Oxford, 2010)

AFRICA

E. Bassani and W. B. Fagg, *Africa and the Renaissance: Art in Ivory* (New York, 1988)

T. F. Earle and K. J. P. Lowe, eds, *Black Africans in Renaissance Europe* (Cambridge, 2005)

PICTURE ACKNOWLEDGEMENTS

The editor and publishers wish to thank the following who have kindly given permission to reproduce the illustrations on the following pages:

4	Courtesy Gordon Campbell
5	© Nacho Calonge/Alamy Stock Photo
7	Musée Unterlinden, Colmar, France. Album/Oronoz/Album/Superstock
8	Kunsthistorisches Museum, Vienna. Album/Oronoz/Album/Superstock
10	© Design Pics Inc/Alamy Stock Photo
15	Ms. A 79 inf.: Virgilian Allegory. Milan, Biblioteca Ambrosiana. Miniatura su pergamena. mm 287 × 198.- © 2016. Photo Scala, Florence
18	Zürich, Zentralbibliothek, Ms. C 74a, f. 201r—Quintiliani Institutionis oratoriae Libri XII
20	Austrian National Library, ÖNB Vienna: Cod. Suppl. Gr. 7 Han, fol. 5r
23	© The British Library Board, shelfmark Harley MS 2493, f 105v
25	Mondadori Portfolio/Contributor/Getty Images
27	Supplied by Royal Collection Trust/© Her Majesty Queen Elizabeth II 2016
32	Royal Collection, Windsor Castle. Supplied by Royal Collection Trust/© Her Majesty Queen Elizabeth II 2016
48	*The Doge Nicolo da Ponte invokes the protection of the Virgin* (oil on canvas), Tintoretto, Jacopo Robusti (1518–94)/Palazzo Ducale, Venice, Italy/Cameraphoto Arte Venezia/Bridgeman Images
50	Rijksmuseum, Amsterdam, SK-A-112
56	DEA/U. COLNAGO/Contributor/Getty Images
57	Rijksmuseum, Amsterdam, SK-A-857
58	World History Archive/Alamy Stock Photo
62–63	Luzern, Korporation Luzern, S 23 fol., p. 200—Illustrated Chronicle by Diebold Schilling of Lucerne (Luzerner Schillling) (http://www.e-codices.unifr.ch/en/list/one/kol/S0023-2)
65	Album/Joseph Martin/Album/Superstock
68	© The Granger Collection/Topfoto
76	All Souls College Library, University of Oxford, n.8.10
78	Courtesy National Gallery of Art, Washington, Widener Collection, 1942.9.4
83	Stanza della Segnatura, Vatican. Leemage/Contributor/Getty Images

174   Florence, Orsanmichele. © 2016. Photo Scala, Florence

175   Florence, Santa Maria Novella. DEA PICTURE LIBRARY/Getty Images

177   © vkstudio/Alamy Stock Photo

178   Florence, Bargello. © 2016. Photo Scala, Florence—courtesy of the Ministero Beni e Att. Culturali

180   © Remo Bardazzi/Mondadori Portfolio/age fotostock

182   Metropolitan Museum of Art, Robert Lehman Collection, 1975 www.metmuseum.org

184   Hampton Court. Supplied by Royal Collection Trust/© Her Majesty Queen Elizabeth II 2016

186   Metropolitan Museum of Art, Purchase, Francis M. Weld Gift, 1948 www.metmuseum.org

187   Florence, Bargello. akg-images

187   Florence, Bargello. akg-images/Erich Lessing

191   Urbino, Palazzo Ducale. DEA/G. DAGLI ORTI/Getty Images

194   *Cardinal Lodovico Trevisano*, 1459 (tempera on panel), Mantegna, Andrea (1431–1506)/Gemäldegalerie, Staatliche Museen zu Berlin, Germany/Artothek/Bridgeman Images

195   Paris, Louvre. Olio su tavola. cm 36,4 × 30.-inv. M.I. 693. - © 2016. Photo Scala, Florence

196   Berlin, Gemäldegalerie. ACME Imagery/Superstock

198   London, National Gallery. © Heritage Image Partnership Ltd/Alamy Stock Photo

199   Giovanni Bellini, The Crucifixion, c.1455. Museo Correr, Venice, Italy/Bridgeman Images

200   Florence, Uffizi. DEA/G. DAGLI ORTI/Getty Images

201   Florence, Uffizi. © Sergio Anelli/Mondadori Portfolio/age fotostock

204   Florence, Galleria Palatina, Palazzo Pitti. © 2016. Photo Scala, Florence—courtesy of the Ministero Beni e Att. Culturali

205   Milan, Brera. DEA/G. CIGOLINI/Contributor/Getty Images

210   DEA/G. DAGLI ORTI/Contributor/Getty Images

212   DEA PICTURE LIBRARY/Contributor/Getty Images

214   © Caroline Blondeau Morizot

215   © Fine Art Images/Superstock

218   Art Collection 3/Alamy Stock Photo

219   *Man with a Roman Coin* (oil on panel), Memling, Hans (c. 1433–94)/Koninklijk Museum voor Schone Kunsten, Antwerp, Belgium/© Lukas—Art in Flanders VZW/Photo: Hugo Maertens/Bridgeman Images

221   *Self Portrait at the Age of Twenty-Eight*, 1500 (oil on panel), Dürer, Albrecht (1471–1528)/Alte Pinakothek, Munich, Germany/Bridgeman Images

INDEX

Note: Figures are indicated by an italic *f* following the page number